AF521709

ITALIAN PAINTINGS

Cover Illustration: Raphael, *Emilia Pia* (cat. no. 13)

ITALIAN PAINTINGS
XIV - XVIIIth Centuries

from the collection of
The Baltimore Museum of Art

Gertrude Rosenthal, Editor

Contents

Foreword

Publication of *Italian Paintings, XIV–XVIIIth Centuries, from the collection of The Baltimore Museum of Art,* marks the thirty-fifth anniversary of Dr. Gertrude Rosenthal's curatorial service to this institution. Trude came to the Museum in 1945 as "Director of Research"; in 1948 she was given the title of "General Curator"; and in 1957 she assumed the position of Chief Curator, a position she held until her official retirement in 1969. By formal action of the Board of Trustees in June of 1970, Dr. Rosenthal was designated Chief Curator Emeritus and—happily for the Museum and for art historical scholarship—Trude has continued her working relationship with the Museum up to the present time. Indeed, we have already elicited from her commitments for future Museum projects that should assure her active engagement for at least another decade!

In the course of her energetic service to The Baltimore Museum of Art, Trude has worked with four Museum directors: Adelyn Breeskin, 1942–1962; Charles Parkhurst, 1962–1970; Tom L. Freudenheim, 1971–1978; and myself, since 1979. Every major aspect of the Museum's operations reflects the wisdom and vision of her professional counsel: most prominently, of course, the collection; the high standards of the publication program; the exhibition history; the conservation facilities; and even the individual staff members, to a very great degree. The Museum paid tribute to Trude's central contribution when it published its *Annual III–IV, Studies in Honor of Gertrude Rosenthal,* in 1968 and 1972 (Parts One and Two, respectively). In the pages of those earlier publications Adelyn Breeskin, Charles Parkhurst, and Tom Freudenheim all had the opportunity to describe Trude's impressive academic background and scholarly accomplishments and to acknowledge her substantial role in shaping The Baltimore Museum of Art and in giving it purpose and direction.

I am deeply privileged to be in a position in 1980 which permits me to renew our tribute to this extraordinary individual by introducing a major monographic publication of a substance and distinction worthy of honoring her. This book represents five years of Trude's life and is a signal achievement in every way. Trude turned her disciplined and passionate attention to the subject of old master Italian paintings with a dedication both fierce and inquiring. She sought out the participation of scholars who would bring to each of the paintings under consideration not only unique expertise but tender concern. She was the most demanding and thus the best of editors. She turned her own prodigious intelligence and discerning eye to the individual studies of five of the most important of the Italian pictures to be published, but I feel certain that all of the contributing authors would also agree that each article indelibly reflects Trude's active and informed involvement.

It is appropriate that the Museum's tribute to Trude is in the form of a publication on one aspect of the Museum's collections and, more specifically, on the Italian pictures. If the intensity of Trude's mind and eye could be distilled to one focus, it would be to acquire for the Museum and thus to preserve for posterity great works of art. Some of the paintings in this catalogue came to the Museum as a direct result of her intercession on the Museum's behalf. The commitment of The Baltimore Museum of Art to publishing its collections is unswerving and has been constant through each administration. There are very few individuals with the breadth of interest and scope of information which would enable them to assume full editorial responsibility for the cataloguing of all the Italian paintings from the fourteenth to the eighteenth centuries in the Museum's collection. We are extremely fortunate that Trude Rosenthal agreed to act in this capacity, since her wide experience in the field and her exacting standards of art connoisseurship and scholarship qualify her uniquely for this role.

In the Preface and Acknowledgments which follow, Trude details the history of the publication and the objects it documents, and offers thanks to the many individuals who have played such an integral part in bringing the book to completion. On behalf of the Board of Trustees of The Baltimore Museum of Art, I can only reiterate, most sincerely, the gratitude expressed in those pages by Dr. Rosenthal. I must, however, add a personal note of acknowledgment to four individuals without whom the publication could not have been realized: Margot Backas, a Washington-based editor who worked with Trude throughout the project, as well as Museum staff members Audrey Frantz, Ann Boyce Harper, and Brenda Richardson. The enormous contribution of each is acknowledged personally by Trude as well, but must be specially noted in this context as comprising an exceptional dedication to the project and to the Museum.

It is with both pride and humble admiration that we offer this, our most recent collection publication, in honor of Dr. Gertrude Rosenthal and her thirty-fifth anniversary with The Baltimore Museum of Art.

Arnold L. Lehman
Director
November 1980

Preface

During the many years I served as Curator of The Baltimore Museum of Art I often wanted to devote more time to research on the permanent collections but was prevented from such an undertaking by the rapid sequence of exhibitions and administrative duties. Rarely is there a second chance to do what one has missed earlier. After a retirement period of six years, spent in part as Consultant to the Honolulu Academy of Arts, I was given this second chance when in 1975 Tom Freudenheim, then Director of the Museum, invited me to consider the possibility of preparing a publication on the Old Master paintings in the Museum's collection.

Initially I envisioned a picture book of the Museum's best European works of the past, with one or two pages of text accompanying each illustration. But when finally the exact nature of the publication had to be determined, my colleagues Ann Boyce Harper and Brenda Richardson convinced me that I should narrow the focus of such a publication and do a comprehensive catalogue of the paintings from one country. I quickly decided to concentrate on the Italian pictures. This choice was probably influenced to some extent by my long-standing wish to study thoroughly the *Portrait of Emilia Pia* (cat. no. 13), perhaps the most controversial of the Museum's major works. Moreover, the publication in 1976 of The Walters Art Gallery's admirable catalogue of its Italian pictures was an important factor in our decision, since our book could be a useful supplement, thus making available complete information on the Italian paintings in both art museums of Baltimore.

In 1976 the Museum was awarded a grant for the Italian catalogue from the National Endowment for the Arts, and we clarified the approach we wanted to take in cataloguing the Italian paintings. What was to be the principal purpose of our undertaking? The answer was simple: it should enable us to learn all that could be known about our Italian Old Masters, for the benefit of the Museum staff, of scholars throughout the world, and of the interested if less specialized Museum visitor. Under no circumstances would there be any embellishment of the facts as to the authenticity, quality or condition of the individual work. This resolve was especially important because we assumed that our Italian collection included not only several controversial items but also a number of erroneous attributions.

Of the thirty-four Italian paintings dating before 1800 six, which had long been suspect, were confirmed to be either fakes, pastiches or so overpainted that they had no claim to authenticity (see Appendix). These were withdrawn for possible future use as study material. Since the two companion pieces presenting views of Venice by Francesco Guardi are discussed in one paper, the number of articles total twenty-seven.

If full research and a written commentary on each picture were to be completed within a relatively short period, it was evident that it could not be a one-person job but would require a variety of experts, familiar with the different periods, to produce an informative, sound, and engrossing study. Thirteen specialists eager to tackle the research of works in the areas of their expertise were chosen, several of them discussing more than one work. All examined the original paintings about which they were to write.

With documentary evidence for old easel paintings at a premium, scientific and technical examinations—which have been greatly improved in the last thirty years—assumed an ever more important role in the attribution of the Italian Old Master works in the Museum's collections. In addition to visual examination, X-radiography, the employment of sophisticated photography, ultraviolet and infrared rays, microscopy, and pigment analysis (if deemed necessary) became vital aids in the research and treatment of art objects. However, these technical tools of examination were not always applicable, and stylistic evidence continued to play an essential part in research.

With the combined results of all these methods it became evident that a relatively large number of previous ascriptions would have to be changed: only fifteen of the twenty-eight could be retained. The attributions of the most important works in the collection were not affected by these recent investigations. Of the reassigned thirteen attributions, some were altered only insofar as they are now considered productions of a master's workshop, circle, or school, whereas before they had been listed as creations by the master's own hand. Here it should be mentioned that several of the authors have examined and explained workshop practices so that the reader might have a better understanding of the reasons for the changed attribution of the work in question.

In some instances new attributions were suggested and frequently confirmed. Since these newly assigned pictures no longer have to "measure up" to the oeuvre of the renowned artist under whose name they were formerly recorded, they can be revaluated on their own merits. In this context it should be mentioned that a painting purchased by its donor as by Jacopo Tintoretto now takes its rightful place as by Palma il Giovane or Palma's circle (cat. no. 12). Obviously this picture is qualitatively more significant when seen within the context of Palma's or even his circle's work than judged as a painting by Tintoretto. Another picture, *A Philosopher with a Book* (cat. no. 27), has been recognized as a copy of a *Head* by Giovanni Battista Tiepolo in the Prague Museum. Accepted as a work by Giovanni Battista's younger son Lorenzo, executed in his father's lifetime and probably in the master's studio, Baltimore's painting is hardly distinguishable from the original but for a slightly pedestrian conception—a feature that is often symptomatic of even the best copies. Among other examples is a *Turkish Scene* (cat. no. 26), successively attributed to Giuseppe Maria Crespi and Francesco Guardi, designations rejected by most specialists who for more than a decade failed to place it, despite an appreciation for the quality of the small canvas. It appears to fit well into the oeuvre of Giovanni Camillo Sagrestani, to whose "circle" it now has been assigned.

It is not always possible to connect a picture with a particular artist: thus some of the Italian paintings are now identified simply by their regions of origin and their approximate dates. The frequent use of these qualifying modifications signals a healthy trend, reversing the attitude of scholars of about two generations ago who more often than not were quick to attach a major artist's name to the object of their inquiry.

The two most extensive articles (cat. nos. 12 and 18) turned out to be discussions of the Italian State Portrait and its evolution in two different art centers. These papers—one dealing with a portrait of a Venetian procurator, the other with a still unidentified "Lady of the Medici Court"—dovetail in a surprising way, though they were conceived and written independently. They not only provide excellent information on the two Baltimore paintings but also make a major contribution to the subject of the Italian State Portrait, an aspect of representation rarely explored.

The small number and often controversial nature of the Museum's Italian holdings suggested an approach slightly different from the usual concise form of catalogue entries. We decided to ask our contributors for an article of between 1500 and 5000 words in which the traditional attribution of the painting with which they were concerned was confirmed or, if persuasively challenged, revised. The intensive study of the material and my work with the authors proved to be stimulating beyond anticipation.

In the course of treating certain pictures, established quality judgments were sometimes questioned. While cleaning and removing nineteenth-century overpaint could demote a picture formerly considered acceptable for exhibition to a mere study piece, some previously neglected works were reinstated as welcome additions to the collection (e.g., cat. nos. 12 and 17). After treatment, a small fresco fragment (cat. no. 2), which in the past was considered practically disposable, turned out to be a fine head of a saint or prophet, probably designed by Agnolo Gaddi and executed in his atelier. The dull color of our earliest panel (cat. no. 1), thought to be from Arezzo, was changed to lively hues under the care of Elisabeth Packard, the dean of conservation of Italian paintings.

Attention was of course paid to subject matter which, in the time span encompassed by our study, was a major element in the artist's creative process. If indicated, the historic climate of the period in which the picture was painted was discussed or at least alluded to. Iconographic interpretation was included if in the author's judgment the picture lent itself to such analysis. We were amazed by the variety existing in the Museum's representations of the Madonna and Child, the theme naturally predominant in early Italian works. Other subjects depicted in our Italian holdings are figures of saints, religious narratives, topographical and fantastic views, genre pictures, and portraits.

As can be seen from the "provenance" section which prefaces each article, The Baltimore Museum of Art has purchased only three of the twenty-eight paintings discussed, a statistic which reflects lack of funds, rather than lack of interest. The works purchased were Strozzi's *St. Apollonia* (cat. no. 19) in 1951, Bacchiacca's *Madonna and Child* (cat. no. 8) in 1959, and Pittoni's *The Presentation in the Temple* (cat. no. 24) in 1965. Five paintings entered the collection as individual gifts; the rest were bequeathed together with other works by three generous donors. The Mary Frick Jacobs bequest dates from 1938, and that of Jacob Epstein from 1951 (part of his collection had been on loan to the Museum since 1929 when the new building in Wyman Park opened). The Saidie A. May bequest also was received in 1951. All three donors at one time or another expressed as the reason for leaving their collections to the Museum the desire to make great art available to their fellow citizens. It is in this spirit that we have undertaken the research and publication of their magnanimous gifts.

Gertrude Rosenthal

ACKNOWLEDGMENTS

In view of the extensive cooperation and assistance received during the various stages of this project, it would be impossible to name all those who have supported this effort both directly and indirectly. We are extremely grateful to them. By design this was an undertaking of collaboration, and thanks must go first of all to the thirteen contributors whose scholarship and perception have given this publication its substance. Their names appear with their respective articles.

All of the authors have expressed their indebtedness to Margot Backas of Washington, D.C. A highly regarded editor and expert in the publishing field, she worked directly with the writers, often clarifying their thoughts and bringing to her task a rare understanding which enabled her to preserve each author's personal style without compromising the laws of language. For me her advice and help were essential; her willingness to share her knowledge and professional experience with me contributed immensely to the realization of this project. When she finished the principal editing and other obligations took her away from virtually full-time work on this publication, I was fortunate to obtain the assistance of Leslie Brubaker for six months before she left for London to complete her dissertation. Anne Derbes then took over the assignment and was a most helpful and informed co-worker.

The project has benefited greatly from the generous counsel received from scholars in the field of Italian art in this country and abroad. Special mention must be made of Federico Zeri, whose early help encouraged me to attempt this book. Familiar with our holdings in this, his specific area of interest, he asked for a set of photographs of the Museum's Italian pictures. In return, he suggested, he would send informative notes on every Italian Old Master painting in the Museum's collection. I have never made a better exchange. Eventually, too, Professor Zeri permitted me to convey his expert opinions to the contributing authors.

Of the many other scholars who were willing to share their knowledge with us, only those few who commented on particularly vexing problems of attribution can be mentioned here: Alice Binion, Boston University; Sydney J. Freedberg, Harvard University; Mojmir Frinta, State University, New York at Albany; Creighton E. Gilbert, Cornell University; Konrad Oberhuber, Harvard University; Rodolfo Pallucchini, Foundation Giorgio Cini, Venice; Terisio Pignatti, University of Venice and Civic Museums, Venice; Donald Posner, New York University; David Rosand, Columbia University; Stella Rudolph, Florence; James Byam Shaw, formerly Christ Church, Oxford; Piero Torriti, Soprintendenza, Provinces of Siena and Grosseto; Harold E. Wethey, University of Michigan; and Sir Ellis Waterhouse, Oxford. W. T. Chase, Head Conservator, Freer Gallery, Washington, D.C. and E. M. Gifford, Conservator, The Walters Art Gallery, Baltimore, most generously made pigment analyses of questionable works. Some of our contributors acknowledge in their papers the special help and information received from colleagues, and I certainly wish to add my thanks to theirs. I am also indebted to the Research Department of Christie's, London, for important data on the provenance of several paintings.

Obviously, this publication could not have been undertaken without the strong support of The Baltimore Museum of Art. I cannot adequately express my gratitude to the staff and Trustees of the Museum. First of all, Tom L. Freudenheim, the former Director, convinced the Museum's Board of Trustees of the need for such a publication. Their approval and financial support enabled me to begin work on the project. Arnold L. Lehman, who assumed the directorship at the end of 1979, has offered much appreciated encouragement.

I am most indebted to my colleagues and friends Brenda Richardson, Assistant Director for Art, and Ann Boyce Harper, Assistant Director for Administration. During the entire course of the project both gave me all the help I asked for, despite their other pressing obligations. For several months, during my prolonged illness, Brenda Richardson took over as the project's director; her careful reading and thoughtful response to the papers were of immense value. Ann Boyce Harper, who in 1976 as the Museum's Managing Editor read my first papers, now has brought the publication to completion. Her critical eye and knowledge of the practical matters of publishing were extraordinarily helpful. Without the continuing enthusiasm, perceptive comments, and professional guidance of Brenda Richardson and Ann Boyce Harper this book would simply not have been possible.

Audrey Frantz, the Museum's Assistant Editor, negotiated the often complicated requests for photographs and publishing permissions for paintings used for comparative purposes in the articles and frequently advised and aided me on complex printing problems. She was also responsible for keeping track of the flow of manuscripts from author to project director, editor, designer, typesetter, and printer, all of which she accomplished with good humor and thorough professionalism. Margaret M. Powell, a scrupulous and perfectionist proofreader, read the final manuscripts as well as various stages of proof. Geoffrey Michael Lemmer, Senior Conservator, handled an important part of the project by not only examining all the Italian paintings before 1800 and treating several of them but also advising the authors on the condition of the pictures under discussion. Both the project director and the authors are most grateful to him. We want to mention the help received from Sona Johnston, Associate Curator of Painting and Sculpture, who researched the provenance of the painting attributed to Chilone. We are also indebted to the conservators, not on the Museum's staff, who have treated a number of the paintings; their names appear under the condition reports of the pictures on which they have worked.

Other members of the Museum's staff gave generously of their time and professional skills. Martha Parkhurst, Director of Development, was instrumental in obtaining the grants which made the publication a reality; Joan Robison confirmed much of the bibliographical data; Linda De Palma assumed many of the duties of copy editor; Duane Suter photographed the majority of the Museum's Italian pictures; and Nancy Press made available the needed photographs of the Museum's paintings to my colleagues and to me.

We feel especially fortunate to have had as graphic designers Alex and Caroline Castro of the Hollow Press, Baltimore, whose craftsmanship, sensitivity, and taste are evident in this publication.

A special note of thanks is due to Elsie Campbell who with infinite patience and at all hours of the day typed and retyped the often almost illegible manuscripts. I am also eager to acknowledge the generous help of Angeline R. Hoen who translated a long, important research paper from Italian into English.

On many occasions we were assisted by the librarians of other institutions. In this regard we are especially grateful to Muriel L. Toppan of The Walters Art Gallery, who also prepared the index and gave the entire manuscript a last proofing. I greatly appreciate the interest and help of Elizabeth R. Usher and her staff at The Metropolitan Museum of Art; of Mildred Steinbach and Helen Sanger of the Frick Art Reference Library; and of Caroline Backlund of the National Gallery of Art, Washington, D.C.

We wish to thank all the owners of the works of art which are reproduced in this publication—both those who are named and those who preferred to remain anonymous. We are particularly grateful to the Soprintendenza per i Beni Artistici e Storici, Florence, which is in charge of many of the works illustrated in this volume. Thanks are also due to the firm of Fratelli Alinari for its generous cooperation in granting permission to reproduce photographs from Italian collections.

Both the research and publication of this catalogue were made possible by grants from the National Endowment for the Arts, to which we are profoundly grateful for having recognized the usefulness of such an undertaking. Further subsidy was received from the Samuel H. Kress Foundation, whose Executive Vice-President Mary M. Davis not only responded to our financial needs but also, because of her deep interest in Italian art, understood the nature of our publication and shared its aims.

G.R.

Sequence

Entries are arranged chronologically, and within the centuries alphabetically by artist's name or region of origin.

Dimensions

Dimensions are given in inches and centimeters, height preceding width. Despite considerable effort, the measurements of several paintings in churches and private collections could not be obtained.

Medium

While not all publications record medium (oil or egg tempera or a mixture of the two), it has been included here, though there exists a margin for error in pictures of the late fifteenth and very early sixteenth centuries (the so-called transition period).

Provenance

Records of provenance of catalogued works vary greatly in thoroughness. There is virtually no information on certain works which were purchased in small shops by dealers or art-struck collectors. In other cases, such as that of Titian's *Portrait of a Gentleman,* the painting's history has been traced in great detail over almost two hundred years. The Titian provenance has only recently become known in its entirety. It is hoped that this publication will help bring to light the histories of other Italian paintings in the Museum's collections.

Condition

Unless otherwise indicated, the condition reports were completed or supervised by the Museum's Senior Conservator Geoffrey Michael Lemmer. A number of the reports were based on examinations by Elisabeth C. G. Packard, former Director of the conservation department, The Walters Art Gallery, and by Victor Covey and Kay Silberfeld, former conservators of The Baltimore Museum of Art (both now at the National Gallery of Art, Washington). All of the Museum's Italian paintings dating before 1800 have been examined. As specified in the individual condition reports, some of the paintings have recently been treated. The name of the conservator who carried out the recent major treatment appears under the condition report of the respective picture. In almost all instances the conservator who handled the treatment also wrote the report. Additional Italian paintings have been scheduled for conservation treatment in the near future.

Selected Bibliographies

The bibliographies frequently include not only publications in which the Baltimore pictures are mentioned but also books and articles which are especially informative about the artist under discussion, or the period or region of the work (some of the authors, however, mentioned only the items which directly refer to the particular entry). Bibliographical entries are cited in chronological order.

Photographic Credits

Unless otherwise indicated works of art are reproduced by courtesy of their respective owners. The credit line "Alinari/Editorial Photocolor Archives" indicates that the photograph and the publishing permission were supplied by Fratelli Alinari, Florence. Permission for illustrations with the credit line "Gallerie Fiorentine" has been granted by the Soprintendenza per i Beni Artistici e Storici, Florence. Occasionally the location or condition of a certain painting made it impossible to obtain a photograph of optimal quality. In several cases a poor photograph has been reproduced, simply to offer a basis for comparison suggested by the author.

Correspondence Files

All correspondence referring to pictures under discussion and addressed to The Baltimore Museum of Art or to Gertrude Rosenthal is retained in the Museum's curatorial files.

XIVth & XVth Centuries

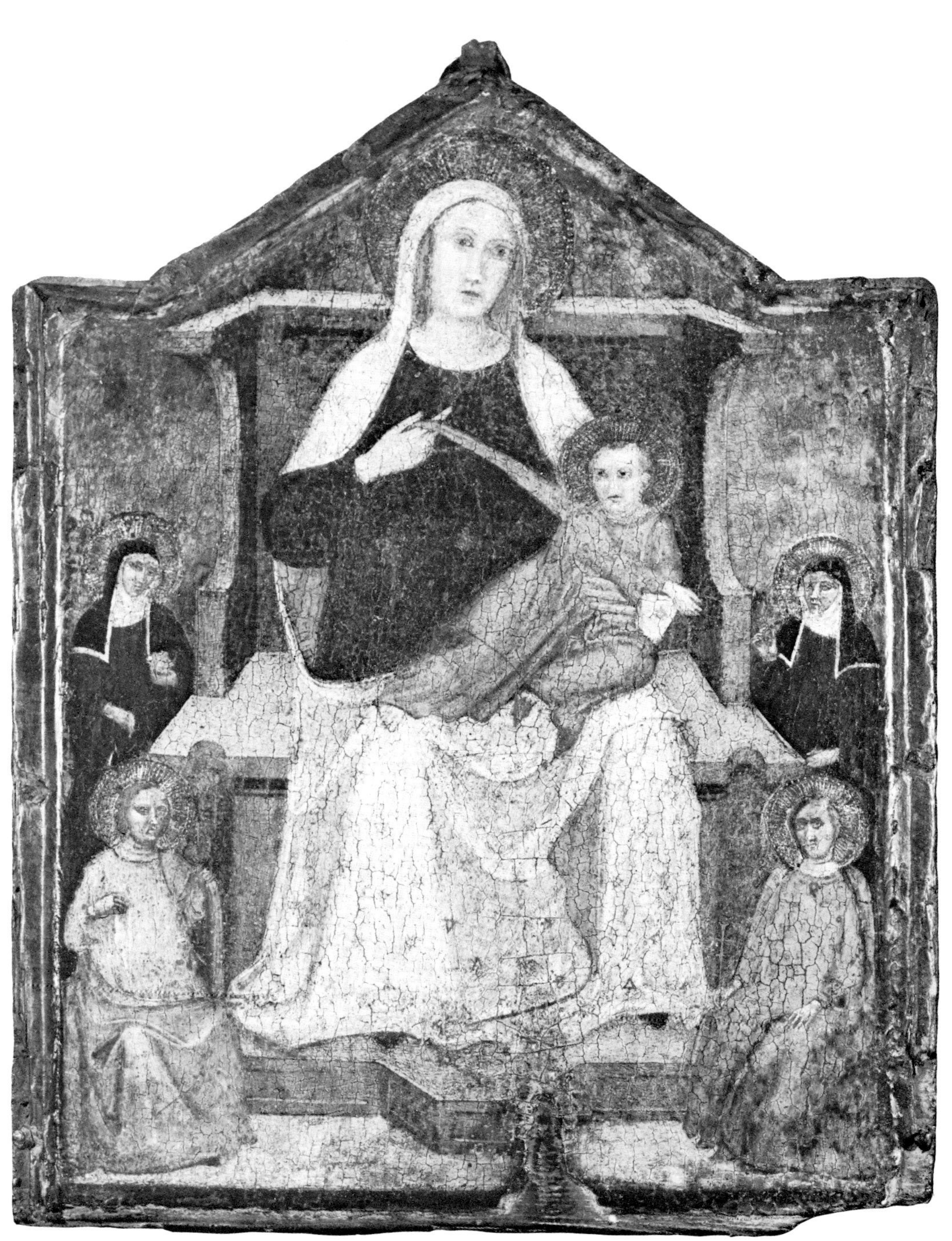

AREZZO (?) (early 14th century)

1. *Madonna and Child Enthroned with Four Saints*

Tempera on wood. 16½ × 12¾ inches (41.9 × 32.3 cm.)
Bequest of Saidie A. May (BMA 51.392)

PROVENANCE

Acquired in Italy by Saidie A. May during the 1920's
Bequeathed to The Baltimore Museum of Art in 1951 by Saidie A. May

CONDITION

This early fourteenth-century panel has a gabled top and engaged molding which is missing at the bottom. Two hinge marks visible on each side suggest that originally the panel had wings or shutters. Although the two vertical battens, attached with nails to the back, show damage by insects, the panel itself is not significantly weakened or warped. The paint surface, however, is marked by protuberances where the heads of the nails fastening the battens have forced the gesso and paint upward. There is a deep burn mark at bottom, slightly right of center, which exposes the wood panel and traces of the fabric under the gesso ground.

The removal of varnish and overpainting, undertaken in 1979, revealed abrasion of paint throughout, as well as many small losses, scratches, and pitted areas. A large loss was discovered on the Madonna's right sleeve under the modern layer of dark blue paint applied to conceal her damaged robe, which was originally of a lighter blue. A dark patch of overpaint had obscured the Child's left foot.

This recent cleaning disclosed a much more colorful painting than its somber appearance had suggested. Delicate tones of rose in the Child's dress became more visible, and mauve, orange, and scarlet appeared in the garments of the saints seated in the foreground. The much damaged mantle of the figure in the right foreground was originally yellow (determined by the presence of scattered particles of yellow pigment which are visible only under the microscope). Even the black robes of the nuns in the background showed variations between the darker veils and lighter habits after removal of dark overpaint revealed drapery folds and the objects held in their hands. Another instance of the refinement of execution displayed in this work was the discovery of traces of a random pattern of minute triangles in red and gold on the Madonna's white mantle. The throne was found to be painted in shades of olive green with its horizontal members in a lighter tone. The simple haloes, consisting of rays and punched dots, bear traces of gold leaf, but the background niche, which is a pinkish-beige, apparently was not gilded.

Elisabeth C. G. Packard
Formerly The Walters Art Gallery, Baltimore

In this small, fascinating, but long overlooked panel one sees the dim reflection of monumental events destined to alter the course of Italian painting. Like several other works from the same period, its importance as a document of style equals its aesthetic merit.

The Madonna wears a blue robe under a white mantle lined with red. The Child's dress is rose-lavender. The two saints at the back are dressed in black habits with white coifs. The nun at the right originally held between thumb and forefinger of her raised hand a small object which might have been a flower but is no longer recognizable. Her companion originally held in her left palm what could have been a pyx.

Of the two saints seated in the foreground, the one at the left wears an orange robe with a mauve mantle. Her right hand is raised to her chest, indicating that she may have held a staff. The saint at the right is dressed in a red garment with a mantle that has become completely abraded and now appears grayish-brown but was originally yellow. In her right hand she holds a red cross. The Madonna's throne is in shades of olive green.

I have been unable to identify the two saints in the foreground. Most saints represented in early Italian painting are common to many locations and are of standard type. Because these two are not readily identifiable, one would suspect that they are local saints little known outside of the town or village where they were venerated.

The nuns to either side of the throne, their black and white habits, their appearance together, and their physical type indicate that they are the saints Flora and Lucilla, who were especially venerated in Arezzo.[1] They were beheaded near Ostia in the third century and their remains were taken to Torrita di Siena (a town not far from Cortona) and then (in 1193?) to Arezzo. Both patrons of Monte Amiata and Torrita, they were worshipped in Arezzo where their remains are housed in the Badia. Because the saints are dressed as Benedictine nuns, it is logical to assume that the commission for the Baltimore panel was in some way tied either to a Benedictine patron or a Benedictine house or church. It seems possible that the two unidentified saints in the foreground are also local figures venerated in Arezzo or in the several other towns devoted to the cult of SS. Flora and Lucilla.

It is quite likely, as P. P. Donati has suggested, that the Baltimore panel originated in Arezzo.[2] Aside from the iconographic connection, it displays the interesting mixture of Florentine and Sienese styles characteristic of that city. Although Donati's ascription of the panel to the Aretine Master of the Nativity of the Baptist is not entirely convincing, it seems to point in the right direction. Given our incomplete knowledge of Aretine painting of the Trecento, the safest attribution for the Baltimore *Madonna and Child* seems to be Arezzo (?), early fourteenth century.

The strong Sienese influence in Arezzo might also account for the Child's posture. The type of active Christ, leaning and gesturing toward the spectator's right (uncommon in early Italian painting), appears to have had its origin and most widespread representation in Siena. There seems to be no other Child exactly like the Baltimore example in fourteenth-century Tuscan painting, but variants of what may be the same type are found in several panels representing the Madonna and Child. The few Florentine depictions of Christ that resemble the Baltimore Child were apparently influenced by Sienese art, another indication that the type originated in Siena.[3] In no comparable work, however, is the Child so active, nor is He restrained by His mother, who in the Baltimore picture holds Him by a leash-like piece of cloth. The vigor and vividness of this splendid Baby do not seem to be the invention of this pleasing but not very original artist. The figure of the Child, in fact, might well be the reflection of a composition by one of the major painters of the Trecento, such as Ambrogio or Pietro Lorenzetti.[4]

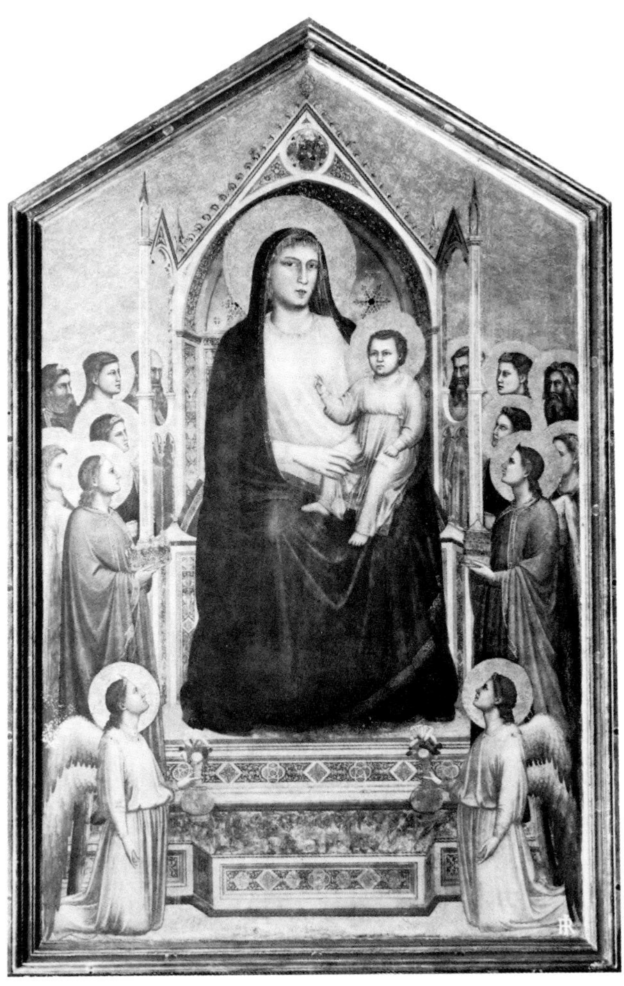

Fig. 1. Giotto, *Ognissanti Madonna* (*Madonna of All Saints*). Tempera on wood. 128 × 80 inches (325 × 204 cm.). Uffizi, Florence. Alinari/Editorial Photocolor Archives

Also suggestive of a Sienese connection is the palette of the Baltimore panel. The particular nature and combination of the scarlet, yellow, mauve, orange, and olive green seem to derive from the remarkable colorists active in Siena during the first decades of the Trecento: Duccio and Simone Martini, among others. There is a clarity and delicacy about the color of the Baltimore panel that appears to be different from anything Florentine.

Yet the basic forms of this picture are not entirely Sienese despite its color and the type of Child. There is a near monumentality and directness about the work which must stem, in one way or another, from Giotto, whose *Ognissanti Madonna* (Uffizi, Florence) was certainly one of the most influential paintings of the entire fourteenth century (fig. 1).[5] Giotto's revolutionary portrayal of the majestic but approachable—and very real—Virgin surrounded by her accessible court of saints and angels sent artistic shock waves throughout all of Tuscany, even to the most remote villages. The effects of Giotto's style can be seen in literally hundreds of frescoes and panels by his contemporaries and by the painters of the next generation.

The artist of the Baltimore panel appears to have been one of a number of painters who grew up while Giotto was still working. His art does not betray any of the highly

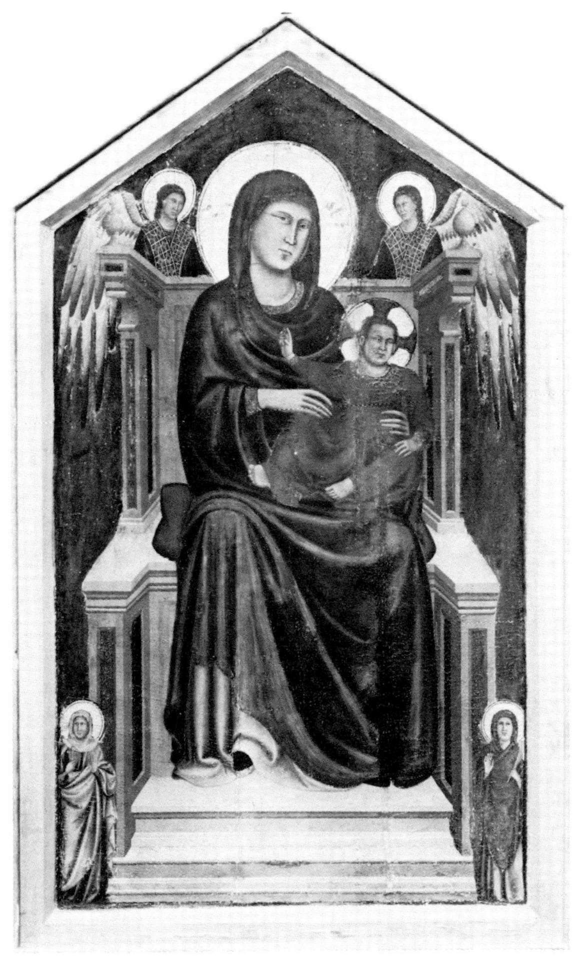

Fig. 2. Santa Cecilia Master, *Madonna and Child with Saints and Angels*. Tempera on wood. 78¾ × 45¼ inches (200 × 115 cm.). Santa Margherita a Montici, Florence. Alinari/Editorial Photocolor Archives

stylized, often geometric characteristics common to the generation of artists trained before Giotto's idiom began to dominate Tuscany. All traits of the artist of the Baltimore panel suggest that he was a close contemporary of Jacopo del Casentino, the Santa Cecilia Master, Pacino di Bonaguida, and a number of other painters active during the early decades of the fourteenth century.[6] These artists were caught in the stylistic wake of Giotto's remarkable inventions. They witnessed the destruction of many of the older principles and conventions of religious art under the force of his new idiom, which was soon to serve as the model for much Tuscan painting. In many ways these men were the interpreters of the new style which they tamed and domesticated, even though they did not fully comprehend it.

Like other artists of the early fourteenth century, the painter of the Baltimore panel seems to have been a rather unwilling follower of Giotto. Possibly he felt slightly ill at ease with Giotto's powerful style, which he grafted onto his own delicate sensibilities. In this respect, the Baltimore panel reminds one of the Santa Cecilia Master's *Madonna and Child with Saints and Angels* at Santa Margherita a Montici, Florence (fig. 2), where the artist is seen at his most uncomfortable Giottesque moment—his innate sense for the easy and the familiar clashing with the monumental tenets of Giotto. Here one sees not a static visual document but an event, a dynamic and tense meeting of two ways of conceptualizing and recording religious imagery. As in the Baltimore picture, the figure types and the architecture of the throne at Santa Margherita a Montici take their inspiration from Giotto, but they have lost nearly all of their original space-defining function; they are translations made from an imperfect understanding of Giotto's pictorial language.

The provincial origin of the Baltimore panel may also have distanced its artist from the revolutionary style of Giotto. Working in the artistically isolated environment of Arezzo, he probably saw Giotto's achievements through the filter of a slightly old-fashioned vision heavily influenced by Sienese painting. It is, however, the hesitancy with which he adopts the idioms of both Siena and Florence which seems to indicate that he really did not belong to either stylistic world. In spite of this, or perhaps because of it, the Baltimore painting remains a charming work of subtle and restrained taste. There is a finesse about it which is shared by a small number of works from the early Trecento done under the influence but not the domination of Giotto.

Bruce Cole
Indiana University,
Bloomington, Indiana

NOTES

1. On SS. Flora and Lucilla, see G. Kaftal, *The Iconography of the Saints in Tuscan Painting* (Florence: Sansoni, 1952), pp. 375–76, 641–42.
2. The picture is published and attributed by Donati to the Master of the Nativity of the Baptist in "Per la pittura aretina del Trecento (III)," *Paragone* 21, no. 247 (1970): 5, fig. 3. Other attributions are: R. Offner, Workshop or School of Giotto (verbally, 1951, to G. Rosenthal); M. Meiss, Florentine, Early Fourteenth Century, but not Workshop or School of Giotto (verbally, October 22, 1959, to G. Rosenthal); F. Zeri, School of Arezzo (letter to G. Rosenthal, December 22, 1975, curatorial files, The Baltimore Museum of Art).
3. On the Child type, see D. Shorr, *The Christ Child in Devotional Images in Italy during the XIV Century* (New York: G. Wittenborn, 1954), pp. 87–98.
4. The fact that the Child leans so vigorously to the right could suggest that the prototype may have come from a panel similar to Ambrogio Lorenzetti's cut-down picture in the church of SS. Peter and Paul at Roccalbegna. Here and in a panel in Budapest, related to the style of Ambrogio, the Child seems to have been in close contact with the surrounding saints. For the *Roccalbegna Madonna,* see B. Berenson, *Italian Pictures of the Renaissance: Central and North Italian Schools* (London: Phaidon Press, 1968), 2:pl. 92. For the Budapest picture, see R. van Marle, *The Development of the Italian Schools of Painting,* 19 vols. (The Hague: Martinus Nijhoff, 1923–1938), 2:fig. 253.
5. For Giotto, see B. Cole, *Giotto and Florentine Painting 1280–1375* (New York: Harper & Row, 1976).
6. For Jacopo del Casentino, see R. Offner, *A Critical and Historical Corpus of Florentine Painting* (New York: New York University, 1930), sec. 3, vol. 2, pt. 2, pp. 87–152. For the Santa Cecilia Master, see ibid. (1931), sec. 3, vol. 1, pp. 15–37. On Pacino di Bonaguida, see ibid. (1930), sec. 3, vol. 2, pt. 1, pp. 1–20.

SELECTED BIBLIOGRAPHY

Richard Offner. *Studies in Florentine Painting: The Fourteenth Century*. New York: F. F. Sherman, 1927. Reprint edition. New York: Junius Press, 1972.

Richard Offner. *A Critical and Historical Corpus of Florentine Painting*. 4 sections. New York: New York University, 1930–1969.

Giulia Sinibaldi and Giulia Brunetti. *Pittura italiana del Duecento e Trecento*. Florence: Sansoni, 1943.

George Kaftal. *The Iconography of the Saints in Tuscan Painting*. Florence: Sansoni, 1952.

Dorothy Shorr. *The Christ Child in Devotional Images in Italy during the XIV Century*. New York: G. Wittenborn, 1954.

Bernard Berenson. *Italian Pictures of the Renaissance: Central and North Italian Schools*. 3 vols. London: Phaidon Press, 1968.

Robert Oertel. *Early Italian Painting to 1400*. New York: Praeger, 1968.

Pier Paolo Donati. "Per la pittura aretina del Trecento (III)." *Paragone* 21, no. 247 (1970):3–11.

Richard Fremantle. *Florentine Gothic Painters from Giotto to Masaccio*. London: Secker and Warburg, 1975.

Bruce Cole. *Giotto and Florentine Painting 1280–1375*. New York: Harper & Row, 1976.

Bruce Cole. *Sienese Painting from its Origins to the Fifteenth Century*. New York: Harper & Row, 1980.

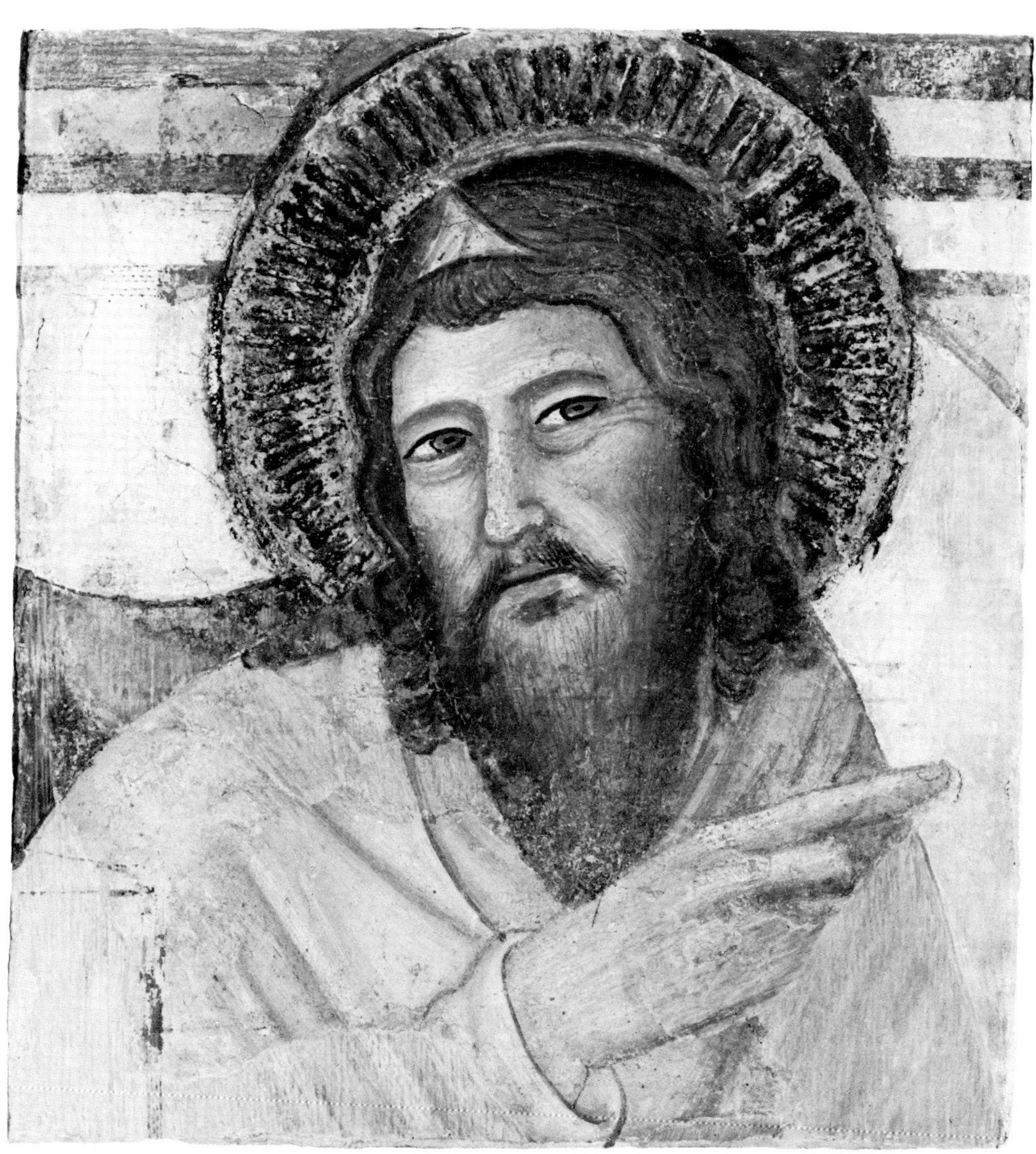

Workshop of
AGNOLO GADDI (active 1369–1396)

2. *Head of a Saint,* last quarter of the 14th century

Fresco fragment. 11¾ × 10½ inches (29.8 × 26.6 cm.)
Bequest of Saidie A. May (BMA 51.395)

PROVENANCE

Brummer Galleries, New York (1925)

Acquired by Saidie A. May in 1925

Bequeathed to The Baltimore Museum of Art in 1951 by Saidie A. May

CONDITION

At an unspecified date, before it entered the Baltimore Museum's collection, the fresco fragment was removed from its original support and mounted onto an auxiliary support of plaster of Paris and reeds. The original lime plaster still adhering was irregular in thickness, varying from 1/16 to 3/8 of an inch (2 mm.–10 mm.). There were two different filling materials used in earlier restorations, one of wax and fillers and the other of hardened plaster of Paris.

The surface of the fresco was covered with grime. It is also likely that the surface had been waxed at least once in the past. While there are large losses around the perimeter, amounting to about 30 percent of the total area, a major part of the original has remained.

The head is well painted and essentially intact. The hair and beard were crisply painted with thin washes of dry earth colors and black onto fresh plaster. The skin tones were painted with thin washes of earth colors and lime water or putty, and the delicate transparency of *buon fresco* can still be observed. The figure's right shoulder was more thickly painted with earth reds, yellows, and lime white, resulting in a texture showing distinct brushstrokes. Even though the hand is severely damaged, the delicate lines of the wrist and finger tip are preserved. The halo was made of lime plaster and at one time was varnished to make it shine.

During its treatment in 1979 the fresco was removed from its unstable support and mounted onto a new support made of styrofoam, birch veneer plywood, and basswood strips. The old fills were replaced. The top coat of the new fills was made of lime, sand, and perlite. The first layer of inpainting was done in fresh plaster. Subsequent layers of inpainting were done with dry pigments and lime water or putty. Gloss match was achieved with a very thin layer of wax brushed onto the areas of new fills.

The areas of loss were inpainted to approximate the colors of the original. The colors are achieved through striation, so that the areas of new paint are obvious to a close observer but do not distract the casual viewer.

Linda Tucker
Cambridge, Massachusetts

The fresco is unpublished and there are no manuscript opinions. There can be little doubt, however, that the fresco is Florentine and that it comes from some larger work. Very likely it once formed part of a painted border around a narrative scene from a fresco cycle, like the one by Agnolo Gaddi discussed below. The figure's hand probably originally pointed toward such a scene. Perhaps the figure also carried a scroll with a text referring to the painted story; such scrolls are common in Trecento painting.[1] The identity of the figure is not certain. Painted borders often contained prophets, but without an identifying scroll one cannot be sure who this is. The halo is, of course, common to both saints and prophets, and the peaked headdress appears to be a generalized one without specific reference to its wearer.[2]

The style closest to this fragment is found in the work of Agnolo Gaddi, one of the most important and popular Florentine painters active during the last quarter of the Trecento.[3] Agnolo, the son of the famous Taddeo Gaddi,[4] a pupil of Giotto, is first documented working in Rome in 1369. His earliest extant paintings date from the 1380's, and until his death in 1396 he produced a number of panels and frescoes of considerable quality. His major commissions were the Castellani Chapel and the Choir of Santa Croce, Florence, and the Chapel of the Sacra Cintola in the Cathedral of Prato, a city close to Florence.

Agnolo Gaddi belonged to a generation of painters destined to make an important contribution to the art of Florence. These artists grew up in a world dominated by the style of Andrea di Cione (called Orcagna) and his brother Nardo.[5] The Orcagnesque idiom resulted in pictures of harsh, aloof, and hierarchical content. Figures were sometimes uncomfortably and ambiguously placed in space; palettes were composed partially of clashing and acidic colors; and the relation of solid to void was frequently jarring. While not every painter working in the decades around the middle of the fourteenth century adhered to this style, most of them were influenced by some aspect of it.[6]

Agnolo Gaddi and his artistic contemporaries were trained by painters under the sway of the Orcagnesque idiom. But Gaddi, Spinello Aretino (an artist from Arezzo), and Antonio Veneziano, who was probably a Florentine, began to move away from this idiom. Although all of their first works naturally betray strong Orcagnesque traits, the paintings of their earliest maturity demonstrate a different spirit. More coherent, stable, and volumetric, they evidence a return to many of the visual values of the first part of the century. The revival of Giotto's style was, in fact, part of the new visual culture created by the generation of artists working in the last quarter of the Trecento. But all of these men forged a personal visual language as they strove to make their pictures more monumental and direct—in both a formal and an iconographic sense—than those of their immediate predecessors. It was the generation of Agnolo Gaddi, Spinello Aretino, and Antonio Veneziano which, in many ways, prepared the path for styles as different as those of Lorenzo Monaco and Masaccio.[7]

Many of these new developments can be seen in Agnolo Gaddi's frescoes in the Cappella Maggiore of Santa Croce, Florence, which belonged to the Alberti, one of the most powerful Florentine banking families. The commission to decorate the walls of the choir was one of the largest and most prestigious of the entire Trecento, and the fact that it was awarded to Gaddi sometime in the 1390's demonstrates that the artist was then at the peak of his fame.[8]

Gaddi's frescoes are devoted to the Legend of the True Cross, a theme most appropriate for the church of Santa Croce. In eight paintings he narrates the complex story—taken from Jacobus de Voragine's *Golden Legend* of the late thirteenth century—which traces the history of the cross from the death of Adam to its recovery by Heraclius.[9] Gaddi's

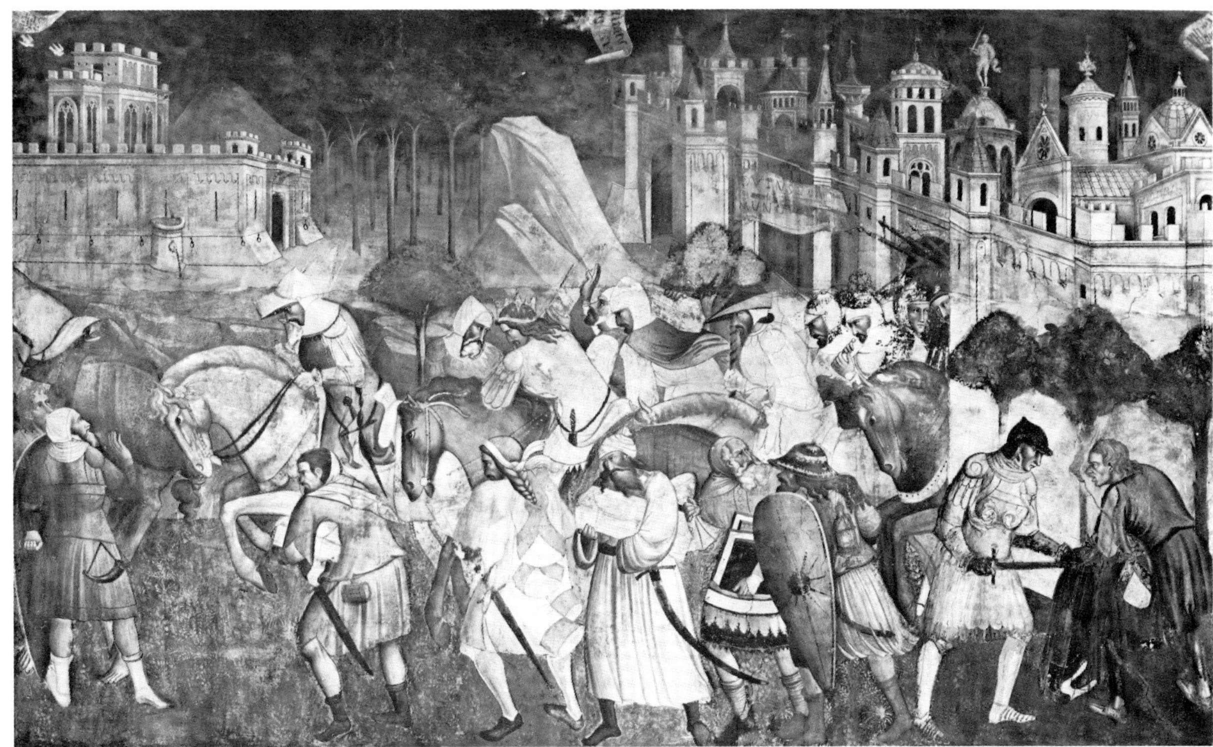

Fig. 1. Agnolo Gaddi, *Flight of Chosroes,* 1390's. Fresco, detail of the *Legend of the True Cross.* Santa Croce, Cappella Maggiore, Florence. Alinari/Editorial Photocolor Archives

series seems to have been the first in a sequence of True Cross cycles (sometimes associated with flagellant societies) which found its apex in Piero della Francesca's frescoes in Arezzo.[10]

The *Flight of Chosroes,* which depicts the stealing of the cross from Jerusalem, is a rather typical example of Gaddi's late style (fig. 1). The frieze-like articulation across the fresco is carefully planned to suggest flight by increasing the spatial intervals between the fleeing figures. From the closely packed crowd bursting out of the city gate to the bounding horses at the far left, Gaddi lengthens the distance between figures. The action even spills out of the picture as the leftmost horseman escapes beyond the painted border, implying that the space continues outside the fresco's painted frame. Further rhythmic emphasis is added by the legs of the running soldiers.

In the foreground of the *Flight of Chosroes* Gaddi reveals his considerable compositional skills. But it is in the background that his real contribution to Florentine art appears. Beyond the twisted rock formations, a type taken up by Lorenzo Monaco,[11] extends a wooded landscape occupied by a large castle and the distant buildings of the city. In its depth, breadth, and atmosphere, the background of the *Flight* is a milestone in Florentine art, for never before had an artist displayed such concern with the construction and details of the far distance. Moreover, it is clear that Gaddi is here trying (not always successfully) to make the background objects move backward rather than upward as is so often the case in the pictures of his immediate predecessors. In short, he shows an embryonic interest in the rational, unified, and convincing space that will become of special concern to Quattrocento painters.

In color, too, Gaddi was an important innovator. The palette of the Ciones often contained a number of dense, highly saturated colors, sometimes combined in a clashing

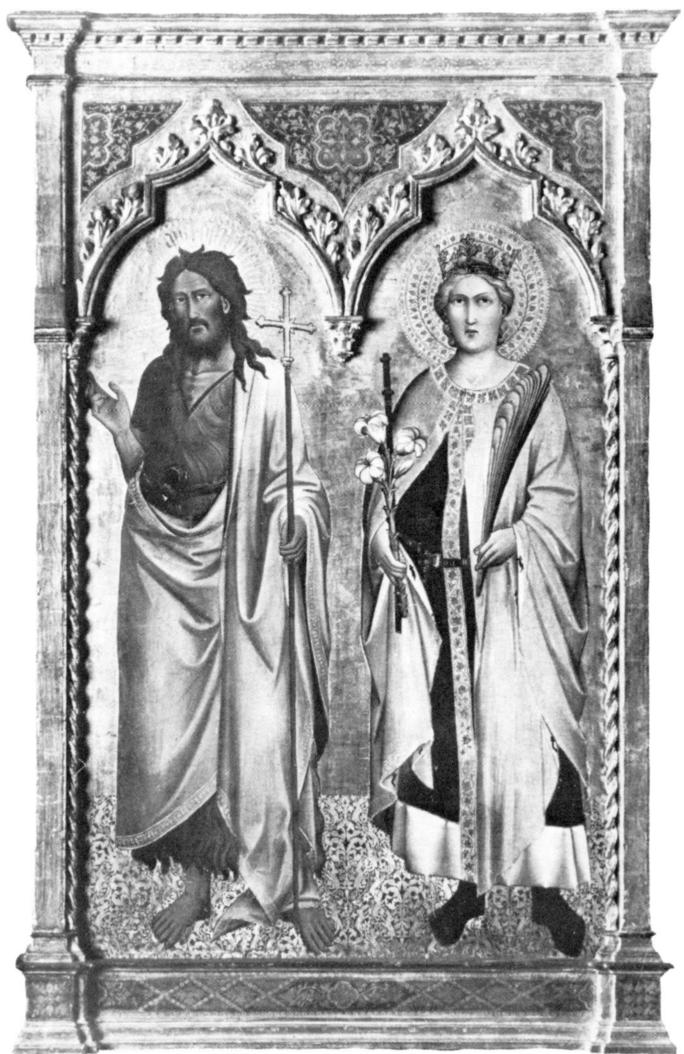

Fig. 2. Agnolo Gaddi, *St. John the Baptist and St. Minias*. Detail of a polyptych. Tempera on wood. Contini Bonacossi Collection, Pitti Galleries, Florence. Alinari/Editorial Photocolor Archives

manner. On the whole, Gaddi's range of color is wide, light, and chorded harmoniously. The large frescoes of the Cappella Maggiore exhibit a brightness and gaiety of color that fill the choir. As Gaddi was perhaps the most distinguished artist of late Trecento Florence and the head of a large workshop, his color was to have a decided influence on both his immediate followers and on the painters of the next generation, the artists of the early Quattrocento.

The pronounced nose, prominent eye sockets, ample mouth, and freely drawn wavy hair of the Baltimore fragment are all characteristic of Agnolo Gaddi. Although the fresco is clearly a product of Gaddi's design, his hand may be absent from its surface. Often frescoes were the product of the many assistants employed to help execute the master's design, and it is quite likely that the more minor parts of the job, such as this head, were left to them.[12]

The facial type and construction of the features of the Baltimore head appear in Gaddi's work from the Castellani Chapel (early 1380's) onward. But because the fragment is so small and not in pristine condition, a precise dating is impossible. It appears, however, to belong to the later part of Gaddi's career. There is less of the influence of Orcagna and Nardo di Cione in it than in earlier works such as the *Coronation* (National Gallery, London) and the large polyptych (Gemäldegalerie, Staatl. Museen PKB, Berlin, West).[13] The work closest to the Baltimore fresco is the Contini Bonacossi polyptych datable to 1394–1396.[14] Formerly in San Miniato al Monte, Florence, it is now in the Contini Bonacossi Collection of the Pitti Galleries. A comparison between the St. John the Baptist from this painting (fig. 2) and the Baltimore fragment demonstrates similarities in the construction of the faces and in the conception of light and shade. Also alike are the tilted heads and direct glances that establish a vivid contact with the onlooker.

It is unfortunate that the original location of the Baltimore fragment is unknown. Certainly it came from a sizeable fresco, probably in Florence or in a neighboring town, the principal sites of Gaddi's late works. It remains an accomplished passage of painting which is now the only record of a work, perhaps once of considerable importance, designed by Agnolo Gaddi.

Bruce Cole
Indiana University,
Bloomington, Indiana

NOTES

1. See, for example, the many figures holding scrolls in Gaddi's *True Cross* frescoes in Santa Croce, Florence. For illustrations, see B. Cole, *Agnolo Gaddi* (Oxford: Oxford University Press, 1977), pls. 26–33.
2. For the iconography of saints in the Trecento, see G. Kaftal, *The Iconography of the Saints in Tuscan Painting* (Florence: G. C. Sansoni, 1952).
3. For Agnolo Gaddi, see R. Salvini, *L'arte di Agnolo Gaddi* (Florence: G. C. Sansoni, 1936), and Cole, *Agnolo Gaddi*.
4. On Taddeo, see P. Donati, *Taddeo Gaddi* (Florence: Sadea, 1966), and R. Oertel, *Early Italian Painting to 1400* (New York: Praeger, 1968), pp. 187–92.
5. For Orcagna, see R. Offner, *A Critical and Historical Corpus of Florentine Painting* (New York: New York University, 1962), sec. 4, vol. 1. On Nardo, see ibid. (1960), sec. 4, vol. 2.
6. For the art of the mid-Trecento, see M. Meiss, *Painting in Florence and Siena after the Black Death* (New York: Harper & Row, 1964), and B. Cole, *Giotto and Florentine Painting 1280–1375* (New York: Harper & Row, 1976).
7. For this generation of painters, see Cole, *Giotto and Florentine Painting*, pp. 121–45.
8. On the Cappella Maggiore, see Cole, *Agnolo Gaddi*, pp. 79–81.
9. For an English translation of *The Golden Legend*, see Jacobus de Voragine, *The Golden Legend*, trans. G. Ryan and H. Ripperger (London: Longmans, Green and Co., 1941; reprint ed., New York: Arno Press, 1969).
10. For Piero's frescoes, see K. Clark, *Piero della Francesca*, 2nd ed., rev. (London: Phaidon Press, 1969).
11. On Lorenzo Monaco, see O. Sirén, *Don Lorenzo Monaco* (Strasbourg: Heitz, 1905).
12. On the problem of workshop collaboration in fresco, see B. Cole, "Some Sinopie by Taddeo Gaddi Reconsidered," *Pantheon* 34 (1976):99–102.
13. For the National Gallery *Coronation*, see Cole, *Agnolo Gaddi*, p. 83; for the Berlin polyptych, see ibid., p. 75.
14. On the Contini Bonacossi altarpiece, see Cole, *Agnolo Gaddi*, pp. 76–77.

SELECTED BIBLIOGRAPHY

Joseph Archer Crowe and Giovanni Battista Cavalcaselle. *A New History of Painting in Italy from the Second to the Sixteenth Century*. 3 vols. London: J. Murray, 1864–1866.

Raimond van Marle. *The Development of the Italian Schools of Painting*. 19 vols. The Hague: Martinus Nijhoff, 1923–1938.

Richard Offner. *Studies in Florentine Painting: The Fourteenth Century*. New York: F. F. Sherman, 1927. Reprint edition. New York: Junius Press, 1972.

Richard Offner. *A Critical and Historical Corpus of Florentine Painting*. 4 sections. New York: New York University, 1930–1969.

Roberto Salvini. *L'arte di Agnolo Gaddi*. Florence: G. C. Sansoni, 1936.

Pietro Toesca. *Il Trecento*. Turin: Unione tipograficoeditrice torinese, 1951.

Bernard Berenson. *Italian Pictures of the Renaissance: Florentine School*. 2 vols. London: Phaidon Press, 1963.

Millard Meiss. *Painting in Florence and Siena after the Black Death*. New York: Harper & Row, 1964.

John White. *Art and Architecture in Italy: 1250–1400*. Harmondsworth and Baltimore: Penguin Books, 1966.

Robert Oertel. *Early Italian Painting to 1400*. New York: Praeger, 1968.

Bruce Cole. *Giotto and Florentine Painting 1280–1375*. New York: Harper & Row, 1976.

Bruce Cole. *Agnolo Gaddi*. Oxford: Oxford University Press, 1977.

Bruce Cole. *Masaccio and the Art of Early Renaissance Florence*. Bloomington: Indiana University Press, 1980.

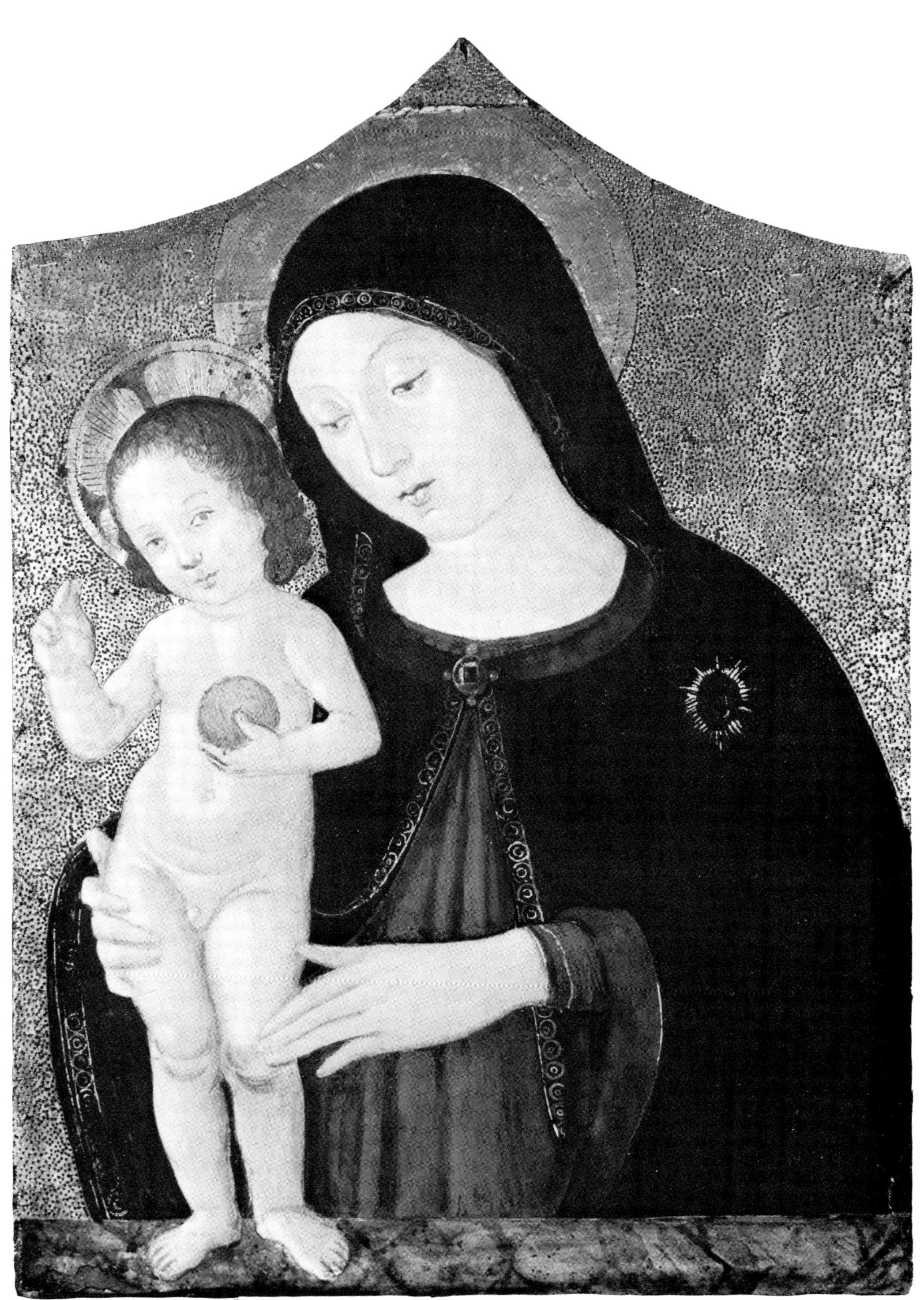

Attributed to
ANTONIAZZO ROMANO (active 1461–1505)
(Antonio di Benedetto Aquilio)

3. *Madonna and Child,* ca. 1480–1490

Tempera on wood. 17⅞ × 13 inches (45.4 × 33 cm.)
The Jacob Epstein Collection (BMA 51.121)

PROVENANCE

Eugenio Ventura, Florence
Acquired by Jacob Epstein, Baltimore
Loaned by Jacob Epstein to The Baltimore Museum of Art in 1932 and bequeathed in 1951

CONDITION

In a conservation treatment prior to entering the Museum's collection, this panel was trimmed on all edges, thinned, cradled, and stained on the reverse with a dark color. The contour of the upper edge of the panel was altered. Two curved pieces were cut away from the upper corners, and a small triangular piece reserved from the excised portion was glued in place to make up the central point. This can be seen on the surface of the painting where the circular pattern of the Virgin's tooled halo is interrupted.

During recent treatment (1979), very discolored varnish layers were removed along with much repaint. The painting had been overcleaned at some time in the past, leaving the original paint very thin in some areas, i.e., the flesh tones, the Virgin's mantle above her forehead, and the border of her left sleeve. Much of the gold decorative border on the Virgin's mantle is a replacement; however, it approximates the original decoration seen at the lower left. The paint of the Virgin's red dress is not original, but there is evidence of a red glaze over a white layer at the neckline of her robe. The final work on this painting included the inpainting of major losses and also the application of a thin, warm-toned glaze over the *terre verte* underpainting of the flesh tones. This glaze is very transparent in order to allow the original underdrawing to be seen.

Sian Jones
The Walters Art Gallery, Baltimore

The stylistic and thematic traits of the *Madonna and Child* (cat. no. 3) bear unmistakable identification with the work of Antoniazzo Romano, a painter active primarily in Rome from 1461 to 1505.[1] The panel would seem to date from the 1480's, a period of extensive productivity for Antoniazzo. His signed works from that decade demonstrate a uniformly high quality marked by the fusion of various artistic trends. While half-length images of the Madonna and Child proliferated in Rome during the last quarter of the fifteenth century, certain characteristics of the Baltimore panel point to the hand of Antoniazzo as the sole master capable of uniting such divergent aspects as the gold-tooled background, the sweet and subtle modulation of the Madonna's face, and, particularly, the more robust body and lively interpretation of the Infant Christ.

Antoniazzo is first documented in 1461 when he was commissioned by Alessandro Sforza to execute a copy, now lost, of the miraculous image of the *Madonna of St. Luke* of Santa Maria Maggiore.[2] Although no earlier record of Antoniazzo's activity survives, he must at that time already have received considerable recognition, and during this same year Alessandro Sforza commissioned a second copy of a miraculous Madonna painting, that of Santa Maria del Popolo, from another promising young artist, Melozzo da Forlì.[3] After 1462 Antoniazzo entered the employ of the popes, and except for a brief period from 1471 to 1474, when his name is not mentioned, he remained active in Rome. An indication of his prominence dates from 1478 with the signing of the statutes of the Corporation of St. Luke.[4] Antoniazzo and two lesser known artists signed the statutes which established a company of painters, formed initially by more than thirty members. His continued presence in Rome during the 1480's is assured by his documented participation in the decoration of the Vatican Palace. During this decade Antoniazzo's influence was felt also in the outlying areas of Velletri and Capua, as it had spread to Fondi by the end of the 1470's and to Bracciano by the early 1490's. In order to accept this last commission for the fresco decoration of the Orsini Castle in Bracciano, Antoniazzo declined the invitation to complete the fresco cycle of the Chapel of San Brizio in the Cathedral of Orvieto in 1491. While accounts of his activity during the 1490's are rather sparse, Rome seems to have remained the center of his operations.[5] Documentation testifies to commissions received by Antoniazzo for the fresco decoration of the major fifteenth-century churches in Rome: Santi Apostoli in 1464–1465, Santa Maria della Consolazione in 1470, San Giacomo degli Spagnoli in 1486, Santa Maria della Pace in 1491, Sant' Agostino in 1496. The final years of Antoniazzo's life show a marked decline in his productivity. His last known painting, the triptych in Santa Maria Assunta, Castelnuovo di Porto (Latium), dates from 1501, and in 1505 he painted a gonfalon for the Confraternity of St. Anthony of Padua in Rieti. He died sometime before September 12, 1512.[6]

The dating of the Baltimore *Madonna and Child* to the 1480's places the work within the period of the artist's maturity. Antoniazzo's first certain, surviving work, the triptych of the Museo Civico, Rieti (signed and dated 1464), reveals the earliest signs of a distinctive painter of the nascent Roman school. The conventionalized composition, the unsure modeling of the figures, and the stiff poses diminished during the following decade as the artist increasingly came into contact with his contemporaries from the north. In 1475 Antoniazzo collaborated with Domenico and Davide Ghirlandaio in the decoration of the Vatican Library. By 1478 he surely felt the influence of prominent Umbrian artists such as Perugino, who had assumed the leading role in the decoration of the Sistine Chapel. In 1479 came his first certain contact with Melozzo da Forlì.[7] Thus by the 1480's Antoniazzo's style had reached a decisive stage of development in which a new monumentality of form was combined with the more archaic features of his youthful works. In the central panel of the triptych at San Pietro, Fondi (signed by the

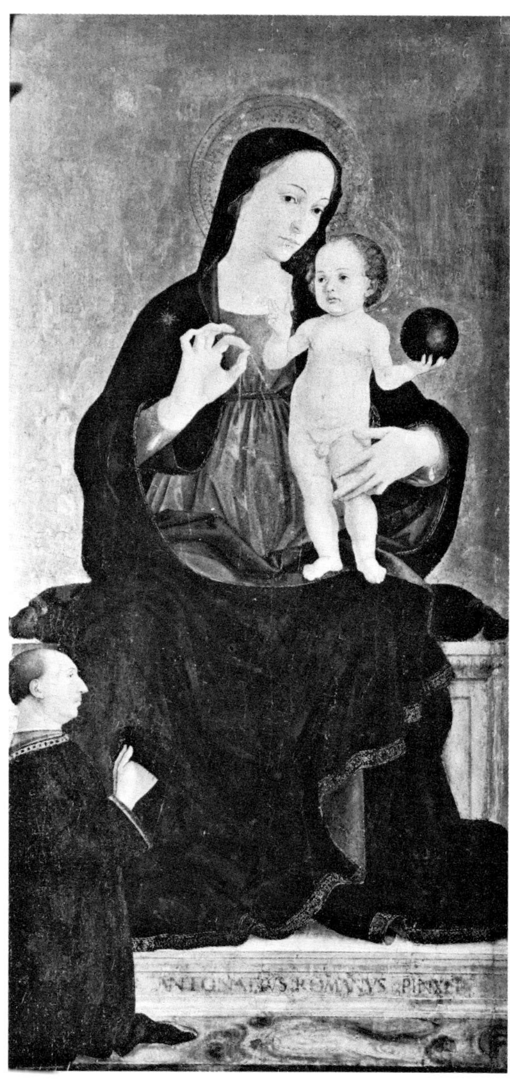

Fig. 1. Antoniazzo Romano, *Madonna and Child*. Tempera on wood. Gaetani Triptych, San Pietro, Fondi. Courtesy Istituto Centrale per il Catalogo e la Documentazione, Rome

painter and produced between 1474 and 1479), the interlocking forms of the Virgin and Child create a sense of spaciousness and naturalism which contrasts with the gilt background and conventional pose of the donor at the lower left (fig. 1). This work heralds the many Madonna images produced by Antoniazzo during the 1480's which frequently consisted of reduced versions of larger altarpieces with the central figures of the Madonna and Child occupying the whole forefront. Often the Madonna supports the Christ Child as He stands on a parapet in the act of blessing, as in the panel in the Museo del Duomo, Velletri.[8] Variants on the theme occur in compositions where the Madonna introduces the recumbent Infant or adores Him, often in the company of St. John.[9]

Antoniazzo's reputation as a painter of the Madonna and Child was clearly established early in his career with the replica of the *Madonna of St. Luke* in 1461. This work and Melozzo's version of the miraculous Madonna image of Santa Maria del Popolo, executed in the same year, may have served as prototypes, or at least acted as stimuli for the production of numerous panels by lesser masters active in the Roman school. All of these Madonna images derive from the panel of the *Madonna of St. Luke,* executed in the

Byzantine manner of the thirteenth century. These works are identifiable in terms of the similar grouping of the figures: the half-length Madonna, the Christ Child seated on the Madonna's left arm with His right hand raised in the gesture of blessing. The clothing of the Madonna varies, but the robes of the Christ Child are uniformly decorated with gold striations, presumably in emulation of the Byzantine prototype. Antoniazzo himself reproduced a noteworthy version in a fresco of the *Madonna Enthroned* in the Velletri Cathedral (signed and dated 1486).[10] Indeed, miraculous images of the Madonna represented a recurring theme in Antoniazzo's oeuvre, and the following, all in Rome, have been attributed to his hand: the Madonnas of Santa Maria della Consolazione (ca. 1470), San Nicola in Carcere (ca. 1470), Santi Apostoli (before 1472), Santa Maria in Cosmedin (date unknown), Santa Maria del Buonaiuto (ca. 1476). He later executed the *Madonna delle Grazie* on canvas now at the Pio Sodalizio dei Piceni, Rome (signed and dated 1494), which reproduces the style and type of the earlier unsigned works.[11]

Although not directly derived from the *Madonna of St. Luke,* the Baltimore *Madonna and Child* recalls a type common to Roman painting of the last quarter of the fifteenth century. The Madonna retains the traditional emblems of the *Mater Amabilis,* the half-length Virgin who introduces the Infant Jesus. She wears a deep blue mantle lined in green and a red undergarment, the colors associated with faith, hope, and charity. On her left shoulder appears the star, the symbol of the *Stella Maris.*[12] The erect figure of the Infant is similarly conventionalized. He blesses with His right hand and in His left holds a golden orb.

The small size of the panel suggests its original function as an object of devotion, either for a private household or as a votive offering for a church. Both Madonna and Child appear parallel to the picture plane, with the body of the Madonna positioned behind the simulated marble parapet of the foreground on which the Infant Christ stands. His gesture and gaze intrude directly into the spectator's space, in contrast to the withdrawn, downcast gaze of the Madonna. The overall impression of immediacy resulting from the artist's concentration on the intimate aspects of the composition differs from the more hieratic attributes of the *Madonna of St. Luke* which had been popularized by Antoniazzo and his circle after 1461. Yet significant signs of this type linger in the Baltimore panel, indications of Antoniazzo's hand. Tendencies toward abstraction persist in the treatment of space where the tooled gold background seems at once to isolate the figures by denying the depth of the picture plane and to refer to Byzantine or hieratic prototypes. Even more distinctly connected with Antoniazzo's own oeuvre is the handling of the Madonna's features. The smooth oval face, almond-shaped eyes, finely arched brows, straight nose, and rounded chin evoke the Byzantine type of Madonna present in the numerous copies of the *Madonna of St. Luke.* No other artist so consistently produced Madonnas of the same type.

To be sure, few of these small devotional images are signed by the master, and thus support for the attribution of the Baltimore *Madonna and Child* to Antoniazzo lies in its similarity to documented altarpieces which were produced contemporaneously. These large works must have served as models for the derivative panels, a corpus of which has been assigned to Antoniazzo.[13] Close to the Baltimore *Madonna and Child* are the central figures of the Barberini altarpiece (signed and dated 1488), Galleria Nazionale, Rome (fig. 2).[14] As befitting a work of more monumental proportions, the full-length figure of the Madonna is enthroned and gazes toward the viewer. The partially draped Christ Child stands on her knee and extends His right hand in a gesture of blessing. The decorative details of the Barberini *Madonna and Child* are more ornate than those of the Baltimore panel: the gilt pattern on the robe of the Madonna and on the border of her cloak is lavish, and there is an elaborate tooling of the halos. Nevertheless, the facial features of the Madonna bear a striking similarity to the Baltimore panel, as do her hands, with

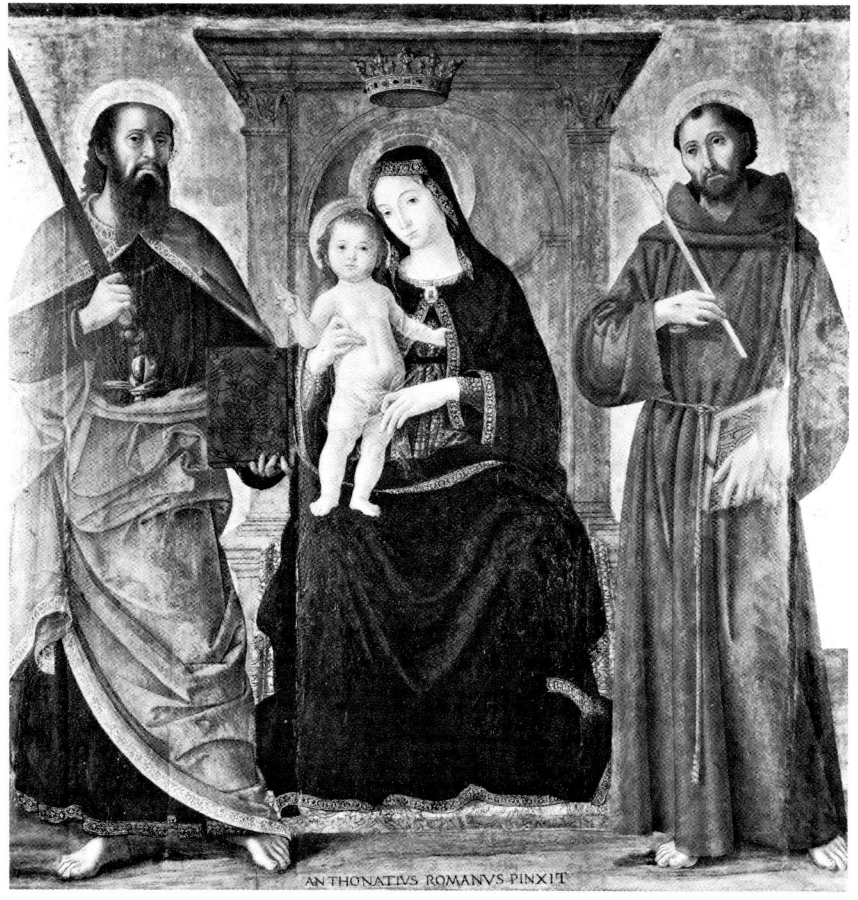

Fig. 2. Antoniazzo Romano, *Madonna and Child Enthroned with Saints Paul and Francis.* Tempera on wood. Galleria Nazionale, Palazzo Barberini, Rome. Courtesy Istituto Centrale per il Catalogo e la Documentazione, Rome

tapering fingers flexed in an elegant and nearly inanimate position. The Christ Child of the Barberini altar, as was typical of this advanced stage of Antoniazzo's development, assumes a vital attitude. His hip slung to one side, the fully modeled body and almost playful gesture in grasping the Madonna's cloak recall the Infant of the Baltimore panel. This contrast between the tendency toward abstraction in the rendition of the Madonna and the three-dimensionality of the Infant Christ remains constant in Antoniazzo's paintings of the 1480's.

The influence of Umbrian painting on local Roman schools may account for Antoniazzo's progressive readiness to incorporate more naturalistic elements into his compositions. The Baltimore panel, in fact, bears strong compositional ties to a group of half-length Madonna and Child paintings which otherwise demonstrate distinct Umbrian characteristics. Among them are, or were, paintings from the following collections: the D. F. Platt Estate, Englewood, New Jersey (22 × 15 inches); formerly Countess Sala Collection, New York (22¾ × 14⅜ inches); formerly Mackley Gallery, London (17 × 10 inches, fig. 3); Museo Nazionale, Naples (dated 1484; 30⅝ × 17 11/16 inches).[15] While the attributes and clothing of the Infant Christ vary, each composition preserves the essential elements of the image: the downcast gaze of the Madonna, the full-figured Christ Child in the act of blessing, the parapet in the foreground, and the gilt

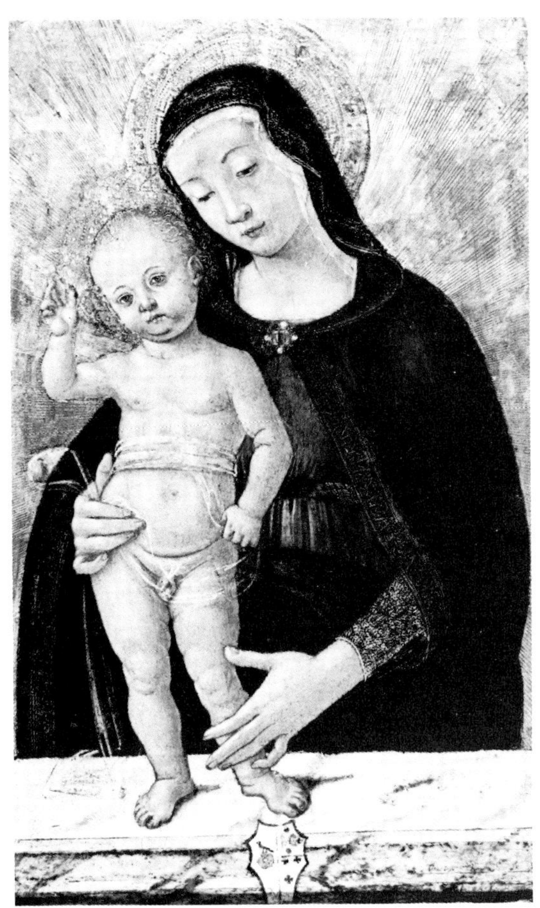

Fig. 3. Fiorenzo di Lorenzo (attributed), *Madonna and Child*. Oil on wood. 17 × 10 inches (43.1 × 25.4 cm.). Formerly Mackley Gallery, London. Courtesy Mackley Gallery, London

background. The attribution of these panels is tentative and their provenance remains unclear, although ties with Umbrian painters, specifically with Fiorenzo di Lorenzo, seem undeniable. Attributed alternately to Fiorenzo di Lorenzo and Antoniazzo Romano, a triptych of the *Madonna and Child with Saints* in the Pinacoteca, Terni (dated 1485) illustrates this fusion of Umbrian and Roman traits.[16] The central figure of the Madonna, gazing tenderly at the standing Infant on her knee, provides an example of the type of model employed by the artists of the smaller devotional panels. Certain features remain constant: the general pose, the gold background, the brooch on the Madonna's robe, and, most significantly, the plump body of the Infant. Although Antoniazzo's documented activity is limited to Latium through the 1480's, contact with Umbrian painters, if not with Fiorenzo di Lorenzo, the leading master of Perugia, may well account for the intrusion of these stylistic traits—specifically the well-modeled Christ Child—in the Baltimore panel.[17] On the other hand, the Baltimore panel reveals the stylistic signature of Antoniazzo, particularly in the figure of the Madonna. Her torso lacks the full-bodied, tapering shape of the Umbrian models and her facial features retain the more flattened, abstracted expression common to Antoniazzo's archaizing types. The Baltimore *Madonna and Child* remains a composite of the retrogressive and progressive tendencies prevalent in Rome in the 1480's, subtly merged by the leading native master, Antoniazzo Romano.

Eunice D. Howe
University of Southern California,
Los Angeles

NOTES

1. Published opinions of the Baltimore *Madonna and Child* include the following (see Selected Bibliography): R. van Marle, Antoniazzo; B. Berenson, Antoniazzo (?); B. Fredericksen and F. Zeri, Follower of Antoniazzo. In a letter of January 27, 1976, to G. Rosenthal, Zeri suggested an Umbrian Follower of Antoniazzo (curatorial files, The Baltimore Museum of Art).
2. For the chronology of Antoniazzo's career, and the dating of the works mentioned below, see F. Negri Arnoldi, "Madonne giovanili di Antoniazzo Romano," *Commentari* 15 (1964):202–12; Negri Arnoldi, "Maturità di Antoniazzo," *Commentari* 16 (1965):225–44; R. van Marle, *The Development of the Italian Schools of Painting* (The Hague: Martinus Nijhoff, 1934), 15:244–304. Additional works are cited in B. Berenson, *Italian Pictures of the Renaissance: Central and North Italian Schools* (London: Phaidon Press, 1968), 1:14–18. For biographical documentation of the artist, see A. Bertolotti, "Der Maler Antonazzo von Rom und seine Familie," *Repertorium für Kunstwissenschaft* 6 (1883):215–33.
3. These important commissions from the Sforza Duke are commemorated by contemporary epigrams. Antoniazzo's copy of the *Madonna of St. Luke* surely played a crucial role in the dissemination of the type. Negri Arnoldi, "Madonne giovanili," p. 207; Bertolotti, "Der Maler Antonazzo," p. 218.
4. E. Müntz, *Les arts à la cour des papes pendant le XVe et le XVIe siècle*, Bibliothèque des Écoles Françaises d'Athènes et de Rome 28 (Paris: E. Thorin, 1878–1882), 3, sec. 1:101–111.
5. Secure works from this decade are: *Madonna and Child,* Sodalizio dei Piceni, Rome (signed and dated 1494); *Madonna Enthroned,* formerly Louvre, now Museum of Le Mans (signed and dated 1494); *Madonna and Child,* Museo Civico, Viterbo (signed and dated 1497).
6. The exact date of his death is unknown. Antoniazzo's will was drawn on March 23, 1508, but actual evidence of death does not appear until 1512. Bertolotti, "Der Maler Antonazzo," pp. 223–25.
7. The date of this significant encounter has been reexamined by Negri Arnoldi, "Madonne giovanili," pp. 209–10.
8. This panel, often confused with the fresco of the *Madonna Enthroned* in the Velletri Cathedral (signed and dated 1486), has been attributed to Antoniazzo and to ca. 1482 by Negri Arnoldi, "Maturità," pp. 232–33.
9. These works are, however, executed in a style quite distinct from the previous group and may depend on an earlier prototype. Among the best known examples are: the *Benson Madonna,* Norton Simon Museum of Art, Inc., Pasadena, and the *Madonna and Child with Little Saint John,* Fogg Art Museum, Cambridge, Mass. (1924.23). For further discussion, see F. Zeri, *Italian Paintings in the Walters Art Gallery,* 2 vols. (Baltimore: The Walters Art Gallery, 1976), 1:164–65.
10. Reproduced in V. Golzio and G. Zander, *L'Arte in Roma nel secolo XV* (Bologna: Licinio Cappelli, 1968), pl. 158, 1.
11. Ibid., pl. 167, 1. For the attribution and dating of the miraculous Madonna paintings, see Negri Arnoldi, "Madonne giovanili," pp. 203–208.
12. For alternate interpretations of the star as a symbol of the Madonna, see Y. Hirn, *The Sacred Shrine* (1912; reprint ed., Boston: Beacon Press, 1957), p. 465.
13. The list is too long to enumerate here, but two superior examples of derivative *Madonna and Child* panels assigned to Antoniazzo are those in The Detroit Institute of Arts (van Marle, *Development of the Italian Schools,* 15: pl. facing p. 250) and the Galleria Nazionale, Perugia (ibid., p. 250).
14. The central groups of the following altars may be associated with the *Madonna and Child* of the Barberini panel, and hence with the same period of Antoniazzo's career: *Madonna of the Rota,* Vatican Pinacoteca, Rome (attributed to Antoniazzo and to ca. 1486–1488); *Madonna and Child with Saints Francis and Anthony,* Sant' Antonio dei Portoghesi, Rome (attributed to Antoniazzo); *Madonna and Child with Saints,* Convent of Santi Giovanni e Paolo, Rome (unpublished).
15. The first two panels have been assigned to the shop of Antoniazzo and to Antoniazzo, respectively. The London *Madonna and Child* carries an attribution to Fiorenzo di Lorenzo, an opinion which is supported by the coat of arms at the base of the painting belonging to a contemporary Perugian family. The Naples *Madonna and Child,* which is the most elaborate of the group and bears an inscription of 1484, has been attributed variously to Bartolomeo Caporali, Fiorenzo di Lorenzo, and Antoniazzo.
16. For a discussion of the attribution, see P. Hendy, "Antoniazzo Romano. A Group of Paintings, 1475–1485." *Art in America* 21, no. 1 (December 1932):2–14.
17. Fiorenzo was active in Perugia during the 1470's, although his earliest surviving painting, the altarpiece from San Francesco, Perugia, dates from 1487. As there is no evidence that the Umbrian master traveled to Rome or that Antoniazzo ever traveled to Perugia, contact between the two artists remains hypothetical. Hendy, "Antoniazzo," pp. 10–14.

SELECTED BIBLIOGRAPHY

Antonino Bertolotti. "Der Maler Antonazzo von Rom und seine Familie." *Repertorium für Kunstwissenschaft* 6 (1833):215–33.

Herbert E. Everett. "Antoniazzo Romano." *American Journal of Archaeology*, 2nd ser., 11 (1907):279–306.

Philip Hendy. "Antoniazzo Romano. A Group of Paintings, 1475–1485." *Art in America* 21, no. 1 (December 1932):2–14.

Raimond van Marle. *The Development of the Italian Schools of Painting*. 19 vols. The Hague: Martinus Nijhoff, 1923–1938.

The Jacob Epstein Collection in The Baltimore Museum of Art. Baltimore: Published by Jacob Epstein, 1939.

Rezio Buscaroli. *Melozzo ed il Melozzismo*. Bologna: Athena, 1955.

Francesco Negri Arnoldi. "Madonne giovanili di Antoniazzo Romano." *Commentari* 15 (1964):202–12.

Francesco Negri Arnoldi. "Maturità di Antoniazzo." *Commentari* 16 (1965):225–44.

Bernard Berenson. *Italian Pictures of the Renaissance: Central and North Italian Schools*. 3 vols. London: Phaidon Press, 1968.

Vincenzo Golzio and Giuseppe Zander. *L'Arte in Roma nel secolo XV*. Bologna: Licinio Cappelli, 1968.

Burton B. Fredericksen and Federico Zeri. *Census of Pre-Nineteenth-Century Italian Paintings in North American Public Collections*. Cambridge, Mass.: Harvard University Press, 1972.

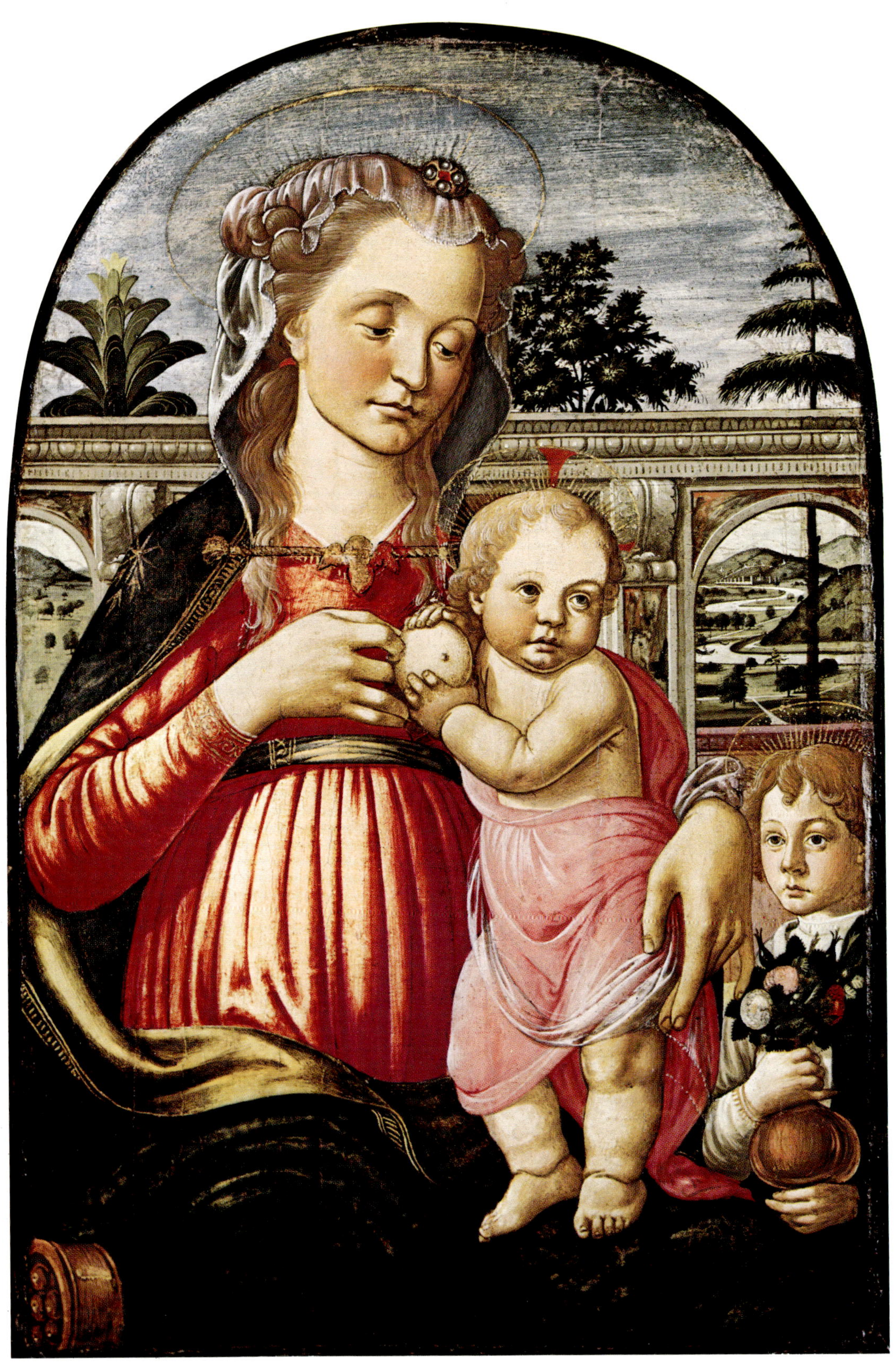

BIAGIO DI ANTONIO (active ca. 1465–1504)

4. *Madonna and Child with an Angel,* ca. 1470–1472

Tempera on wood. 27½ × 18½ inches (69.3 × 46.4 cm.)
The Jacob Epstein Collection (BMA 51.120)

PROVENANCE

Dr. Benedict & Co., Berlin, 1928
Advertisement in *Pantheon,* 1928

Ehrich Galleries, New York

Purchased by Newhouse Galleries, New York

Acquired by Jacob Epstein, Baltimore, in 1931

On the back of the panel is an old inscription in ink, "Philippe Lippi 1472 474" (some further marks are illegible), which might be taken to mean that the picture was once in a French collection.

CONDITION

Before its acquisition by the Museum it seems likely that this panel by Biagio was slightly cut down to accommodate four narrow (3/8 to 3/4 inch; 0.9 × 1.8 cm.) strips of oak that were attached to the sides of the painting. Open worm tunnels, bisected when the panel was trimmed, can be seen on the right edge. The gesso and gold paint outside the arched upper perimeter were added to cover the join with the new wood. The panel has been weakened by extensive insect damage, particularly in the center. The wood is desiccated and numerous splits run vertically, parallel to the grain. Traces of two battens, now missing, run horizontally across the grain. At some time in the past, seven oak butterfly battens were sunk into the panel from the reverse to rejoin splits; areas of worm damage were filled with a dense putty.

Removal in 1980 of severely discolored varnish and overpainting revealed relatively little loss. Aside from minor abrasion, the most extensive damage was found in the gold-leafed areas and in the Virgin's blue robe. The halos and details in the Virgin's costume were originally modeled in gesso and gilded. Most of the modeling has been lost, and the gold has been regilded in the past at least twice, once with gold leaf and once with powdered gold paint. Further embellishments, such as the inner rays of the Virgin's halo, were added during earlier treatments. Abrasion in the Virgin's robe and traces of insoluable repaint have resulted in a mottled appearance. For the most part the flesh tones, the Madonna's headdress, the Child's tunic, the wall and the trees behind it are well preserved.

After this recent treatment, only the relatively few areas of complete paint loss were inpainted and the severe abrasions were lightly toned.

E. Melanie Gifford
The Walters Art Gallery, Baltimore

Accustomed to look for originality in art, we may be surprised by Vasari's account of how Renaissance artists developed. The artists whose biographies make up the *Lives* evolved their styles, according to Vasari, by acquiring and adapting other artists' manners.[1] Indeed taking into account the majority of works of art produced during the Renaissance, it becomes clear that, as in any other period, imitation far outweighed invention. Having thus acknowledged the large role that sources played in the creative process of a Renaissance artist, we are in a position to appreciate such a genuinely interesting figure as Biagio di Antonio, whose work is a barometer of the artistic climate in Florence in the last third of the fifteenth century. He seems to have attached himself in turn to the leading masters of the time: first Pesellino (d. 1457) and Pollaiuolo, then Verrocchio, and finally Domenico Ghirlandaio.

Modern connoisseurs, including Berenson, brought together a group of stylistically consistent paintings which they attributed to a certain Giovanni Battista Utili, active in the town of Faenza. Later, Utili was identified as Giovanni Battista Bertucci, whose paintings are different in style from those originally attributed to Utili. Eventually it was discovered that the true author of the group first given to Utili was Biagio di Antonio, a Florentine painter already mentioned, who was recorded in Faenza in 1476, 1483, and again in 1504.[2] The documented works and others in Biagio's mature style are easily recognized: they identify him as a follower of Ghirlandaio.[3] But his earlier pictures, those made before 1476, have continued to pose problems for scholars seeking to explain his development.[4] The early works are mainly dependent upon Verrocchio, the pre-eminent painter-sculptor in Florence in the 1470's in whose workshop Biagio must have been employed. They differ enough from Biagio's later pictures that some scholars have attributed one or another of them to other artists from Verrocchio's circle, like Botticini, or even to the master himself.[5]

When the Baltimore *Madonna and Child with an Angel* was acquired by Jacob Epstein it was ascribed to Botticini.[6] Though incorrect, this attribution is better than the one to Filippo Lippi (or Filippino), recorded in an old inscription on the back of the panel. Botticini and Biagio di Antonio were contemporaries, and their development was parallel in relation to Verrocchio. Berenson included the Baltimore *Madonna* among the series he designated as "Utili," in other words, as Biagio di Antonio,[7] and his attribution has been accepted by Everett Fahy and by Federico Zeri.[8] There are, in fact, many similarities of type and motif between the Baltimore painting and such documented works by Biagio as the *Madonna and Child Enthroned with Angels and Saints* of 1483, now in the Pinacoteca in Faenza.[9] Konrad Oberhuber, however, recently expressed doubts about Biagio's authorship of the Baltimore picture, preferring to give it instead to an anonymous follower of Verrocchio.[10] Thus, to determine whether the Baltimore painting is by Biagio di Antonio, it will be necessary to establish a sequence of those works generally accepted as his. Into such a sequence, the Baltimore picture, if by Biagio, ought to fit. In the case of this eclectic artist we need to identify consistent traits in each of his works that remain constant despite his changing attachments to the great masters.

We begin with Biagio's first extant documented work, the *Adoration of the Child with Saints and Donors* (fig. 1), ordered by the Ragnoli family for the church of S. Michele in Faenza and now in the Kress Collection at the Philbrook Art Center, Tulsa.[11] Berenson wrote on the back of a photograph of this altarpiece that it was the artist's "masterpiece, still close to Verrocchio." Yet, as Zeri has observed, by the time this picture was painted, ca. 1476, Biagio was already influenced by the young Ghirlandaio, even though that artist was probably his junior.[12] We detect this influence in Biagio's marked simplification of Verrocchio's modeling, shapes, and types. Corresponding to the change in form is a change in expression from Verrocchio's overrefined delicacy of feeling to the less

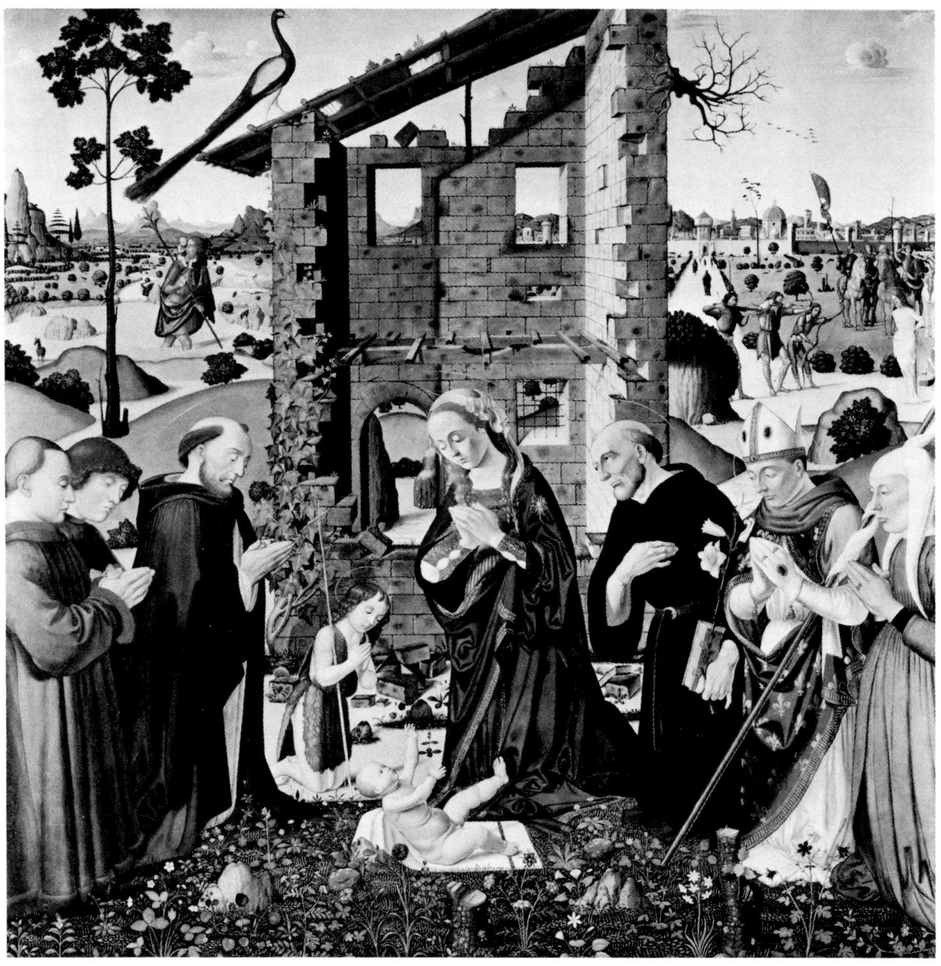

Fig. 1. Biagio di Antonio, *Adoration of the Child with Saints and Donors.* Tempera on wood. 73 × 71¼ inches (185.4 × 181 cm.). Philbrook Art Center, Samuel H. Kress Collection, Tulsa, Oklahoma

sophisticated mood of Ghirlandaio.[13] Though he was encouraged in this simplifying process by the example of Ghirlandaio, Biagio carried it much further.

A little less than a decade may separate the Tulsa altarpiece of ca. 1476 from the *Madonna and Child with an Angel* (fig. 2) in the Kress Collection in Ponce, Puerto Rico.[14] Though the panel has been catalogued as "Florentine School,"[15] it is, in my opinion, one of Biagio's earliest works, antedating his close association with Verrocchio.[16] The rose hedge behind the figures recalls Pesellino and his imitators. As for the figures themselves, their facial types, elongated proportions, and angular draperies more nearly resemble those of Pollaiuolo to whom the painting once was attributed. Though at first glance details in the painting in Ponce seem to be rendered as Pollaiuolo would have done, with great finesse, closer inspection reveals that they are treated rather mechanically. The regular highlights on the hair, for instance, or the emphasis on facial and bodily contours betray that the artist's basic impulse was to simplify, not to elaborate, and that he was here working in a manner which may not have been entirely congenial to him. The outlining that we find in this and other early works by Biagio is generally characteristic of the host of Pesellino imitators; and the way in which Pesellino's models were

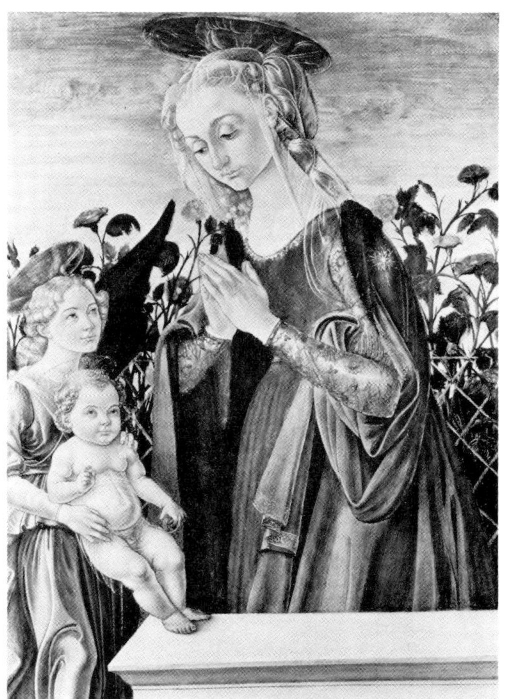

Fig. 2. Biagio di Antonio, *Madonna and Child with an Angel*. Tempera on wood. 27¼ × 19⅜ inches (69.2 × 49.2 cm.). Museo De Arte De Ponce, Kress Study Collection, Ponce, Puerto Rico

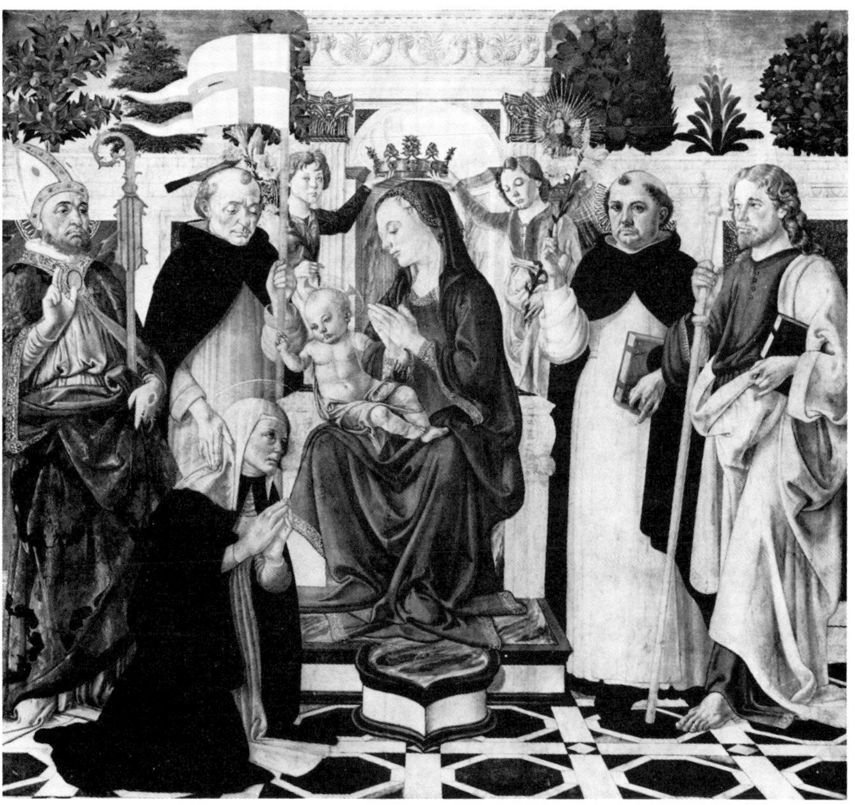

Fig. 3. Biagio di Antonio, *Madonna and Child Enthroned with Saints*. Tempera on wood. 66⅛ × 69⅞ inches (168 × 177.5 cm.). Museum of Fine Arts, Budapest

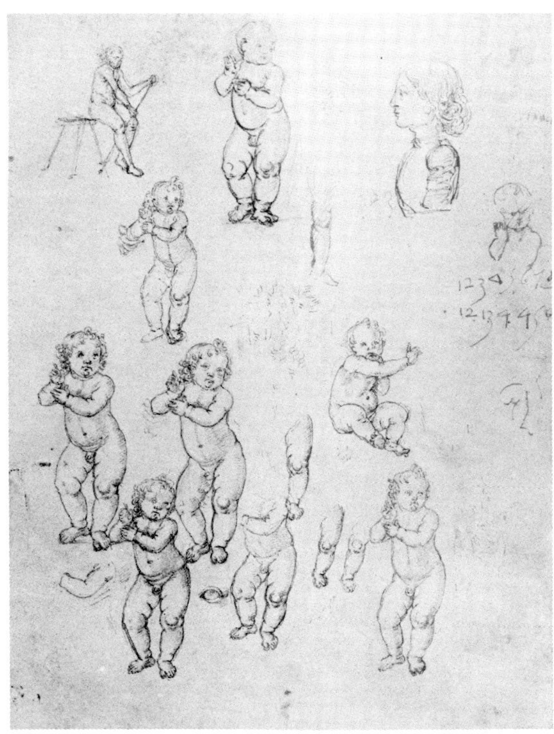

Fig. 4. Attributed to Francesco di Simone, *Studies of the Christ Child*. Pen and ink on paper. 10 × 7¼ inches (25.5 × 18.5 cm.). The British Museum, London. Courtesy of the Trustees, The British Museum

schematized may have had a strong and lasting effect on Biagio di Antonio's own approach to sources.[17] Other idiosyncrasies marking the picture are the way the hair of the Madonna and of the angel is reflected in their halos; the ruddy flesh tones; and the imprecise drawing of the ledge on which the Christ Child stands. The Child is shown leaning backward in a pose that the artist must have adapted from that of a recumbent infant, perhaps the one in his contemporary *Madonna Adoring the Child* in the Ringling Museum in Sarasota, equally indebted to Pollaiuolo.[18]

Not long after the Ponce *Madonna* of the late 1460's, Biagio di Antonio completed the much discussed altarpiece from the church of S. Domenico del Maglio in Florence (fig. 3), now in the Museum of Fine Arts, Budapest.[19] This *sacra conversazione* is high enough in quality to have been recently ascribed to Verrocchio, and indeed it was given to Verrocchio by Vasari.[20] Nevertheless, certain shortcomings seem to indicate that, whatever role Verrocchio may have played as head of the workshop in which it was made, the picture was painted by a young and relatively inexperienced assistant, namely Biagio. The ruddy complexions, the outlined facial features and hands, the stiff postures, and the angular draperies, even a detail such as the Child hanging off balance on His mother's arm link this picture with the one in Ponce. Berenson related the Madonna's head in near-profile to that in a Verrocchiesque drawing in the Uffizi, which he then attributed, like the altarpiece itself, to "Utili."[21] Though the drawing, pricked for transfer, does not exactly correspond to this or any other Madonna by Biagio, the relation is undeniable and serves to show the new stylistic orientation of Biagio's work around 1470 toward Verrocchio rather than Pesellino and Pollaiuolo. Also revealing Biagio's authorship is the Madonna's rather awkward sideways position. As Miklòs Boscovits has observed, it seems to have been derived from a kneeling attitude of the kind found in Biagio's

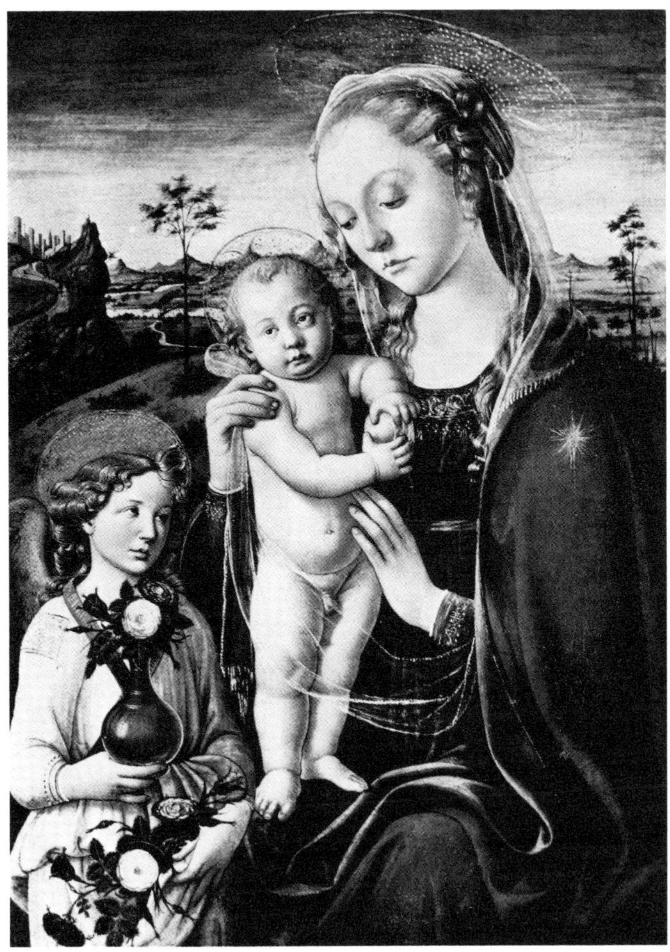

Fig. 5. Biagio di Antonio, *Madonna and Child with an Angel*. Tempera on wood. 29⅞ × 20⅞ inches (76 × 53 cm.). Museo Poldi-Pezzoli, Milan

contemporary *Madonna* in the National Gallery of Ireland, Dublin, in which the Child, lying on the ground, is adored by His mother.[22]

Close in style to the Budapest altarpiece is the *Madonna* in Baltimore. The dense figure compositions and sober, monumental air of both pictures seem to show an awareness on Biagio's part of the work of Andrea del Castagno (d. 1457), possibly through Verrocchio, who was himself influenced by the older master. The elaborately coiled and veiled headdress of the Baltimore *Madonna* recalls Verrocchio, as well as Pollaiuolo. Moreover, as with the Budapest altarpiece, a Verrocchiesque sheet of drawings can, in my opinion, be associated with the painting in Baltimore. The sheet, in the British Museum (fig. 4), attributed to an assistant of the master named Francesco di Simone, contains numerous studies of an infant whose facial type and *contrapposto* resemble those of the Child in the Baltimore picture.[23] The infant in the drawing makes a blessing gesture, whereas Biagio's rests His hands on His mother's breast.[24] Behind the figures are towering trees and an arched wall, unusual in a picture of this scale and probably derived from the Budapest altarpiece. Through the openings in the wall we glimpse a placid distant landscape which resembles the backgrounds of certain of Biagio's other early works.[25]

Representing a somewhat later moment in Biagio's early development is a *Madonna and Child with an Angel* (fig. 5) in the Museo Poldi-Pezzoli in Milan.[26] In contrast to the broad square face of the Baltimore *Madonna,* the features of her counterpart in Milan seem more refined and girlish. Significantly, the Madonna's smoothly rounded oval face in the Milan picture resembles more nearly that of the Madonna in the Tulsa *Adoration.* And the Child appears to be of the same mold too. Even the fall of the draperies is similar. Yet, despite the way it anticipates the Tulsa altarpiece and thus follows the Baltimore painting in Biagio's oeuvre, the *Madonna* in Milan, with its awkward foreshortening and unclear spatial relations, is still the work of a young artist striving to emulate the complex achievement of Verrocchio. The attitude of the Child is revealing. He stands stiffly on His mother's lap, placing His hands on her breast, in a pose apparently of Biagio's own invention. Comparison with the Baltimore *Madonna,* where the composition is reversed, shows how much more effectively the Child is balanced there, even though that painting is earlier. The reason is that the Baltimore Child is based, as we have seen, on a Verrocchiesque prototype. In the same way, in the Milan painting, the hands, again seemingly of Biagio's design, are flaccid and poorly drawn, whereas those of the Virgin in Baltimore are rendered in a more articulate, Verrocchiesque manner.

Thus, we can understand Biagio's dilemma: he had a keen eye and a considerable talent, but he lacked the ability to invent significant forms like those he imitated. Apart from his shortcomings, Biagio's own tendency as an artist was to simplify and schematize. Accordingly, in the painting in Ponce he failed to capture Pollaiuolo's refinement. Then, while working in Verrocchio's elaborate, painstaking manner, he seems to have been led to an awareness of Castagno's contribution to the monumental tradition of painting in Florence. Some such attraction to Castagno, or at least to that side of the early Verrocchio which was indebted to Castagno, is suggested by the Budapest altarpiece and by the Baltimore *Madonna.* Finally, when the young Ghirlandaio began to react against the excesses of Verrocchio's work, predictably enough Biagio followed, as we see in the Tulsa *Adoration.* Each in its own way, Biagio di Antonio's early paintings document his search for an appropriate model on which to base his style.

David Alan Brown
National Gallery of Art,
Washington, D.C.

NOTES

1. G. Vasari, *Le Vite de' più eccelenti pittori, scultori ed architettori,* ed. Gaetano Milanesi (Florence: G. C. Sansoni, 1878–1885).
2. The documents relating to Biagio di Antonio were published by C. Grigioni in *La Pittura Faentina dalle Origini alla Metà del Cinquecento* (Faenza: Fratelli Lega, 1935), pp. 194–219, 721–25. The most complete treatment of the artist is E. Golfieri and A. Corbara, "Biagio d'Antonio pittore fiorentino in Faenza," in *Atti e Memorie dell'Accademia Fiorentina. La Colombaria,* n.s. 1 (Florence, 1947): 435–54. For a summary of this difficult-to-find article, see A. Corbara, "Un pittore tosco-romagnolo del Quattrocento," in *Emporium* 107, no. 637 (January 1948):30–31.
3. E. Fahy, *Some Followers of Domenico Ghirlandajo* (Ph.D. dissertation, Harvard University, 1968; New York: Garland, 1976), pp. 204–11.
4. Berenson was the first to draw attention to what he called the "striking if crude" early works of Biagio di Antonio (*Catalogue of a Collection of Paintings. I. Italian Paintings* [Philadelphia: Published by John G. Johnson, 1913], cat. no. 62, pp. 35–36). The outlines of Biagio's career were sketched by R. Longhi in C. Gnudi and L. Becherucci, *Mostra di Melozzo e del Quattrocento Romagnolo* (Bologna: Stabilmenti poligrafici editori de "Il Resto del Carlino," 1938), pp. 85–88. See also for the early period G. Passavant, *Verrocchio* (London: Phaidon Press, 1969), p. 212.
5. K. Oberhuber, "Le problème des premières oeuvres de Verrocchio," *Revue de l'Art* 42 (1978): 63–76. Several pictures now generally given to Biagio were ascribed to a "compagno di Botticini" by E. Kühnel (*Francesco Botticini* [Strasbourg: Heitz, 1906], pp. 18–20 and pls. XII.1 and XIII.1).
6. The picture was called "Francesco Botticini" in a reproduction in *Pantheon* in 1928, when it was with Dr. Benedict in Berlin. Though acquired as by that artist, the painting was unaccountably labeled "Raffaello di Francesco Botticini" in the booklet of the Epstein collection (*The Jacob Epstein Collection in the Baltimore Museum of Art* [Baltimore: Published by Jacob Epstein, 1939], n.p.). The booklet further records R. van Marle's opinion that the picture, for him by Francesco Botticini, shows the influence of Verrocchio.
7. B. Berenson, "Tre Disegni di Giovan Battista Utili da Faenza," *Rivista d'Arte* 15 (1933):28 and 26, fig. 5; *Pitture Italiane del Rinascimento* (Milan: U. Hoepli, 1936), p. 502; *The Drawings of the Florentine Painters,* 2nd rev. ed. (Chicago: University of Chicago Press, 1938), 1:69; *Italian Pictures of the Renaissance, Florentine School* (New York and London: Phaidon Press, 1963), 1:210. Even after the existence of Biagio di Antonio was known, Berenson retained the designation "Utili."
8. Fahy, *Some Followers of Domenico Ghirlandajo,* p. 204; B. B. Fredericksen and F. Zeri, *Census of Pre-Nineteenth-Century Italian Paintings in North American Public Collections* (Cambridge, Mass.: Harvard University Press, 1972), p. 28. Zeri wrote to the Museum confirming the attribution on December 22, 1975.
9. Compare the cherub ornament on the Madonna's robe and the angels holding vases of flowers to the same motifs in the Faenza altarpiece (Berenson, *Italian Pictures of the Renaissance. Florentine School,* 2; fig. 1041). On the other hand, the position of the Madonna's left hand, used for the Madonna in the altarpiece and in other works by Biagio, is found as well in other products of the Verrocchio workshop and does not necessarily identify its user as Biagio di Antonio.
10. Oberhuber, "Le problème des premières oeuvres de Verrocchio," p. 65.
11. F. R. Shapley, *Paintings from the Samuel H. Kress Collection. Italian Schools XIII–XV Century* (London: Phaidon Press, 1966), no. K1088, p. 131; and the Addenda to vol. 1 in *Paintings from the Samuel H. Kress Collection. Italian Schools XVI–XVIII Century* (London: Phaidon Press, 1973), p. 386. Heraldic evidence suggests a date of 1472 for Biagio's so-called Morelli-Nerli *cassoni* in the Courtauld Institute Galleries in London (Berenson, *Italian Pictures of the Renaissance. Florentine School,* 2; fig. 1031).
12. F. Zeri, *Italian Paintings in the Walters Art Gallery* (Baltimore: Walters Art Gallery, 1976), 1:99. Biagio is presumed to have been born in the early 1440's; Ghirlandaio's birth date is 1449.
13. Contrast Verrocchio's *Madonna* in Berlin (Passavant, *Verrocchio,* cat. no. 18, p. 187, and figs. 69–71).
14. Museo de Arte de Ponce, Puerto Rico, no. 64.0269. See J. Held, *Paintings of the European and American Schools,* Catalogue (Ponce, Puerto Rico: Museo de Arte de Ponce, 1965), p. 10.
15. Shapley, *Kress Collection. Italian Schools XIII–XV Century,* no. K369, pp. 119–20. See also Oberhuber, "Le problème des premières oeuvres de Verrocchio," n. 32, p. 75.
16. For the attribution to Biagio di Antonio see Held, *Paintings of the European and American Schools,* p. 10; G. Passavant, *Andrea del Verrocchio als Maler* (Düsseldorf: L. Schwann, 1959), pp. 93–94 and n. 287, pp. 196–97; Berenson, *Italian Pictures of the Renaissance. Florentine School,* 1:211; Fredericksen and Zeri, *Census of Pre-Nineteenth-Century Italian Paintings in North American Public Collections,* p. 28; and Fahy, *Some Followers of Domenico Ghirlandajo,* p. 208.

17. Compare, for instance, Zeri, *Italian Paintings in the Walters Art Gallery,* 1:80–85, cat. nos. 50–52, and pl. 43.

18. See P. Tomory, *Catalogue of the Italian Paintings before 1800* (Sarasota, Fla.: John and Mable Ringling Museum of Art, 1976), cat. no. 2, pp. 9–10. For a reproduction see Passavant, *Andrea del Verrocchio als Maler,* fig. 82. The picture is accepted as Biagio's work by Fredericksen and Zeri (*Census of Pre-Nineteenth-Century Italian Paintings,* p. 28) and by Fahy (*Some Followers of Domenico Ghirlandajo,* p. 209). The Child stands properly upright in a variant of the Ponce painting and is related to Verrocchio in style (sold at Sotheby's on June 24, 1964, lot 51, and reproduced in R. van Marle, *The Development of the Italian Schools of Painting* [The Hague: Martinus Nijhoff, 1931], 13:fig. 122, p. 188).

19. Museum of Fine Arts, Budapest, no. 1386. See A. Pigler, *Katalog der Galerie Alter Meister* (Tübingen: E. Wasmuth, 1968), 1:750–52.

20. Oberhuber, "Le problème des premières oeuvres de Verrocchio," pp. 63–76.

21. Like the Tulsa altarpiece and the Baltimore *Madonna,* the Budapest *sacra conversazione* was first attributed to "Utili" or Biagio di Antonio by Berenson (Johnson Collection *Catalogue,* pp. 35–36). About the Uffizi drawing (no. 1254E), see the literature cited in note 7. The Budapest picture has been attributed to Biagio by, among others, Passavant (*Verrocchio,* App. 52, pp. 212–13) and Fahy (*Some Followers of Domenico Ghirlandajo,* p. 205).

22. M. Boscovits, *Toskanische Frührenaissance Tafelbilder,* trans. G. Engl, 2nd rev. ed. (Budapest: Corvina, 1978), commentary to pls. 36 and 37. Boscovits dates the Budapest painting, which he gives to Biagio, to around 1470, a few years before his documented activity in Faenza, and notes the strong influence of Verrocchio. About the Dublin painting, see the *Catalogue of Pictures of the Italian Schools* (Dublin: National Gallery of Ireland, 1956), no. 842, p. 22. It is reproduced in Berenson, "Tre disegni di Giovan Battista Utili," fig. 2. The Dublin picture is close in composition to the one in Sarasota, cited in note 18, except that the Madonna's near-profile head is here taken from Verrocchio rather than Pollaiuolo.

23. A. E. Popham and P. Pouncey, *Italian Drawings in the Department of Prints and Drawings in the British Museum* (London: Trustees of the British Museum, 1950), 1: cat. no. 56, pp. 38–40.

24. Following upon the Baltimore painting is a similar but full-length *Madonna and Child Enthroned,* formerly in the De Stuers Collection and then with French & Co., New York (*Connoisseur* 142, no. 571 [September 1958]:xlix). In the ex-De Stuers picture, the Child is shown seated, not standing, on His mother's lap. She has the same attitude as in the Baltimore painting, except that her waist has been shortened to accommodate the change in the position of the Child. The motif of the vase of flowers, favored by Biagio, is found here too.

25. Compare the early Verrocchiesque Madonnas by Biagio in the Louvre (van Marle, *The Development of the Italian Schools of Painting,* 11: fig. 347, pp. 568–69) and in São Paulo (*Catálogo* [São Paulo: Museu de Arte, 1963], no. 8, p. 10 with repro.).

26. F. Russoli, *La Pinacoteca Poldi-Pezzoli* (Milan: Electa Editrice, 1955), no. 581, pp. 226–27.

SELECTED BIBLIOGRAPHY

Bernard Berenson. "Tre disegni di Giovan Battista Utili da Faenza." *Rivista d'Arte* 15 (1933):21–33.

Carlo Grigioni. *La Pittura Faentina dalle Origini alla Metà del Cinquecento.* Faenza: Fratelli Lega, 1935.

Bernard Berenson. *The Drawings of the Florentine Painters.* 2nd revised edition. Chicago: University of Chicago Press, 1938.

Roberto Longhi in Cesare Gnudi and Luisa Becherucci. *Mostra di Melozzo e del Quattrocento Romagnolo.* Bologna: Stabilmenti poligrafici editori de "Il Resto del Carlino," 1938.

Ennio Golfieri and Antonio Corbara. "Biagio d'Antonio pittore fiorentino in Faenza." *Atti e Memorie dell'Accademia Fiorentina. La Colombaria* n.s. 1 (Florence, 1947).

Antonio Corbara. "Un pittore tosco-romagnolo del Quattrocento." *Emporium* 107, no. 637 (January 1948):30–31.

Bernard Berenson. *Italian Pictures of the Renaissance. Florentine School.* 2 vols. New York and London: Phaidon Press, 1963.

Ennio Golfieri. "Biagio d'Antonio da Firenze." In *Dizionario Biografico degli Italiani.* Rome: Istituto della Enciclopedia Italiana, 1968.

Burton B. Fredericksen and Federico Zeri. *Census of Pre-Nineteenth-Century Italian Paintings in North American Public Collections.* Cambridge, Mass.: Harvard University Press, 1972.

Everett Fahy. *Some Followers of Domenico Ghirlandajo.* Ph.D. dissertation, Harvard University, 1968. New York: Garland, 1976.

Konrad Oberhuber. "Le problème des premières oeuvres de Verrocchio." *Revue de l'Art* 42 (1978): 63–76.

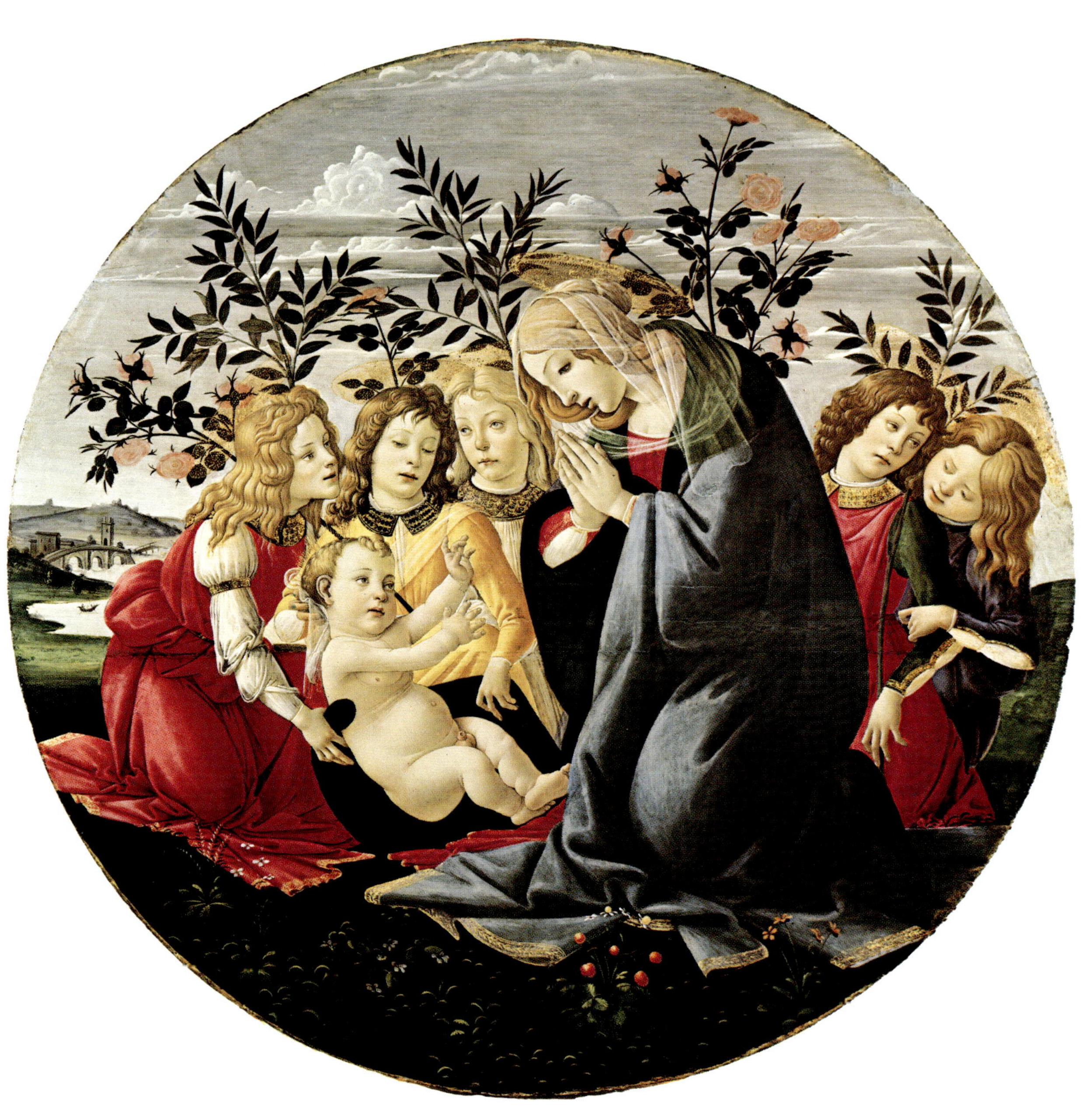

SANDRO BOTTICELLI (1445–1510) and Studio

5. *Madonna Adoring the Child with Five Angels,* ca. 1485–1490

Tempera on wood with touches in oil. Tondo, diameter 52¼ inches (132.7 cm.)
The Mary Frick Jacobs Collection (BMA 38.226)

PROVENANCE

Joseph, Cardinal Fesh, Rome

The Reverend Walter Davenport Bromley, London

Rev. Walter Davenport Bromley Collection Sale Catalogue, Christie's, London: June 12, 1863, p. 15, lot 85

G. F. Waagen, *Treasures of Art in Great Britain* (London: John Murray, 1854), 3:376

Acquired by Sir William Bingham Baring, Lord Ashburton, at the Bromley Sale, 1863

C. N. Plunkett, *Sandro Botticelli* (London: George Bell & Sons, 1900), p. 101

Lady Louisa Ashburton

The painting passed to Lady Ashburton and was included in the sale of her collection in 1905, but it was apparently bought in and returned to Thomas Agnew & Sons Ltd., acting on behalf of the executors of Lady Ashburton's estate.

Lady Louisa Ashburton Collection Sale Catalogue, Christie's, London: July 8, 1905, lot 12

A. Graves, *Art Sales from Early in the Eighteenth Century to Early in the Twentieth Century* (London: Graves, 1918), 1:57

Letter to Russell Sale from Margaret Christian of the Research Department of Christie's, April 24, 1978

From 1905 until 1912 the panel was apparently in a private collection.

Acquired by Mary Frick Jacobs, Baltimore, in 1912 from the Blakeslee Galleries, New York

Henry Barton Jacobs, *The Collection of Mary Frick Jacobs* (Baltimore: Prepared and published by Dr. Henry Barton Jacobs, 1938), no. 29

Bequeathed to The Baltimore Museum of Art in 1938 as part of The Mary Frick Jacobs Collection

CONDITION

Before the painting of the *Madonna and Child with Five Angels* entered The Baltimore Museum of Art in 1938, the worm-damaged panel had been treated to stabilize climatically-caused warping of its horizontally placed members. The original thickness of the support had been planed down to approximately one-half inch and a wooden cradle attached to the reverse. Most of the damage to the panel and painted surface was caused by the cradle, which prevented normal movement of the wood. As a result of this restraint, a number of new horizontal splits had developed, one running through the Virgin's head, and others following the grain of the wood in the area of the Virgin's waist and the Child's head and shoulders. Missing pigment, caused by flaking, blistering, and the movement of the wooden support, was here most serious. The lacunae had been overpainted, covering original paint unnecessarily in several areas, as can be seen in the infrared photographs. In addition, a disfiguring aspect of this earlier treatment was the removal of a wedge-shaped piece of the panel, ranging in width from 6 to 15 mm., from the area of the Christ Child's right shoulder and arm. This loss has caused an interruption in the painted contour of the Child's form and has altered the proportions of the arm to an unnatural thinness.

In 1954 additional treatment was carried out by the laboratory of The Walters Art Gallery under the direction of Elisabeth Packard. The wooden cradle was removed and the reverse of the panel was impregnated with a melted wax resin to provide resistance to changes in humidity. For mechanical support, slotted aluminum channels were attached to the back. The painted surface was cleaned, blisters set down, old overpaint removed, and the losses inpainted.

The recurrence of flaking and blistering of the paint and the discoloration of the varnish used in the 1954 treatment necessitated additional stabilization and conservation measures. In 1977–1978 the painting was treated by the Art Conservation Laboratory, Inc., of Raymond, New Hampshire. The aluminum channels on the reverse were replaced by a flexible, multi-layered support consisting of synthetic resin, fiberglass cloth, and balsa wood blocks. The active flaking and blistering were stabilized, old fillings, inpaintings, and varnish coatings were removed, and the losses were refilled and inpainted. The panel was then coated with multiple layers of non-yellowing, synthetic polymer solutions.

In spite of past usage and the extensive treatments the panel has undergone, the painted surface is in relatively good condition. Aside from the sliver of the panel actually removed, most of the pigment losses are confined to the areas along the horizontal cracks and joint lines, most extensively just below the center of the painting. Several scratches and scars have been inpainted, and there are also some losses apparent around the panel's edge.

For a more detailed history, see:

Elisabeth Packard, "The Restoration of Two Paintings in the Jacobs Collection," *Baltimore Museum of Art News* 18, no. 2 (December 1954):3–12.

Barbara Beardsley, "A Flexible Balsa Back for the Stabilization of a Botticelli Panel Painting," *Conservation of Wood in Painting and the Decorative Arts* (London: International Institute for Conservation of Historic and Artistic Works, September 1978), pp. 153–55.

Art Conservation Laboratory, Inc.
Raymond, New Hampshire

The high quality and charm of Botticelli's *Madonna Adoring the Child with Five Angels* are immediately apparent. Contained within the circular format and set off by an exceedingly rich frame is one of the most beautiful variations of the popular fifteenth-century devotional image of the Madonna kneeling in adoration of the newborn Christ. At first the eye is attracted by the sensuous warmth of the sunlight and gaiety of the bright red and yellow robes of the five angels, three to the left of the Madonna, two to the right. Richly dressed, with gilded collars and cuffs, their artfully arranged tresses in alternate shades of blond and brown, the angels along with the branches of olive and roses create a frieze-like, slightly concave foil to the Virgin and the sacred Child. Their youthful motions and glances enhance the exuberance of the colors, as do the decorative silhouettes of the plants and the white puffs of clouds in the cool grayish-blue sky behind them. They are beautified earthlings full of youthful vigor, not the otherworldly beings of a Fra Angelico. These angels serve to announce the joy of the birth by attracting the eye. Once seduced by them, by the springtime plants in the foreground, and by the glimmer of a landscape behind, the spectator's mind and eye slowly perceive the subtly different mood presented by the picture's protagonists.

The interrelation of the Madonna and Child occupies the center of the composition. Christ, a human baby here rather than a precocious divinity, looks longingly toward His mother and reaches out for her. Although He is easy to overlook at first because the tone of His flesh and His gestures compete with difficulty with the more aggressive colors and linear movements of the angels, He is touching in the longing of His hands and eyes, the more so as His seeking is not reciprocated.

Dominating the other figures by her size and by the heaviness of her ashen-blue mantle lined with green, Botticelli's Virgin is lost to the present, to the Child, and to the angels, in a timeless inner reverie. She kneels over the Child but does not look at Him. Her gaze is unfocused. Her face, with its delicate, idealized features and its softened and continuous modeling, has all the fragility of the finest porcelain. She is absorbed in a visionary trance, with a sibylline gaze into the threatening future that was also to characterize the Madonnas of the youthful Michelangelo several decades later. Her mood is imbued with that wistful melancholy characteristic of Botticelli. Her entire being is possessed of it, from the sombre hue of her too massive cloak, the unbroken, lyrical contour of her elongated back, the restrained diagonals and curves of the veils about her head, to the single tress of hair that falls loosely on the right side of her face. Abandoned by any moving will, the Virgin's body succumbs to her vision. What she sees is not the joyous moment of her Child's birth, but the mystery of the Savior's future death. She and the passion of her Child are inextricably bound together by a beautiful formal solution on the part of the artist. The inner lining of her mantle is green, symbolic of hope, a color in harmony with the promises of the Savior's birth. But this is not a joyful green. It is extremely dark, introducing a sombre note in the center of the painting. In its darkness it is close to black, symbolic of death and sin, a color that a few years later will dominate the Virgin's dress as she receives her dead son in the artist's moving *Pietàs* in Milan and Munich. In this painting the deep green of the mantle flows around her shoulders, setting off the whiteness and the fragility of her skin. A large fold of the mantle falls from her right arm, seeming to engulf the Child. Where He is free of it, He is active. Where it touches Him, He is quiet, one leg upon the other as though already on the cross.

The moving but delicate balance the painting offers between the sensuous pleasures and delights of the physical world on the one hand and the religious emotion of the Madonna's reverie on the other suggests a date in the 1480's, before Botticelli's work became gripped by that more fervid emotionalism of the Savonarola period. Indeed, because of its strong connections with other more firmly dated works, we can be certain that the Baltimore panel was produced in Botticelli's studio in the 1480's, probably in the second half of the decade. The smooth-faced adolescent angels on either side of the Madonna find their closest cognates in Botticelli's great works of the period, in the *Madonna of the Magnificat,* the *Madonna of the Pomegranate,* and in the *Saint Barnabas Altarpiece,* all in the Uffizi.[1] Virtually the same face appears on the leftmost angel in the Baltimore painting and on the one immediately to the right of the Virgin in the *Madonna of the Pomegranate* (fig. 1), and the latter's immediate neighbor appears in two slightly varied poses in the Baltimore work, the second angel in from the edge on either side. The Virgin's inward preoccupation is in varying degrees common to all of these paintings, as is the too large mantle, which gives her the appearance of physical shrinking in harmony with her mental detachment. In the *Madonna and Child* in the Poldi-Pezzoli Museum in Milan, usually dated to the early 1480's, the Virgin's head bows in a similarly exaggerated, and therefore expressively pathetic, angle.[2] There too a lock of hair falls downward to reinforce the delicate gaze. And there too Christ's passion is the motivation of the Madonna's vision; the Child bears the crown of thorns and three nails in His left hand. In the *Bardi Altarpiece* of 1485 from Santo Spirito, now in the Gemäldegalerie, Staatl. Museen, PKB, Berlin (West), the Christ Child is very close in type to that of the Baltimore painting, and the positioning of the upper part of the body in each case is extremely similar, though reversed.[3]

The strength of these connections of the Baltimore tondo with Botticelli's chief productions of the 1480's serves to reinforce its dating to the same period and suggests that the panel's execution was close to the master's own hand. Recognition of the panel's quality has been slow in coming, however, and the problematic questions connected with it, such as its unevenness in execution and its failure as a whole to come up to the quality expected in a work by the master, have never been discussed in detail.

Although it had appeared with the ascription to Botticelli in nineteenth-century collection lists, the Baltimore panel was first attributed to the artist by G. N. Plunkett, a Botticelli scholar, in his monograph of 1900, where it is simply listed in the catalogue of works.[4] Crowe and Cavalcaselle included it in their catalogue of Botticelli's oeuvre, saying that "it is in the raw system of tone peculiar to some of the master's works."[5] Herbert Horne left it out of his monumental study, and in this he was followed by most other authors of monographs on Botticelli. Yashiro considered it to be no more than a "faithful copy" of another painting, now in the Pitti Gallery, one which itself was in his view a contemporary variation on a Botticellian original.[6] In his 1932 *Italian Pictures of the Renaissance* Berenson indicated the superiority of the Baltimore tondo to that in the Pitti.[7] He made the important suggestion that both were derived from a lost Botticelli original, that in the Pitti being a copy, the one in Baltimore a version produced in the master's studio. The distinction is important, for a version could entail direct intervention or at least supervision by Botticelli. In the 1963 edition of his lists, Berenson seems to have lowered his estimation of the work, for it is called simply a "studio work."[8] Salvini ignored both the Baltimore and the Pitti paintings in his 1958 catalogue, but he did include as an autograph work a related image of the *Nativity with the Child Saint John* in the National Gallery of Scotland in Edinburgh, dating it 1488.[9] To include the latter painting, which in this author's view (based on a photograph) is a schoolwork of no higher quality than the Pitti panel and far below that of the Baltimore work, is to ignore the problem posed by all three. The more recent catalogue of Gabriele Mandel and Carlo Bo includes the Baltimore tondo, calling it a replica of a Botticelli invention produced in the studio.[10] And, most recently, Federico Zeri considered the panel to have come from Botticelli's atelier, not up to his autograph production but based on his drawings and perhaps including some of his own touches.[11]

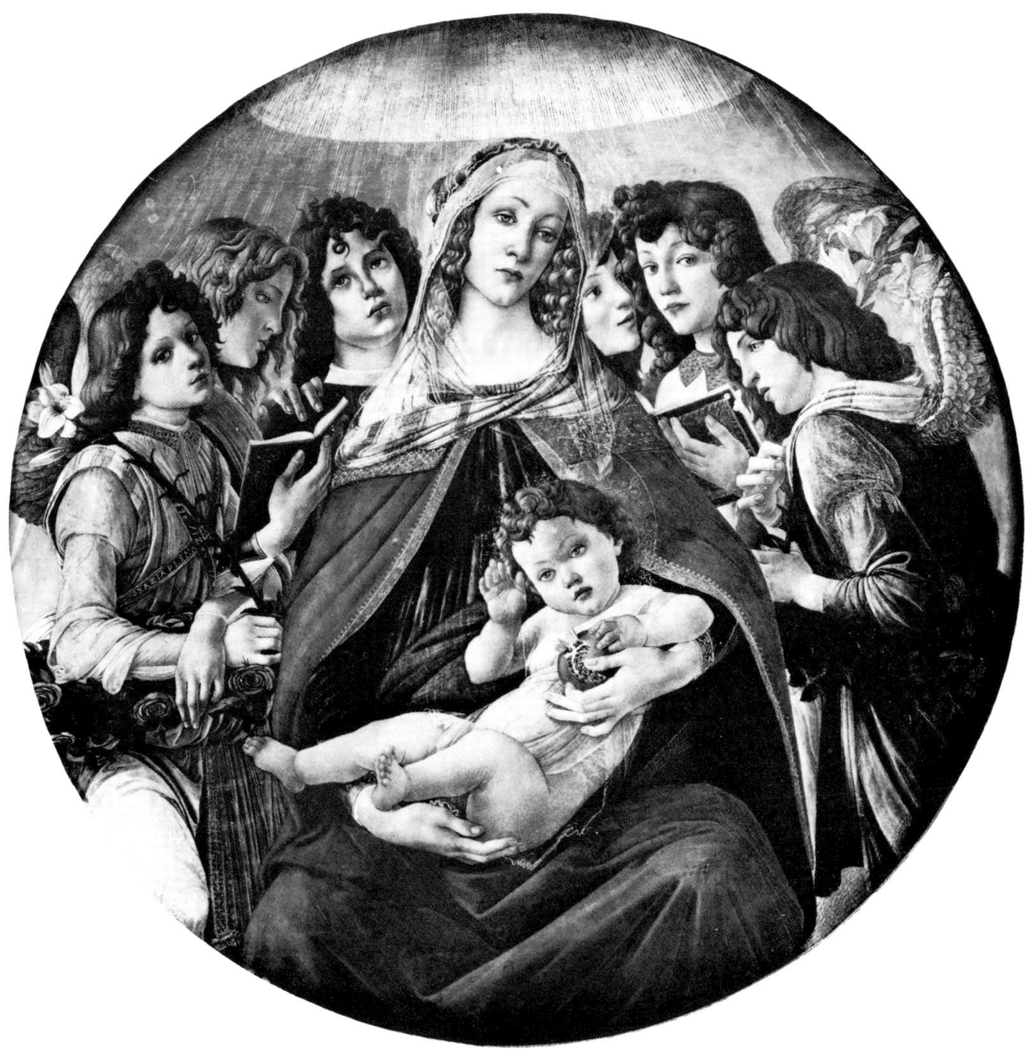

Fig. 1. Sandro Botticelli, *Madonna of the Pomegranate,* ca. 1486. Tempera on wood. Tondo, diameter 56½ inches (143.5 cm.). Uffizi, Florence. Alinari/Editorial Photocolor Archives

Scholarly opinion on the Baltimore panel has thus been mixed. But the question involving authorship of the work is not whether there was any participation by Botticelli, but how much. Those who have seen the painting firsthand, while recognizing its unevenness, nevertheless consider it to be of high quality, a sensitive production of the master's studio. It was certainly produced with the aid of his drawings and cartoons, and parts of it appear to have been worked on directly by him, especially the fresh faces and luxuriant hair of the three angels on the left, and the face of the Madonna (fig. 2).[12] The exquisite modeling of the latter, so delicately continuous, is rare in Botticelli and may be the result of Leonardo's influence, an influence also apparent in the body of Venus and in the face of the Hora receiving her in the *Birth of Venus* of the mid-1480's in the Uffizi. But we should not carry too far the attribution of the painting's every stroke, for it must be remembered that not a single one of the pictures of the Madonna ascribed to the master is securely documented, and that not one of them is entirely free from questions regarding authorship of every part.[13]

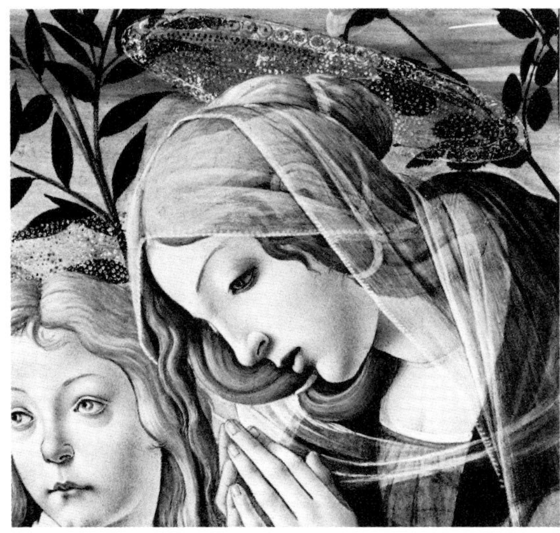

Fig. 2. Sandro Botticelli, *Madonna Adoring the Child with Five Angels,* detail of cat. no. 5

The greater vitality and spontaneity of touch of the Baltimore Adoration is evident at once in a direct comparison with the closely related tondo in the Pitti Gallery (no. 580).[14] Aside from an early attribution to Botticelli, modern scholarship has uniformly recognized the Pitti version (fig. 3) of the Baltimore painting to be a rather mediocre production of the shop, or by an imitator.[15] But it is obviously based on the same model as the Baltimore work. They are exactly similar in composition, although there are differences in some of the accoutrements of the angels' dress, in their hair, their number, and in the size of the two paintings, that in Baltimore measuring 132.7 cm., that in the Pitti 110 cm. Another obvious difference is that in the Pitti panel roses alone fill the sky above the group, and there is only the slightest hint of a landscape to the left. More telling, however, are the qualitative differences. Whereas the foliage, the lighting, the expressions of the angels and the richness of their hair in the Baltimore panel bespeak a creative vitality and absolute ease of execution, these same elements are dry and lifeless in the Pitti example. They bear the mark of the copyist, a mentality of dependence upon another's design and a determination to "get it right," rather than a creative freedom. The roses fill the sky with insistence, a *horror vacui,* and there is an inexplicable gap between the Child's head and the hand of the angel ostensibly supporting it. In the Baltimore panel this gap does not exist, the space being filled by a delicate gossamer cloth. The angel second from the right in the Baltimore tondo holds a branch of olive in the left hand. This same hand in the Pitti version is empty and without function. The folds of cloth of all the figures in the Baltimore panel have become in the Pitti picture rather rigid black channels. And the Madonna's mantle falls in a lifeless pile around her, the artist completely misunderstanding the plunge of the material along her back, its adherence to her hips as she sinks, its being cast into highlight as it curves over her protruding knee, and finally its shadowed tension as it is drawn in and over the left foot on which she rests.

As we have seen, the Baltimore tondo is the superior painting of the two versions, and undoubtedly it was done on Botticelli's direction, in his studio, even, in part, executed by him. And yet there is something about the painting as a whole that does not meet the standard expected of the artist, something in which the Pitti version is actually more effective. This something is the concentration of the painting on its central theme, the interrelation of the Madonna and her Child.

In both the *Madonna of the Magnificat* and the *Madonna of the Pomegranate* the figures occupy nearly all of the available space. They are large, placed in the immediate foreground, even cut off by the frame. In each, the Madonna dominates the composition

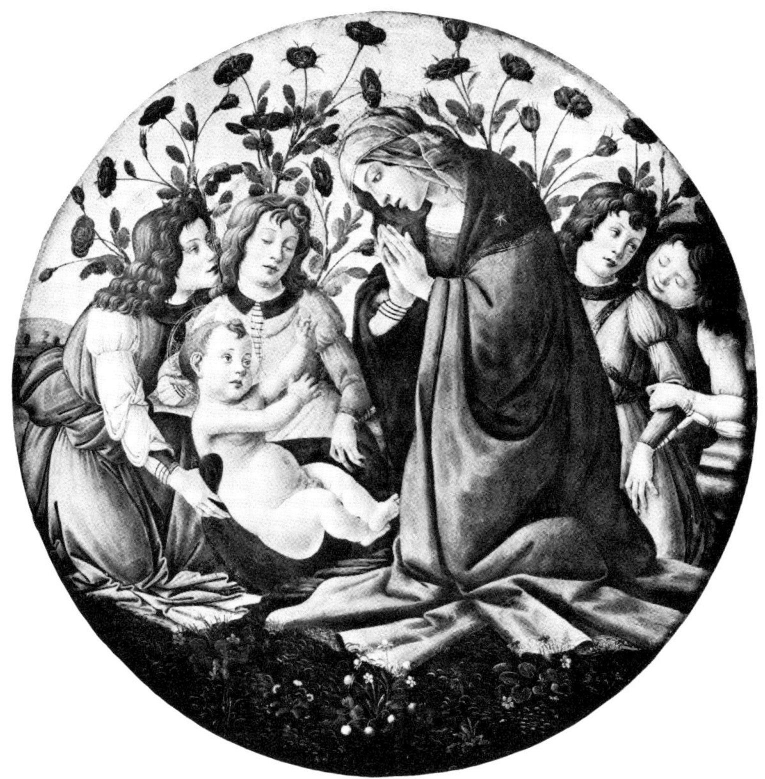

Fig. 3. Copy after Botticelli, *Madonna Adoring the Child with Four Angels,* ca. 1485–1490. Tempera on wood. Tondo, diameter $43^{5}/_{16}$ inches (110 cm.). Pitti Palace, Florence. Alinari/Editorial Photocolor Archives

by her size and expression, along with the Child. Part of the marvelous effect of each is this compositional close-up and focusing in on the leading participants. When we look at the Baltimore and the Pitti versions of the *Adoration of the Child,* the Pitti copy, for all its dryness, has this same riveting focus, which the Baltimore panel does not possess nearly to the same extent. The reason for this is that the Baltimore tondo is larger by nearly 23 centimeters and there is more space around the periphery. For the size of the panel, the figures are relatively smaller and thus appear at a greater remove from the surface plane, and thereby from the attention of the spectator.

From these observations the following hypothesis for the origin of the Baltimore Museum painting can be proposed. There existed a tondo of the *Adoration of the Child* executed by Botticelli himself, a painting now lost, but which is reflected quite accurately, even in its size, in the Pitti Gallery work. A commission came to Botticelli for a rather large devotional image of the theme. Since the commission was not a major one calling for something absolutely new and was probably from an out-of-town client, Botticelli set his assistants to work on a somewhat larger version of the painting already completed. From an anecdote recorded by Vasari we know that assistants in the studio painted panels based on the master's work which were later sold under his name.[16] The same drawings and cartoon used on the first example could economically be used again, with Botticelli's direction. Since the new panel was to be larger than the other, the artist simply added a landscape view, clouds, more space all around, and the additional head of an angel between the Madonna and the two angels on the left. The result would be the Baltimore painting, a version of the presumed original, yet one bearing the stamp of creative variation and ease of execution rather than slavish copying. Such a hypothesis might explain the slight dissolution of focus from the central group and its escape into the attractive but not necessary details of landscape and sky. It would also provide some rationale for the abrupt appearance of the blond-haired angel in the center of the composition. This angel looks like an afterthought, not like an organic part of the design, and its gaze distracts attention from the Madonna. All of these features might then explain the lack of ready acceptance of the painting as an original by Botticelli. It may well be a variation directed by Botticelli after one of his own inventions, a variation of high quality, but one that does not bear the full intensity of the creative impulse.

The iconographical theme of which the Baltimore tondo is a refreshingly beautiful example originated nearly a century before the panel's execution. The Madonna kneeling in adoration of her newborn Son and accompanied by angels grew out of a new type of nativity representation that appeared in the late fourteenth century.[17] Replacing an earlier Byzantine formula which showed the Madonna in a recumbent position for the birth of her Child, the new type presented her kneeling. This so-called Bridgetine nativity was directly inspired by the mystic writings of St. Bridget of Sweden. Among the many favors she had promised the saint, the Virgin told Bridget in a vision that she would herself witness the manner of Christ's birth and His death on the cross. And while the saint was on a pilgrimage to the Holy Land in 1370, the promise was fulfilled in a vision of the Savior's birth.[18] In the revelation she saw Mary great with child, dressed in a white mantle, her hair flowing loosely over her shoulders. When the Virgin had prepared everything, she knelt down and began to pray.

> With her hands and eyes raised to heaven, she remained as though suspended in the ecstasy of contemplation, as though drunken with divine sweetness.[19]

While thus kneeling she bore the Child who glowed with an ineffable light. The angels joined in celebration with their chorus.

> And when the Virgin realized that she had given birth, immediately, with her head bowed and her hands joined, she adored the child with great respect and reverence. . . . Then as the child was whining and trembling from the cold and from the hardness of the floor where he was lying, he stretched out his arms imploring her to raise him to the warmth and to the motherly love, the mother then took him in her arms and pressed him to her breast, and with her cheek and her breast she warmed him with great joy and tender maternal compassion.[20]

By the beginning of the fifteenth century, the Bridgetine nativity with the kneeling Virgin had almost completely replaced the earlier type in both the north and the south. St. Bridget's revelation contained many other details not mentioned above which were incorporated into nativity representations. But more important here is the development from the larger birth narrative to a separate theme, the adoration of the Child by the Virgin, sometimes accompanied by angels, sometimes by Joseph, John the Baptist, or other saints.[21] For these various representations the passages cited above from St. Bridget's vision were very important, but they were not followed in exact detail or in precise sequence by all artists. By the time the Baltimore tondo was painted, the theme, either in its more limited form or in the wider nativity context, was extraordinarily popular. Botticelli was no doubt introduced to it when he entered Fra Filippo Lippi's studio as a youth. The Fra's very tender Adorations in the Gemäldegalerie, Berlin (West), formerly in the Medici Palace chapel (fig. 4); in the Uffizi; and in the Prato Gallery; provided types that were followed by many others.[22] Almost every Florentine artist of the second half of the century painted at least one Adoration, and some, such as Jacopo del Sellaio or Francesco Botticini, did many.[23] The so-called Pseudo-Pier Francesco Fiorentino who worked in the following of Fra Filippo and Pesellino seems to have specialized in

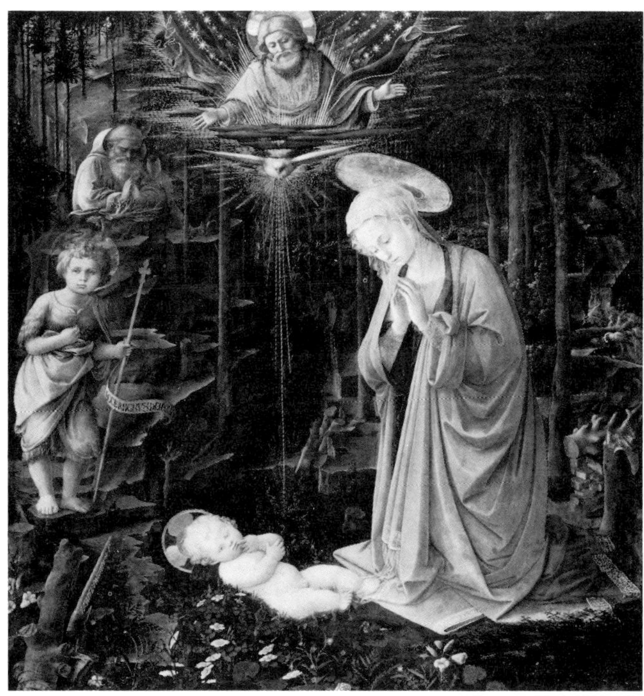

Fig. 4. Fra Filippo Lippi, *Madonna Adoring the Child with the Young St. John,* ca. 1455–1460. Tempera on wood. 50 × 45$^{11}/_{16}$ inches (127 × 116 cm.). Gemäldegalerie, Staatl. Museen, PKB, Berlin (West)

producing derivative paintings with this subject.[24] The central motif of all these images was the Madonna kneeling before her Child, hands joined in prayer, as St. Bridget had described. The Child sometimes lies directly on the ground, sometimes on a bundle of straw, or, as in the Baltimore Museum panel, on an extended fold of the Virgin's cloak. Fra Filippo's Uffizi *Adoration* provided a model for the latter detail, as did Domenico Ghirlandaio's *Sassetti Altarpiece* which was painted in 1485, about the same time as the Baltimore Botticelli.[25]

The very multitude of images of adoration was in itself a challenge to the artist to devise a new and striking invention. Botticelli evidently looked very hard at Lippi's compositions, especially at their emphasis on the contemplative Madonna. But he seems also to have returned to St. Bridget's vision for inspiration. He concentrated his energies on capturing the Virgin's pre-delivery psychic state, St. Bridget's moving words describing her "as though suspended in the ecstasy of contemplation, as though drunken with divine sweetness." The Madonna in the Baltimore panel not merely "adored the child with great respect and reverence," as Lippi's Virgin in the Berlin painting can be said to do; rather, she is completely possessed by her reverie, her body swaying in big curves, her head pendulous, her gaze pensive. By thus combining the textually separate incidents of the Virgin's rapture and her adoration of the Child, the artist heightened the emotional content and gave the panel a decidedly mystical effect. And by including St. Bridget's description of the Holy Child's imploring and helpless gesture toward the Madonna, he broadened the content of the Virgin's ecstasy from the Bridgetine "divine sweetness" to foreboding pity. The use of the dark green lining of Mary's cloak to unite her with the Child and to suggest at one instant the hope and expectation of His birth and the tragedy of His death appears to be Botticelli's own addition to the iconography.

The tender sentiment of the Madonna and Child is set off by the five angels. Their moods lyrically enhance that of the Virgin, as do the delicate silhouettes of the branches of olive and roses. The light in the panel has a tinge of eternity, and the presence of the angels and the plants, and their arrangement in a frieze closing off the distance may all be intended to suggest the heavenly realm, removing the image from the world of tragedy to that of contemplation. An allusion to the image of the enclosed garden or *hortus conclusus,* symbolic of the Immaculate Conception and borrowed from the Song of Solomon, is perhaps intended in the delimited space in the foreground of the painting.[26] The rose, flower of the Virgin, and the olive, symbolic of divine peace, are among the flora of the heavenly paradise.[27] The delicately rendered plants in the lower foreground may allude to both the passion of Christ and His victory over death, or to virtuous action on the part of the Christian beholder.[28] The bridge in the left distance might possibly bear a symbolic content, suggesting the journey of the soul from this world to the next, as it does in the *Moralia* of Gregory the Great.[29] But since the bridge appears to be broken, it offers a dangerous passage at best. The small boat below the bridge would seem to provide a better crossing as it heads out from shore. If intended to convey symbolic content, this boat participates in the ancient iconographic tradition of the Ship of the Church, guided by Christ, as it travels over the perilous waters of this world and on to the next.[30] With this image of a journey into eternity, the painting's arresting formal presentation is joined to its thematic content, thus serving the devotional function of guiding the eye, the mind, and the heart of the pious to the contemplation of divinity.

J. Russell Sale
National Gallery of Art,
Washington, D. C.

NOTES

1. R. Salvini, *All the Paintings of Botticelli,* 4 vols. (New York: Hawthorn Books, 1965), 3:pls. 1, 25, 29.
2. Ibid., pl. 5.
3. Ibid., pl. 20.
4. G. N. Plunkett, *Sandro Botticelli* (London: George Bell & Sons, 1900), p. 101. The painting is listed as a Botticelli in G. F. Waagen's *Treasures of Art in Great Britain* (London: John Murray, 1854), 3: 376.
5. J. A. Crowe and G. B. Cavalcaselle, *A History of Painting in Italy* (New York: Charles Scribner's Sons, 1911), 4:261, 266.
6. Y. Yashiro, *Sandro Botticelli* (London: The Medici Society, 1925), 1:238.
7. B. Berenson, *Italian Pictures of the Renaissance* (Oxford: Clarendon Press, 1932), pp. 101, 102.
8. B. Berenson, *Italian Pictures of the Renaissance: Florentine School* (London: Phaidon Press, 1963), 1:33.
9. Salvini, *Botticelli,* 3:131, and pl. 28.
10. G. Mandel and C. Bo, *L'Opera completa del Botticelli* (Milan: Rizzoli, 1967), p. 99, no. 92.
11. B. B. Fredericksen and F. Zeri, *Census of Pre-Nineteenth-Century Italian Paintings in North American Public Collections* (Cambridge, Mass.: Harvard University Press, 1972), p. 33; and in a letter of January 27, 1976, from Zeri to G. Rosenthal.
12. In his letter of January 27, 1976, to G. Rosenthal, Zeri suggested the possible intervention of Botticelli in the last stage of execution, and he underlined the fine quality of the Virgin's face and the first and third angels from the left.
13. In their monograph on Botticelli the Ettlingers discuss the imitable character of Botticelli's style, the mass-producing of paintings, and the lack of documents "for any of Botticelli's genuine *Madonnas*": L. D. and H. S. Ettlinger, *Botticelli* (New York: Oxford University Press, 1977), pp. 8, 17, 80.
14. Mandel and Bo, *L'Opera completa del Botticelli,* p. 99, no. 92.
15. A. Streeter, *Botticelli,* rev. ed. (London: George Bell & Sons, 1905), pp. 147–48, gives the painting to Botticelli with the extensive aid of assistants. For the negative view, see Crowe and Cavalcaselle, *A History of Painting in Italy,* 4:261; Berenson, *Italian Pictures of the Renaissance* (1932), p. 102; J. Mesnil, *Botticelli* (Paris: A. Michel, 1938), p. 229; and Mandel and Bo, *L'Opera completa del Botticelli,* p. 99, no. 92.
16. Giorgio Vasari, *Le Vite de' più eccellenti pittori, scultori ed architettori,* 9 vols. ed. Gaetano Milanesi, 2nd ed. (Florence: G. C. Sansoni, 1906), 3:319.
17. For a discussion of the development of the new nativity type, see Henrik Cornell, *The Iconography of the Nativity of Christ* (Uppsala: A.-B. Lunde-

quistska Bokhandeln, 1924), passim; Louis Réau, *Iconographie de l'art chrétien,* 3 vols. (Paris: Presses Universitaires de France, 1957), 2, pt. 2:219–20; W. Braunfels, "Das Marienbild in der Kunst des Westens bis zum Konzil von Trient," *Lexikon der christlichen Ikonographie,* E. Kirschbaum, ed. 8 vols. (Rome: Herder, 1968–1976), 3:190–91.

18. The vision in its Latin text and translation is in Cornell, *The Iconography of the Nativity of Christ,* pp. 9 ff.
19. Ibid., p. 9: Erectis igitur manibus et oculis in celum intentis, stabat quasi in exstasi contemplationiis suspensa, inebriata divina dulcedine.
20. Ibid., p. 10: Cum igitur virgo sensit se iam peperisse statim inclinato capite et iunctis manibus cum magna honestate et reverentia adoravit puerum. . . . Et tunc puer plorans et quasi tremens per frigore et duricia pavimenti ubi iacebat, voluebat se paululum et extendebat membra querens invenire refrigerium et matris favorem, quem tunc mater suscepti in manibus et strinxit eum ad pectus suum et cum maxilla et pectore calefaciebat eum cum magna leticia et tenera compassione materna.
21. The new type is radically different from the Byzantine images of the Madonna adoring the Child. See Braunfels, "Das Marienbild in der Kunst des Westens," *Lexikon der christlichen Ikonographie,* 3:190.
22. Cf. Giuseppe Marchini, *Filippo Lippi* (Milan: Electa, 1975), figs. 147, 157, 160; Alfred Neumeyer, *Filippo Lippi: Anbetung des Kindes* (Stuttgart: Reclam, 1964).
23. For these, see the lists in Berenson, *Italian Pictures of the Renaissance: Florentine School,* 1:195–96, 39–40.
24. Ibid., pp. 171–72. The designation of Pseudo Pier Francesco Fiorentino has been changed to Lippi-Pesellino Imitator. See F. R. Shapley, *Italian Paintings* (Washington, D.C.: National Gallery of Art, 1979), 1:266.
25. For Ghirlandaio's painting, see Ernst Steinmann, *Ghirlandajo* (Leipzig: Velhagen & Klasing, 1897), fig. 26.
26. As suggested by B. Carroll in "Floral Symbolism in an Early Florentine Painting," *Baltimore Museum of Art News* 18, no. 2 (December 1954):1–3.
27. For the rose and olive, see *Lexikon der christlichen Ikonographie,* 3:564–65, 341.
28. Carroll has identified the five plants in the foreground as, from left to right: the plantain, symbolic of the well-trodden path to righteousness; the bluet (perhaps), associated by its faintly blue color with the Madonna; the violet, symbolic of humility and mourning ("it drooped in sorrow when the shadow of the crucifixion passed over it"); the strawberry, whose fruit may symbolize the virtuous works of man; the scarlet pimpernel or shepherd's weatherglass, its red color alluding to the passion of Christ; "Floral Symbolism in an Early Florentine Painting," pp. 2–3.
29. L. Ettlinger, "Virtutum et Viciorum Adumbracio," *Journal of the Warburg and Courtauld Institutes* 19 (1956):156. See also *Lexikon der christlichen Ikonographie,* 1:330.
30. For the image of the Ship of the Church, see *Lexikon der christlichen Ikonographie,* 4:61–63.

SELECTED BIBLIOGRAPHY

Gustav Friedrich Waagen. *Treasures of Art in Great Britain.* 3 vols. London: John Murray, 1854.

Rev. Walter Davenport Bromley Collection Sale. Catalogue. Christie's, London: June 12, 1863.

George N. Plunkett. *Sandro Botticelli.* London: George Bell & Sons, 1900.

Lady Louisa Ashburton Collection Sale. Catalogue. Christie's, London: July 8, 1905.

A. Streeter. *Botticelli.* Revised edition. London: George Bell & Sons, 1905.

Joseph A. Crowe and Giovanni Battista Cavalcaselle. *A History of Painting in Italy.* 6 vols. New York: Charles Scribner's Sons, 1911.

Algernon Graves. *Art Sales from Early in the Eighteenth Century to Early in the Twentieth Century.* 3 vols. London: Graves, 1918.

Yukio Yashiro. *Sandro Botticelli.* 3 vols. London: The Medici Society, 1925.

Bernard Berenson. *Italian Pictures of the Renaissance.* Oxford: Clarendon Press, 1932.

Douglas H. Gordon. "A Rich Gift to Baltimore: The Mary F. Jacobs Collection Presented to the Art Museum." *Art News* 36, no. 33 (May 14, 1938):7–9.

Henry Barton Jacobs. *The Collection of Mary Frick Jacobs.* Baltimore: Prepared and published by Dr. Henry Barton Jacobs, 1938.

Bette Carroll. "Floral Symbolism in an Early Florentine Painting." *Baltimore Museum of Art News* 18, no. 2 (December 1954):1–3.

"The Madonna and Child through the Centuries." *Baltimore Sun: Sunday Sun* (December 22, 1957), Magazine Section, pp. 8–9.

Bernard Berenson. *Italian Pictures of the Renaissance: Florentine School.* 2 vols. London: Phaidon Press, 1963.

Gabriele Mandel and Carlo Bo. *L'Opera completa del Botticelli.* Milan: Rizzoli, 1967.

Burton B. Fredericksen and Federico Zeri. *Census of Pre-Nineteenth-Century Italian Paintings in North American Public Collections.* Cambridge, Mass.: Harvard University Press, 1972.

Leopold D. and Helen S. Ettlinger. *Botticelli.* New York: Oxford University Press, 1977.

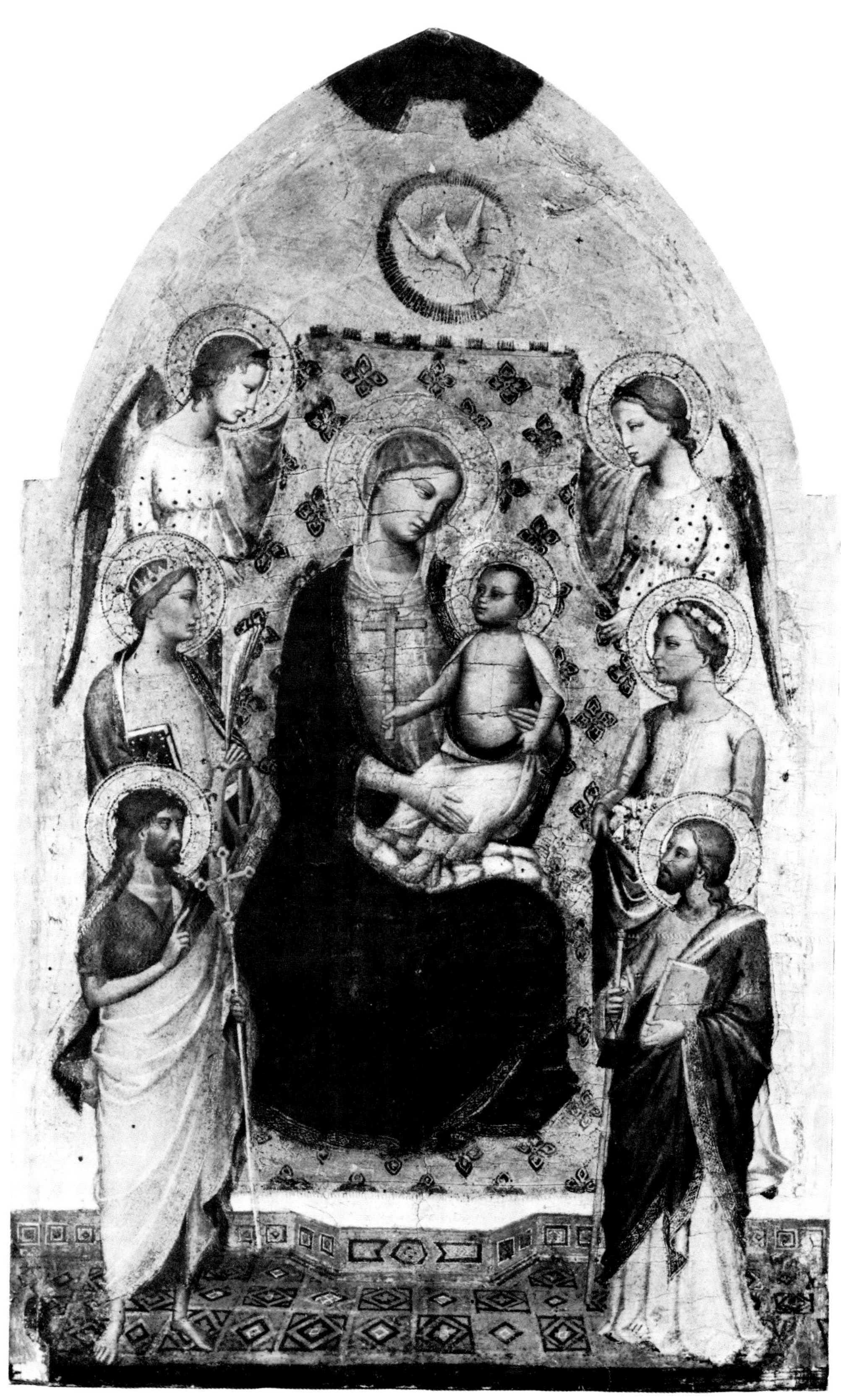

Circle of
NICCOLÒ DI PIETRO GERINI (active 1368–1415)

6\. *Madonna and Child Enthroned with Two Angels and Four Saints,* ca. 1400

Tempera on wood. 30¼ × 18⅛ inches (76.8 × 46 cm.)
Bequest of Saidie A. May (BMA 51.390)

PROVENANCE

Pazzagli & Nesi, Florence

Purchased by Saidie A. May in 1925

Bequeathed to The Baltimore Museum of Art in 1951 by Saidie A. May

CONDITION

In the past this painting of the *Madonna and Child Enthroned* had been "transferred," i.e., its original wood panel support was cut away from the reverse, and subsequently the paint and ground layers were attached to a fabric layer which then was fastened to another panel. The extant panel, which is worm-eaten, was reduced in thickness to about 9/16" (1.5 cm.) and was cradled. Additional wooden strips have been attached to the left and right edges, and another piece was added to the top. There is some delamination between the fabric layer and the wood panel at the present time. Previous records indicate that the separation between layers is a recurrent problem as was evident when the painting was treated for blisters in 1965.

Up to this time the painting has not been cleaned. Present X-radiography, ultraviolet and infrared examinations suggest that there are few areas of complete paint loss but much abrasion. The actual condition of the paint layer is difficult to assess due to concealing layers of discolored varnish.

Proposed conservation treatment for this painting includes both the removal of the discolored varnish layers and structural work to stabilize the support.

Sian Jones
The Walters Art Gallery, Baltimore

Illustrations of this work in this publication are from photographs taken prior to treatment.

In this painting, purchased as a work by Niccolò di Pietro Gerini,[1] the Madonna sits against a gold cloth of honor patterned in red and black. Her cloak, originally a light blue, has been covered with darker paint, but the red of her tunic is well preserved. The Child, who holds a cross, is partially covered by a yellow garment. At the base of the throne stand SS. John the Baptist and James the Greater. John the Baptist, at the left, wears a pink cloak over a brownish hair shirt and, at the right, James the Greater is dressed in a blue cloak with a yellow lining draped over a pink robe. The two middle figures, SS. Catherine of Alexandria and Dorothy, wear, respectively, a purple mantle over a red robe and a purple cloak over a pink robe. The angels wear white robes with brown and black decoration and have red mantles draped over their shoulders.

The choice and combination of saints in the Trecento are not accidental. Often much can be learned about the circumstances surrounding a particular altarpiece from the saints it depicts.[2] Each of the saints in the Baltimore panel was popular during the Tuscan Trecento. St. John the Baptist, who holds his attribute, the long cross, was one of the patron saints of Florence. His inclusion in the most important heraldic position of the painting (to the Madonna's right) may well indicate that the panel was originally intended for a location in Florence. St. James the Greater was the patron of medieval pilgrims, and his appearance in the Baltimore panel, carrying his attributes, the pilgrim's staff and bell, may indicate that the altar on which this painting originally stood held a famous and often visited relic, but this is only speculation. The two female saints, Catherine of Alexandria and Dorothy, are both virgin martyrs. Catherine holds the martyr's palm and the wheel on which she was tortured, while Dorothy is shown crowned with and carrying roses, the flowers she sent from heaven to a pagan scribe who mockingly asked the saint to send them to him from paradise. Although each of the four saints has a clearly defined legend and tradition, their inclusion together does not allow us to determine why they were chosen or exactly where the painting comes from. The choice of saints, their physical type, their costumes and attributes are, however, all typically Florentine.

One unusual feature of the picture is the cross held by Christ. This is an extremely rare motif and its significance is not entirely clear. It is possible that Christ, surrounded by martyrs, exhibits a sign of his own future martyrdom. It may also be that he shows the cross to St. Catherine, at whom he appears to gaze, perhaps an indication that the altar where the picture originally was located was dedicated to her or, possibly, that the donor bore that name. In any case, the Christ holding the cross is a surprising departure from the firmly established type to which the Baltimore panel belongs.[3]

Niccolò di Pietro Gerini (active 1368–1415) was one of the most prolific and popular Florentine artists of the last quarter of the fourteenth century. His entry into the *Arte dei Medici e Speziali* (the guild to which the Florentine painters belonged) is dated 1369, and one can assume that his earliest independent activity must date from around that same time.[4]

The identity of Niccolò's teacher is unknown, though in all likelihood it was Taddeo Gaddi or someone from his close circle. Taddeo Gaddi (ca. 1300–1366) was, in turn, a pupil of Giotto (ca. 1267–1337).[5] Throughout Gerini's career his work also demonstrated a dependence upon the style of Nardo di Cione, an extremely influential painter active around the middle of the century.[6]

Gerini was a member of the generation of artists who helped bring the style of Florence from the decades of the mid-Trecento into the next century. This generation of painters was to replace the often aloof and hierarchical idiom of Nardo di Cione and his brother Orcagna with a more open pictorial world. Gerini, along with Agnolo Gaddi, Spinello Aretino, Jacopo di Cione (Nardo's brother), and Antonio Veneziano, were the painters who formed the idiom of the crucial early years of the Quattrocento.[7]

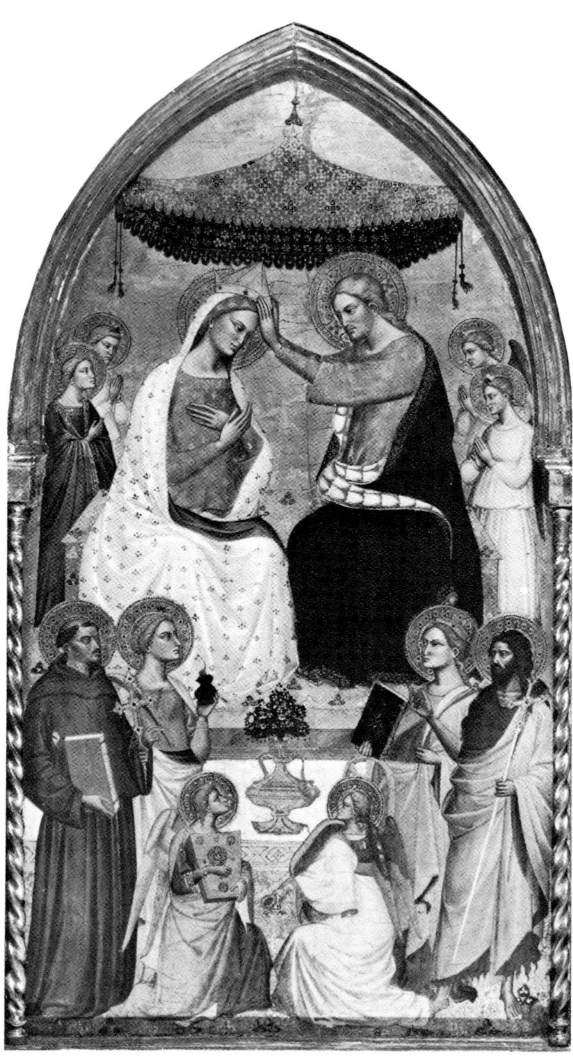

Fig. 1. Attributed to Niccolò di Pietro Gerini, *The Coronation of the Virgin.* Tempera on wood. 35⅜ × 20¹⁵⁄₁₆ inches (89.9 × 53.2 cm.). The Montreal Museum of Fine Arts, John W. Tempest Fund

An understanding of Gerini's style can be obtained by studying a body of homogeneous works which he painted over a period of about four decades. Almost all of them display strong traces of Nardo's style, including the dark, mask-like faces and jagged profiles so characteristic of mid-fourteenth-century painting. Also apparent are the blunt and rotund forms derived from Taddeo Gaddi. The general articulation and massing of the figures come from Taddeo as well.

Each of Gerini's securely attributed Madonnas exhibits a ponderous, somewhat clumsy, stolid form and presence. This important trait of his style can be seen, for example, in the large *Virgin and Child* in Boston[8] or, closer to the Baltimore picture, in *The Coronation of the Virgin* in Montreal (fig. 1). The Montreal panel is a good example of Gerini's particularly robust style. Highly characteristic of the artist are the rather awkward disposition of the figures across and into the picture's space and the static and stiff construction of each of the saints. One has only to look at the standing angels to see how inelegant are Gerini's arms and torsos. The lower figures, while slightly more fluid, are

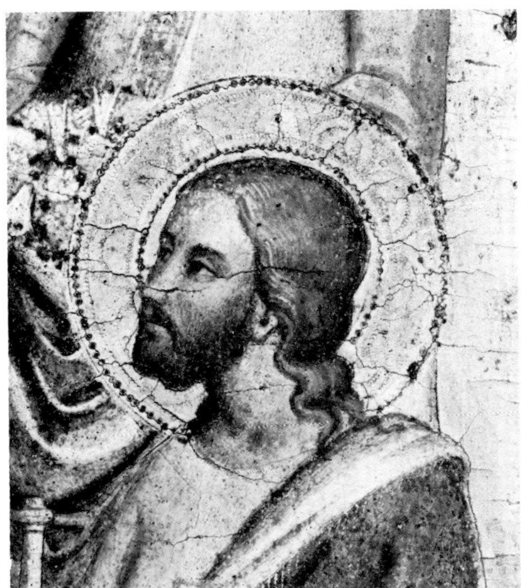

Fig. 2. Circle of Niccolò di Pietro Gerini, *Madonna and Child Enthroned with Angels and Saints,* detail of cat. no. 6

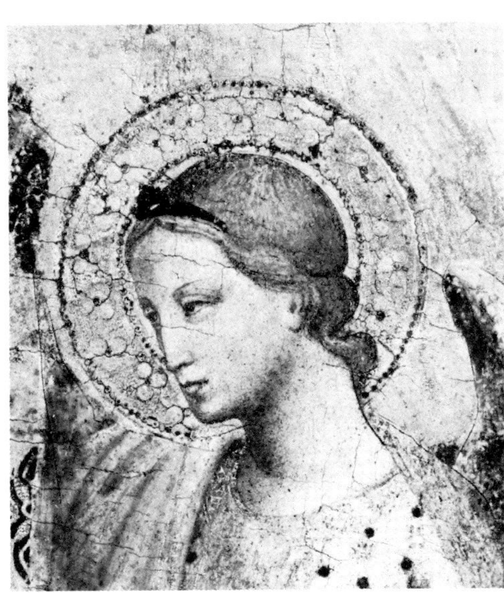

Fig. 3. Circle of Niccolò di Pietro Gerini, *Madonna and Child Enthroned with Angels and Saints,* detail of cat. no. 6

also typical. All of Gerini's faces are marked by a sharp nose, sloping forehead, and large chin. The jerky articulation of the holy figures is paralleled by the patterns which break up the surface of the Montreal panel: the sharply folded robes, the carpet, the cloth of honor, the embroidered cloak of the Madonna, and the decorated canopy all lead the eye from one part of the picture to another in a hurried, uneven fashion.

The Baltimore panel, while surely closely connected with works like the Montreal *Coronation,* seems to lack the ponderous, heavy quality of Madonna panels by Gerini himself. There is, throughout it, a lightness and delicacy slightly foreign to his personal style. There is also a buoyancy and agility about the figures that is absent in all of Gerini's secure works, from the earliest known paintings (*Baptism of Christ,* National Gallery, London; *Crucifix,* Santa Croce, Florence)[9] to the last frescoes in San Francesco, Prato.[10] The halting, tender expression of the saints and angels in the Baltimore panel (figs. 2 and 3) is not found in Gerini's works, where one is confronted with a much more serious, direct, and harsh encounter between the holy figures.

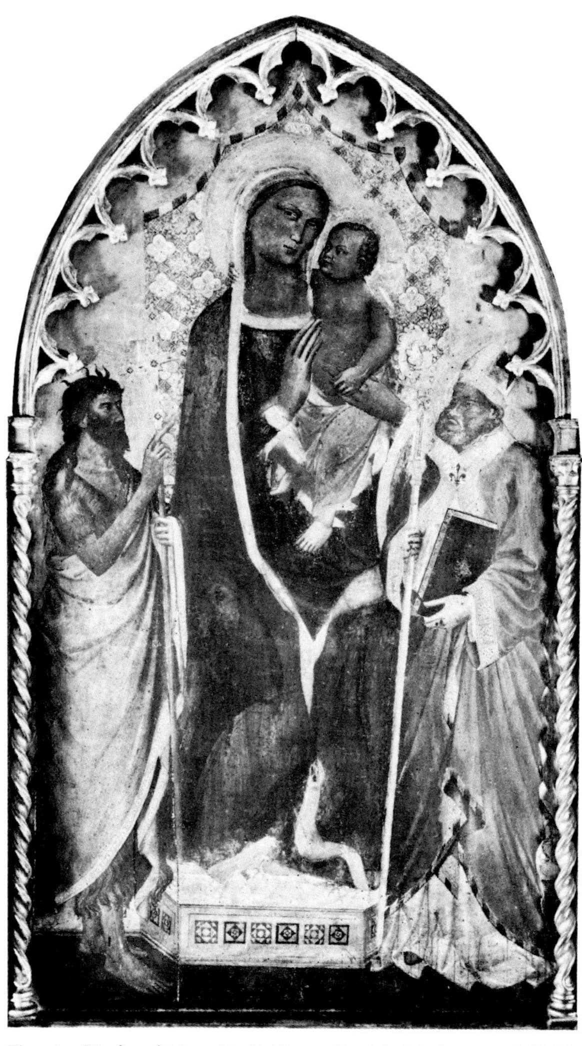

Fig. 4. Circle of Niccolò di Pietro Gerini, *Madonna and Child with Saints John the Baptist and Zenobius*. Tempera on wood. 70⅞ × 39⅜ inches (180 × 100 cm.). Museo Civico, Pistoia Alinari/Editorial Photocolor Archives

A *Madonna and Child with Saints John the Baptist and Zenobius* in the Pinacoteca Communale, Pistoia (fig. 4), is close to the style of the Baltimore panel.[11] It is possible that the artist responsible for this, who seems to have been among Gerini's best followers, was the author of the Baltimore picture.

Whatever the artist's name, his use of numerous light reds and pinks interspersed with white, blue, and black demonstrates that he was a talented colorist. In fact, this charming little work must be classified as one of the better paintings from the circle of Niccolò di Pietro Gerini.

The Baltimore panel cannot be dated with certainty, but on the basis of analogous compositions by Gerini and his school, a date of around 1400 seems most acceptable.

Bruce Cole
Indiana University,
Bloomington, Indiana

NOTES

1. In a letter to G. Rosenthal of December 22, 1975, F. Zeri attributes the panel to Gerini (curatorial files, The Baltimore Museum of Art). M. Boskovits also gives the picture to Gerini and dates it around 1400 (*Pittura fiorentina alla vigilia del Rinascimento* [Florence: Edam, 1975], p. 403). The picture is attributed by R. Fremantle to the Master of the Arte della Lana (*Florentine Gothic Painters from Giotto to Masaccio* [London: Secker and Warburg, 1975], p. 330, no. 684).
2. For saints in Florentine Trecento painting, see G. Kaftal, *The Iconography of the Saints in Tuscan Painting* (Florence: G. C. Sansoni, 1952).
3. I cannot find a single example of Christ holding the cross in D. Shorr, *The Christ Child in Devotional Images in Italy during the XIV Century* (New York: G. Wittenborn, 1954). The only other example I know is found in a Madonna and Child panel (formerly in the Santa Croce Museum, Florence) attributed to Lorenzo di Niccolò.
4. On Gerini, see R. Offner, *Studies in Florentine Painting: The Fourteenth Century* (New York: F. F. Sherman, 1927; reprint ed., New York: Junius Press, 1972), pp. 83–95, and B. Berenson, *Italian Pictures of the Renaissance: Florentine School* (London: Phaidon Press, 1963), 1:158–61.
5. On Taddeo Gaddi, see P. P. Donati, *Taddeo Gaddi* (Florence: Sadea, 1966), and R. Oertel, *Early Italian Painting to 1400* (New York: Praeger, 1968).
6. For Nardo di Cione, see R. Offner, *A Critical and Historical Corpus of Florentine Painting: Nardo di Cione* (New York: New York University, 1960), sec. 4, vol. 2.
7. For this generation of Florentine painters, see B. Cole, *Giotto and Florentine Painting 1280–1375* (New York: Harper & Row, 1976), pp. 121–45.
8. For the Gerini panel in the Museum of Fine Arts, Boston, see Offner, *Studies in Florentine Painting: Gerini*, pl. 1.
9. For the *Baptism*, see Berenson, *Italian Pictures of the Renaissance: Florentine School*, 1:pl. 366; for the *Crucifix* see ibid., 1:pl. 363.
10. On the Prato frescoes, see U. Baldini, *La Cappella Migliorati nel San Francesco di Prato* (Florence, 1965).
11. For the Pistoia panel, see L. Marcucci, *I dipinti toscani del secolo XIV: Gallerie nazionali di Firenze* (Rome: Istituto Poligrafico dello Stato, 1965), p. 113.

SELECTED BIBLIOGRAPHY

Joseph Archer Crowe and Giovanni Battista Cavalcaselle. *A New History of Painting in Italy*. 3 vols. London: J. Murray, 1864–1866.

Raimond van Marle. *The Development of the Italian Schools of Painting*. 19 vols. The Hague: Martinus Nijhoff, 1923–1938.

Richard Offner. *Studies in Florentine Painting*. New York: F. F. Sherman, 1927. Reprint edition. New York: Junius Press, 1972.

Richard Offner. *A Critical and Historical Corpus of Florentine Painting*. 4 sections. New York: New York University, 1930–1969.

Pietro Toesca. *Il Trecento*. Turin: Unione tipografico-editrice torinese, 1951.

Bernard Berenson. *Italian Pictures of the Renaissance: Florentine School*. 2 vols. London: Phaidon Press, 1963.

John White. *Art and Architecture in Italy 1250–1400*. Baltimore: Penguin Books, 1966.

Robert Oertel. *Early Italian Painting to 1400*. New York: Praeger, 1968.

Bruce Cole. *Giotto and Florentine Painting 1280–1375*. New York: Harper & Row, 1976.

Bruce Cole. *Agnolo Gaddi*. Oxford: Oxford University Press, 1977.

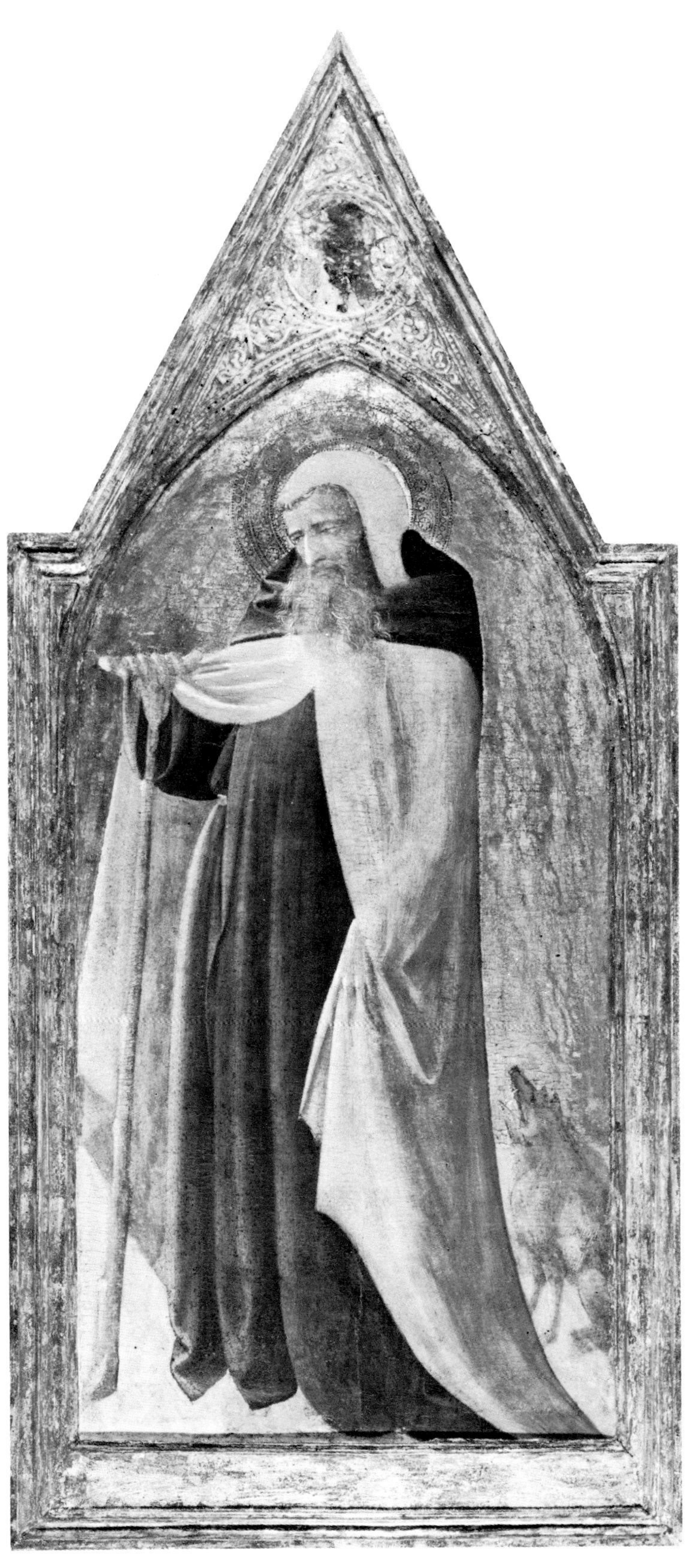

GIOVANNI DAL PONTE (1385–1437)
(Giovanni di Marco)

7. *Saint Anthony Abbot,* ca. 1430

Tempera on wood. 52¼ × 22¾ inches (132.7 × 57.8 cm.)
Bequest of Saidie A. May (BMA 51.391)

PROVENANCE

Acquired from Alberto and Costantino Citernesi, Florence, by Saidie A. May in 1925

Bequeathed to The Baltimore Museum of Art in 1951 by Saidie A. May

CONDITION

The panel representing St. Anthony Abbot consists of two members joined vertically near the center of the painting. The join was originally reinforced by a horizontal wood batten attached to the reverse. At some time in the past the panel was thinned and the batten removed, leaving only the batten channel visible on the reverse. The present panel has new wooden inserts added to the pinnacle and along the bottom edge. There are also narrow wooden strips of framing added around the entire perimeter. All of these later structural additions were incorporated into the design as part of the engaged frame on the front of the painting.

The support shows extensive insect damage. The worm tunnelling is noticeable throughout and makes the panel appear sponge-like. The panel also has been affected by unstable environmental conditions which have caused desiccation that severely weakened the wood and contributed to warping and separation of the join.

The image had been obscured by heavy layers of discolored varnish for years, but recent cleaning has revealed a strong, though abraded, painting. The folds of St. Anthony's robe now suggest a left arm underneath and traces of his left hand. Details of the animal's fur, teeth, and snout are now more visible and give the appearance of a boar rather than of a pig. Much of the gilt background is missing, revealing the underlying red bole. There are major losses along the lower edge and surrounding the vertical join in St. Anthony's light colored cloak. The engaged frame was probably re-gilded when the additions were incorporated into the structure.

Conservation treatment has included consolidation of the fragile wooden support and removal of the grimy varnish layers.

Sian Jones
The Walters Art Gallery, Baltimore

Modern scholarship has correctly rescued this panel from anonymity and recognized its author as Giovanni dal Ponte. Giovanni di Marco, called dal Ponte by Vasari because of his residence near the Ponte Vecchio, was a lesser master of the early Quattrocento.[1] Working in Florence and its environs, he maintained the conservative traditions of the fourteenth-century painters but was open to the swiftly changing artistic developments of the new century. His first works reveal the overwhelming effect upon him of the International Gothic style as transmitted by Ghiberti, Lorenzo Monaco, and the Master of the Bambino Vispo. Absorbed as he was by the abstractly ornamental play of cursive lines, colors, and materials, Giovanni still managed to give his adaptation of the style a personal stamp. He infused his figures with a distinctive psychological presence, at times a fierce intensity, but more often an inwardness of spirit that ranged from delicate passivity to brooding preoccupation tinged with melancholy. In the later 1420's Giovanni came to grips with the revolutionary innovations of Masaccio, and his art was slowly penetrated by a new character.[2] He did not abandon his Gothic inheritance, but he modified it substantially. Eliminating the decorative complexity of his earlier works after the example of Masaccio's grand simplicity, Giovanni's mature paintings of the later 1420's and 1430's achieved a monumentality that asserted the new-found significance of the individual. They expressed this monumentality by adapting some of the plasticity of Masaccio's sculpted drapery and modeling, but more particularly by means of Giovanni's lyrical eloquence of line and delicate sensitivity to shapes. These are the qualities that distinguish this panel depicting St. Anthony Abbot.

There has been some doubt concerning the attribution of the panel since it came to public attention. Philip Pouncy first suggested Giovanni dal Ponte in 1958,[3] but in 1961 Cesare Gnudi and Cesare Brandi disagreed, putting it in the mass of works associated with the school of Lorenzo Monaco.[4] Berenson in his 1963 lists ascribed it, with a question mark to provoke discussion, also to Lorenzo Monaco.[5] More recently, Miklòs Boskovits and Federico Zeri have both given it, without hesitation, to Giovanni, and that is the view of this writer.[6]

Despite its damaged state which tends to obscure detail, the panel exhibits specific features identifying it as Giovanni's work. The physiognomic details of St. Anthony's face are typical of the artist, especially the prominent, sharply highlighted nose, the flattened forehead, and the nearly horizontal, deeply cut ridge of the brow. These features, along with the brooding mood of the whole head which unites them, are recurrent traits in Giovanni's art from the early *Coronation of the Virgin* in the Musée Condé, Chantilly, to the late *Annunciation* of 1435 in the Vatican, and particularly in the remains of his documented frescoes of 1434 in Sta. Trinità, Florence.[7] Similarly recurrent in Giovanni's oeuvre is the crude approach to the hands, the right one with its wide-spread, claw-like fingers resting on the crutch, and the left with its unnaturally elongated fingers shown drawing a fold of the saint's cloak to his side. Such hands appear on St. Anthony's support and on St. Thomas's book to the far left and right, respectively, of the Chantilly painting, and in the Virgin's hands in the Vatican *Annunciation*.

The proportions of the figure and the rhythmic sway of the masses of the body find their equivalents in figures from Giovanni's later works and suggest a dating to the later 1420's or even early 1430's but not to the early teens as has been suggested.[8] The cursive movement of the linear elements, in particular the elegant sweep of the cloak's contour, reflects Giovanni's knowledge of the decorative and expressive potential of the International Gothic style. And yet there is nothing of the superficial application of complex drapery and linear movement to essentially rigid figures that is so evident in the standing saints of the Chantilly *Coronation*. Nor is there the artificial attenuation of the figures manifested in *The Mystic Marriage of St. Catherine* of 1421 in the Museum of Fine Arts,

Budapest, and in the large altarpiece of the *Ascension of St. John the Evangelist with Saints* in the National Gallery, London, of a few years later.[9] Rather, in the restrained and disciplined simplicity of St. Anthony's forms one detects the decisive example of Masaccio. Under the latter's influence, or even possibly through its mediation by Fra Angelico, Giovanni combined his native lyricism with a new dignity of form and subdued color. The saint is now more of an individual, possessing a physical presence that underscores his spiritual depth. His physical being and spiritual presence seem to demand and confidently to inhabit the surrounding ambience rather than merely existing on a flat surface against a gold background. The emphasis on lucidity and monumentality is characteristic of Giovanni's mature work. Accompanying these qualities is the flattening of the pointed arch immediately above the saint's head, a subtle change which eliminates some of the vertical stress of the earlier pictures while providing more ample freedom for the head and shoulders of the figure below. These marks of the artist's mature style can be followed in four triptychs: the *Coronation of the Virgin* of the late 1420's in the Accademia in Florence; and an *Annunciation* in the Badia di Poppiena of about 1431, in the Church of the Annunciate Virgin in Rossano of 1434, and in the Vatican, dated to 1435.[10]

The Baltimore panel was most likely the right wing of a triptych, of which the left wing and central panel are missing.[11] Federico Zeri has suggested that three panels now in the Musées Royaux des Beaux-Arts in Brussels and long attributed to Giovanni originally formed the predella to this triptych, since one of the panels illustrates an incident from the legend, *St. Anthony Tempted by a Pile of Gold* (fig. 3), the other two showing *The Adoration of the Magi* and *St. Francis Receiving the Stigmata* (figs. 2 and 1).[12] The correctness of Zeri's proposal is supported by the size of the predella panel of St. Anthony in relation to the presumed wing above it.[13] All three of the Brussels panels may be placed, like the Baltimore *St. Anthony,* late in the artist's career.[14] They also agree compositionally in that the pose of St. Anthony in the predella would seem to require a placement on the right, the one with St. Francis on the left. Furthermore, the uncommon attribute of the skullcap in the Baltimore painting agrees with this same unusual feature on the St. Anthony figure in Brussels.[15]

The missing panels of the triptych from which our St. Anthony came would probably have been a Madonna and Child in the center and a standing figure of St. Francis to the left. Some idea of the latter's appearance might be obtained by references to two quite similar images Giovanni dal Ponte painted of him, one on the lower part of the left pilaster of the London triptych, the other on the left side of the Accademia altarpiece. In each the saint stands in a three-quarter view, like the Baltimore St. Anthony, but facing right and holding a cross in his left hand while indicating with his right the wound in his side. An impression of the shape of the whole lost triptych can also be obtained by comparing Giovanni's intact triptych now in the Columbia Museum of Art, Columbia, South Carolina (fig. 4).[16] There, the measurements differ slightly, but the style of the frame, including the roundel and gilded gesso-work of the pinnacles, is very close. Like that in the Columbia painting, the roundel in the Baltimore panel might originally have contained the image of the annunciate Virgin.

St. Anthony Abbot (ca. 250–356) was the great patriarch of the desert hermits in the Early Christian period.[17] One of the fathers of monasticism, his constant battles with demons were legendary. In the late Middle Ages his cult spread far and wide. In Italy themes of the hermitic life away from the cities were especially popular after the ravages of the Black Death. Venerated as a hermit and, like SS. Roch and Sebastian, as a healer of contagious diseases, St. Anthony was highly regarded toward the end of the fourteenth century and the beginning of the fifteenth. The cult in Florence radiated from the huge monastery and hospital of Sant'Antonio di Vienna, now destroyed.[18] Giovanni dal Ponte

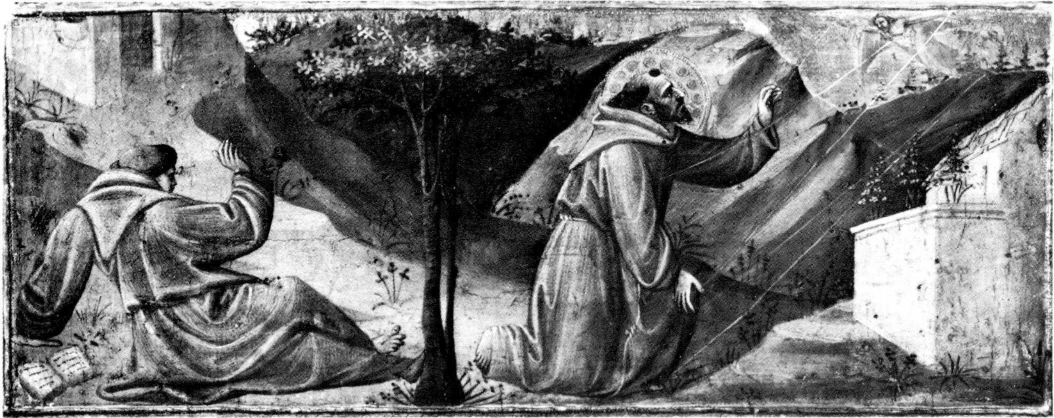

Fig. 1. Giovanni dal Ponte, *St. Francis Receiving the Stigmata*, ca. 1430. Tempera on wood. Predella panel. 7⅞ × 19½ inches (20 × 50 cm.). Musées Royaux des Beaux-Arts, Brussels

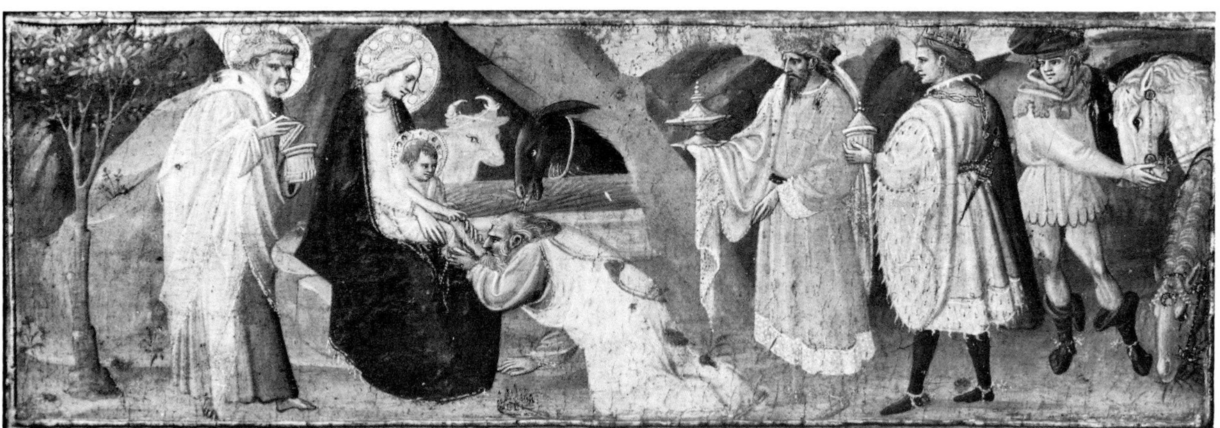

Fig. 2. Giovanni dal Ponte, *The Adoration of the Magi*, ca. 1430. Tempera on wood. Predella panel. 7⅞ × 22⅝ inches (20 × 57.5 cm.). Musées Royaux des Beaux-Arts, Brussels

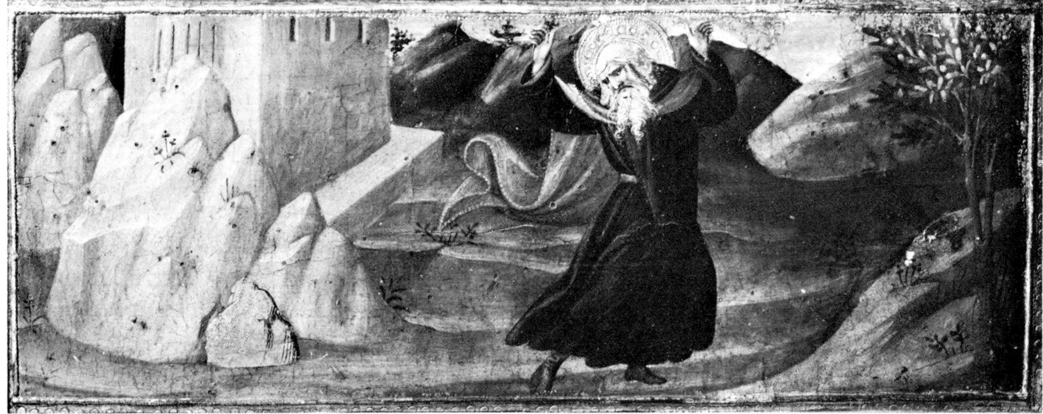

Fig. 3. Giovanni dal Ponte, *St. Anthony Tempted by a Pile of Gold*, ca. 1430. Tempera on wood. Predella panel. 7⅞ × 19½ inches (20 × 50 cm.). Musées Royaux des Beaux-Arts, Brussels

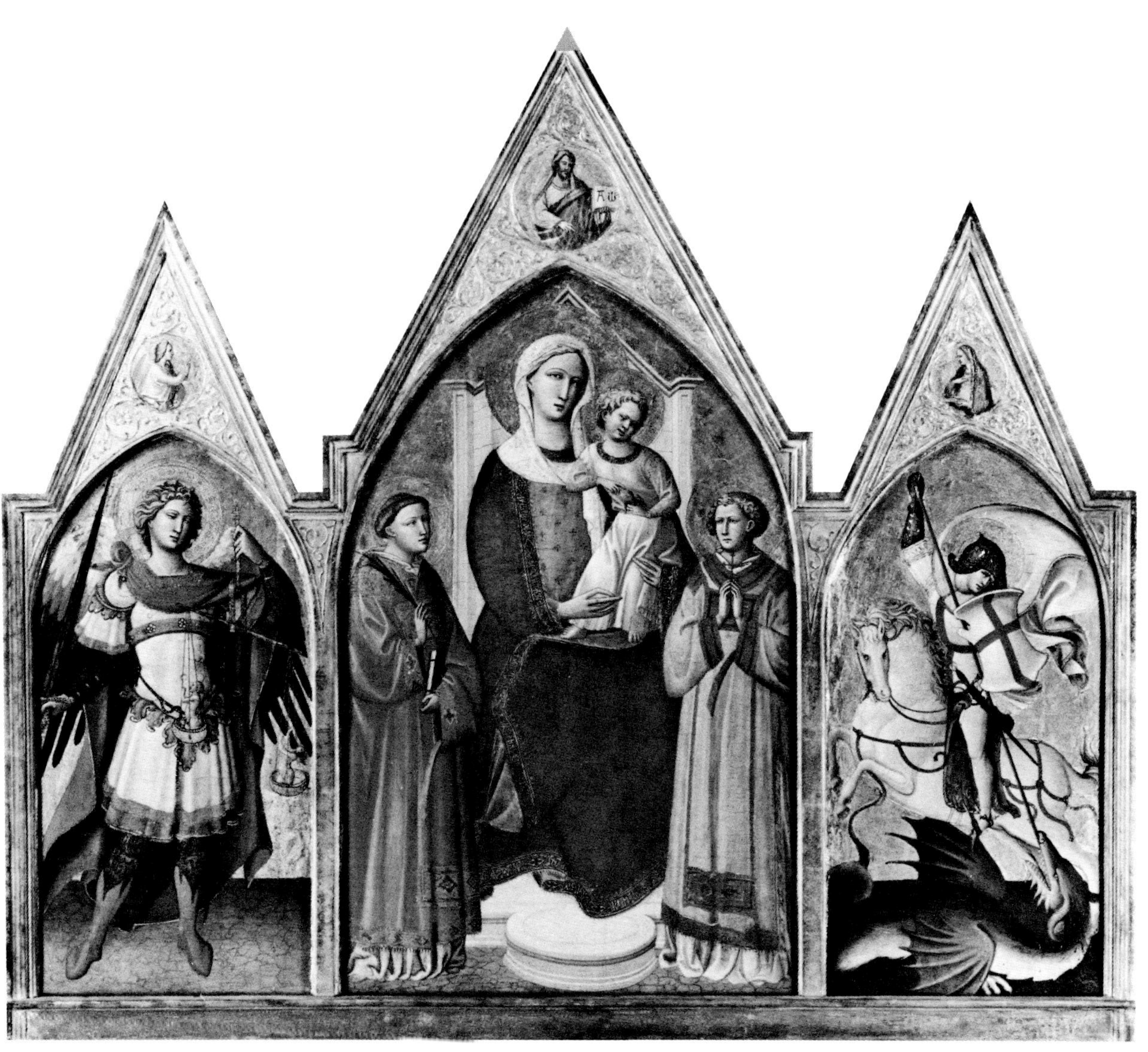

Fig. 4. Giovanni dal Ponte, *Madonna and Child with Saints Michael and George,* ca. 1430–1435. Tempera on wood. Central panel, 36½ × 23 inches (92.7 × 58.4 cm.). Side panels, 28 × 13⅞ inches (71.1 × 35.2 cm.). Columbia Museum of Art, Columbia, South Carolina

painted images of the saint or scenes from his life numerous times, as did nearly every artist of the day. In most of these representations he is shown as he is here, a heavily bearded old man, dressed in the black habit and light cloak with black cowl of the Antonite order. One of his customary attributes is the healing sign of the tau-shaped crutch, shown here in his right hand. Behind him is another of his attributes, the pig, in this instance with mouth agape in an expressive contrast to the saint's tight-lipped countenance. The pig is often considered a symbol of evil and of the demons against which Anthony combatted.[19] But since the Antonite order had a special privilege to raise swine for its livelihood and because lard was a remedy for one of the diseases Anthony was invoked to prevent or cure, the pig accompanying the saint was more often portrayed as his companion than as his adversary.[20] Here the seated animal, oddly canine in form but provided with boar-like tusks, raises its head tensely, awaiting some response from the grieving figure before it.

J. Russell Sale
National Gallery of Art,
Washington, D. C.

NOTES

1. For Giovanni dal Ponte, see the two studies by F. Guidi: "Per una nuova cronologia di Giovanni di Marco," *Paragone* 19, no. 223/43 (September 1968): 27–46; "Ancora su Giovanni di Marco," *Paragone* 21, no. 239 (January 1970):11–23.
2. C. Shell has stressed the reaction of Giovanni to Masaccio in the late 1420's: "Two Triptychs by Giovanni dal Ponte," *Art Bulletin* 54, no. 1 (March 1972):41–46.
3. In a letter to G. Rosenthal of October 22, 1958.
4. Gnudi and Brandi examined the painting with G. Rosenthal on September 20, 1961.
5. B. Berenson, *Italian Pictures of the Renaissance: Florentine School* (London: Phaidon Press, 1963), 1:117.
6. Miklòs Boskovits' attribution is contained in a letter to G. Rosenthal of December 12, 1968; that of Federico Zeri in the *Census of Pre-Nineteenth-Century Italian Paintings in North American Public Collections* (Fredericksen and Zeri, Cambridge, Mass.:Harvard University Press, 1972), p. 91, and again in a letter of December 22, 1975 from Zeri to G. Rosenthal.
7. For all three works, see Guidi, "Per una nuova cronologia," figs. 25, 35, 24.
8. Boskovits, in his letter to G. Rosenthal of December 12, 1968, put the panel in the "comparatively little known early activity of the painter."
9. For the Budapest panel, see Guidi, "Per una nuova cronologia," p. 32, and fig. 27. For the London triptych, see Guidi, "Ancora su Giovanni di Marco," p. 16, fig. 11.
10. For the three *Annunciations,* see Guidi, "Per una nuova cronologia," figs. 33, 32, 35. For the Accademia *Coronation,* see the Academy Gallery's *Catalogue of the Principal Paintings* (Florence, 1932), p. 28, no. 44, and pl. 44.
11. As Zeri suggested in his letter to G. Rosenthal of December 22, 1975.
12. Ibid. The panels are numbers 631a, 631b, 631c: Musées Royaux des Beaux-Arts, Brussels, *Catalogue de la Peinture Ancienne,* new ed. (Brussels: Editions de la Connaissance, 1957), p. 82. The panels are discussed, with earlier literature, by Guidi, "Ancora su Giovanni di Marco," pp. 12, 19, n. 9, and figs. 4a, 4b, 4c.
13. The St. Anthony panel in Brussels (631c) is 50 cm. wide, that in Baltimore 46.4 cm. These dimensions are compatible and would allow the placement of the standing saint above the incident from his legend.
14. Guidi ("Ancora su Giovanni di Marco," p. 12) suggests a very early dating for the Brussels panels, to about the middle of the second decade, preceding the Chantilly *Coronation of the Virgin.* This would seem to be impossible in view of the

remarkably advanced state of anatomy, naturalistic detail, suggestion of space, and dramatic accentuation evident in the three Brussels panels when compared with the predella scenes of St. Catherine from the Budapest *Mystic Marriage of St. Catherine* of 1421 (Guidi, "Per una nouva cronologia," figs. 27–30). By the time he did the Brussels predella panels, Giovanni certainly was aware not only of Ghiberti's North Portal for the Baptistry but also of Gentile da Fabriano's achievement in the Strozzi *Adoration of the Magi* of 1423. In the slow dignity and composure of figures in the Brussels *Adoration* there seems to be a distinct echo of Masaccio's predella *Adoration,* now in the Gemäldegalerie, Staatl. Museen, PKB, Berlin (West), from the Pisa Polyptych of 1426. The motif of the horse bending down for food in the Brussels *Adoration* certainly recalls the same motif in the Masaccio. Both Gamba and Salvini considered the Brussels panels to be a late work: C. Gamba, "Ancora di Giovanni dal Ponte," *Rivista d'Arte* 4 (1906):166; R. Salvini, "Lo sviluppo stilistico di Giovanni dal Ponte," *Atti e Memorie della Reale Accademia Petrarca* 16 (Arezzo, 1935):41.

15. This was first mentioned by Zeri in his letter to G. Rosenthal of December 22, 1975. This type of cap is uncommon for St. Anthony. It seems to appear in one of Giovanni's earlier representations of the saint which is on the right pilaster of the Budapest *Mystic Marriage of St. Catherine* (Guidi: "Per una nuova cronologia," fig. 27). It appears again in an altarpiece close to, but more likely derivative from, Giovanni dal Ponte, the triptych of the *Annunciation with Saints Eustace and Anthony Abbot* in the church of S. Andrea in Brozzi; R. van Marle, *The Development of the Italian Schools of Painting* (The Hague: Martinus Nijhoff, 1927), 9:43, fig. 24. Van Marle attributes the painting to Paolo di Stefano with the influence of Giovanni.
16. F. R. Shapley, *Paintings from the Samuel H. Kress Collection: Italian Schools XIII–XV Century* (London: Phaidon Press, 1966), p. 92, no. K300, figs. 246–48.
17. L. Réau, *Iconographie de l'art chrétien* (Paris: Presses Universitaires de France, 1958), 3, pt. 1:101–102.
18. Walter and Elisabeth Paatz, *Die Kirchen von Florenz* (Frankfurt a/M.: V. Klostermann, 1955), 1: 199 ff.
19. Réau, *Iconographie de l'art chrétien,* 3, pt. 1: 105.
20. Ibid.

SELECTED BIBLIOGRAPHY

Carlo Gamba. "Giovanni dal Ponte." *Rassegna d'Arte* 4, no. 12 (1904):177–86.

Carlo Gamba. "Ancora di Giovanni dal Ponte." *Rivista d'Arte* 4 (1906):163 ff.

Raimond van Marle. *The Development of the Italian Schools of Painting*. 19 vols. The Hague: Martinus Nijhoff, 1923–1938.

Academy Gallery, Florence. *Catalogue of the Principal Paintings*. Florence, 1932.

Roberto Salvini. "Lo sviluppo stilistico di Giovanni dal Ponte." *Atti e Memorie della Reale Accademia Petrarca* 16 (Arezzo, 1935):37 ff.

Louis Réau. *Iconographie de l'art chrétien*. 3 vols. Paris: Presses Universitaires de France, 1955–1959.

Musées Royaux des Beaux-Arts, Brussels. *Catalogue de la Peinture Ancienne*. New edition. Brussels: Editions de la Connaissance, 1957.

Martin Davies. *National Gallery Catalogues: The Earlier Italian Schools*. 2nd edition, revised. London: National Gallery, 1961.

Bernard Berenson. *Italian Pictures of the Renaissance: Florentine School*. 2 vols. London: Phaidon Press, 1963.

Fern Rusk Shapley. *Paintings from the Samuel H. Kress Collection: Italian Schools XIII-XV Century*. London: Phaidon Press, 1966.

Fabrizio Guidi. "Per una nuova cronologia di Giovanni di Marco." *Paragone* 19, no. 223/43 (September 1968):27–46.

Fabrizio Guidi. "Ancora su Giovanni di Marco." *Paragone* 21, no. 239 (January 1970):11–23.

"The Saidie A. May Collection: The Baltimore Museum of Art." *Baltimore Museum of Art Record* 3, no. 1 (1972).

Curtis Shell. "Two Triptychs by Giovanni dal Ponte." *Art Bulletin* 54, no. 1 (March 1972):41–46.

Burton B. Fredericksen and Federico Zeri. *Census of Pre-Nineteenth-Century Italian Paintings in North American Public Collections*. Cambridge, Mass.: Harvard University Press, 1972.

XVIth Century

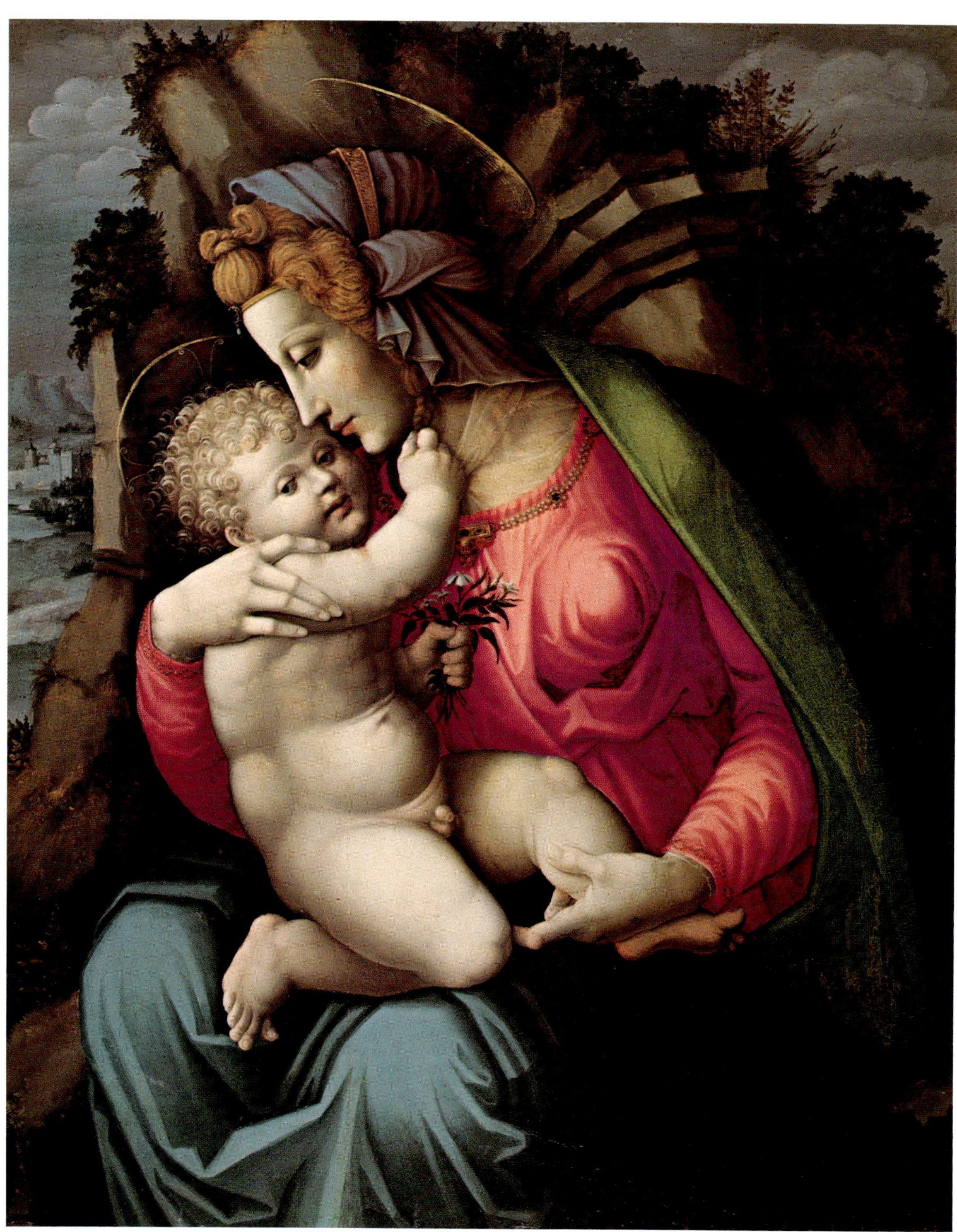

BACCHIACCA (1494–1557)

(Francesco Ubertini)

---

8. *Madonna and Child in a Landscape,* ca. 1540

Oil, possibly with tempera, on wood. 34 × 27 inches (86.4 × 68.6 cm.)
Museum Purchase (BMA 59.87)

PROVENANCE

Benigno Crespi, Milan
A. Venturi, *La Galleria Crespi in Milano* (Milan: U. Hoepli, 1900), p. 211
Crespi Collection Sale Catalogue, Galerie Georges Petit, Paris: June 4, 1914, p. 4, no. 2

Sold on June 4, 1914, in Paris to a M. Feral
Frick Art Reference Library, New York, information printed with the photograph of the painting

Galerie Trotti et Cie., Paris
Frick Art Reference Library, New York, undated photograph from the Galerie Trotti

Heilbuth Collection, Copenhagen
A. McComb, "Francesco Ubertini: Bacchiacca," *Art Bulletin* 8, no. 3 (March 1926):158

Ehrich Galleries, New York
Frontispiece, *International Studio* 82, no. 343 (December 1925)
A. McComb, "Francesco Ubertini: Bacchiacca," *Art Bulletin* 8, no. 3 (March 1926):158

William Randolph Hearst, San Simeon, California
Art Objects and Furnishings from the William Randolph Hearst Collection, Catalogue, Hammer Galleries, Inc., New York (New York: Publishers Printing Co., 1941), p. 15, lot 52, no. 36

Sold in April 1941 to William Thornton, Jr., Baltimore
Memo, curatorial files, The Baltimore Museum of Art

The painting passed to Mrs. Florence B. Thornton, from whose estate it was acquired by The Baltimore Museum of Art on September 29, 1959.
Memo of Gertrude Rosenthal, curatorial files, The Baltimore Museum of Art

CONDITION

Bacchiacca's *Madonna and Child* was painted on a wood panel consisting of two vertical members. The join line is about 9$^9/_{16}$ inches (24.3 cm.) from the left edge, bisecting the Madonna's face and the Child's body. The paint medium is oil, perhaps with some tempera underpainting, laid onto a gesso ground. Prior to its acquisition by the Museum the picture apparently had undergone major treatment. Probably at that time the panel was reduced in thickness to ½ inch (1.3 cm.) and then cradled. On all four sides new wooden strips were added of ¾ inch (1.9 cm.) width.

The painting had deteriorated prior to major treatment by the conservation laboratory of The Walters Art Gallery in 1960. The wood panel was worm-eaten and cracked in several places. The original join had opened, and the right panel member had two major splits extending down from the top edge; there were also several small splits extending into both members of the panel from both the top and the bottom. During its earlier restoration, losses and wormholes had been filled in and overpainted, covering large areas of original paint. The visual aspect was distorted by a heavy, discolored varnish, either stained or tinted.

In 1960, after the painting had been acquired by the Museum, the overpaint and the darkened varnish were removed. The cradle was taken off, as was the white lead filling the worm channels. The panel was infused from the reverse with approximately one pound of wax-resin adhesive. A ¼ inch (0.6 cm) sheet of cork impregnated with wax resin was then attached to the reverse, and five aluminum strips were affixed horizontally across the panel to provide stiffness. The losses were filled with gesso and inpainted with tempera, and the painting was given two coats of non-yellowing varnish.

The paint film has developed normal age cracks, and the green copper resinate of the Madonna's cloak shows a brownish cast. Aside from this and the losses associated with the splits the picture is in good condition.

Were the *Madonna and Child in a Landscape* the only surviving work of Francesco Ubertini, called Bacchiacca, our interpretation of the man and his achievement would be fundamentally different.[1] The usual perception of him as a quaint and rather humorous artist of the Mannerist period, one possessing an archaizing Quattrocento soul wedded uncomfortably to a Cinquecento body, does not apply here.[2] Instead of a narrative picture composed of bits and pieces by Vasari's "most diligent master of little figures,"[3] Bacchiacca presents us with a monumental composition that has the power to grip the viewer. The panel is a major creation of a convinced Mannerist, intending to create a highly expressive work and capable of doing so. In the process, he subverts both the form and the content of High Renaissance art. The nature of Bacchiacca's expressive idea is felt instantly. The image is a disturbing one, evoking through artistic means an impression of strangeness and eccentricity. It offers a view of the darker side of Mannerist art.

The strident pink of the Madonna's dress first catches the spectator's eye and then draws him into the painting. The quality of this hue and the others surrounding it reveal that the world embodied within the picture's frame has nothing to do with normal reality. The colors are entirely subjective, and they are chilling in the emotional tenor they evoke. Combined with the picture's forms, its colors suggest the portentous atmosphere of a ghostly world, one visited only in a troubling dream or hallucination. The pink is chalky and flat, denying richness to the deeper crimson tones of the drapery folds surrounding it. The warmth of the green lining of the Virgin's mantle and of the browns in the rocks behind are more than subdued by the darker blue near them, and above all by the blue-green highlights of the drapery covering the Madonna's knees. This tint occurs again in the highlights of the cloth entwined in her hair, where it turns to an even cooler violet, and a wash of the same blue-green hue casts a pall over the landscape view to the left, destroying its arcadian potential.

Most startling of all in this alien yet compelling color scheme are the flesh tones of the Madonna and Child. The artist here deliberately confounds one's expectations, and in so doing achieves a more pervasive effect of strangeness. For where his monumental figures are bound together in the ostensibly tender embrace of mother and child, and where one might expect a heightened sense of vitality from the athletic force and grace of the Child's pose, all intimacy and vitality are stripped away by the lifeless tints of their flesh. Their skin, created by a return to Gothic technique,[4] is not simply pallid, but unnatural. Their red lips and the Madonna's rouged cheek serve only to heighten the spectral effect.

This chilling array of hues is Bacchiacca's primary means of achieving disquieting effects, but it is not the only means. Though not immediately apparent, the same desire to disturb lies behind the artist's manipulation of every element of the painting's formal structure, beginning with the figural composition. In this arrangement Ubertini successfully disciplines his propensity for an abundance of picturesque and distracting detail, and instead concentrates on the monumental figures of the Madonna and Child. The grouping is felicitous: the bodies of the two figures are placed in opposite three-quarter views and locked together in complementary curves. The unity and lucidity of this composition, combined with its formal complexity, recalls the achievement of the High Renaissance from which it derives. Yet how different from the spirit of that period is the result. Though grand in dimension, the Virgin's body is without substantive bulk. The draperies covering her form are the abstracted renderings of actual fabric. The highlights about her breast, arms, and knees do not describe folds; they are facets of an abstract pattern. The lighting of the whole is excitant in its intent and completely arbitrary in its application. It is instrumental in the flattening of the drapery, but at the same time it exaggerates the volume of the Child's vigorous forms, leaving Him insufficiently supported and floating.

Bacchiacca's devices center on contrasting form and content. In spite of His pale flesh, the Child's glance toward the spectator possesses an innocence and a spontaneity. His right arm reaches touchingly toward one of His mother's braids, and in His left hand is an offering of a posy. The contrast with the Madonna, if she can be so called, is frightening. She is neither loving nor innocent. A calculated deliberation determines the placement of her arms about the Child. What maternal lyricism of line the composition could afford is obviated by a distinct tension in her arms and by the artificial preciousness of her hands.

The strain of the disquieting figures reverberates throughout the painting. The Madonna sits on a rocky ledge. Her precise position in space, however, cannot be determined. Her feet are cut off by the frame, and there is no visible means for measuring the distance between her seat and the primordial forms of the rocky outcrop behind. These lithic masses create a far more effective emphasis on the figures than do their halos, and the crevices and broken planes of the rocks' abstracted forms suggest by their centrifugal arrangement some of the tension ready to burst from the Madonna and Child. The boulders appear to be immediately behind the figures, but such close proximity is impossible. Full-sized trees, not small plants, inhabit the crevices. By such ambiguity Bacchiacca enhances the apparent figural scale at the expense of all logic, and such dimensional contradiction is a trick he uses repeatedly in his art. The Madonna and Child appear gargantuan, increasing the viewer's apprehension. One is allowed no escape. The cold landscape to the left and the leaden-gray turbulence of the sky above complete the painting by casting over it a quality of brooding melancholy.

From the consistency and singular direction of all elements in the painting, there can be no doubt that Bacchiacca fully intended the image of the Madonna and Child to be disturbing. It is not a haphazard creation. It possesses a striking expressive capacity. Bacchiacca was in complete control of all his resources, and he has achieved a compelling work. The subversion of the traditional representation of the subject relates the painting to similar experiments by some of his contemporaries, such as Rosso's shocking Adonis-like *Dead Christ* in the Boston Museum of Fine Arts or the tense *Noli Me Tangere* by Michelangelo and Pontormo.[5]

Not to lessen Bacchiacca's achievement, but to comprehend it fully and to put his creative abilities in proper perspective, one must realize that in this painting as in so much of his other activity he has freely taken over for his own ends the discoveries of others.[6] In the *Madonna and Child,* compositional details and motifs from at least three different masters have been selectively employed.

The exact figural composition goes back to about 1515, although precedents for it have been traced even earlier. In his *Madonna and Child* in the Palace of the Legion of Honor, San Francisco (fig. 1), dating to the middle of the second decade of the century, Francesco Granacci presents the same grouping of the figures.[7] There are some differences, such as Granacci's three-quarter pose of the Madonna's head and the different arrangement of her left hand. And Bacchiacca's infant holds a bouquet of jasmine instead of the small bird. Yet the two compositions are remarkably close, even in their size.[8] They are so close that one can hypothesize either that the Granacci was the model for Bacchiacca, or that a third source, a painting or a cartoon by a different master, was the model for both artists. The latter was probably the case. In the first place, the plastic complexity, grandeur, and clarity of the design are beyond Granacci's capacity and must result from a greater talent.[9] In the second place, even the discrepancies between the Granacci and the Bacchiacca point to a different source. Through wear, the transparency of the flesh tones in the California *Madonna* now reveals that the work's cartoon had her head in profile, like the head in the Baltimore picture, with the nose close to the Infant's forehead just above His left eye.[10] Furthermore, pentimenti now visible in the paint around the left hand of

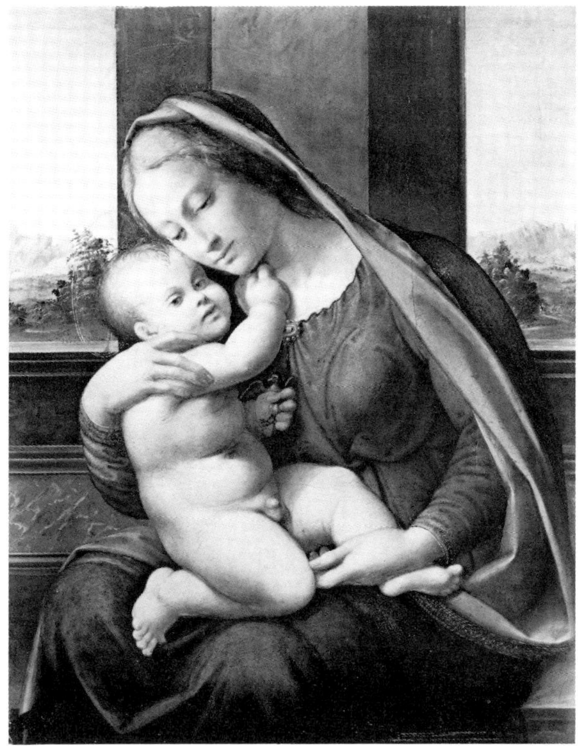

Fig. 1. Francesco Granacci, *Madonna and Child,* ca. 1515. Oil on wood. 33¼ × 25³/₁₆ inches (84.4 × 63.9 cm.). California Palace of the Legion of Honor, San Francisco. Published by permission of The Fine Arts Museums of San Francisco

Bacchiacca's Virgin indicate that her thumb initially extended horizontally, like the same hand in the San Francisco work. These details indicate the respective artists' changes on an original design, a design which included the Madonna's profile and a left hand that extended with the thumb and first finger to the Infant's right knee. Granacci did what might be a more faithful version of the original composition in his *Madonna and Child* formerly in the Hardy Collection, London, from the 1520's.[11] Although Granacci here has altered only the placement of the Child's hand on the Madonna's neck, this small change also indicates that Bacchiacca did not use this work as his source. It is a simplified variant of the presumed original, as is, to a lesser extent, the San Francisco painting. It seems likely that Bacchiacca and Granacci both had access to the original, perhaps in the middle years of the second decade when they both worked on paintings for the *camera* of Pierfrancesco Borgherini.[12] Since the Baltimore panel and that in California use the same color scheme of reddish tunic and blue mantle with green lining, the model could have been a painting or a cartoon with color indications.[13]

Unless it should come to light in the future, we cannot be certain what the original composition used by both Granacci and Bacchiacca looked like. Nevertheless, considering the date of Granacci's San Francisco painting as around 1515, and the surprising nature of its appearance within his oeuvre, one can assume that it is far closer in spirit to the original than is the Bacchiacca. That first and influential composition was undoubtedly the creation of a High Renaissance master. Because of the complexity and vigor of the design, Michelangelo has been put forward as the originator.[14] To this writer, however, the intimacy of the relation between mother and child, the cursive fluidity of the design as a whole and in detail, and the serene corporeal existence of the two figures, all suggest

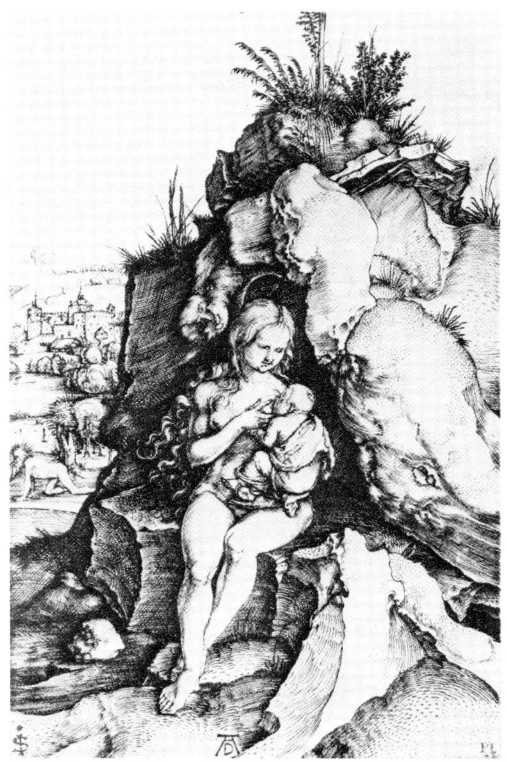

Fig. 2. Albrecht Dürer, *Penance of Saint John Chrysostom* (B.63), ca. 1497. Engraving. 7¼ × 4¹¹⁄₁₆ inches (18 × 11.9 cm.). National Gallery of Art, Rosenwald Collection, Washington, D.C.

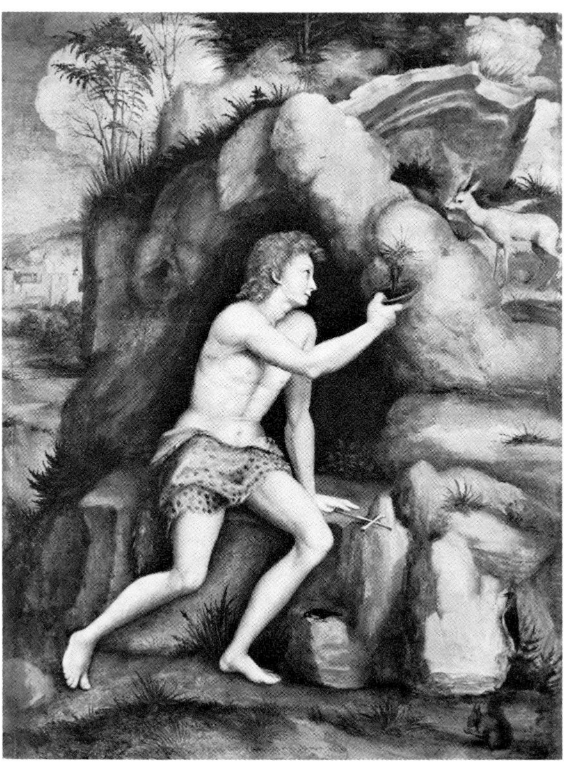

Fig. 3. Bacchiacca (Francesco Ubertini), *St. John the Baptist in the Wilderness,* ca. 1530. Oil on wood. 18¼ × 13½ inches (46.3 × 34.2 cm.). Kunsthalle Bremen

the art of Raphael or someone closer to him, perhaps even Leonardo.[15] But whoever the author was, it is important to recognize how radically Bacchiacca reinterpreted him. The Baltimore panel injects tension and angularity into the design, and replaces the easy serenity with a nervous agitation, reinforced by the arbitrary, dramatic lighting. Bacchiacca took the design from someone else, certainly, but he creatively transformed it to new ends.

The same approach characterizes Bacchiacca's use of two other sources. He has adapted the rocky background and the view opening onto a landscape at the left from Dürer's engraving of the *Penance of St. John Chrysostom* (fig. 2).[16] Throughout his career Bacchiacca loved to combine the more unruly landscapes of the North with Italian figural designs, capitalizing on the tensions arising from such a juxtaposition.[17] He had already used this same Dürer background for his *St. John the Baptist in the Wilderness* in the Kunsthalle Bremen (fig. 3).[18] In that work he was relatively faithful to the naturalistic indications of Dürer's rocky cave, to its scale and placement within the print, and to the figure's relation to the whole. But already one can perceive Bacchiacca's efforts to make the setting more picturesque and to aggrandize its apparent scale. Whole trees, their limbs covered with delicately patterned leaves contrasted with the gnarled forms of dead branches, replace Dürer's grasses and frondy weeds. The flattened rocky plates to the upper right in the engraving are accentuated, giving them an added upward and outward thrust. And Bacchiacca has even added a full-grown deer beneath these plates, turning the relatively small scale of Dürer's curving rock into an entire meadow. The effect of these changes on the figure is disconcerting, for St. John seems almost a giant—a hearkening back to irrational Gothic scale. Something of the same impression applies to

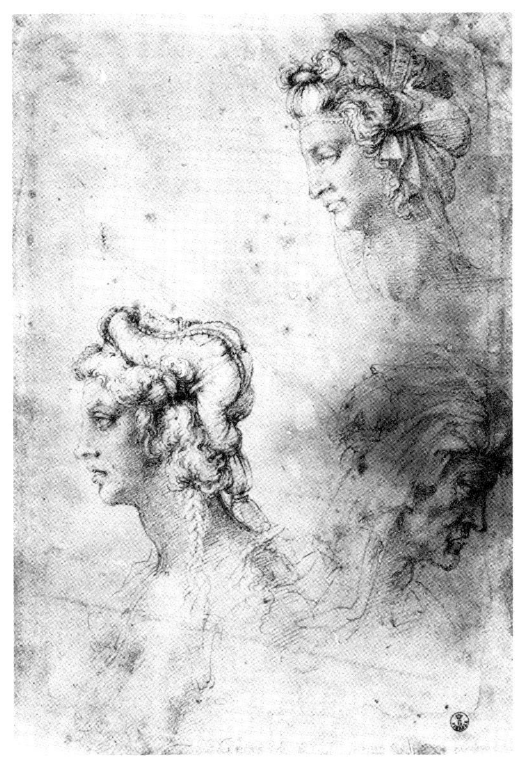

Fig. 4. Follower of Michelangelo, *Three Studies of Female Heads,* ca. 1520's. Black chalk. 13⅜ × 9¼ inches (34 × 23.5 cm.). Uffizi (no. 599E recto), Florence. Alinari/Editorial Photocolor Archives

the rocky backdrop behind the Baltimore *Madonna and Child.* There is a dimensional ambiguity between the figures and the background. But in this painting the artist achieves a different and more impressive result, for the scale of monumentality of the figures has been concordantly increased with the now highly abstracted forms of the stony mass. The still existent tensions between the figures and the ground operate in favor of the former, giving the two figures a superhuman scale. The troubling content of the group is consequently accentuated.

To attain the eccentric result he sought, Bacchiacca adopted a type of female head used by Michelangelo in the 1520's and 1530's, the so-called *teste divine,* intended, according to Vasari, for Gherardo Perini.[19] Several of these drawings in the Uffizi (598E recto, 599E recto), their attribution to Michelangelo in dispute, were known by Bacchiacca and have even been cited as his works, copying Michelangelo's designs (fig. 4).[20] These drawings, and a number of others like them, exhibit a masculine structure in the classicized female face and suggest a certain austere remoteness of character. They also present each head with a coiffure of elaborate complexity involving braids, ringlets, waves, entwined cloths, applied ornaments of a curving sumptuousness, and jewels. However marvelously inventive these headdresses are, they do not, at least to this writer, agree in their expressive effect with the character of the face to which they are applied. The treatment of the face and the hair are disjunctive, the minute attention to the ornamental accompaniment competing with, rather than complementing, the face as the major expressive vehicle.

Bacchiacca liked these heads and used them again and again in his paintings. In most instances he brought the remote character of the faces down to a more accessible level of ordinary expression. But he retained the elaborate headdress. The combination of the commonplace face and the ornate artificial hairdo seems to be less disjunctive in his paintings than in the drawings. He employed the new type in his *Portrait of a Lady* in the Springfield Museum of Fine Arts and in the rather coy *Woman with a Cat* in a private collection in Italy, neither one a portrait likeness, each more of a type.[21] When such a head appears in his religious works, it is for Salome and her attendants in the *Decapitation of St. John* in the Gemäldegalerie, Staatl. Museen, PKB, Berlin (W.), or for the women in the highly decorative pageants of *Moses Striking the Rock,* whose location is unknown, and in the *Gathering of Manna,* National Gallery of Art, Kress Collection.[22] In all of these works the spirit is secularizing, even sensual, with few overtones of a more elevated spiritual realm. To judge best the associations the type of head may have had for Bacchiacca and his contemporaries, or at least for his audience, we need only look at his most faithful representation of one of these *teste divine,* his so-called *Portrait of a Lady and Child* at the University of Southern California, Los Angeles.[23] Her coiffure and dress are very close to Uffizi 599E.[24] Because of her luxury, the satyric grin of the young child, and the open purse that she fingers, the woman in the painting quite appropriately has been called a courtesan and the picture titled *Portrait of a Courtesan with Eros.*[25] And Bacchiacca did have firsthand knowledge of such gaudy ladies if we are to believe Cellini's account of the artist's shabby treatment at the hands of the notorious Pantasilea in Rome.[26]

Whatever associations the *teste divine* had for Michelangelo, Bacchiacca's adaptations of them express little in the way of divinity, at least in a traditional Christian sense. It is precisely for this reason that the appearance of such a head on the Madonna in the Baltimore painting is so disturbing. Such obvious ornamentation had a visual history of association with beguiling deceit, not with the Virgin. We need only think of the moral overtones attached to such conspicuous display in Botticelli's *Calumny of Apelles* in the Uffizi, where virtuous Truth is naked and unadorned.

The indecorous overtones are present in the Baltimore Madonna's head, yet as we have seen, all aspects of the painting possess a sense of strangeness. The headdress of the figure in the upper right corner of Uffizi 599E is close to that in the painting, but the face is not. Nor is any face in the known drawings sufficiently exact to be called a direct source. Bacchiacca has taken something of the drawn figures' remoteness by adopting the rigid profile and the strong features. He has, however, transformed their plastic structure into a cameo thinness. By using pale flesh tones and sharpening the contour, he has hardened the face considerably. Skillfully combining the drawings' strength of character with his own selective transformations, he has created a head of ominous impact.

The sureness with which he utilized all the means of his art to achieve the discomfiting *Madonna and Child* in Baltimore suggests that Bacchiacca executed the painting at the height of his powers. Aspects of the work occur elsewhere in his art, but rarely with such effect or with such obvious seriousness of purpose. The monumentality and intensity are equally rare. They present a side of his achievement unrecorded in Vasari and in all later scholarship. With this realization of his capabilities, other works of the period heretofore considered beyond his talents may yet appear or be returned to him. But such recognition is hampered by our severe lack of information on his career. It is, in fact, impossible to date the Baltimore picture with any precision. All the extant works mentioned by Vasari come before 1525, or relatively early in Bacchiacca's artistic life. Only one dated painting, a portrait of 1533, documents his career's development for the next thirty-two years, until his death in 1557.[27] A stylistic analysis and arrangement of his paintings are complicated further by his frequent re-use of individual figures and motifs and by the repetition of whole compositions. This is true also of the Baltimore *Madonna and Child,* for Bacchiacca made use of the same figural composition at least three other times. These appear to be earlier than the painting under discussion, and they are likewise undated.

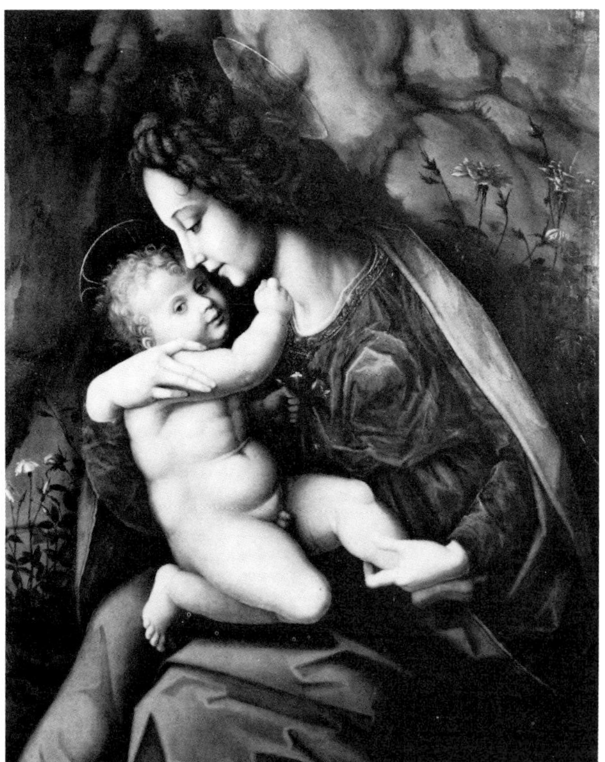

Fig. 5. Bacchiacca (Francesco Ubertini), *Madonna and Child,* ca. 1530. Oil on wood. 34 × 26¾ inches (86.4 × 67.9 cm.). Collection of Jack Linsky, New York

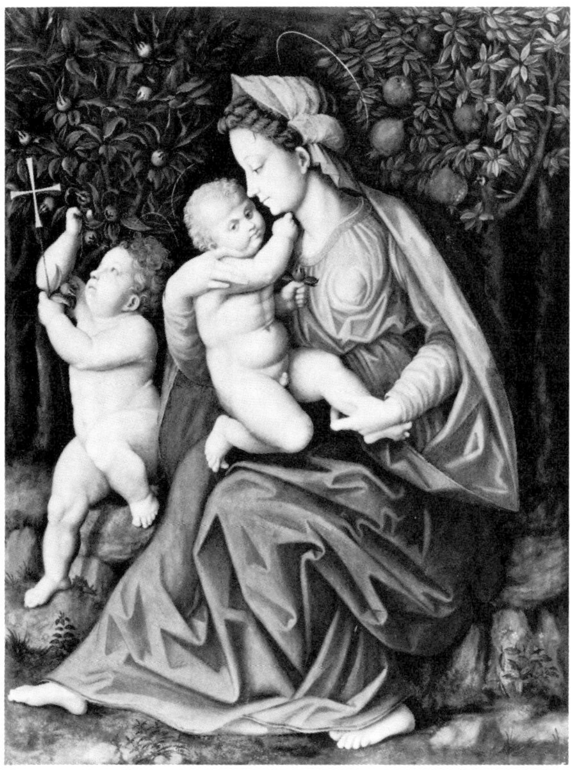

Fig. 6. Bacchiacca (Francesco Ubertini), *Madonna and Child with the Infant St. John,* ca. 1550–1555. Oil on wood. 45 × 34¼ inches (114 × 87 cm.). P. & D. Colnaghi & Co. Ltd., London

What might be the first occurs as an apparition in the small *Vision of St. Bernard* in the Palazzo Venezia in Rome, dated in the 1520's by Nikolenko.[28] The two other works are similar in size to the Baltimore picture. These are the *Madonna and Child* in the Linsky collection, New York (fig. 5), and the *Madonna and Child with the Infant St. John* which recently appeared at Colnaghi's in London (fig. 6).[29]

From its retention of a sfumato atmosphere, chiaroscuro, and a more humane face for the Madonna, the Linsky version was probably executed while Bacchiacca was still under the influence of Andrea del Sarto, in the 1520's.[30] The gesture of the Child's right hand is unmotivated in the Linsky picture, but the use of the Dürer engraving for the background is already evident, in this instance a magnified close-up. The third version, the Colnaghi picture, shares with the Linsky painting the placement of the Madonna's legs parallel to the surface rather than orthogonally as in Baltimore. Since the Colnaghi picture includes the Virgin's feet and the motif of the young St. John reaching into a tree, it appears less concentrated and less monumental than the Linsky panel and therefore might seem earlier. But the lessening of the Madonna's bulk through the abstracting pattern of the drapery, along with the changing type of head and more arbitrary lighting, put it closer to the painting in Baltimore. The latter's sophistication and subversion of the traditional image of the Virgin—compare the Linsky Madonna—would seem to necessitate a date later in the artist's career. The artist is aware of the explorations in color, form, and content of Rosso and Pontormo, and of some of the tensions in Michelangelo, but he is no longer dependent on these masters for complete guidance. Most scholars have put the Baltimore *Madonna and Child* later in Francesco Ubertini's career, and a dating around 1540 seems reasonable.[31]

Since the Madonna of Bacchiacca's image sits directly on the ground, she may be said to belong to the general iconographical type of Madonna of Humility. While the character of the Virgin's head does not suggest that virtue, the artist's knowledge of the type and his willful twisting of it seem more probable and poignant than a purely arbitrary collection of iconographical motifs. Every aspect of the picture was executed with deliberation. The Child's innocent gestures, especially the left hand with the bouquet, contrast with the calculated placement of the arms of His mother. The bouquet itself might be interpreted as echoing the same combination of sweetness and tension. Several writers have mentioned that the flowers are jasmine,[32] often symbolic of the Virgin and also, because of their form, of grace and elegance.[33] In another example of its use, the Christ Child reaches for a sprig of the plant in the hands of Leonardo's gracious *Benois Madonna*.[34] Looking more closely at Bacchiacca's bouquet, the central blossom appears to be different from the surrounding jasmine. It could be sweetbriar, and if such, could allude, because of its five petals, to the five wounds of Christ, thus prefiguring in the Child's youth, in the very arms of His mother, the tragedy of His future passion.[35]

Such symbolic interpretations are difficult to pin down and easily seem overdone, but one cannot avoid the foreboding atmosphere of the entire picture. Much of this comes from the chilling colors and from the character of the Madonna. She is large and made even larger by the primeval rocky mass behind her. There is a strange congruence of the curves, masses, and shapes of the stony pile and those of the Madonna herself. She and the craggy mountain are closely identified. There was an ancient tradition linking major events of Christ's life to earthen grottoes: His birth, entombment, and resurrection.[36] The emotional and religious allure of such *loci* of the supernatural and divine epiphany led the Renaissance to specific manifestations. We need only remember the gaping mouth of the cave in Mantegna's *Adoration of the Magi* (Uffizi), the dark mystery surrounding Leonardo's *Madonna of the Rocks* (Louvre) and the fad for artificial grottoes in the late fifteenth and in the sixteenth centuries.[37] Bacchiacca himself painted frescoes in the grotto in the Pitti Palace gardens in Florence.[38] Rocks rise up in the Baltimore painting, but the cave seen in Dürer's print is largely suppressed. The works by Mantegna and Leonardo demonstrate the association of the Madonna and Child with the cave, and also, though not so directly, with the rocky outcrop surrounding it. A less prominent tradition did, however, make a specific symbolic link between a mountain of stone and the Divine Mother and her Child.

This usage traces its origin to the Book of Daniel in the Old Testament. There, under threat of death if he should fail, Daniel undertook to interpret the troubling dream-vision of Nebuchadnezzar, king of Babylon, who was then persecuting the Jews. In the dream the king saw a mighty human image of frightening size, fashioned of gold, silver, iron, and bronze. But as he looked at the image, it was destroyed before his very eyes by another power whose appearance in the dream made no clear sense:

> Thus thou sawest, till a stone was cut out of a mountain without hands: and it struck the statue upon the feet thereof that were of iron and of clay, and broke them in pieces.
>
> Then was the iron, the clay, the brass, the silver and the gold broken to pieces together, and became like the chaff of a summer's thrashing floor . . . but the stone that struck the statue, became a great mountain, and filled the whole earth. (Daniel 2:34–35)

The prophet revealed the message of the dream to signify the certain downfall of Nebuchadnezzar's kingdom and many others at later times. The image of the stone "cut from the mountain by no human hand" represents the power of God to destroy the symbolic idols of earthly power. It also signifies the divine establishment of an eternal kingdom, one that would, to continue the metaphor, become a great mountain and fill the whole earth.

> And in the days of those kingdoms the God of heaven will set up a kingdom that shall never be destroyed, and his kingdom shall not be delivered up to another people, and it shall break in pieces, and shall consume all these kingdoms, and itself shall stand forever. According as thou sawest that the stone was cut out of the mountain without hands . . . (Daniel 2:44–45)

The apocalyptic and promissory nature of Daniel's interpretation was naturally turned by Early Christian biblical exegesis into a prophecy of the coming of Christ and His Kingdom, and it was used as such in the Renaissance.[39] The mountain became symbolic of the Virgin in Hrabanus Maurus's popular *Allegoriae in Sacram Scripturam* of the ninth century, the stone cut from the mountain a prophecy of the Virgin Birth of Christ.[40] These symbolic associations of mountain and stone easily come to mind in front of the Mantegna and Leonardo paintings mentioned above. A second Mantegna painting, moreover, has been convincingly interpreted as just such an allegory of the Virgin Birth and the promise of Christ's reign[41]—the small *Madonna of the Rocks,* also in the Uffizi.[42]

Mantegna's finely executed little work, though worlds apart in the character of its expression, is remarkably close in iconographic detail to Bacchiacca's *Madonna and Child.* With the Mantegna example as a precedent, the mountain of rock in the Baltimore panel no longer appears so exceptional, and we can be reasonably confident that a similar religious allegory of the Virgin Birth and of the promise of Christ's victory lies behind it.

J. Russell Sale
National Gallery of Art,
Washington, D. C.

NOTES

1. For general literature on Bacchiacca, see L. Nikolenko, *Francesco Ubertini called Il Bacchiacca* (Locust Valley, N.Y.: J. J. Augustin, 1966).

   For discussion of the painting, see: ibid., pp. 24, 26, 57, no. 66, and fig. 66; B. Berenson, *The Florentine Painters of the Renaissance,* 2nd ed. (New York: G. P. Putnam's Sons, 1901), p. 102; A. Venturi, *Storia dell'Arte Italiana* (Milan: U. Hoepli, 1925), 9, pt. 1: 473; A. McComb, "Francesco Ubertini (Bacchiacca)," *Art Bulletin* 8, no. 3 (March 1926):158; H. S. Merritt, "Bacchiacca Studies: The Uses of Imitation" (unpublished dissertation, Princeton University, 1958), p. 127; H. S. Merritt, "Francesco Ubertini called Il Bacchiacca, 1494–1557," in *Bacchiacca and His Friends: Florentine Paintings and Drawings of the Sixteenth Century,* exhibition catalogue, in *Baltimore Museum of Art News* 24, no. 2 (Winter 1961):26–27, 30; G. Rosenthal, "Bacchiacca and His Friends: Comments on the Exhibition," in *Bacchiacca and His Friends,* p. 7, and cat. p. 41, no. 16; G. Rosenthal, "Bacchiacca: Mannerist with Perfect Manners," *Art News* 59, no. 9 (January 1961):42–44, 61–63; G. Rosenthal, "Il Bacchiacca at Baltimore," *Connoisseur* 149, no. 599 (January 1962):58–63.
2. For Bacchiacca as a playful artist, see L. Marcucci, "Contributo al Bacchiacca," *Bollettino d'Arte* 43, no. 1 (January–March 1958):29–30, and S. J. Freedberg, *Painting in Italy 1500 to 1600,* rev. ed. (Harmondsworth, England: Penguin Books, 1975), pp. 239–40.
3. Giorgio Vasari, *Le Vite de' più eccellenti pittori, scultori ed architettori,* 9 vols., ed. G. Milanesi, 2nd ed. (Florence: Sansoni, 1906), 3:592.
4. Bacchiacca's technique of laying in the flesh tone with a cool green or blue-gray on which modeling followed in pale pink recalls that of Italian Trecento painters; Nikolenko, *Francesco Ubertini,* p. 28.
5. For Rosso's Boston picture, see Freedberg, *Painting in Italy,* p. 201, and fig. 82. We have several versions of the lost *Noli Me Tangere* that Michelangelo designed and Pontormo painted for Alfonso d'Avalos in 1531. For one, attributed to Bronzino and now in the Casa Buonarotti in Florence, see E. Baccheschi, *L'Opera completa del Bronzino* (Milan: Rizzoli, 1973), p. 88, no. 19, and pl. 4.
6. Ubertini is probably one of the few artists about whom a dissertation has been written on his

derivations from others: Merritt, "Bacchiacca Studies: The Uses of Imitation."

7. S. J. Freedberg recognized the painting, formerly attributed to Fra Bartolommeo, as a work by Granacci of about 1515. He related the composition to nearly contemporary works by Alonso Berruguete and to a precedent established by Donatello: *Painting of the High Renaissance in Rome and Florence* (Cambridge, Mass.: Harvard University Press, 1961), 1:491. For Granacci's picture in San Francisco, see C. von Holst, *Francesco Granacci* (Munich: Bruckmann, 1974), p. 141, no. 19, and pls. 38, 39; Merritt, "Francesco Ubertini called Il Bacchiacca," p. 26.
8. The San Francisco painting measures 84.4 × 63.9 cm. compared with the 86.4 × 68.6 cm. of the Baltimore panel: von Holst, *Francesco Granacci,* p. 141.
9. This is recognized by von Holst, *Francesco Granacci,* pp. 27, 141.
10. Ibid., p. 27, and fig. on p. 29.
11. Von Holst, *Francesco Granacci,* pp. 27, 157, no. 47, and pl. 78.
12. Vasari, *Le Vite,* 5:342–43.
13. Von Holst, *Francesco Granacci,* p. 27.
14. Ibid., pp. 27, 141. For the presumed influence of Michelangelo on Bacchiacca's composition, see Nikolenko, *Francesco Ubertini,* pp. 24, 57, and McComb, "Francesco Ubertini," p. 158.
15. Only G. Rosenthal has described the composition of Bacchiacca's painting as Raphaelesque: "Bacchiacca and His Friends: Comments on the Exhibition," p. 7. For earlier and contemporary works by Raphael and his circle which may be related in general to the composition in question, see the *Tempi Madonna* in Munich, the *Madonna di Foligno* in the Vatican, the *Sistine Madonna* in Dresden, the *Madonna of the Chair* in the Pitti Gallery, the *Madonna della Tenda* in Munich, and the *Madonna del Pesce* in Madrid: Paolo de Vecchi, *L'Opera completa di Raffaello* (Milan: Rizzoli, 1968), p. 99, no. 83; p. 108, nos. 97, 105; p. 111, nos. 109, 110, 111.
16. Merritt, "Bacchiacca Studies," p. 127.
17. Ibid., p. 123.
18. Nikolenko, *Francesco Ubertini,* p. 52, and fig. 51. Nikolenko dates the panel to 1525–1530.
19. Vasari, *Le Vite,* 7:276.
20. For the relationship of these drawings to Michelangelo, and their history, see L. Dussler, *Die Zeichnungen des Michelangelo* (Berlin: Mann, 1959), p. 230, no. 491; p. 231, no. 492; and F. Hartt, *The Drawings of Michelangelo* (London: Thames and Hudson, 1971), p. 383. Merritt believes that Bacchiacca used Uffizi 599E recto for the Baltimore panel: "Bacchiacca Studies," p. 127, and "Francesco Ubertini called Il Bacchiacca," p. 26.
21. For the two paintings, see Nikolenko, *Francesco Ubertini,* p. 61, and fig. 76; p. 52, and fig. 50.
22. Ibid., p. 58, and fig. 69; p. 59, and figs. 70, 71.
23. Ibid., p. 51, and fig. 49.
24. I. Berge, "Un dipinto sconosciuto del Bacchiacca e il suo modello," *Rivista d'Arte* 17 (1935):85.
25. Ibid.
26. Benvenuto Cellini, *The Life,* trans. J. A. Symonds, 3rd ed. (London: John C. Nimmo, 1899), p. 69.
27. The location of the portrait of the philosopher, Origene Salecchi, is unknown; Nikolenko, *Francesco Ubertini,* p. 54, and fig. 57.
28. Ibid., p. 45, and fig. 31.
29. The Linsky collection painting (see fig. 5) measures 86.4 × 67.9 cm., while the Colnaghi picture is slightly larger, 114 × 87 cm. For the Linsky *Madonna,* see Nikolenko, *Francesco Ubertini,* p. 57, and fig. 67. For the Colnaghi work (see fig. 6), see "Old Masters at Colnaghi's," *Apollo* 108, no. 197 (July 1978): 71; and *Paintings by Old Masters,* catalogue (London: P. & D. Colnaghi & Co., 1978), p. 13, no. 11.
30. Nikolenko, *Francesco Ubertini,* p. 57, dates it later, to ca. 1533–1540.
31. McComb, "Francesco Ubertini," p. 158, considered it a "late work." Merritt, in his dissertation ("Bacchiacca Studies," p. 127), gave it a date of "sometime after about 1525"; but in his later article ("Francesco Ubertini," p. 30) he dates it with reserve to 1530–1535. Rosenthal ("Bacchiacca and His Friends," p. 7) suggested a date after 1520. Nikolenko (*Francesco Ubertini,* p. 57) considered it to belong to the last period of Ubertini's life, to 1540–1557.
32. A. Venturi, *La Galleria Crespi in Milano* (Milan: U. Hoepli, 1900), p. 211; M. Levi D'Ancona, *The Garden of the Renaissance: Botanical Symbolism in Italian Painting* (Florence: Leo S. Olschki, 1977), p. 193.
33. Levi D'Ancona, *Garden of the Renaissance,* p. 193.
34. Kenneth Clark, *Leonardo da Vinci,* rev. ed. (Baltimore: Penguin Books, 1963), pl. 8.
35. Levi D'Ancona, *Garden of the Renaissance,* p. 368.
36. E. Benz, "Die heilige Höhle in der alten Christenheit und in der Östlich-Orthodoxen Kirche," *Eranos Jahrbuch* 22 (1953):365–432.
37. For the artificial grottoes, see E. Battisti, "Natura artificiosa to Natura artificialis," in *The Italian Garden,* ed. D. R. Coffin (Washington, D.C.: Dumbarton Oaks, 1972), pp. 32–33; and E. MacDougall, "Ars Hortulorum: Sixteenth Century Garden Iconography and Literary Theory in Italy," in *The Italian Garden,* pp. 56–57.
38. Vasari, *Le Vite,* 6:456.
39. Jerome, *Commentaria in Danielem Prophetam,* in J. P. Migne, *Patrologiae cursus completus . . . Series*

Latina, vol. 25 (Paris: J. P. Migne, 1884), col. 504; E. Kirschbaum, ed., *Lexikon der christlichen Ikonographie*, 8 vols. (Rome: Herder, 1968–1976), 2: 24–25.

40. Hrabanus Maurus, *Allegoriae in Sacram Scripturam*, in Migne, *Patrologia Latina*, vol. 112 (Paris: J. P. Migne, 1878), col. 1001; "Mons, virgo Maria, ut in Daniele: Abscissus lapis de monte sine manibus quod Christus de Maria sine virili semine."

41. F. Hartt, "Mantegna's Madonna of the Rocks," *Gazette des Beaux-Arts*, ser. 6, 40 (July–December 1952):333 ff.

42. N. Garavaglia, *L'Opera completa del Mantegna* (Milan: Rizzoli, 1967), p. 113, no. 68, and pl. 50.

SELECTED BIBLIOGRAPHY

Adolfo Venturi. *La Galleria Crespi in Milano*. Milan: U. Hoepli, 1900.

Bernard Berenson. *The Florentine Painters of the Renaissance*. 2nd edition. New York: G. P. Putnam's Sons, 1901.

Adolfo Venturi. *Storia dell'arte italiana*. 11 vols. Milan: U. Hoepli, 1901–1939.

Adolfo Venturi. "La Quadreria Sterbini in Roma." *L'Arte* 8 (1905):422–40.

Adolfo Venturi. *La Galleria Sterbini in Roma*. Rome: Casa Editrice de L'Arte, 1906.

Roberto Salvini. "Francesco Ubertini." In Thieme-Becker, *Allgemeines Lexikon der Bildenden Künstler*. 37 vols. Leipzig: E. A. Seemann, 1907–1950.

Karl Madsen. *Catalogue of a Collection of Paintings Exhibited in the Danish Museum of Fine Art, Autumn 1920*. Copenhagen: H. Heilbuth, 1920.

International Studio 82, no. 343 (December 1925). Frontispiece.

Arthur McComb. "Francesco Ubertini (Bacchiacca)." *Art Bulletin* 8, no. 3 (March 1926):141–67.

Inge Berge. "Un dipinto sconosciuto del Bacchiacca e il suo modello." *Rivista d'Arte* 17 (1935):85.

Bernard Berenson. *The Drawings of the Florentine Painters*. 3 vols. Chicago: University of Chicago Press, 1938.

Art Objects and Furnishings from the William Randolph Hearst Collection. Catalogue. Hammer Galleries, Inc., New York. New York: Publishers Printing Co., 1941.

Frederick Hartt. "Mantegna's Madonna of the Rocks." *Gazette des Beaux-Arts*, ser. 6, 40 (July–December 1952):329–42.

Luisa Marcucci. "Contributo al Bacchiacca." *Bollettino d'Arte* 43, no. 1 (January–March 1958):26–39.

Howard S. Merritt. "Bacchiacca Studies: The Uses of Imitation." Unpublished dissertation, Princeton University, 1958.

Luitpold Dussler. *Die Zeichnungen des Michelangelo*. Berlin: Mann, 1959.

"Accessions of American and Canadian Museums." *Art Quarterly* 23, no. 1 (Spring 1960):93–94.

Baltimore Museum of Art News 24, no. 1 (Fall 1960). Frontispiece.

"La Chronique des Arts." In *Gazette des Beaux-Arts*, ser. 6, 57 (February 1961):25.

Sydney J. Freedberg. *Painting of the High Renaissance in Rome and Florence*. 2 vols. Cambridge, Mass.: Harvard University Press, 1961.

Howard S. Merritt. "Francesco Ubertini called Il Bacchiacca, 1494–1557." In *Bacchiacca and His Friends: Florentine Paintings and Drawings of the Sixteenth Century*. Exhibition catalogue. In *Baltimore Museum of Art News* 24, no. 2 (Winter 1961):19–34.

Gertrude Rosenthal. "Bacchiacca and His Friends: Comments on the Exhibition." In *Bacchiacca and His Friends: Florentine Paintings and Drawings of the Sixteenth Century*. Exhibition catalogue. In *Baltimore Museum of Art News* 24, no. 2 (Winter 1961):7–18.

Gertrude Rosenthal. "Bacchiacca: Mannerist with Perfect Manners." *Art News* 59, no. 9 (January 1961): 42–44, 61–63.

Gertrude Rosenthal. "Il Bacchiacca at Baltimore." *Connoisseur* 149, no. 599 (January 1962):58–63.

Bernard Berenson. *Italian Pictures of the Renaissance: Florentine School*. 2 vols. London: Phaidon Press, 1963.

Lada Nikolenko. *Francesco Ubertini called Il Bacchiacca*. Locust Valley, N.Y.: J. J. Augustin, 1966.

Burton B. Fredericksen and Federico Zeri. *Census of Pre-Nineteenth-Century Italian Paintings in North American Public Collections*. Cambridge, Mass.: Harvard University Press, 1972.

Christian von Holst. *Francesco Granacci*. Munich: Bruckmann, 1974.

Sydney J. Freedberg. *Painting in Italy 1500 to 1600*. Revised edition. Harmondsworth, England: Penguin Books, 1975.

"Old Masters at Colnaghi's." *Apollo* 108, no. 197 (July 1978):71.

Paintings by Old Masters. Catalogue. London: P. & D. Colnaghi & Co., 1978.

Charles Colbert. *Bacchiacca in the Context of Florentine Art*. Cambridge, Mass.: Unpublished dissertation, Harvard University, 1978.

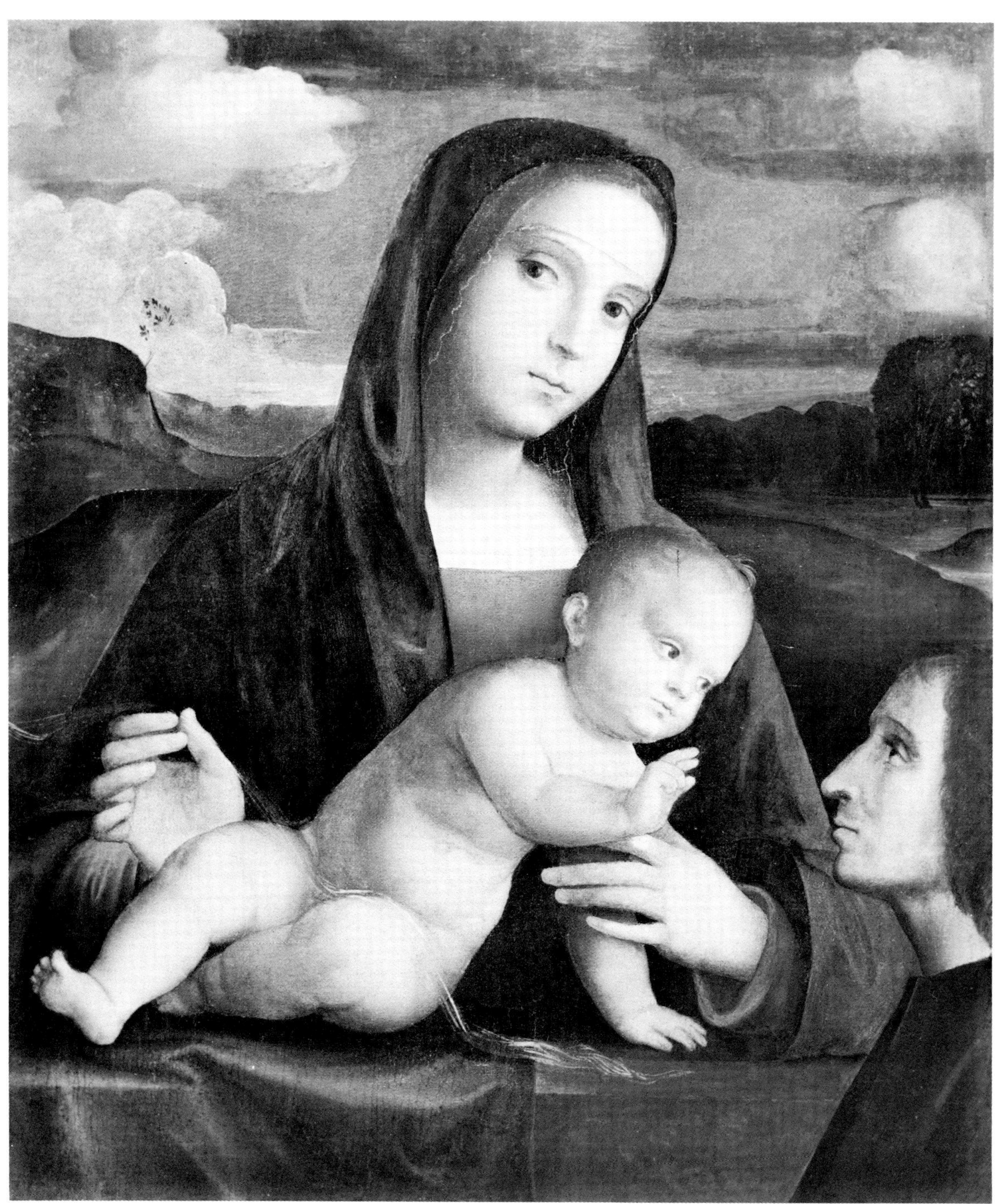

Workshop of
FRANCESCO FRANCIA (ca. 1450–1517)
(Francesco Raibolini)

---

9. *Madonna and Child with Donor,* ca. 1515

Oil and probably some tempera on canvas, transferred from wood. 24 × 19½ inches (60.9 × 49.5 cm.)

The Jacob Epstein Collection (BMA 51.118)

PROVENANCE

Probably Ehrich Galleries, New York

Acquired by Jacob Epstein, Baltimore

It is likely that Mr. Epstein purchased the painting from or through the Ehrich Galleries at least four years before the firm was discontinued around 1935. Records from the Ehrich Galleries, which include a certificate from Hermann Voss attributing the painting to Francia, are on file at the Newhouse Galleries, New York. Labels from the Newhouse Galleries are also affixed to the back of the picture. An old label on the front of the picture frame, identifying the painting in French, suggests that the painting may once have been in a French collection.

Loaned by Jacob Epstein to The Baltimore Museum of Art in 1931 and bequeathed in 1951

CONDITION

The painting had suffered considerably before its acquisition by Jacob Epstein. It had been transferred from its original support, probably a wooden panel, to a new support consisting of a triple layer of fabric mounted on a cradled wood structure. Examination revealed that because of poor adhesion between the new wooden support and the triple layer of fabric, vertical ridges and unsightly "buckles" had developed. The woven pattern of the modern fabric support had become imprinted on the surface of the painting and is still visible. There were numerous pinpoint paint losses and some major ones along a vertical band extending from top to bottom to the right of the Madonna. These losses include a long, V-shaped section of sky and landscape; a narrower strip to the right, running down through the pupil of the donor's eye; parts of the Madonna's left cuff and the Child's left hand; and the donor's praying hands, of which traces were later discovered by X-radiography during a 1957–1961 treatment. The losses had been filled in with a reddish ground which was also extended over much of the original paint in an effort to conceal surface irregularities. This ground had been applied to the reverse of the paint film during the transfer before acquisition by Mr. Epstein.

During treatment in 1957–1961 by Elisabeth Packard of The Walters Art Gallery, the modern repaint was removed, as were the modern wooden structure and two layers of fabric. The third layer of fabric (a thin gauze) and the reddish ground were left on and the painting was lined with a linen fabric and wax-resin adhesive. Traces of the donor's hands found after cleaning were too fragmentary to justify reconstruction and were overpainted to provide a continuity of design. The other losses described above were inpainted.

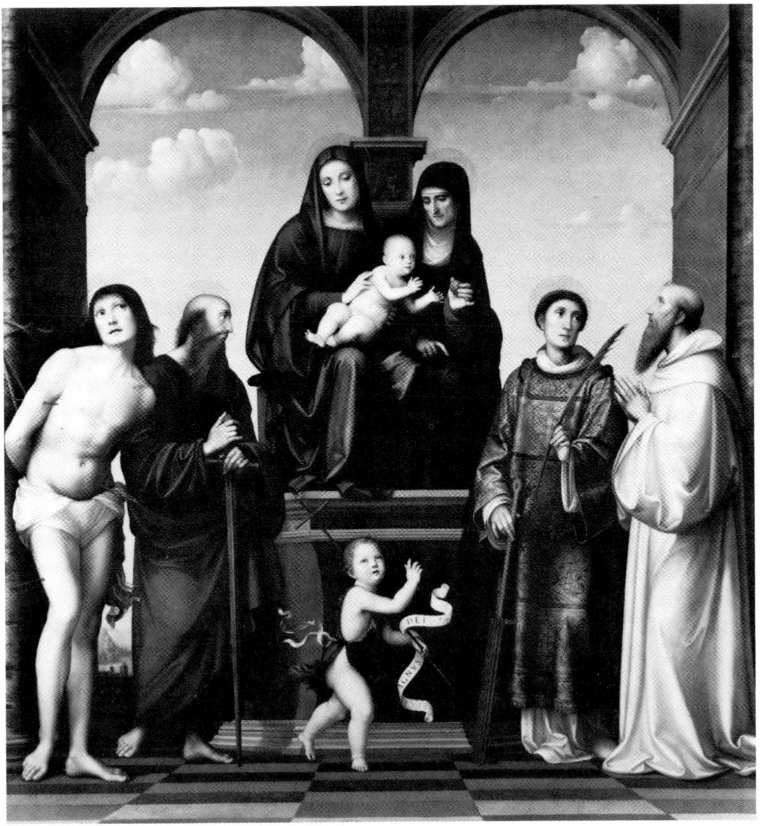

Fig. 1. Francesco Francia, *Madonna and Child and St. Anne Enthroned with Saints.* Oil with tempera on canvas, transferred from wood. 78½ × 72 inches (199 × 182 cm.). The National Gallery, London. Reproduced by courtesy of the Trustees, The National Gallery, London

In the *Madonna and Child with Donor,* the Madonna's dull gray-blue mantle (possibly changed with age and also with the transfer of the painting from wood to canvas) partly covers a transparent veil over her light brown hair and red dress. The Child rests on a leaf-green cloth draped over a brown parapet. The donor's hair is brown, and he wears a dark blue garment. The figures are set against a bleak landscape in which, behind a lake, trees and woods merge in the distance into bluish hills. A dull, greenish-blue sky, heavy with clouds, is enlivened on the left at the horizon by pink sunset streaks.

Aside from the 1939 Epstein catalogue entry, there is no known reference to this painting in the literature on Francia, who was a goldsmith and medalist to Pope Julius II as well as the leading Bolognese painter of his day. The Epstein brochure reported that the picture had been endorsed as an authentic work of Francia by Hermann Voss, then Curator of the Kaiser Friedrich Museum in Berlin.[1] Berenson does not mention it.[2] Gertrude Coor supported the Francia attribution in 1958.[3] In 1976 Federico Zeri suggested that it was rather the work of one of Francia's sons.[4]

Gertrude Coor's proposed date of ca. 1515 is convincing. The heavily cloaked Madonna with an energetically twisting Child occurs in several later works by Francia, such as the Buonvisi altarpiece of the *Madonna and Child and St. Anne Enthroned with Saints* in the National Gallery, London (fig. 1), and the altarpiece of the *Madonna and Child with Saints,*

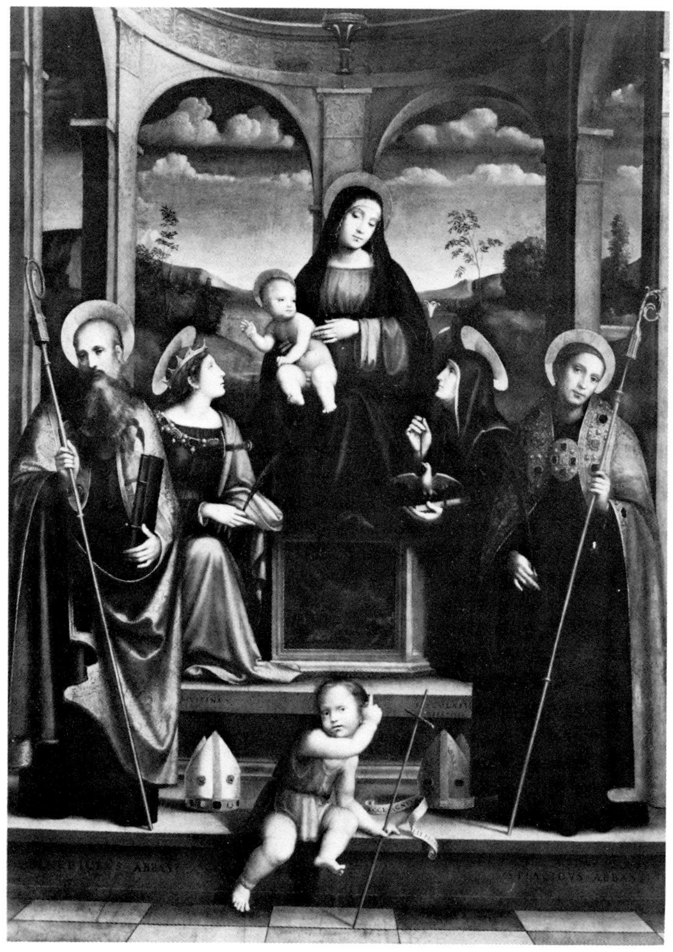

Fig. 2. Francesco Francia, *Madonna and Child with Saints*. Oil on wood. 88 15/16 × 63 13/16 inches (226 × 162 cm.). Galleria Nazionale, Parma

dated 1515, in the National Gallery, Parma (fig. 2). But the question of whether our painting was actually executed by Francia himself or by a close follower may have to remain open. A great number of Madonnas with widely differing stylistic features have been assigned to him; few have received unanimous acceptance. As he was legendary for his legion of assistants, secure attributions for his Madonnas are particularly elusive.[5] The problem is compounded here because the picture has suffered much, to the detriment of such meticulous surface finish and subtle modeling as might have supported the Francia attribution.

The Madonna, while in general type close to Francia's Virgins, seems unusually slender, narrow-faced, and geometric for him, and lacks his characteristic soft plumpness around the neck, jaw, and eyes. Francia's typical slow-swelling curves are missing in some usual places (the veil edge, neckline, eye contours); here instead lines are almost straight and corners turned sharply. The flat red dress also differs from Francia's usual custom of modeling the gown in loose gathered folds to suggest the rounded form underneath. The Child is closely comparable in proportions, type, and energetic movement to the children in the London and Parma altarpieces, and very similar in pose to the Christ Child twisting toward the infant John the Baptist in a Madonna of fine quality attributed to Francia in the National Gallery, Parma (fig. 3). According to the

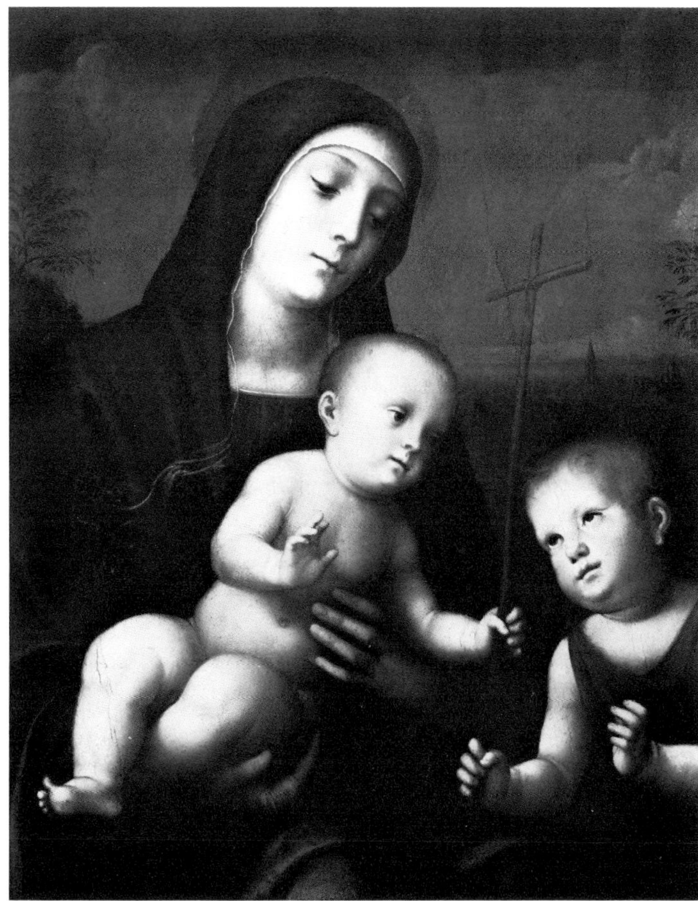

Fig. 3. Francesco Francia, *Madonna and Child with the Infant St. John the Baptist.* Oil on wood. 23⅝ × 19⁵⁄₁₆ inches (60 × 49 cm.). Galleria Nazionale, Parma

treatment report, the contour lines defining the Child's left arm, the Madonna's cheek and chin, and other areas are original and are characteristic of Francia's technique. The Child's expression, however, is exceptionally intent and intelligent for a Francia *bambino*.

If the work is by a follower of Francia, he appears to be a more sensitive one than either of the master's sons. Although there is little reliable information on their oeuvre, it appears that in many works attributed to them the figures are stiffer, more artificially elegant, and less animated (see fig. 4) than those in the Baltimore picture.[6] The name of Jacopo Boateri, "one of the most scrupulous and at the same time one of the best" of Francia's followers,[7] should perhaps be tentatively considered. Boateri's style is known through a signed *Holy Family* in the Pitti Gallery in Florence. A *Madonna and Child with Saints Jerome and Catherine* attributed to him in the Borghese Gallery in Rome has the child twisting to His left in a manner comparable to the Baltimore picture, with the Madonna's hands in nearly identical positions, and a similarly summary landscape.

Small half-length Madonna paintings like this one, with the Child presented on a parapet as if offered on an altar, were usually private devotional images for homes or convents.[8] The presence of a donor (placed in a zone in front of the parapet, thus sharing the viewer's removal from the holy figures) is unusual in a picture of this kind and would presumably have been requested by the patron himself. Francia's small Madonnas often include additional figures, but they are generally saints or angels.

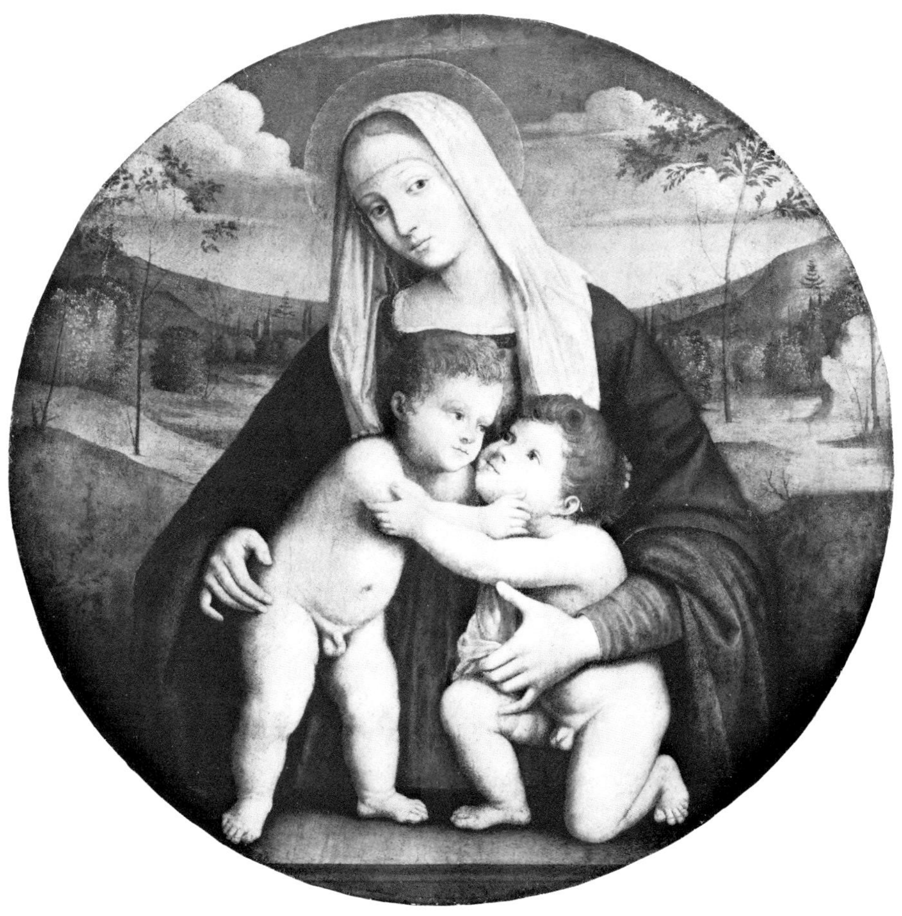

Fig. 4. Giacomo (or Giulio) Francia, *Madonna and Child and St. John the Baptist*. Oil with tempera on wood. Tondo, diameter 33¹⁵/₁₆ inches (86.2 cm.). The Walters Art Gallery, Baltimore

The Virgin, with her low coif, her large eyes, and with her head isolated against the sky high above the other figures, may reflect Venetian experience,[9] or at least acquaintance with Giovanni Bellini's type of the iconic half-length Madonna in a landscape. The Child's lively spiraling pose, on the other hand, suggests the influence of such Florentine works as Leonardo da Vinci's cartoon of the *Madonna and Child with St. Anne and the Infant St. John the Baptist* in the National Gallery, London.[10]

Alison Luchs
National Gallery of Art,
Washington, D.C.

NOTES

1. *The Jacob Epstein Collection in The Baltimore Museum of Art* (Baltimore: Published by Jacob Epstein, 1939).
2. Berenson must have known the painting as he knew Mr. Epstein at various stages, but he omits it from both *Italian Pictures of the Renaissance* (Oxford: Clarendon Press, 1932), pp. 206–9, and *Italian Pictures of the Renaissance: Central and North Italian Schools,* 3 vols. (London: Phaidon Press, 1968), 1:145–49.
3. Letter of May 23, 1958, to Elisabeth Packard: ". . . I consider it fairly certain that the Baltimore picture is a late product by Francesco Francia, executed close to 1515. The composition and execution of Mary's veil, the rectangular Virgin face, glance out of the corners of the eyes, pursed mouth, and shape of hands, as well as the Child type are all characteristic of this artist, and the summary style and strong contrast of light and shadow are characteristic of his last period. Compare especially with the work under consideration the Parma altarpiece of 1515 (G. C. Williamson, *Francesco Raibolini Called Francia* [London: G. Bell & Sons, 1901], pl. 38) and the contemporary Buonvisi altarpiece in the National Gallery, London (ibid., pl. 34). . . . The main figures in the Baltimore panel are less sentimental than in most examples by Francia and more alive than in most late works by this artist, yet I see no really good reasons for taking it away from him."
4. Letter of Janaury 27, 1976, to G. Rosenthal: "The surface is in such bad state that it is difficult to read it clearly. However, from the type of the clouds, and from the psychological feeling, I would exclude Francia's hand: very likely this is a work painted in his studio by one of his sons, either Giacomo or Giulio Francia, during their period of apprenticeship. Also the gesture of the Child reminds one of Francia's two sons (see panel in Budapest)."
5. See Williamson, *Francesco Raibolini Called Francia,* p. 100; see also G. Lipparini, *Francesco Francia* (Bergamo: Istituto italiano d'arti grafiche, 1913), p. 101, on the problem of Francia's Madonnas.
6. For illustrations of works assigned to Francia's sons, see A. Venturi, *Storia dell'arte italiana* (Milan: U. Hoepli, 1914):7, pt. 3, 968 ff.; see also Lipparini, *Francesco Francia,* pp. 115 ff.
7. A. Venturi, *North Italian Painting of the Quattrocento: Emilia* (New York: Harcourt Brace & Co., 1931), p. 64.
8. R. Goffen, "Icon and Vision: Giovanni Bellini's Half-Length Madonnas," *Art Bulletin* 57, no. 4 (December 1975):487–518; see pp. 511–14.
9. Venturi in *Storia,* 7, pt. 3, p. 862, suggests that Francia visited Venice.
10. For Leonardo's cartoon, see cat. no. 10, fig. 1.

SELECTED BIBLIOGRAPHY

George C. Williamson. *Francesco Raibolini Called Francia.* London: G. Bell & Sons, 1901.

Giuseppe Lipparini. *Francesco Francia.* Bergamo: Istituto italiano d'arti grafiche, 1913.

Adolfo Venturi. *Storia dell'arte italiana.* 11 vols. Milan: U. Hoepli, 1901–1939.

Georg Gronau. "Francesco Francia (Francesco di Marco di Giacomo Raibolini)." In Thieme-Becker, *Allgemeines Lexikon der Bildenden Künstler.* 37 vols. Leipzig: E. A. Seemann, 1907–1950.

The Jacob Epstein Collection in The Baltimore Museum of Art. Baltimore: Published by Jacob Epstein, 1939.

Arthur McComb. "Francesco Francia (Francesco di Marco di Giacomo Raibolini)." In *Encyclopedia of World Art.* 15 vols. New York: McGraw-Hill, 1959–1968.

Michael Baxandall and E. H. Gombrich. "Beroaldus on Francia." *Journal of the Warburg and Courtauld Institutes* 25 (1962):113–15.

Creighton Gilbert. "Francia (Raibolini)." In *McGraw-Hill Dictionary of Art.* 5 vols. New York: McGraw-Hill, 1969.

Jacques Thuillier. "Francia (Francesco Raibolini)." In *Praeger Encyclopedia of Art.* 5 vols. New York: Praeger, 1971.

Emmanuel Bénézit. "Francia (Francesco di Marco Raibolini)." In *Dictionnaire des Peintres, Sculpteurs, Dessinateurs et Graveurs.* 10 vols. 3rd ed. Paris: Librairie Gründ, 1976.

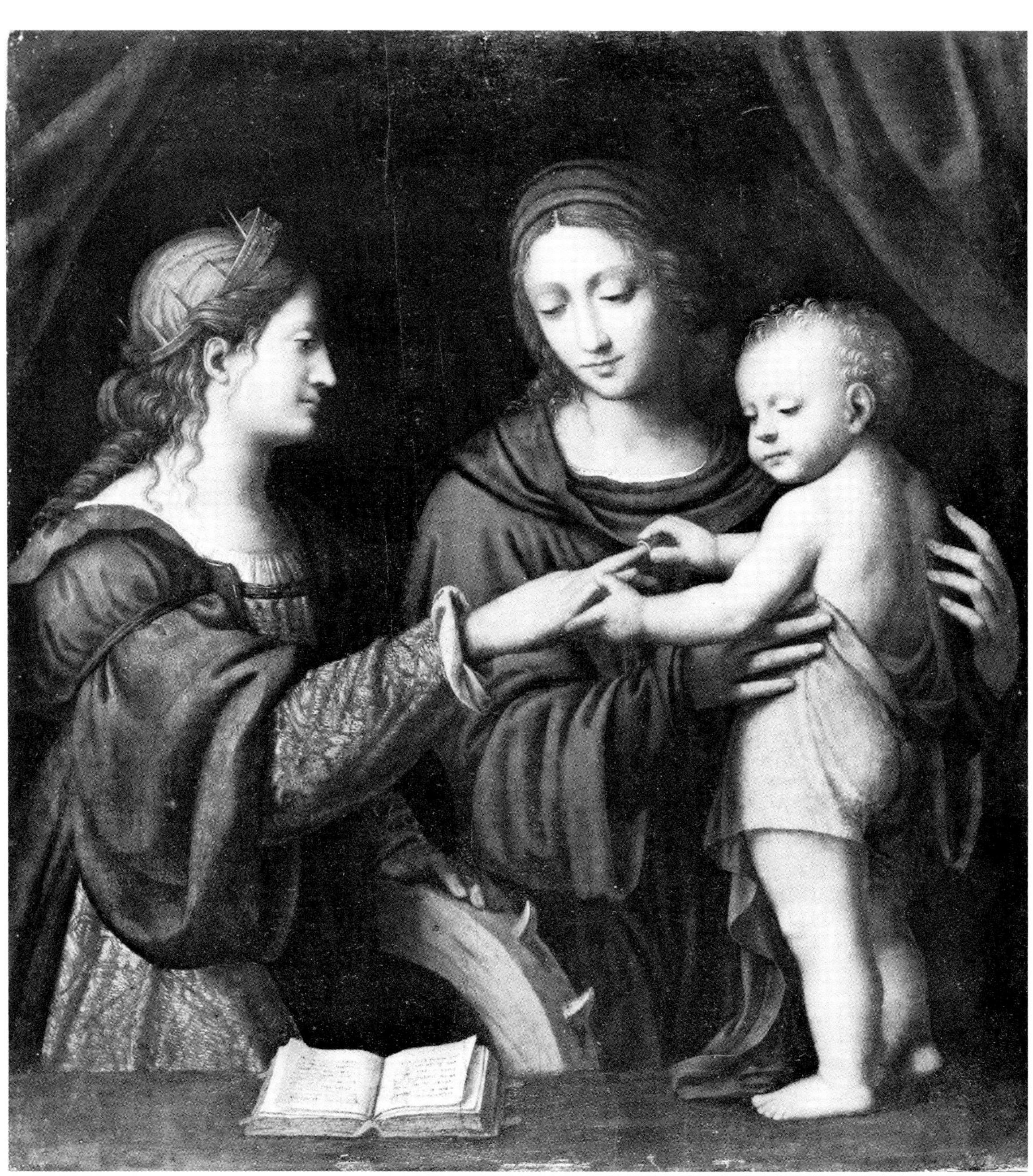

BERNARDINO LUINI (ca. 1480–1532)

10. *The Mystic Marriage of Saint Catherine,* ca. 1520–1525

Oil on wood. 23⅛ × 20⅜ inches (58.7 × 51.7 cm.)
The Mary Frick Jacobs Collection (BMA 38.227)

PROVENANCE

G. Cornwall Legh, Eaton Place, London
Catalogue of the Art Treasures of the United Kingdom Collected at Manchester in 1857 (London: W. H. Smith & Son, 1857), no. 204, p. 27
G. F. Waagen, *A Walk through the Art-Treasures Exhibition at Manchester* (London: J. Murray, 1857), p. 11
G. F. Waagen, *Galleries and Cabinets of Art in Great Britain* (London: J. Murray, 1857), pp. 181–82
W. Burger [E. J. T. Thoré], *Trésors d'Art Exposés à Manchester en 1857* (Paris, 1857), p. 38
National Exhibition of Works of Art at Leeds. Official catalogue (Leeds: Baines, 1868), no. 269, p. 29

Colonel H. Cornwall Legh, High Legh Hall, Knutsford
Illustrated Catalogue of Pictures by Masters of the Milanese and Allied Schools of Lombardy, exhibition catalogue, Burlington Fine Arts Club, 1898 (London: Burlington Fine Arts Club, 1899), no. 30, p. 8

R. Langton Douglas, London
Lionello Venturi, *Italian Paintings in America,* 3 vols. (New York: E. Weyhe, 1933), 3: pl. 490

Sedelmeyer Gallery, Paris
Illustrated Catalogue of 100 Paintings by Old Masters (Paris: Sedelmeyer Gallery, 1905), no. 51, p. 62

Eugène Fischhof, Paris
Henry Barton Jacobs, *The Collection of Mary Frick Jacobs* (Baltimore: Prepared and published by Dr. Henry Barton Jacobs, 1938), no. 33

Acquired by Mary Frick Jacobs, Baltimore
The back of an old photograph of the painting at Villa I Tatti was inscribed by Bernard Berenson: "Dr. Jacobs, Baltimore. Luini."

Bequeathed to The Baltimore Museum of Art in 1938 as part of The Mary Frick Jacobs Collection

CONDITION

Though said to be in "good preservation" in the mid-nineteenth century (G. F. Waagen, *Galleries and Cabinets of Art in Great Britain* [London: J. Murray, 1857], pp. 181–82), the condition of *The Mystic Marriage of St. Catherine* today could be described as only fair but stable. The picture is painted in oil over a gesso ground on wood. Warping of the panel was reduced in 1958–1959 by Elisabeth Packard at The Walters Art Gallery: the battens were removed and the painting was exposed to humidity. After this treatment, beeswax and gum elemi were ironed into the back of the panel, the grooves which formerly were occupied by the battens were filled with wax, and a linen fabric was attached to the back with wax. X-radiographs show many small paint losses through flaking, notably in the flesh areas. The facial features of the Madonna and Child may have been slightly altered by these losses. Moreover, there is much abrasion throughout the entire surface which has unfavorably affected the appearance of the panel. The picture has not been cleaned since it came into the possession of The Baltimore Museum of Art, but in addition to the work done in 1958–1959 it received minor treatment in 1966 at the conservation department of the Baltimore Museum. It is anticipated that the panel will be cleaned and treated in the near future to remove discolored varnish and overpaint and to make the abrasions less visible.

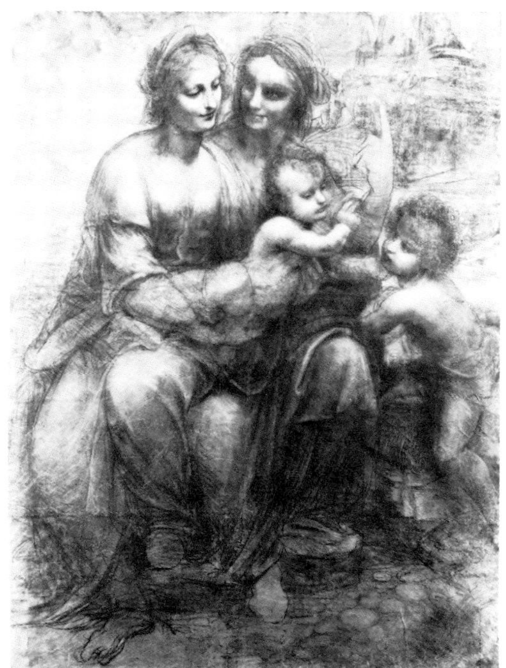

Fig. 1. Leonardo da Vinci, *Madonna and Child with St. Anne and the Infant St. John the Baptist*. Cartoon. Charcoal heightened with white on brown paper. 54¾ × 39⅜ inches (135 × 100 cm.). The National Gallery, London. Reproduced by courtesy of the Trustees, The National Gallery, London

The painting of *The Mystic Marriage of St. Catherine* is the product of Bernardino Luini's mind, if not entirely of his own hand. To judge from his production, Luini headed a workshop that included many assistants, one of whom may have worked on the Baltimore painting. The question of whether Luini himself executed the picture is complicated by its somewhat abraded condition, which does not permit us to assess its quality with any precision.

For a discussion of the painting to be meaningful, we must first take into account our image of the artist and his work. Though now unfamiliar, Luini was a great favorite with the picture-viewing public in the latter half of the nineteenth century. The English art critic John Ruskin, who claimed to have discovered him, even ranked Luini for his sincerity and spirituality above Leonardo da Vinci.[1] Luini's reputation as the major Lombard painter of the Renaissance peaked when in 1911 the Milanese architect-scholar Luca Beltrami published an exhaustive monograph on the artist that is still worth consulting.[2]

But by this time the reaction had already begun. Luini's works, however appealing, lacked the qualities of form, movement, and space that Bernard Berenson admired in Italian painting.[3] Berenson's stern disapproval of this "least intellectual of famous painters" has echoed down the twentieth century,[4] though by now it seems as one-sided as Ruskin's adulation.

If in the past scholars saw Leonardo as the chief source of inspiration for Luini,[5] modern art historians have tended to dissociate him from the master. Now Luini is made to depend upon Bramantino, who, among Milanese painters active in the early sixteenth century, bears no obvious relation to Leonardo.[6] Bramantino, moreover, appeals to the current taste for Mannerism. Nevertheless, adhering to the traditional view, I believe that it was Leonardo, and not Bramantino, who was Luini's real artistic mentor.

Those scholars who rightly stressed Leonardo's relevance unfortunately went on to criticize Luini for lack of imagination. The lingering Romantic concept of originality, of

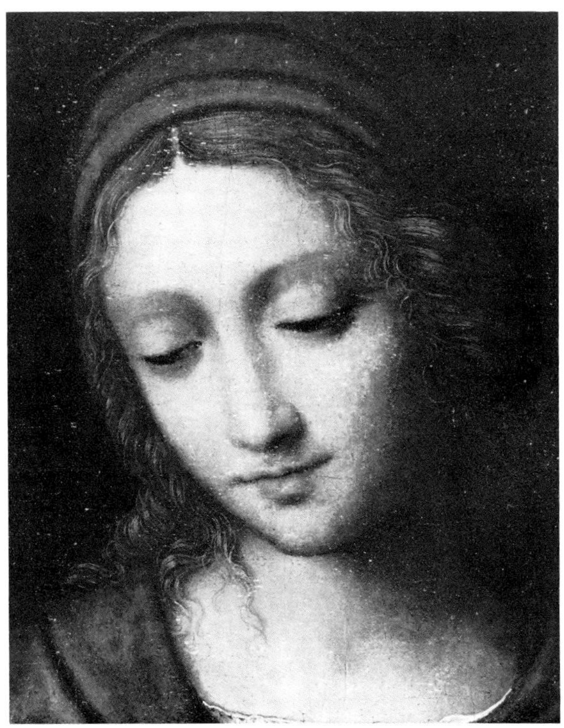

Fig. 2. Bernardino Luini, *The Mystic Marriage of St. Catherine,* detail of cat. no. 10

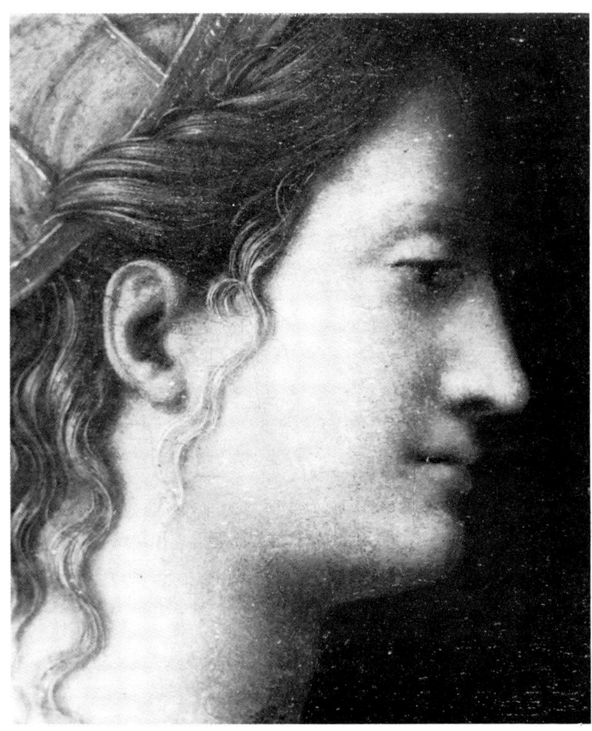

Fig. 3. Bernardino Luini, *The Mystic Marriage of St. Catherine,* detail of cat. no. 10

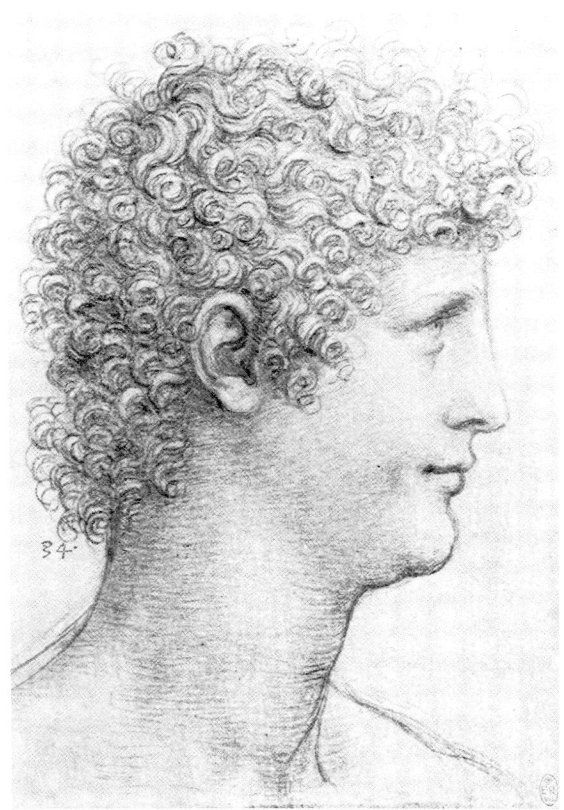

Fig. 4. Leonardo da Vinci, *Profile of a Youth with Curly Hair.* Chalk on paper. Royal Library, Windsor Castle

art as self-expression, has, in fact, prevented us from admiring Luini's resourcefulness. His achievement consists of a successful fusion of what he gained from Leonardo, whose works were, after all, far more advanced in style than anything else to be seen in Milan, and of the native Lombard tradition of Foppa and Bergognone in which he was trained. Luini made a special study of Leonardo's cartoon or full-scale preparatory drawing, now in the National Gallery, London, showing the *Madonna and Child with St. Anne and the Infant St. John the Baptist* (fig. 1). He adapted the cartoon in his painting now in the Pinacoteca Ambrosiana in Milan.[7] Luini's adaptation reveals that he grasped Leonardo's aim, which was to introduce the large scale of form and feeling of *The Last Supper* into the mainstream of Madonna painting.

With a more balanced view of Luini's style and sources, we are now prepared to evaluate *The Mystic Marriage of St. Catherine* in Baltimore. Leonardo seems never to have treated this subject, taken from the *Golden Legend* and symbolizing the union of the soul with Christ. Thus, Luini was obliged to turn to his Lombard predecessors for guidance. His version of the theme, like theirs, follows a standard iconography. Painted for private devotion, the picture omits the attendant saints often included as witnesses to the mystical event. Instead, the protagonists are shown in three-quarter length against a dark unspecified background. St. Catherine is identifiable by her attributes of the crown, book, and spiked wheel, standing for her high birth, knowledge, and martyrdom. She extends her right hand to receive the ring from the Infant Christ. Their union is watched over approvingly by the Madonna, who supports her Son physically as well, as He stands on a ledge.

Like Luini's other works, *The Mystic Marriage* is broadly painted. The brushwork lacks refinement, though the forms are not summary either. Luini's paint handling in easel pictures such as this one is perhaps best compared to the technique of fresco, in which he excelled. As for color, the Baltimore painting shows the artist's typical preference for secondary hues. The curtains are green, as is the dress of St. Catherine, ornamented with gold brocade. The Madonna wears a red dress with gray-blue sleeves and veil, while the Child's drapery is cream-colored.

Lacking an exact prototype for his composition, Luini was led to adapt Leonardo's treatments of other subjects to the requirements of his theme. The Madonna's facial type (fig. 2) and smiling expression derive from *The Madonna of the Rocks,* while Luini's other great model, the London cartoon already cited (fig. 1) provided the idea of juxtaposing two female heads, as well as the *contrapposto* of the Child, seen partly from behind. The closing of the group with a figure in emphatic profile stems, perhaps, from *The Last Supper.* St. Catherine's brightly lit profile featured against the dark background (fig. 3) bears a still more cogent relation to Leonardo. The type to which she belongs was created by Leonardo and used by him and his followers interchangeably for youths and young women, as, for instance, in a drawing by the master at Windsor Castle (fig. 4).[8] Luini's effort to recapture Leonardo's monumentality results in a design that is impressive, if static. The ponderous movement of his figures lacks Leonardo's animation, except for the touching behavior of the Child, who places the ring on the saint's finger with an air of youthful concentration.

Where does the Baltimore painting belong in Luini's career? Discussions about his stylistic development have been plagued by misattributions. A glance through any book on Luini demonstrates that not all the works given to him could possibly be by the same artist. In particular, paintings wrongly attributed to the young Luini, like the well-known altarpiece in the Musée Jacquemart-André in Paris, have distorted our view of his formation.[9] This altarpiece and another work mistakenly attributed to Luini, a fresco of the Madonna enthroned with saints in a church near Milan, differ from each other and from his signed or otherwise certain pictures.[10]

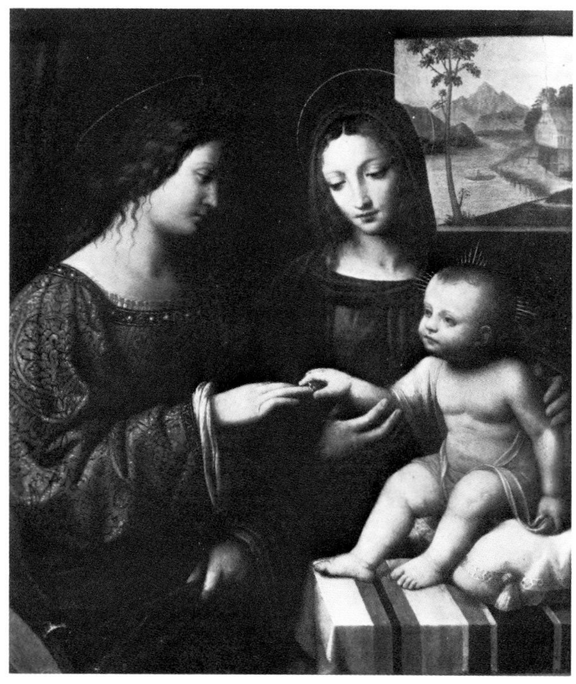

Fig. 5. Bernardino Luini, *The Mystic Marriage of St. Catherine*. Oil on wood. 23¼ × 21¼ inches (59 × 54 cm.). Museo Poldi-Pezzoli, Milan

Both the altarpiece and the fresco are dated 1507. Writers who accept those works have proposed a birth date for Luini of around 1480 or even earlier. But Luini's first signed picture, a fresco of the Madonna in Chiaravalle, is dated 1512.[11] If we reject the attributed works of 1507 and accept the signed fresco of 1512 as the hallmark of Luini's early style, then the artist may not have been born before the last decade of the fifteenth century. The importance of a later birth date for Luini's chronology is that it alters our view of his stylistic development. Though it does reflect Leonardo's presence in Milan from 1506 to 1513 and draws upon his visual ideas as well as his paintings and studies, the early Chiaravalle fresco is only superficially Leonardesque. Other works by Luini that are more fundamentally indebted to Leonardo evidently result from a renewed study of the master's models.

Luini's chance to reconsider Leonardo came after the master's death in France in 1519, when certain of his works were brought back to Milan by his disciple Melzi. At this time, in the 1520's, Luini produced the adaptation already mentioned of the London cartoon. He also took up specifically Leonardesque themes, as in the *Madonna with the Two Holy Children* in the Prado Museum in Madrid. And a fresco like the *Christ in the Temple* at Saronno shows that Luini considered anew how Leonardo had grouped figures in *The Last Supper*. Thus, the relation to Leonardo—slight or profound—provides us with a fairly reliable means of dating Luini's pictures, before or after 1520.

The Mystic Marriage of St. Catherine in Baltimore has often been likened to another version of the theme by the artist in the Poldi-Pezzoli Museum in Milan (fig. 5).[12] Scholars have duly noted that the Milan painting differs in motifs, such as the window opening onto a landscape, the placing of the Child on a cushion, and the omission of St. Catherine's crown and book. But they have failed to observe that the Baltimore painting also differs in style and presumably in date from the one in Milan to which it has been compared. As the more naive and youthful facial types of the figures indicate, the Milan picture belongs to the earlier phase of Luini's career. It may be compared to a work like *The Madonna of the Carnation* of about 1515 in the Kress Collection, National Gallery of Art, Washington, D.C.[13] The Baltimore painting, on the other hand, with its more doctrinaire types, dark background, and naturalistic handling of details and surfaces, pertains to the later, more thoroughly Leonardesque phase of Luini's career in the 1520's. If the Milan picture is fresher in spirit, in better condition, and of higher quality than the one in Baltimore, the latter does allow us to see how Luini returned to and definitively treated a theme he had depicted before.

David Alan Brown
National Gallery of Art,
Washington, D.C.

NOTES

1. *The Works of John Ruskin,* 39 vols., ed. E. T. Cook and A. Wedderburn (London: G. Allen and New York: Longmans, Green & Co., 1903–1912), 4:355, and 37:463–64.
2. L. Beltrami, *Luini 1512–1532: Materiale di studio* (Milan: Tipografia U. Allegretti, 1911).
3. B. Berenson, *The North Italian Painters of the Renaissance* (New York: G. P. Putnam's Sons, 1907), pp. 117–19.
4. S. J. Freedberg, *Painting in Italy 1500 to 1600* (Harmondsworth and Baltimore: Penguin Books, 1971), pp. 264–65.
5. See, for example, G. C. Williamson, *Bernardino Luini* (London: G. Bell & Sons, 1899), passim. Adolfo Venturi offered a more balanced view (*Storia dell'arte italiana,* 11 vols. [Milan: U. Hoepli, 1926], 9, pt. 2:742–68). Though he did not underestimate Leonardo's impact on Luini, W. Suida's examples in proof of it were badly chosen (*Leonardo und sein Kreis* [Munich: F. Bruckmann, 1929], pp. 233–38).
6. About Bramantino (Bartolommeo Suardi, ca. 1465–1530), see Freedberg, *Painting in Italy,* pp. 262–64. For his relation to Luini, see A. Ottino della Chiesa, *Bernardino Luini* (Novara: Istituto geografico De Agostini, 1956). Her views are incorporated in F. Mazzini, "Bernardino Luini," chap. 3 of "La Pittura del Cinquecento," in *Storia di Milano,* 17 vols. (Milan: Fondazione Treccani degli Alfieri, 1953–1966), 8:615–38.
7. Ottino della Chiesa, *Bernardino Luini,* no. 132, p. 104.
8. For Leonardo's invention of this type, see K. Clark, *The Drawings of Leonardo da Vinci in the Collection of Her Majesty the Queen at Windsor Castle,* 3 vols., 2nd ed. rev. (London: Phaidon Press, 1968–1969), 1: nos. 12508, 12554 (fig. 4 of this paper), 12557. The type was used for ideal heads of women, inspired by the Antique, in two engravings from Leonardo's circle (M. Hind, *Early Italian Engraving,* pt. 2, vol. 5 [London: B. Quaritch, 1948], nos. 12 and 13, pp. 90–91; and vol. 6, pl. 620). The type was favored by the Leonardo follower called the Pseudo-Boltraffio (Suida, *Leonardo,* figs. 227, 231, 234).
9. Ottino della Chiesa (*Bernardino Luini,* pp. 128–30) summarized the arguments in favor of the attribution to Luini, which she accepted.
10. About the fresco, located in the town of Gerenzano, see S. Stefani, "La giovinezza del Luini in uno sconosciuto affresco del 1507," *Commentari* 12, no. 2 (April–June 1961):108–19. See also A. Bertini, "La giovinezza di Bernardino Luini. Revisioni critiche," *Critica d'Arte* 9, nos. 53–54 (September–December 1962):20–61; and M. L. Ferrari, "Zenale, Cesariano e Luini," *Paragone* 28, no. 211 (September 1967):18–38.
11. Ottino della Chiesa, *Bernardino Luini,* no. 32, p. 171.
12. For references to the Poldi-Pezzoli painting, comparing it to the one in Baltimore, see Ottino della Chiesa, *Bernardino Luini,* no. 141, p. 107, and color pl. opp. p. 72.
13. F. R. Shapley, *Paintings from the Samuel H. Kress Collection: Italian Schools XV–XVI Century* (London: Phaidon Press, 1968), no. K297, and fig. 335.

SELECTED BIBLIOGRAPHY

Gustav Friedrich Waagen. *Galleries and Cabinets of Art in Great Britain.* London: J. Murray, 1857.

George C. Williamson. *Bernardino Luini.* London: G. Bell & Sons, 1899.

Luca Beltrami. *Luini, 1512–1532: Materiale di studio.* Milan: Tipografia U. Allegretti, 1911.

Bernard Berenson. *Italian Pictures of the Renaissance.* Oxford: Clarendon Press, 1932.

Henry Barton Jacobs. *The Collection of Mary Frick Jacobs.* Baltimore: Prepared and published by Dr. Henry Barton Jacobs, 1938.

Angela Ottino della Chiesa. *Bernardino Luini.* Novara: Istituto geografico De Agostini, 1956.

Bernard Berenson. *Italian Pictures of the Renaissance: Central and North Italian Schools.* 3 vols. London: Phaidon Press, 1968.

Burton B. Fredericksen and Federico Zeri. *Census of Pre-Nineteenth-Century Italian Paintings in North American Public Collections.* Cambridge, Mass.: Harvard University Press, 1972.

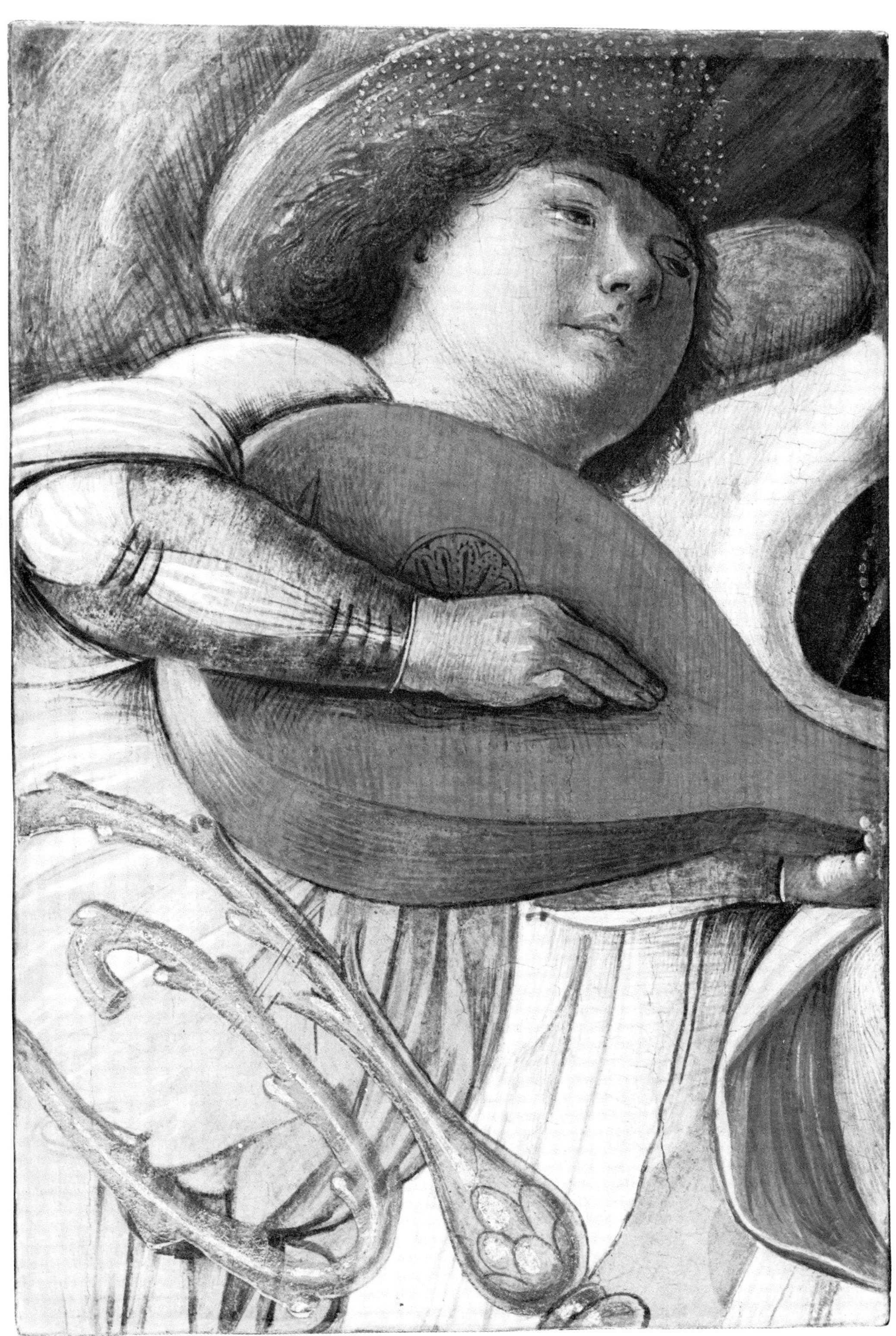

GIACOMO PACCHIAROTTO (1474–ca. 1540)

11. *Angel Playing a Lute,* ca. 1495–1510

Fragment from an Altarpiece of the Assumption
Tempera with oil on wood. 12¾ × 8½ inches (32.3 × 21.6 cm.)
Gift of M. Knoedler & Co. in Honor of Adelyn D. Breeskin (BMA 62.16)

PROVENANCE

M. Knoedler & Co., New York

The Knoedler Gallery stated only that the panel was found in southern France near Avignon. At present nothing else appears to be known about the history of this particular panel.

Obviously a fragment, the little painting is thought to have been part of a large altarpiece of *The Assumption of the Virgin* from which other panels also seem to have survived. (For the provenance of two of these panels, see notes 18 and 20.) However, no information exists concerning the original location of the now dismembered altarpiece or of the patron who commissioned it.

Presented to The Baltimore Museum of Art in 1962 by M. Knoedler & Co.

CONDITION

Prior to its acquisition by the Museum, the painting, which is a fragment, had undergone major treatment. It had been transferred from its original wooden support to a new cradled wooden support.

A visual examination of the picture suggests that the medium is tempera with some oil passages. The design layer has a network of fissures and small cracks which in some areas reveal a discolored resinous substance. The green underpainting (probably *terre verte*) used for shadows shows through the surface mainly in the flesh layers where the surface has become transparent. The gold tones of the crosier and sash have lost their sparkle and have become very light brown, and the metal clasps on the angel's sleeve have darkened.

X-radiography shows old filled losses of two different types along the edges, particularly at the lower right corner. There are also losses from insect tunneling scattered throughout, but none of the losses are of consequence and the general condition of the painting is good.

In 1962 the small panel of an *Angel Playing a Lute* was presented to The Baltimore Museum of Art as a work by Melozzo da Forlì (1438–1494). It had previously been lent to the Museum with the same attribution.[1] Shortly after the picture's acquisition it was recognized by Gertrude Coor as a fragment from an *Assumption of the Virgin,* a dismembered altarpiece by the Sienese Giacomo Pacchiarotto.[2] The initial, erroneous ascription seems to have been based to some extent on the subject matter, that recalls Melozzo's famous fresco fragments of angels making music which were originally part of the ceiling decorations of SS. Apostoli in Rome and were later transferred to the Vatican Museum. In addition, certain obvious but superficial similarities between the celestial figures in the respective paintings must have contributed to the wrong attribution. Most conspicuous of these similarities is the unusual rendering of the halos, which consist of small light dots, giving the appearance of stippled disks. Another feature found in the robes of the Melozzo angels as well as in those of the Baltimore figure is the rendering of the sleeves; in both instances they are puffed and slashed longitudinally, revealing the lighter fabric of the garment beneath. On the angels' sleeves are ornaments of gold or silver that add to the elegance of their fashionable attire. These similarities between the Baltimore panel and the Vatican fresco fragments may have suggested Melozzo as the artist of the Baltimore picture, but more convincing considerations have subsequently refuted such a hypothesis.

More basic stylistic comparisons reveal the three-dimensional quality of the Melozzo angels, their vitality, the force of their movement, and the beauty of their expressive faces. The smaller Baltimore figure, now ascribed to Pacchiarotto, indicates a more linear conception, almost like that of a colored drawing; even though the angel is sturdy and heavy set, he conveys a lyrical and dreamy mood.

Giacomo Pacchiarotto is known to have spent the major part of his life and career in Siena, but, as is frequently the case with many of his fellow Italian artists, his paintings have eluded precise documentation: none are signed or dated, and hardly any records of his commissions are known to exist. Moreover, various scholars have become aware of a contradiction for which no explanation has been found and which could throw some doubt on the research done so far on Pacchiarotto. Federico Zeri gives the following description: "The only authenticated work by Pacchiarotto is a fresco from around 1520 in the Palazzo Pretorio at Casole d' Elsa, but it does not seem to be by the same hand as the large group of paintings that modern criticism accepts under his name. This group, which is plainly homogeneous, shows an artistic personality formed in the workshop of Matteo di Giovanni or of Guidoccio Cozzarelli and later influenced by Francesco di Giorgio Martini and by the Umbrian painters Perugino and Pinturicchio who were active in Siena."[3] Since the problem posed by the "dual personality" of the painter who executed the documented fresco at Casole d' Elsa and the artist of the altarpieces on wood cannot be resolved at this time, this text will follow the path taken by experts from Vasari to Coor, when considering Pacchiarotto's oeuvre.

G. H. Edgell names as Pacchiarotto's teacher Matteo di Giovanni who is often considered the major native Sienese artist of the second half of the fifteenth century. Pacchiarotto appears at times to have emulated Matteo, as some of his works have been confused with those of the older master. Frequently mentioned as Pacchiarotto's mentor is Pinturicchio, though Pacchiarotto "never became his slavish imitator." [4] Certain works by Pacchiarotto show a mixture of Umbrian and Sienese trends that may have resulted from the kinship he felt for Pinturicchio. The influence of the earlier Pietro di Domenico as well as that of the avant-gardist Signorelli has been noticed in some of Pacchiarotto's major works, and artists as different as Vecchietta, Neroccio, Pacchia, Fungai, Ghirlandaio, and Perugino are said to have had an impact on Pacchiarotto's art.[5] In view of this

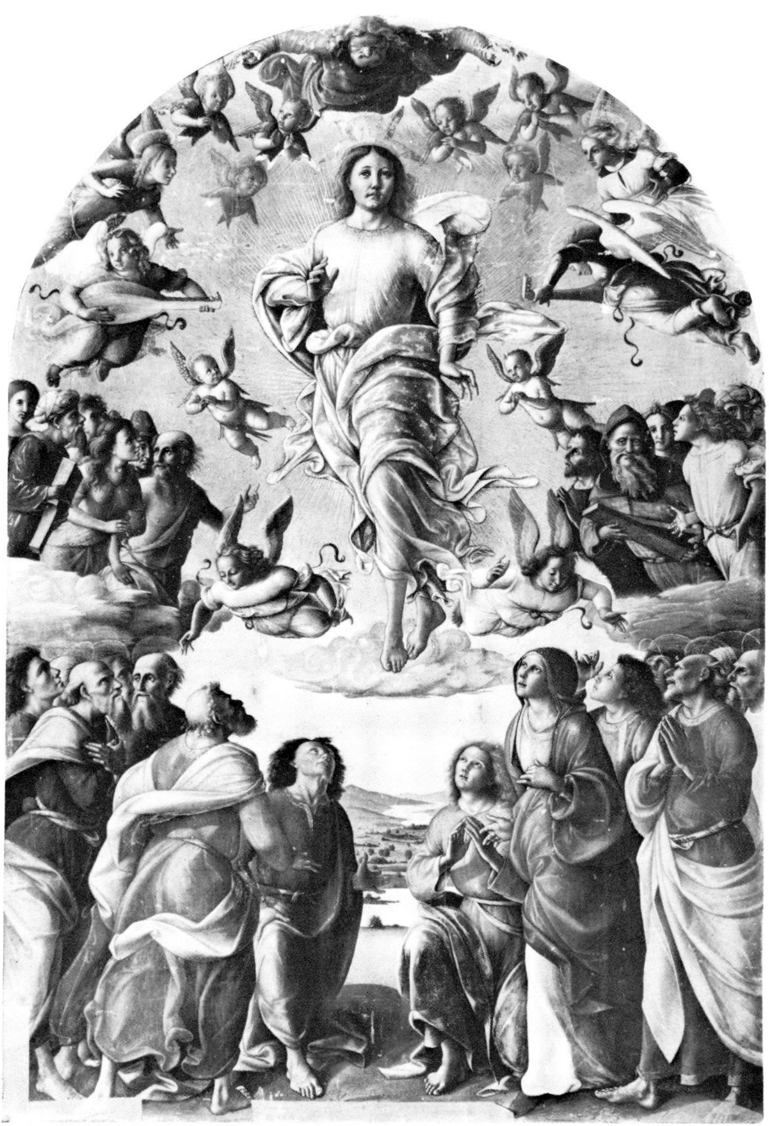

Fig. 1. Giacomo Pacchiarotto, *Ascension of Christ*. Tempera with oil on wood. 102½ × 90½ inches (260.4 × 230 cm.). Pinacoteca Nazionale, Siena

eclecticism, it is not surprising that earlier art historians from Vasari to Rumohr have confounded his paintings with works by others, such as Fungai and especially Pacchia with whom he is said to have collaborated occasionally.[6] Only in our time has a serious attempt been made to isolate Pacchiarotto's work from those of his Sienese confrères and to identify his style.

Less scant than our knowledge of Pacchiarotto's activities as a painter is our information on his personal life, mainly thanks to an outline provided by G. Milanesi in his comments on Vasari,[7] and to the lively descriptions given by Crowe and Cavalcaselle as well as Edgell.[8] They tell a wild tale of Pacchiarotto's disorderly life which reputedly contributed to the loss of many of his pictures. His lawlessness resulted in various confrontations with the city government which, nonetheless, employed him—apparently continuously—for the decoration of churches and public buildings. He supposedly plotted against his city yet courageously defended Siena when it was attacked by outside enemies. He belonged to a brotherhood of pranksters who were said to have made Siena unsafe by day and by night. Politically active, he took part in an insurrection and belonged to a faction called the Libertini. Twice Pacchiarotto was exiled from his city but pardoned after a few months and called home by the authorities. The city administration sought his opinion and asked him to evaluate paintings by such highly regarded artists as Perugino and Beccafumi. He was married and had two daughters. Biographical comments mention that he died peacefully in bed like a good, law-abiding citizen, instead of in a street brawl which his contemporaries thought would have been more fitting to his style of life.

There is no reflection of his turbulent, ribald life in his paintings, which have justly been called lyrical and tender, delicate and mystical.[9] Known to exist are at least forty Pacchiarotto paintings, some in poor condition. They are altarpieces, single panels, and predellas—mainly pictures in the Umbro-Sienese tradition of the late Quattrocento. Especially remarkable are the *Holy Family with Four Angels,*[10] now in a private collection in Parma; a *Nativity*[11] in the National Gallery, London; two impressive renderings of *The Visitation,*[12] a *Madonna with Saints Onofrio and Bartholomew,*[13] and his masterwork, the *Ascension of Christ* (fig. 1),[14] all four in the Siena Pinacoteca. His very large *Assumption of the Virgin* (102 x 89 inches) in the storerooms of the Siena Pinacoteca is in deplorable condition, far beyond restoration; yet its sad remnants still suggest a work of once high quality.[15]

The Baltimore *Angel Playing a Lute* is thought to have been part of another *Assumption* by Pacchiarotto, who seems to have treated this favorite theme of the Sienese Trecento and Quattrocento at several different periods.[16] No trace of documentary evidence concerning such an altarpiece has come to light. However, an excellent case for its former existence has been made by Gertrude Coor on the basis of the close connection between four fragments that, on the evidence of style, she attributed to Pacchiarotto.[17]

In the past these pieces had been given various attributions, sometimes even to Pacchiarotto, but until Coor's successful research no one had ever suggested that they once had belonged to the same altarpiece, an opinion generally accepted today. The most important of these fragments is the tall standing figure of the *Virgin Mary with Seven Cherubim* (fig. 2),[18] which has informed us on the subject matter of the unknown altarpiece. This figure can easily be related to two small oblong panels (figs. 3 and 4), each of which shows three angel musicians.[19] It is especially to these small fragments that the Baltimore *Angel* reveals a close kinship.

In 1967, two years after the posthumous publication of Coor's article, Luisa Vertova added two more fragments to Pacchiarotto's cut-up *Assumption.* One represents *St. John the Baptist and Three Saints* (fig. 5), the other *King David, Moses, and Two Saints* (fig. 6).[20] Originally, these two fragments must have been at right and left of the altarpiece, symmetrically placed on either side of the *Assunta.* While these panels appear less closely connected in composition and figure style to the other fragments from the dismembered altarpiece, they are undoubtedly by Pacchiarotto. There are resemblances to details of other paintings by the artist. The most obvious is the figure of King David wearing a turban (see fig. 6), which recurs in the *Ascension* (see fig. 1) among the cloud-borne group at the left.

Vertova estimates that the entire altarpiece originally measured approximately ten feet, six inches in height and seven feet in width, dimensions only partially accounted for by the existing fragments. Since Vertova's findings,[21] no further panels or data have turned up that could be connected with the dismembered altarpiece. Avoiding mere speculation—tempting whenever the reconstruction of a work of art is involved—the existing fragments have been carefully explored and described by the scholars mentioned previously. The Baltimore Museum's *Angel* has received less attention than the rest of the panels, for two

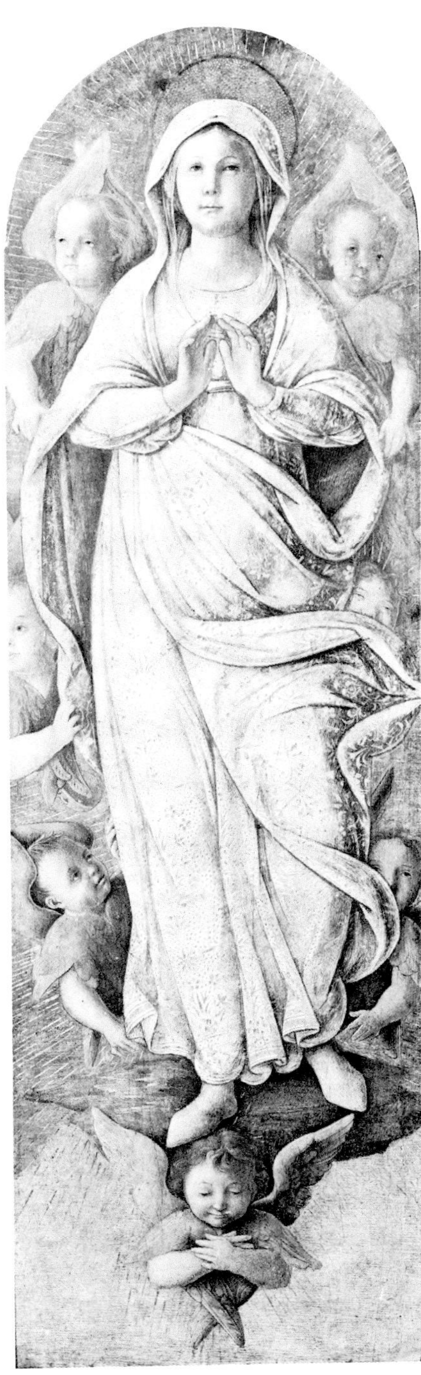

Fig. 2. Giacomo Pacchiarotto, *Virgin Mary with Seven Cherubim* (fragment). Tempera with oil on wood. 56 × 17¾ inches (142.2 × 45.1 cm.). Whereabouts unknown. Courtesy of the Frick Art Reference Library, New York

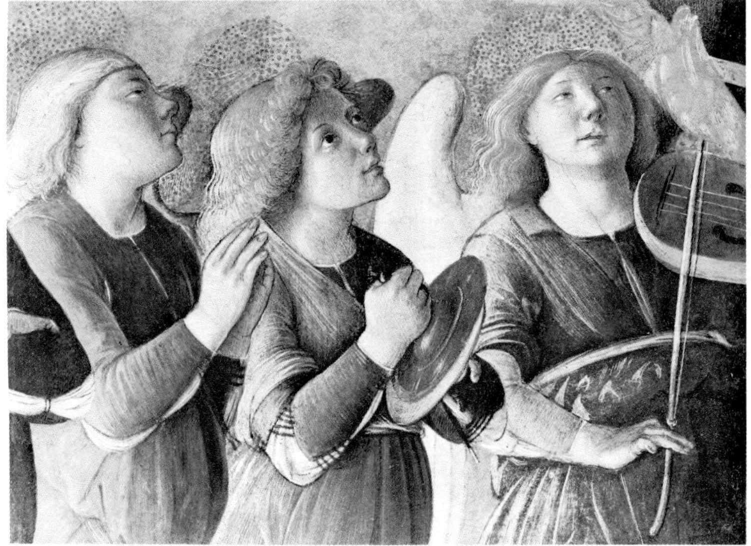

Above: Fig. 3. Giacomo Pacchiarotto, *Angel Musicians* (fragment). Tempera with oil on wood. 14 × 17¼ inches (35.5 × 43.8 cm.). El Paso Museum of Art, Samuel H. Kress Collection, El Paso, Texas

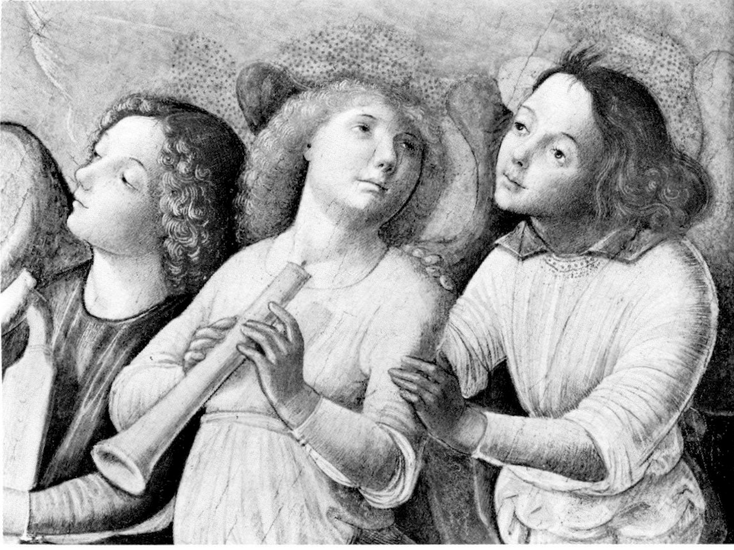

Below: Fig. 4. Giacomo Pacchiarotto, *Angel Musicians* (fragment). Tempera with oil on wood. 14 × 17¼ inches (35.5 × 43.8 cm.). El Paso Museum of Art, Samuel H. Kress Collection, El Paso, Texas

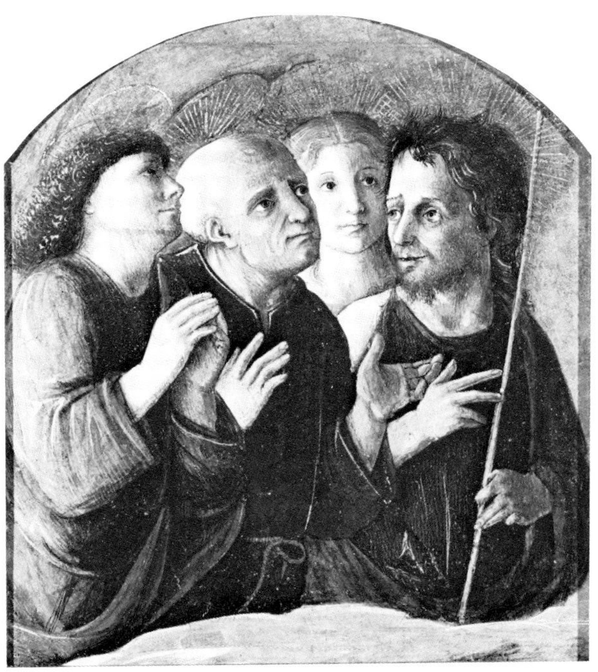

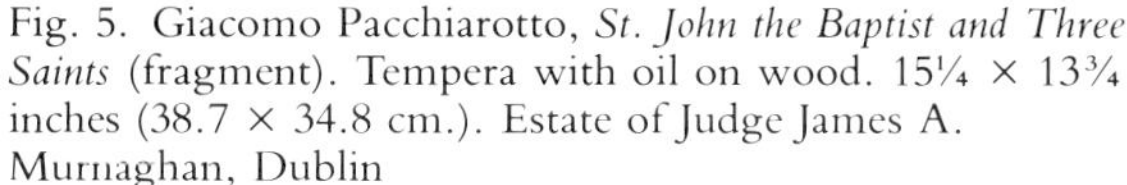

Fig. 5. Giacomo Pacchiarotto, *St. John the Baptist and Three Saints* (fragment). Tempera with oil on wood. 15¼ × 13¾ inches (38.7 × 34.8 cm.). Estate of Judge James A. Murnaghan, Dublin

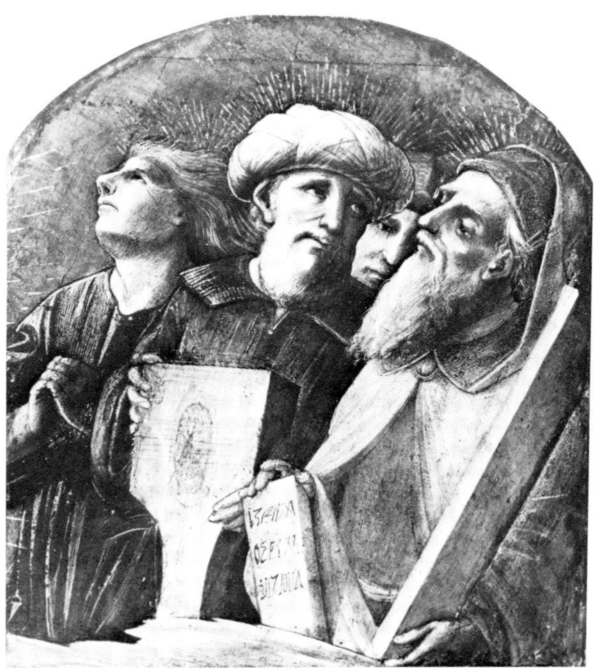

Fig. 6. Giacomo Pacchiarotto, *King David, Moses, and Two Saints* (fragment). Tempera with oil on wood. 16 × 15 inches (40.6 × 38 cm.). Collection of Anthony Post, London

possible reasons. Unlike the other fragments, the *Angel Playing a Lute* had not previously been in any well-known English collection. In the records of Knoedler & Co., which purchased it, there is nothing about its provenance except that it was "found in Southern France near Avignon." Moreover, Coor was less familiar with this piece than with the others. Though already convinced that it was part of the dismembered painting, she came to Baltimore to study it in detail but could not finish her project.

Any uncertainty about the attribution of the *Angel Playing a Lute* is at once eliminated by comparison with other works established as by Pacchiarotto. The relationship of the Baltimore picture to the two Kress paintings (see figs. 3 and 4) is obvious and especially apparent in the facial types of two of the six angel musicians—the one with the lute and the other, of the companion panel, holding a *chalumeau* (predecessor of the modern clarinet). Moreover, the ruddy flesh tones of all the figures, the rendering of the hands, the hair, and the halos leave no doubt that the Baltimore *Angel* and the Kress panels are the work of the same artist and very likely derive from the same painting. The head of the *Assunta,* once the central figure of the lost altarpiece, also can easily be associated with the Baltimore panel, as can a number of figures in other works by Pacchiarotto not connected with the dismembered altarpiece. Among these should be mentioned the praying angel standing behind the Virgin, and the seated one in the right foreground, both from the *Holy Family with Four Angels* (fig. 7).[22]

The apparent complexity of the design of the Baltimore picture—partly due to its fragmentary condition—makes it hard to "read," but its intricacy, together with the strange, pastel-like color, not unusual in Pacchiarotto's oeuvre, contributes to the attractiveness of the little panel. The angel's head is slightly tilted back. He seems to look toward the center where the figure of the *Assunta* was originally located.

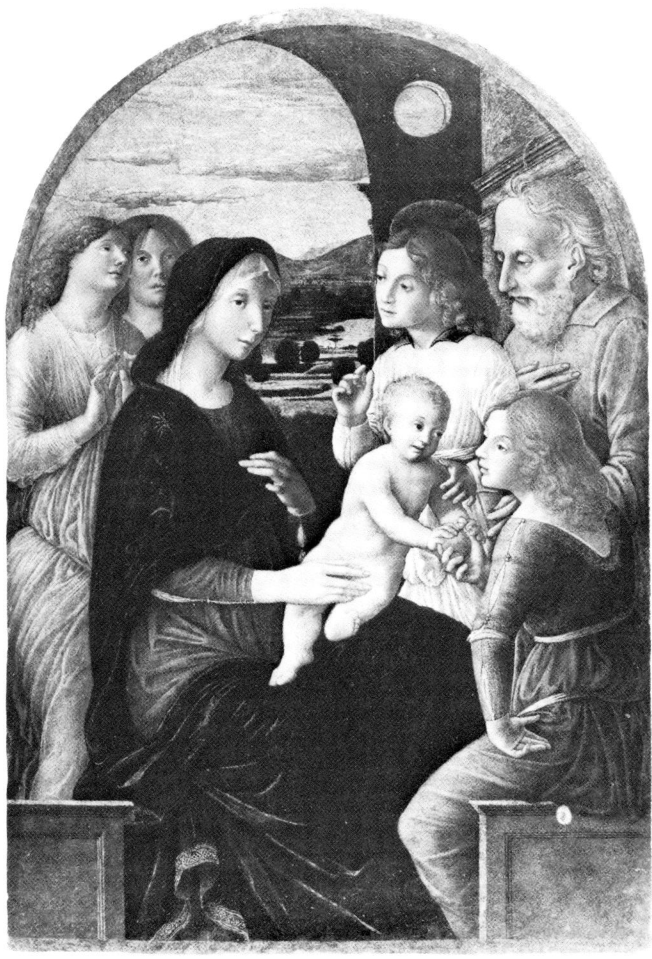

Fig. 7. Giacomo Pacchiarotto, *The Holy Family with Four Angels.* Tempera with oil on wood. 33¹³/₁₆ × 22⅜ inches (85.9 × 56.8 cm.). Private collection, Parma

The angel's garment is of a light grayish-blue, which is enlivened by the colors of the sleeve, wings, and by a gold sash attached to the lute and superimposed on a blue background (probably suggesting the sky). The azure fabric of the over-sleeve, held together by metal clasps, affects a subtle color combination with the lighter garment. More striking is the mauve of the angel's wings, only portions of which are visible. Next to them at the upper left corner appears a small red area, obviously part of a second angel's wing. At the right of the figure, a large section of a white wing, bordered with a faint Venetian red, makes it evident that the Baltimore *Angel* was flanked by other angel figures which, unlike the figures in the Kress panels, were not arranged in a straight row.

The design of the fragment is further complicated by the large crook of a bishop's staff in front of the angel. The holy figure carrying the crosier may be standing in the foreground, though in other Sienese representations of the Assumption of that period, saints are often rendered floating in the air, a position that might better explain the spatial relationship of the angel and the bishop's crook. The shape of the crook is reminiscent of earlier designs by Mantegna, Crivelli, and Giovanni Bellini. Thus, such a minor detail confirms Edgell's observation that ". . . Pacchiarotto despite his date was really a child of the Quattrocento."[23] S. J. Freedberg concurs when he writes: "Pacchiarotto who lived long into the sixteenth century seems not to have acquired more than an occasional and superficial coloration of sixteenth-century style."[24] With his dependence on Quattrocento art, Pacchiarotto shared the characteristics of most Sienese sixteenth-century painters who rarely progressed into the realm of the High Renaissance. As even so small a fragment as the *Angel Playing a Lute* reveals, it was hardly an avant-garde quality that distinguished Pacchiarotto's pictures, but competent craftsmanship, a certain inventiveness, and a particular lyrical charm.

Gertrude Rosenthal
The Baltimore Museum of Art

NOTES

1. The attribution to Melozzo was made by W. E. Suida, "Mantegna and Melozzo," *Art In America* 34 (April 1946):72. For illustrations of *Angels Making Music* by Melozzo da Forlì, Vatican Gallery, Rome, see. R. Buscaroli, *Melozzo da Forlì* (Rome: Reale Accademia d'Italia, 1938), pp. 67–76.
2. G. Coor, "Notes on Six Parts of Two Dismembered Sienese Altarpieces. II—Four Fragments from an Assumption of the Virgin," *Gazette des Beaux-Arts* 65 (March 1965): cover and pp. 132–36 (published posthumously). Her tentative date of 1495–1510 for the altarpiece has been accepted by other scholars of Sienese art.
3. F. Zeri, *Italian Paintings in the Walters Art Gallery* (Baltimore: The Walters Art Gallery, 1976), 1: 134. B. Berenson, "Lost Works of the Last Sienese Masters," *International Studio,* pt. 3 (April 1931): 19–21. M. Salmi, "Renaissance," in *Encyclopedia of World Art* (New York: McGraw-Hill, 1967), 12: 56, states that Pacchiarotto first followed Matteo di Giovanni but that his later manner was closer to the styles of Perugino and Pinturicchio, an opinion that is generally accepted today. F. Russell, "The Evolution of a Sienese Painter: Some Early Madonnas of Pacchiarotto," *Burlington Magazine* 115 (December 1973):802, believes that Pacchiarotto was the pupil of Guidoccio Cozzarelli but that he freed himself early from Cozzarelli's influence. See also M. Davies, *National Gallery Catalogues: The Earlier Italian Schools,* 2nd ed. (London: National Gallery, 1961), p. 399.
4. G. H. Edgell, *A History of Sienese Painting* (New York: Dial Press, 1932), p. 268.
5. Coor, "II—Four Fragments from an Assumption of the Virgin," p. 132.
6. J. A. Crowe and G. B. Cavalcaselle, *A New History of Painting in Italy from the Second to the Sixteenth Century* (London: J. Murray, 1864–1866), 3:374, n. 2, and p. 383.

   Karl Friedrich von Rumohr (1785–1843), famous early art historian, was the first to discuss separate artistic problems in essays or articles. His investigations of source material and his *Italienische Forschungen* (1827–1831) established his international reputation.
7. G. Vasari, *Le Vite de' più eccellenti pittori, scultori ed architettori,* ed. G. Milanesi, 2nd ed. (Florence: G. C. Sansoni, 1906; reprint ed., 1973), 6:415–28.
8. Crowe and Cavalcaselle, *New History of Painting in Italy,* 3:377–78. Edgell, *History of Sienese Painting,* p. 268.
9. Coor, "II—Four Fragments from an Assumption of the Virgin," p. 132.
10. Ibid., p. 133, fig. 5.
11. L. Vertova, "On Pacchiarotto's Dismembered Assumption," *Gazette des Beaux-Arts* 69 (March 1967):162, fig. 7.
12. Edgell, *History of Sienese Painting,* figs. 405 and 407.
13. Ibid., fig. 408. B. Berenson, *Italian Pictures of the Renaissance: Central and North Italian Schools* (London: Phaidon Press, 1968), pl. 921.

14. Edgell, *History of Sienese Painting,* fig. 406. Vertova, "On Pacchiarotto's Dismembered Assumption," p. 159, fig. 1. R. van Marle, *The Development of the Italian Schools of Painting* (The Hague: Martinus Nijhoff, 1937), 16: fig. 291.

15. Van Marle, *The Development of the Italian Schools of Painting,* 16:500. "Siena, Gallery . . . No. 576, *Assumption of the Virgin,* formerly ascribed to Gerolamo del Pacchia but restored to Pacchiarotto by L. Olcott" (*Guide to Siena* [1904], p. 332). Photograph and letter of June 11, 1977, received from Piero Torriti, Soprintendente of Art and History for the Provinces of Siena and Grosseto, with excerpt from catalogue by C. Brandi, *La Regia Pinacoteca di Siena* (Rome: La Libreria dello Stato, 1933).

16. H. Beenken, "Das Urbild der sienesischen Assuntadarstellungen im XIV. und XV. Jahrhundert," *Zeitschrift fur Bildende Kunst* 62 (1928–1929): 73–85. M. Meiss, *Painting in Florence and Siena after the Black Death* (Princeton: Princeton University Press, 1951), pp. 21 ff. Representations of the Assumption of the Virgin by Sienese artists of the fifteenth and sixteenth centuries were rendered by, among others, Benvenuto di Giovanni (The Metropolitan Museum of Art, New York) and Matteo di Giovanni (National Gallery, London, and Cathedral, Grosseto). Girolamo di Benvenuto supposedly painted five pictures of the Assumption, of which the one at Montalcino is considered the finest. Pietro di Domenico and Fungai also painted the Assumption of the Virgin.

17. Coor, "II—Four Fragments from an Assumption of the Virgin," pp. 131–36.

18. Ibid., pp. 131–32 (with provenance), and figs. 3 and 4. Listed as by Matteo di Giovanni in Sale Catalogue no. 1378 (New York: Parke-Bernet Galleries, November 12, 1952), p. 5, lot 15, repro. After this sale the large fragment disappeared. In June 1977 Sotheby Parke-Bernet informed me that they did not know the present whereabouts of the *Assunta* panel.

19. Coor, "II—Four Fragments from an Assumption of the Virgin," pp. 134–35, figs. 6, 7, and cover. F. R. Shapley, *Paintings from the Samuel H. Kress Collection: Italian Schools XV–XVI Century* (London: Phaidon Press, 1968), pp. 111 ff. (with bibliography).

20. Vertova, "On Pacchiarotto's Dismembered Assumption," pp. 160–61 and figs. 2 and 3. The panel showing *St. John the Baptist and Three Saints* is owned by the Estate of Judge James A. Murnaghan, Dublin. The related panel depicting *King David, Moses, and Two Saints* is in the possession of Anthony Post, London; it has been in his family since the mid-nineteenth century (ex colls.: William Graham [sale London, April 1886], Lord Muir Mackenzie, and Mrs. Donnel Post).

21. Ibid., pp. 160–61. In addition, Vertova attempts to connect a predella of five panels with the dismembered *Assumption.* F. Zeri, "A Predella by Giacomo Pacchiarotto," *Journal of The Walters Art Gallery* 27–28 (1964–1965):79–86, figs. 6–10, has no doubt that the attribution to Pacchiarotto is correct. However, before accepting Vertova's hypothesis that the predella pieces were part of the cut-up *Assumption,* he thinks more proof will be needed. (See also Zeri, *Italian Paintings in the Walters Art Gallery,* 1:139.)

22. Coor, "II—Four Fragments from an Assumption of the Virgin," p. 133, fig. 5.

23. Edgell, *History of Sienese Painting,* p. 272.

24. S. J. Freedberg, *Painting in Italy: 1500–1600,* rev. ed. (Harmondsworth and Baltimore: Penguin Books, 1975), p. 117.

SELECTED BIBLIOGRAPHY

Joseph Archer Crowe and Giovanni Battista Cavalcaselle. *A New History of Painting in Italy from the Second to the Sixteenth Century.* 3 vols. London: J. Murray, 1864–1866.

Giorgio Vasari. *Le Vite de' più eccellenti pittori, scultori ed architettori.* 9 vols. Edited by Gaetano Milanesi. 2nd edition. Florence: G. C. Sansoni, 1906; reprint edition, 1973.

Cesare Brandi. "Pacchiarotto." In Thieme-Becker, *Allgemeines Lexikon der Bildenden Künstler.* 37 vols. Leipzig: E. A. Seemann, 1907–1950.

Gustav Friedrich Hartlaub. *Matteo da Siena und seine Zeit.* Strasbourg: J. H. E. Heitz, 1910.

Raimond van Marle. *The Development of the Italian Schools of Painting.* 19 vols. The Hague: Martinus Nijhoff, 1923–1938.

Herman Beenken. "Das Urbild der sienesischen Assuntadarstellungen im XIV. und XV. Jahrhundert." *Zeitschrift für Bildende Kunst* 62 (1928–1929):73–85.

Bernard Berenson. "Lost Works of the Last Sienese Masters." *International Studio* 3 (April 1931):19–21. The same article appeared in Italian in *Dedalo* 3 (1931):753–57.

Bernard Berenson. *Italian Pictures of the Renaissance.* Oxford: Clarendon Press, 1932.

George Harold Edgell. *A History of Sienese Painting.* New York: Dial Press, 1932.

William E. Suida. "Mantegna and Melozzo." *Art In America* 34 (April 1946):66–72.

John Pope-Hennessy. *Sienese Quattrocento Painting.* Oxford: Phaidon Press, 1947.

Millard Meiss. *Painting in Florence and Siena after the Black Death.* Princeton: Princeton University Press, 1951.

4000 Years of Modern Art. Exhibition catalogue. Baltimore: Baltimore Museum of Art, 1956.

Mario Salmi. "Renaissance." In *Encyclopedia of World Art.* 15 vols. New York: McGraw-Hill, 1959–1968.

Alberto Tailetti. *Guida artistica illustrata di Siena e provincia.* Siena, 1959.

Martin Davies. *National Gallery Catalogues: The Earlier Italian Schools.* 2nd edition. London: National Gallery, 1961.

Federico Zeri. "A Predella by Giacomo Pacchiarotto." *Journal of The Walters Art Gallery* 27-28 (1964–1965): 79–86.

Gertrude Coor. "Notes on Six Parts of Two Dismembered Sienese Altarpieces. II—Four Fragments from an Assumption of the Virgin." *Gazette des Beaux-Arts* 65 (March 1965):132–36.

Luisa Vertova. "On Pacchiarotto's Dismembered Assumption." *Gazette des Beaux-Arts* 69 (March 1967): 159–63.

Bernard Berenson. *Italian Pictures of the Renaissance: Central and North Italian Schools.* 3 vols. London: Phaidon Press, 1968.

Fern Rusk Shapley. *Paintings from the Samuel H. Kress Collection: Italian Schools XV–XVI Century.* London: Phaidon Press, 1968.

Francis Russell. "The Evolution of a Sienese Painter: Some Early Madonnas of Pacchiarotto." *Burlington Magazine* 115 (December 1973):801–805.

Federico Zeri. *Italian Paintings in the Walters Art Gallery.* 2 vols. Baltimore: Walters Art Gallery, 1976.

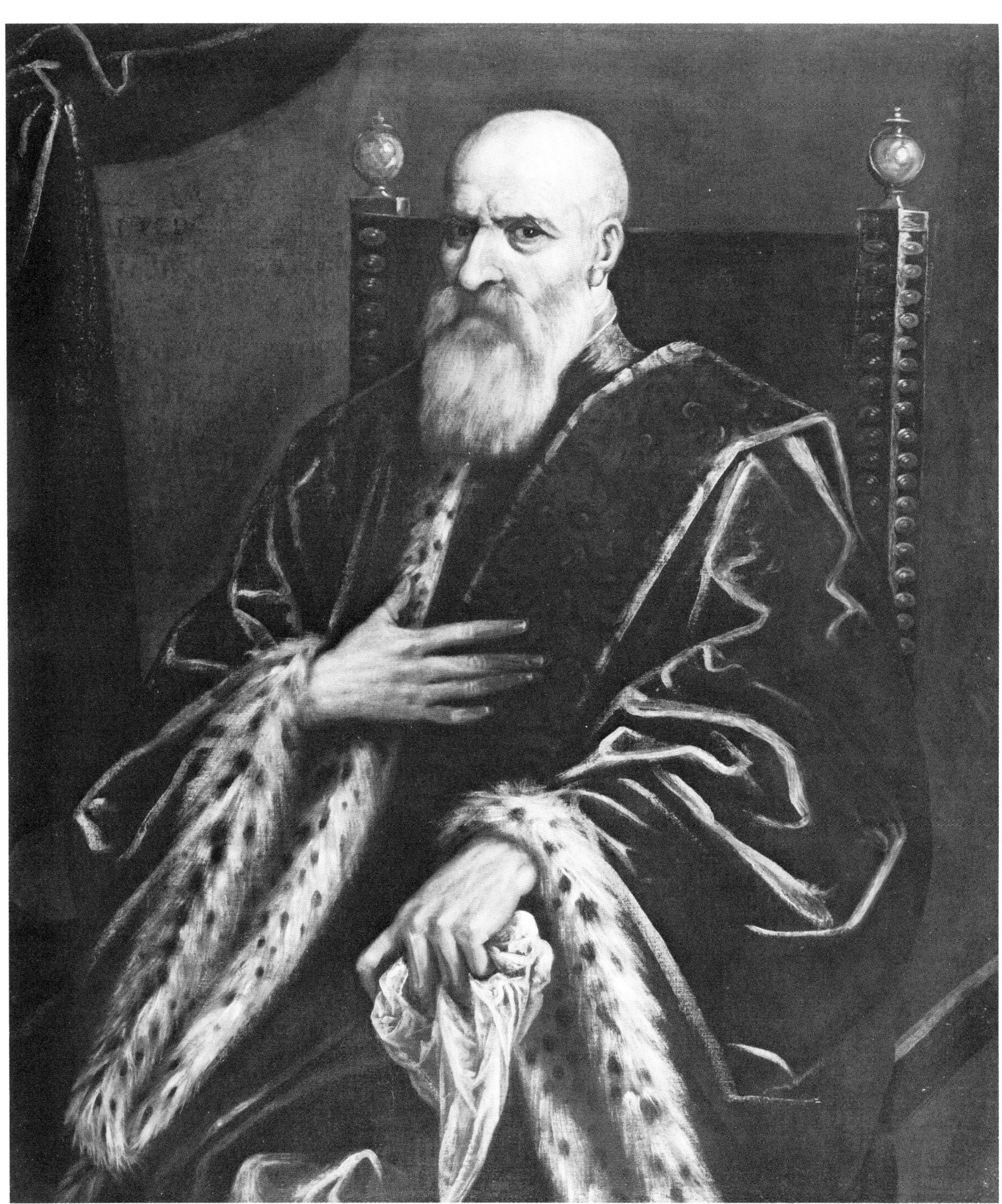

Circle of
PALMA IL GIOVANE (1548–1628)
(Jacopo Negretti)

---

12. *Portrait of a Venetian Procurator,* ca. 1590–1600

Oil on canvas. 47⅜ × 39 inches (120.3 × 99 cm.)
The Jacob Epstein Collection (BMA 51.116)

PROVENANCE

Wurtemberg Royal Collections, Stuttgart (?)

Collection of Arthur J. Sulley, Middleton, Berkshire (pre-1926)

Wildenstein & Company, London and New York (1927)

Purchased by Jacob Epstein, Baltimore, in 1928

Loaned by Jacob Epstein to The Baltimore Museum of Art in 1929 and bequeathed in 1951

CONDITION

The condition of the painting is fair in the essential parts, such as the face and figure of the sitter, but examination has shown that surrounding areas and background had been badly damaged. At an uncertain date, perhaps early in its history, the entire lower left corner of the canvas was lost, and at the right margin a vertical strip of an irregular shape, 7 to 23 cm. wide and 62 cm. high, of which the right edge is about 1.5 cm. from the right margin, was also lost. These lacunae were filled in with two pieces from another painting with a canvas weave very similar to that of the original. When cleaned, the fragment at the lower left corner showed the figure of a winged putto and part of a second putto (fig. 1); the vertical strip at the right showed clouds and other figural fragments. The fragments seem to have been Venetian of the period ca. 1590–1630 and probably were taken from a damaged painting selected because its texture and weave matched thóse of the original canvas. These inserts had been overpainted to complete the missing passages of the original.

The picture, which had been lined and had gone through various restorations before its purchase by Mr. Epstein, was reported by its previous owner, A. J. Sulley (letter of August 25, 1927; curatorial files, The Baltimore Museum of Art), to have been very dirty prior to cleaning in 1926 or 1927, but there is no indication that the insertions were made at that time. There are local losses, notably at the tip of the index finger of the right hand, and the surface has a rather regular pinpoint abrasion throughout. An inscription at the left which had been overpainted has suffered serious losses. It appears to have been added subsequent to the original paint surface but very close in date to it. At that time the neutral tone of the back wall was extended to cover a portion of the original curtain at left, in order to accommodate the inscription, which has become illegible.

During the treatment in 1978–1979 the painting was relined and most of the later inpainting was removed. The inscription was left in its impaired state. Local losses were inpainted, as were the added pieces of canvas which were left in place to maintain the continuity of texture and composition.

Geoffrey Michael Lemmer
The Baltimore Museum of Art

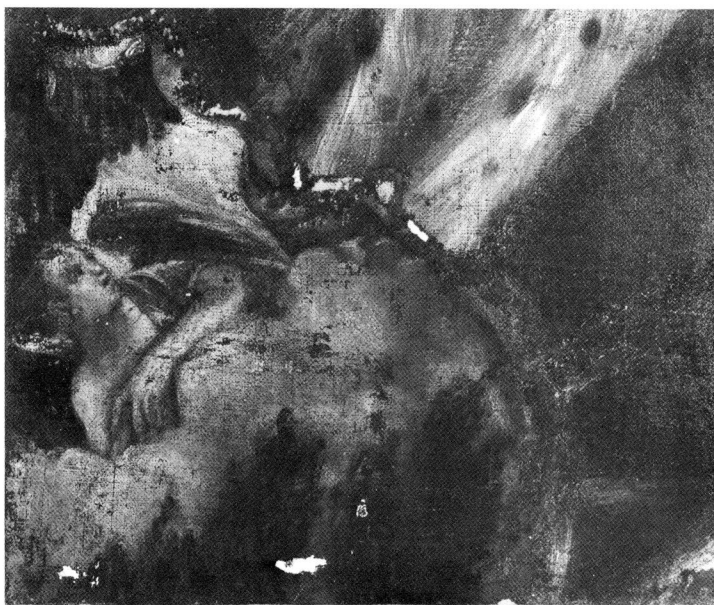

Fig. 1. Fragment of lower left corner, overpainted insert, cat. no. 12

Venetian Renaissance portraiture is perceptibly distinct in patronage and format from that of other Italian city states.[1] This is evident not only in the obvious contrast with either Papal Rome or small dukedoms and marquisates such as Urbino and Mantua, but also in comparison with Florence which made the transition from a republican society resembling that of Venice to a Grand Duchy during the same period. Until the rise of Humanism official portraits were rare in Florence and private examples seem nonexistent; only in the years paralleling the rise of Medici power did easel portraits become popular, and in public projects they were limited to *staffage* in a religious context, seemingly excluded by intention from civic decorations.[2]

This was not the case in Venice where the mosaic of the *Transport of the Body of Saint Mark* over the left portal of San Marco contains images of the Doge and his retinue which come as close to portraiture as Italo-Byzantine convention allowed in the years around 1260.[3] More naturalistic in conception and in a similar civic-religious context, small scale portraits appear almost simultaneously with the earliest examples of panel painting in Venice, such as that of the Muranese administrator and his wife in *Donato Memmo and His Wife in Adoration of Saint Donato* (SS. Maria e Donato, Murano) dated 1310.[4] Slightly later, now in a funerary context, Paolo Veneziano depicted *Doge Francesco Dandolo and His Wife with Saints Francis and Elizabeth in Adoration of the Virgin* (Santa Maria Gloriosa dei Frari, sacristy, Venice), in which the clearly characterized portraits are represented on the same scale as the religious figures.[5] From the time of this example, ca. 1339, official portraits appear, not frequently but with a certain regularity, not only in a religious setting but probably also in a secular framework, in the lost decorations of the Palazzo Ducale. In this cycle of paintings the naturalistic tradition of Altichiero, imported from Padua, must have played a significant role. To the best of our knowledge, however, private easel portraits were unknown in either Venice or Florence until they were introduced in both cities by Gentile da Fabriano, who probably developed his formulation on the basis of Lombard prototypes, executing pendant male and female portraits in Venice in the years around 1408, and no doubt doing such portraits also in Florence about 1423–1426.[6]

During the following half century the strict profile portrait against a neutral dark ground prevailed throughout Italy, its use for private patrons—of no apparent civic importance—increasing greatly toward the middle of the century.[7] In Venice the practice of according each doge an official portrait was expanded to include a significant number of doge portraits for private patrons as well as occasional depictions of other civic officials. Gentile Bellini, in his semi-official role as chief painter to the Serenissima, seems to have enjoyed the lion's share of these commissions, executing them in the old-fashioned profile format until after the turn of the century when he essayed the three-quarter view of certain eminent sitters such as *Caterina Cornaro* (Museum of Fine Arts, Budapest).[8] The three-quarter view, the bust, and later the half-length portrait began to supplement the profile in the years around 1460–1475 under the direct influence of Flemish prototypes. Mantegna's *Cardinal Lodovico Mezzarota* (Gemäldegalerie, Staatl. Museen, PKB, Berlin W.),[9] Pollaiuolo's *Young Man* (National Gallery of Art, Mellon Collection, listed by the Gallery as by Andrea del Castagno)[10] and Giovanni Bellini's *Joerg Fugger* (Norton Simon, Inc. Museum of Art, Pasadena)[11] are among the earliest known examples. Of these, only the Florentine work puts the figure against a naturalistic setting of sky, though no landscape is indicated in these early pictures. Important examples of Antonello da Messina's three-quarter view portraits were, as a result of his peregrinations, dispersed through several Italian artistic centers in the years before his death in 1479.[12] All of these portraits in the new format seem to have been commissioned by a Humanistic circle of patrons; official portraits usually retained the more conservative profile type for quite a long period.

The range and format of Venetian portraiture expanded into innovative areas during the first decade of the sixteenth century. Giovanni Bellini established a new imagery for the doge's portrait with his painting of *Leonardo Loredano* (National Gallery, London) of ca. 1507,[13] and he created an entirely new group portrait of purely civil import with the *Doge Loredano with Four Counselors* (formerly Baron Marczell von Nemes Collection, Munich), an important if ruined picture dated 1507.[14] In unofficial, Humanist portraiture the role of Leonardo da Vinci, who visited Venice in early 1500, remains obscure,[15] and the importance of Giorgione's portraits is still a matter of discussion;[16] by 1512 it is clear that Titian had assumed leadership with a series of masterful pictures, establishing a standard which most Venetian portraitists observed for more than a generation.[17]

Before 1500, senators, procurators, and chancellors sat for their portraits only rarely and then usually in the modest bust-length format favored by Humanists.[18] They appear in quantity as spectators in the various canvases commissioned by the *scuole* between the last decade of the century and about 1510,[19] but the first independent portrait in which a state official appears in the new expanded setting is Titian's *Portrait of a Procurator* (Mrs. Rush H. Kress Collection), a little known but important work of ca. 1510–1511 whose attribution has been a matter of controversy.[20] It is, in fact, a combination of a Humanist type with its book and allegorical landscape, and an official one with its conscious emphasis on the red robe and black stole of office. Later, Titian would give the Humanist elements, such as the window into a landscape, the book, and other still-life details, less emphasis or, more often, would omit them altogether. Perhaps the most significant surviving example of this more austere format is the portrait of the *Senator Giacomo Dolfin* (Messrs. Agnew, London), executed ca. 1532 (fig. 2). Its economy, rather forbidding characterization, and concern with the garb of office established a type which would provide the model for such pictures for the remainder of the century.[21] But the earlier formulation, which retained the Humanist motifs, also continued for several decades in the work of Titian's followers.

Toward 1560, an element of dramatic characterization may be detected in the impressive *Senator* (H. J. Ralph Bankes Collection, Kingston Lacy, England) where the energetic sitter grasps the chaperon with his right hand and pulls it across his robe to create a diagonal which is paralleled by his raised left arm and which contrasts with the aggressive turn of his head to gaze in the opposite direction.[22] In the years after his appointment to the Sensaria in 1517, Titian was required to paint an official portrait of each new doge upon his election to the office. Most of the originals were lost in one or another of the conflagrations that swept the Palazzo Ducale in 1574 and 1577, but in many cases replicas, either autograph or from the shop, survive to document their appearance.[23] These, too, conform, with varying degrees of emphasis on official pomp, to Titian's restrained type, although late in his career, in the *Doge Francesco Venier* (Thyssen-Bornemisza Collection, Lugano) of ca. 1555, he reintroduced the window at left with a distant seascape, and a draped curtain at right, elements which suggest a conservative and perhaps nostalgic evocation of his earliest official portraits.[24] This Humanist formula would soon be endowed with a monumental solemnity in the so-called *Palma* (Staatliche Gemäldegalerie, Dresden) of 1561, a portrait of a physician in the guise of either St. Cosmas or St. Damian, but probably, given his garb, of a state official as well (see in this publication cat. no. 14, fig. 1 and n. 9).[25] It is clearly an expansion of the concept already established by the Kingston Lacy portrait.

Titian's example provided a model for official portraits from which his Venetian contemporaries rarely departed. During the first half of the century those few portraits of doges which did not originate in Titian's shop show virtually no progressive innovations, but instead often remain rooted in the late Quattrocento mode.[26] Portraits of senators, procurators, and other office holders are surprisingly rare until after mid-

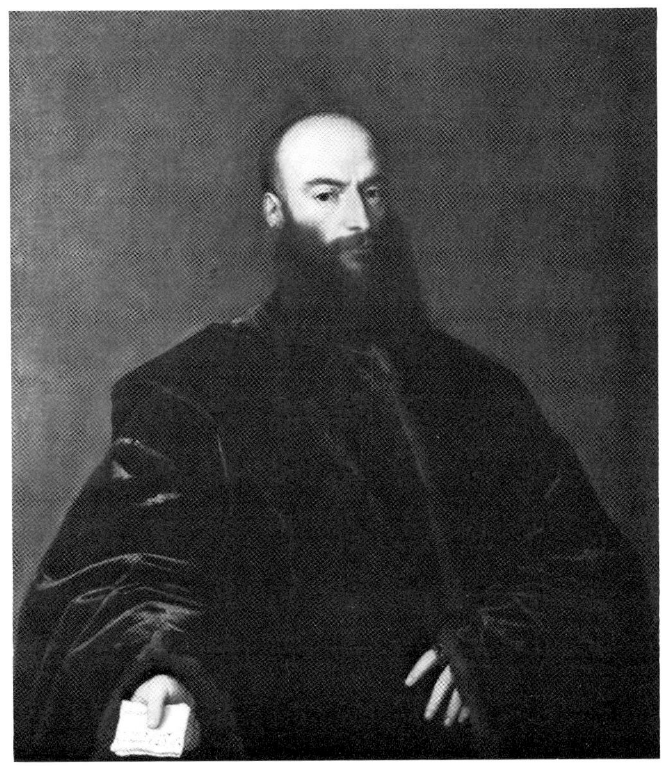

Fig. 2. Titian, *Portrait of Senator Giacomo Dolfin.* Oil on canvas. 40½ × 35¼ inches (102.9 × 90.2 cm.). Messrs. Thos. Agnew, London

century. Palma Vecchio, it would seem, worked exclusively for Humanist patrons;[27] Bonifazio avoided portraiture altogether;[28] Paris Bordone depicted officials only in the larger context of *istorie* for the Scuola di San Marco;[29] and Lorenzo Lotto's oeuvre does not, despite some fanciful attributions, include any portraits of Venetian secular office holders.[30] The splendid *Portrait of Bernardo Morosini* in the Kunstsammlungen Cassel, attributed by the museum to Lotto, is by Jacopo Bassano and dates to about 1542.[31]

After the middle of the Cinquecento, in the years which saw a vigorous new generation of painters reach maturity, one finds a startling increase in the number of portraits of senators, procurators, and other state officials. They do not, however, originate with the artist whose distinction as a portraitist and whose bravura technique might have been well matched for the depiction of splendidly robed officials. Indeed, Paolo Veronese seems never to have painted a Venetian government personage, nor did artists of his circle and following make a specialty of such pictures. Their patrons seem to have been exclusively from Humanist circles, and Paolo is a true heir to the tradition of Palma Vecchio.[32]

The patronage for civic portraits centered instead almost entirely on one workshop, which appears to have held a virtual monopoly on this trade—that of Jacopo Tintoretto (1518?–1594). Although this volcanic orchestrator of swirling visions would seem the least gifted portraitist of the Venetian painters, Tintoretto executed individual portraits of at least four doges, from Francesco Donato in about 1552 through Alvise Mocenigo in about 1571. Indeed, there is some evidence that his ducal patronage in portraiture was limited to this twenty-year span and that it overlapped significantly with that of Titian, who still held the responsibility for each doge's official portrait. Tintoretto's portraits of the heads of state are scant, however, in comparison with the proliferation of pictures of senators and procurators which issued from his shop. He began to attract official portrait patronage only in his mature years, his earliest depiction of a procurator dating to the late 1540's and his earliest documented representation of a senator to the period just before 1562.[33] Aside from his commissions for the doges, the great majority of his official portraits evidently originated from the 1570's or later. The crest of the wave of popularity for such portraits seems to have come during the years of Tintoretto's most intense activity for the state in the Palazzo Ducale, that is between 1578 and 1590.

Jacopo Tintoretto, his son Domenico, and other members of the family shop painted at least thirty-six surviving portraits of senators and some dozen more of procurators of various types in the same format.[34] Jacopo does not seem to have painted a state official full length except in the votive iconography of which a great many examples survive, all of them in one way or another indebted to Titian's *Vendramin Votive* (National Gallery, London). Taking into account that most canvases of the period have lost some part of their margins, usually along the bottom, it seems that Tintoretto frequently planned his official portraits to a measure of about 110 × 90 centimeters. One may conclude that while Tintoretto and his collaborators made but slight contributions to the evolution of the official portrait in Venice, they did dominate the genre and in sheer quantity appear to have been virtually its only practitioners.

Given the almost automatic attribution to Tintoretto of any Venetian portrait which fell generically into this type, it is hardly surprising that the Epstein picture bore a traditional ascription to that master when it entered the Epstein collection in 1928.[35] However, despite its persistence in the Berenson lists under the name of Jacopo as late as 1957, The Baltimore Museum of Art had already recognized that this attribution was untenable and had modified it, first to Domenico and later to the Venetian School, sixteenth century, an opinion confirmed by Paola Rossi in her study of Tintoretto's portraits.[36] No recent author has attempted a more precise definition of its artistic origin.

The Epstein portrait (cat. no. 12) conforms, with several significant variations, to the conventions established by Tintoretto and his followers. The figure is turned slightly toward its right and wears a deep red velvet robe, probably floor length, open down the front with a low, round fitted collar and widely belled sleeves falling from fitted shoulders. The robe is lined with fur of a type usually described as marten but which perhaps is snow leopard. In many portraits such fur appears as a mere edging on the sleeves and down the front seam, but in the Epstein picture there seems to be a full lining of a type used in winter. The sitter has a red chaperon with a stylized floral design over his left shoulder; a white handkerchief is grasped in his left hand. He is portrayed seated in a high-backed chair with brass finials, against a neutral interior. He is bareheaded, since the fashion of being painted wearing the pileus was already out of style by mid-century.

Unfortunately, the lengthy inscription at left is of little value in establishing the sitter's identity, his official status, the picture's date, or its authorship.[37] Although some portraits of the period bear inscriptions which were part of the original design and must have been painted before the picture left the artist's studio, the vast majority of such inscriptions were added subsequently, usually at the sitter's death when it was deemed necessary to record his identity and office or to preserve salient information on the sitter for his heirs. This was almost certainly the case in the Epstein picture, since the inscription was placed between the sitter's right shoulder and the left edge of the canvas in an arrangement that is cramped and awkward, requiring that some words at the left overlap the curtain. Some overpainting of the ground must have been required to effect an even setting for the inscription. This addition, however, seems to have occurred at a date close to that of the original painting since it cannot be removed without causing damage to the original background. Despite its near contemporaneity, the inscription has suffered far more than the original surface and has been reduced to virtual illegibility, a scattered pattern of isolated letters and fragments which, with infrared and other technical examination, has yielded only one clearly legible word—*procuratore,* which appears just above the sitter's right shoulder. While it is tempting to discover the word *opera* following this, and the name *Quirini* above, this must remain pure speculation.

The inclusion of the term "procurator" in the inscription confirms what the robe of office has already suggested about the sitter's civic rank. This is, however, only a beginning in the complex process of sorting out the formula of Venetian civil costume. It is, indeed, startling to observe the confusion in the art historical literature about such distinctions, the terms "senator," "procurator," "chancellor," etc., being used almost interchangeably and often simultaneously for such pictures. In the case of the Epstein portrait, the inscription confirms that the sitter was a procurator, for whom the red robe was standard. The color and position of the chaperon are more specific. Since the red patterned stole worn over the right shoulder is that of a *Procuratore de Citra,* its position here on the left shoulder indicates a procurator who was also a regular member of the Senate, although representatives of specific offices such as *tesoriero, avogadro,* etc., wear the chaperon over the left shoulder as well. There seems to have been some modification in official robes during the sixteenth century, and seasonal fashions as well as occasional license on the part of painters, who worked from life only for the heads and enjoyed some freedom of invention in the costume, account for the difficulty in identifying state offices.[38] In any case, we may identify the present subject as a procurator.

How closely does the Epstein *Procurator* relate to Jacopo Tintoretto's official portraits? The powerful portrait of *A Procurator of St. Mark's* (National Gallery of Art, Kress Collection) provides an apt comparison (fig. 3).[39] The seated but restless figure conveys an expressive tension which dramatizes the sitter's vitality and authority. By contrast, the Baltimore *Procurator* is relaxed, even prosaic, despite the more self-consciously rhetorical position of the hands. The pictorial character is equally distinct, the former richly textured, with sweeping slashes of assured brushstrokes, where the latter is timidly descriptive, with labored patterns of highlight. Tintoretto's vibrant color is saturated in tonality and reveals dense impasto, but that of the Baltimore picture is grayed toward a monochrome and rather dry and thready in texture. One must, however, raise the ever present question of participation by Tintoretto's workshop in the Baltimore painting. Only a handful of his portraits are masterpieces of the first rank; the vast majority show that his febrile imagination grew impatient with the restrictions of the genre, and in many cases, especially after about 1570, that he tended to interest himself with the sitter's head and to relegate the remainder of the picture to one or several assistants, in some pictures to specialists in velvet, fur, curtains, landscape, etc.

The Baltimore *Procurator* is not, however, such a collaboration. It is thinly and evenly painted with a fluent if dry touch and with absolute security about the desired form and effect. The absence of *pentimenti* and the seeming sureness with which every stroke of paint serves its illustrative function raise the possibility of the painting's being an early copy. The professional handling of the paint and the secure balances of light and color, however, suggest an original work by an artist who uses his medium in a somewhat pedestrian way. There is no evidence that more than one hand was involved in the picture's execution. We may, therefore, rule out not only Tintoretto's own authorship but also a collaborative effort of his shop. It is even more obvious that his son Domenico had nothing to do with its creation.[40] His pedestrian temperament allowed, indeed demanded, a more reportorial naturalism in his portraits, but it is not of the order seen here. His predilection for harsh contrasts of blood-red and black with a cold blue, set off by lacy skeins of yellow or white highlights over sooty shadows, has no resemblance to

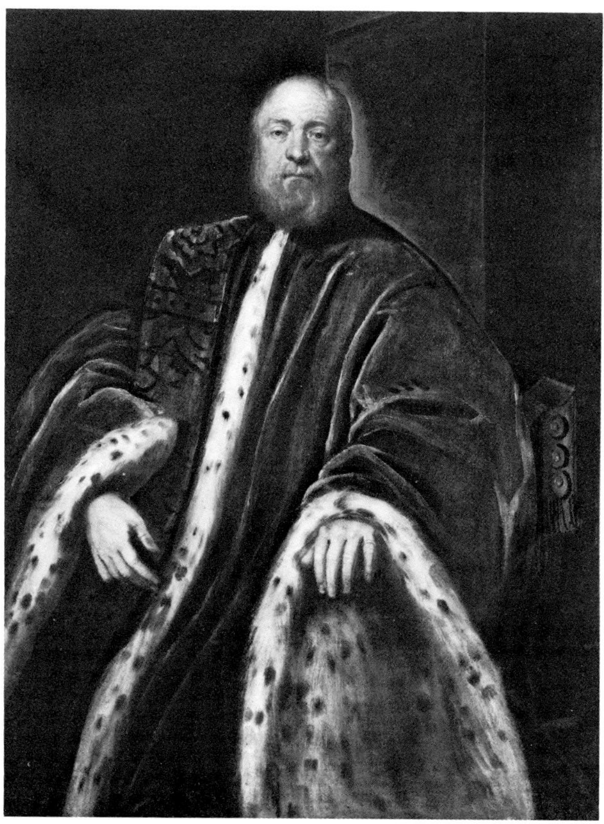

Fig. 3. Jacopo Tintoretto, *A Procurator of St. Mark's*. Oil on canvas. 54½ × 39⅞ inches (138.4 × 101.3 cm.). National Gallery of Art, Samuel H. Kress Collection, Washington, D.C.

the even color of the Baltimore *Procurator*. Nor do Domenico's vivid accents of sharp color dabbed with a sticky impasto around facial features resemble the smooth execution of this painting. Among the other members of the Tintoretto family, Marco remains indistinct as a portraitist; son-in-law Sebastian Casser (called Cassieri) employs a singularly harsh, red-yellow-blue color in a ribbony, long line brushstroke, and Marietta, the master's adored daughter, has been given an image of a painter that is devoid of reality.[41]

There is evidence to suggest that the Epstein portrait must date from very late in the sixteenth if not into the seventeenth century. Earlier, and in every known authentic portrait by Jacopo Tintoretto and his immediate shop, the chair depicted is of the familiar Renaissance type usually called a Roman chair. A folding, double-arch type with volute arms, it usually has a velvet or tooled leather back, though these elements are only occasionally visible in portraits of voluminously robed officials. The high-backed chair depicted here is leather with brass-nailed binding on front and sides, and its arms, not visible, are probably flat. Its most prominent feature are the two brass balls which serve as corner finials to the back. This type of chair, of Spanish origin, had become familiar in other parts of Italy during the last quarter of the century, but it does not seem to have come into common use in Venice until about 1600. It would be widely popular for about fifty years thereafter.

As Tintoretto began to withdraw from the field of civic portraiture, a genre he had essentially created twenty years earlier, patronage tended to shift to his shop and also to the studio of Leandro Bassano (Leandro dal Ponte) who had migrated from his home

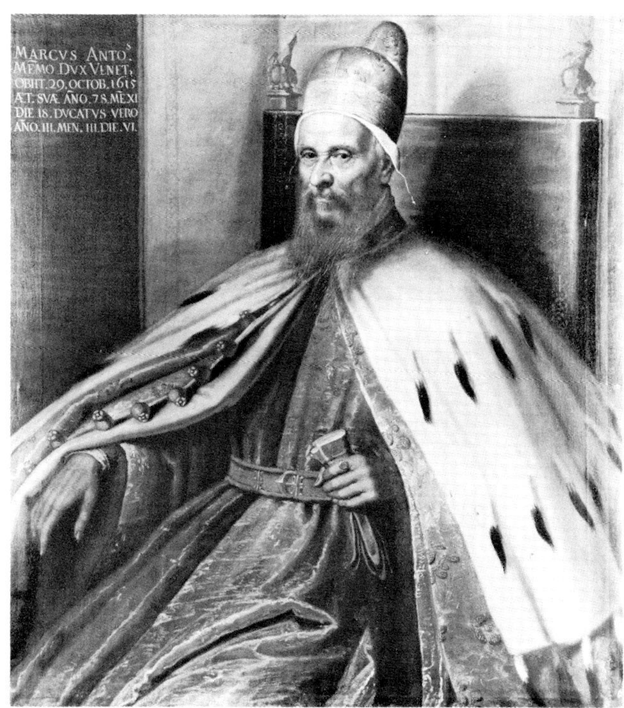

Fig. 4. Leandro Bassano, *Portrait of Doge Marcantonio Memmo.* Oil on canvas. 49¼ × 43⅛ inches (125 × 109.5 cm.). Museo Civico, Padua. Photograph courtesy Museo Civico, Padua

base to Venice about 1584 and had become the preferred portraitist to several doges and to numerous senators and procurators.[42] His *Doge Marcantonio Memmo* (Museo Civico, Padua), which dates from Memmo's term of office, 1612–1615, is characteristic and related to the Baltimore picture in format and to some degree in style (fig. 4). In both paintings the seated figure is shown in a relaxed pose on a slight diagonal against a neutral ground which is relieved by an understated curtain. Both paintings have a dry, stringy texture, a grayed chromatic range, and a niggling, descriptive handling of detail. Furthermore, the chairs in the two pictures are rather similar. But the Epstein *Procurator* cannot be by Leandro or any other member of the prolific Bassano (dal Ponte) clan since its brushwork is broader and more fluent and its color tonality darker. It does, however, originate from approximately the same period.

It is, in fact, to the principal heir to the tradition of Tintoretto and the dominant painter at the beginning of the new century that we should look for the proper ambience of the Baltimore picture. Jacopo Negretti, called Palma il Giovane to distinguish him from his great-uncle, Palma Vecchio, as well as from his father, Antonio Palma, was born in Venice in 1548 but received his major training in Urbino and, more important, in Rome before resuming a career in Venice in 1570.[43] From then until his death in 1628 he absorbed a diverse range of artistic experiences. Accepting Tintoretto's stifling influence on the classical native tradition, he eventually came to emulate the older master's example by producing yards of canvas peopled by athletic mannequins disposed according to mechanical convention. While in his late works this would descend into a ghostly Mannerism, during his mature years Palma developed a personal style in which Tintoretto's dramatic formula was modified by a preference for a candid naturalism—a style akin to the eclectic formulation of the Carracci during these same years.[44] Some order has recently been made of Palma's paintings and drawings, but his career as a

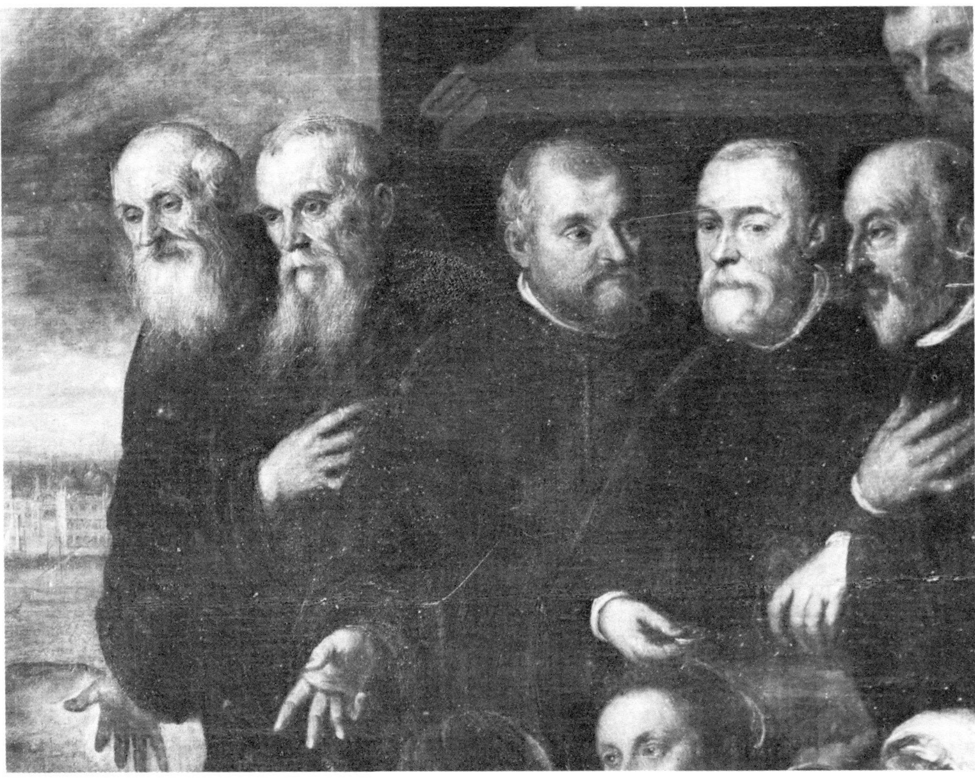

Fig. 5. Palma il Giovane, *Doge Renier Zen Blessed by the Redeemer,* detail. Oil on canvas. Overall, 154¾ × 141⅜ inches (393 × 359 cm.). Oratorio dei Crociferi, Venice. Photograph courtesy Osvaldo Böhm, Venice

portraitist remains sparsely documented. Although portraiture must always have held a minor place in his industrious production, there are Palma portraits of a distinct character from all periods of his activity whose importance and quality have yet to be adequately evaluated.

Palma's approach to portraiture shortly after his return to Venice may be deduced from the group of souls in limbo to the right of the *Christ in Limbo* (Accademia, Venice), an early work of ca. 1573. The prosaic, descriptive character of these heads clearly indicates that they are portraits from life, and their clumsy disjuncture from the rest of the composition is emphasized by a rather thick texture, a dull black and yellow color range, and a tentative devotion to surface detail.

In little more than a decade the artist demonstrates an entirely mature assurance in the numerous portraits which appear in the guise of historic personages such as Doge Zen as well as in the direct representation of contemporaries, Doge Pasquale Cicogna, his retinue, and the friars in the cycle of canvases done between 1585 and ca. 1593 for the Oratorio dei Crociferi.[45] The idealized portrait of the medieval Doge Zen, who founded the Oratorio, is accompanied at left and right by portraits done from life of the lay and religious benefactors of the Oratorio during the years in which Palma painted these pictures to decorate its halls. In the group at right (fig. 5) the elderly man at left shows characteristics comparable in the rendering with those of the *Portrait of an Old Man* (National Gallery of Victoria, Melbourne, Australia; fig. 6). The portraits of Doge Cicogna and his clerical entourage (fig. 7) are undoubtedly done from life and illustrate the nervous vitality of Palma as a portraitist. His grasp of form is now sure, his brushwork looser and more spontaneous, and the balance and variety of color and texture fresh and

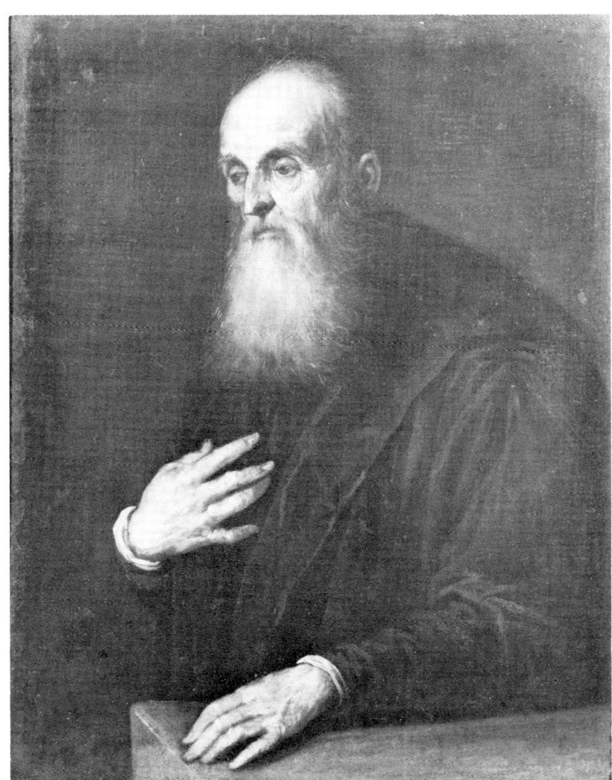

Fig. 6. Palma il Giovane, *Portrait of an Old Man.* Oil on canvas. 37⅛ × 29 inches (94.2 × 73.6 cm.). National Gallery of Victoria. Bequeathed by Howard Spensley, 1939. Reproduced by permission of the National Gallery of Victoria, Melbourne, Australia

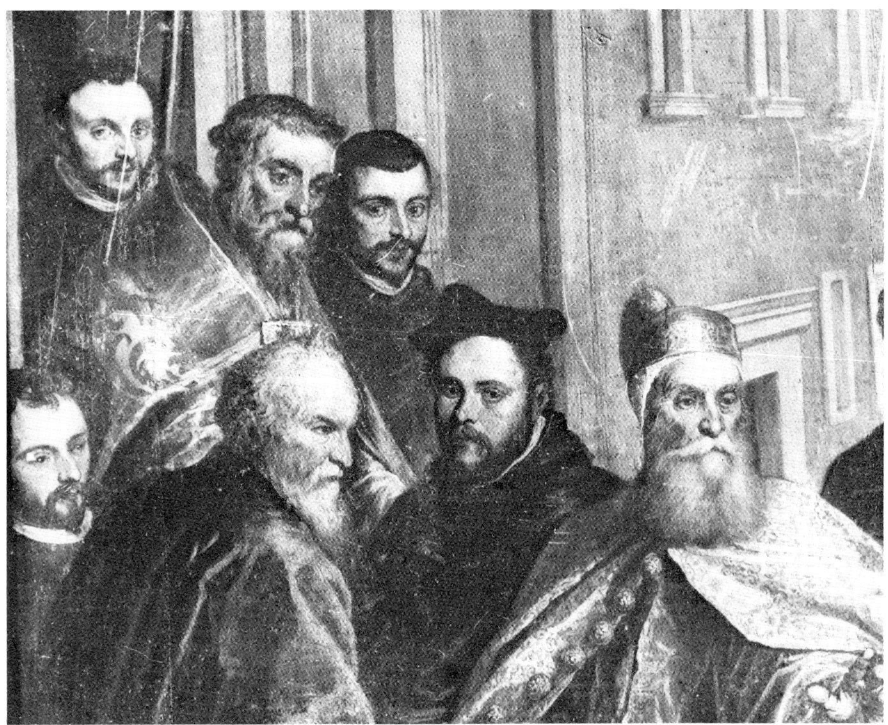

Fig. 7. Palma il Giovane, *Doge Cicogna Visits the Oratorio dei Crociferi,* detail. Oil on canvas. Overall, 145¼ × 103⅛ inches (369 × 262 cm.). Oratorio dei Crociferi, Venice. Photograph courtesy Osvaldo Böhm, Venice

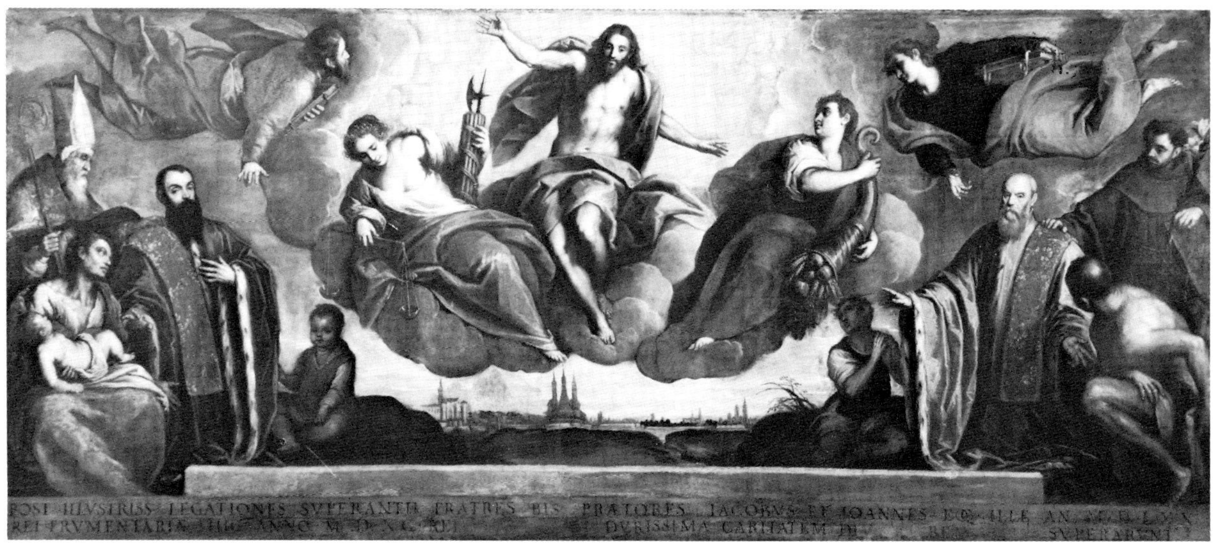

Fig. 9. Palma il Giovane, *Soranzo Votive* (*Podestà Jacopo and Giovanni Soranzo in Adoration of the Redeemer*). Oil on canvas. $91\frac{5}{16} \times 218\frac{1}{2}$ inches (232×555 cm.). Museo Civico, Padua. Photograph courtesy Museo Civico, Padua

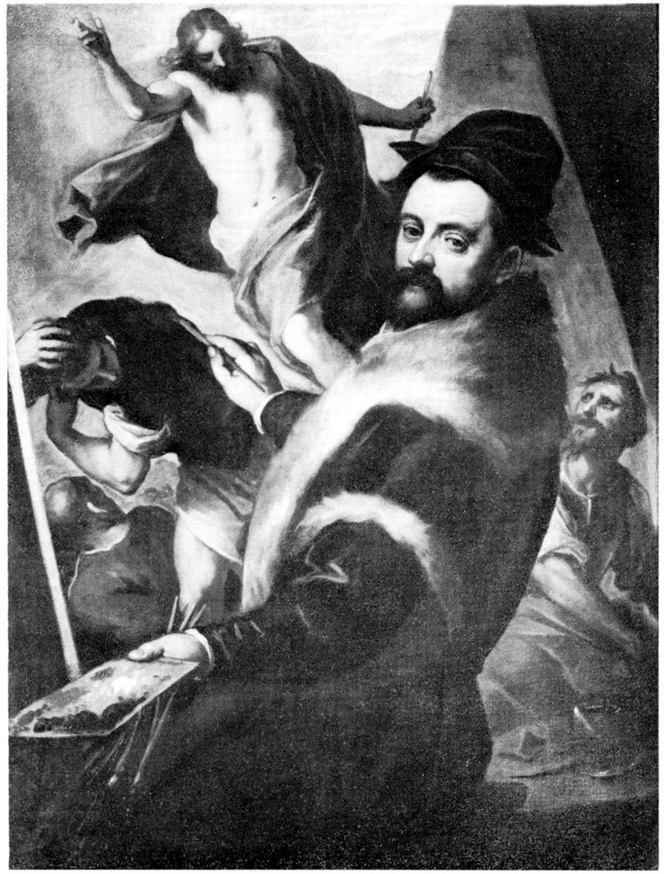

Fig. 8. Palma il Giovane, *Self-Portrait*. Oil on canvas. $50\frac{3}{8} \times 37\frac{13}{16}$ inches (128×96 cm.). Brera Gallery, Milan. Alinari/ Editorial Photocolor Archives

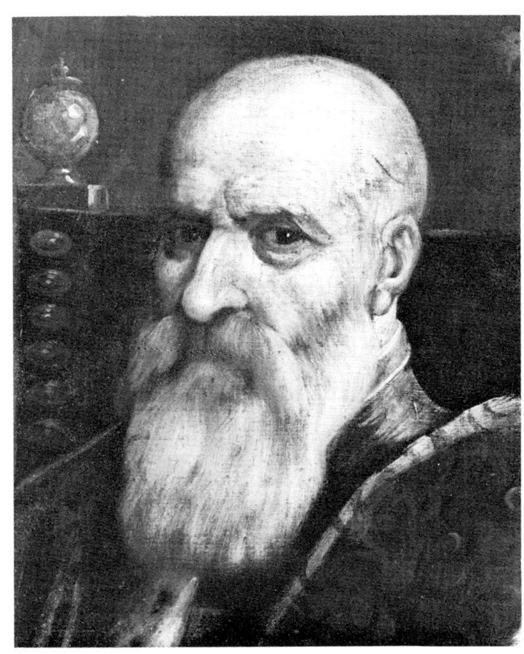

Fig. 10. Circle of Palma il Giovane, *Portrait of a Venetian Procurator,* detail of cat. no. 12

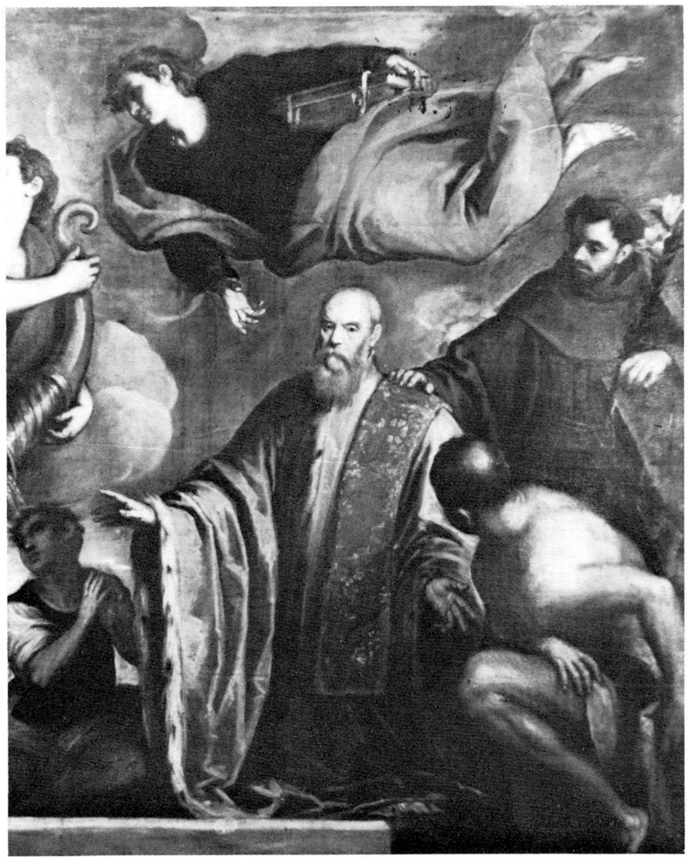

Fig. 11. Palma il Giovane, *Soranzo Votive,* detail of fig. 9 (Giovanni Soranzo). Oil on canvas. Museo Civico, Padua

decorative. In the Oratorio commission Palma most closely approximates the candid naturalism which appeared only shortly before in the work of the Carracci brothers, who were, in all probability, present in Venice in 1586 at the inception of the project. It is in this context that one should see the remarkable portrait of a *Sculptor* (City Museum and Art Gallery, Birmingham, England), a work once attributed to Annibale Carracci and one of Palma's most relaxed and vivacious portraits. It may, indeed, date to about 1586, shortly after the Oratorio dei Crociferi paintings were begun.[46]

The *Padre Giuliano Cirno* of ca. 1588–1590 (Brera Gallery, Milan) is related to this cycle, and as an independent portrait shows Palma's sharp but faintly sentimental observation of the old man's wrinkled countenance, which still evokes the optical intensity of Titian; but now, transposed into a naturalistic key, it stresses the physical topography of the face to the exclusion of an idealizing abstraction. The *Portrait of an Old Man,* with its similarities to the *Cirno* portrait, has been attributed to Jacopo Bassano, but is, when compared with the *Cirno,* clearly by Palma (see fig. 6).[47] Its stark black and white harmony is relieved by a feathery brushstroke which suggests that it could be dated about ten years later. Perhaps the most remarkable of Palma's portraits is his *Self-Portrait* (Brera Gallery, Milan), in which the painter is shown at work on a picture of the Resurrection (fig. 8). It has plausibly been dated to about 1590.[48] Stylistically very close, not only in its two portraits of the Soranzo brothers but also in the figure of the Redeemer (fig. 9), the *Soranzo Votive* (Museo Civico, Padua) may be dated to 1590 or perhaps to 1591.[49] After the turn of the century Palma gradually retreated to a threadlike texture, minute attention to detail, and an almost monochromatic gray tonality most evident in the dispirited *Sculptor* (Kunsthistorisches Museum, Vienna) or the even later *Self-Portrait* (Uffizi, Florence).

The Epstein *Procurator* (cat. no. 12 and fig. 10) is closely related to the portrait of Giovanni Soranzo (fig. 11) in the Padua votive in the general disposition of the figure; to the Brera *Self-Portrait* (see fig. 8) in the careful construction of the head and the description of the facial features; to the Oratorio dei Crociferi portrait figures (see figs. 5 and 7) in the handling of drapery; and to the numerous portraits of spectators in the cycle of murals in the sacristy of the Gesuiti church, Venice, datable to the late 1590's, in details such as hands. Its rather arid paint quality, thin impasto, and muted color do not suffer from the gloomy, monochromatic black and white tonality of Palma's latest portraits, nor is its illustrative naturalism subject to the niggling, stringy surface which after 1610 gives his portraits an enervated air. It is, therefore, in Palma portraits of the years between 1590 and 1600 that we find the closest stylistic analogies for the Baltimore picture.

The attribution of the Epstein *Procurator* to Palma Giovane himself is tempting, and it is certainly in this general ambience that the painting finds its most convincing associations. However, it must be recognized that our knowledge of Palma as a portraitist is still limited to relatively few examples and that stylistic contradictions exist among these pictures which leave many unanswered questions. I prefer, therefore, to venture only a suggestion that the *Procurator* is a work of the circle of Palma Giovane until further clarification of the complex problems surrounding his career in this genre is forthcoming.

W. R. Rearick
University of Maryland,
College Park

NOTES

1. Portrait patronage has yet to be given thorough study, in particular in respect to the political, social, and economic conditions which helped to determine distinctions from one geographical area to another.
2. See J. Alazard, *Essai sur l'évolution du portrait peint à Florence de Botticelli à Bronzino* (Paris: H. Laurens, 1924; *The Florentine Portrait,* trans. B. Whelpton, reprint ed. [New York: Schocken Books, 1968]), and J. Pope-Hennessy, *The Portrait in the Renaissance* (New York: Pantheon Books, for the Bollingen Foundation, 1966). Masaccio is known to have included portraits of his contemporaries in the *Sagra* fresco which he painted in the Carmine cloister to commemorate the consecration of the church in 1422. This tradition continued through Domenico Ghirlandaio's fresco cycle in the choir of Sta. Maria Novella of 1485–1490. None of the various fresco programs in the Palazzo Vecchio is known to have contained portraits until the patently propagandistic decorations presided over by Vasari in the years between 1556 and 1570 where the Medici and their minions appear in quantity. Although members of the Medici family were included in paintings of religious subjects and in rather veiled form in the frescoes of their own palace chapel, they were apparently reticent about family portraits until the establishment of the Grand Duchy. At that time Pontormo had to rely on a medallion for the features of *Cosimo il Vecchio* (Uffizi, Florence).
3. O. Demus, *The Church of San Marco in Venice: History, Architecture, Sculpture* (Washington, D.C.: Dumbarton Oaks Research Library and Collection, 1960), pp. 103–104.
4. M. Muraro, *Paolo da Venezia* (University Park and London: Pennsylvania State University Press, 1970), pp. 141–43, fig. 148.
5. Ibid., pp. 126–27, pl. 25. In both tomb effigies and in a secular context, as in the kneeling *Antonio Venier* (Doge 1382–1400), in the Museo Correr, Venice, portrait sculpture in Venice generally attempted a more explicit realism than comparable work in Florence during the Trecento.
6. M. Michiel, *Le notizie d'opere del disegno,* 1800 (quoted in E. Micheletti, *Gentile da Fabriano* [Milan: Rizzoli, 1976], pp. 83, 87, nn. 16 a, b) mentioned what might be the first independent panel portraits executed in Venice, images by Gentile of a fat man and a young priest (now lost) which were probably profiles, half-length with arms and hands, against a dark neutral background. Michiel reported that they were commissioned by Antonio Pasqualino, and we may date them to ca. 1409. Gentile also painted a donor in profile in the *Madonna with Saints Nicholas and Catherine* (Gemäldegalerie, Staatl. Museen, PKB, Berlin W.), a work of ca. 1408 which was also painted in Venice. His influence is dominant in the earliest Tuscan examples of the genre as well.
7. Of the Tuscan examples, only the Uccellesque pendants of *Matteo Olivieri* (National Gallery of Art, Mellon Collection) and of his brother *Michele Olivieri* (formerly John D. Rockefeller Collection) are clearly identified by inscriptions. Neither brother is known to have held a civil office which might have occasioned these portraits.
8. Gentile Bellini seems not to have made extensive use of the more progressive approach until after the turn of the century when he painted *Caterina Cornaro* half-length, possibly in response to a new expanded format employed by Giorgione, as in the so-called *Laura* (Kunsthistorisches Museum, Vienna) of 1506.
9. Mezzarota might have been portrayed in Mantua during the Church Council of 1459–1460. The portrait is significantly similar to Jan van Eyck's *Cardinal Albergati* (Kunsthistorisches Museum, Vienna), a work painted almost thirty years before but which might then have been accessible to Mantegna in the Cardinal's home city of Bologna.
10. Once attributed to Antonio Pollaiuolo but now given to Andrea del Castagno, this innovative work accords best with Pollaiuolo's early, Castagno-influenced paintings of ca. 1460–1465. Although the open-air setting suggests an awareness of a Flemish prototype, the absence of landscape underlines Pollaiuolo's independence of approach, as does the inclusion of one hand in the composition.
11. Inscribed on the reverse of the panel *"Joerg Fugger a di XX di Zugno MCCCCLXXIIII"* (1474). None of Giovanni Bellini's three-quarter-view, bust-length portraits may be securely dated earlier than 1474. Although it is tempting to see the Fugger portrait as responsive to the sitter's native South German tradition, there are no portraits from there of that approximate date which resemble it in significant details or concept.
12. Antonello's presence in Venice is probable in 1475 and certain in the spring of 1476. It is noteworthy, however, that his Flemish-inspired portraits were in several cases once in Venetian collections and bear the dates 1474, 1475 (on three examples) and perhaps 1478. The landscape in the *Young Man* (Gemäldegalerie Staatl. Museen, PKB, Berlin West), a picture which once bore the date 1478, was painted over a standard black background, possibly by a later Venetian Quattrocento artist.
13. Frequently dated to the first year of Loredano's dogeship, 1501, its style suggests that it might better be dated to 1507, the year of Gentile's death and the most logical moment for Giovanni to have assumed his role as official portraitist.

14. Despite damage which has left little if any of the original surface visible through repeated restorations, and although the picture has been inaccessible for study in recent decades, the signature and date are thought to be authentic. It might once have been in the Palazzo Ducale where fire damage in 1574 could have occasioned its early ruin and removal. Its composition remains unique in the context of Venetian portraits.

15. Leonardo was in Venice in the early spring of 1500 and may have had his drawing of *Isabella d'Este* (Louvre, Paris) in his baggage.

16. Only two portraits generally accepted as by Giorgione survive: the *Young Man* of ca. 1501 (Gemäldegalerie, Staatl. Museen, PKB, Berlin West) and the *Portrait of a Man,* the so-called "Terris" portrait (Fine Arts Gallery, San Diego), on which the inscribed date probably should be read as 1510. It seems clear that his patronage lay almost exclusively with the circle of Humanists and that he never received significant state portrait commissions, with the exception of an enigmatic document of 1508 in which he is mentioned as being at work on a large canvas for the Palazzo Ducale. The *Portrait of Francesco Maria della Rovere* (Kunsthistorisches Museum, Vienna) is by Sebastiano del Piombo and may be dated ca. 1509–1510.

17. Titian's impulse toward a more dynamic expansion of the Quattrocento portrait type is evident by about 1508 in the Goldman Portrait (National Gallery of Art, Kress Collection, listed by the Gallery as *Portrait of a Venetian Gentleman* and attributed to Giorgione and Titian). In this painting traditional elements such as the parapet, the window, etc., are given a large scale and enlivened by the aggressive pose and the inclusion of the hand in the composition.

18. It should be noted that most of the rather scarce portraits of civic officials which may be dated prior to about 1510 are of uncertain authorship and frequently of mediocre quality.

19. The familiar red robe with black chaperon and pileus is frequently seen in the canvases done by Gentile Bellini, Carpaccio, Mansueti, etc., for the Scuola di San Giovanni Evangelista. *Scuole* such as those of the Carità, Saint Ursula, and others contain similar group portraits of civic officials. For the Scuola di San Marco, Gentile, and after his death Giovanni Bellini, painted the *Preaching of Saint Mark* (Brera Gallery, Milan) in which an interesting variety of officials appears.

    The characteristic Cinquecento spectrum of crimson, violet, purple, and black damask robes are not found in these early examples, but a veritable encyclopedia of types and colors appears in Paris Bordone's *The Presentation of the Ring to the Doge* (Accademia, Venice), painted in 1534 for the Scuola di San Marco. This would seem to document a significant change of fashion among procurators, senators, etc., between about 1515 and 1520 when members of the Pesaro family appear in their votive (Santa Maria Gloriosa dei Frari, Venice) in rich cut-velvets. Early sources are explicit in describing the cycle of murals in the Sala del Maggior Consiglio of the Palazzo Ducale as filled with portraits of civic officials. The murals, which spanned more than two centuries, unhappily were destroyed in the fire of 1577.

20. Published as *Portrait of a Man with a Book,* or simply as *Portrait of a Man,* the red robe, black chaperon and pileus, belt and gloves are all characteristic of procurators in the years between about 1490 and 1515. Variously attributed to Girolamo Romanino, Paris Bordone, and Giovanni Cariani, the name of Titian was confirmed by A. Morassi, verbally, at the time of the Giorgione exhibition (as quoted by P. Zampetti, *Giorgione e i Giorgioneschi. Catalogo della mostra,* 2nd rev. ed. [Venice: Arte Veneta, 1955], no. 97, p. 212). The painting is listed in the catalogue under Cariani. F. Valcanover, *L'Opera completa di Tiziano* (Milan: Rizzoli, 1969), no. 15, p. 91, accepts it as a possible Titian, while H. Wethey, *The Paintings of Titian,* vol. 2: *The Portraits* (London: Phaidon Press, 1971), no. x47, p. 166, and F. R. Shapley, *Paintings from the Samuel H. Kress Collection: Italian Schools XV–XVI Century* (London: Phaidon Press, 1968), pp. 168–69, retain the attribution to Cariani.

21. Giacomo Dolfin, born about 1490, occupied many offices in Venice; perhaps the most prestigious—that of Podestà of Treviso in 1532—might have occasioned this portrait. Stylistically, it fits well with this date. W. E. Suida, *Tizian* (Zurich: Orell Fussli, 1933), pl. CXCV, published this picture when its overpainted state did not encourage its acceptance as by Titian. A recent successful cleaning confirms its authenticity and has revealed on a letter held by the sitter the inscription: *AL.CL^{mo} S. iacomo delfino.*

22. Identified, on rather fragile grounds, as Francesco Savorgnan della Torre who died in 1547.

23. It would seem that Titian was absolved of his obligation to paint the doge's official portrait after 1556, and no portraits of the four doges who held office during the remaining twenty years of the artist's life are known. Each of these doges was, in fact, portrayed by Tintoretto. Sebastian Veniero, Doge 1577–1578, was portrayed by Jacopo Bassano.

24. Only this, the last of Titian's surviving doge portraits, is cast in the older Humanist format with the window at left. The historical significance of the burning city seen on the horizon has not been satisfactorily explained.

25. The sitter cannot, for reasons of date, be the painter Jacopo Palma il Giovane, who was born in 1548, nor is there any basis for the idea that

Titian painted his father Antonio Palma, although he would have been about fifty in 1561, an age which accords with that of the sitter.

See also H. E. Wethey. *The Paintings of Titian.* 2:48.

26. A characteristic example of a doge portrait is Catena's *Andrea Gritti* (National Gallery, London) of ca. 1530, with its awkward expansion of the old profile format to include the body seen from the front and the addition of the hands. Catena also painted, at about the same time, a *Senator* (Metropolitan Museum of Art, New York), in which the type is simply that of Giovanni Bellini somewhat enlarged in size and setting. Perhaps Catena's private wealth and social position brought him such official commissions.

27. Very few of Palma Vecchio's subjects can be identified, but many seem to have been poets or men of letters and none wears robes of civic office.

28. Portrait figures appear as spectators in many of Bonifazio's paintings in which a genre element predominates, but the only quasi-portrait is that of a *Courtesan* (El Paso Museum of Art, Texas) which follows the example of his master Palma Vecchio and is, in any case, in the realm of the decorative fancy picture and not a true portrait.

29. Given the splendid quality of the numerous portraits of state and *scuola* officials in *The Presentation of the Ring to the Doge,* it is surprising that Paris Bordone seems not to have enjoyed official patronage. Titian's open hostility might have prevented such commissions. Paris Bordone seems to have worked for wealthy private patrons, both local and foreign.

30. The single possible exception, the *Portrait* (formerly Marquess of Sligo Collection, Westport, Ireland) dated 1519, is probably an autograph by Lotto, but since I have not seen the original I cannot even discuss the significance of the robe which might be either red, purple, or black. The format follows that of Titian's *Procurator* of ca. 1510–1511 (cf. n. 20). Pictures given to Lotto, such as the *Senator* (Marchwood Collection, Ashford, England), are clearly not his and seem more closely dependent on the example of Catena. Nor does the ruined *Procurator* (Washington University, Saint Louis) justify an attribution to Lotto. It must date from after his death, perhaps based on an earlier picture by him.

31. The sitter, Bernardo Morosini, Podestà of the Serenissima to his native village, is depicted in his robes of office, seated in an informal, neutral interior. See W. R. Rearick, "The Portraits of Jacopo Bassano," *Artibus et Historiae* 1 (1980):107.

32. Only at the very end of his life did Veronese receive a commission for a civic decoration that was intended to include portraits of senators, procurators, etc. There is one drawing (Albertina, Vienna, no. 24476) for the mural *Alexander III Receiving Pope Ziani at the Scuola della Carità* (Palazzo Ducale, Sala del Maggior Consiglio, Venice) in which civic officials are clearly indicated in their robes of office, but the master died in 1588 before beginning the painting, and it was his son Carletto who was delegated to draw and paint the individual portraits.

33. Neither of these attributions to Tintoretto nor their dates are a matter of absolute certainty.

34. This tabulation is generally based on the portraits included in P. Rossi, *Jacopo Tintoretto: I Ritratti* (Venice: Alfieri, n.d. [1974?]). A few portraits known to the author but not found in Rossi have also been taken into account.

35. A photograph in the Berenson Photographic Archive, Villa I Tatti, Florence, indicates a provenance from the Royal Collection in Stuttgart. (I am grateful to Paola Rossi for this information.) It has not been possible to confirm this provenance, but it is clear that by 1926 the presumably traditional attribution to Jacopo Tintoretto was already current.

36. Rossi, *Jacopo Tintoretto,* p. 137, pl. 276.

37. Inscriptions of the artist's name are usually autograph, those of dates somewhat less frequently so, and those of the sitters' names and ages sometimes in the artist's hand. Longer inscriptions with biographical information are generally the work of a hack.

38. W. N. Hargreaves-Mawdsley, *A History of Legal Dress in Europe Until the End of the Eighteenth Century* (Oxford: Clarendon Press, 1963), pp. 8–9, gives some information on the costume of Venetian procurators in the sixteenth century, but not in sufficient detail to identify the various subdivisions of the office or to clarify exactly the meaning of elements such as the position of the chaperon. Rossi, *Jacopo Tintoretto,* has defined certain sitters as holding particular offices, but she did not discuss the general question of costume in official portraits. It deserves a serious and comprehensive treatment.

39. Rossi, *Jacopo Tintoretto,* pp. 131–32, pl. 152. The subject has been variously identified as Francesco Duodo, which would indicate a dating between his election as *Procuratore de Ultra* in 1587 and his death in 1592, or as Giovanni Donato, based on an early copy or replica inscribed with his name and dated 1560. Rossi does not accept either proposal and dates the picture ca. 1572. Tintoretto's official portraits of ca. 1562, such as *Andrea Cappello* (Accademia, Venice), are generally rather formal and reserved in gesture. The Washington picture fits better with his more dramatized types such as the portrait of Michele Bon as donor in the *Saint Michael* (San Giuseppe di Castello, Venice) which must date shortly before 1584. I would, therefore, propose a date of ca. 1580–1583.

40. Domenico Tintoretto's oeuvre as a portraitist is not clearly defined. Although some portraits convincingly attributed to him on the basis of stylistic analogies with his established paintings of nonportrait character have been dated, we do not have a single signed portrait by Domenico, much less one securely dated and signed. Many of his portraits still pass as by Jacopo.

41. *Portrait of a Man* (El Paso Museum of Art, Texas) is a notable work which bears a fragmentary inscription of the name Tintoretto. Clearly not by either Jacopo or Domenico, it is a possible candidate for the work of Marco, although it more closely resembles the only secure painting by Sebastian Casser, *Saint George and the Dragon* (San Giorgio Maggiore, sacristy, Venice). Casser (Tintoretto's son-in-law) is supposed to have used Tintoretto as surname and sometimes also as his signature. Thus it is possible that the El Paso picture is by him. None of the pictures attributed to Marietta can be substantiated as hers; and the series of *Courtesans* (Prado, Madrid; Worcester Art Museum) are evidently by Domenico.

42. Leandro painted the *Grand Chancellor Andrea Frigerio* (Museo Civico, Padua) in 1581, about two years after Tintoretto had portrayed him (Palazzo Pitti, Florence).

43. Palma il Giovane's date of birth, believed to be 1544, recently was corrected to 1548 in accord with an inscription by the artist on the drawing of his *Self Portrait* of 1606 in the Pierpont Morgan Library, New York. See D. Rosand, "Palma il Giovane as Draughtsman: The Early Career and Related Observations," *Master Drawings* 8 (1970): 148–49. For other recent literature on Palma il Giovane, see D. Rosand's dissertation, "Palma Giovane and Venetian Mannerism" (Columbia University, 1965; University Microfilms International, 1967); also S. Mason Rinaldi, "Disegni preparatori per dipinti di Jacopo Palma il Giovane," *Arte Veneta* 26 (1972): 92–110; S. Mason Rinaldi, "Il libro dei disegni di Palma il Giovane del British Museum," *Arte Veneta* 27 (1973): 125–43; S. Mason Rinaldi, "Tre momenti documentati dell'attività di Palma il Giovane," *Arte Veneta* 29 (1975):197–204.

44. S. J. Freedberg, *Painting in Italy 1500–1600* (Harmondsworth and Baltimore: Penguin Books, 1971), pp. 384–85.

45. See S. Mason Rinaldi, "Jacopo Palma il Giovane all' Ospedaletto dei Crociferi: una nuova cronologia," *Arte Veneta* 31 (1977):240–50.

46. S. Mason Rinaldi, "Un ritratto di Palma il Giovane a Birmingham," *Per Maria Cionini Visani* (Turin: G. Canale & Cia, 1977), pp. 96–99. (The present writer recognized Palma's authorship of the Birmingham *Sculptor* in 1961).

47. E. Arslan, *I Bassani,* 2 vols. (Milan: Ceschina, 1960), 1:143–44, 171, pl. 12; and 2, fig. 194. Comparison with the portraits in the Oratorio dei Crociferi suggests a date of ca. 1590–1593.

48. Giovanni Mariacher et al., *La Pittura del Seicento a Venezia* (Venice, 1959), pp. 3–4.

49. Lucio Grossato, *Il Museo Civico di Padova* (Venice: Neri Pozza editore, 1957), no. 169, pp. 113–14.

SELECTED BIBLIOGRAPHY

Bernard Berenson. *Italian Pictures of the Renaissance.* Oxford: Clarendon Press, 1932.

The Jacob Epstein Collection in The Baltimore Museum of Art. Baltimore: Published by Jacob Epstein, 1939.

Bernard Berenson. *Italian Pictures of the Renaissance: Venetian School.* 2 vols. London: Phaidon Press, 1957.

John Pope-Hennessy. *The Portrait in the Renaissance.* New York: Pantheon Books, for the Bollingen Foundation, 1966.

Pierluigi de Vecchi. *L'Opera completa del Tintoretto.* Milan: Rizzoli, 1970.

Sydney J. Freedberg. *Painting in Italy 1500–1600.* Harmondsworth and Baltimore: Penguin Books, 1971.

Paola Rossi. *Jacopo Tintoretto: I Ritratti.* Venice: Alfieri, n.d. [1974?].

Terisio Pignatti. *The Golden Century of Venetian Painting.* Exhibition catalogue. Los Angeles: Los Angeles County Museum of Art, 1979.

Fern Rusk Shapley. *Catalogue of The Italian Paintings.* 2 vols. Washington, D.C.: National Gallery of Art, 1979.

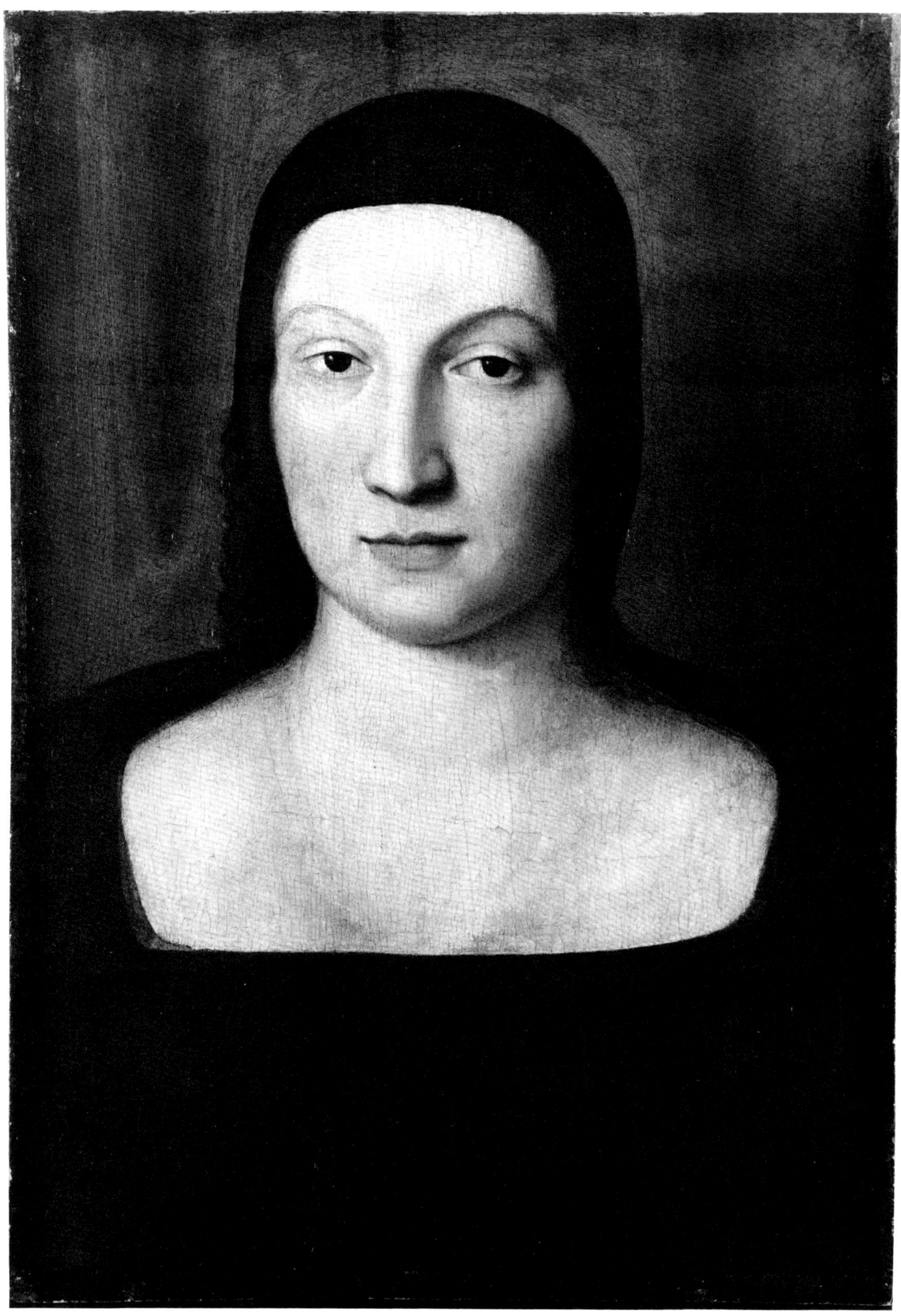

RAPHAEL (Raffaello Santi, 1483–1520)

13. *Portrait of Emilia Pia da Montefeltre,* 1502–ca. 1504

Oil and probably some tempera on wood. 16¾ × 11¼ inches (42.5 × 28.5 cm.)
The Jacob Epstein Collection (BMA 51.114)

PROVENANCE

Storerooms of Urbino ("guardarobba d'Urbino"), registered as no. 224(?)

The Archivio di State Urbino, cl. II, Div. A. F. III., mentions "a painting on wood with a portrait of a widow," according to G. Gronau, "I ritratti di Guidobaldo da Montefeltro . . . ," *Bollettino d'Arte,* ser. 2, 4, no. 2 (1924–1925):458.

Inventory of the Medici, Florence, 1654(?)

Fondaco dei Tedeschi, Venice

Before having been cradled, the panel had on its back the fragment of a seal on which the name of the building, the Fondaco dei Tedeschi ("ntico tedescho di V"), could be deciphered. This led to the assumption that the picture might have been kept there at some time in its history.

Vienna, early 1920's

In the early 1920's the portrait turned up on the Vienna art market.

Coray-Stoop Collection, Erlenbach (near Zurich), 1925

Acquired by Jacob Epstein, Baltimore, from the Kleinberger Galleries, New York in November 1925

Loaned by Jacob Epstein to The Baltimore Museum of Art in 1929 and bequeathed in 1951

CONDITION

The wood support of the *Portrait of Emilia Pia* shows splits in three places and signs of past insect activity. There is abrasion throughout. According to Georg Gronau and Ettore Camesasca (see bibliography), the painting was treated in Vienna in the early 1920's by a Professor Sikora, a restorer. In 1925 the reverse of the panel was shaved smooth by Marcel J. Rougeron (to prepare it for cradling). It is not known whether any further treatment was given to the painting at that time.

In 1954 the condition of the picture was investigated in the laboratory of The Walters Art Gallery where it was examined by X-radiography and infrared photography. This examination suggested that the neckline of the dress has been altered and that probably the shoulders were originally covered. The veil surrounding the face seems to be of a later date. A band across the forehead, visible only in the X-radiograph (fig. 1), cannot be explained, unless there was a lower veil across the forehead. There are paint losses: major ones on the shoulders and some minor losses on the left side of the face around the nose and lips. The dress, veil, and hair exhibit extensive repainting which may have been applied to obscure abrasion and earlier alterations.

Since its examination by The Walters Art Gallery, the condition of the painting has been closely watched. In 1964 the conservation department of The Baltimore Museum of Art conducted a thorough visual review which confirmed the findings of The Walters Art Gallery laboratory. At that time some minor inpainting along the edges was done and several small discolored retouchings on the face and neck were corrected. In 1975 the painting was seen by the Painting Conservation Studio, Inc., Newark, N.J. (Bernard Rabin). The results of this examination were similar to those of the laboratories of The Walters Art Gallery and the Baltimore Museum. Another thorough visual examination by the Baltimore Museum's conservation department in 1976 reiterated the earlier findings.

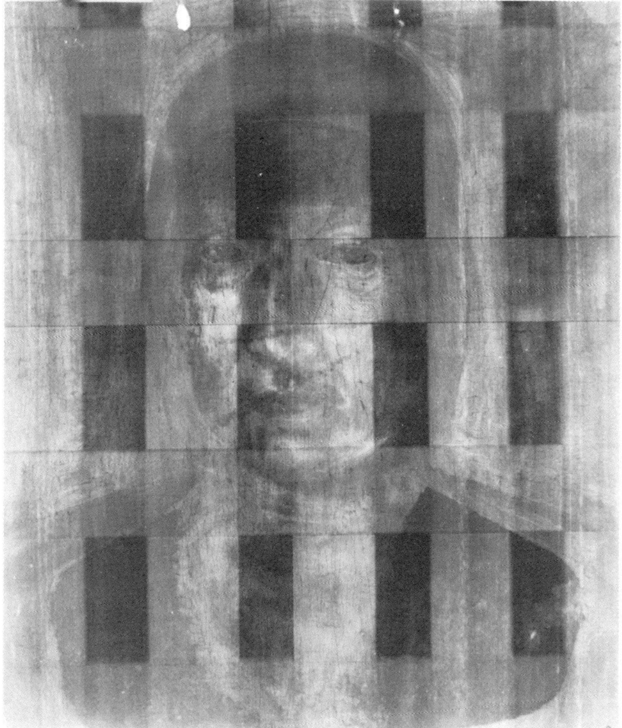

Fig. 1. Raphael, *Portrait of Emilia Pia da Montefeltre,* X-radiograph of cat. no. 13

The portrait has been examined by conservators here and abroad. Those abroad have seen the X-radiographs and infrared photographs. All agree with scholars of Italian Renaissance painting that the portrait dates from the sixteenth century.

Like many easel paintings ascribed to Raphael, the *Portrait of Emilia Pia* (cat. no. 13) has posed a problem of attribution. From the time the picture came to light in the early 1920's and was recognized as a work of the young Raphael by the well-known German scholar, Georg Gronau,[1] it has been a matter of controversy. Always acknowledged as an Italian sixteenth-century painting, it was and still is attributed to different artists by various scholars of the Italian Renaissance. On the other hand, the identification of the sitter has been generally accepted, since it is based on what might be considered documentary evidence: an inscription on the back of the painting in a late sixteenth- or early seventeenth-century script that read "Emilia Pia da Montefeltro." The inscription is no longer extant; it was obliterated when the panel was shaved down in order to accommodate a cradle. It has, however, been preserved in a photograph (fig. 2) which was kept by the late Jacob Epstein, former owner and donor of the painting.[2] In this photograph, just above the lettering, a fragment of a seal is visible which was also lost by the application of the cradle. According to Gronau, the seal's "coat-of-arms" shows the two-headed Imperial eagle, and the inscription can be completed as follows: "[Fo]*ntico tedescho di V*[enezia]."[3] While such a stamp is often helpful in tracing the history of an art object, this seal has not as yet furnished an explanation for the change of location of the *Portrait of Emilia Pia* from Florence to Venice and then to Vienna. Below the photograph of the back panel is the following statement of certification signed by the restorer Rougeron: "I certify herewith that this photograph reproduced the back of this panel before the cradling. In order to affix the cradling, I was, of course, obliged to eface [*sic*] the name 'Emilia Pia da Montefeltro' which was written on this panel. New York, Nov. 24, 1925." [4]

The identity of the sitter is further indicated by a bronze medallion executed by Adriano Fiorentino.[5] Though it shows Emilia in profile, it suggests her strong features as they can be observed in the painting. The inscription surrounding the relief of the bust portrait reads "AEMYLIA PIA FELTRIA." The back of the medallion shows a tall pyramid topped by an urn and inscribed: "CASTIS CINERIBUS" ("chaste until death").[6]

Emilia Pia (ca. 1470–1528), represented in her portrait (apparently the only painted one in existence) wearing a black dress and a widow's veil, was one of the most remarkable women of the Renaissance. The youngest daughter of Marco Pio, Seigneur of Carpi, a small town near Modena, she married in 1487 Antonio da Montefeltre, illegitimate son of Federico da Montefeltre[7] and half-brother of Guidobaldo da Montefeltre, Duke of Urbino. After her husband's early death in 1500, Emilia remained at the court of Urbino, sister-in-law and intimate friend of Duke Guidobaldo's wife, Elisabetta Gonzaga, a princess from Mantua.[8] Emilia has been described as the vitalizing spirit of the Urbino court, elegant and vivacious, with a quick, skeptical mind, never at a loss for a repartee or witty comment.[9] Pietro Bembo, cardinal, courtier, poet, and arbiter of Italian letters, feared for his biting tongue, had only admiring words for Emilia, calling her a magnanimous and prudent lady, as remarkable for her wisdom as for her warm affections. He as well as Baldassare Castiglione, the author of *The Courtier,* never ceased "to praise her in poetry and prose."[10] "Sister by reason of affection to Elisabetta who took her with her everywhere . . . Lady Emilia is certainly among the most amiable and most honored women of our Renaissance."[11] Considered "the chief ornament of Urbino when its court was the model of intellectual refinement,"[12] and often mentioned as the embodiment of the Renaissance personality, she died supposedly discussing a point in *The Courtier* rather than asking for the Holy Sacraments. *The Courtier,* one of the most celebrated and influential Italian books of its era, consisted of conversations between the Duchess Elisabetta and a group of her friends and dealt with matters of etiquette, social problems, and intellectual questions and achievements.[13] Emilia's great prestige and brilliant

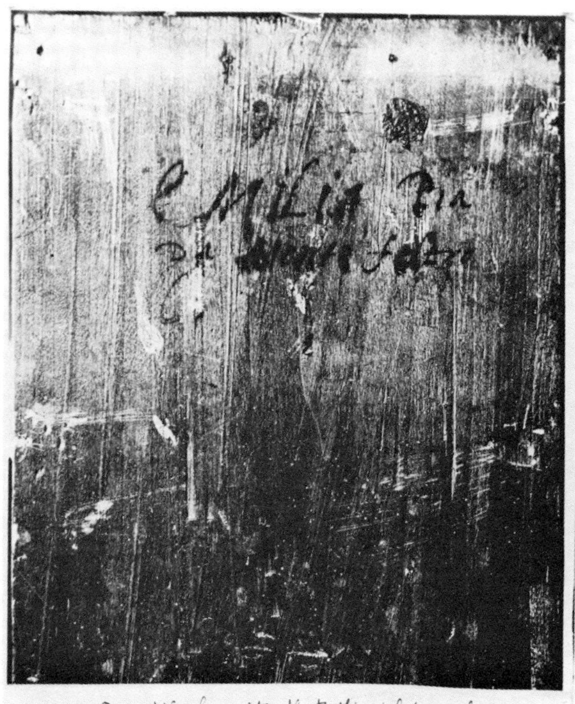

Fig. 2. Raphael, *Portrait of Emilia Pia da Montefeltre,* reverse of cat. no. 13, before cradling

reputation are still remembered largely because of her role as stimulating guide and skillful moderator in the discussions immortalized by Castiglione.

From the time of its rediscovery and attribution by Gronau, the *Portrait of Emilia Pia* has been connected with that of Elisabetta Gonzaga (fig. 3).[14] Frequently the *Portrait of Guidobaldo, Duke of Montefeltre*[15] has been thought to belong with these two female portraits, but because of its marked difference in size, support, and to some degree in technique, its inclusion in the group is more often rejected. On the other hand, most scholars involved in research on Raphael conclude that the portraits of Elisabetta and Emilia were painted by the same artist (whoever he may have been) and in the same period. This opinion is based on similarities in conception, style, and technique. As Gronau observes, the completely frontal arrangement of the figure in the picture space is almost identical in the two works. He regards the draftsmanship in both paintings as similar and finds a great resemblance in the expression of the sitters' eyes.[16]

The author of the most extensive recent investigation concerning the three Montefeltre pictures is Ursula B. Schmitt who has attributed the two female portraits to Francesco Bonsignori (1455–1519), an artist from Verona, active mainly at the court of Mantua. While completely refuting Gronau's ascription to the young Raphael, she equally strongly supports his opinion that both pictures are by the same hand and were painted at the same time.[17] Using practically the same reasoning as Gronau to establish both portraits

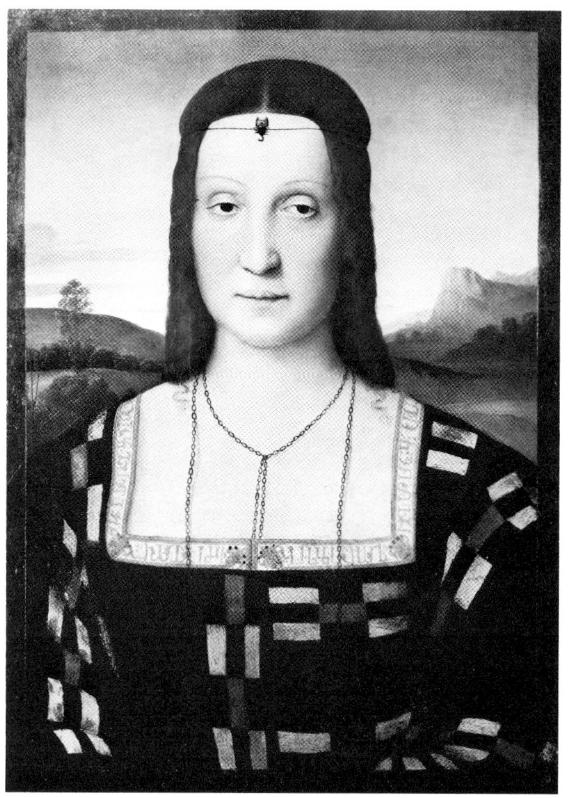

Fig. 3. Raphael, *Portrait of Elisabetta Gonzaga*. Oil on wood. 22⅞ × 14⅜ inches (58 × 36 cm.). Gallerie fiorentine, Florence

as the works of one artist, she emphasizes the resemblance of the facial features in the portraits of these women.[18] In her discussion of the portrait of Elisabetta (and thus of Emilia), Schmitt argues that it lacks the nobility which Raphael "through his own genius" would have bestowed upon it. She believes that the painter was a minor artist, such as Bonsignori, who could have reproduced merely the features of his sitters without having been capable of suggesting their elevated personality and distinguished character.[19] Though Schmitt mentions in very general terms that stylistic elements have been a factor in her attribution of the two female portraits to Bonsignori, she does not specify these elements. Her rejection of Raphael and attribution to Bonsignori thus rely mainly on her very subjective judgment of the paintings' lack of interpretive and artistic merits.[20] Her hypothesis, still not completely discarded by all Raphael specialists, yet rejected by most,[21] leads her to date the paintings to 1509, hardly a year after Duke Guidobaldo's death, when Elisabetta and Emilia visited Mantua where Bonsignori was at work for the court.

Gronau, to promote his attribution of the Montefeltre portraits to Raphael, emphasized such a negative factor as the absence of any documentary evidence. He rejected the then frequent ascription to Bonsignori or to any other artist active in Mantua at that time by pointing out that a commission of such importance, from another court, would certainly have been recorded in the comprehensive compilation of source material published later by A. Luzio and R. Renier in *Mantova e Urbino* (1893). However, it must be admitted that neither is such a commission mentioned in regard to Raphael. One could argue that in the first few years of the sixteenth century Raphael was still a very young and little-known artist whose commissions, perhaps, did not warrant being recorded. In this case, one might wonder why these two women would not have chosen an artist of greater repute. However, it was no secret that the friendship which the Urbino court had shown Raphael's father, Giovanni Santi,[22] had been transferred to his son, making it only natural that the father's patrons would sit for the young painter. A number of facts reveal the amicable relationship of the Ducal Court to Raphael: Giovanna della Rovere, Guidobaldo's sister and the mother of Francesco Maria della Rovere, the Duke's presumptive successor, in October 1504 recommended Raphael to Piero Soderini, the Gonfaloniere of Florence, in a letter full of personal warmth and affection for the young artist;[23] and four years later Raphael appealed to Prince Francesco Maria himself to help him obtain a commission from the Florentine Signoria.

Raphael's contemporary, the famous architect and theoretician Sebastiano Serlio (1475–1554), in his treatise on architecture described Duchess Elisabetta's role in the life of the young painter as follows: "Had the virtuous Duchess Isabella [*sic*] of Urbino not first raised and placed the divine Raphael so well when he was still young, had then Pontiff Julius II not rewarded him so generously as did also Leo, the Holy Father, protector of all the arts and of all artists of merit, indeed, he would not have been able to raise painting to such splendor or to leave such a large number of masterpieces in painting and architecture. . . ."[24] In view of Elisabetta's patronage of Raphael it can be surmised that the portrayal of his benefactors was a matter of course. Indeed, contemporary sources record portraits of Elisabetta and Guidobaldo by Raphael; in a letter of April 19, 1516, Bembo mentions a portrait by Raphael of the late Duke,[25] and Antonio Beffa Negrini, an eighteenth-century writer, in his *Eulogy of Castiglione* makes reference to a portrait of the Duchess by the hand of Raphael, said to have been owned by Castiglione.[26] Though this latter vague reference does not permit identification of the portrait mentioned by Negrini as the Uffizi likeness of the Duchess,[27] it establishes at least that a special relationship, namely that of artist and sitter, existed between Raphael and Elisabetta.

Elimination of artists such as Bonsignori, Caroto, Costa, Francia, Viti, and others as potential painters of the portraits of Elisabetta, Guidobaldo, and also Emilia is not a valid basis on which to attribute these paintings to Raphael. Moreover, the often raised question of whether these pictures reveal the nobility and dignity inherent in Raphael's works is meaningless since the response depends primarily on the observer's personal interpretations and idiosyncracies.

There is another point which is often made by those who reject Raphael's authorship of the female portraits. They emphasize that these works stand outside Raphael's oeuvre, with which, in the judgment of some writers, they have nothing in common.[28] Yet should not these two youthful paintings be regarded as important steps in the master's development? There is no doubt that they date from the first decade of the sixteenth century. From the activities of the Ducal couple, and thus those of Emilia Pia, only three periods emerge during which they could have sat for the portraits: shortly before 1502 (when Elisabetta, accompanied by Emilia, went to Ferrara for the wedding of Duke Alphonso I to Lucrezia Borgia); in 1504; or in the spring and early summer of 1506.[29] Of these dates, the earliest seems to this writer the most probable for the execution of Elisabetta's and Emilia's portraits, although the year 1504 should not be excluded. A date later than 1506 is unlikely for stylistic reasons.

Most writers on Raphael have mentioned that the works of Piero della Francesca, in whose ambience Raphael had grown up, must have had a profound impact on him. Moreover, the Master from Sansepolcro was no stranger to the Santi family; it is reported that in 1469 Piero, while in Urbino, even stayed in Giovanni Santi's house.[30] It is likely that Piero's concept of frontality, a significant element in his compositions, inspired the young Raphael to make use of it in several of his early works,[31] among them perhaps the portraits of Elisabetta and Emilia.

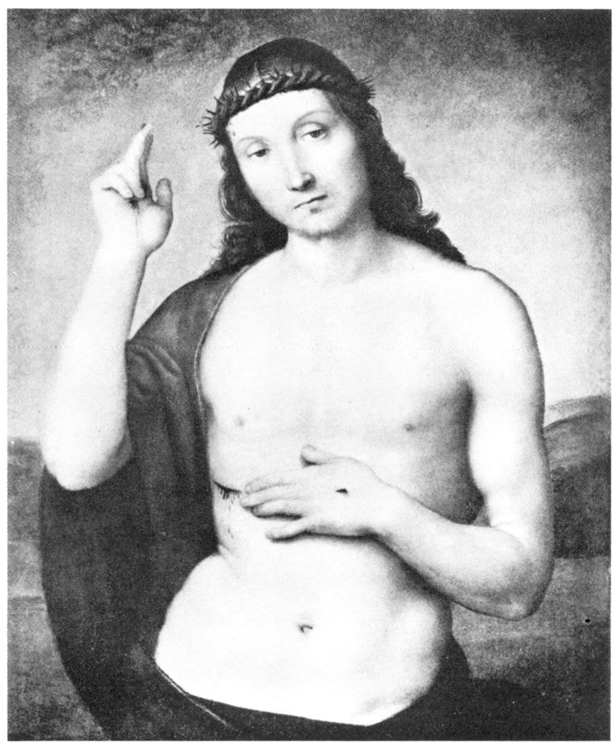

Fig. 4. Raphael, *Christ Blessing*. Oil on wood. 11¹³/₁₆ × 9¹³/₁₆ inches (30 × 25 cm.). Pinacoteca Tosio-Martinengo, Brescia. Alinari/Editorial Photocolor Archives

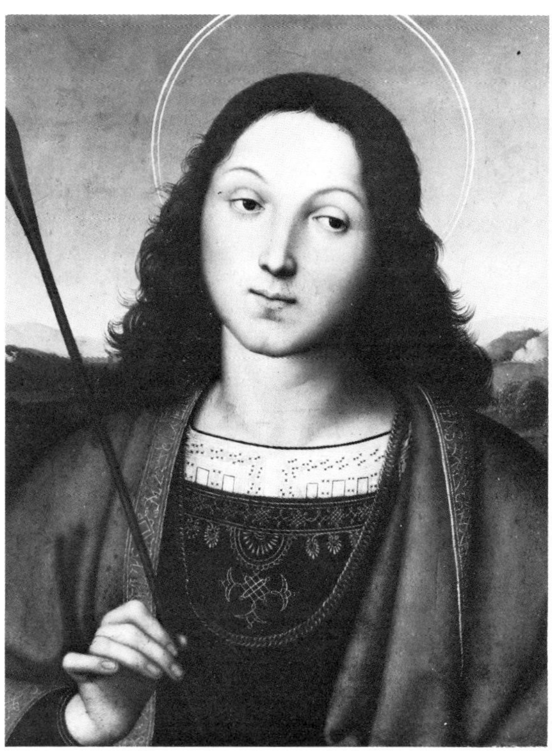

Fig. 5. Raphael, *St. Sebastian*. Oil on wood. 16¹⁵/₁₆ × 13⅜ inches (43 × 34 cm.). Accademia Carrara, Bergamo. Alinari/Editorial Photocolor Archives

A careful stylistic examination of the *Portrait of Emilia Pia* may disclose additional similarities with accepted works from Raphael's youth (figs. 4 and 5). Such an analysis has to be limited to the face, since the exact extent of restoration on the neck, veil, and dress in the Emilia painting remains a matter of conjecture (see condition report). Emilia radiates the serene calm and quietness which can be seen in *Christ Blessing* (Pinacoteca, Brescia) and in *St. Sebastian* (Accademia Carrara, Bergamo), both of about the same date as the Baltimore picture.[32] The wide oval of Emilia's face, beneath which the strong bone structure is suggested, with the slightly accentuated chin, appears again in the two religious panels mentioned above. Common to them as well as to *Emilia* are the delicate, carefully applied brushwork, the homogeneous texture of the skin, the even lighting, and the precise contours that are characteristic of Raphael's style during this period. Even single features show a resemblance: for example, compare Emilia Pia's nose, which seems so individual with its rather wide nostrils, with that of St. Sebastian and even with the nose of Christ in the Brescia painting, though here the similarity is less evident. By far the strongest resemblance exists in the rendering of the eyes, noticed by this writer many years ago when standing in the Uffizi in front of *Elisabetta Gonzaga* with a detail photograph of the Emilia portrait in hand. Since then, a repetition of this comparison has always convinced this writer that the treatment of the eyes in the two portraits is almost identical (figs. 6 and 7). This observation can be extended to other Raphael paintings of this period such as the *Portrait of a Young Man with an Apple* (Uffizi, Florence), *Christ Blessing* (see fig. 4), and *St. Sebastian* (see fig. 5), the latter two paintings mentioned before as sharing other similarities with the portraits of Elisabetta and Emilia. In all these works the eyes are set in the face in the same manner, the upper lids are similarly shaped,

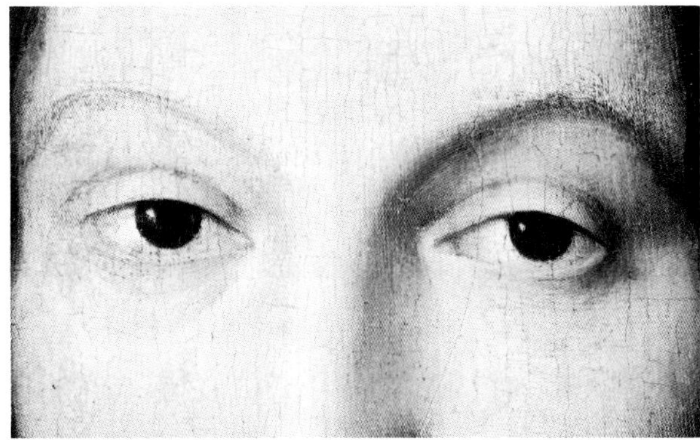

Fig. 6. Raphael, *Portrait of Emilia Pia da Montefeltre,* detail of cat. no. 13

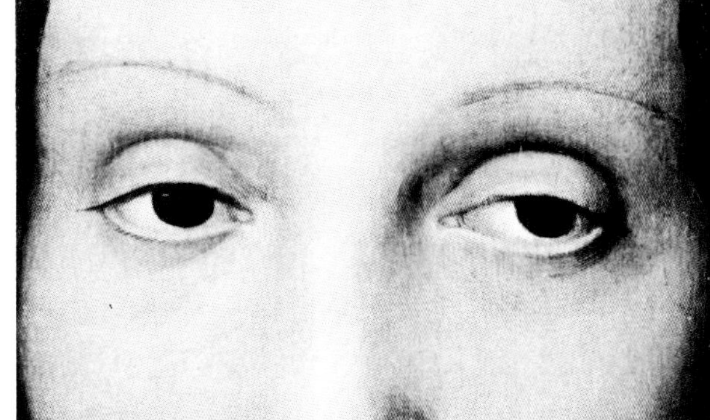

Fig. 7. Raphael, *Portrait of Elisabetta Gonzaga,* detail of fig. 3

and the irises are placed in the eyeball in much the same way, a treatment that endows the various faces with "the marvellous, distant gaze."[33]

As must be obvious from the preceding comments, this writer accepts the attribution of the *Portrait of Emilia Pia* to Raphael, being aware of the damages inflicted on the picture which account for some of its shortcomings. It is extremely fortunate that the face of Emilia Pia has suffered relatively little and remains in good condition.

However, opposing the attribution to Raphael are a number of experts on Italian Renaissance painting. Luitpold Dussler, following Ursula B. Schmitt in her article on Bonsignori, rejects Raphael as the painter of the Emilia panel; Anna Maria Brizio concurs, stating: ". . . the attribution to Raphael . . . of *Emilia Pia di Montefeltre* . . . cannot be sustained. . . ."[34]

Jan Lauts accepts the identification of the sitter as Emilia Pia but doubts that Raphael painted the portrait.[35] In a letter of October 1975, on file at the Baltimore Museum, he outlined these doubts. Oskar Fischel, in his entry on "Raphael" in Thieme-Becker, reveals an ambiguous attitude. He states that the attribution to Raphael would be acceptable if supported by some documentary evidence. In his later monographs on Raphael the painting is not mentioned.[36]

Three scholars express their disbelief in the ascription of *Emilia Pia* to Raphael in letters kept in the curatorial files of The Baltimore Museum of Art:

The late Fernanda Wittgens, after having studied the painting at the Baltimore Museum, and later from photographs, wrote (Milan, March 24, 1954) that she and her colleagues were convinced that it is "a very important work by Lorenzo Costa," Raphael's contemporary who for a time worked at Isabella d'Este's court.

John Shearman, not having seen the painting since 1961, had to make his judgment from photographs. He is certain, for a number of reasons, that it is not by Raphael, while he accepts the *Portrait of Elisabetta Gonzaga* as an autograph work by the master. He does "not doubt that *Emilia Pia* is an Umbro-Marchigian painting of the period" and suggests as attribution: "Imitator of Raphael c. 1510" (letter from London, December 31, 1975).

After a long acquaintance with the picture and a careful study of recent photographs and X-radiographs, Creighton Gilbert suggests that the picture probably was executed by Timoteo Viti (1467–1523) who resided in Urbino and at one time was thought to have been Raphael's early teacher, an opinion refuted by recent scholarship. Because of certain similarities of Viti's style with the work of the young Raphael, several specialists over the years have ascribed the Baltimore portrait to him, an attribution, however, that has not been convincing (correspondence with Creighton Gilbert, November 5, 1975–February 7, 1976).

On the other hand, the affirmative opinion that the Baltimore portrait should be included in the oeuvre of the young Raphael has been voiced by a number of scholars well known in the field of Renaissance art.[37] Gronau, of course, whose article in the *Bollettino d'Arte* of 1924–1925 has been frequently quoted here, did important preliminary work on the Montefeltre portraits. On October 16, 1925, Bernard Berenson recommended the acquisition by cabling Jacob Epstein that "the portrait is one of Raphael's highest achievements." In a letter to Epstein of November 22, 1925, after the painting's purchase, Berenson again endorsed the painting stating that it has all the characteristics of Raphael's early works.[38] Accordingly, Berenson lists the *Portrait of Emilia Pia* as by Raphael in his index, *Italian Pictures of the Renaissance*.[39]

W. E. Suida takes Raphael's authorship for granted and dates the Emilia portrait to 1504; Roberto Longhi similarly accepts the attribution, as do Carlo Volpe and Ettore Camesasca.[40]

More recently, several experts, either orally or by letter, have voiced their acceptance of *Emilia Pia* as a portrait by Raphael, but have at the same time expressed concern about the condition of the picture. Visiting Baltimore on November 25, 1968, Mina Gregori, Florence, commented that she had no doubt that the original part of the portrait is by Raphael.

Konrad Oberhuber, in a letter dated September 19, 1975, states: ". . . I have always been interested in the *Portrait of Emilia Pia* and have always upheld the opinion that it and *Elisabetta Gonzaga* are by the young Raphael . . ." Oberhuber explains that he has had no opportunity to examine the Uffizi portraits very thoroughly and therefore wants his remarks concerning them "more as a kind of suggestion than an absolutely reliable statement." Upon having received photographs of the X-radiographs and condition report of *Emilia Pia,* Oberhuber on November 6, 1975, wrote again: "The X-ray confirms my original notion that the portrait could really be a work by Raphael, as it seems to have all the sharp and clear outlines and the traces of painting stroke typical for his work." The letter continues: "The Baltimore portrait and the two connected portraits in the Uffizi, the *Elisabetta Gonzaga* and the *Guidobaldo di Montefeltre* are in my eyes the earliest portraits by Raphael known to us, probably dating from around 1502. . . ."

Sydney J. Freedberg commented in a letter: "I spent some time pondering the problem portrait. Very reluctantly, I am inclined to admit the attribution to Raphael should be correct. I do so with reservations and some misgiving. No coincidence with undoubted early Raphaels is quite exact, and the kinds of damage and alteration that have been suffered by the picture are a grave impediment to judgment. It is not a valid argument in support of the attribution to Raphael that I can find no painter to whom the painting could be more convincingly assigned" (Cambridge, Mass., February 10, 1976).

In Baltimore, November 1974, Federico Zeri, who had studied the *Portrait of Emilia Pia* repeatedly, stated that he considered the painting, though damaged, still a major work by Raphael. In a letter from Rome of December 22, 1975, he wrote that "the sensational beauty of this early masterpiece still glitters, in spite of the unsatisfactory condition. A most extraordinary work showing the remote influence of Piero della Francesca."

SUMMARY

The opinions of outstanding experts on the Emilia portrait have been brought together here; they range from acceptance to doubt to rejection of Raphael's authorship. While a casual viewing of the panel may result in a less favorable response, a thorough study of the face frequently has convinced the onlooker of the painting's Raphaelesque properties and high artistic quality.

The time of execution, which without doubt was within the first decade of the sixteenth century, the likelihood that the picture went from Urbino to Florence as part of the artistic patrimony of the Della Rovere, the Urbino court's warm relationship with and proven concern for Giovanni Santi's son, and a number of obvious stylistic features all speak for Raphael's authorship of the portrait. Accordingly, and despite missing documentary evidence, this writer is convinced that Raphael was the painter of *Emilia Pia*.

Gertrude Rosenthal
The Baltimore Museum of Art

NOTES

1. G. Gronau, "I ritratti di Guidobaldo da Montefeltro e di Elisabetta Gonzaga in Firenze," *Bollettino d'Arte,* ser. 2, 4, no. 2 (1924–1925):443–60. In source material as well as in later references, "da" Montefeltre is used, as are "di" and "de" Montefeltre; also Montefeltro.
2. Ibid., p. 459. The photograph is now in the Jacob Epstein Archives, The Baltimore Museum of Art.
3. Ibid., p. 458. *Fontico* (*Fondachi* in Venetian dialect) was the name of the business and storage buildings of foreign nations engaged in trade with the Republic of Venice.
4. I am indebted to Sheldon Keck for deciphering Mr. Rougeron's signature and informing me that he was "a Belgian restorer of paintings, active in the New York area in the 1920's and 30's." Gronau, "I ritratti di Guidobaldo da Montefeltro," p. 458, names a Professor Sikora as having restored the portrait in Vienna and mentions various minor details of the treatment.
5. C. von Fabriczy, *Jahrbuch der preussischen Kunstsammlungen* 24 (1904):71–98, and also F. Knapp, "Adriano Fiorentino," in Thieme-Becker, *Allgemeines Lexikon der Bildenden Künstler* (Leipzig: E. A. Seemann, 1907), 1:91–92. Adriano Fiorentino was a well-known sculptor and medalist. He was born in the 1440's and died in 1499. In 1495 he stayed in Urbino and was recommended by the Duchess Elisabetta to her brother Gianfrancesco, Marchese of Mantua.
6. G. F. Hill, *A Corpus of Italian Medals of the Renaissance before Cellini* (London: British Museum, 1930), 1:no. 345, p. 86; 2:no. 345, pl. 56. The medallion representing Elisabetta Gonzaga (vol. 2, no. 344, pl. 56) is treated very similarly to that of Emilia and shows a close resemblance to Emilia's features. The medallion of Emilia Pia is also reproduced in J. Dennistoun, *Memoirs of the Dukes of Urbino Illustrating the Arms, Art and Literature of Italy from 1440 to 1630* (London: Longman, Brown, Green and Longmans, 1851), 2:69, 263.
7. Duke Federico early legitimized Antonio, who accompanied his father on several of his campaigns.
8. Dennistoun, *Memoirs of the Dukes of Urbino,* 1:278: "The Duchess Elisabetta, whose friend and companion she [Emilia] had been alike during the bright days of wedlock and the blight of widowhood, bequeathed to her in 1527 the life-rent of Poggio d'Inverno and appointed her an executrix of her will."
9. J. Lauts, *Isabella d'Este, Fürstin der Renaissance, 1474–1539* (Hamburg: M. von Schröder, 1952), p. 132.
10. A. Luzio and R. Renier, *Mantova e Urbino* (Turin and Rome: L. Roux et cie., 1893), p. 88, n. 1.
11. Ibid.
12. Dennistoun, *Memoirs of the Dukes of Urbino,* 1:278.
13. B. Castiglione, *The Book of the Courtier,* intro. and trans. G. Bull (Baltimore: Penguin Books, 1967).
14. *Portrait of Elisabetta Gonzaga,* oil on wood, 22⅞ × 14⅜ inches (58 × 36 cm.), Uffizi, Florence. The verso of the panel is inscribed: "Duchessa Isabetta [*sic*] Mantovana moglie del Duca Guido." In May 1976 the painting was removed for restoration. At that time Dr. Emma Micheletti, Curator of Painting, Uffizi, expressed the opinion that the portrait of Elisabetta Gonzaga is by Raphael.
15. *Portrait of Guidobaldo, Duke of Montefeltre,* oil on canvas, 27⅜ × 20½ inches (69 × 52 cm.), Uffizi, Florence. Attributed to Raphael. For repro., see

Gronau, "I ritratti di Guidobaldo da Montefeltro," fig. p. 445; M. Salmi et al., *The Complete Work of Raphael* (New York: F. Reynal, 1969), p. 38, fig. 33; L. Berti, *The Uffizi* (Florence: Becocci, 1971), p. 79, fig. 8. A casual study of this painting suggested to this writer that the very controversial attribution of Gronau and several other scholars to Raphael might be correct (see in addition to the general conception, facial details, especially the eyes). The condition of the surface might suggest a transfer from wood to canvas, undertaken perhaps as early as the seventeenth or eighteenth century.

16. Gronau, "I ritratti di Guidobaldo da Montefeltro," p. 456.
17. U. B. Schmitt, "Francesco Bonsignori," *Münchner Jahrbuch der Bildenden Kunst*, ser. 3, 12 (1961): 101–2. The *Portrait of Emilia Pia* (fig. 27, p. 99) is discussed on pp. 101–2 and as no. 1, p. 113. See also *Portrait of Elisabetta Gonzaga* (fig. 26, p. 98), p. 101 and no. 4, p. 116.
18. Ibid., pp. 100–101; no. 1, p. 113; no. 4, p. 116; figs. 26 and 27.
19. Ibid., pp. 102 and 116–17.
20. Ibid., pp. 116–17.
21. L. Dussler, *Raphael, A Critical Catalogue of his Pictures, Wall-Paintings and Tapestries,* trans. S. Cruft (London and New York: Phaidon Press, 1971), pp. 56 and 59, is one of the few scholars who still finds Schmitt's attribution convincing. Among the scholars who have recently rejected this attribution either by letter (curatorial files of the Baltimore Museum) or orally are the following: Creighton Gilbert, letter of December 13, 1975; John Shearman, Courtauld Institute, University of London, letter of December 18, 1975; Konrad Oberhuber, Fogg Art Museum, Harvard University, orally, Fall 1972; W. R. Rearick, University of Maryland, orally, Fall 1975; Federico Zeri, orally, October 1975.
22. In a letter of October 13, 1494, shortly after Giovanni Santi's death, Elisabetta wrote to her brother, the Marchese of Mantua, that Giovanni Santi because of ill health had not been able to finish his portrait or do the one of her she had commissioned. She added that she intended to have her portrait painted by another skillful artist. E. Müntz, *Raphael, His Life, Works and Times* (rev. ed.; London: Chapman & Hall, 1888), pp. 10 and 11, quoting the original letter after G. Campori, *Notizie e documenti per la vita di Giovanni Santi e di Rafaello Santi da Urbino* (Modena, 1870), p. 4. One may speculate whether eight or ten years later the Duchess asked Giovanni Santi's son to paint her portrait.
23. Giovanna's letter to the Gonfaloniere is quoted by J. D. Passavant, *Raphael of Urbino and His Father Giovanni Santi* (London and New York: Macmillan, 1872), pp. 49–50. Müntz, *Raphael,* p. 95, also discusses this recommendation.
24. "Et se la uirtuosa Duchessa Isabella [*sic*] d'Urbino non hauesse prima alzato, et messo su il diuin Raphaello ne la sua giouentù, et poi Julio, pur secondo Pontefice, che gli fu gran remuneratore, et ultimamente Leone padre, et protettore di tutte le belle arti, et di tutti i buoni operatori, certo ch'ei non harebbe potuto alzare la pittura a quel splendore ou'egli la condusse; nè hauria lasciate tante opere così mirabil di Pittura, et d'Architettura come si vedeno. . . . " Sebastiano Serlio, *Regoli generali de architettura,* Libro Quarto di architettura (Venice, 1540), p. IIa, quoted from V. Golzio, *Raffaello, nei documenti, nelle testimonianze dei contemporanei e nella letteratura del suo secolo.* Pontificia Insigne Accademia Artistica del Virtuosi al Pantheon (Vatican City: Panetto & Petrelli, 1936), p. 284.
25. Golzio, *Raffaello,* p. 44.
26. A. B. Negrini, *Elogj de'Castiglione* (Padua, 1733), p. 329; see Passavant, *Raphael of Urbino,* pp. 67, 68.
27. Dussler, *Raphael, A Critical Catalogue,* p. 59, rejects the possibility that the painting mentioned by Negrini could be the Uffizi portrait, but he states "there is no doubt that Raphael made a portrait of the Duchess."
28. Ibid., pp. 56 and 59.
29. See Dennistoun, *Memoirs of the Dukes of Urbino,* and Luzio and Renier, *Mantova e Urbino,* for the whereabouts of Elisabetta from 1502 to 1508. It is known that while working in Perugia (1500–1504) Raphael maintained his close ties to Urbino. W. E. Suida, *Raphael* (London: Phaidon Press, 1948), p. 6, records that Raphael spent the greater part of 1504 in Urbino.
30. Stefan Bottari, "Piero della Francesca," in *Encyclopedia of World Art* (New York, Toronto, London: McGraw-Hill, 1966), 11:344.
31. Very slightly deviating from complete frontality are the following early paintings: *St. Sebastian,* 1501–1502, Accademia Carrara, Bergamo (O. Fischel, *Raphael,* 2: fig. 11); *Christ Blessing,* ca. 1502, Pinacoteca, Brescia (ibid., 2:fig. 19); *Portrait of a Young Man with an Apple* (formerly called *Francesco Maria della Rovere*), 1500 or 1504, Uffizi, Florence (Suida, *Raphael,* fig. 19).
32. See n. 31.
33. The phrase used by Fischel, *Raphael,* 1:21, to describe the facial expression of *Horatius Cocles,* a painting which he attributes to Raphael within Perugino's decorations in the Cambio, Perugia. In date it is related to the works by Raphael mentioned in n. 31.
34. Dussler, *Raphael, A Critical Catalogue,* p. 56; A. M. Brizio, "Raphael," in *Encyclopedia of World Art* (New York, Toronto, London: McGraw-Hill, 1966), 11:845.
35. J. Lauts, *Isabella d'Este,* fig. 35.
36. O. Fischel, "Raphael Santi," in Thieme-Becker,

Allgemeines Lexikon der Bildenden Künstler (Leipzig: E. A. Seemann, 1935), 29:435; *Raphael*, trans. B. Rackham (London: K. Paul, 1948); *Raphael* (Berlin: Gebr. Mann, 1962).

37. E. Durand-Gréville, "Trois Portraits méconnus de la jeunesse de Raphael," *Revue de l'art ancien et moderne* 17 (1905):377–86, was the first to attribute to Raphael the Montefeltre portraits, then in the galleries of the Pitti Palace, Florence.

38. The full text of Berenson's letter to Jacob Epstein reads as follows:

I Tatti, Settignano, Florence
November 22nd. 1925.

Dear Sir,

I am happy to learn from Mr. Kleinberger that you have purchased Raphael's portrait of Emilia Pia da Montefeltro.

Mr. Kleinberger further tells me that you have been flattering enough to wish to know my opinion of this painting.

In the first place, I desire to assure you that the attribution of this picture to Raphael himself is, for me, a matter beyond dispute. It has all the characteristics and marks of his early works, such as the two portraits in the Pitti of the Duke and Duchess of Urbino—relatives of the sitter of your panel—and of other young works, as, for instance, the famous Gran' Duca Madonna also in the Pitti, all painted on his first return to the Court of Urbino as a young but already recognized great Master, about 1504.

As a work of art, apart from any question of authorship, this portrait is as simple, as direct and as convincing as any masterpiece by Antonello da Messina or Piero della Francesca, two of the very greatest names in Renaissance Art. The design offers an admirable instance of simplification, without smoothing away or flattering the objective appearance of the person represented.

I am sure you will take great pleasure in reading about the subject of this picture, namely Emilia Pia, in Baldassare Castiglione's book on the Court of Urbino ("Il Cortegiano"), which happily exists in two English translations. The one, an Elizabethan translation, has been republished in the Tudor Classics, and the other, which may be more to your purpose, is a beautiful illustrated edition—"The Book of The Courtier, by Count Baldesar Castiglione" translated by Opdyke, and published in 1901 by Scribner's of New York.

With congratulations upon owning a masterpiece by Raphael, and the portrait of a fascinating Renaissance Court Lady.

I am,

Yours truly,
(Signed) Bernhard Berenson

To Mr. Jacop [sic] Epstein,
Baltimore.

39. B. Berenson, *Italian Pictures of the Renaissance* (Oxford: Clarendon Press, 1932), p. 479.

40. Suida, *Raphael*, p. 6; R. Longhi, "Percorso di Raffaello giovine," *Paragone* 6, no. 65 (May 1955): 22; C. Volpe, "Due questioni Raffaellesche," *Paragone* 7, no. 75 (March 1956):17, n. 12; E. Camesasca, *All the Paintings of Raphael*, trans. L. Grosso (New York: Hawthorne Books, 1963), 1: 44–45. Camesasca also comments on the provenance of the picture.

SELECTED BIBLIOGRAPHY

Baldassare Castiglione. *Libro del Cortegiano*. Venice: Aldus Manutius, 1528 (first English translation, 1561). Edition consulted: *The Book of the Courtier*. Introduced and translated by George Bull. Baltimore: Penguin Books, 1967.

Antonio Beffa Negrini. *Elogj de'Castiglione*. Padua, 1733.

James Dennistoun. *Memoirs of the Dukes of Urbino, Illustrating the Arms, Arts and Literature of Italy from 1440 to 1630*. 3 vols. London: Longman, Brown, Green and Longmans, 1851.

Giuseppe Campori. *Notizie e documenti per la vita di Giovanni Santi e di Rafaello Santi da Urbino*. Modena, 1870.

Johann David Passavant. *Raphael of Urbino and His Father Giovanni Santi*. London and New York: Macmillan, 1872.

Eugène Müntz. *Raphael, His Life, Works and Times*. Revised by Walter Armstrong. London: Chapman & Hall, Ltd., 1888.

Alessandro Luzio and Rodolfo Renier. *Mantova e Urbino*. Turin and Rome: L. Roux et cie., 1893.

E. Durand-Gréville. "Trois Portraits méconnus de la jeunesse de Raphael." *Revue de l'art ancien et moderne* 17 (1905):377–86.

Oskar Fischel. "Raphael Santi." In Thieme-Becker, *Allgemeines Lexikon der Bildenden Künstler*. 37 vols. Leipzig: E. A. Seemann, 1907–1950.

Joseph Archer Crowe and Giovanni Battista Cavalcaselle. *A History of Painting in North Italy, Venice, Padua, Vicenza, Verona, Ferrara, Milan, Friuli, Brescia, from the Fourteenth to the Sixteenth Century*. Edited by T. Borenius. 2nd edition. New York: C. Scribner's Sons, 1912.

Georg Gronau. "I ritratti di Guidobaldo da Montefeltro e di Elisabetta Gonzaga in Firenze." *Bollettino d'Arte*, ser. 2, 4, no. 2 (1924–1925):443–60.

Francesco Filippini. "Raffaello a Bologna." *Cronache d'Arte* 2 (1925):201–34.

Ella S. Siple. "Recent Acquisitions by American Collectors." *Burlington Magazine* 51 (December 1927): 297–309.

J. Scott Taylor. "A New Portrait of Elisabetta Gonzaga?" *Burlington Magazine* 52 (March 1928):143–44. (The portrait of Emilia Pia is confused with that of Elisabetta Gonzaga.)

George Francis Hill. *A Corpus of Italian Medals of the Renaissance before Cellini.* 2 vols. London: British Museum, 1930.

Alfred M. Frankfurter. "Thirty-five Portraits from American Collections." *Art News,* Supplement, May 16, 1931.

Bernard Berenson. *Italian Pictures of the Renaissance.* Oxford: Clarendon Press, 1932.

Vincenzo Golzio. *Raffaello, nei documenti, nelle testimonianze dei contemporanei e nella letteratura del suo secolo.* Pontificia Insigne Accademia Artistica del Virtuosi al Pantheon. Vatican City: Panetto & Petrelli, 1936.

The Jacob Epstein Collection in The Baltimore Museum of Art. Baltimore: Published by Jacob Epstein, 1939.

Alfred M. Frankfurter. "Great Renaissance Portraits." *Art News* 38, no. 24 (March 16, 1940):7–9.

"Ladies of the Renaissance." *New York Times,* Supplement, March 10, 1940.

Sergio Ortolani. *Raffaello.* 2nd edition. Bergamo: Istituto italiano d'arti grafiche, 1945.

Oskar Fischel. *Raphael.* 2 vols. Translated by B. Rackham. London: K. Paul, 1948.

W. E. Suida. *Raphael.* London: Phaidon Press, 1948.

Jan Lauts. *Isabella d'Este, Fürstin der Renaissance, 1474–1539.* Hamburg: M. von Schröder, 1952.

Roberto Longhi. "Percorso di Raffaello giovine." *Paragone* 6, no. 65 (May 1955):22.

A Picture Book: 200 Objects in The Baltimore Museum of Art. Baltimore: The Baltimore Museum of Art, 1955.

Carlo Volpe. "Due questioni Raffaellesche." *Paragone* 7, no. 75 (March 1956):17, n. 12.

Anna Maria Brizio. "Raphael." In *Encyclopedia of World Art.* 15 vols. New York: McGraw-Hill, 1959–1968.

Ursula B. Schmitt. "Francesco Bonsignori." *Münchner Jahrbuch der Bildenden Kunst,* ser. 3, 12 (1961): 73–152.

Ettore Camesasca. *All the Paintings of Raphael.* Translated by L. Grosso. 2 vols. New York: Hawthorne Books, 1963.

Mario Salmi, et al. *The Complete Work of Raphael.* New York: F. Reynal, 1969.

Luitpold Dussler. *Raphael, A Critical Catalogue of His Pictures, Wall-Paintings and Tapestries.* Translated by S. Cruft. London and New York: Phaidon Press, 1971.

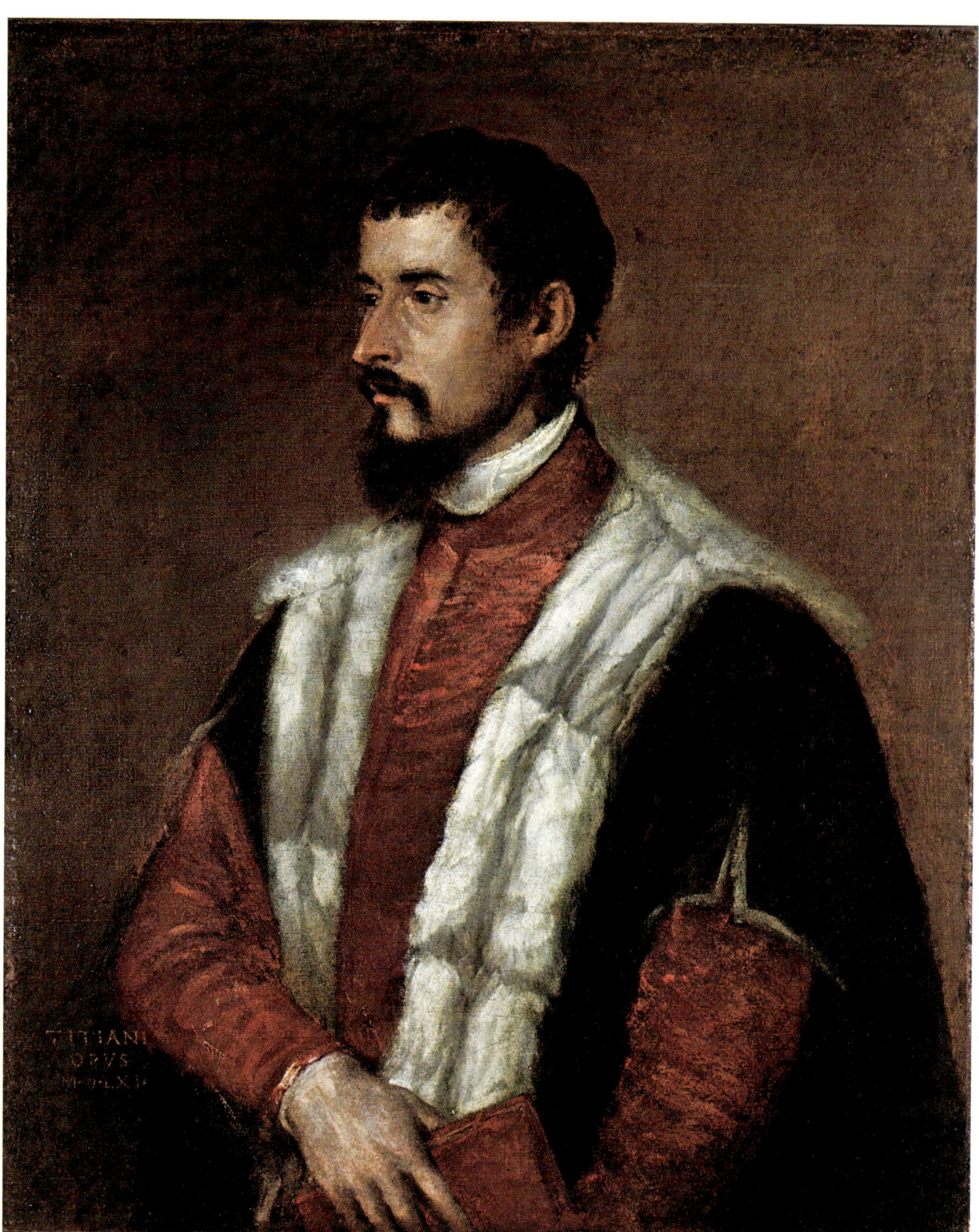
TITIANI
OPVS

TITIAN (Tiziano Vecellio, ca. 1488–1576)

14. *Portrait of a Gentleman,* 1561

Inscribed and dated, lower left: TITIANI OPVS MDLXI
Oil on canvas. 34¼ × 28 inches (87 × 71.1 cm.)
The Jacob Epstein Collection (BMA 51.115)

*PROVENANCE**

Probably Collection of Sir Joshua Reynolds
Reynolds Sale, Christie's, London, March 16, 1795 (third day of sale), lot 70

Collection of Philip Metcalfe, probably acquired at the Reynolds Sale

Bequeathed (?) to Henry Metcalfe by Philip Metcalfe
Henry Metcalfe Sale, Christie's, London, June 15, 1850, lot 35

Acquired in 1850 by Farrer as a signed and dated (1561) work by Titian

Collection of Thomas B. Brown
Thomas B. Brown Sale at Phillips, London, May 20, 1856, lot 67

Acquired by Maynard at Phillips, London, May 20, 1856
Herman de Zoete Sale, Christie's, London, May 8 and 9, 1885, lot 324

Bought by P. & D. Colnaghi at the de Zoete Sale, Christie's, London, May 9, 1885

Collection Charles Brinsley-Marlay

Bequeathed in 1912 to The Fitzwilliam Museum, Cambridge, by Charles Brinsley-Marlay

Anonymous Sale ("Property of a Gentleman deceased"), Christie's, London, February 1, 1924, lot 43

Acquired at Christie's in 1924 by Max Rothschild of the Sackville Gallery, London

Acquired in 1925 by Jacob Epstein, Baltimore, from M. Knoedler & Co., New York
Portrait of a Man by Tiziano Vecelli (New York: M. Knoedler & Co., 1925), sale brochure in curatorial files, The Baltimore Museum of Art

Loaned by Jacob Epstein to The Baltimore Museum of Art in 1932 and bequeathed in 1951

**NOTE:*

The provenance of the Baltimore Titian is complicated by the fact that two different paintings attributed to Titian and referred to as *Portrait of Nicholas Orsini* existed or perhaps still exist.

Information on Reynolds's ownership of the portrait, its subsequent sale to Philip Metcalfe, and the Phillips sale of 1856 is based on annotations in sale catalogues in the National Gallery, the Courtauld Institute of Art, and the Victoria and Albert Museum, all in London. The discovery of the one-time Joshua Reynolds ownership was made by Francis Broun of the Art Gallery of Ontario, who kindly supplied this information (letters of June 25, 1979, July 31, 1979, and January 11, 1980, curatorial files, The Baltimore Museum of Art). Philip Metcalfe was one of Reynolds's three executors; Mr. Broun has also discovered catalogue notes stating that the Metcalfe collection was assembled largely on the advice of Sir Joshua. Reynolds also bequeathed to Metcalfe and his other two executors £200 each, with the suggestion that they buy pictures from his (Reynolds's) art collection at the posthumous sale of his possessions.

Sir Ellis Waterhouse was the first to bring to our attention the history of the Baltimore painting, starting in the eighteenth century (letter to G. Rosenthal, June 22, 1976, curatorial files, The Baltimore Museum of Art). His data were confirmed by Christie's, London (letters to G. Rosenthal, May 16, 1976, and October 18, 1977).

CONDITION

After its purchase by Jacob Epstein in 1925 the portrait by Titian was treated only once, in 1962, by the late Russell J. Quandt of Washington, D.C. Since then it has been examined at regular intervals by the Baltimore Museum's conservation department, most recently in 1976 when X-radiographs were taken.

The following comments are drawn from the 1962 report of Russell Quandt as no new developments in the condition of the picture have been observed:

> In the past [before 1962] the original linen support was reinforced by an auxiliary linen support attached with aqueous adhesive. The painting is abraded more in the figure than in the background. The abrasions are typical of those which frequently occur if surface varnish is removed too radically. There are a number of old tack holes at the edges with some resulting paint loss.

According to Quandt, the Baltimore painting has been "under" rather than "over" retouched (letter of June 13, 1962).

The history of the painting indicates that it underwent thorough cleaning in 1924, and probably it was at that time that much of the abrasion damage occurred and that some paint was applied to the darkest passages of the costume. Horizontal strokes of rose-colored paint in the upper part of the doublet very likely date from the same period. In 1962 a major part of the old surface varnish was removed by a mild solvent, mainly from the light areas, with special attention to skin tones. Four tiny, conspicuously bright spots which were located under the sitter's left eye, on the bridge of his nose, and in the background at left and right center, were toned down.

An inscription containing the name of the artist and a date appears at the lower left, but does not seem to have been done by Titian's hand. Concerning this question, see main section of this article and also Wethey, *The Paintings of Titian* (vol. 2, no. 68, p. 120).

At various times during its history attempts have been made to identify the sitter of the Titian portrait in the Baltimore Museum, but none could be supported by documentary evidence. Harold E. Wethey in his catalogue raisonné of *The Paintings of Titian* lists the picture as "Niccolò Orsini (so-called)" but in the text of his entry states that "the identification of the sitter is highly doubtful."[1] Sometimes referred to as a portrait of "Duke Orsini," it was called "Count Orsini" in Christie's sale catalogue of February 1, 1924 (lot 43). In the brochure on the portrait prepared by Raymond Henniker-Heaton for the firm of M. Knoedler & Co., the possibility is advanced that the subject may have been Fulvio Orsini (1529–1600),[2] an art collector and antiquarian, said to have been advisor to the Farnese family on its art collections and library. As intriguing as this hypothetical identification may be, no facts are available to substantiate it. Thus, even in the Knoedler publication, the title used is *Portrait of a Man.* In other references the picture is called *Portrait of a Bearded Gentleman* or *Portrait of a Nobleman* or, most frequently, *Portrait of a Gentleman,* as it is catalogued by The Baltimore Museum of Art.

Against a dark grayish-brown background the sitter is shown in three-quarter length, a view that Titian seems to have preferred for the portraits executed in his old age.[3] The face is seen in near profile, rarely employed by the artist in his late works. He wears the standard aristocratic dress of the time: a red doublet, the luminous texture of which is achieved by a masterful blending of several different tones of red. His black mantle, trimmed with ermine, has short sleeves revealing the red sleeves of the doublet, thus enlivening the restrained color scheme of the painting. An accent of white is provided by a piece of cloth (part of a shirt?) folded around the man's neck. His eyes are very dark and have a pensive expression.

Titian's unsurpassed ability to modulate color can be observed in the subtle distinction of reds used for the velvet-bound book held in the sitter's right hand, and of those seen in the vibrant hues of his doublet. Less conspicuous but still noticeable is the change from the warm black of the hair and beard to the cold black of the gentleman's mantle.

There is general agreement about the authenticity of the painting. It has been accepted as an autograph work of Titian by all experts who have discussed it in their writings.[4] In addition, unpublished comments by other notable scholars, also affirming the genuine character of the Baltimore picture, can be found in the Museum's curatorial files. Among these records are two letters dated July 8, 1926, and January 26, 1928, from Bernard Berenson assuring the owner, Jacob Epstein, that the Titian portrait was to be included in his forthcoming index of Italian Renaissance paintings. At the same time, Berenson encouraged Mr. Epstein to continue collecting works of the quality of his Raphael and his Titian.

Before Mr. Epstein's acquisition of the painting the late August L. Mayer endorsed the *Portrait of a Gentleman* as follows:

> I have studied very carefully the male portrait reproduced by this photograph [the Epstein Titian]. It is in my opinion a very fine genuine work by Titian and one of the most artistic and powerful examples of the later Titian which appeared during the last years. The signature and date seem to be all-right. The style and technique betray the wonderful free pictorial manner of Titian in 1560 untill [*sic*] his death. There is the great and noble feeling of the master which nobody else among the other Venetian painters had but he alone.

Signed and dated: August L. Mayer, March 24, 1924. These remarks echo Mayer's evaluation of the picture which appeared in the same year in the Austrian art journal *Belvedere.*[5]

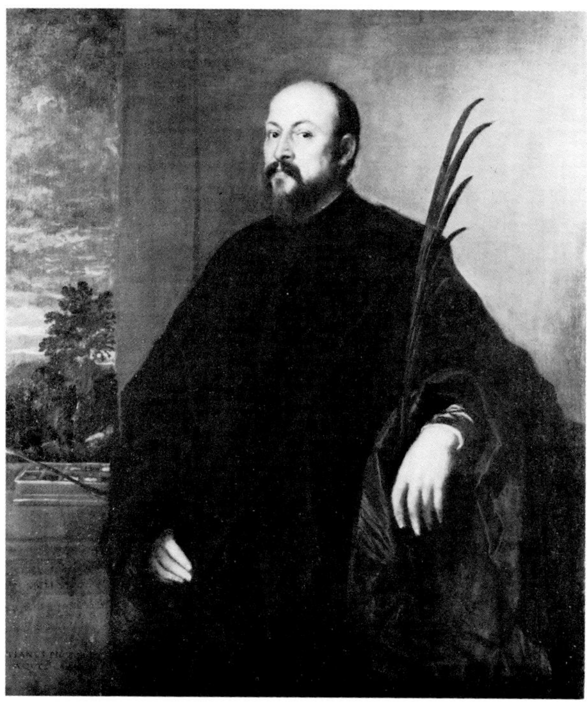

Fig. 1. Titian, *Portrait of a Painter with a Palm (Antonio Palma).* Oil on canvas. 54⅜ × 45¾ inches (138 × 116 cm.). Staatliche Gemäldegalerie, Dresden

In 1925, in an article entitled "An Uncatalogued Titian," R. R. Tatlock described the first reaction to the painting when in 1924 it appeared for auction at Christie's:

> The portrait . . . gave rise to a great deal of speculation. At that time the surface was heavily repainted and the original brushwork was much obscured. There seemed to be little faith in London that the attribution to Titian was justified and the canvas changed hands without unusual competition. After the right degree of cleaning, however, no doubt remained that only Titian could have painted it. There is practically universal agreement about it. The decision was arrived at, not on the strength of documentary evidence, but on account of the impression made on the experienced eye by the picture itself. . . . A study . . . will, we think, convince scholars that the picture must be added to the list of Titian's authentic work. . . .[6]

When visiting the Baltimore Museum in June 1966, Terisio Pignatti, after careful study of the Titian painting, stated that he had "no doubt that this is an autograph by Titian and quite a beautiful work." He noticed that part of the costume in front had suffered, and he also wondered about a certain weakness around the mouth, perhaps due to restoration. He mentioned especially the painting of the hand as typical of Titian and also "the beauty of the head in general."

As recently as 1976 three experts on the art of Titian reiterated their opinions on the Baltimore portrait. Harold E. Wethey, author of the critical catalogue of the master's paintings, in a letter of April 29, 1976, restated his belief in the authenticity of the picture—already mentioned in his catalogue entry[7]—as follows: "I have no doubt that your portrait is a late work by Titian." This conviction was echoed in May 1976 by W. R. Rearick (orally) and by Federico Zeri, who in a letter of January 27, 1976, wrote in reference to the Museum's Titian: "Much abraded and battered but still showing the lion's claw. A splendid work, surely by Titian; signature doubtful."

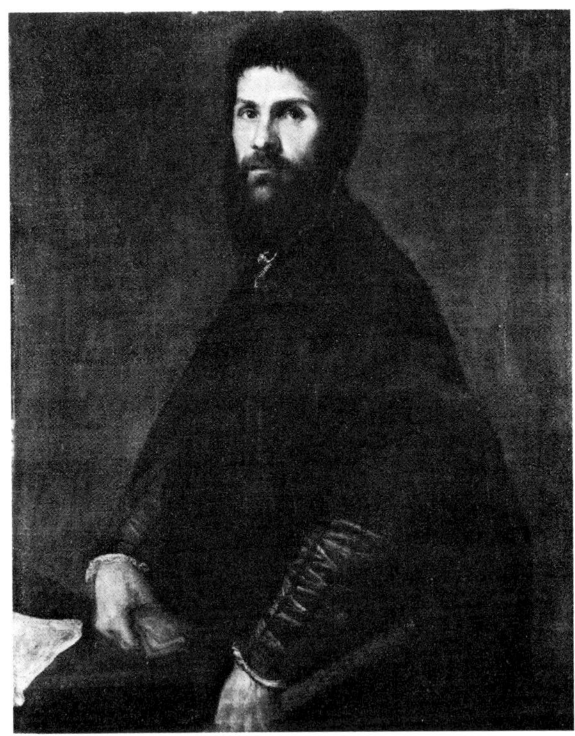

Fig. 2. Titian, *Man with a Flute*. Signed on table at left: TITIANVS F. Oil on canvas. 38½ × 30 inches (97.8 × 76.2 cm.). The Detroit Institute of Arts, Gift of the Founders Society

Professor Zeri's doubts concerning the signature[8] are shared by many Titian experts. In gold leaf at the lower left of the picture is an inscription which reads: TITIANI OPVS MDLXI. Since Titian did not sign in this fashion, the inscription has frequently been thought by many to have been added by another hand, though generally it is believed to be of the period. When in May 1962 Russell Quandt examined the signature, he reported that: "The solubility of the inscription was tested under magnification in a microscopically small area at the end of the initial T of 'TITIANI'. After surface varnish had been dissolved away, the gold was observed to be unaffected by the solvent, a reaction which indicates that the gold is not floating on a resinous layer." This points out that the inscription in gold leaf is on the original paint film, a fact that has encouraged some specialists to suggest that the signature was original and not a later addition. However, the possibility cannot be ruled out that after removal of the original varnish, which could have occurred at any time, the signature could have been applied and the painting then revarnished. Another factor, until now overlooked, also suggests that the signature was not inscribed by the artist: it spreads over the right sleeve of the figure. It is hard to believe that such a placement would have been chosen by the master himself. Despite the problematic signature, the various scholars who have concerned themselves with this painting have neither doubted the picture nor its date of 1561 which, judged on stylistic evidence, appears correct.

It is not known whether in Titian's later years the princes of State and Church preferred younger artists for their portrait commissions, or whether the master no longer sought such official tasks. From approximately 1560 on, he devoted himself much less to portraiture, and the relatively few portraits painted during this late period are mainly likenesses of men of his own circle.

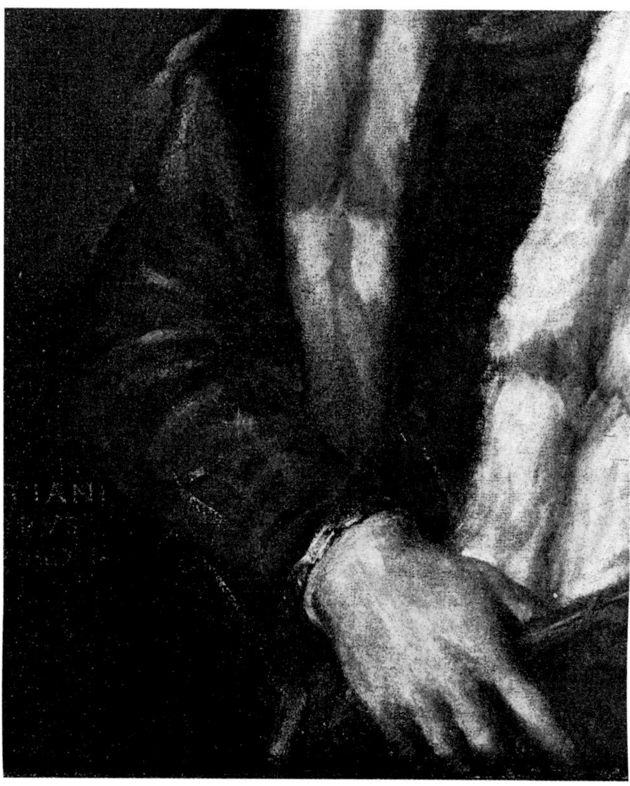

Fig. 3. Titian, *Portrait of a Gentleman,* detail of cat. no. 14

Portraits near in date, technique, and spirit to the Baltimore *Gentleman* are *Antonio Palma* (fig. 1), listed as *Portrait of a Painter with a Palm* by its owner, the Staatliche Gemäldegalerie, Dresden[9] and *Man with a Flute* (fig. 2), dated between 1560 and 1565 (Detroit Institute of Arts).[10] Both these paintings share with the Epstein picture restraint in the use of color[11] and an almost brooding mood. In the austere *Man with a Flute* the impressionist technique is especially conspicuous in the rendering of the sitter's left sleeve, reminiscent of the treatment of the sleeves in the Baltimore picture, but even more accentuated (compare figs. 3 and 4). Vasari noted Titian's use of this technique and described the master's style of his old age as follows:

> Titian's methods in these [late] paintings differ widely from those he adopted in his youth. His first works are executed with a certain finesse and diligence, so that they may be examined closely, but these [the late works] are done roughly in an impressionist manner, with both strokes and blobs to obtain the effect at a distance. . . . The method is admirable and beautiful if done judiciously, making paintings appear alive and achieved without labor.[12]

Vasari's comments support the assumption that Titian painted his late works *alla prima,* directly on the canvas.[13] "Titian reportedly used brushes 'big as broomsticks' or even his fingers—'like God when he created man,' as he used to say himself."[14]

The late style of the great masters, as interpreted by Walter Friedlaender, shows "a deepening, a condensation, an increasing harmony of the underlying artistic concept,"[15] qualities that are characteristic of Titian's late manner. Contours are no longer emphasized; instead the brushstrokes are so skillfully manipulated that they miraculously take on the shape of the object they are supposed to represent, as they do in the late works of Rembrandt who presumably was influenced by Titian's old-age style.

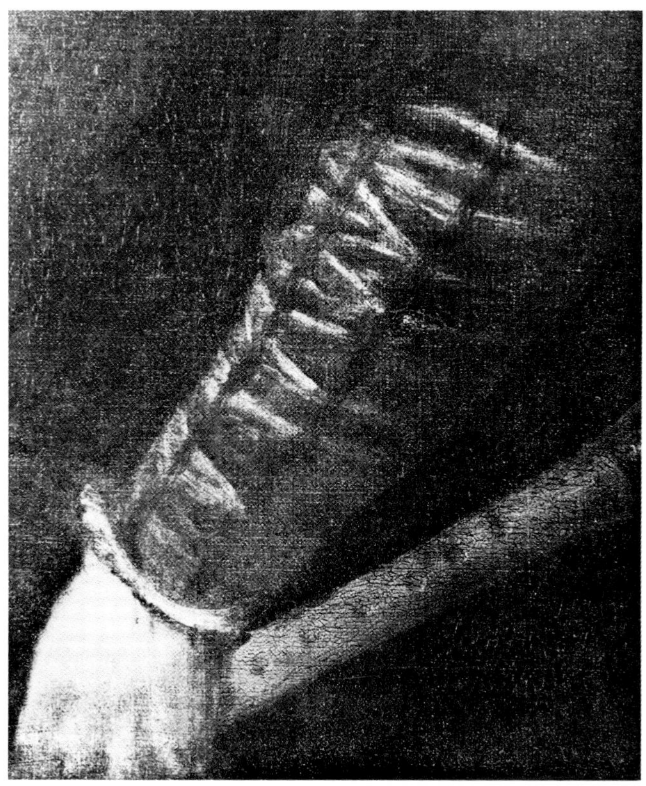

Fig. 4. Titian, *Man with a Flute,* detail of fig. 2

The aging master's portraits reveal his unique grasp of reality, a brilliant intellectualism, profound spirituality, and a sensuousness for which color has become the vehicle. The different personalities of his sitters are observed and rendered with great psychological insight that is perhaps more finely honed than in his earlier works. Thus the adjectives "elegant," "gentle," and "sensitive" have been used appropriately for the Baltimore portrait.

As in the case of Picasso in our time, Titian's tremendous productivity and his international reputation "deepened the natural isolation of the aging artist in regard to the younger generation."[16] Panofsky, in his own later years, found the simplest but most illuminating words to express the enigma of Titian's creations of his old age: "Titian's latest style—like the latest style of most great masters—amounts to a coincidence of opposites: intense emotion and outward stillness, color and non-color, the broadest and apparently almost chaotic technique of execution and the most rigid order and density of composition."[17]

Gertrude Rosenthal
The Baltimore Museum of Art

NOTES

1. H. E. Wethey, *The Paintings of Titian* (New York: Phaidon Press, 1969), 2:120, no. 68, pl. 202. Wethey states that the picture after 1794 was cut down 19 cm. This does not apply to the Baltimore painting but probably to the other portrait, referred to as "Niccolò Orsini," whose history often has been confused with the picture under discussion and whose present location is not known. In a letter to this writer, Wethey explains: "When a name like Orsini is attached to a picture, I have the feeling that there must be some reason for it" (April 29, 1976).
2. *Portrait of a Man by Tiziano Vecelli* (New York: M. Knoedler & Co., 1925), brochure.
3. Wethey, *The Paintings of Titian,* 2:47. Examples of Titian's use of the three-quarter length figure are also found in the following portraits: *Fabrizio Salvaresio* (1558), *Antonio Palma* (1561), *Man with a Flute* (1560–1565). See Wethey, 2:nos. 92, 69, and 63; pls. 199, 205, and 201, respectively.
4. The names of these scholars and the publications pertaining to the Epstein portrait by Titian are listed in the Bibliography.
5. A. L. Mayer, "Zwei Unbekannte Gemälde aus Tizians Spätzeit," *Belvedere* 5 (1924):184, repro. facing p. 184.
6. R. R. Tatlock, "An Uncatalogued Titian," *Burlington Magazine* 47 (November 1925):222, frontispiece and repro. facing p. 222.
7. Wethey, *The Paintings of Titian,* 2:120, no. 68.
8. See discussion of placement of signatures by C. E. Gilbert, "Some Findings on Early Works of Titian," *The Art Bulletin* 62, no. 1 (March 1980): Appendix II, pp. 73–75.
9. This portrait is considered one of Titian's finest late portraits. As with the Baltimore picture, the signature is not by Titian, according to Wethey, *The Paintings of Titian,* 2:120, no. 69, pl. 205. For a discussion of the identity of the sitter, see cat. no. 12, n. 25 of this publication.
10. According to Wethey, the *Man with a Flute* was "cut down at the lower edge, eliminating part of the left hand; . . . the signature has been restored." *The Paintings of Titian,* 2:117, no. 63, pl. 201.
11. E. Panofsky speaks about Titian's color in the master's late work as follows: ". . . after about 1560 . . . we have those authentic creations which show the ultimate in lateness, particularly the final triumph of spatial over local color resulting in what may be called a colorful monochrome." *Problems in Titian, Mostly Iconographic,* The Wrightsman Lectures (New York: New York University Press, 1969), p. 24.
12. G. Vasari, *The Lives of the Painters, Sculptors and Architects,* 4 vols., trans. A. B. Hinds (London: J. M. Dent & Sons, Ltd.; New York: E. P. Dutton, Inc., 1927), 4:208–9. It is interesting to recall that Titian's late works were rarely appreciated until toward the end of the nineteenth century when they became famous and most desirable—perhaps in connection with the Impressionist movement.
13. R. Wittkower, *Masters of the Loaded Brush: Oil Sketches from Rubens to Tiepolo* (New York: Columbia University Press, 1967), p. xviii.
14. Panofsky, *Problems in Titian,* p. 16 (quoted from M. Boschini, *Le minere della pittura* [Venice, 1664; enlarged edition, 1674, entitled *Le ricche minere della pittura Veneziana*], fols. b4v. ff.).
15. W. Friedlaender, *David to Delacroix,* trans. R. Goldwater (Cambridge, Mass.: Harvard University Press, 1952), p. 131.
16. H. Tietze, *Titian, Paintings and Drawings* (Vienna and London: Phaidon Press, 1937), p. 7.
17. Panofsky, *Problems in Titian,* p. 25.

SELECTED BIBLIOGRAPHY

Lodovico Dolce. *Dialogo della Pittura . . . .* Venice, 1557. (English translation by Mark Roskill. *Dolce's Aretino and Venetian Art Theory of the Cinquecento.* New York: New York University Press, 1968.)

Carlo Ridolfi. *Le Maraviglie dell'arte o vero le vite degl'illustri pittori Veneti . . . .* 2 vols. Venice: G. B. Sgaua, 1648.

Matteo Boschini. *Le minere della pittura . . . di Venezia.* Venice, 1664.

Joseph Archer Crowe and Giovanni Battista Cavalcaselle. *Titian: His Life and Times.* 2 vols. London: J. Murray, 1877.

Georg Gronau. *Tizian.* Berlin: E. Hofmann, 1900. (English translation, London and New York: Duckworth & Co., 1904.)

Theodor Hetzer. "Tiziano Vecellio." In Thieme-Becker, *Allgemeines Lexikon der Bildenden Künstler.* 37 vols. Leipzig: E. A. Seemann, 1907–1950.

Charles Ricketts. *Titian.* London: Methuen & Co., 1910.

Detlev von Hadeln, editor. *Carlo Ridolfi. Le Maraviglie dell'arte o vero le vite degl'illustri pittori Veneti . . . .* 2 vols. Berlin: G. Grote, 1914–1924.

August L. Mayer. "Zwei Unbekannte Gemälde aus Tizians Spätzeit." *Belvedere* 5 (1924):184–85.

Robert Rattray Tatlock. "An Uncatalogued Titian." *Burlington Magazine* 47 (November 1925):222.

Paintings by Titian. Exhibition catalogue. Detroit: Detroit Institute of Arts, 1928.

Oskar Fischel. *Tizian.* Klassiker der Kunst. 5th edition. Stuttgart: Deutsche Verlagsanstalt, 1929.

Bernard Berenson. *Italian Pictures of the Renaissance.* Oxford: Clarendon Press, 1932.

Wilhelm Suida. *Tizian.* Zurich: Orell Füssli, 1933.

Theodor Hetzer. *Tizian: Geschichte seiner Farbe.* Frankfurt a/M.:Von Klostermann, 1935.

A Picture Book: 200 Objects in The Baltimore Museum of Art. Baltimore: The Baltimore Museum of Art, 1935.

Hans Tietze. *Titian, Paintings and Drawings.* Vienna and London: Phaidon Press, 1937.

Venetian Masters. Exhibition catalogue. New York: M. Knoedler & Co., 1938.

The Jacob Epstein Collection in The Baltimore Museum of Art. Baltimore: Published by Jacob Epstein, 1939.

Eugène Delacroix. *The Journal of Eugène Delacroix.* Translated by Walter Pach. New York: Crown Publishers, 1948.

Walter Friedlaender. *David to Delacroix.* Translated by Robert Goldwater. Cambridge, Mass.: Harvard University Press, 1952.

Man and His Years. Exhibition catalogue. Baltimore: The Baltimore Museum of Art, 1954.

Old Masters from American Collections. Exhibition catalogue. Newark: Newark Museum, 1956.

Bernard Berenson. *Italian Pictures of the Renaissance: The Venetian School.* 2 vols. London: Phaidon Press, 1957.

Antonio Morassi. "Titian." In *Encyclopedia of World Art.* 15 vols. New York, Toronto, London: McGraw-Hill, 1959–1968.

Ernst H. Gombrich. *Art and Illusion.* New York: Pantheon Books, 1960.

Francesco Valcanover. *Tutta la Pittura di Tiziano.* 2 vols. Milan: Rizzoli, 1960. (English translation by S. J. Tomalin. *All the Paintings of Titian.* 2 vols. New York: Hawthorn Books, 1964.)

Antonio Morassi. *Titian.* Milan and Greenwich, Conn.: New York Graphic Society, 1964.

Kent Roberts Greenfield. *The Museum: Its First Half Century.* Annual I. Baltimore: The Baltimore Museum of Art, 1966.

Rudolf Wittkower. Introduction. *Masters of the Loaded Brush: Oil Sketches from Rubens to Tiepolo.* Exhibition catalogue. New York: Columbia University Press, 1967.

Rodolfo Pallucchini. *Tiziano.* Florence: Sansoni, 1969.

Erwin Panofsky. *Problems in Titian, Mostly Iconographic.* The Wrightsman Lectures. New York: New York University Press, 1969. (See also the bibliography on Titian recommended by Panofsky, pp. 172–76.)

Harold E. Wethey. *The Paintings of Titian.* 3 vols. New York: Phaidon Press, 1969–1971.

Johannes Wilde. *Venetian Art from Bellini to Titian.* Oxford: Clarendon Press, 1974.

Terisio Pignatti. *The Golden Century of Venetian Painting.* Exhibition catalogue. Los Angeles: Los Angeles County Museum of Art, 1979.

Fern Rusk Shapley. *Catalogue of The Italian Paintings.* 2 vols. Washington, D.C.: National Gallery of Art, 1979.

Creighton E. Gilbert. "Some Findings on Early Works of Titian." *The Art Bulletin.* 62, no. 1 (March 1980): 36–75.

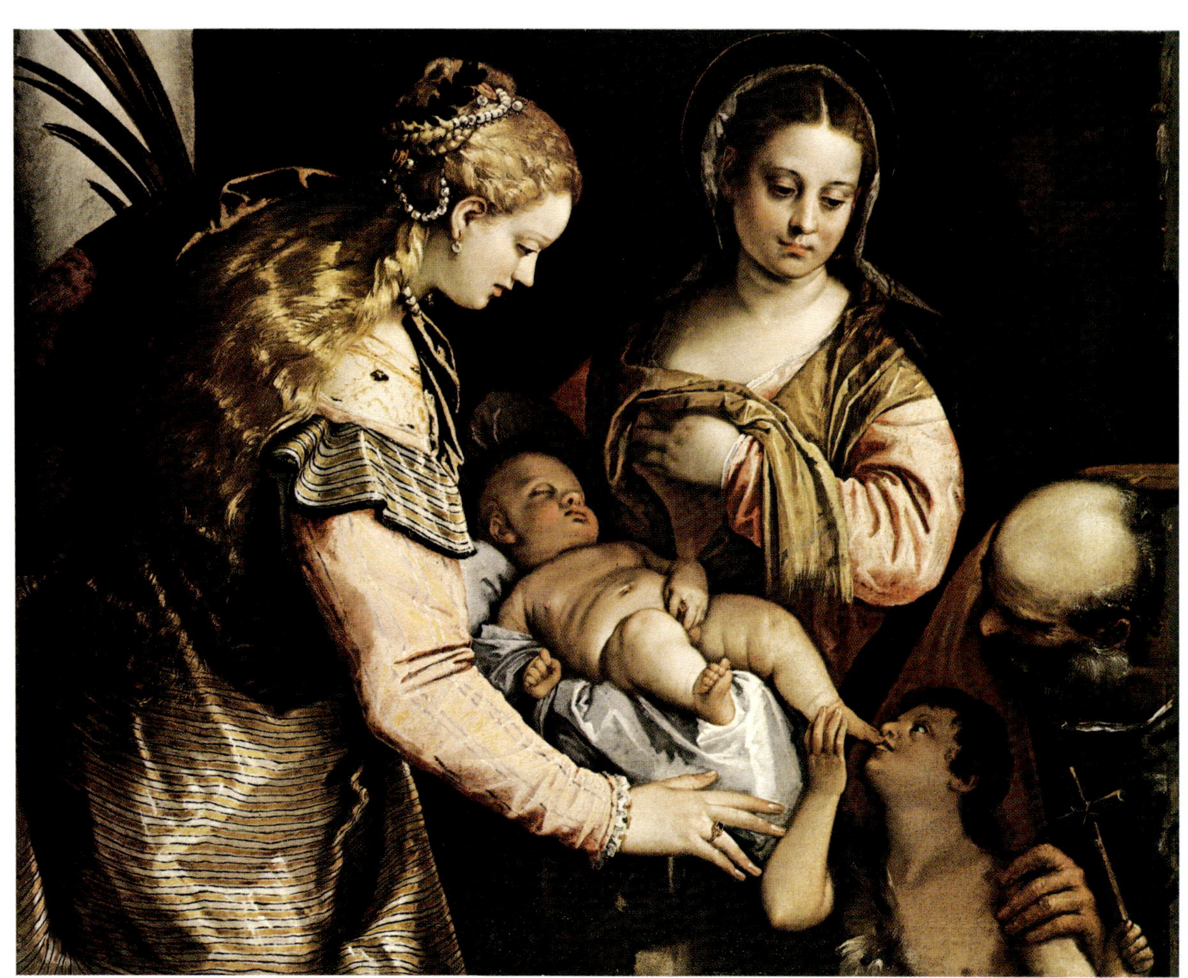

Workshop of
PAOLO VERONESE (1528–1588)
(Paolo Caliari)

---

15. *Holy Family with Saint Barbara and Young Saint John the Baptist,* before 1600

Oil on canvas. 39 × 46 inches (99 × 118 cm.)
The Jacob Epstein Collection (BMA 51.119)

PROVENANCE

Probably Collection of John, Third Duke of Rutland (1696–1779)

According to letters from Christie's, London, of October 19, 1976, and November 8, 1976 (curatorial files, The Baltimore Museum of Art). However, no definite information on this matter could be obtained.

In a letter of April 28, 1977, Sir Ellis Waterhouse informed Gertrude Rosenthal that the picture was listed, apparently for the first time, in The Reverend Irvin Ellery, *History of Belvoir Castle* [seat of the Duke of Rutland] (London, 1841), p. 238.

Sale, Christie's, London, April 16, 1926

Recorded as Paolo Veronese, *The Holy Family with St. Catherine and the Infant St. John*, 39 × 46 inches, in Christie's auction catalogue, *Old Pictures: The Property of His Grace, the Duke of Rutland . . .*, no. 42.

Acquired by Leger Galleries, London, on April 16, 1926

In a letter of May 31, 1977, the Leger Galleries, London, confirmed that "*The Holy Family with St. Barbara* from the Workshop of Paolo Veronese" had been in their possession, having been purchased at Christie's on April 16, 1926. The Leger Galleries further reported that "our records for this period are no longer in existence, and we have no way of telling to whom we sold the painting. . . ." (curatorial files, The Baltimore Museum of Art). In a letter of September 14, 1977, the Leger Galleries informed the Baltimore Museum that a branch of their gallery existed at 57th Street, New York, "from approximately 1926 until 1935, and it seems fairly certain that the Veronese Workshop painting was sold direct to a client from that address." Undoubtedly this client was Jacob Epstein.

Acquired by Jacob Epstein, Baltimore, before 1932

The painting was mentioned as being in Mr. Epstein's possession in an article in the Baltimore *Sun*, March 19, 1933.

Loaned by Jacob Epstein to The Baltimore Museum of Art in 1932 and bequeathed in 1951

CONDITION

The canvas of straight weave, nine threads per centimeter warp by nine threads per centimeter weft, is mounted on an auxiliary support of fabric with aqueous based adhesive. It appears that the picture received major treatment in the early nineteenth century when a stretcher was applied which was replaced in 1976–1977, the time of the most recent treatment.

The top and bottom edges of the original support still retain the selvedge thread, i.e., the vertical dimension of approximately one meter is the original loom width. The design layer extends around onto the tackover edges on both sides, but not on top and bottom.

The exact size of the original support of the Baltimore painting cannot be precisely determined because of the dimensional instability of fabric on a wooden frame; however, X-radiography indicates that no appreciable size change has occurred. Examination of the paint film by visual, photographic, and X-radiographic methods has shown that the painting has survived in remarkably good condition. The surface texture is rather irregular in areas, particularly in the blues, probably due to the coarsely ground ultramarine pigment. In the course of time the paint film cracked and cupped slightly. Pressure of the previous hot gluelining methods pushed the paint film particles back into place causing minute crushing and wear along the edges. Actual losses to the design layer are minimal. Before recent treatment they consisted of a puncture at the extreme bottom center, a tear through the cross, a small tear in the neck of St. John, and losses through flaking along the edges, particularly at the bottom and corners. There are also minute pinpoint losses in the flesh tones. The only area of extensive overpaint was the addition of drapery between the Child's legs. Microscopic and ultraviolet examinations showed this piece of drapery to have been a later addition, perhaps of the nineteenth century.

When the painting underwent treatment in 1976–1977, the horizontal dimension was extended to encompass the entire design layer. The drapery between the Child's legs was removed, leaving the original surface completely intact.

Removal of the discolored varnish—which before treatment softened the outlines, flattened the overall composition, and imparted a warm golden tone to the picture—revealed a cooler silvery tonal quality and a contrast of colors. However, the color of the Madonna's sleeve, for which madder lake was used, has faded through exposure to light so that the play of the once brilliant red against the blue is now lost. Preliminary analysis of a few paint samples shows pigments characteristic of the sixteenth century.

Geoffrey Michael Lemmer
With assistance from Margaret R. Ash
The Baltimore Museum of Art

Fewer scholarly books have been written about Paolo Veronese than about any of the other illustrious Italian Renaissance masters, despite the fact that his works were greatly appreciated during his lifetime and remained sources of influence through the following centuries. Artists such as Rubens, Poussin, the Carracci, Sebastiano Ricci, Giovanni Battista Tiepolo, the Guardis, Watteau, Delacroix, Turner, Cézanne, Bonnard, and even Matisse acknowledged in their work and/or their writings the inspiration received from Veronese's paintings.[1] A possible explanation for the absence (recently remedied) of a comprehensive monograph or catalogue raisonné of Veronese's oeuvre may be that relatively few of his commissions are documented and many of his paintings are only circumstantially datable, which results in a "vexed chronology."[2] Moreover, the lack of knowledge of his everyday life, of his personality, and of those of his thoughts and goals which cannot be surmised from his paintings and drawings was not conducive to the task of a definitive Veronese publication. Nevertheless, these obstacles to modern scholarship were finally overcome by Terisio Pignatti in his comprehensive work (1976) on the master.[3] Together with Carlo Ridolfi's biography of Veronese (a chapter in his *Le Maraviglie dell'arte . . .* of 1648), Pignatti's publication constitutes an essential tool for any research on Veronese.

An additional factor that has complicated the dating and the attribution of a great number of Veronese's works was the special role his workshop played during his life and after his death. It has been known that frequently the master worked out only the composition and determined the colors, while the execution was left to his most skillful assistants. After Paolo's death the large workshop was directed by his brother Benedetto (1538–1598), who for many years had been Veronese's recognized collaborator, and by Paolo's sons Gabriele (1568–1631) and the precocious, gifted Carletto (1570–1596). His nephew Alvise Benfatto del Friso was also a distinguished member of the *bottega.* Many artists' workshops in Venice, unlike those in other Italian art centers, traditionally were family enterprises, but Veronese's posthumous studio furnished a unique example of this type of collaboration. Well organized under the leadership of three of Paolo's relatives, the firm worked under the name of "Haeredes Pauli" or "Haeredes Paoli" ("Heirs of Paolo"),[4] a name that even appears as a signature[5] on a number of pictures, though by no means on the entire production of the atelier of Veronese's heirs. The firm functioned at least until the turn of the century by which time Benedetto and Carletto had died. Upon Benedetto's death in 1598, Gabriele is said to have given up painting and to have devoted himself to selling his father's works and, it can be assumed, also those by his uncle and brother, as well as the paintings that were produced under the name of "Haeredes Paoli."[6]

During the approximately ten years of their activity, the "Heirs of Paolo" applied themselves in various ways. There were first of all the orders left unfinished at the time of the master's death which had to be completed; also, paintings based on Veronese's drawings and *modelli* were very much in demand. Moreover, Benedetto and his nephews produced compositions of their own invention, sometimes individually, sometimes jointly.[7] However, the atelier's main commissions seem to have been for copies of pictures Veronese himself had painted. It is in this latter category that the Baltimore Museum's *Holy Family with St. Barbara and Young St. John* obviously belongs: the painting is a very close replica of the original in the Uffizi, Florence.[8] Before discussing the relationship of the Baltimore painting to the Uffizi canvas, it seems obligatory first to analyze the original picture.

So far as is known, the original painting (fig. 1), now called *Holy Family with St. Barbara and Young St. John* (Uffizi no. 1433), was first mentioned by Carlo Ridolfi in his 1648 biography of Veronese as *The Mystic Marriage of St. Catherine.*[9] From that time on

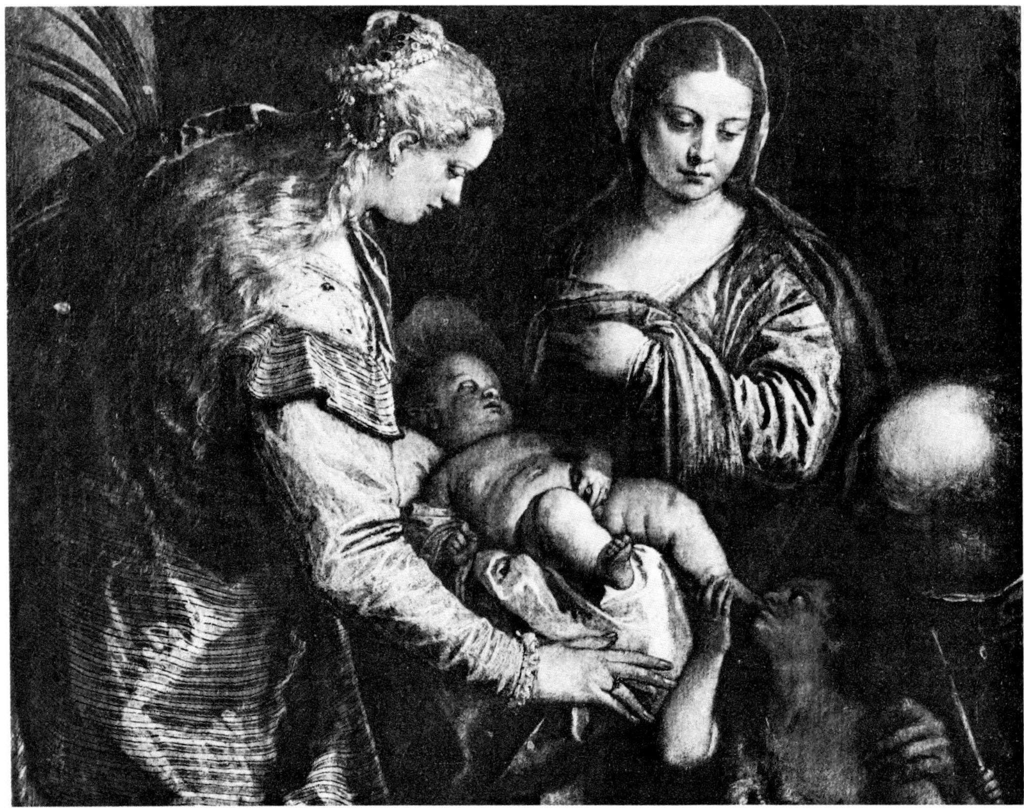

Fig. 1. Paolo Veronese, *Holy Family with St. Barbara and Young St. John.* Oil on canvas. 33⅞ × 48¹/₁₆ inches (86 × 122 cm.). Uffizi, Florence. Alinari/Editorial Photocolor Archives

the picture's whereabouts can be traced without interruption. Ridolfi referred to it as being owned by the Counts Widman of Venice and described "the pleasing composition with the Virgin and the Baby in her lap, whose tender feet the Boy Baptist kisses; on one side is St. Joseph, supporting himself on his right arm,[10] while St. Catherine Martyr stands by, admiring her Husband and Lord," all of whom, Ridolfi stated, "are admirable figures."[11] The picture then was in the possession of the painter and art collector Paolo del Sera who at one time resided in Venice; it was bought in 1654 by Cardinal Leopoldo de' Medici as part of the del Sera Collection. In 1675 it passed into the Ducal collection in Florence, and on July 30, 1798, it was transferred to the Uffizi and was hung in the Tribuna[12] where it remained for many years.

In the literature on this painting, beginning with Ridolfi (1648) and Boschini (1660) and continuing through the 1920's, the accompanying female saint is always identified as St. Catherine (of Alexandria), and the picture is entitled *The Mystic Marriage of St. Catherine.*[13] However, in his book on Paolo Veronese, Fiocco,[14] one of the foremost Veronese scholars of the recent past, rejects this interpretation as erroneous and calls the female martyr St. Barbara. His identification has been accepted and the title for the Uffizi original has been changed to *Holy Family with St. Barbara and Young St. John* (*Sacra Famiglia con Santa Barbara e San Giovannino*). Almost all collections owning early copies of the painting have adopted the new title,[15] although none of the versions shows the saint with her identifying attribute (a miniature tower), unless one regards her superb clothes and rich jewelry as indication of the wealth supposedly possessed by this completely legendary martyr.

The type of composition seen in the Uffizi *Holy Family with St. Barbara* and its versions does not seem to recur—not even in a modified form—in any other work by Veronese. The two majestic figures of the Virgin and St. Barbara stand out from the dark background, which is relieved at the left by a light silvery-gray column against which a palm branch, the symbol of martyrdom, is placed. On the right, there is a suggestion of spatial depth where a leafy shrub can be barely recognized; the indistinct shapes next to it (which recur in all versions but one)[16] have resisted explanation. As St. Barbara is shown in three-quarter view from the back and the Virgin in three-quarter view from the front, they create a dell-like space in which the Christ Child rests in His cradle.

In addition to this imaginative structural design of balance and counterbalance provided by the regal figures of the two women, attention should be paid to another rare compositional feature—the absence of a focal point. The Baby's head, which ordinarily would serve as a pictorial and spiritual center of the painting, is in deep shadow, a device that could have created a hole in the composition and thus compromised it; instead, the shadowed head intensifies the mood of peace and serenity. The crouched figure of St. Joseph and the bust of the young St. John squeezed into the lower right corner appear almost as fillers in the composition and accentuate the grandeur of the group formed by the two women and the Baby.

Though Veronese's art has often been considered exclusively representative of the Renaissance and proclaimed as the last great statement of that style,[17] the Uffizi's *Holy Family* contains certain Baroque features which should not be overlooked. In the intimate setting of an easel painting, the monumentality of the two women anticipates seventeenth-century shapes rather than revealing Renaissance forms. Even more in the Baroque spirit is the strong diagonal movement that goes from the light column in the upper left corner of the canvas to the lower right where the two male saints are wedged in and where St. Joseph's bald head in strong light appears as a counterbalance to the column on the other side.

An analysis of this picture gives rise to other questions. Does this work also reveal the Mannerist tendencies obvious in Veronese's early pictures, which showed the influence of Giulio Romano and Parmigianino? Did the impact of Mannerism continue throughout Veronese's career? This issue can never be completely clarified. In many of Veronese's paintings certain Mannerist elements can be discerned, but rarely are they dominant enough to produce a picture in the Mannerist style. Thus, in the *Holy Family with St. Barbara* a lack of deep space,[18] showing the main group strongly projecting from the shallow background, can be observed as well as a nearly all-over design; both features can be considered Mannerist—but do they make this picture a Mannerist piece? Without being eclectic, the mature artist, endowed with an abundance of imagination, has made discriminating and deliberate use of the artistic ideas and techniques his epoch could offer, absorbing and refining them.

In addition to Ridolfi and Boschini, many writers through the centuries have voiced their appreciation of the unusual design of the Uffizi picture. Among them was Pietro Caliari who expressed his praise by quoting from a publication on the Gallery of Florence in which the authors refer to this painting as having been executed "in the most exquisite manner, truly worthy of Paolo's brush"; the work is then praised for "the beautiful contrast and variety of movements and the ingenious grouping of the fine figures, large as life, arranged in restricted but well-apportioned space—neither narrow nor crowded—so that the grouping does not appear artificial but spontaneous."[19] Among the laudatory comments by several twentieth-century writers is Adolfo Venturi's observation that we are "far removed from Titian in this extraordinarily original composition which projects from its background in a daring but powerful three-dimensionality."[20]

Ridolfi has recorded that Veronese "revered Titian as the father of art."[21] There were periods when Titian's influence made itself strongly felt in certain aspects of the younger master's work; but as a colorist Veronese remained independent, always finding new ways of making color the most expressive and seductive instrument of his art. Unlike Titian's followers, who strove for "the golden tone" which their master so incomparably had employed, Veronese's colors generally are more silvery, monochromatic rather than tonal. However, the Uffizi painting with its relatively warm colors constitutes, to a certain extent, an exception to Veronese's usually cooler and clearer color scheme.

Attempts to describe what has been called "the miracle of Veronese's color" have been made by a number of scholars of Venetian painting, among them Theodor Hetzer[22] whose unusual treatment of the subject should be mentioned. Without reference to individual pictures, he offers a thought-provoking philosophical discussion of Paolo's concepts and achievements in regard to color, at the same time interpreting the artist through the medium of color.

Rodolfo Pallucchini's approach to the same theme is a different one. A few of his observations follow here: "At an early age Veronese absorbed, in the artistic atmosphere of Verona, the teachings of a pictorial culture backward in comparison with that of Venice but nonetheless quite original in its coherent taste, tending to heighten color by juxtaposition and by breaking up of light."[23] Paolo continued this early manner of treating color, refining it and making it more and more complex. Pallucchini also states that Veronese's "figures . . . create clearly distinct zones of color that when juxtaposed generate . . . luminosity in which shadow itself becomes color. . . ."[24] His figures "are articulated according to a principle . . . fundamental to the style of Veronese: a dilation of the surfaces with controlled exaggeration so that the figures present the greatest possible areas of color. . . ."[25] These comments by Pallucchini are applicable to the use of color in the Uffizi *Holy Family*. It is especially the last remark that is pertinent in explaining the amazing effect of this work with its sumptuous but restrained color. The stark contrast between the almost uniformly dark background and the clearly defined figures of the women in the foreground—a contrast rarely seen in sixteenth-century Venetian painting except in Veronese's works—heightens the shimmer and glow of the picture. In trying to recollect the color scheme of the painting, one recalls immediately St. Barbara's golden hair and her robe which, though striped in white, blue, and yellow, leaves the impression of being gold-colored. These areas, together with the Virgin's fringed shawl in greenish gold, seem to outweigh the various reds, blues, pale rose tones, and whites that make up a large part of this canvas. In this context it may be worth quoting Percy H. Osmond's reaction to the Uffizi picture: ". . . it is a most beautiful and interesting piece of painting. . . . There is not much positive colour: a few blues (in the Madonna's cloak for instance), rich reds in her dress, while St. Catherine's [i.e., St. Barbara's] hair and robe are golden. The painting of the lower part of that robe is especially superb, with the most dexterous brushwork over the whole figure. The execution is thicker than was Paolo's usual practice."[26] The color differences between the Uffizi painting and the Baltimore Museum version will be discussed later.

In dating the Uffizi *Holy Family with St. Barbara* no agreement among the experts has yet been reached. Opinion still runs the gamut from considering the painting an early work to considering it a very late one. Ridolfi does not mention the date of its execution, and Pietro Caliari likewise avoids this subject. Osmond assumes that it is an early work, and Ingersoll-Smouse refers to "the beautiful *Holy Family* . . . of the Uffizi" as part of "the series of Holy Families, a beloved subject of the young Veronese."[27]

Adolfo Venturi in his publication in honor of the four-hundredth anniversary of Veronese's birth connects the Uffizi *Holy Family* stylistically with the ceiling paintings of ca. 1556 in the Church of S. Sebastiano in Venice. Fiocco in the catalogue part of his book on Veronese declares it a youthful work, while mentioning it in the same publication under the chapter heading of "Maturity."[28] Salvini, on the other hand, catalogues it as late, and Berti calls the painting "a rather late work . . . presented with great pictorial skill. . . . And in the serene nobility of the figures, there is also to be found a subtle lyricism, a meditative note particularly evident in the painter's last phase."[29]

Pignatti in his catalogue raisonné relates the Uffizi *Holy Family* in date to the *Altarpiece of St. Zaccaria* of 1562 (Accademia, Venice) and to *The Mystic Marriage of St. Catherine* (Hampton Court).[30] Fiocco and also W. R. Rearick have termed this *Mystic Marriage* an early canvas, while Pignatti dates it ca. 1565. If dated in the early 1560's the Uffizi picture is placed in time with what is perhaps Paolo's greatest accomplishment of his middle period—the frescoes for the Villa Maser. For this writer, it has been difficult to see the close connection Pignatti makes between the *Mystic Marriage* at Hampton Court and the *Holy Family with St. Barbara* in the Uffizi, but the relationship between the latter and the St. Zaccaria Altarpiece can easily be observed. There is an obvious resemblance between the Virgin of the *St. Zaccaria Altarpiece*[31] and the one of the Uffizi painting. Furthermore, in these two pictures the figures of St. Joseph are very similar and seem to have been rendered after the same model. A close relationship is also apparent between the Uffizi canvas and the *Madonna and Child with St. Peter and a Female Martyr* (Pinacoteca Civica, Vicenza)[32] if one compares the representations of the Virgin and of the male saint in the two works. Fiocco[33] again sets an early date for the Vicenza picture, an opinion shared by Rearick, while Pallucchini sees it as a work of the 1560's, and Pignatti perceives it as a great accomplishment of the years 1555–1560—dates that would explain the resemblances to the Uffizi canvas.[34] In this context Rearick cautions that one must be careful in dating on the basis of similarities of motif as Paolo drew on the same repertory of subjects over a long span of time.

The *Holy Family with St. Barbara* apparently was one of Veronese's most appreciated easel paintings: a large number of workshop copies must have existed, of which five have been preserved. Of these, the closest to the original and the only one that approximates it in size is the version in The Baltimore Museum of Art's Jacob Epstein Collection.[35] At first glance differences between the two paintings are hardly noticeable, and even after thorough examination such distinctions might be considered minor.

Thus it is not surprising that in 1926 at Christie's auction of the Duke of Rutland's Collection the Baltimore picture was listed as Veronese and that, together with other respected experts, Wilhelm von Bode, the famous German Renaissance scholar, endorsed it as an autograph work.[36] However, the assumption that it may be a replica by the master's own hand cannot be sustained. It would have been quite out of character for Veronese to busy himself making replicas when frequently he only worked out the design and color scheme even of a new commission, leaving the execution to his experienced assistants. On the other hand, the possibility that the Baltimore version was painted during the master's life and under his supervision cannot be completely ruled out, though most, if not all, experts consider it a work of the "Haeredes Pauli Veronensis," the official name of the firm established by Veronese's heirs. David Rosand has pointed out that whenever this signature was used "the surviving relatives affirmed that they were still producing the genuine product as it were. The Master was dead, but the style lived on. . . . The functioning of the workshop depended upon their ability to paint in the official studio style. . . ."[37]

Obviously, it was the goal of the "Haeredes" to follow the original as closely as possible, and thus only a few details of the replica deviate from the Uffizi *Holy Family*. What are these differences? The most noticeable can be discerned in the Madonna's face, which in the Baltimore version (fig. 2) appears as a wide oval, almost child-like, while in the original (fig. 3) her features are more modeled and more complex; the Uffizi

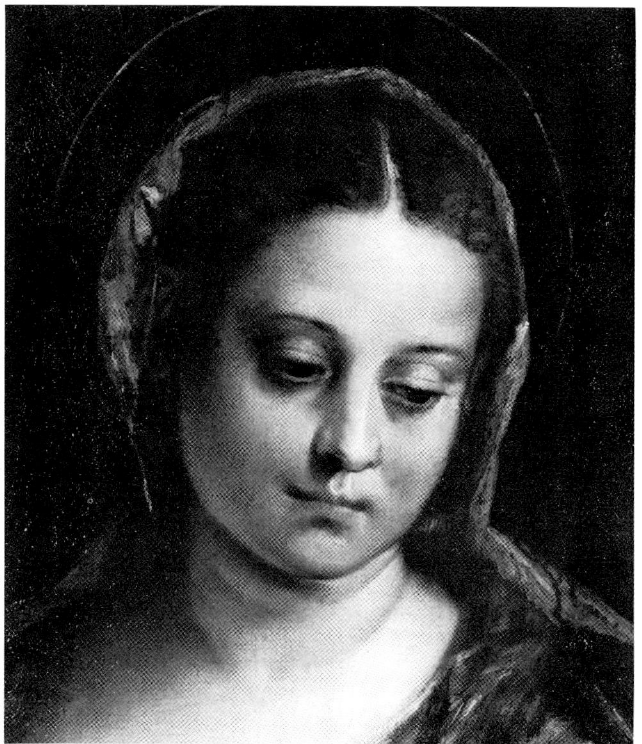

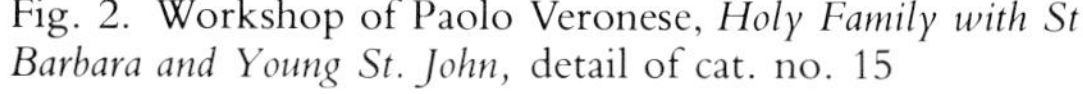

Fig. 2. Workshop of Paolo Veronese, *Holy Family with St. Barbara and Young St. John,* detail of cat. no. 15

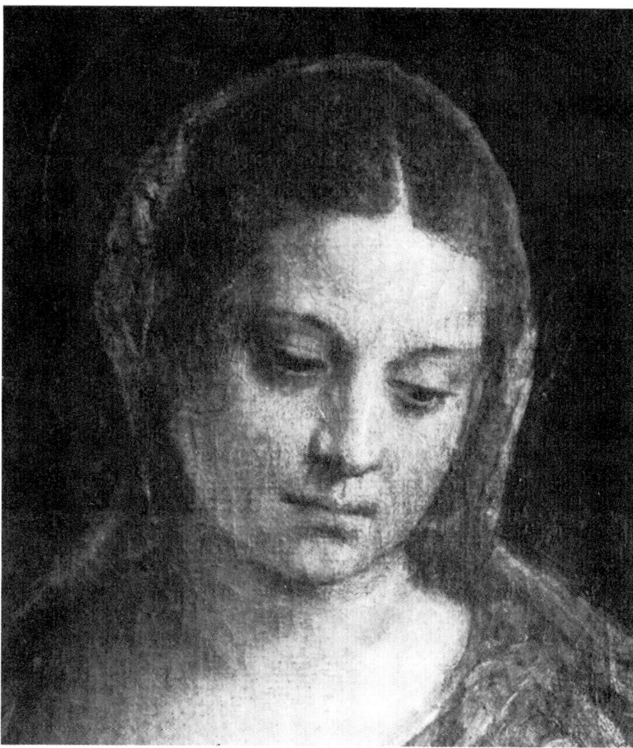

Fig. 3. Paolo Veronese, *Holy Family with St. Barbara and Young St. John,* detail of fig. 1

Madonna's expression combines the serenity of a young mother with the anticipation of her Son's death. The Baby's position, His head, torso, and limbs are identical in the two paintings, and yet the weight of His small body (in the only slightly suggested cradle) can be felt in the original and much less in the Baltimore picture—a difference that is symptomatic of a copy.

Perhaps harder to detect are some other small variations that only slightly affect the quality of the copy: the folds and shadows of St. Barbara's sleeveless silken mantle are a bit more mechanically handled in the Baltimore painting than in the Uffizi picture. Also, the strong contrast of light and shade which can be observed here does not occur in the original. Moreover, the sleeves of the women's garments are rendered with less care in the replica where the folds are rather superficially suggested.

Whereas these differences can be seen as very minor shortcomings typical of a replica, one wonders about the ugly shape of the Virgin's left hand which, one realizes, is almost equally clumsy in the Uffizi original. There is an explanation for this poorly drawn form that becomes especially convincing when it is compared with St. Barbara's sensitive hand and with the well-shaped fingers of young St. John: the Virgin's hand must have been executed by one of Paolo's less competent assistants. Although a blemish in both pictures, this inferior piece of painting does point out the dangers inherent in the methods of Veronese's studio.

While the composition of the Baltimore picture follows the Uffizi original exactly, the former's colors are cooler. This became especially apparent after the cleaning of the Baltimore version which became much lighter with the removal of the dirty varnish.[38]

In the Baltimore painting the background appears an almost black wall behind the two women and the Baby, who as a group stand out from it as if cast in relief. Contrasting

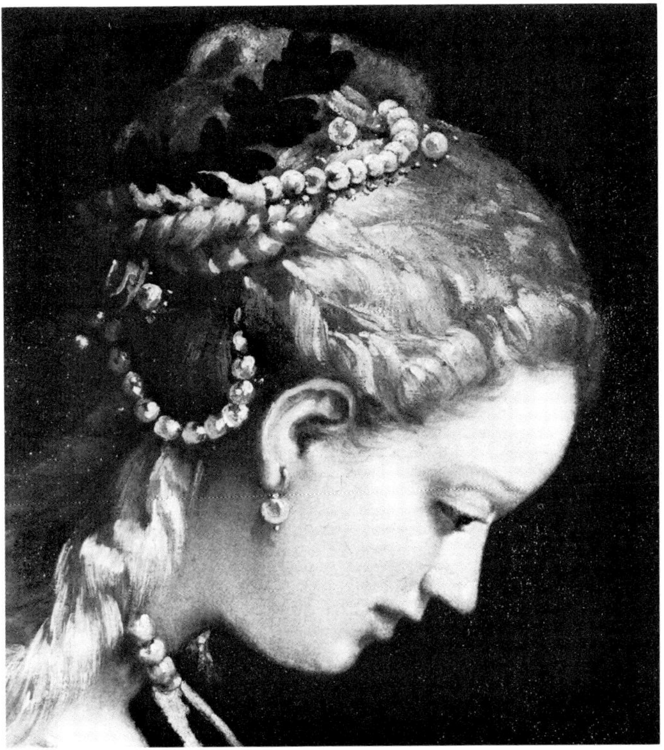

Fig. 4. Workshop of Paolo Veronese, *Holy Family with St. Barbara and Young St. John,* detail of cat. no. 15

with the light column at the left is the darkness on the right, where elements of a landscape background with a very faint pinkish cloud formation might be recognized along with some foliage.[39] These elements could indicate that this area at one time was planned as a landscape setting.

Fiocco calls the saint of the Uffizi painting "the gorgeous St. Barbara," and Adolfo Venturi and Pallucchini both pay homage to her beauty. The martyr of the Baltimore version warrants similar admiration. Her skin is very light and her honey-colored hair, set off with highlights, is loosely painted, emphasizing the individual brushstrokes (fig. 4). Interwoven with the glittering jewelry in her hair are dark leaves. The strands of pearls around her neck and in her hair, as well as her earrings, are accentuated by highlights. The pattern of her satin garment shows gold and white stripes separated from each other by thin blackish-blue lines. The undergarment, of which only the right sleeve is visible, is also of silk. It is lighter in color than the corresponding sleeve in the original—almost white, with a pink cast and light blue vertical stripes. Above the ruffle, over the material of the sleeve, can be seen a piece of white silk netting with drawn-work pattern. A dark cape or voluminous shawl hangs over the saint's left shoulder and to the front of her neck.

The Virgin, more simply dressed, wears a garment of which mainly the left sleeve shows. It is painted in the celebrated Venetian red tones which in the course of time have turned into fugitive rose and here appear less deep than the reds in the Uffizi canvas. A small area of this rose garment is visible on her right. Slung over her lower left arm and covering part of her hand is a fringed, gold-colored shawl (which in the Uffizi picture has a greenish cast). The Virgin also wears a cape in ultramarine, which in the original is of a slightly different hue. A white veil hangs down from the back of her head. Her hair is brown and her flesh tones are darker than those of St. Barbara, creating an interesting pictorial contrast.

St. Joseph's robe is ultramarine, repeating the color of the Virgin's cape, but his cloak introduces a reddish brown, close to burnt sienna and different from the hues of his mantle which are of a deeper red in the Uffizi picture. Over his naked chest the young St. John wears a small piece of animal fur suggesting his future life in the desert. The healthy-looking sleeping Baby rests on a white silken drapery that has a slightly bluish cast.

While, as stated before, in most instances the individual colors of the Baltimore version are similar to those in the Uffizi original, certain differences can be observed in the overall handling of color and light. Since its cleaning the Baltimore picture appears to this writer cooler in tone and more chromatic, with its color juxtapositions more markedly separated from each other and with more emphasis on chiaroscuro in some areas. Moreover, the brushwork is less liquid than Veronese's and results in a harder, glossier surface in certain parts.

To David Rosand, the Baltimore canvas seemed to be "a very high quality work of the studio" (letter of January 5, 1977). Terisio Pignatti in his catalogue raisonné has called the Baltimore painting "luministico,"[40] a term indicating contrast of light and shadow and the use of spotlighting. These features are not typical of Veronese, as Pignatti explains, but can be encountered in the works of Jacopo Bassano and in those of Carletto Caliari, Paolo's younger son, who was trained not only by his father but also by Jacopo Bassano. Though it is tremendously difficult to ascribe a workshop replica that is very close to the original to one specific member of the *bottega,* Pignatti has attributed the Baltimore *Holy Family with St. Barbara,* at least tentatively, to Carletto. On the other hand, Rearick has remarked that Carletto's tonality and his Bassano-influenced attention to precise detail of surface description are not to be found in the Baltimore painting. It is rather with Paolo's brother Benedetto that Rearick finds a probable association.[41] Until these questions can be resolved the picture will have to be listed simply as a work by the "Haeredes Pauli Veronensis," or even in a more general manner, "Workshop of Paolo Caliari, called Veronese."

RELATED VERSIONS

In addition to the Baltimore Museum painting, four other early versions of the Uffizi *Holy Family with St. Barbara* have come to the attention of this writer. So far no information has surfaced concerning additional replicas. In any case the Veronese picture must have been very popular to have prompted such a large number of repetitions.

For various reasons I could not see the four copies themselves, but at least two of the versions have been thoroughly examined by well-known experts, and the various data, photographs, and transparencies were scrutinized by the present writer.

In a letter of December 22, 1975 (curatorial files, The Baltimore Museum of Art), Federico Zeri refers to a relatively small replica (fig. 5) in a Swiss private collection which he considers to be of an early date and of special merit. This replica is distinguished by unusual freshness of color and a directness and spontaneity that are difficult to explain in view of its similarity to the other renditions. It differs markedly in only one aspect: the face of the Virgin appears greatly changed in comparison with the original and with all other versions; the Swiss painting shows a younger and even more serene Madonna. The question has sometimes been raised whether this small painting might have been a *modello.* However, certain features, among them its highly finished condition, refute the idea that it could have served as a sketch before the completion of the original.

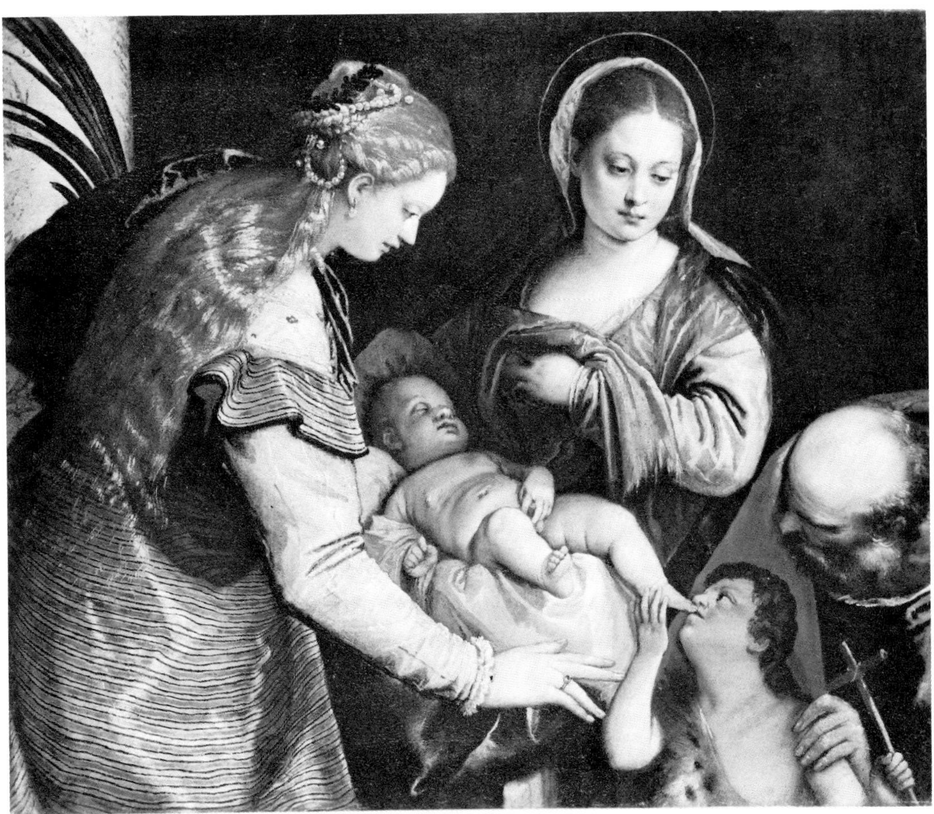

Fig. 5. Attributed to Paolo Veronese, *Holy Family with St. Barbara and Young St. John.* Oil on canvas. 20⅞ × 24¹³⁄₁₆ inches (53 × 63 cm.). Private collection, Switzerland

To judge from a photograph in the Frick Art Reference Library, another copy of the *Holy Family with St. Barbara* (oil on canvas; 19¾ × 26¾ inches; 50.2 × 67.9 cm.) seems to be of good quality and very similar to the Swiss version except for the expression on the Virgin's face. The information provided on the back of the Frick Library photograph (16C-427 Mus) refers to the picture as "a very exact copy of the Uffizi painting." The canvas originally was part of the James Jackson Jarves Collection with which it was first exhibited in New York in 1860 and then in 1863 at the New-York Historical Society. According to information received from The Cleveland Museum of Art, the picture is listed as no. 35, *Marriage of St. Catherine,* in James Jackson Jarves, *Handbook for Visitors to the Hollenden Gallery of Old Masters* (Cleveland, 1884). In the same year it was bought by Liberty E. Holden of Cleveland and was given in 1916 to The Cleveland Museum of Art by Mrs. Liberty E. Holden as part of her collection. It is listed as *Marriage of St. Catherine* in the publication by Stella Rubinstein, *Catalogue of a Collection of Paintings Presented by Mrs. L. E. Holden to the Cleveland Museum* (Cleveland, 1917), no. 42. The picture is accurately described by the author of the catalogue who explains the awkward pose of the Virgin's left hand by saying that the Madonna might have just closed her bodice after nursing her Child. In 1929 the painting with other works from the Holden Collection was returned to members of the family; its present location is not known.

Still another copy which seems to have disappeared is known today only through color reproductions, one of which is in the Frick Art Reference Library (707-11 j). It is called *Study for the Sacra Conversazione in the Uffizi.* Medium, support, and size are given as oil on paper, applied to panel, 14⅞ × 16⅞ inches (37.7 × 42.3 cm.). In its overall appearance

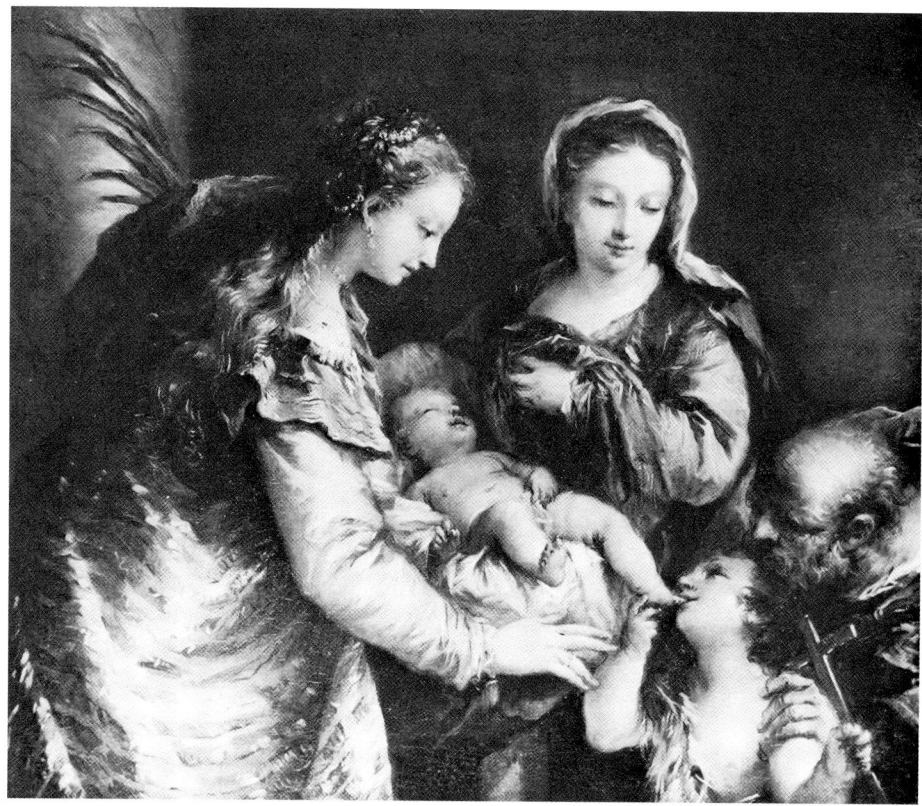

Fig. 6. Gian Antonio Guardi, *Holy Family with St. John and a Female Martyr (Holy Family with St. Barbara)*. Oil on canvas. 23⅞ × 27 inches (60.6 × 68.5 cm.). Seattle Art Museum, Samuel H. Kress Collection, Seattle, Washington

and in all details except for the Virgin's face (different in all versions) and a brown tone which seems to cover the entire picture, this small painting closely follows the original. Whether the brown color is due to dirty varnish cannot be determined from the photograph. The picture was in the Augusto Lurato Collection, Milan, which on April 18–21, 1928, was sold at the Galleria Pesaro, Milan. Since then no trace of the picture has been found. At the time of the sale it was reproduced in color in the "Illustrated Supplement of Sale" (of the Lurato Collection), p. 6, pl. 5, and was referred to as a "color study for the Madonna with St. Barbara and the Infant Baptist in the Uffizi." The accuracy of this claim can only be determined if the picture is rediscovered. Until then it must be considered a copy, and at best, one produced by the "Haeredes Paoli."

The Seattle Art Museum, Samuel H. Kress Collection, possesses the latest version of the Uffizi *Holy Family with St. Barbara.* This painting[42] (fig. 6) dates from the eighteenth century and is the work of a major Venetian painter, Gian Antonio Guardi (1699–1769), to whose brother Francesco it was formerly ascribed. Though the picture follows generally the composition of the original, it is not a copy in the usual sense; because of its differences in technique and color from the Uffizi canvas, it could possibly be termed a variation on a Veronese theme. As Rubens's renderings after Titian and Manet's copies of Velázquez or Goya illuminate special characteristics of both the originator of the painting and the "imitator," so does Guardi's version point up various features of his own style and, by contrast, qualities typical of Veronese which are not inherent in Guardi's version. Guardi has achieved a true Rococo painting, based on Veronese's invention, by making the figures, especially their facial expressions, more relaxed. He has altered the color scheme which has become warmer, more tonal than in the original or in any of the other copies. Here gold and Venetian rose in deep hues predominate, whereas Veronese's juxtapositions of color areas to assure great brilliance have been abandoned. Moreover, in Guardi's painting the brushwork is much looser, more spontaneous, and almost impetuous, often looking as if the paint had been squirted onto the canvas.

The various renditions of the Uffizi *Holy Family* have scrupulously followed Veronese's composition except for a single deviation occurring in the Guardi painting. While in all other versions St. Joseph has been pushed into the lower right-hand corner, here he has been given more space. It is in accordance with a Rococo painter's preference that Gian Antonio has opened up the Mannerist construction of the originally crowded area, thus achieving a charming eighteenth-century work.

Gertrude Rosenthal
The Baltimore Museum of Art

NOTES

1. For the impact of Veronese on Delacroix, see *The Journal of Eugène Delacroix,* trans. W. Pach (New York: Crown Publishers, 1948), pp. 170–71, 247, 249, 284, 298–99, 366–67, 528, 571, 627, 710–11; on Turner, see J. Ziff, ed., "Backgrounds, Introduction of Architecture and Landscape: A Lecture by J. M. Turner," in *Journal of the Warburg and Courtauld Institutes* 26 (1963):138–39; on Cézanne, see J. Gasquet, *Cézanne* (Paris: Bernheim Jeune Editions, 1921), p. 101, and (Berlin: Bruno Cassirer, 1930), pp. 128–29; on Matisse, see A. Barr, *Matisse, His Art and His Public* (New York: Museum of Modern Art, 1951), p. 129.
2. M. Levey, "An Early Dated Veronese and Veronese's Early Work," *Burlington Magazine* 102 (March 1960):105–11.
3. T. Pignatti, *Veronese,* 2 vols. (Venice: Alfieri, 1976). This publication contains a major critical discussion of Veronese's oeuvre as well as the first comprehensive catalogue raisonné of the artist's paintings.
4. For an excellent exposition of the "Haeredes Paoli," see H. Tietze and E. Tietze-Conrat, *The Drawings of the Venetian Painters in the 15th and 16th Centuries* (New York: J. J. Augustin, 1944), pp. 352–54; also H. Tietze, "Meister und Werkstätte in der Renaissance Malerei Venedigs," *Alte und Neue Kunst, Wiener Kunstwissenschaftliche Blätter* 1, no. 3 (1952):89–91.
5. Though there are some minor differences, the usual signature reads as follows: *Haeredes Paoli Caliari Veronensis fecerunt.* See, for example, the *Baptism of Christ* in the Cathedral of St. John the Divine, New York; for provenance, see W. E. Suida, "Paolo Veronese and His Circle: Some Unpublished Works," *Art Quarterly* 8 (1945): fig. 7, p. 187, n. 12.
6. L. C. Larcher, "Per Gabriele Caliari," *Arte Veneta* 18 (1964):175.
7. Their collaboration on a specific painting is described in a letter of Benedetto, in which he states that Paolo had devised the subject: "Benedetto made the first sketch, apparently on paper, Carletto sketched this idea on canvas, while the final execution fell to Gabriele." Quoted from Tietze and Tietze-Conrat, *The Drawings of the Venetian Painters,* p. 352; the authors of this book point out that certainly not all the paintings of the workshop were produced in this manner.
8. Pignatti, *Veronese,* 1: no. A6; 2: fig. 723. So far, the existence of four additional versions is known to the present writer; these pictures will be briefly discussed in Related Versions.
9. D. von Hadeln, ed., *Carlo Ridolfi: Le Maraviglie dell'arte . . .* (Berlin: G. Grote, 1914–1924), 1:340. Pignatti, *Veronese,* 1: no. 128; 2: fig. 372.
10. Von Hadeln, ed., *Carlo Ridolfi,* 1:340. Ridolfi's description is not completely accurate: St. Joseph's right arm is not visible in the picture; Ridolfi has interchanged the saint's right and left arms.
11. Ibid.
12. The writer Pietro Caliari saw the picture in the Tribuna, as he reports in his study of *Paolo Veronese, sua vita e sue opere* (Rome: Forzani & Co., 1888), p. 352.

13. Various experts have remarked that St. Joseph does not usually appear in representations of *The Mystic Marriage of St. Catherine*.

14. G. Fiocco, *Paolo Veronese* (Rome: Casa Editrice d'Arte, 1934), p. 112. R. Marini, *L'opera completa del Veronese* (Milan: Rizzoli, 1968), no. 85, p. 104, agrees with Fiocco.

15. See Related Versions for a brief discussion of the other early copies. *Holy Family with St. John and a Female Martyr* is the title used for the Kress Collection version: see F. R. Shapley, *Italian Art: Samuel H. Kress Collection* (Seattle: Seattle Art Museum, 1952), no. 25, p. 22. F.R. Shapley states correctly that the saint has no distinctive attributes.

16. The exception is the version by Guardi in the Kress Collection at the Seattle Art Museum. In regard to the shrub, see n. 39.

17. R. Pallucchini, *Veronese* (Rome: W. Krenn, 1941), p. 35.

18. A similar lack of deep space occurs in a variety of Veronese's works, notably in the *St. Zaccaria Altarpiece,* Accademia, Venice; see Fiocco, *Paolo Veronese,* pl. 24; Pignatti, *Veronese,* 1: no. 127; 2: fig. 370.

19. Caliari, *Paolo Veronese, sua vita e sue opere,* p. 352, n. 4, quotes fully Zannoni and Montalvi, *Nel opera della Galleria di Firenze* (ser. 1, vol. 2, pp. 85–88).

20. A. Venturi, *Storia dell'arte italiana* (Milan: U. Hoepli, 1929), 9, pt. 4:808.

21. C. Ridolfi, *Le Maraviglie dell'arte . . .* (Venice: G. B. Sgaua, 1648), 1:335.

22. T. Hetzer, *Tizian. Geschichte seiner Farbe* (Frankfurt a/M: Von Klostermann, 1935), p. 191.

23. R. Pallucchini, "Paolo Veronese," in *Encyclopedia of World Art* (New York, Toronto, London: McGraw-Hill, 1967), 14:746.

24. Ibid., p. 747. Pallucchini's observation on Veronese's handling of shadows may partly explain the Impressionists' admiration for Paolo.

25. Ibid.

26. P. H. Osmond, *Paolo Veronese: His Career and Work* (London: Sheldon Press, 1927), p. 32.

27. Osmond, *Paolo Veronese,* p. 31. F. Ingersoll-Smouse, "L'oeuvre peinte de Paul Véronèse en France," *Gazette des Beaux-Arts* 16, no. 5 (1927): 221.

28. A. Venturi, *Paolo Veronese per il IV centenario dalla nascita* (Milan: U. Hoepli, 1928), p. 62. Fiocco, *Paolo Veronese,* pp. 112, 41.

29. R. Salvini, *La galleria degli Uffizi. Catalogo dei dipinti* (Florence: Arnaud, 1964). L. Berti, *The Uffizi* (Florence: Scala Books, 1975), p. 109.

30. Pignatti, *Veronese,* 1: no. 127; 2: figs. 370, 371 (*St. Zaccaria Altarpiece*); 1: no. A125; 2: fig. 830 (*Mystic Marriage of St. Catherine*).

31. R. Pallucchini, *Mostra di Paolo Veronese.* Exhibition catalogue (Venice: Libreria Serenissima, 1939), no. 39, pp. 99–100; Pignatti, *Veronese,* 1: no. 127; 2: fig. 370.

32. Pallucchini, *Mostra di Paolo Veronese,* no. 27, pp. 76–77; Pignatti, *Veronese,* 1: no. 55, p. 34, pl. 4; 2: fig. 111.

33. Fiocco, *Paolo Veronese,* p. 111.

34. Pallucchini, *Mostra di Paolo Veronese,* no. 27, pp. 76–77. Pignatti, *Veronese,* 1: p. 34.

35. The Uffizi canvas measures 33⅞ × 48¹⁄₁₆ inches (86 × 122 cm.). The Baltimore version is 39 × 46½ inches (99 × 118 cm.). According to Fiocco, *Paolo Veronese,* p. 112, the Uffizi canvas was cut at some time. The Baltimore painting has also been trimmed: see Condition Report.

36. *The Jacob Epstein Collection in The Baltimore Museum of Art* (Baltimore: published by Jacob Epstein, 1939).

37. D. Rosand, "Veronese & Co.: Artistic Production in a Venetian Workshop," in *Veronese and His Studio in North American Collections.* Exhibition catalogue (Birmingham, Ala.: Birmingham Museum of Art, 1972).

38. So far as could be learned, the Uffizi painting has not been cleaned in the recent past. Thus the comparative comments on the colors of the original and the Baltimore Museum painting must be taken with caution. The eventual cleaning of the Uffizi canvas may reveal substantial color changes.

39. Similar foliage, also used purely decoratively, can be found in Veronese's *Allegory of Peace,* Capitoline Gallery, Rome: see reproduction in Levey, "An Early Dated Veronese," p. 106. Cf. Pignatti, *Veronese,* 2: figs. 57, 58.

40. Pignatti, *Veronese,* 1: no. A6; also explanatory letter of October 13, 1976, from Pignatti concerning the meaning of the term "luministico" (curatorial files, The Baltimore Museum of Art).

41. W. R. Rearick's comments quoted throughout this paper were made orally in December 1976.

42. See n. 15 for title and bibliographical reference concerning Seattle Art Museum version.

SELECTED BIBLIOGRAPHY

Carlo Ridolfi. *Le Maraviglie dell'arte o vero le vite degl'illustri pittori Veneti. . . .* 2 vols. Venice: G. B. Sgaua, 1648.

Marco Boschini. *La Carta del navegar pitoresco . . . in l'alto mar de pitura.* Venice: Baba, 1660.

Gustav Friedrich Waagen. *Treasures of Art in Great Britain.* 3 vols. London: J. Murray, 1854.

Pietro Caliari. *Paolo Veronese, sua vita e sue opere. Storico-Estetici.* Rome: Forzani & Co., 1888.

Giovanni Morelli Lermolieff. *Italian Painters.* 2 vols. London: J. Murray, 1892–1893.

Adolfo Venturi. *Storia dell'arte italiana.* 11 vols. Milan: U. Hoepli, 1901–1939.

Detlev von Hadeln. "Paolo Caliari (Paolo Veronese)." In Thieme-Becker, *Allgemeines Lexikon der Bildenden Künstler.* 37 vols. Leipzig: E. A. Seemann, 1907–1950.

Detlev von Hadeln, editor. *Carlo Ridolfi. Le Maraviglie dell'arte o vero le vite degl'illustri pittori Veneti. . . .* 2 vols. Berlin: G. Grote, 1914–1924.

Stella Rubinstein. *Catalogue of a Collection of Paintings Presented by Mrs. L. E. Holden to the Cleveland Museum.* Cleveland: The Cleveland Museum of Art, 1917.

Joachim Gasquet. *Cézanne.* Paris: Bernheim Jeune Editions, 1921 (Berlin: Bruno Cassirer, 1930).

Florence Ingersoll-Smouse. "L'oeuvre peinte de Paul Véronèse en France." *Gazette des Beaux-Arts* 16, no. 5 (1927):211–35.

Percy H. Osmond. *Paolo Veronese: His Career and Work.* London: Sheldon Press, 1927.

Adolofo Venturi. *Paolo Veronese per il IV centenario dalla nascita.* Milan: U. Hoepli, 1928.

Bernard Berenson. *Italian Pictures of the Renaissance.* Oxford: Clarendon Press, 1932.

Giuseppe Fiocco. *Paolo Veronese.* Rome: Casa Editrice d'Arte, 1934.

Theodor Hetzer. *Tizian. Geschichte seiner Farbe.* Frankfurt a/M: Von Klostermann, 1935.

Alan Burroughs. *Art Criticism from a Laboratory.* Boston: Little, Brown & Co., 1938.

The Jacob Epstein Collection in The Baltimore Museum of Art. Baltimore: Published by Jacob Epstein, 1939.

Rodolfo Pallucchini. *Mostra di Paolo Veronese.* Exhibition catalogue. Venice: Libreria Serenissima, 1939.

Rodolfo Pallucchini. *Veronese.* Rome: W. Krenn, 1941.

W. G. Constable. "Two Paintings of the Venetian Cinquecento." *Bulletin of the Museum of Fine Arts, Boston* 41, no. 244 (June 1943):25–28.

Hans Tietze and Erika Tietze-Conrat. *The Drawings of the Venetian Painters in the 15th and 16th Centuries.* New York: J. J. Augustin, 1944.

The Venetian Tradition. Exhibition catalogue. Cleveland: The Cleveland Museum of Art, 1956.

Rodolfo Pallucchini. "Paolo Veronese." In *Encyclopedia of World Art.* 15 vols. New York: McGraw-Hill, 1959–1968.

Luciana Crosato Larcher. "Per Gabriele Caliari." *Arte Veneta* 18 (1964):174–75.

Roberto Salvini. *La galleria degli Uffizi. Catalogo dei dipinti.* Florence: Arnaud, 1964.

Luciana Crosato Larcher. "Per Carletto Caliari." *Arte Veneta* 21 (1967):108–24.

Bernard Berenson. *Italian Pictures of the Renaissance: Central and North Italian Schools.* 3 vols. London: Phaidon Press, 1968.

Remigio Marini. *L'opera completa del Veronese.* Milan: Rizzoli, 1968.

David Rosand. "Veronese & Co.: Artistic Production in a Venetian Workshop." In *Veronese and His Studio in North American Collections.* Exhibition catalogue. Birmingham, Ala.: Birmingham Museum of Art, 1972.

Rodolfo Pallucchini. "La Pittura veronese tra 'maniera' e 'natura.' " *Arte Veneta* 28 (1974):133–56.

Luciano Berti. *The Uffizi.* Florence: Scala Books, 1975.

Sydney J. Freedberg. *Painting in Italy 1500 to 1600.* Revised edition. Harmondsworth and Baltimore: Penguin Books, 1975.

Terisio Pignatti. *Veronese.* 2 vols. Venice: Alfieri, 1976.

Terisio Pignatti. *The Golden Century of Venetian Painting.* Exhibition catalogue. Los Angeles: Los Angeles County Museum of Art, 1979.

XVIIth Century

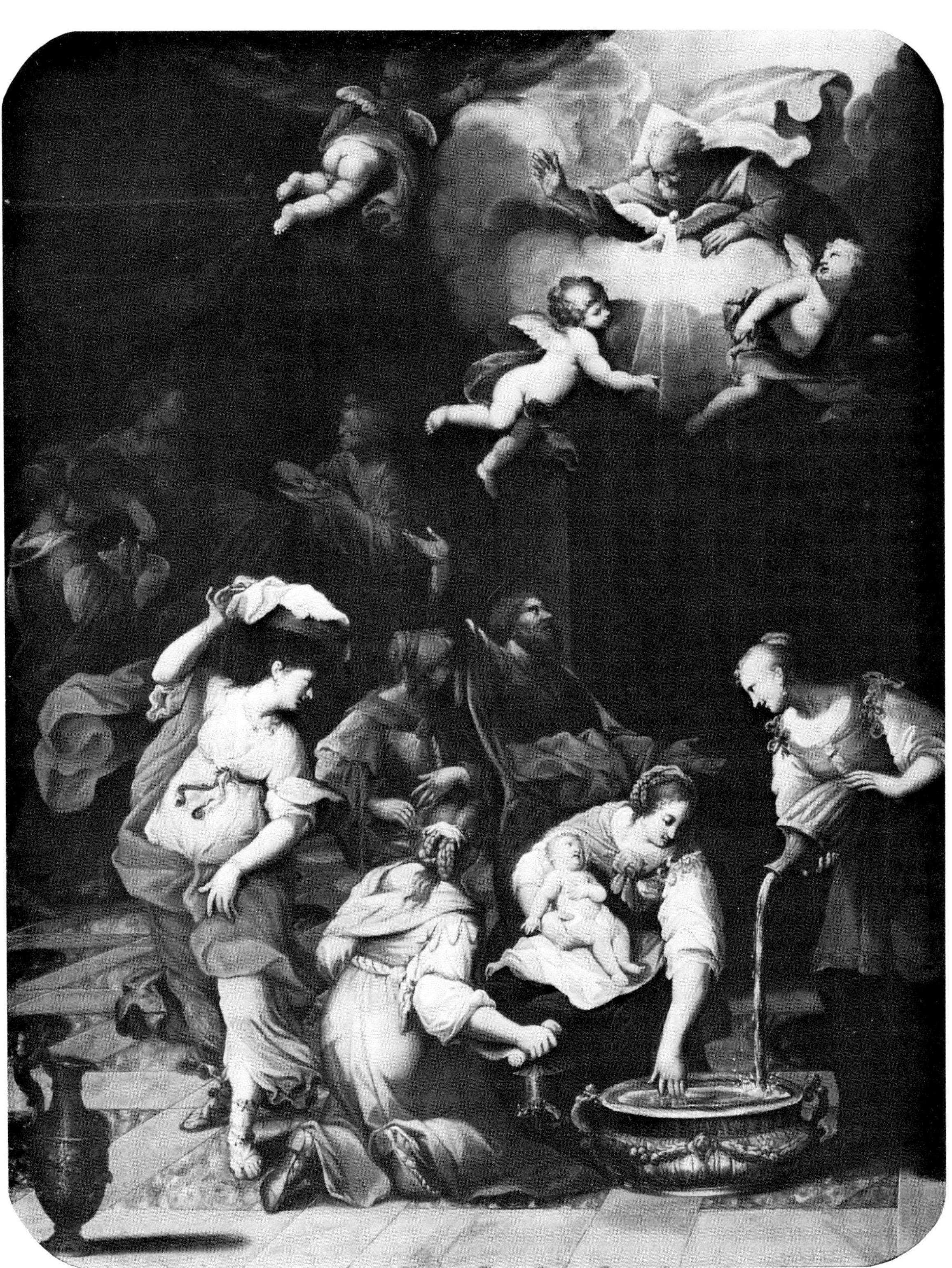

CENTRAL ITALY
THIRD QUARTER OF THE SEVENTEENTH CENTURY

16. *Nativity Scene*

Oil on canvas. 53½ × 40 inches (135.8 × 101.6 cm.)

Gift in Memory of Mr. and Mrs. William G. Read by her son, James Morris Howard, and his sisters, Miss Lilly Howard and Mrs. Alfred E. Hipsley (BMA 24.12.1)

PROVENANCE

Cornelia Read Howard

Mrs. Howard was the widow of John Eager Howard, Jr. (eldest son of the Revolutionary War hero, John Eager Howard), who, according to family tradition, is said to have bought the picture at a sale of the paintings left to an illegitimate son by Joseph Bonaparte, former King of Spain. No documentation to verify this association of the painting with Joseph Bonaparte has been found.

The following information, received February 9, 1979, from the Maryland Historical Society, perhaps may suggest the early possession of the picture by the Howard family: "There is a clipping of an ad in the *Baltimore Daily Gazette* dated June 20, 1863, listing an executor's sale of the effects of Mrs. Cornelia R. Howard which includes 'a valuable collection of oil paintings'." Our painting might have been in this collection but may not have been sold.

Given to The Baltimore Museum of Art in 1924 by James Morris Howard, Miss Lilly Howard, and Mrs. Alfred E. Hipsley

CONDITION

The fabric support of the *Nativity* is a plain open weave. The ground is comprised of two distinct layers: the lower one is red, the upper one is white. The paint film was applied as a moderately thin opaque paste with a somewhat low impasto in the whites, and transparent glazes for the details.

The picture received thorough examination and extensive treatment in the Museum's conservation laboratory in 1968–1969. Before treatment several old layers of varnish and dirt had made the surface appear very dark. There were a number of large blisters throughout and flaking had occurred in the dark areas. Along the original right edge approximately 1 to 1¼ inches are missing and were replaced during a previous treatment with a matching fabric that has since been removed. Upon removal of two old glue linings and cleaning the true condition could be assessed. Besides the losses from flaking, there was a large vertical tear (repaired) to the left of center starting by the handmaiden's left hand and extending up into the canopy of the bed. A horizontal extension of this tear went across the background and through the figures of the two lower putti.

There is also a repaired diagonal tear above the gesturing male in the center of the painting. In addition to the large loss along the right side, further losses due to flaking had occurred along the other three sides, particularly the left one. After the removal of old repairs, the picture was relined using a multi-layer fabric support and synthetic wax-resin adhesive. The paint losses were filled and inpainted.

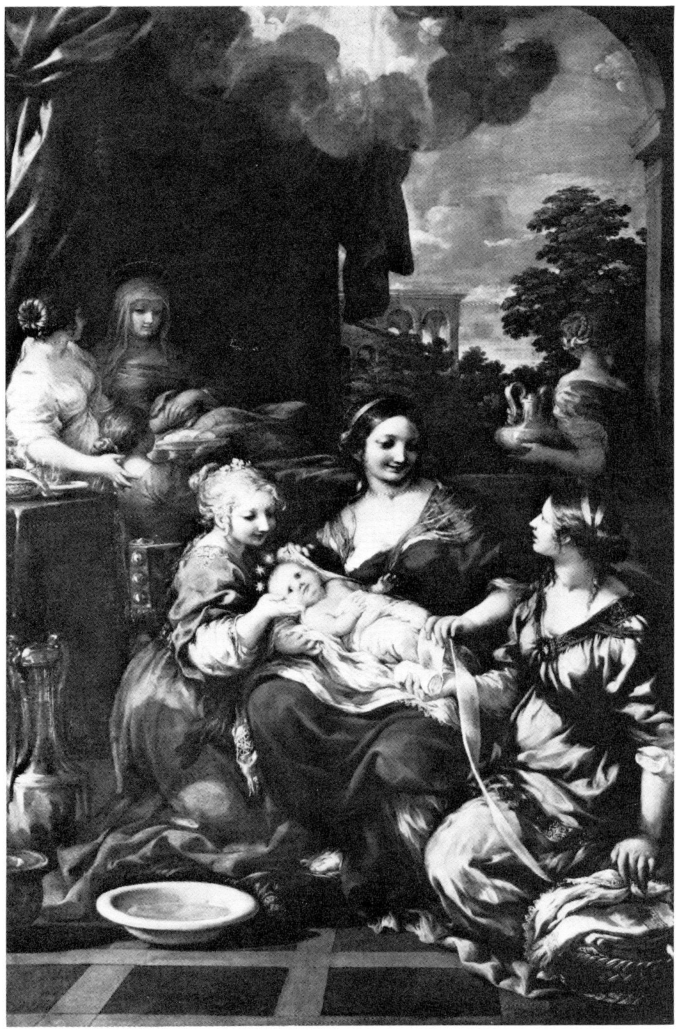

Fig. 1. Pietro da Cortona, *Nativity of the Virgin*. Oil on canvas. 97⅝ × 64⁹⁄₁₆ inches (248 × 164 cm.). Galleria Nazionale, Perugia. Alinari/ Editorial Photocolor Archives

Interest in this painting derives in part from the fact that it was one of the earliest gifts received by The Baltimore Museum of Art and that it was acquired in the nineteenth century by a member of a family associated with the events of the American Revolution.

The Baltimore *Nativity* has always been considered an Italian seventeenth-century work. There is no reason to challenge this assessment; however, an early attribution of the painting to Pietro da Cortona and the later relegation to his workshop must both be withdrawn. Comparison of the Baltimore picture with a *Nativity of the Virgin* of 1643 by Cortona (fig. 1) unequivocally demonstrates the considerable differences, both stylistic and qualitative, that separate Cortona from this modest craftsman. No firm attribution can as yet be offered in substitute, but general suggestions can be made. The painting is probably the product of a provincial artist working in central Italy (Tuscany as well as Lazio, Umbria, and the Marches). Although the situation is far from clear, this would seem to be the work of an artist of roughly the same generation as the Sienese Raffaello

Vanni (1587–1673).[1] A date for the Baltimore painting before 1650 seems doubtful despite the fact that the picture does not reflect developments associated with the Late Baroque style, such as the impact of the French Academy in Rome, of Antiquarianism, or a sophisticated exploitation of theatre design.[2] The beribboned shoulder ties worn by two of the serving maids reflect late seventeenth-century fashion and support a date in the third quarter of the century.[3]

Before attempting to interpret the problematic subject of this painting, it will be useful to consider the stylistic qualities and the formal organization of the scene. The space described in the painting is palatial. It is also unsettling. This is caused in large part by the fact that the floor—composed of brilliant white strips framing variegated marble rectangles within which are set alternately octagons of veined marble and circles of *verde antico*—improbably aligns with several disparate vanishing points located along the right edge of the painting. It is revealing that the artist does not attempt a three-point perspective system—the construction of which (whether drafted with mathematical precision or merely roughed in) was an essential skill of a seventeenth-century artist well grounded in the basics of his profession. A close look at the individual figures makes it clear that the artist was no more an anatomist than an architect.

What saves this painting is the enthusiastic embrace of color; what the artist lacks in *disegno* is, if not actually compensated for, at least obfuscated by the panache with which he adds color to the scene and by the enlistment of certain chiaroscuro effects to minimize the visual uncertainties of his architecture. In the far left portion of the scene, partially obscured by darkness, we note the presence of two maids and a woman who has just given birth and reclines in a bed placed beneath a baldachin (fig. 2). On the right-hand side of the painting, the background darkness is all but impenetrable, save for an area of half-light that reveals the termination of the marble pavement and the presence of a brick floor that continues back into the darkness. The line of demarcation between marble and brick would seem to be aligned with the gray wall section visible near the middle of the painting, suggesting two distinct spaces: one, an interior with polished marble floor, and another paved with brick and perhaps out-of-doors. But color rather than chiaroscuro constitutes the redeeming feature of this ingenuous work. God the Father appears elegantly attired in a soft gray robe and a cloak of rich purple. Below him, head raised and arms held open to the heavens, appears a bearded male, certainly identifiable as the newborn's father, who wears a long brown tunic and a gray cloak. It is, however, in the ladies' fashions that the power of the artist's palette is fully displayed. The handmaiden, holding a basket on her head, wears a *changeant* silk garment of pink, off white, and blue toned in gray. Her waistband is brilliant green and her cloak a bright red. Her large pearl earrings, her necklace consisting of strings of pearls and a jeweled pendant, and her gold bracelets pass scarcely noticed in this array of colors. She is the most resplendent, but the other women are scarcely less richly hued. The various accoutrements of the newborn infant's toilette are as sumptuous as the fashions of the women to whom the child has been entrusted. Bath water pours from a brass or golden jug into a silver basin ornamented with garlands and handles of gold. Nearby a gold-throated silver jug rests on the marble floor. In the lower left corner stands a lavishly ornamented gold pitcher. It is hardly surprising that the artist, aware of his artistic strengths and weaknesses, has bathed the foreground group of women in full light, thus concentrating the observer's attention on them and on their colorful garments.

Who is the newborn infant attended by such fashionable midwives and so auspiciously blessed by the Heavenly Father and Holy Ghost? Obviously, the birth of Christ is ruled out by the setting. This palatial room is no stable. The candidates are either the Virgin Mary or John the Baptist. A strategic fall of drapery obscures the infant's sex, eliminating anatomical clues. In reviewing the alternative identifications we must bear in mind the

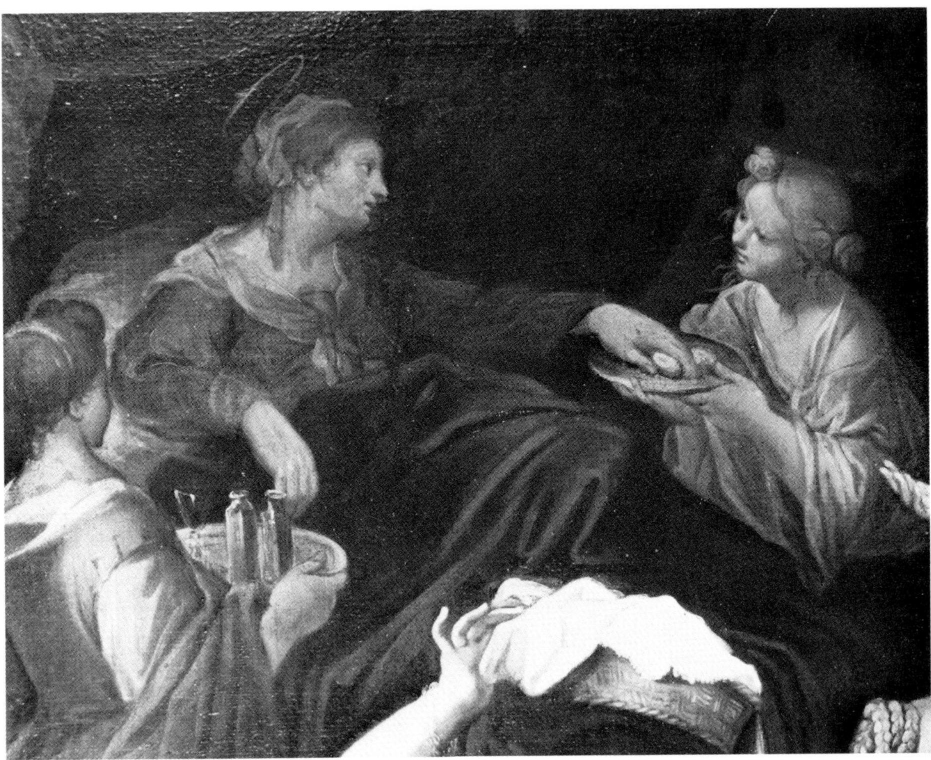

Fig. 2. School of Central Italy, *Nativity Scene,* detail of cat. no. 16

artist's untutored rendering of perspective; his command of the iconography of either of these events may be similarly confused. It is possible that he has assembled his scene from canonical depictions of both nativity scenes as well as from a variety of other visual sources. To attempt identification of this scene we will need to examine the principal textual sources for both events. When we do so, it will be apparent that certain features of the painting are particularly relevant to our inquiry. These include the presence of the Deity and the Holy Ghost, the presence of both parents, the ages of the parents, and the pose of the father.

The chief literary sources for the life of the Virgin's parents, Anna and Joachim, and the circumstances of her birth are to be found in the New Testament apocrypha, specifically in the Protoevangelium Jacobi and the Gospel of the Nativity of Mary.[4] These accounts indicate that Joachim was a man of great wealth and that he and his wife were childless. Although they do not expressly state that the couple was old when Mary was born, it is several times implied. In both texts Anna's circumstances are compared to those of Sarah, who gave birth to Isaac at a great age, and in the Gospel of the Nativity of Mary the couple is described as having lived childless for twenty years in their own house. In neither account is there mention of Joachim's presence at the moment of birth, and although he has several conversations with the angel of the Lord, he receives no direct revelation from the Deity. However, in the Gospel of the Nativity of Mary, the angel of the Lord expressly states that Mary "shall be filled with the Holy Spirit, even from her mother's womb."[5] The artist might have included the dove in order to stress the Virgin's investment by the Holy Spirit, thus providing as well an adumbration of the frequent manifestations of the Deity and the Holy Spirit in depictions of the Annunciation. Certainly the painting can be associated with the visual conventions of the Virgin's birth. An Antonio Salamanca print attests to essentials of this tradition (fig. 3).[6] This scene,

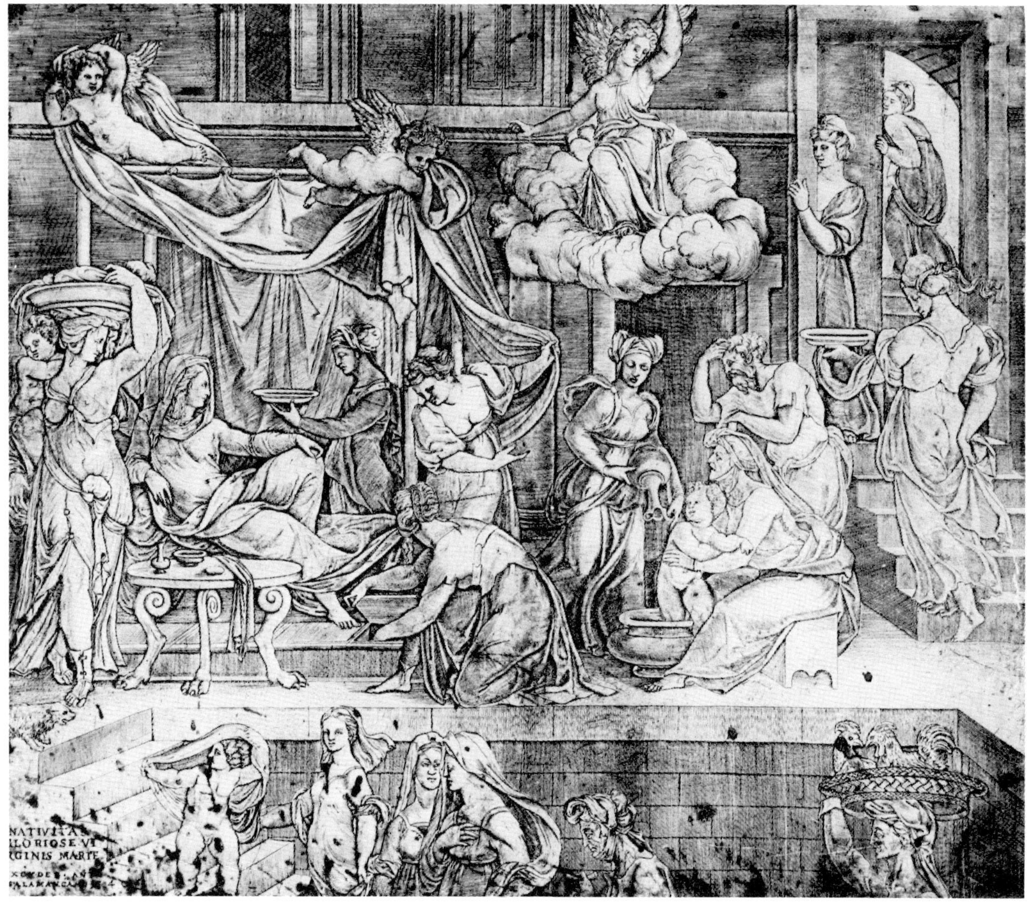

Fig. 3. Antonio Salamanca, *Nativity of the Virgin* (after Baccio Bandinelli). Engraving. 14⅞ × 17 inches (37.8 × 43.2 cm.). University of London, The Warburg Institute, London

apparently derived from a drawing by Baccio Bandinelli, is inscribed NATIVITAS GLORIOSE VIRGINIS MARIE EXCUDEB. ANT. SALAMANCA. 1540, leaving no doubt of the intended subject. Furthermore, the nude baby is unambiguously female. Above the infant an angel of the Lord appears. To the left, a rather youthful Anna is assisted by her maids, one of whom, holding a basket of linen on her head and a child in her arm, recalls the woman who pirouettes with a basket of linen in the Baltimore painting. The twin motifs of pouring bath water and testing its temperature are commonplace in nativity scenes; however, the latter motif is presented in such similar terms (albeit with pose reversed) in Lodovico Cigoli's *Nativity of the Virgin* in SS. Annunziata, Pistoia (fig. 4), that it is very likely that the artist of the Baltimore *Nativity* knew this work or an engraving of it.[7] Joachim does not appear in Cigoli's painting which is dated 1608. And this we might expect, for he was expunged from the Breviary in 1572 and does not reappear as a principal in the drama of the nativity until the second decade of the seventeenth century, when he is permitted even to witness celestial revelations, as in Andrea Sacchi's version of this event now in the Prado.[8]

What makes determination of subject matter in the case of the Baltimore *Nativity* frustrating is the fact that of the motifs we have inventoried, not one is exclusively associated with the Virgin's birth. The Gospel of St. Luke states that the parents of John the Baptist, Elizabeth and Zacharias, are "both stricken with age," and John too was

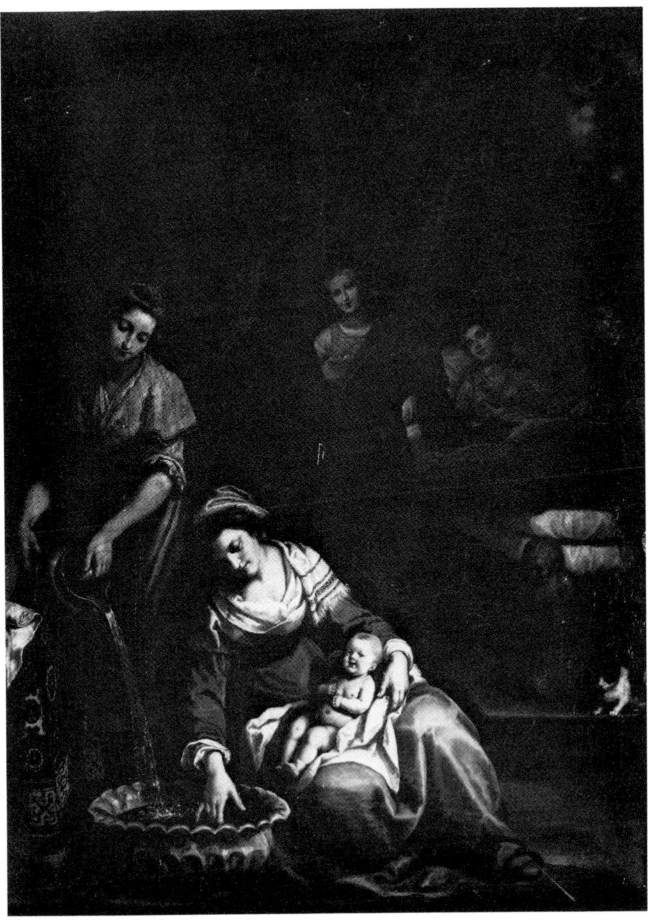

Fig. 4. Lodovico Cigoli, *Nativity of the Virgin.* Oil on canvas. 116¼ × 78¾ inches (295 × 200 cm). Gallerie fiorentine, Florence

"filled with the Holy Ghost even from his mother's womb."[9] The text for the Birth of John the Baptist and the Baltimore painting do share one important feature—namely, the prominent role assigned to the father of the newborn child. When the angel Gabriel announced the forthcoming birth of a son, Zacharias doubted and was therefore struck dumb until after the birth of his son.[10] Zacharias remained mute until the eighth day, when, on the occasion of John's circumcision, Zacharias wrote his son's name on a tablet, regained the power of speech, and, filled with the Holy Ghost, foretold John's future accomplishments.[11]

In keeping with his role in these events, Zacharias, when he is depicted at the nativity of his son, is given a markedly dramatic pose. He witnesses divine manifestations—a burst of light, often accompanied by joyous angels—which are not visible to others in the scene: this occurs, for example, in paintings of the birth of John the Baptist painted by Lodovico Carracci and by Andrea Sacchi.[12] It is a longstanding tradition in the visual arts that Zacharias be depicted as an active witness to the birth of his son. In medieval representations, the Baptist's birth, his naming, and Zacharias's prophecy were sometimes conflated into a single image. In the Drogo Sacramentary, for example, Zacharias in an orant pose makes the prophecy of his son's mission within a single illuminated letter and in close juxtaposition to the birth scene.[13] The male figure, nimbed and bearded, who stands with arms outstretched, gazing toward the heavens in the Baltimore painting, may

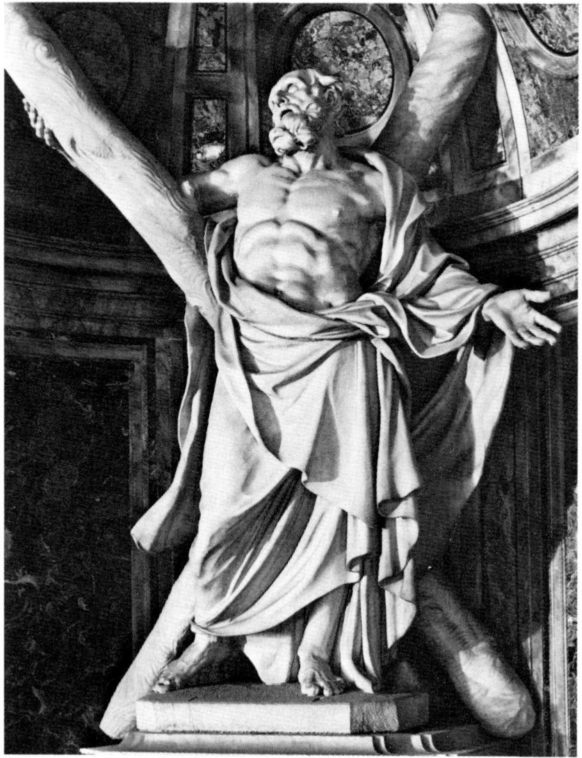

Fig. 5. François Duquesnoy, *St. Andrew*. Marble. Over life-size. St. Peter's, Rome. Alinari/Editorial Photocolor Archives

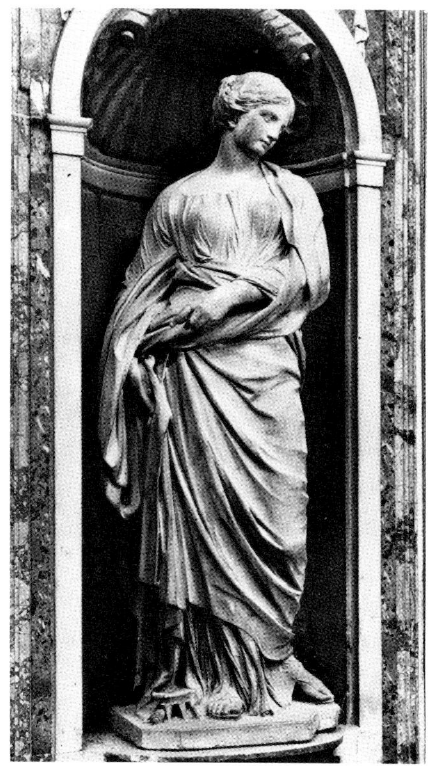

Fig. 6. François Duquesnoy, *St. Susanna*. Marble. Over life-size. Sta. Maria di Loreto, Rome. Alinari/Editorial Photocolor Archives

be a direct descendant of this traditional portrayal of Zacharias. A desire to present him in an emphatic, declamatory pose would seem to have led the artist to use a pose Gianlorenzo Bernini had created for his *St. Longinus* (1629–1638) and for the design of François Duquesnoy's *St. Andrew* (1629–1640; fig. 5) at the crossing in St. Peter's, Rome.[14] The female next to this figure is also derived from a sculptural source: in this case the association with Duquesnoy is clearly the ever popular *St. Susanna* (1629–1633) in Sta. Maria di Loreto (fig. 6). The emphatic gesture of the male figure argues for the interpretation of this scene as a nativity of John the Baptist. The simultaneous appearance of the Lord and the Holy Ghost in a nativity scene seems to be a unique event. God the Father can be found in nativities of the Virgin, such as those by Sebastiano del Piombo and Annibale Carracci.[15] In these examples, however, Joachim is placed in the background and the Holy Ghost is not in evidence. God the Father, cloudborne and accompanied by angels but without the Holy Dove, also appears in a print after Giulio Romano of the *Nativity of John the Baptist,* but Zacharias is not present.[16]

The subject of the Baltimore painting remains perplexingly ambiguous. Its iconographical motifs do not decisively clarify the subject. As we have noted, the sex of the child is hidden. The actions of bathing the child, testing the water, pouring water from a jug, carrying linens, unrolling a belly band are generic to depictions of the nativity of both John the Baptist and the Virgin, as are the ages of the parents or the fact that they and their child are nimbed. The presence of the Deity has no corroboration in the text of either nativity, but there are precedents for His appearance in the visual traditions of both, although in no other example is the Holy Dove included. Of those particulars that most cogently suggest the birth of John the Baptist, the fact that both parents are portrayed as "stricken with years" and the pose of the father carry special weight. The fact that the artist derived his pose for the male from a Bernini-Duquesnoy figure type intended to depict a figure enraptured by a revelation, together with the placing of this figure in such a way as to render unambiguous his witness to the arrival of the Deity and Holy Ghost, suggest that he is Zacharias rather than Joachim. The account of John's birth records, albeit after the actual birth but in close association with it, the fact that Zacharias, like John, was "filled with the Holy Spirit" and that he did then prophesy the future accomplishments of his newborn son. Thus identification of the painting as the *Nativity of John the Baptist* would seem slightly favored, but by a scarcely significant margin.

The fact that the painting leaves its precise subject in doubt may be in part the fault of its creator, but we should not judge him harshly on this account, for far superior artists such as Lodovico Carracci and Andrea Sacchi produced scenes of the same subject no less ambiguous. It may be that the picture was one of a narrative series and that the preceding scenes (Joachim in the Wilderness or Zacharias in the Temple) and the following ones (Presentation of Mary in the Temple or the Naming of John the Baptist) would have eliminated all doubt of the identity of the newborn child and of the proud parents.[17]

Malcolm Campbell
University of Pennsylvania,
Philadelphia

AUTHOR'S ACKNOWLEDGMENTS

Several colleagues have kindly offered advice in matters stylistic and iconographic. I would especially like to thank Marco Chiarini, Mina Gregori, Philip Pouncey, and Ellis Waterhouse for examining photographs of the painting. Several others have discussed the iconography of the work, most notably and patiently Rosalie Green, Charles Minott, and Jennifer Montegu. The tentative conclusions concerning attribution and interpretation of subject matter are, however, the responsibility of the author.

NOTES

1. Cf. A. Marabottini and L. Berti, *Mostra di Pietro da Cortona,* exhibition catalogue (Rome: De Luca, 1956), p. 80, pl. 84. Indeed, paintings attributed to Vanni in places like Spoleto and Collescipoli but which are probably the production of local artists (perhaps working out of Narni) bear a slight resemblance to the Baltimore painting. See, for example, V. Casale et al., *Pittura del settecento.* (Treviso: Libreria editrice Canova, 1976–), 1: figs. 65, 335 (Vanni), and fig. 245 (Francesco Refini). Future publications in this series will provide systematic illustration and documentation of paintings in the Italian provinces. These studies will be valuable for resolving attribution problems posed by paintings by minor seventeenth- and eighteenth-century Italian artists such as this one.
2. For comment on the Late Baroque style, see R. Wittkower, *Art and Architecture in Italy 1600 to 1750,* 3rd rev. ed. (Harmondsworth and Baltimore: Penguin Books, 1973), pp. 363–68.
3. I wish to thank Dr. Aileen Ribeiro for this observation.
4. *Apocryphal Gospels, Acts, and Revelations,* trans. A. Walker (Edinburgh: T. and T. Clark, 1870), passim.
5. Ibid., p. 55.
6. A. Bartsch, *Le peintre graveur,* 21 vols. (Vienna: J. V. Degen, 1802–1821), 15:13.1.
7. M. Bucci, A. Forlani, L. Berti, and M. Gregori, eds., *Mostra del Cigoli e del suo ambiente,* exhibition catalogue (S. Miniato: Stampato a iniziativa della

Cassa di Risparmio, 1959), no. 40, pp. 101–2, pl. 37.

8. For a discussion of the suppression of Joachim, his return to popularity, and further references to this problem, together with illustration and discussion of Sacchi's painting, see A. Sutherland Harris, *Andrea Sacchi* (Princeton: Princeton University Press, 1977), no. 14, pp. 55–56, pl. 20, where further bibliography for the problem of Joachim's presence at the nativity will be found.
9. Luke 1:7, and 1:15.
10. Luke 1:11–20.
11. Luke 1:67–79.
12. For Lodovico Carracci's painting, see H. Bodmer, *Lodovico Carracci* (Burg: A. Hopfer, 1939), p. 125, and pl. 69. The Andrea Sacchi picture is reproduced and discussed in Harris, *Andrea Sacchi,* no. 56, p. 88, and pl. 118. Zacharias as a dramatic figure is also a feature of versions of the subject by Francesco Albani (Capitoline Museum, Rome), Pietro Paolini (Pinacoteca, Lucca), and Francesco Solimena (Bowes Museum, Durham, England).
13. See *Drogo Sakramentar, Ms. Lat. 9428, Bibliothèque Nationale, Paris,* ed. F. Mütherich (Graz: Akademische Druck- und Verlagsanstalt, 1974).
14. For the attribution of the design of both statues to Bernini, see I. Lavin, *Bernini and the Crossing of Saint Peter's* (New York: New York University Press, 1968), pp. 28–32.
15. For an illustration of Sebastiano del Piombo's *Nativity of the Virgin* in S. Maria del Popolo, see A. Venturi, *Storia dell'arte italiana,* 11 vols. (Milan: U. Hoepli, 1901–1939), 9, pt. 5:fig. 28; and for Annibale's painting, formerly at the Sacra Casa di Loreto and now at the Louvre, see D. Posner, *Annibale Carracci,* 2 vols. (London: Phaidon Press, 1971), 2:no. 110, p. 48, pl. 110a.
16. Bartsch, 15:443.26.
17. For examples of seventeenth-century cycles of the life of the Virgin and of John the Baptist, see, respectively, the series by Luca Giordano in Vienna (O. Ferrari and G. Scavizzi, *Luca Giordano,* 3 vols. [Naples: Edizioni scientifiche Italiane, 1966], 2:201–2, and 3:figs. 394–99, 402, 403, 405) and those in the Lateran Baptistry by Andrea Sacchi (Harris, *Andrea Sacchi,* cat. nos. 54–61, figs. 116–23).

SELECTED BIBLIOGRAPHY

Hermann Voss. *Die Malerei des Barock in Rom.* Berlin: Propyläen-Verlag, 1924.

Arthur McComb. *The Baroque Painters in Italy.* Cambridge, Mass.: Harvard University Press, 1934. Reprint edition. New York: Russell and Russell, 1968.

Alessandro Marabottini and Luciano Berti. *Mostra di Pietro da Cortona.* Exhibition catalogue. Rome: De Luca, 1956.

Vincenzo Golzio. *Il Seicento e Settecento.* Turin: Unione tipografico-editrice torinese, 1960.

Giuliano Briganti. *Pietro da Cortona o della pittura barocca.* Florence: Sansoni, 1962.

Ellis K. Waterhouse. *Italian Baroque Painting.* London: Phaidon Press, 1962.

Mina Gregori. *70 pitture e sculture del '600 e '700 Fiorentino.* Florence: Vallecchi, 1965.

Marco Chiarini. *Artisti alla Corte Granducale.* Florence: Centro Di, 1969.

Joan Nissman. *Florentine Baroque Art from American Collections.* Exhibition catalogue. New York: The Metropolitan Museum of Art, 1969.

Rudolph Wittkower. *Art and Architecture in Italy 1600 to 1750.* 3rd revised edition. Harmondsworth and Baltimore: Penguin Books, 1973.

V. Casale, G. Falcida, F. Pansecchi, and B. Toscana. *Pittura del settecento. Ricerca in Umbria.* Treviso: Libreria editrice Canova, 1976–

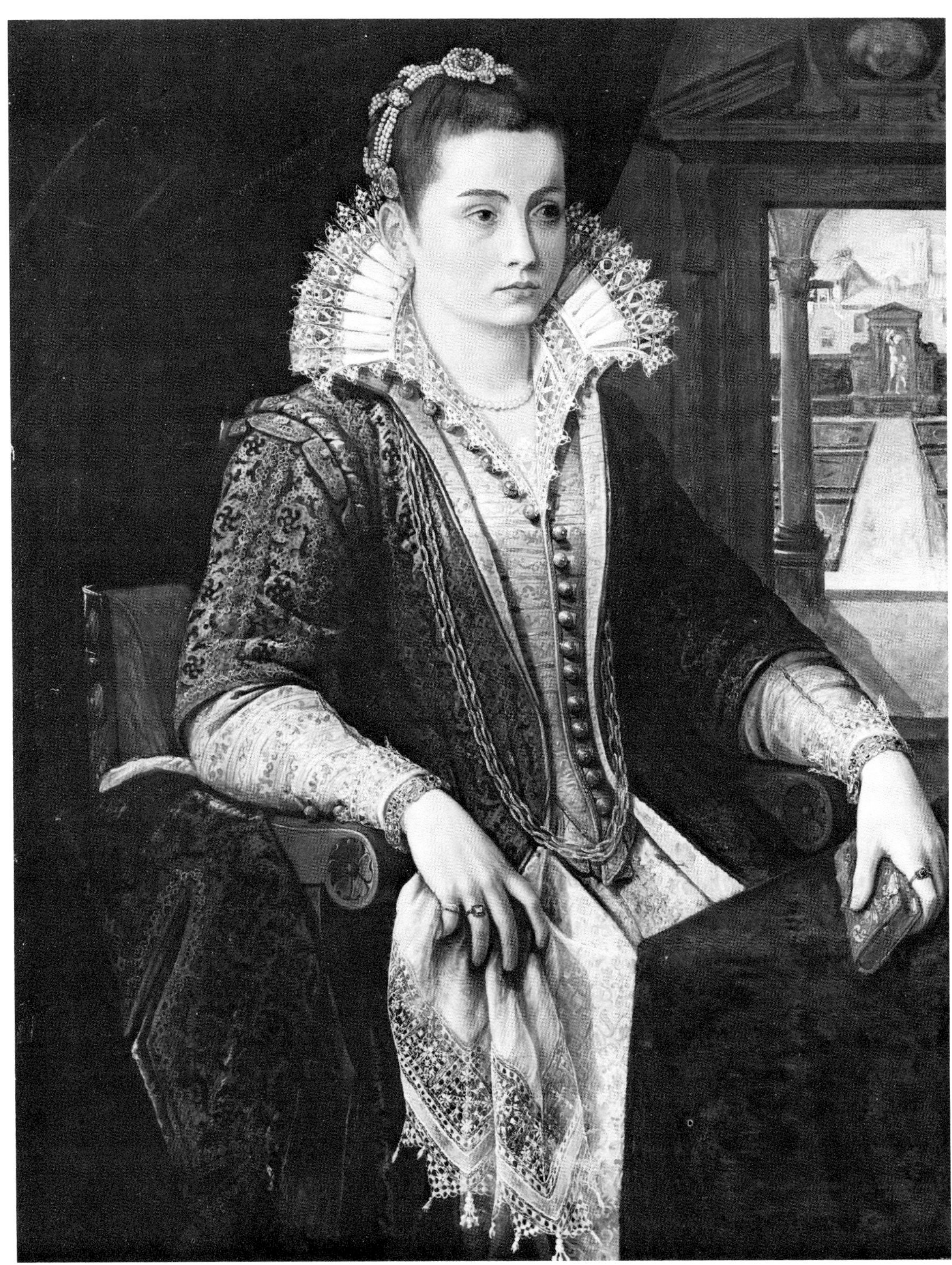

FLORENCE, EARLY SEVENTEENTH CENTURY

17. *Portrait of a Young Lady,* ca. 1600–1610

Oil on wood. 45⅞ × 34¼ inches (116.5 × 86.7 cm.)
The Mary Frick Jacobs Collection (BMA 38.173)

PROVENANCE

Mary Frick Jacobs, Baltimore
The previous ownership, said to be that of the Earls of Dudley, could not be verified.
Bequeathed to The Baltimore Museum of Art in 1938 as part of The Mary Frick Jacobs Collection

CONDITION

The panel, *Portrait of a Young Lady,* is made up of three vertical members held together by two horizontal dovetailed battens. Over the years, climatic conditions have caused the panel members to warp, resulting in a slight convex curvature. The left seam has opened up about one-third of its length from the top, and the right seam for the entire length. This movement of the panel has also caused separation and loss of some of the paint film. The losses are most noticeable along the splits and in the upper left corner. There are also losses across the top and bottom in the background, to the right of the head and scattered throughout the drapery.

Prior to its acquisition by the Museum, the painting had undergone some treatment. The panel had been infused from the reverse with a wax-resin mixture, and strips of fabric had been fastened along the joins, loose paint set down, and losses filled and inpainted. Detailed examination by the Museum's conservation department in 1978 indicated that during some previous cleaning, modeling and/or tonal glazing had been removed from the face, which now appears rather flat compared to the rest of the picture. Recent surface treatment has consisted of removal of the discolored varnish layer and overpaint from several different prior treatments, paring down fillings that are too high, filling in low spots, inpainting the losses, and resurfacing with a non-yellowing synthetic varnish.

Geoffrey Michael Lemmer
The Baltimore Museum of Art

This painting was first published in 1938 as the *Portrait of a Venetian Lady* by Sofonisba Anguissola (1528–1625) in a catalogue prepared by Henry Barton Jacobs, husband of the donor. According to this source, the painting was acquired "at the Earl of Dudley's sale at Christie's, London." However, neither inquiries at Christie's nor a search of sales catalogues at the libraries of the Courtauld Institute and the Victoria and Albert Museum have produced the description of an item similar to this painting in the catalogues of the various sales of property belonging to the Earls of Dudley at Christie's or other locations occurring between 1791 and 1938, the year the painting was bequeathed to The Baltimore Museum of Art. After its arrival at the Museum the painting came under closer scrutiny which led to a precipitous decline in its reputation. The attribution to Sofonisba was changed, the identification of the sitter as a Venetian was questioned, and the presence of repainting, then considered to be very extensive, was noted. The painting was withdrawn from public view.

Recently the painting was subjected to a more thorough review. Federico Zeri, whose wide-ranging expertise was sought, commented on this work as a "remarkable" portrait and urged that it be cleaned.[1] The cleaning revealed that damage and repainting were not as extensive as had previously been assumed, and the portrait has emerged from restoration as a work of modest originality, competent technique, and considerable art historical interest.

The painting depicts a young woman, probably eighteen to twenty-five years of age, seated in an interior space and turned to the spectator's right. A dark brown drapery fringed in gold braid and tied at the left corner of the painting provides a backdrop for the figure. To the lady's left in the background is a doorway surmounted by a broken pediment which is partially supported by consoles, of which the left-hand one is visible. At the center of the pediment, before an oval niche, is a bust of a nude female truncated at the shoulders.

It may be assumed that the bust over the door was once intact, and its decapitation points to losses along the top edge of the panel support, an assumption that is given credence by visible worm damage in this area on the back of the panel and along the right-hand edge of the support. To accommodate the missing head of the bust would require an additional strip at the top of the panel. It is also likely that a slightly narrower strip is missing along the right-hand edge of the support, a loss which exaggerates the awkward thrust of the left arm and hand of the sitter.

Through the doorway we can see across a loggia to the open air (fig. 1). The presence of a loggia is indicated by the appearance of one of its supports, an unfluted Corinthian column set on a plinth. The loggia is vaulted and enough of the vault springing is visible above the column to indicate that it is groin-vaulted in a manner common to Italian Renaissance architectural practice, especially in Tuscany. Beyond the loggia appears a series of predominately green parterres and a walk of reddish material (whether brick, crushed stone, or earth is unclear). At the end of this walk is a garden *aedicula* of gray stone, consisting of a niche with a pediment supported by pilasters of the Tuscan Order and flanked by wall sections topped by a pair of volutes. A marble statue of Bacchus accompanied by a panther is set in the *aedicula*. On either side the garden is defined by a high curb behind which there is a close-cropped hedge that partially hides a garden wall. Beyond the garden, the upper stories of simple city dwellings appear. These buildings are beige in tone and have pink-hued tile roofs. One of them has an attic loggia from which laundry flutters in the breeze, and from whose chimney gray smoke curls into a pale blue sky. In the far background can be discerned a tall structure which may be the campanile of a church or, more likely, one of the fortified towers built in the Middle Ages by powerful Italian families, especially in the cities of central Italy.

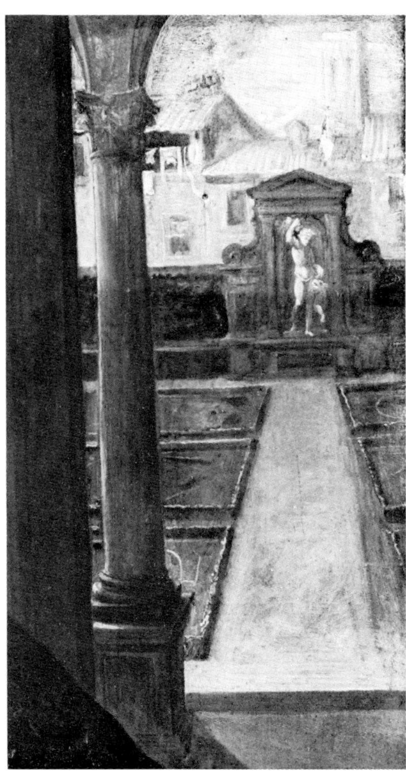

Fig. 1. Florence, Early Seventeenth Century, *Portrait of a Young Lady,* detail of cat. no. 17

The sitter is posed in a chair of a type popularly referred to as a Savonarola chair, a cross-legged folding armchair often, as in this case, with seat and back of leather fixed to the frame with brass nails. In front of the sitter is a table covered with a bottle-green cloth. The young woman wears her auburn hair swept up and held at the back of her head by an elaborate headpiece composed of strands of pearls embellished at nodal points by gold rosettes set with pearl clusters. Over her right ear is a rose, and at the crown of her head a daisy with petals of pale pink and white. The cheeks of the sitter appear rouged; her eyebrows are unplucked. Her pearl headdress is complemented at the base of her neck by a short strand of pearls. Around her neck, hanging to below her waist, she wears a double chain of oval gold links. At her wrists are matching gold bracelets set with red stones and what appear to be small cameos. On her left index finger she wears a small gold ring set with a red stone. A similar ring on the third finger of her right hand contains a clear stone, perhaps a rock crystal or a diamond, and on the little finger of this hand she wears a ring decorated with clasped hands. In her left hand the sitter holds a book, presumably a missal, covered in red leather ornamented in gold and closed by two silver clasps, one of which is visible; in her right hand she carries a handkerchief bordered with lace. A striking feature of her dress is the starched lace collar which is attached to a bodice unbuttoned at the neck. The buttons intricately worked of gold resemble acorns and, like the lace design of her collar, are repeated at her wrists. Over her bodice and chemise, which are predominately white and gold, the young woman wears an overgown of burgundy cut velvet. The costume of the sitter will be of further concern to us when we consider the date and place of origin of this painting.

Our consideration of the portrait's iconography (in the original descriptive sense of that term) provides a basis for its appraisal. The portrait does not require an interpretive analysis of its content: it is an essentially unambiguous image and its accumulation of signs and symbols are bereft of hidden meaning, for things are what they appear to be.

We are left with such basic but not so easily answered questions as the identity of the sitter, the authorship of the painting, and when and where it was executed. We will consider these questions in reverse order, being prepared to accept the fact that our analysis will yield diminishing results at each sequential stage. It is to be hoped that further research, initiated by this publication, may provide fuller answers to these questions.

When the portrait is approached in most general terms it is evident that it adheres to a formula that is Florentine in its essentials. It was in Florence that this type of seated pose, first developed in the Renaissance for the depiction of popes, and a vista viewed through portal or window, a motif initiated by the Venetians, were combined in portraits of secular figures, men and women of the mercantile as well as the patrician class. The Florentine artist in whose hands this formula was most perfectly compounded was Agnolo Bronzino (1503–1572), whose brilliant, seemingly effortless delineations and enameled surfaces were the epitome of the courtly style of the high *Maniera* as practiced during the reigns of Grand Dukes Cosimo I and Francesco I de' Medici in Tuscany. Every essential motif of the iconography of this portrait—pose, accoutrements of the sitter, and features such as the statue incorporated in the vista—is found in Bronzino's work.[2] The stylistic properties and also the architectural details discussed above point to the portrait as a work of Florentine origin, by a Florentine painter or by an artist deeply influenced by that school, and specifically by Bronzino or his followers.

Comparative analysis of Florentine portraiture in the second half of the sixteenth century and early seventeenth century is hampered by the lack of documented portraits. Portraits have been grouped and attributed in highly arbitrary fashion, and the situation has been exacerbated by an art market that gives progressively greater esteem to a work in this genre the more closely it is associated with Bronzino or his principal pupil, Alessandro Allori (1535–1607), no matter how tenuous or even farfetched that association may appear on the basis of visible evidence. Comparison of the Baltimore portrait with the work of Alessandro Allori, Girolamo Macchietti, Mirabello Cavalori, Scipione Pulzone, to name only a few artists, Florentine and non-Florentine, suggested by colleagues as candidates for authorship or close association with this work, produced no convincing leads. The *Portrait of a Young Lady* resembles in a general way many portraits of the period, such as the one from the Villa Poggio a Caiano, Florence, illustrated here (fig. 2). Presumed to represent Bianca Cappello, mistress and later morganatic wife of Grand Duke Francesco I, the painting is often stated to be in the "manner of Alessandro Allori." However, this painting and others like it differ from the *Portrait of a Young Lady* in the consistency with which visual forms have undergone an idealizing and stylizing process. The effects of this process, although not as evident in the portrait of *Bianca Cappello* as they had been in the portraits by Bronzino, are nevertheless recorded in practically every area of the painting. In contrast, the Baltimore portrait is painted in two styles: one meticulously records, with supererogatory perception, the details of costume and accessories; the other, freer and more sketch-like, describes, with a winning if at times awkward naturalism, the features of the sitter and more successfully captures, with disarming immediacy and painterly freedom, the vista seen through the doorway. Whereas in portions of the painting, particularly in the architecture, the impressed line of a stylus used to transfer the artist's design from cartoon to panel is readily visible to the naked eye, neither the face nor the vista bears traces of its application. In these areas the artist, painting *alla prima,* has captured the natural effects of light and shade on form. We note especially the reflected light along the left edge of the loggia column and the shadow cast by the column. In the depiction of the sitter, the effect of light and shade is also recorded, though less felicitously, as coming from a point outside the painting and falling upon the sitter from above and to the left. These touches of a nascent naturalism

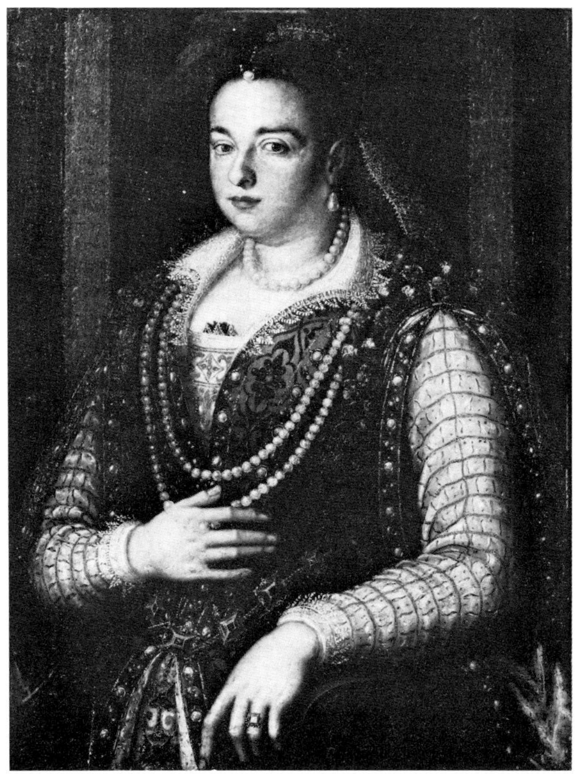

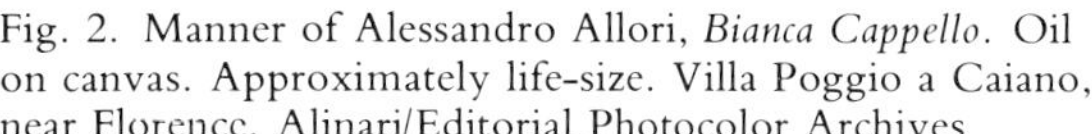

Fig. 2. Manner of Alessandro Allori, *Bianca Cappello*. Oil on canvas. Approximately life-size. Villa Poggio a Caiano, near Florence. Alinari/Editorial Photocolor Archives

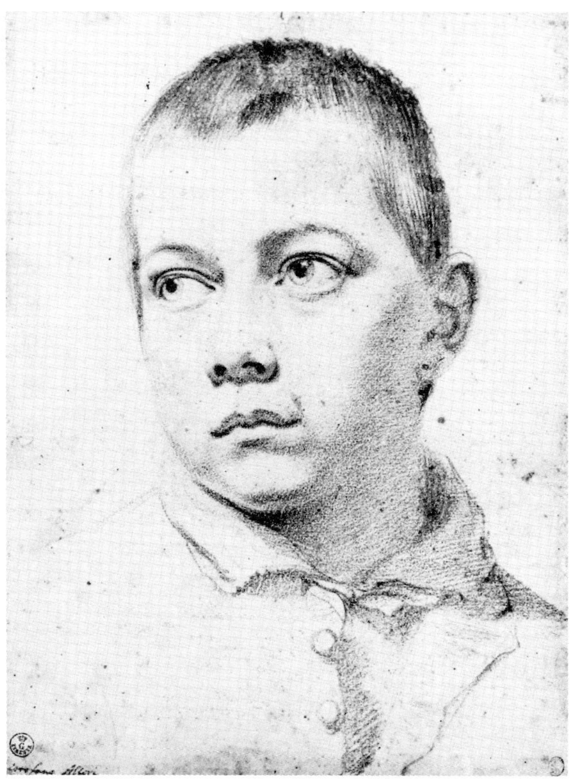

Fig. 3. Cristofano Allori, *Head of a Boy*. Red chalk on paper. $10^{13}/_{16} \times 8^{1}/_{4}$ inches (27.4 × 20.6 cm.). Gallerie fiorentine, Florence

suggest a date later than that conventionally attached to paintings of this Bronzinesque genre.

The handling of the sitter's facial features suggests an effort to establish form through the effects of light and shade. The artist seems to be attempting the qualities of illumination found in the work of the youngest member of the Allori clan, Cristofano (1577–1621), particularly in his drawings.[3] An example is a drawing, *Head of a Boy,* in the Gabinetto Disegni of the Uffizi (inv. no. 1505 5) which contains passages similar to those found in the Baltimore portrait (fig. 3). Although our knowledge of Cristofano's portraits is limited, nevertheless, certain idiosyncratic passages in the Baltimore picture—e.g., the definition of nostrils, the short chin, the pursed turning of the lips, the modeling of the ears, and a tendency to flatten the planes of the face nearest the spectator—suggest that the painter had possible connections with Cristofano or with his shop. The device of the averted gaze, used by both Cristofano Allori and the artist of the Baltimore panel, is not innovative: it appears occasionally in formal Renaissance portraits by such major sixteenth-century masters as Raphael, Titian, and Sebastiano del Piombo. What is new in Cristofano's sketch is the way the artist has captured the sense of movement in the youth's head, and the way he has convincingly described a momentary pose. The Baltimore portrait presents us with an unsuccessful attempt to use the same device in a formal setting. Unfortunately, here the figure seems immobilized, and the head, stiffly held in line with the torso, does not convey a sense that the sitter's attention has been only momentarily diverted. The portrait is like an effigy which the cosmetics of naturalism have failed to bring to life, suggesting that it may be posthumous, with the face derived from a miniature or similar source.

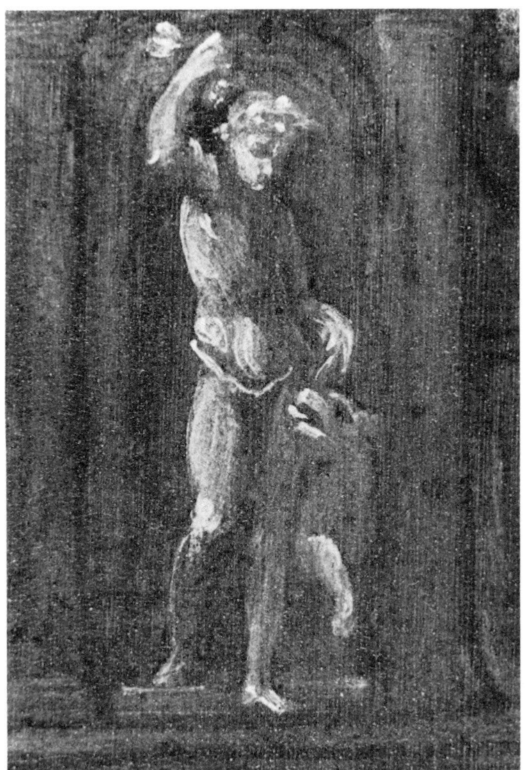

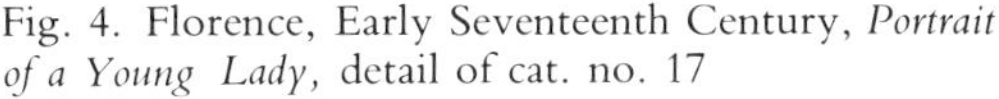

Fig. 4. Florence, Early Seventeenth Century, *Portrait of a Young Lady,* detail of cat. no. 17

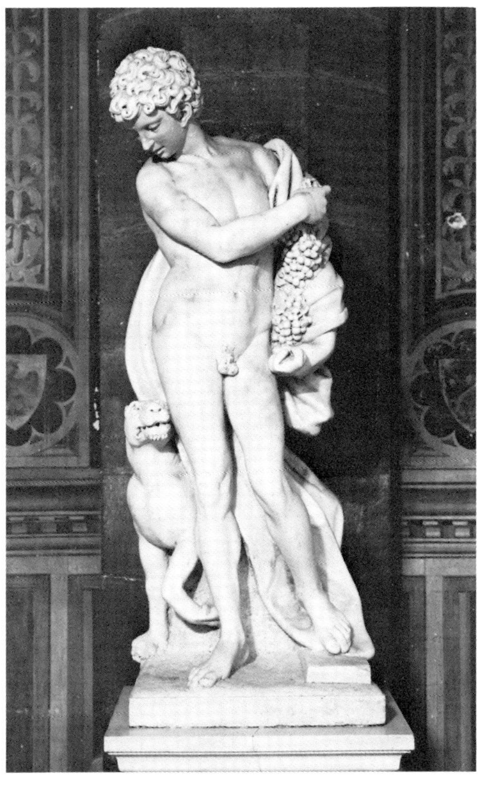

Fig. 5. Follower of Giambologna (?), *Bacchus with Panther.* Marble. Height, $53^{15}/_{16}$ inches (137 cm.). Gallerie fiorentine, Florence

To date, consensus has been that the Baltimore portrait is probably a work of the third quarter of the sixteenth century. The degree of naturalism present in the painting of face and garden vista suggests, however, that a later dating is warranted. To assign the portrait to the late sixteenth century is to attribute to the painter progressive and innovative capacities that neither the sharp dualities of style nor the weaknesses in design will allow. Rather, the portrait would seem the work of a capable but somewhat conventional early seventeenth-century artist who is responding to the innovations of his immediate predecessors and more adventurous contemporaries.

Several additional details in the painting support the proposal of an early seventeenth-century date. These include the garden *aedicula,* whose heavy volutes suggest the architecture found in Florence and Tuscany after the death of Grand Duke Francesco and during the reigns of Grand Dukes Ferdinand I and Cosimo II. Even the statue of Bacchus supports such a date. Antique figures of Bacchus are generally shown standing at ease. Their movement consists of no more than a slight *contrapposto,* and interaction with their feline companion is usually limited to dousing the creature with wine from a jug or proffering grapes.[4] In contrast, the Bacchus in the Baltimore painting appears to step forward, simultaneously turning to regard the panther whom he teases with a bunch of grapes held aloft in his right hand (fig. 4). This complex action has no precise prototype in antique or Renaissance sculpture. However, a little-studied work in the Bargello, Florence, stylistically datable to the late sixteenth century and perhaps by a follower of Giambologna, provides the essential elements: Bacchus's teasing interaction with the panther and, reversed, the spiraling attitude and suggestion that the figure is stepping downward and forward (fig. 5).[5] The Bacchus in the painting may derive from a similar

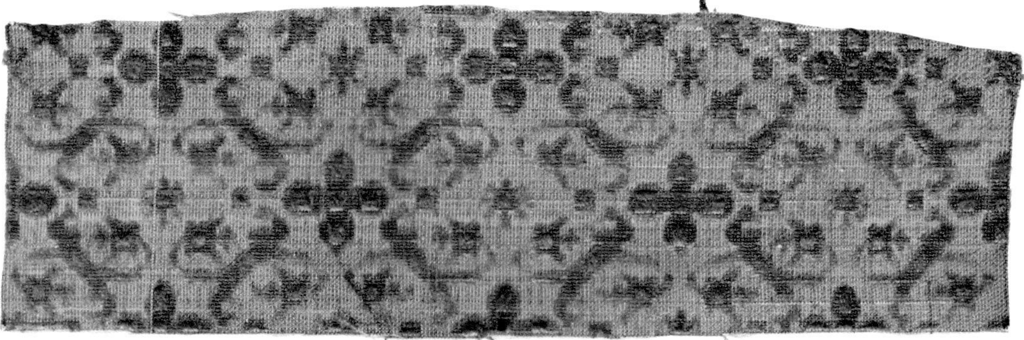

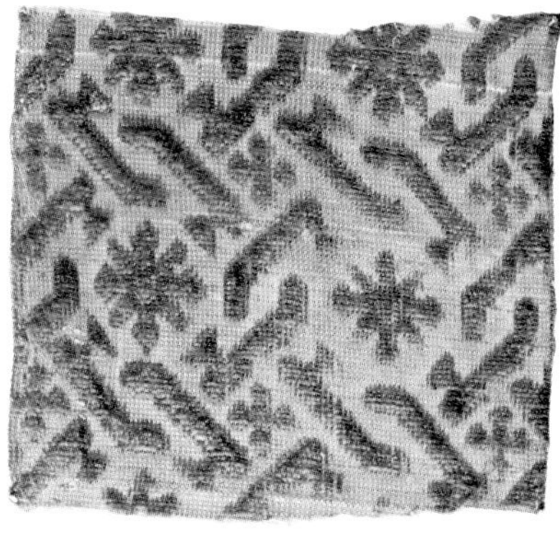

Fig. 6. Two fragments of Cut and Uncut Red Silk Velvet. Italian, Early Seventeenth Century. 3½ × 3 inches (8.9 × 7.6 cm.) and 9 × 3 inches (22.8 × 7.6 cm.). Victoria and Albert Museum, London

contemporary piece of sculpture, or it may be a free reworking of this much smaller and more juvenile figure. In any event, the painted version combines the playful interaction of Bacchus and panther, an action that is more contained in the Bargello sculpture group, and the suggestion that the principal figure is about to step forth from his plinth.[6]

The costume of the sitter and her hair style offer further support for an early seventeenth-century date. The same hair style and a similar costume appear among the drawings of Ottavio Leoni (1578–1630), now in the National Gallery of Scotland, one of which is inscribed with the name of the sitter and a date of 1617.[7] The costume worn by the sitter in the Baltimore painting derives from a fusion of Spanish and Venetian high fashion, just the combination of influences to be expected in Florence in the late sixteenth and early seventeenth centuries. A number of late sixteenth-century portraits approach the style of the sitter's costume, but none precisely repeat it.[8] The young lady wears an open overgown of cut velvet. This garment, known in Italian as a *sopravveste,* and generally described by its Spanish name as a *ropa,* has half sleeves, shoulder tabs, and wings. The young woman has raised this heavy garment and dropped it over her chair. One of the deep vertical slits made along its hem to facilitate movement is visible. Under the *ropa* the sitter wears a bodice that is partially unbuttoned at the top. This garment, stiffened with stays, terminates in a sweeping curved point called a *panchetta* in Italian, or in English, a peasecod. Under this she wears a chemise.

With the assistance of the staff and the facilities of the Department of Textiles of the Victoria and Albert Museum, London, it has been possible to compare the fabrics rendered with such care in the portrait with dated examples in the museum collection and to identify the materials depicted and their approximate dates of manufacture. The material of the chemise can be compared to types of silk damask produced in Italy ca. 1600.[9] The bodice and the matching lining of the overgarment are of woven silk, French or Italian manufactury, and of a kind produced in the first half of the seventeenth century.[10] It is, however, a comparison of the sitter's overgarment with fragments of

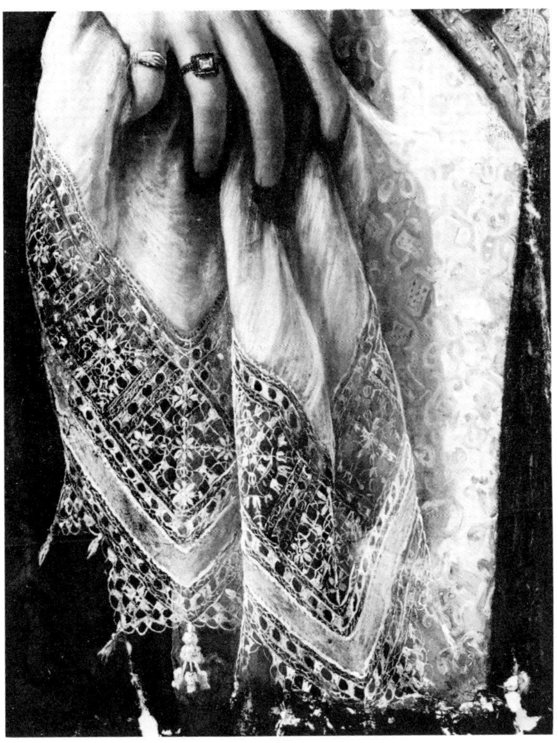

Fig. 7. Florence, Early Seventeenth Century, *Portrait of a Young Lady,* detail of cat. no. 17

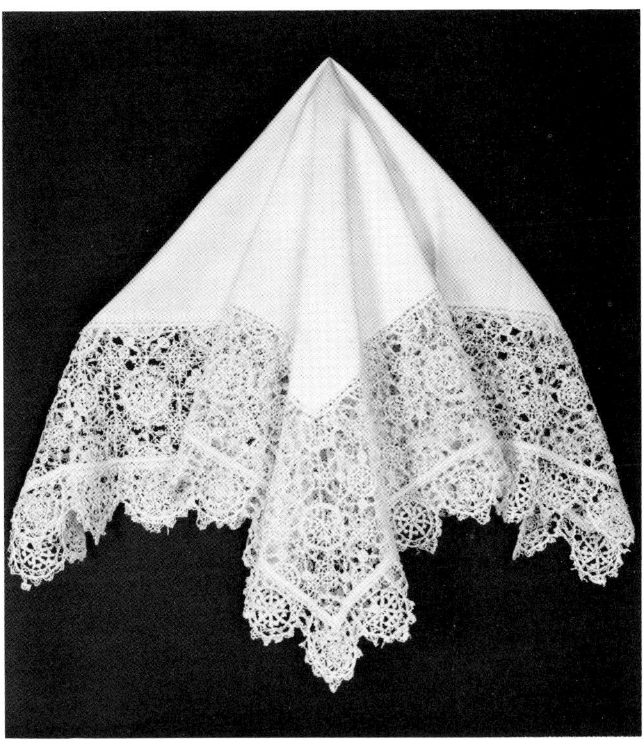

Fig. 8. Handkerchief Bordered with *Reticella* Needle Lace. Italian, Early Seventeenth Century. Maximum depth of lace 5¾ inches (14.6 cm.). Victoria and Albert Museum, London

Italian cut and uncut silk velvet that offers the most striking evidence. Two examples in the collection of the Victoria and Albert Museum (fig. 6) are especially close in color and pattern. The size of the pattern is of considerable significance for dating the Baltimore portrait,[11] as small-patterned velvets began to come into fashion around 1580 and were in vogue during the early seventeenth century. Before the late sixteenth century the patterned velvet used by dressmakers was actually produced for furnishings, and consequently the patterns were enormous, as in the famous Bronzino portrait of *Eleanor of Toledo and Her Son Giovanni de' Medici*[12] in the Uffizi, or at least large, as in the late sixteenth-century portrait of *Bianca Cappello* (fig. 2). In contrast to these earlier sixteenth-century works, the pattern in the cut velvet overgarment of the *Young Lady* is as small in size as the seventeenth-century examples and markedly similar in design. The lacework at the neck and wrists of the young woman in the portrait and on her handkerchief is of a quality commensurate with the bravura technique and fidelity to detail with which the artist has recorded it for us. The *punto-in-aria* needle-lace borders on the collar and the matching lace worn in her open bodice and at her wrists are recognizable as Italian of the late sixteenth or early seventeenth century.[13] And her handkerchief (fig. 7) compares favorably with a very similar early seventeenth-century Italian one in the Victoria and Albert Museum (fig. 8). The borders of both these handkerchiefs are of *reticella* needle lace; the painted example is rather more elaborate with its large and small tassels.

At this point we can return to the stylistic properties of the work, for the artist realizes in his rendering of the handkerchief two important concerns of the early seventeenth century: the dual artistic responsibility of producing an exact descriptive document of things and also of recording how light and shade actually reveal them to the eye. Thus he has painted the lace in such meticulous detail that it could be reproduced by a skilled lace-maker; at the same time he has recorded such optical phenomena as the way the light passes through the translucent linen handkerchief and through the intricacies of its lacework to reveal portions of the overgown and chemise which the handkerchief partly obscures.

For now, the identity of the young lady portrayed in her finery is unknown, as is the author of her portrait. Even without such desirable information, the painting is a valid period document and an attractive costume piece.

Malcolm Campbell
University of Pennsylvania,
Philadelphia

AUTHOR'S ACKNOWLEDGMENTS

The writer has benefited from the observations of numerous colleagues and friends. Luisa Vertova and Claudio Pizzorusso have been especially helpful. Aileen Ribeiro, History of Dress Department, Courtauld Institute of Art, provided generous counsel concerning problems of costume. The cooperation of the Department of Textiles of the Victoria and Albert Museum is gratefully acknowledged and, in particular, Santina M. Levey, Assistant Keeper of the Department, is thanked for her kind assistance and advice. Information gathered on short notice by Fiorella Superbi Gioffredi, Fototecaria at Villa I Tatti, and by Josephine Dunn is gratefully acknowledged.

NOTES

1. Written communication, based on examination of a photograph, to G. Rosenthal, December 22, 1975 (curatorial files, The Baltimore Museum of Art).
2. Cf., especially, Bronzino's portraits of *Ugolino Martelli* (Gemäldegalerie, Staatl. Museen, PKB, Berlin [West] and *Lucrezia Panciatichi* (Uffizi, Florence), illustrated in E. Baccheschi, *L'opera completa del Bronzino* (Milan: Rizzoli, 1973), pls. 13 and 21, and A. McComb, *Agnolo Bronzino: His Life and Works* (Cambridge, Mass.: Harvard University Press, 1928), figs. 2 and 5.
3. For consideration of Cristofano's portraiture, see C. Del Bravo, "Su Cristofano Allori," *Paragone* 18, no. 205 (1967):68–83, and G. Ewald, "Studien zur Florentiner Barockmalerei," *Pantheon* 23 (1965):306–307.
4. There are examples in the Villa Borghese, Rome (where the panther is missing), and in the Palazzo Pitti, Florence. See also the example in the Capitoline Museum which was bought by Pius IV in 1565 (G. Franzini, *Icones . . .* [Rome, 1599], E-4).
5. For a recent discussion of this work, see H. Utz, "Giambologna e Piero di Giovanni Fiammingo: Una proposta per 'il Bacco con la pantera' ed altre opere," *Paragone* 22, no. 251 (1971):80–83. For more comparative material, see M. Horster, "Antike Vorstufen zum Florentiner Renaissance Bacchus" in *Festschrift Ulrich Middeldorf*, A. Kosegarten and P. Tigler, eds., 2 vols. (Berlin: De Gruyter, 1968), 1:218–24; 2:pls. 115–17.
6. Very recently, a print by Marcantonio Raimondi that is similar to the sculpture group came to this writer's attention. (For illustration, see "Marc Antoine Raimondi. Illustrations du catalogue de son oeuvre gravé par Henri Delaborde publié en 1888," *Gazette des Beaux-Arts*, ser. 6, 92 [1978]: no. 336, p. 50). Depicting a satyr teasing a panther, this engraving provides a prototype for the combination of raised right arm and head turned toward the panther who stands at the left of his tormentor. Even the suggestion of some forward motion, a salient feature of the Bacchus in the painting, is present in the engraving.

7. Cf. K. Andrews, *Catalogue of Italian Drawings: National Gallery of Scotland*, 2 vols. (Cambridge: Cambridge University Press, 1968), 1:66 (D. 1754 and D. 2995), and 2: figs. 462 and 465.

8. See, for example, Federico Barocci, *Duchess of Urbino*, Museo Filangeri, Naples (R. Levi Pisetzky, *Storia del costume in Italia* [Milan: Istituto editoriale italiano, 1966], 3:fig. 109), and a portrait of a gentlewoman attributed to Scipione Pulzone in the collection of Victor Spark, New York (F. Cappi Bentivegna, *Abbigliamento e costume nella pittura italiana. Rinascimento* [Rome: Bestetti, Edizione d'Arte, 1962], figs. 454 and 455).

9. Cf. Victoria and Albert Museum, Department of Textiles, mus. nos. 1030–1888 and 503–1884.

10. Cf. Victoria and Albert Museum, Department of Textiles, mus. no. T. 68-1959.

11. Victoria and Albert Museum, Department of Textiles, mus. nos. 918-1887 and T. 143-1932.

12. For illustrations, see E. Baccheschi, *L'opera completa del Bronzino*, pls. 45 and 46, and A. McComb, *Agnolo Bronzino*, fig. 39.

    Eleanor's son Giovanni is sometimes referred to as Don Garcia.

13. Cf. Victoria and Albert Museum, Department of Textiles, mus. nos. T. 300 and 302-1912.

SELECTED BIBLIOGRAPHY

Adolfo Venturi. *Storia dell'arte italiana*. 11 vols. Milan: U. Hoepli, 1901–1939.

Arthur McComb. *Agnolo Bronzino: His Life and Works*. Cambridge, Mass.: Harvard University Press, 1928.

Henry Barton Jacobs. *The Collection of Mary Frick Jacobs*. Baltimore: Prepared and published by Dr. Henry Barton Jacobs, 1938.

Craig Hugh Smyth. "The Earliest Works of Bronzino." *Art Bulletin* 31, no. 3 (September 1949): 184–210.

Maria Luisa Becherucci. "Cristofano Allori." In *Dizionario biografico degli italiani*. 22 vols. Rome: Istituto della Enciclopedia italiana, 1960–1979.

Andrea Emiliani. *Il Bronzino*. Busto Arsizio: Bramante, 1960.

F. Cappi Bentivegna. *Abbigliamento e costume nella pittura italiana. Rinascimento*. Rome: Bestetti, Edizione d'Arte, 1962.

Janet Cox Rearick. "Some Early Drawings by Bronzino." *Master Drawings* 2 (1964):363–82.

Gerhard Ewald. "Studien zur Florentiner Barockmalerei." *Pantheon* 23 (1965):306–307.

R. Levi Pisetzky. *Storia del costume in Italia*. 5 vols. Milan: Istituto editoriale italiano, 1964–

John Pope-Hennessy. *The Portrait in the Renaissance*. New York: Pantheon Books, for the Bollingen Foundation, 1966.

C. Del Bravo. "Su Cristofano Allori." *Paragone* 18, no. 205 (1967):68–83.

Sydney J. Freedberg. *Painting in Italy: 1500 to 1600*. Harmondsworth and Baltimore: Penguin Books, 1971.

Craig Hugh Smyth. *Bronzino as Draughtsman, with Notes on His Portraiture and Tapestries*. Locust Valley, N.Y.: J. J. Augustin, 1971.

E. Baccheschi. *L'opera completa del Bronzino*. Milan: Rizzoli, 1973.

Mina Gregori. "Note on Cristofano Allori." In *Scritti di storia dell'arte in onore di Ugo Procacci*. Milan: Electa, 1977.

Claudio Pizzorusso. "Un documento e alcune considerazioni su Cristofano Allori." *Paragone* 29, no. 337 (1978):60–75.

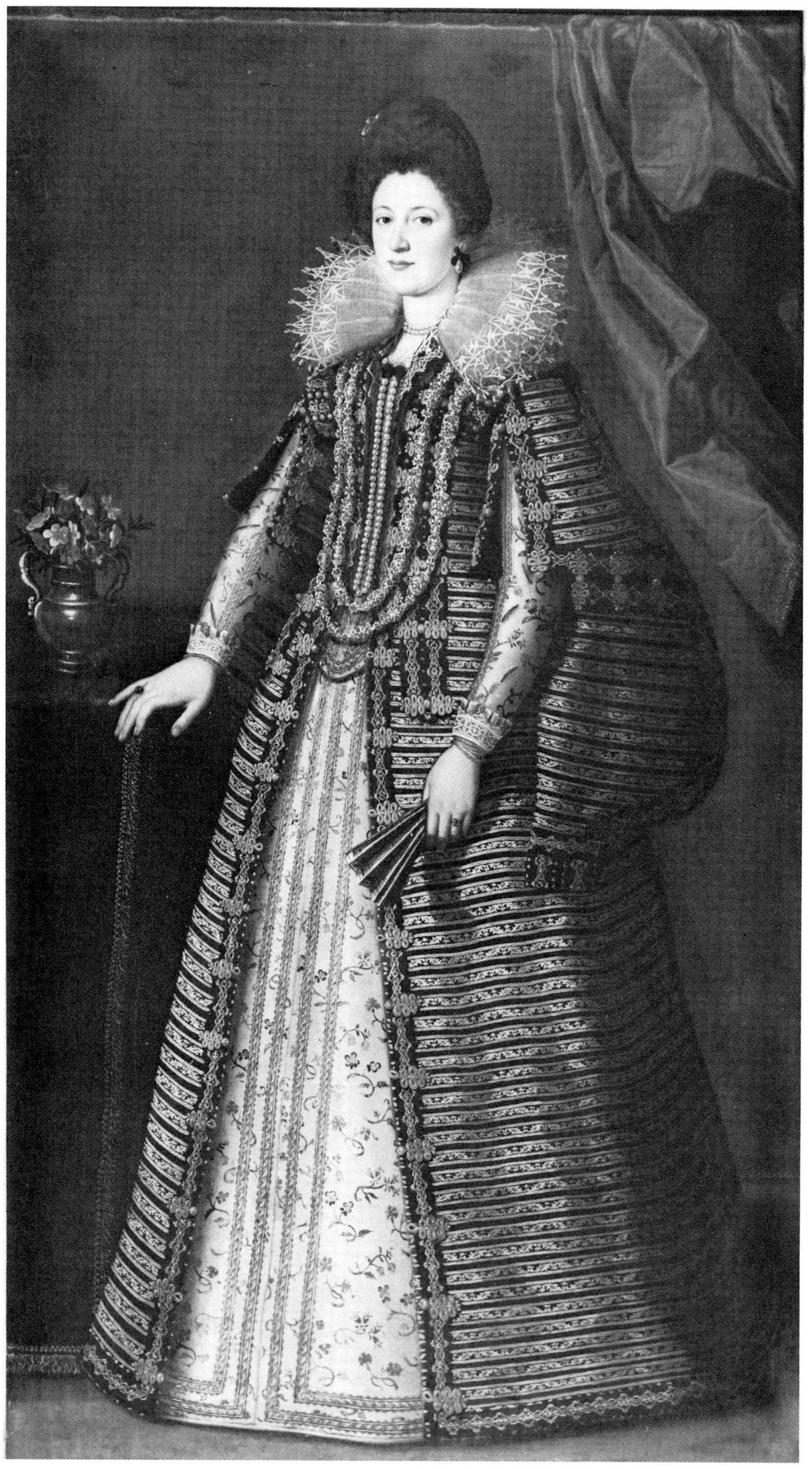

FLORENCE, EARLY SEVENTEENTH CENTURY

18. *Portrait of a Lady of the Medici Court,* ca. 1600–1620

Oil on canvas. 81⅝ × 43⅞ inches (207.3 × 111.4 cm.)
The Jacob Epstein Collection (BMA 51.102)

PROVENANCE

Lieut.-Col. Sir George Lindsay Holford by 1913
Sale at Christie's, London, May 17–18, 1928
Purchased by Jacob Epstein, Baltimore, before 1932
Loaned by Jacob Epstein to The Baltimore Museum of Art in 1932 and bequeathed in 1951

CONDITION

The fabric support of this portrait, which has a reddish-orange ground, is typical of the period. The paint film is for the most part opaque and thinly applied, allowing the texture of the canvas to show through. At some time prior to its acquisition by the Museum, the painting underwent major treatment. It was lined, probably with a glue-type adhesive, and backed with what appears by its stiffness to be a multiple layered auxiliary support. The original tack-over edges are missing, indicating that the painting may have been cut down during the course of the early lining. The added weight of this heavy lining has caused a ripple effect at all four corners of the support. At the time the painting was lined, two tears were repaired. One is at the edge of the red drapery on the right; the other, a large zigzag tear, starts on the right side of the lace collar, continues into the red drapery and ends in the upper right corner. There is marked abrasion from previous cleaning throughout the design layer. Retouching and overpaint associated with the repair of the tears and also abraded areas in the background have turned dark, particularly at the upper left side and across the top. The natural resinous varnish applied at the time of the earliest treatment has yellowed and darkened.

Since its acquisition by the Museum, the picture has not undergone any major treatment; this, however, is being contemplated for the near future.

The portrait traditionally entitled *Lady of the Medici Court* poses problems regarding the artist, the identification of the lady, and the provenance. Although these questions must remain essentially unanswered, the painting is of interest as a reflection of a specific moment in the history of the state portrait in Florence. As will be discussed, the portrait reflects a taste often associated with Late Mannerism in which physiognomical description was subordinated to style and to courtly conventions characterized by elaborate dress and a studied grace in bearing and expression.

The Mannerist costume—distinguished by the symmetry of its design and the profusion of contrasting textures, patterns, and colors—is a telling attribute of the lady's status and important evidence for the identification of the artist's period. The stiff, bell-shaped underskirt and the sleeves of her dress are of a shimmering silvery white material embroidered with stylized flowers that appear to be carnations, touch-me-nots, and pansies arranged in an irregular, open pattern. Small slashes in the sleeves reveal coral-red undersleeves whose color harmonizes with the carnations and the drape at the right. In strong contrast are the overgarment and the split and ballooned oversleeves of black velvet embroidered with a dense, horizontal pattern of silver and gold stitchery. In addition, the overgarment and oversleeves are ornamented with vertical borders of a lozenge pattern sewn in gold and silver threads, overlaid at intervals with gold frogged fastenings. The conical shape of the gown is emphasized by the two gold stripes which encircle the lower hem of the underskirt and rise in a bold quartet of lines up the center to the waist. This centrality is maintained by the pattern of fastenings on the bodice and by the studied arrangement of jewelry. A thick chain of silver openwork set with coral hangs in two heavy ropes from the shoulders across the bodice to the waist. Centered between them and joined with a black ribbon at the top of the bodice is a long rope of pearls which echoes the double collar of pearls at her neck. The symmetry of the lady's costume is further enhanced by the large, starched and embroidered open ruff spreading over her shoulders and framing her face. Her costume is comparable to gowns seen in Florentine portraits of the early seventeenth century. The bell-shaped, trainless gown, somewhat open bodice, and ruched lace collar are typical of the graceful Florentine adaptation of the rigid, tailored Spanish fashions of the late sixteenth century.[1] Other Florentine adaptations of European conventions are seen in the composition, setting, and pose.

The lady stands rather rigidly in a shallow space against a neutral background, holding in her left hand a painted fan, while her right hand rests upon the corner of a draped table. On the table is a silver or pewter urn of flowers, among which are varieties of buttercups and carnations that repeat some of the floral motifs in her costume. Her pose is one of diffident grace, in keeping with the restraint of her smile and gaze. As a display of virtuosity, the picture presents a portrait of a portrait, a kind of trompe l'oeil comparable to the play-within-a-play motif of Renaissance dramas (such as in *Hamlet*). The portrait has tacks painted near the top to suggest the attachment of a canvas to a stretcher (fig. 1). A covering drape of red silk is presented as having been thrown over the upper right corner of the simulated portrait.

Features such as the splendid gown, the rigid yet graceful stance, the impersonal expression, the high figure-ground relationship, the shallow spatial setting, and the levels of illusion, are artistic choices influenced by specific traditions and tastes. The pose, dress, and composition can be recognized as conventions from a highly codified vocabulary employed in state portraiture in late sixteenth- and early seventeenth-century Florence. We will return to the artistic and historical significance, the attribution, and the interpretation of the portrait after considering the provenance and earlier suggestions of authorship.

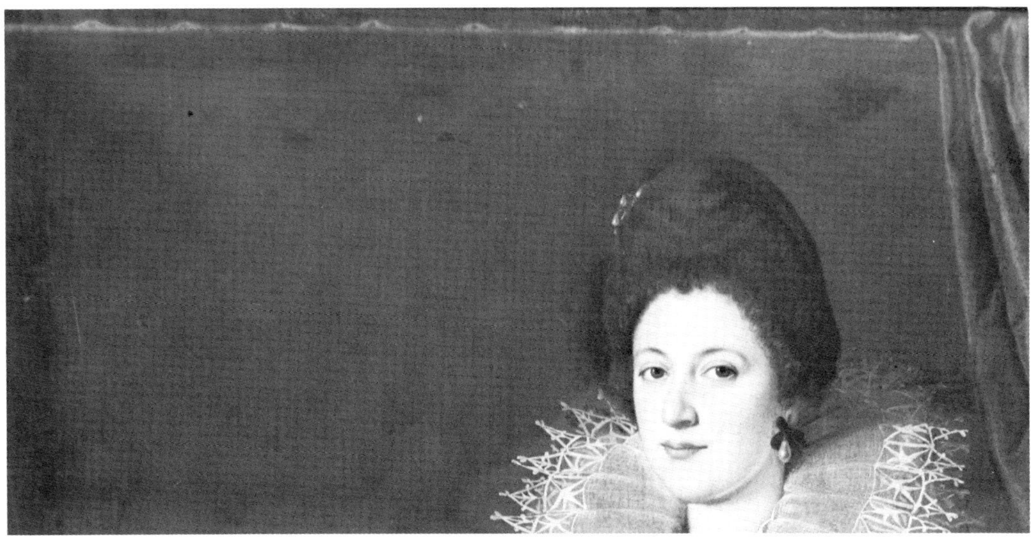

Fig. 1. Florence, Early Seventeenth Century, *Portrait of a Lady of the Medici Court*, detail of cat. no. 18

No records seem to exist to document when or from what source the *Lady* was acquired for the Holford Collection. The portrait could have been obtained after 1854, as in that year a brief description of the collection of Robert Stayner Holford (1808–1892), then displayed at his London house on Russell Square, was published, without reference to the portrait, by Gustav Friedrich Waagen who praised Holford for the quality of the newly formed collection and for its accessibility to persons interested in art.[2] But neither Waagen's omission of the portrait nor the fact that the portrait is not included in the notes and sketches (unpublished) made by Sir George Scharf during his visit to the Holford Collection at Dorchester House on September 13–14, 1858,[3] are in themselves proof that the painting had not yet been acquired by Holford. The earliest published association of the *Portrait of a Lady* with the Holford Collection was in 1913, the year in which the painting was cited as "not previously exhibited."[4] Thus it is likely that the portrait was acquired by Lieut.-Col. Sir George Lindsay Holford (1860–1926), from whose collection it was then auctioned at Christie's in London in 1928.

The identification of the *Lady* is equally uncertain. Exhibited in 1913 as a portrait of an unknown lady, the painting was entitled in the 1927 catalogue of the Holford Collection *Portrait of a Lady of the Medici Court* and illustrated as "A Medici Princess?". The source of these identifications was not specified, but the knowing eye of the collector may have led to this first published association with Florence. It is indicative of the taste that shaped the Holford Collection that the portraits at Dorchester House were predominantly court portraits, and that the majority of these were of members of the Medici family and of Florentine ladies and gentlemen of the Grand Ducal court.[5]

Attributions of the portrait have ranged from Spanish to Flemish to Italian artists. In 1913, the painting was ascribed to the Spanish court painter Alonso Sánchez Coello (ca. 1531–1588).[6] In the 1927 catalogue of the Holford Collection, the portrait was attributed to the Flemish painter Justus Sustermans (1597–1681). This attribution may postdate the 1912 monograph on Sustermans' paintings by Pierre Bautier, who does not mention the *Portrait of a Lady* in his citations of works in the Holford Collection.[7] The attribution to Sustermans was continued in 1928 in the catalogue of the Holford Collection Sale at Christie's, in an article in *Apollo* by William Gibson, and again in 1939 in the booklet published by the Baltimore collector Jacob Epstein.[8]

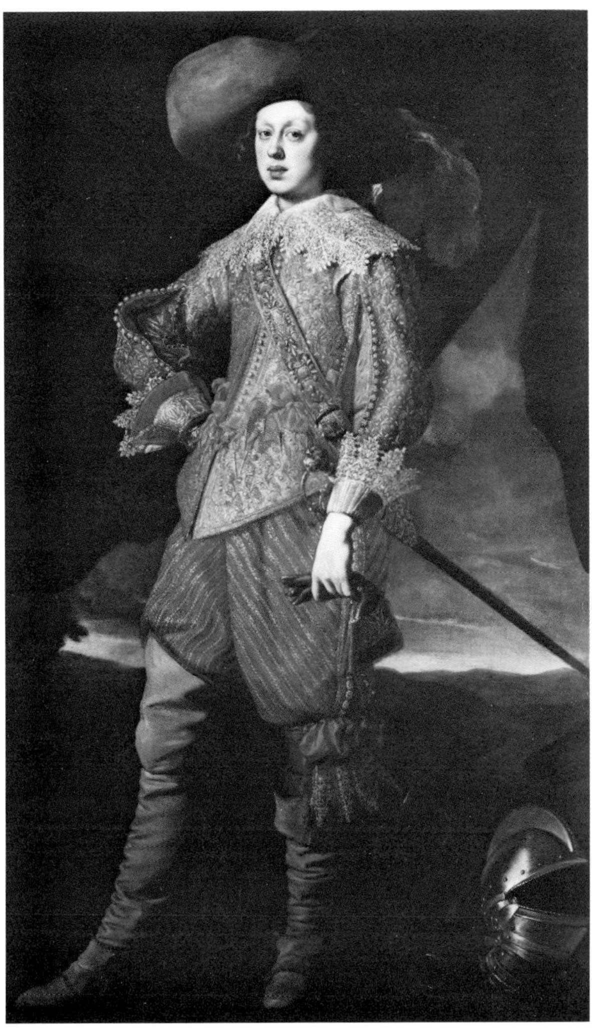

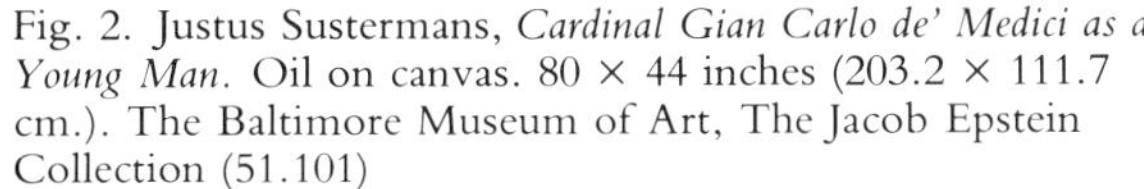

Fig. 2. Justus Sustermans, *Cardinal Gian Carlo de' Medici as a Young Man*. Oil on canvas. 80 × 44 inches (203.2 × 111.7 cm.). The Baltimore Museum of Art, The Jacob Epstein Collection (51.101)

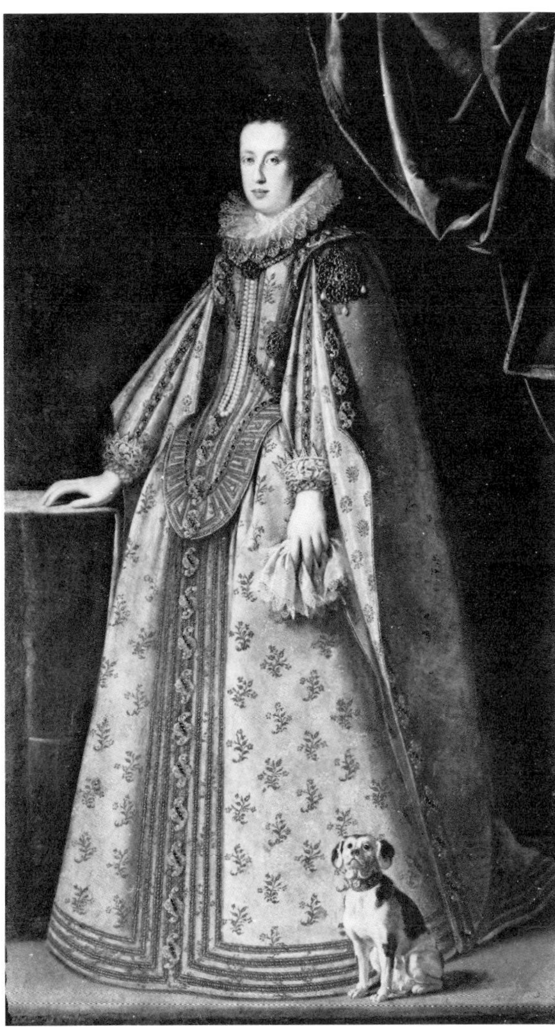

Fig. 3. Justus Sustermans, *Claudia de' Medici*. Oil on canvas. $80^{5}/_{16}$ × $45^{11}/_{16}$ inches (204 × 116 cm.). Gallerie fiorentine, Florence (Inv. 1890, no. 2267)

Only recently has the Sustermans attribution been seriously questioned. In 1951 the *Portrait of a Lady* was newly catalogued at The Baltimore Museum of Art as the work of a follower of Sustermans.[9] Subsequently, in 1976, Federico Zeri stated that an attribution to Sustermans, or even to his circle, was not tenable. His observation is readily confirmed by the contrast of style between the *Lady* (cat. no. 18) and Sustermans' *Gian Carlo de' Medici* of ca. 1630 in The Baltimore Museum of Art (fig. 2) or his *Claudia de' Medici* of ca. 1626 in the Palazzo Pitti, Florence (fig. 3). Zeri proposed that the *Lady* was the work of an earlier artist and that, judging by composition, dress, and arrangement of the hair, it seemed to compare with portraits produced at the Medici Court in Florence of either the late sixteenth century, or around 1600–1605. He also noted that the trompe-l'oeil motif of the painting-within-a-painting was related to late sixteenth-century international tendencies in portraiture as seen in pictures by François Clouet (ca. 1510–1572) and by Scipione Pulzone (ca. 1550–1598). He further mentioned a kinship to works by Frans Pourbus the Younger (1569–1622).[10]

Although the identification as a "Medici Princess" cannot be verified, the Holford and Zeri associations of the painting with Florentine court portraiture appear from style and dress to be correct. I would propose that the portrait is by a Florentine artist, perhaps dated as late as 1620, and that it is an example of a preference for long-established conventions which can be described as Mannerist, in a Florence that was turning more and more to Baroque tastes in portraiture.

To place the picture in this historical context and to suggest an artistic circle for its authorship, one must consider the developments in Florentine portraiture from the mid-sixteenth-century activity of Agnolo Bronzino (1503–1572) to the arrival in Florence of Justus Sustermans in 1620.[11] During this period, portraiture was strongly patronized and influenced by the Medici rulers and their courts: Cosimo I, Duke from 1537 and Grand Duke from 1569 until 1574; Francesco I, ruling 1574–1587; Ferdinando I, ruling 1587–1609; and Cosimo II, ruling 1609–1621.

During the rule of Cosimo I, Florentine portraitists differed significantly from their counterparts in North Italy in their approach to rendering a likeness. In Venice, Titian painted portraits in which description and interpretation were held in equilibrium through the subtle mitigation of the accidents of nature and the designing of pose and expression in a manner appropriate to the character of the individual portrayed (see Titian's *Portrait of a Gentleman* in this volume, cat. no. 14). Figures moving easily from translucent depths to atmospheric light, warm color, lustrous textures, and also a painterly quality (sometimes suggesting rather than delineating form) characterize his execution. In Titian, likeness, decorum, and a profound portrayal of character were combined so harmoniously that his portraits determined Venetian and ultimately international tastes in state portraiture.

During the same period in Medici Florence, Bronzino produced likenesses which emphasized artful design and interpreted the sitter in a fashion now considered illustrative of the style and ideas of Mannerist portraiture. A superb draftsman, with a great ability to render detail and create the tactile suggestion of material surfaces, Bronzino subordinated verism to an expression of aristocratic status. Often shown in plain and seemingly shallow spatial settings, his figures were illuminated from the front by a cool, strong, but diffused light. His subjects were delineated by firmly defined contours that created a silhouette effect, enhancing the impressiveness of the image, and were dressed in elaborate costumes depicted with some of the most realistic rendering of material surfaces in Italian art. In contrast to this surface realism, the likeness followed a courtly ideal of beauty. Physiognomical characteristics were less important than regular and smoothly modeled features (perhaps in emulation of Classical sculpture), attenuated proportions, and calculated graceful poses. Through such interpretive choices, Bronzino's likenesses, which have been characterized by H. W. Janson as "prestige portraits," became images of ideal beauty, status, and, when appropriate, power. They visually embody *sprezzatura* (a certain gracefulness in all things), and *virtù,* two concepts long considered appropriate and desirable in the courtier. In portraits such as *Cosimo I* and *Eleanor of Toledo and Her Son Don Giovanni* of ca. 1545 (both in the Uffizi, Florence), Bronzino can be said to have created the quintessential expression of what it meant to be a Florentine and a member of the Medici court. His portraiture seems to have been influenced by diverse artistic developments: the Florentine tradition of *disegno,* which accorded much weight to highly proficient drawing and studied design; his thorough training in this tradition by his teacher Pontormo; and the Mannerist concern with technical virtuosity and stylized gracefulness. In addition, there was the desire to give visual expression to the monarchical and aristocratic aspirations of the Medici ruler and his court. Having made the successful translation of the ideas of his patrons into art, Bronzino established the ideal and direction for later sixteenth-century portraiture in the Medici court.[12]

Portraiture in Florence between Bronzino's death in 1572 and Justus Sustermans's arrival in 1620 remains to be studied in detail with respect to individual painters, their careers and styles, and their specific portraits. Nevertheless, a general history of later Florentine portraiture has emerged. Portraiture in Florence during this period developed on a pattern somewhat comparable to that of various other European courts: a transitional phase, which combined new interest in veristic likeness and setting with established conventions of pose and dress, gradually replaced the stylization of Bronzino's Mannerism and anticipated the Baroque. This transitional development paralleled naturalistic tendencies in narrative painting in the late sixteenth-century Italy, which have been variously described as Late Mannerist, relating to the Counter Reformation or the Tridentine Style; Counter-Reformation realism; Late Counter-Maniera; the Style Sixtus V; pre-Baroque, or early Baroque. No single descriptive term for this phase in Italian art has yet found general acceptance in art criticism.[13] One might think of this period of around 1570 to the early 1600's as a Late Mannerist recursion in which artists combined Mannerist ideas with a return to the aims and means of Renaissance art to produce a style and an artistic climate that created the basis for the Baroque. The Mannerist emphasis on style was combined with a renewed interest in more descriptive portraits, and the works produced anticipated the unequivocal and persuasive portrayal of likeness, character, and status that characterizes Baroque portraiture. Over a fifty-year period the Italian pattern became an international one. The Mannerist style—exemplified by Bronzino in Medici Florence, the Fontainebleau School of Valois France, and the painters of the "English Icons" at the Elizabethan court[14]—gave way between 1570 and 1620 to the more descriptive or "reformed" Late Mannerist portraiture based in part on Titian's conventions. This synthesis was made by artists such as Scipione Pulzone, Antonio Mor, François Clouet, Alonso Sánchez Coello, Frans Pourbus the Younger, and the Dutch, Flemish, and British painters of the early Stuart court.[15] In turn, "reformed" Late Mannerist portraiture was replaced by the Baroque portraiture of Rubens and Anthony Van Dyck. Justus Sustermans, the Fleming associated with Rubens's circle, introduced Baroque portraiture to Florence when he was named court painter to the Medici in 1620.[16]

The Baltimore *Portrait of a Lady* is a late example of this transition to the Baroque in Florentine art. It could be said to illustrate the end of the limited but observable development in portraiture produced between the 1570's and 1620's by two generations of "reformer" painters: the first generation of Bronzino's immediate successors, led by his own pupil Alessandro Allori (1535–1607), included Maso di San Friano (1536–1571), and Santi di Tito (1536–1603); the younger generation consisted of Jacopo Chimenti da Empoli (1554–1640), Lodovico Cigoli (1559–1613), Cristofano Allori (1577–1621), and Tiberio Titi (1573–1627).

Although the "reformer" artists reveal individual styles, their portraits share certain conventions. Surviving from Bronzino's powerful example are the use of splendid dress and a limited repertoire of formal poses and aloof expressions. New are the subtle modifications of the figure and setting: the traditionally limited stage space is made more plausible by a warm light, atmospheric shadow, and perspective drawing; there is a greater integration of the figure in space; the plain setting is embellished with a table and attributes, and often with a drawn curtain; and there is a preference for three-quarter or full-length figures which are slightly turned to one side. With respect to the figure, proportions become more normal and physiognomical description is a matter of greater concern. While Alessandro Allori and Santi di Tito define figures, forms, and surfaces with a crisp, bright light, Empoli and particularly Cigoli (known for naturalism and color) and his followers reintroduce chiaroscuro and sfumato to the painter's vocabulary in Florence.[17]

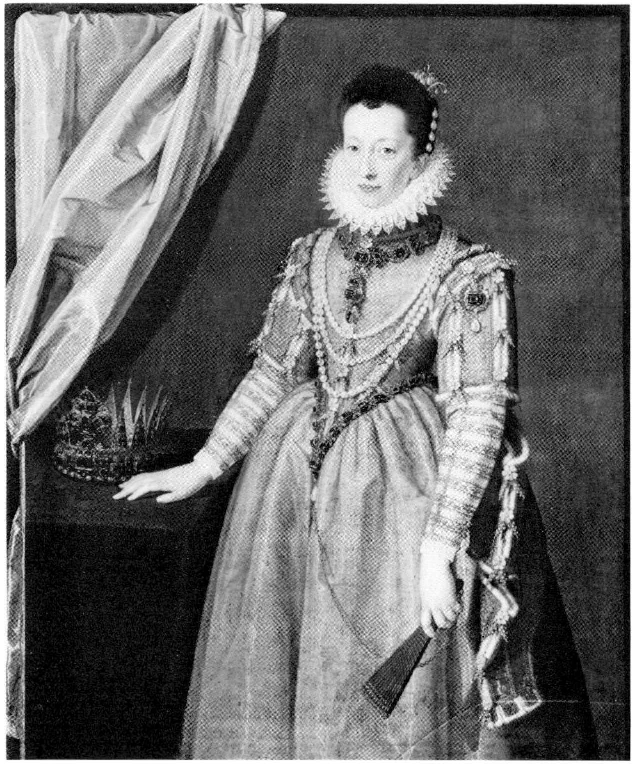

Fig. 4. Scipione Pulzone, *Christine of Lorraine as Grand Duchess of Tuscany*. Oil on canvas. 56 5/16 × 46½ inches (143 × 118 cm.). Gallerie fiorentine, Florence (Inv. 1890, no. 9161)

Many of these innovations were already international and had been disseminated by traveling artists such as the influential court painters Antonio Mor and Frans Pourbus the Younger; by the exchange of portraits as gifts and diplomatic presentations; by the commissioning of original portraits, replicas, or copies; and by the greatly increased production in the sixteenth century of reproductive engravings.[18]

The introduction of international conventions in Florentine portraiture was influenced in no small way by the political aspirations and activities of the Medici Grand Dukes. Cosimo I set the dynasty's pattern for political and cultural ties with foreign courts through negotiations and marriages. His son Francesco I was married to Giovanna of Austria in 1565; another son, Ferdinando I, to Christine of Lorraine in 1589; and Cosimo II to Maria Maddalena of Austria in 1608—ties which were complemented by Ferdinando's negotiation of the marriage of Marie de' Medici to Henry IV of France in 1600. Such relationships with northern European courts contributed much to taste and fashion and, through the presence of foreign artists and foreign art works, to the international style of portraiture in Florence.

In terms of patronage, too, the Medici played an important role in the development of portraiture. Cosimo I ordered the copying of Paolo Giovio's extensive collection at Como of portraits of prominent men and women. Cosimo further enlarged the Medici collection through individual commissions, acquisitions, and gifts. His descendants continued in this vein, collecting or commissioning such series as the "Beauties of Florence" and the "Self-Portraits of the Artists." Thus in early seventeenth-century Florence both patrons and painters had access to examples by foreign contemporaries such as Holbein, Mor, Clouet, and Pourbus the Younger.[19] In Florence, Antonio Mor

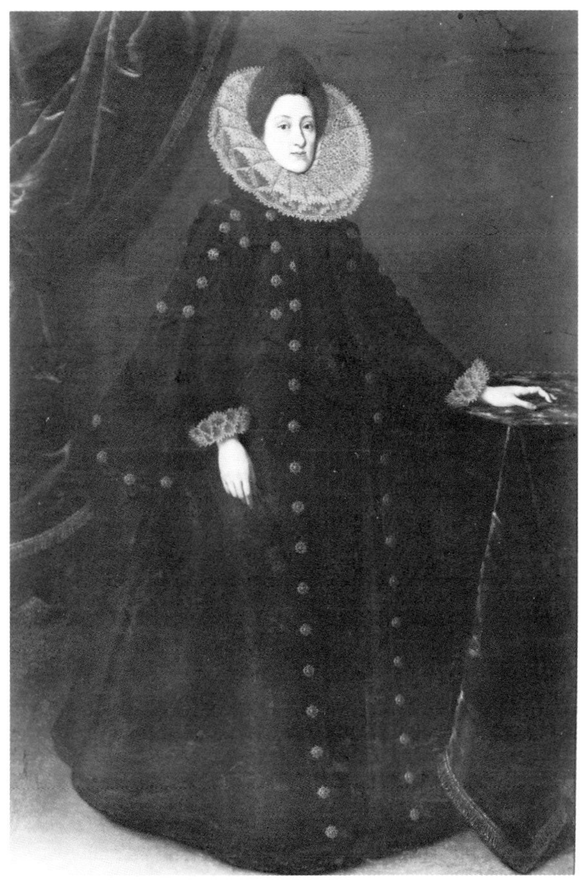

Fig. 5. Cristofano Allori, *Christine of Lorraine* or *Maria Maddalena of Austria*. Oil on canvas. 85¹³/₁₆ × 55⅛ inches (218 × 140 cm). The Prado Museum, Madrid

had his counterparts in Alessandro Allori and Santi di Tito, while Frans Pourbus the Younger may be seen as the counterpart of Pulzone, Cigoli, Cristofano Allori, and Tiberio Titi.

The Baltimore *Portrait of a Lady* belongs in this context of Tuscan artistic tradition modified by new, more descriptive artistic intentions and by foreign influences; it provides a good example of the transitional style in early seventeenth-century Florentine portraiture.[20] Indeed, it seems most to resemble portraits of Christine of Lorraine's daughter-in-law Maria Maddalena of Austria (1587–1629) and certain portraits of Christine's own daughter, Claudia de' Medici (1604–1648). The composition follows a type apparently established for Florentine portraiture by Scipione Pulzone's *Christine of Lorraine as Grand Duchess* of 1590 in the Palazzo Pitti (fig. 4), in which the figure is seen standing in ornate court dress by a table on which is conspicuously placed the crown, symbol of her status.[21] Also similar is the trompe l'oeil of the drapery-over-the-stretcher motif employed here and in other portraits by Pulzone.[22] The placement of the figure, with her right hand resting on a table and the left holding a fan, seems to have been a pose preferred by Christine of Lorraine, possibly in imitation of the portraits painted by Mor and Coello for the French, German, and Spanish courts.[23] Indeed, this pose, with only slight variations, was employed so often in portraits of Christine and of ladies of her court that it is often difficult to identify with certainty either the sitter or the portraitist.

The Baltimore picture seems closest to Florentine portraits that can be dated in the first third of the seventeenth century. In stance and gesture the figure compares with Cristofano Allori's portrait in the Prado Museum traditionally identified as *Christine of Lorraine* and more recently by Karla Langedijk as *Maria Maddalena of Austria* (fig. 5).[24] While the Baltimore *Lady* is similar in pose and hair style to Cristofano's portrait,[25] some details of her gown are reminiscent of the elaborate dress and precious jewelry that appeared first in Bronzino's portraiture and continued in Pulzone's *Christine of Lorraine* (fig. 4) and in the Uffizi *Caterina Strozzi* (fig. 6).[26] The pose of the *Lady* is retained in two portraits of *Claudia de' Medici,* one painted around 1626 by Sustermans (fig. 3) and the other associated with Tiberio Titi (fig. 7).[27] The similarities in composition and possibly in execution suggest that it is probably among the Italian portraitists of Claudia de' Medici that one may eventually identify the artist of the Baltimore *Lady*.

The identity of the Baltimore *Lady* remains unknown. There is nothing to affirm or deny the Holford identification as a Medici princess or a lady of the Medici court. A precise identification cannot be suggested solely on the basis of likeness. Florentine portraits of the same person often show great disparity in likeness, as can be seen by comparing the Titi (?) and Sustermans portraits of *Claudia de' Medici* (figs. 7 and 3). Conversely, different persons are portrayed by Florentine artists in a strikingly similar manner as a result of stylistic conventions. This can be seen in the Pulzone and Titi (?) portraits of *Christine of Lorraine, Claudia de' Medici,* and the Baltimore *Lady* (figs. 4, 7, and cat. no. 18). One must resist the temptation to overstate the similarities between the portrait of *Caterina Strozzi* and that of the Baltimore *Lady* (fig. 6 and cat. no. 18) as these may be only a coincidence deriving from the stylization of the features.

Perhaps the *Portrait of a Lady* was intended to form part of a now dispersed series of portraits of beautiful women comparable to the series of court beauties still preserved from the Medici collections.[28] Alternatively, the painting could be related to a betrothal or marriage, as the carnations on the sitter's dress and in the bouquet suggest sentiments related to marriage.[29] The interpretation can be proposed that an allusion to a particular moment in the life of the subject may be intended by the motif of the painting-within-a-painting, which suggests an impromptu or informal exhibit of the unframed canvas.[30] The painting could be understood as commemorating an event, possibly the presentation of the portrait to the lady's betrothed. However, far too much remains to be discovered to consider this interpretation as more than a hypothesis.

The identification of the artist also remains problematic and inconclusive. That his composition is influenced by Pulzone seems clear. But the costume, atmospheric light, and warm color are comparable with the early seventeenth-century works by Cigoli and his pupils such as Cristofano Allori. The artist of the Baltimore painting differs, however, from these painters in his style of execution. He seems to be more capable of producing a type of image than of rendering details with the finesse of a Bronzino, a Pulzone, or a Cigoli. His limitations are apparent in the generalized modeling of the face, in the heavy rendering of the repeated patterns of the gown, and in the schematic treatment of the flowers in the vase. The identity of the artist whose specialty possibly was the "costume piece" (the state portrait in court dress) will remain unknown until the patronage of portraiture at the Grand Ducal court is studied in detail.[31] Until this has been accomplished, it would be premature to propose a precise attribution for the Baltimore *Lady*. As a result of our research it may be suggested on the basis of style that the portrait dates from the first two decades of the seventeenth century and seems particularly close to the Uffizi *Claudia de' Medici* (fig. 7). It is certainly the work of a Florentine "reformer," perhaps identifiable with or close to Tiberio Titi, an artist yet to be studied but one recorded as very active in Florence as a painter of portraits.[32]

Despite our lack of information on the identities of both artist and sitter, the *Portrait*

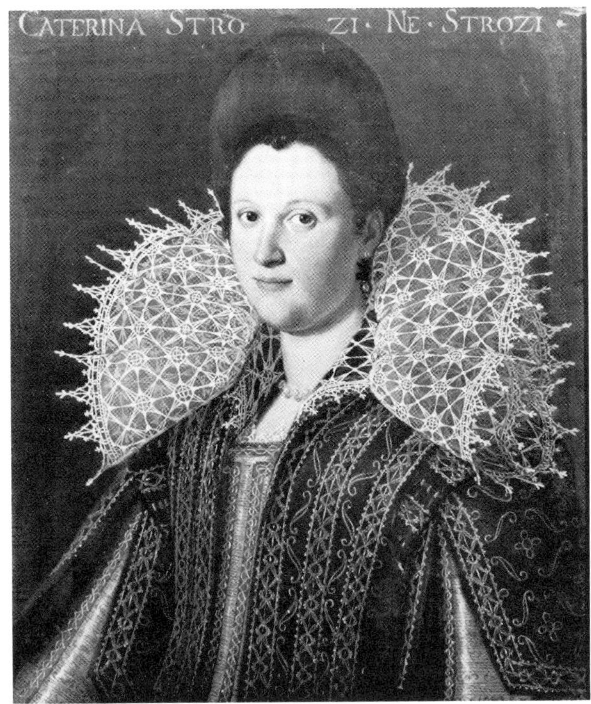

Fig. 6. Florence, Early Seventeenth Century, *Caterina Strozzi*. Oil on canvas. 33½ × 67½ inches (85 × 71.5 cm.). Gallerie fiorentine, Florence (Inv. 1890, no. 2292)

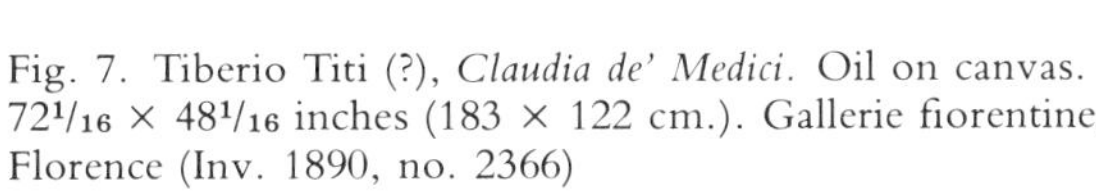

Fig. 7. Tiberio Titi (?), *Claudia de' Medici*. Oil on canvas. $72^{1}/_{16} \times 48^{1}/_{16}$ inches (183 × 122 cm.). Gallerie fiorentine, Florence (Inv. 1890, no. 2366)

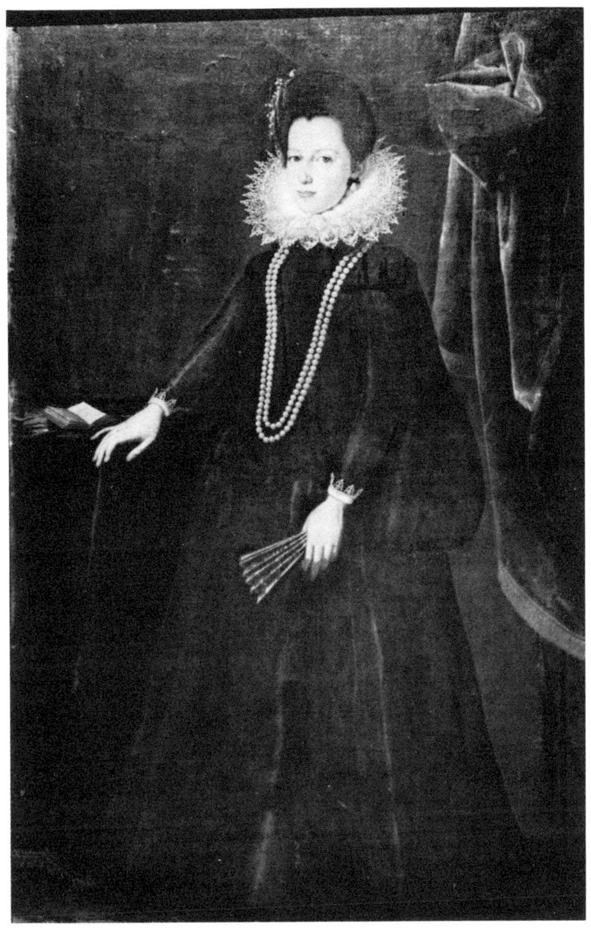

of a Lady is of great interest for what it can tell us of the history of the state portrait in Florence. The painting may usefully be contrasted with another Florentine portrait in The Baltimore Museum of Art, Sustermans' *Cardinal Gian Carlo de' Medici* of ca. 1630 (fig. 2), with its unmitigated literalism, strong color, forceful turning movement, assertive swagger, and incisive characterization. The *Lady* and *Gian Carlo* can be considered reflections of the change in style and taste in seventeenth-century Florence. The Baltimore picture's levels of illusion, the splendor and detail of dress, the restraint of movement, and the stylization of the likeness reveal the survival of Mannerist conventions just prior to the development, created in large part by Sustermans, of a more Baroque style of portraiture in Florence.

Miles Chappell
College of William and Mary,
Williamsburg, Virginia

AUTHOR'S ACKNOWLEDGMENTS

Expressions of gratitude for generous assistance and responses to requests for information are due to Ulrich Middeldorf at the Kunsthistorisches Institut, Florence; Marco Chiarini, Director of the Pitti Gallery, Florence; Sylvia Meloni of the Soprintendenza per i Beni Artistici e Storici, Florence; Alfonso E. Pérez Sánchez of the Prado Museum; Karla Langedijk; Rupert Hodge at the Witt Library of the Courtauld Institute; and Stewart A. Ware of the College of William and Mary.

NOTES

1. On dress in Florence, see C. Köhler, *A History of Costume*, ed. and augmented by E. von Sichart, trans. A. K. Dallas (London: George G. Harrap and Company, 1928; reprint ed. New York: Dover Publications, 1963), pp. 280–85; and F. Cappi Bentivegna, *Abbigliamento e costume nella pittura italiana: Barocco e Impero*, 2 vols. (Rome: Bestetti, Edizioni d'Arte, 1964), 2:2–23, and figs. 29–30, which belong to the same portrait series as the *Caterina Strozzi* (fig. 6).
2. G. F. Waagen, *Treasures of Art in Great Britain*, 3 vols. (London: J. Murray, 1854), 2:193.
3. The notebooks of Sir George Scharf (1820–1895) are preserved at The National Portrait Gallery, London. I am grateful to Malcolm Rogers, Assistant Keeper, for his informative response (letter of April 20, 1979) to my request for information on Scharf's notes on the Holford Collection (contained in notebook no. SSB 53).
4. *Exhibition of Spanish Old Masters in Support of National Gallery Funds and for the Benefit of the Sociedad de Amigos del Arte Española, Oct. 1913 to Jan. 1914*, exhibition catalogue, 2nd ed. (London: Grafton Galleries, 1913), no. 78, pp. 82–83.
5. R. H. Benson, *The Holford Collection, Dorchester House* (Oxford: The University Press, 1927), 2: no. 121 (*Portrait of a Lady of the Medici Court*). For portraits of other Florentine and Medici personages, see nos. 101–7, and 122.
6. *Exhibition of Spanish Old Masters*, no. 78, pp. 82–83.
7. Benson, *The Holford Collection*, 2:no. 121, p. 18. On Sustermans's paintings in the Holford Collection, see P. Bautier, *Juste Suttermans: Peintre des Médicis* (Brussels: G. van Oest & Cie, 1912), pp. 87, and 123.
8. *Final Portion of the Collection of Important Pictures by Old Masters, Chiefly of the Dutch, Flemish, French, Spanish and British Schools, the Property of the Late Sir George Lindsay Holford*, sale catalogue (London: Christie, Manson and Woods, 1928), no. 46, p. 35; W. Gibson, "The Holford Collection," *Apollo* 7 (1928):203; *The Jacob Epstein Collection in The Baltimore Museum of Art* (Baltimore: Published by Jacob Epstein, 1939).
9. Curatorial files, The Baltimore Museum of Art (catalogue card for inventory number 51.102).
10. Letter from F. Zeri to G. Rosenthal of January 27, 1976.
11. The history of later sixteenth-century Florentine portraiture and its relationship to conventions in state portraiture at the royal courts outside of Italy has yet to be written. For general and specific treatments of this interesting topic, see J. Alazard, *The Florentine Portrait*, trans. B. Whelpton, reprint ed. (New York: Schocken Books, 1968), pp. 195–220; J. Pope-Hennessy, *The Portrait in the Renaissance* (New York: Pantheon Books, for the Bollingen Foundation, 1966), pp. 155–204; and E. Battisti, "Portraiture," *Encyclopedia of World Art* (New York: McGraw-Hill, 1959–1968), 11: 477–93.
12. See M. Jenkins, *The State Portrait: Its Origin and Evolution*, Monographs on Archaeology and Fine Arts, vol. 3 (New York: College Art Association of America in conjunction with *The Art Bulletin*, 1947), pp. 13 ff; H. W. Janson, "A Florentine Sixteenth Century Portrait of a Nobleman," *St. Louis Museum Bulletin* 29 (November 1944):1–7; A. Hauser, *Mannerism: The Crisis of the Renaissance and the Origins of Modern Art*, 2 vols. (London: Routledge & Kegan Paul, 1965), 1:197–201; J. Shearman, *Mannerism* (Harmondsworth and Baltimore: Penguin Books, 1967), p. 176; F. Hartt, *History of Italian Renaissance Art: Painting, Sculpture, Architecture* (New York: Harry N. Abrams, 1969), p. 592.
13. On the problem of defining late sixteenth-century Italian art, see R. Wittkower, *Art and Architecture in Italy 1600–1750*, 3rd rev. ed. (Harmondsworth and Baltimore: Penguin Books, 1973), pp. 22–28. See also E. Battisti, "Counter Reformation," *Encyclopedia of World Art*, 11:907; S. J. Freedberg, *Painting in Italy 1500 to 1600* (Harmondsworth and Baltimore: Penguin Books, 1971), pp. 455–60.
14. On Mannerist portraiture outside Italy, see Hauser, *Mannerism*, pp. 240–58; C. D. Cuttler, *Northern Painting from Pucelle to Bruegel: Fourteenth, Fifteenth, and Sixteenth Centuries* (New York: Holt, Rinehart and Winston, 1968), pp. 461–66. On portraiture in England, see E. Waterhouse, *Painting in Britain 1530 to 1790* (Harmondsworth and Baltimore: Penguin Books, 1953), pp. 19–32 and figs. 23–24 (portraits showing compositional conventions similar to those of the Baltimore *Lady*); see also R. Strong, *The English Icon: Elizabethan and Jacobean Portraiture* (New Haven: Yale University Press, 1969).
15. On late sixteenth-century portraiture, see Jenkins, *The State Portrait*, pp. 17 ff; G. T. Faggin, *La pittura ad Anversa nel Cinquecento* (Florence: Marchi & Bertolli, 1969); P. Philippott, *Pittura fiamminga e rinascimento italiano*, trans. P. Argan (Turin: Giulio Einaudi, 1970), pp. 218–30; A. Blunt, *Art and Architecture in France 1500 to 1700*, 2nd rev. ed. (Harmondsworth and Baltimore: Penguin Books, 1973), pp. 116–19, and 189–90. On Mor and Pulzone, see F. Zeri, *Pittura e controriforma: L'arte senza tempo di Scipione da Gaeta* (Turin: Giulio Einaudi, 1957), pp. 17 ff.
16. On Sustermans in Florence, see M. Chiarini, *Artisti alla corte granducale* (Florence: Centro Di, 1969), p. 43. For bibliography and discussion of *Gian Carlo de' Medici* (fig. 2 of this paper), see J. Nissman, *Florentine Baroque Art from American Collections* (New York: Niles & Phipps, 1969), no. 34, pp. 39–40.

17. On late sixteenth-century portraiture in Florence, see C. Gamba, "Il ritratto fiorentino," in *Il ritratto italiano dal Caravaggio al Tiepolo alla Mostra di Palazzo Vecchio nel MCMXI* (Bergamo: Istituto italiano d'arti grafiche, 1927), pp. 63–67; and Alazard, *The Florentine Portrait,* p. 227. On specific Florentine artists, see S. de Vries, "Jacopo Chimenti da Empoli," *Rivista d'arte* 15 (1933): 273–75; M. Bucci, *Mostra del Cigoli e del suo ambiente* (San Miniato: Tipografia Palagini, 1959), no. 10; and C. Thiem, *Gregorio Pagani, ein Wegbereiter der Florentiner Barockmalerei* (Stuttgart: Galerie Valentien, 1970), pp. 37–39. For a general discussion of Florentine painters in the late sixteenth century, see Freedberg, *Painting in Italy 1500 to 1600,* pp. 428–36.

18. On the international character of state portraiture (reflected in the Baltimore *Portrait of a Lady*), see Pope-Hennessy, *The Portrait in the Renaissance,* pp. 185 ff; and Jenkins, *The State Portrait* (see figs. 32, 45, 51, and 55). This increased production of reproductive engravings and of engraved portraits in single prints and in series influenced the standardization of conventions in state portraiture: see A. M. Hind, *A History of Engraving and Etching,* 3rd ed. (New York: Houghton Mifflin Company, 1923), chap. 4. On the production and patronage of portrait engravings, see A. H. Mayor, *Prints and People: A Social History of Printed Pictures* (Greenwich, Conn.: The New York Graphic Society, 1971), figs. 282–89.

19. On the later history and culture of Florence, see E. Cochrane, *Florence in the Forgotten Centuries, 1527–1800* (Chicago: University of Chicago Press, 1973). On the patronage and collecting of portraits, see Alazard, *The Florentine Portrait,* pp. 225–27. For a study of the patronage and the iconography of portraits of the first Medici Grand Dukes and their families, see K. Langedijk, *De Portretten van de Medici tot omstreeks 1600* (published dissertation, University of Amsterdam, 1969), and the forthcoming catalogue of Medici portraits by the same scholar. For early examples of the collecting of foreign portraits at the Medici court (such as portraits of English rulers), see M. Webster, *Firenze e L'Inghilterra, rapporti artistici e culturali dal XVI al XX secolo* (Florence: Centro Di, 1971), "Introduzione," and especially nos. 6–10 (portraits of *Elizabeth I* and *James I* by John de Critz, then in Florence). The apparent relationship of Frans Pourbus the Younger (and possibly of Rubens) to early seventeenth-century portraiture in Florence has yet to be studied. A useful discussion with bibliography for such a study is J. Müller Hofstede, *Peter Paul Rubens: Rubens in Italien* (Cologne: Greven & Bechtold, 1977), pp. 68–75.

20. *The Portrait of a Lady of the Medici Court* can be said to be the work of an artist of the second generation of "reformers" in Florentine painting and may usefully be contrasted with The Baltimore Museum of Art's *Portrait of a Young Lady,* which seems to be the work of an artist of the first generation of "reformers" more directly influenced by Alessandro Allori and Santi di Tito (see the discussion in this publication, cat. no. 17, fig. 2).

21. Uffizi, Florence, Inv. 1890, no. 9161; 143 × 118 cm.; now exhibited in the Museo degli Argenti, Palazzo Pitti. See U. Ojetti et al., *Mostra Medicea, Palazzo Medici, Firenze,* 2nd ed. (Florence: Casa editrice Marzocco, 1939), no. 10, p. 51; Zeri, *Pittura e controriforma,* pp. 105–6; and Langedijk, *De Portretten,* p. 101; Luciano Berti et al., *Gli Uffizi Catalogo Generale* (Florence: Centro Di, 1979), p. 701, Ic 638.

22. See Zeri, *Pittura e controriforma,* p. 18, and figs. 7, 10, and 87.

23. For discussion of the origin of the pose in Titian and its extensive use in the portraiture of Mor and Coello, see Jenkins, *The State Portrait,* pp. 19 ff, and figs. 32, 35, and 51.

24. The Prado portrait appears in nineteenth-century and subsequent catalogues of the collection as *Christine of Lorraine* by Cristofano Allori (see *Museo del Prado, Catalogo de las Pinturas* [Madrid: Blass, S. A. Tipográfia, 1963], no. 8, p. 6). Dr. Alfonso E. Pérez Sánchez of the Prado Museum has kindly informed me that although the attribution to Allori does not appear in the old inventories, the traditional identification is correct (letter of July 14, 1978). In her study of Medici portraits, however, Langedijk observed that the Prado portrait actually depicts Maria Maddalena of Austria (*De Portretten,* p. 153, n. 124). This observation is borne out by three comparable likenesses identified as Maria Maddalena in the Uffizi: (1) The replica of the Prado portrait (Inv. 1890, no. 2471), which is catalogued as a portrait by an unidentified artist; Langedijk has suggested the attribution of this portrait to Cristofano Allori (letter of March 21, 1979); (2) Inv. 1890, no. 2358, by an unidentified painter (attributed to Cristofano Allori, ca. 1600); see Silvia Meloni Trkulja in Berti, *Gli Uffizi,* p. 752 (Ic 988); (3) Inv. 1890, no. 2285, by an unidentified artist, ca. 1615; see Meloni Trkulja in Berti, *Gli Uffizi,* p. 752 (Ic 990). See also the portrait of *Maria Maddalena* by an unidentified artist discussed by Cappi Bentivegna, *Abbigliamento e costume,* 2:fig. 31.

25. As was kindly pointed out to me by Karla Langedijk in a letter of March 21, 1979, Christine of Lorraine and Maria Maddalena are commonly portrayed with this hairstyle and in this pose.

26. There are two nearly identical series of some twenty portraits of the "Beauties of Florence," one consisting of bust-length portraits and the other of half-length portraits. The *Caterina Strozzi* (Uffizi, Inv. 1890, no. 2292) was part of a series of twenty portraits documented as having arrived at the Medici Villa Artimino on July 9, 1601; a

bust-length replica is also preserved in the Uffizi (Inv. 1890, no. 2283). I am grateful to S. Meloni of the Soprintendenza per i Beni Artistici e Storici, Florence, for information on these paintings (letter of October 31, 1978). Both portraits were displayed recently in the exhibition "Firenze e la Toscana dei Medici nell'Europa del Cinquecento," sponsored by the Council of Europe; see Emanuela Fiori in *Palazzo Vecchio: committenza e collezionismo medicei, 1537–1610* (Florence: Edizioni Medicee s.r.l., 1980), nos. 623–24. For the history of the series known as "Le Bellezze d'Artimino," see L. Bigalli in Berti, *Gli Uffizi*, pp. 710 and 716 (Ic737). Other paintings from the series are illustrated in Cappi Bentivegna, *Abbigliamento e costume,* 2:figs. 29–30. Such series must have inspired the taste in Italy, England, and elsewhere for similar collections of portraits.

27. On the Sustermans portrait of *Claudia de' Medici* of ca. 1626, see Ojetti, *Mostra Medicea,* no. 9, p. 61. The portrait (cat. no. 18, fig. 7) of *Claudia de' Medici* (Uffizi, Inv. 1890, no. 2366; 183 × 122 cm.) is catalogued as by an unidentified artist (repeated by Langedijk, letter of March 21, 1979); it has also been associated with Tiberio Titi (files of the Gabinetto Fotografico, Soprintendenza alle Gallerie, Florence). The Baltimore *Portrait of a Lady* is also comparable in composition and possibly even in execution with the unpublished *Portrait of a Lady with a View of the Palazzo Pitti* (Uffizi, Inv. 1890, no. 2415; 193 × 128 cm.; now stored in the Palazzo Pitti; Alinari E.P.A. no. 717).

    An apparent comparison with another portrait, made on the basis of photographs, raises as yet unanswerable questions. The Baltimore *Lady* seems to resemble in composition, costume, and physiognomy the portrait formerly in the David Citroen Collection, advertised in 1940 by Tomas Harris, Ltd. of London as a *Portrait of Maria de' Medici* by Juan de la Cruz (1553–1608), who is generally known as Pantoja de la Cruz (see *Art News* 39, no. 2 [October 12, 1940]:p. 2). The identification of the artist as Pantoja de la Cruz (who usually signed his works) and the identity of the lady as Maria de' Medici need further investigation. The present whereabouts of the Citroen portrait is not known, and thus a close comparison with the Baltimore *Lady* cannot yet be made. It is not impossible that the Citroen portrait was painted by a Florentine artist and was a marriage portrait of a Medici princess such as Claudia de' Medici. The physiognomical comparison may indeed represent important evidence for the identification of The Baltimore Museum of Art's portrait.

28. See n. 26 above on such series of portraits.

29. See M. Levi D'Ancona, *The Garden of the Renaissance: Botanical Symbolism in Italian Painting* (Florence: Leo S. Olschki, 1977), p. 81.

30. In his discussion of the Pulzone *Portrait of a Lady* formerly owned by Victor Spark (*Pittura e controriforma,* p. 81, fig. 87), Zeri relates the picture-within-a-picture motif suggested by the gathered drape that is not part of the portrait itself to an intellectual play on levels of illusion.

31. Rich material exists for such a study of Florentine portraiture between ca. 1575 and ca. 1625. Portraits, inventories, and many records of payment survive in Tuscan collections and archives.

32. Tiberio Titi, who was trained by his father Santi di Tito, was described briefly by F. Baldinucci as specializing in portraits of the Medici family and of many other Florentines (*Notizie de' professori del disegno da Cimabue in qua,* ed. and augmented by D. M. Manni, 21 vols. [Florence: Gio. Battista Stecchi e Anton Giuseppe Pagani, 1767–1774], 7: 86). Titi's name has thus come to be associated with a number of Medici and other Florentine portraits such as the *Claudia de' Medici* (fig. 7) discussed in n. 27 above. See Gamba, "Il ritratto Fiorentino," pp. 67 ff. It may be observed that the Titi portrait (traditional attribution) of *Giovanni Battista Strozzi and His Family* (L. Ginori Lisci, *I Palazzi di Firenze nella storia e nell'arte,* 2 vols. [Florence: Cassa di Risparmio di Firenze, 1972], 1:184, pl. 158) shows a certain similarity, in the treatment of the vase of flowers and of the figure and dress of Maria del Bali Strozzi, with the Baltimore *Portrait of a Lady*.

SELECTED BIBLIOGRAPHY

Exhibition of Spanish Old Masters in Support of National Gallery Funds and for the Benefit of the Sociedad de Amigos del Arte Española, Oct. 1913 to Jan. 1914. Exhibition catalogue, 2nd edition. London: Grafton Galleries, 1913.

Robert H. Benson. *The Holford Collection, Dorchester House.* 2 vols. Oxford: The University Press, 1927.

Carlo Gamba. "Il ritratto fiorentino." *Il ritratto italiano dal Caravaggio al Tiepolo alla mostra di Palazzo Vecchio nel MCMXI.* Bergamo: Istituto italiano d'arti grafiche, 1927.

Final Portion of the Collection of Important Pictures by Old Masters, Chiefly of the Dutch, Flemish, French, Spanish and British Schools, the Property of the Late Sir George Lindsay Holford. Sale catalogue. London: Christie's, 1928.

The Jacob Epstein Collection in The Baltimore Museum of Art. Baltimore: Published by Jacob Epstein, 1939.

Marianna Jenkins. *The State Portrait: Its Origin and Evolution.* Monographs on Archaeology and Fine Arts, vol. 3. New York: College Art Association of America in conjunction with the *Art Bulletin,* 1947.

Jean Alazard. *The Florentine Portrait.* Translated from the French by Barbara Whelpton, 1948. Reprint edition. New York: Schocken Books, 1968.

Federico Zeri. *Pittura e controriforma: L'arte senza tempo di Scipione da Gaeta.* Turin: Giulio Einaudi, 1957.

Eugenio Battisti. "Portraiture." In *Encyclopedia of World Art.* 15 vols. New York: McGraw-Hill, 1959–1968.

John Pope-Hennessy. *The Portrait in the Renaissance.* New York: Pantheon Books, for the Bollingen Foundation, 1966.

Charles D. Cuttler. *Northern Painting from Pucelle to Breugel: Fourteenth, Fifteenth, and Sixteenth Centuries.* New York: Holt, Rinehart and Winston, 1968.

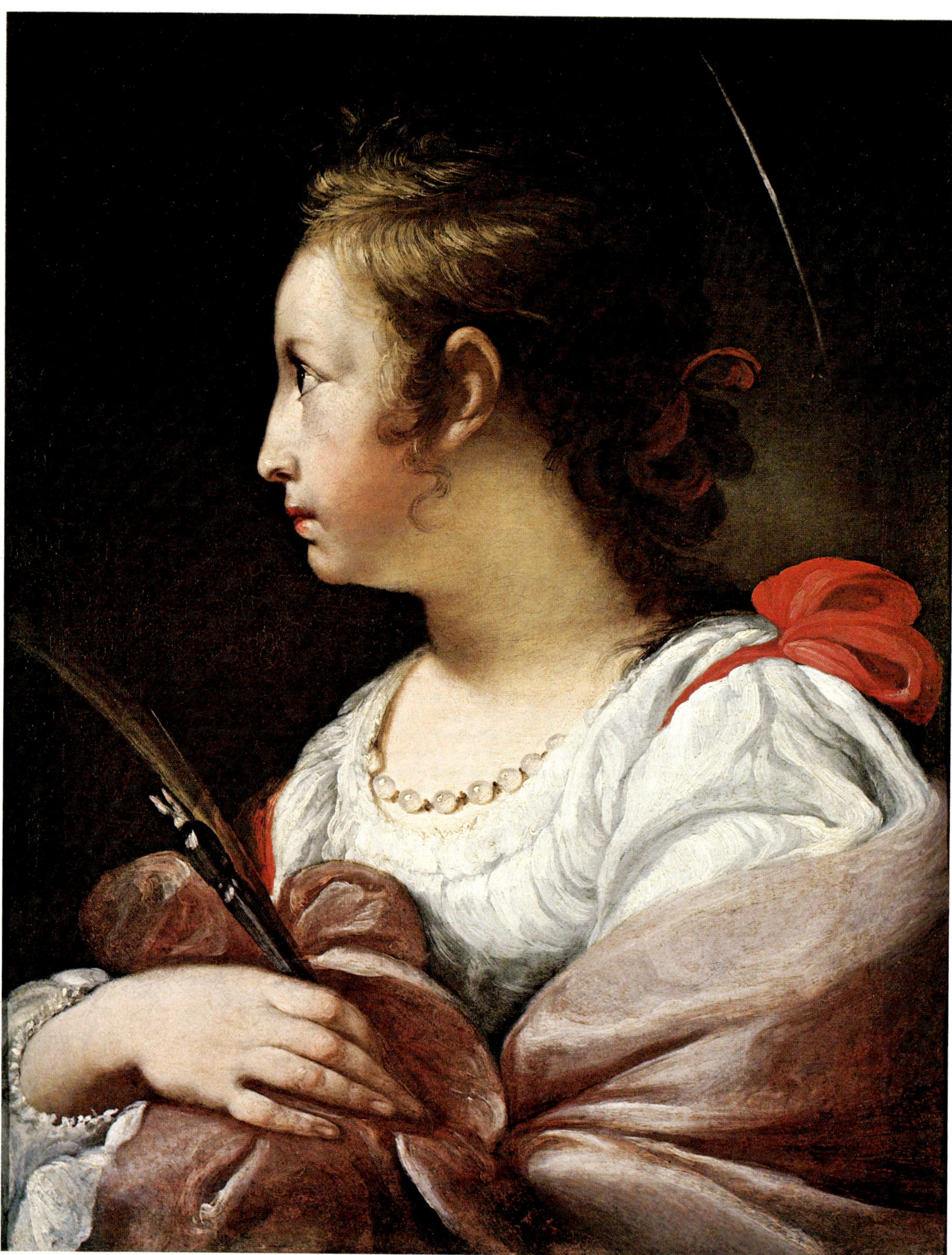

BERNARDO STROZZI (1581–1644)

19. *Saint Apollonia,* 1627–1629

Oil on canvas. $28^{7}/_{16} \times 21^{7}/_{8}$ inches (72.2 × 55.5 cm.)
Museum Purchase (BMA 51.158)

PROVENANCE

Italico Brass, Sr., Venice

In a letter to Gertrude Rosenthal of May 18, 1951, Adolph Loewi, from whom The Baltimore Museum of Art bought the painting, stated: "I know the history of the painting only as far back as about 1925 when it was in the collection of Prof. Italico Brass in Venice" (curatorial files, The Baltimore Museum of Art). Italico Brass Sr. (1870–1943) was a noted dealer and collector of Italian art who had assembled over the years a particularly fine collection of Strozzi's works.

Adolph Loewi, Los Angeles

A photograph of the painting taken sometime before March 29, 1943 indicates that the work was in Mr. Loewi's possession by that date (Frick Art Reference Library, Supply Photographs).

Purchased from Adolph Loewi by The Baltimore Museum of Art in 1951

CONDITION

The original support of *St. Apollonia* is linen composed of single threads, unevenly spun and loosely woven in a plain weave. The painting, which at an unknown date had been lined with glue, was in 1967 relined with linen and microcrystalline wax and mounted on an expansion bolt stretcher. The old tack pulls on the original linen indicated that the painting had undergone only very slight dimensional changes over the years.

The ground is a moderately thick, dark red single layer. The paint is an opaque oil medium, rather thickly applied on the figure with marked brushstrokes, and more thinly and smoothly brushed in the background. In 1967 a thorough treatment of the picture was undertaken by Kay Silberfeld, then Conservator of the Baltimore Museum, now Head, Conservation of Paintings, National Gallery of Art. Disfiguring layers of darkened varnish and discolored, old restorations were removed. As a result of cleaning, a lowering of the neckline, made by the artist, became more noticeable. The condition of the paint layer was found to be as follows: the face had suffered markedly from abrasion along the jaw line, and somewhat less around the eye, along the back of the neck, and on the top of the head. Fortunately, the only severe damage was a strip of about 4.5 cm. of almost total loss due to flaking along the right and the bottom edges, with a few small scattered losses along the other edges and background.

In the 1967 treatment the flaked losses were inpainted with pigments in a non-yellowing synthetic medium, and the abraded losses were touched in enough to minimize their disfiguring effect. The painting was revarnished with a non-yellowing, clear synthetic resin.

The art of Bernardo Strozzi occupies an important place in the history of two major centers of artistic production, Genoa and Venice. Strozzi was born in Genoa in 1581 and may have had his first artistic training with the little-known Cesare Corte (1550–ca. 1613) before entering the studio of the Tuscan Mannerist Pietro Sorri (1556–1622) who was working in Genoa between 1595 and 1597.[1] Strozzi's biographer, Raffaello Soprani, reported that the young man made prodigious progress in Sorri's studio, but almost as soon as his apprenticeship was completed he became a Capuchin monk in the convent of St. Barnaba in Genoa.[2] He continued to paint small devotional pictures, and in about 1610 was given permission to leave the monastery in order to care for his mother and younger sister. He was also allowed to wear secular religious dress and thus earned his nicknames of "il cappuccino" and, later, "il prete Genovese."[3] He quickly made a name for himself and was recognized as one of the strongest Italian painters of his generation. Through his own work and as a teacher of the younger generation, Strozzi's influence was pervasive. His interests apparently included a concern with urban development, for in 1619 he presented to the Commune of Genoa a study dealing with the problems of the city's major harbor.

In 1630 Strozzi's mother died, and he was ordered to return to the monastery. He rebelled against this order to take up once again the duties and restrictions of the conventual life and refused to return. A warrant was eventually issued for his arrest, but he fled to Venice where he remained until his death in 1644. The work which he executed in Venice exerted a great influence on the art of his contemporaries, and though he himself was drawn to the art of Titian, Tintoretto, and especially Veronese, Strozzi's work contributed substantially to the shift of Venetian painting away from the late Cinquecento tradition and toward the idiom of the Baroque.

Many of Strozzi's works, like the Baltimore *St. Apollonia,* are medium-sized, half-length representations of saints which were probably intended for private devotional purposes. St. Apollonia is one of the more commonly represented saints in the Baroque period. Very little is known of her life. She apparently died in an anti-Christian riot in Alexandria around the middle of the third century, and the earliest account of her death is contained in a letter written by Dionysius, Bishop of Alexandria from ca. 247 until ca. 264, to the Bishop of Antioch and published in *The Ecclesiastical History* of Eusebius, Bishop of Caesarea in Palestine (263–339). In his description of those who suffered martyrdom in Alexandria, Dionysius wrote: "Moreover, they seized then that marvelous aged virgin Apollonia, broke out all her teeth with blows on her jaws, and piling up a pyre before the city threatened to burn her alive, if she refused to recite along with them their blasphemous sayings. But she asked for a brief respite, and, being released, without flinching she leaped into the fire and was consumed."[4] Dionysius's account was embellished by Jacobus de Voragine in *The Golden Legend,* a thirteenth-century compilation of hagiographical legends which was enormously popular during the late Middle Ages. He stated that her persecutors "began by tearing out all her teeth. . . . But when she saw the mounting flames, she first paused for a moment, praying within herself; and then, slipping from the grasp of her persecutors, she cast herself into the fire, striking terror even into the cruel hearts of her tormentors."[5] Although both Dionysius and Jacobus de Voragine explicitly mention St. Apollonia's venerable age, she is usually represented as a young woman. Her customary attributes are the palm of martyrdom and a dental forceps which holds a large tooth. Both of these are visible in the Baltimore painting, although at one time, before the painting entered The Baltimore Museum of Art, the subject was mistakenly identified as "St. Cecilia."[6]

The painting is not signed, but the attribution of *St. Apollonia* to Strozzi has not been questioned, for it clearly exhibits distinctive elements of his personal style. The facial

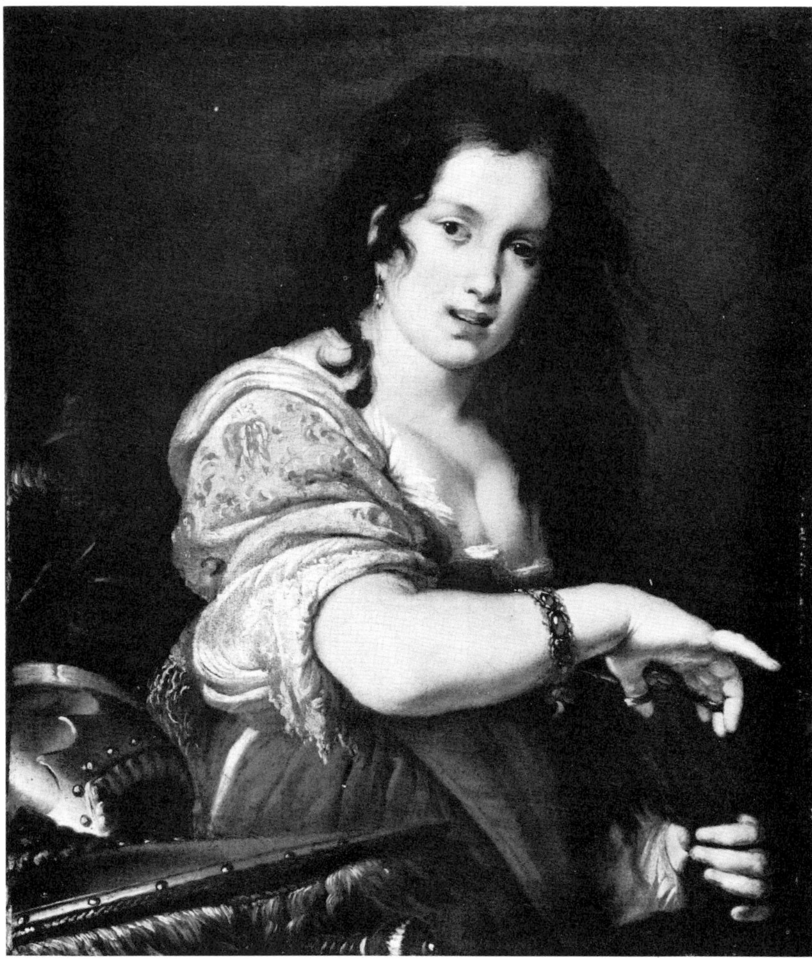

Fig. 1. Bernardo Strozzi, *Berenice Cutting Her Hair*. Oil on canvas. 34 × 28½ inches (86.3 × 72.4 cm.). Los Angeles County Museum of Art, William Randolph Hearst Collection

type, wide-eyed, with an elongated nose, and the long, pointed fingers are characteristic, as are the warm tonality of the flesh tones and the chromatic contrasts. As in the Los Angeles County Museum of Art's *Berenice Cutting Her Hair* (fig. 1), the paint is loosely and thinly worked in the background, in contrast with the elegant handling of the figure, where the paint is applied with a fluidity that is typical of Strozzi's love of richly textured surfaces (see figs. 2 and 3).

Establishing a precise date for the painting, however, is more difficult. Strozzi is one of the least documented of the major Italian Baroque painters, and there are few dated works with which to establish his artistic chronology. Between ca. 1610, when he presumably left the convent of St. Barnaba,[7] and his departure for Venice in 1630 there are only two firmly dated works. The earlier of these is the cycle of frescoes in the Palazzo Centurione di Carpineto at San Pier d'Arena near Genoa, which was executed between 1623 and 1625.[8] The other is the altarpiece of the *Madonna and Child with St. Lawrence and Young St. John the Baptist* (fig. 4) in the Chiesa dei Sordomuti, Genoa, which is signed and dated 1629.[9]

Strozzi shows a bewildering variety of artistic influences during the early part of his career, vacillating between the work of late Tuscan Mannerists, contemporary Lombard

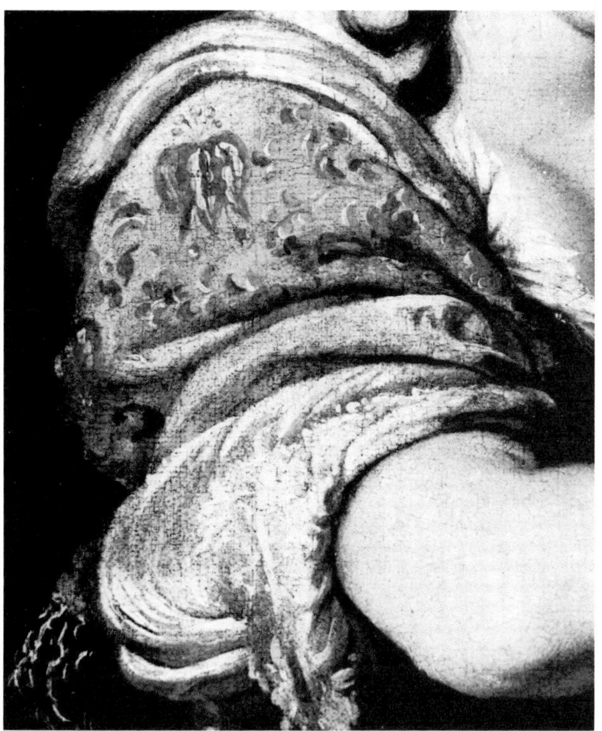

Fig. 2. Bernardo Strozzi, *Berenice Cutting Her Hair,* detail of fig. 1

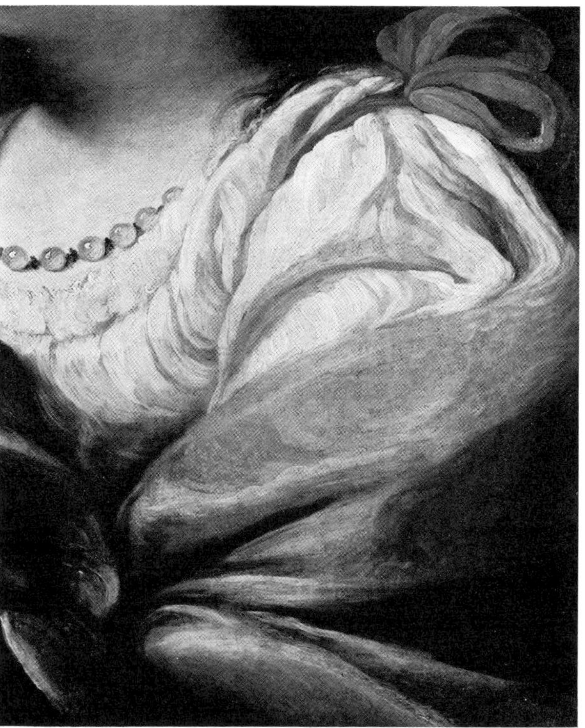

Fig. 3. Bernardo Strozzi, *St. Apollonia,* detail of cat. no. 19

painters, and the styles of Barocci and Rubens. Nevertheless, there is general agreement that the Baltimore *St. Apollonia* was executed during the Genoese period and probably during the 1620's, with a majority of scholars favoring a date toward the end of the decade. In his catalogue of the Binghamton exhibition of Strozzi's works from American collections, Milkovich assigned the painting to the late Genoese period,[10] and his conclusion was not questioned by Matteucci in her review of the exhibition.[11] Antonov also accepted a dating in the late 1620's and drew attention to the similarities between the Baltimore painting and a representation of an unidentified female saint in the Musée des Beaux-Arts, Caen.[12] Matteucci has published a version of the Baltimore painting in a private collection in Florence, dating the picture in the late 1620's (see Related Versions, 3).[13]

Luisa Mortari, on the other hand, who knew only the Genoese version of the painting (see Related Versions, 2), suggested that it might be as early as 1620–1625,[14] but this seems to me to be too early for the Baltimore picture. Toward the end of the decade, Strozzi's work acquired a greater luminosity, a new richness in the brushstrokes, and a greater freedom in the handling of the pigment, quite probably as a result of his renewed study of Flemish and Venetian masters.[15] The climax of this development is his altarpiece for the Chiesa dei Sordomuti (1629) which, in spite of the difference in size, shows the fluid impasto and luminous flesh tones that recall the Baltimore painting.[16] There are also parallels in both handling and pose between the Baltimore picture and the *St. Cecilia and the Angel* in Dijon, a painting which Mortari dates toward the end of the decade.[17] In both paintings there are transparent shadows along the cheek and also the flashing, scattered highlights in the hair which are characteristic of his works that are generally dated in the late 1620's.

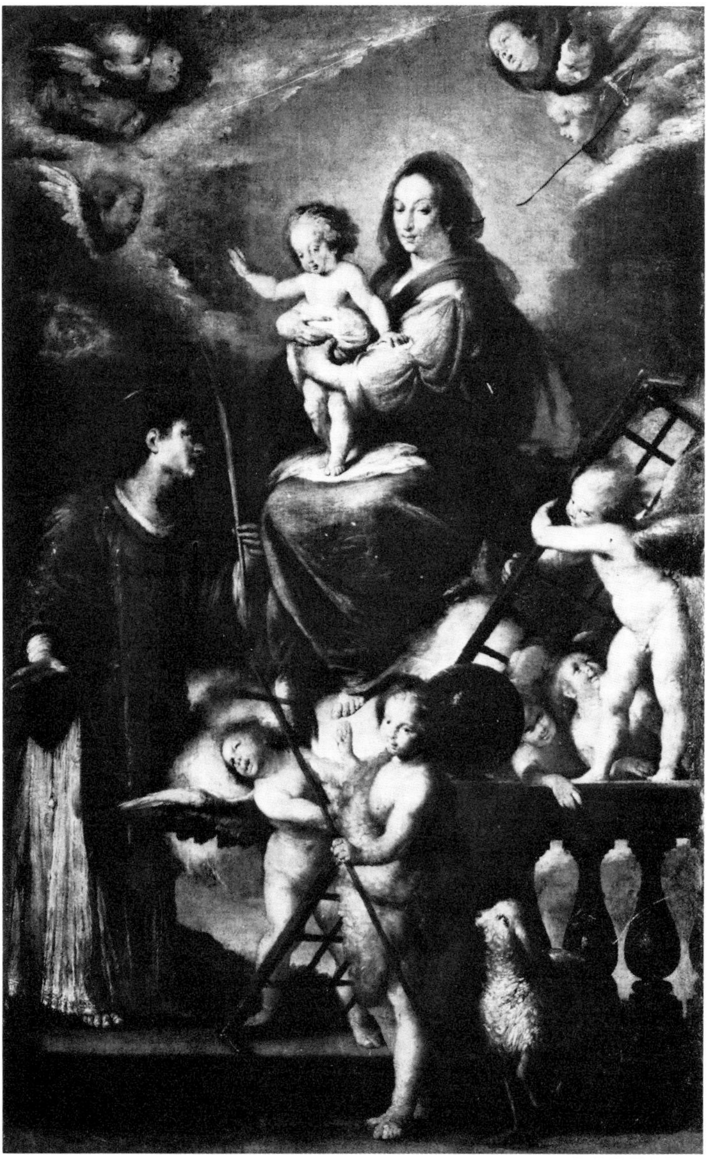

Fig. 4. Bernardo Strozzi, *Madonna and Child with St. Lawrence and Young St. John the Baptist.* Oil on canvas. 125⅛ × 75⅝ inches (318 × 192 cm.). Chiesa dei Sordomuti, Genoa. Courtesy Soprintendenza per i Beni Artistici e Storici della Liguria, Genoa

Strozzi's large, public commissions in Genoa were few and far between. Soprani wrote that not many of his paintings were to be seen in public because he usually painted works commissioned by private patrons for the decoration of their palaces.[18] Half-length figures of female saints were popular subjects. One of the earliest of these is certainly the *St. Catherine of Alexandria* in the Palazzo Reale, Genoa, which may have been painted before 1607.[19] The *Unidentified Female Martyr*—who is certainly St. Apollonia, since she carries the dental forceps in her left hand—in the Gardella Collection, Milan, is Strozzi's earliest known representation of the saint, probably preceding the Baltimore painting by some years.[20] It is tempting to think that Baltimore's *St. Apollonia* may at one time have been part of a series of paintings of saints, but so far no such series has been identified. The painting may, however, once have had a pendant and been one of a pair of paintings, such as the *St. Peter* and the *St. Paul,* which were formerly in the Rovelli Collection in Florence.[21] This possibility receives some confirmation from the fact that a *St. Cecilia* and a version of the Baltimore painting were sold together in 1950 (see Related Versions, 5).[22] The two paintings were the same size and both had frames with the Chigi coat of arms. As yet, however, such a hypothetical pendant for the Baltimore painting has not been verified.

The power of the monumental works of Strozzi's Genoese period has often been noted, but more modest works such as the Baltimore *St. Apollonia* are far more characteristic of his Genoese oeuvre and show how well he could inject a note of compelling drama into smaller works. There is an almost feverish intensity in the stare of the young female martyr, and this is beautifully echoed in the restless movement of the brush and of the undulant contours which define the forms. Works such as this must be counted among the best productions of Strozzi's maturity.

Strozzi was a prolific painter who often duplicated his compositions,[23] and the existence of several versions of the *St. Apollonia* raises questions about the practices of his Genoese workshop. He evidently ran a large studio in which a number of important younger artists were trained, among them Giovanni Andrea de' Ferrari (1598–1669) who, as Soprani reported, was able to imitate Strozzi's work very closely,[24] and Antonio Travi (1608–1665),[25] as well as a host of lesser figures such as Giuseppe Badarocco (1588–1657),[26] and Clemente Bocciardo (1620–1658).[27] In Strozzi's atelier the execution of important commissions was often entrusted to assistants and collaborators, a practice which has a long history in Italian art and was followed by most of the successful seventeenth-century artists.[28] Sometimes, as in the case of Rubens, the price of the work reflected the extent of the master's participation.[29] Certain masters employed specialists to execute parts of the work, such as the representation of architecture or landscape backgrounds.[30] Seventeenth-century connoisseurs were well aware of these procedures, and the artistic biographies of the period are filled with accounts of pupils or assistants who were said to have been able to copy their master's work to perfection.[31]

It is possible that when a particular painting was executed, several versions, either partially or completely painted, might have been retained by the artist in hopes that a buyer could be found. Stechow has suggested that these studio replicas "may have assumed the role of 'clean copy' for the fastidious client who was less bent upon evidence of the painter's 'handwriting' than is his modern counterpart."[32] Such practices may, perhaps, explain the existence of the various replicas of the *St. Apollonia.*

Any assessment of the exact degree of the master's participation in a medium-sized painting such as the Baltimore *St. Apollonia* must remain a matter of individual judgment among connoisseurs, but the quality of the Baltimore painting argues for a high percentage of Strozzi's involvement. The small change made by the artist in the neckline of the dress would also support the conclusion that the Baltimore painting does not depend upon a pre-existing version, for such changes are seldom found in copies. The *St. Apollonia* in The Baltimore Museum of Art is a splendid example of the master's style, executed with the astonishing bravura which Strozzi's contemporaries so admired.

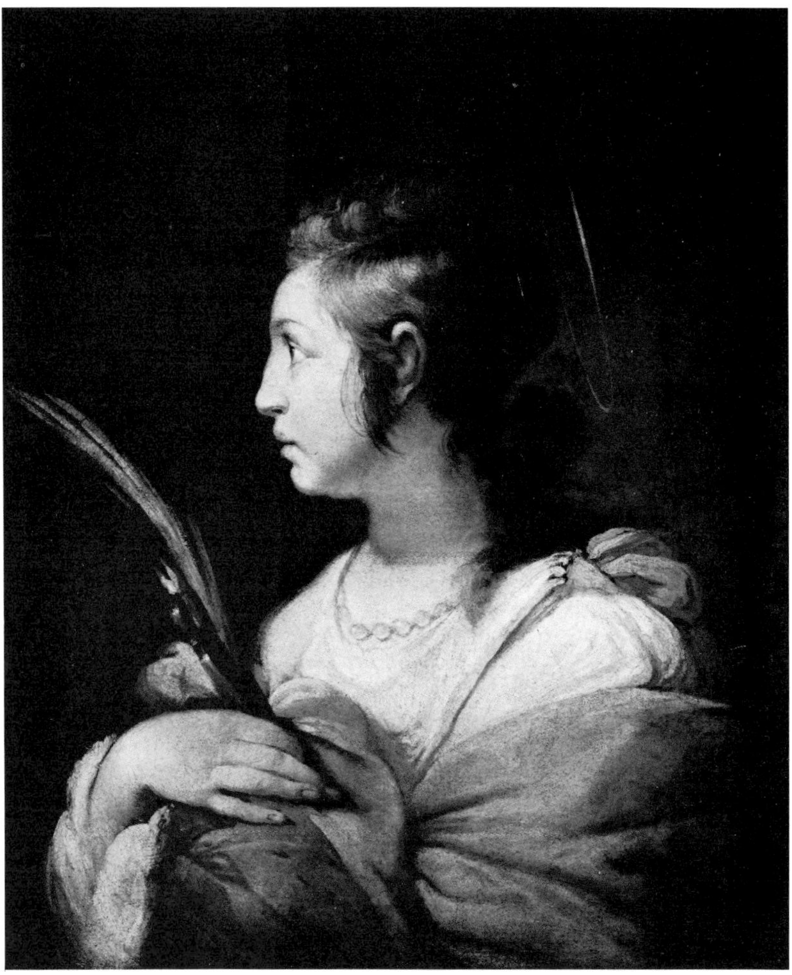

Fig. 5. Bernardo Strozzi, *St. Apollonia*. Oil on canvas. 33⅞ × 27 15/16 inches (86 × 71 cm.). Private collection, Copenhagen

RELATED VERSIONS*

1. Private Collection, Copenhagen
   Oil on canvas. 33 7/8 × 27 15/16 inches (86 × 71 cm.)
   This painting (fig. 5) had been attributed to the "eighteenth-century Italian School," but was correctly recognized as "clearly Strozziesque" by Harald Olsen, who wrote that "although not an important work the painting is more likely to be by the master himself than by one of the imitators (Ermanno Stroiffi)."[33] Professor Olsen, who saw the Baltimore version in November 1961, wrote to G. Rosenthal on May 15, 1962 that the Copenhagen painting "is somewhat more sketchy and less elaborately painted than your version. Moreover, a little more of the figure is shown and there are some minor differences in the treatment of hair and dress. . . . I believe there can be no doubt that Strozzi himself has painted replicas of his own paintings. On the other hand, replicas and copies of inferior quality must be from his studio or by his imitators. I have not seen the version published in *Arte Veneta* [see 3 below]: as for the others I would suppose that the picture in Copenhagen is the earliest one."[34] Luisa Mortari considered this work to be a product of Strozzi's Genoese workshop.[35]

2. Dr. Angelo Costa Collection, Genoa
Oil on canvas. 27 3/16 × 19 11/16 inches (69 × 50 cm.)
Mortari dated this painting ca. 1620–1625 and felt that it might be the same painting as that published by A. M. Matteucci in 1955 as being in a "private collection, Florence" (see 3 below).[36] In his notes on the Baltimore painting, Federico Zeri commented that it was "slightly inferior to an almost identical version in the Collection of Dr. Angelo Costa in Genoa (perhaps the one published by A. M. Matteucci in *Arte Veneta*)."[37]

3. Private Collection, Florence
Published by A. M. Matteucci in 1955 as a work executed by Strozzi before his departure from Genoa.[38] On September 18, 1956, Rodolfo Pallucchini wrote to G. Rosenthal that Miss Matteucci had informed him that the painting was still in an Italian private collection.[39] Mortari felt that this was probably the painting which Matteucci listed as being in a private collection, Genoa (see 2 above).[40] It is also possible that this painting could be no. 4 or no. 5 below.

4. Formerly Galerie Charpentier, Paris
Oil on canvas. 26 3/4 × 22 1/16 inches (68 × 56 cm.)
Sold at the Galerie Charpentier, Paris, on March 24, 1952.[41] In the sale catalogue it was erroneously suggested that this painting was the one exhibited at Baltimore in 1944 (i.e., The Baltimore Museum of Art version). This misinformation led Mortari to suggest that the Charpentier painting was once in the Loewi collection,[42] or that it might be the version which was sold from the Navarra Viggiani Collection in 1950 (see 5 below).[43]

5. Formerly Marchese Navarra Viggiani Collection
Oil on canvas. 27 15/16 × 22 1/16 inches (71 × 56 cm.)
This painting of *St. Apollonia* and its possible companion piece of the same size, a *St. Cecilia,* appeared at a 1950 sale in Rome with the Chigi coat of arms on the gilded frames.[44] Mortari felt that this may have been the painting sold two years later at the Galerie Charpentier, Paris (see 4 above). She considered it a work of Strozzi's Genoese period, datable to ca. 1620–1625.[45]

*For the paintings mentioned in the section on Related Versions, the author had to rely on reproductions.

Eric Van Schaack
Colgate University,
Hamilton, New York

NOTES

1. R. Soprani, *Le Vite de'pittori, scultori ed architetti genovesi . . . seconda edizione riveduta . . . da Carlo Giuseppe Ratti,* 2 vols. (Genoa: Casamara, 1768–1769), 1:104 and 422. See also the biographical summary published by L. Mortari, *Bernardo Strozzi* (Rome: DeLuca Editore, n.d. [1966]), pp. 83–85.
2. Soprani, *Le Vite,* 1:184 ff.
3. Ibid., 1:195.
4. Eusebius, *The Ecclesiatical History,* 2 vols., trans. K. Lake and J. E. L. Oulton (Loeb Classical Library; New York: G. P. Putnam's Sons, 1926–1932), 2:Bk. 6, chap. 41, sec. 7.
5. *The Golden Legend of Jacobus de Voragine,* trans. G. Ryan and H. Ripperger (New York: Arno Press, 1969), p. 164.
6. *Three Baroque Masters: Strozzi, Crespi, Piazzetta* (Baltimore: The Baltimore Museum of Art, 1944), no. 4, ill. p. 16.
7. L. Mortari, *Bernardo Strozzi,* p. 83.
8. Ibid., p. 172, figs. 241–43.

9. Ibid., p. 110, fig. 303.

10. M. Milkovich, *Bernardo Strozzi: Paintings and Drawings,* exhibition catalogue (Binghamton: University Art Gallery, State University of New York at Binghamton, 1967), no. 15, ill. p. 43.

11. A. M. Matteucci, "Bernardo Strozzi a Binghamton (New York)," *Arte Veneta* 22 (1968):264.

12. V. Antonov, "Aggiunte allo Strozzi," *Antichità viva* 11, no. 3 (1972):18.

13. Matteucci, "L'Attività veneziana di Bernardo Strozzi," *Arte Veneta* 9 (1955):141.

14. Mortari, *Bernardo Strozzi,* p. 128.

15. V. Antonov, "Un quadro inedito di Bernardo Strozzi e il problema di quattro Pietri," *Paragone* 19, no. 223 (1968):75 and 77.

16. Mortari, *Bernardo Strozzi,* p. 110 and fig. 303.

17. Ibid., p. 102 and fig. 206.

18. Soprani, *Le Vite,* 1:186. For a list of Strozzi's destroyed fresco commissions, see Matteucci, "L'Attività veneziana di Bernardo Strozzi," p. 138, n. 3.

19. Mortari, *Bernardo Strozzi,* p. 115, fig. 56. Mortari has suggested that this painting may actually be a copy of the version which is now in a Genoese private collection.

20. Ibid., p. 148, fig. 35.

21. Ibid., p. 107, figs. 123 and 124.

22. Ibid., p. 166.

23. Mortari lists, in various locations, ten replicas of *The Supper at Emmaus,* the best known of which is in the Chiesa della SS. Annunziata del Vastato, Genoa (*Bernardo Strozzi,* p. 37).

24. Soprani, *Le Vite,* 1:164 and 267.

25. Ibid., 1:267.

26. Ibid., 1:212.

27. Ibid., 1:328.

28. See H. Tietze and E. Tietze-Conrat, *The Drawings of the Venetian Painters of the 15th and 16th Centuries* (New York: J. J. Augustin, 1944), pp. 352–54. H. Tietze, "Meister und Werkstätte in der Renaissance Malerei Venedigs," *Alte und Neue Kunst, Wiener Kunstwissenschaftliche Blätter* 1, no. 3 (1952):89–91. I am grateful to G. Rosenthal for bringing this article to my attention.

29. Regarding workshop replicas, Rubens wrote to Sir Dudley Carleton in 1618: "Your Excellency must not think that the others are mere copies, for they are so well retouched by my hand that they can hardly be distinguished from originals. Nevertheless, they are rated at a much lower price." *The Letters of Peter Paul Rubens,* trans. and ed. R. S. Magurn (Cambridge, Mass.: Harvard University Press, 1955), pp. 61–62.

30. In the studio of Francesco Albani (1578–1660) there were many such specialists, Filippo Veralli was retained as a painter of landscapes, and the same task was carried out by Giovanni Antonio Maria del Sole and Giovanni Maria Galli Bibiena, whom Albani called "il fontaniere" because he generally painted rivers, lakes, and seascapes. See C. C. Malvasia, *Felsina Pittrice: Vite de pittori bolognesi . . .,* 2 vols. (Bologna: Erede di Domenico Barbieri, 1678), 2:267, 273, and 293.

31. See, for example, the material collected by F. Mendax, *Art Fakes and Forgeries,* trans. H. S. Whitman (New York: Philosophical Library, 1956), pp. 129 ff. Studio copies were rarely distinguished as such in the older inventories. An interesting exception is the studio inventory made after the death of El Greco. As many as four or five versions of some paintings are noted, some expressly distinguished by the words, "This is an original." H. van de Waal, "Forgery as a Stylistic Problem," *Aspects of art forgery; papers read by H. van de Waal, Th. Würtenberger, W. Froentjes at a symposium organized by the Institute of Criminal Law and Criminology of The University of Leiden* (The Hague: Martinus Nijhoff, 1962), p. 5, n. 2.

32. W. Stechow, *Hendrick Terbrugghen in America,* exhibition catalogue, The Dayton Art Institute and The Baltimore Museum of Art (Dayton, Ohio: Printing Service, n.d. [1965]), p. 10.

33. H. Olsen, *Italian Painting and Sculpture in Denmark* (Copenhagen: Munksgaard, 1961), p. 90, pl. 47a.

34. Olsen, see curatorial files, The Baltimore Museum of Art.

35. Mortari, *Bernardo Strozzi,* pp. 100–101.

36. Ibid., p. 128, fig. 130; L. Mortari, "Su Bernardo Strozzi," *Bollettino d'Arte,* ser. 4, 40 (1955):330.

37. Letter to G. Rosenthal of December 22, 1975, in the curatorial files, The Baltimore Museum of Art.

38. Matteucci, "L'Attività veneziana di Bernardo Strozzi," p. 141, fig. 152.

39. Curatorial files, The Baltimore Museum of Art.

40. Mortari, *Bernardo Strozzi,* p. 106.

41. Galerie Charpentier, Paris (March 24, 1952), sale catalogue, no. 64, pl. 25.

42. Mortari, *Bernardo Strozzi,* pp. 101 and 159–60, fig. 138.

43. Ibid., p. 166.

44. Jandolo Sale, Rome (December 1950), sale catalogue, no. 344, pl. 2A.

45. Mortari, *Bernardo Strozzi,* p. 166.

SELECTED BIBLIOGRAPHY

Raffaello Soprani. *Le Vite de' pittori, scultori ed architetti genovesi . . . seconda edizione riveduta . . . da Carlo Giuseppe Ratti.* 2 vols. Genoa: Casamara, 1768–1769.

Victor Lasareff. "Beiträge zu Bernardo Strozzi." *Münchner Jahrbuch der Bildenden Kunst,* N.S. 6, no. 1 (1929):11–30.

Three Baroque Masters: Strozzi, Crespi, Piazzetta. Exhibition catalogue. Baltimore: The Baltimore Museum of Art, 1944.

The Gallant Style. Exhibition catalogue. Columbus, Ohio: Columbus Gallery of Fine Arts, 1947.

Anna Maria Matteucci. "L'Attività veneziana di Bernardo Strozzi." *Arte Veneta* 9 (1955):138–54.

Luisa Mortari. "Su Bernardo Strozzi." *Bollettino d'arte,* serie 4, 40 (1955):311–34.

Harald Olsen. *Italian Painting and Sculpture in Denmark.* Copenhagen: Munksgaard, 1961.

Anna Maria Matteucci. "Per Bernardo Strozzi." *Arte antica e moderna* 19 (1962):292–93.

Luisa Mortari. "Aggiunte allo Strozzi." *Paragone* 13, no. 153 (1962):22–28.

Anna Maria Matteucci. "Un Libro Sullo Strozzi." *Arte Veneta* 20 (1966):296–97.

Luisa Mortari. *Bernardo Strozzi.* Rome: De Luca Editore, n.d. [1966].

Michael Milkovich. *Bernardo Strozzi: Paintings and Drawings.* Exhibition catalogue. Binghamton: University Art Gallery, State University of New York at Binghamton, 1967.

Victor Antonov. "Un quadro inedito di Bernardo Strozzi e il problema di quattro Pietri." *Paragone* 19, no. 223 (1968):74–78.

Anna Maria Matteucci. "Bernardo Strozzi a Binghamton (New York)." *Arte Veneta* 22 (1968):264–65.

Hugh McAndrew. "A Silver Basin Designed by Strozzi." *Burlington Magazine* 113 (January 1971): 4–11.

Victor Antonov. "Aggiunte allo Strozzi." *Antichità viva* 11, no. 3 (1972):18–22.

Rudolf Wittkower. *Art and Architecture in Italy 1600–1725.* 3rd edition revised. Harmondsworth and Baltimore: Penguin Books, 1973.

XVIIIth Century

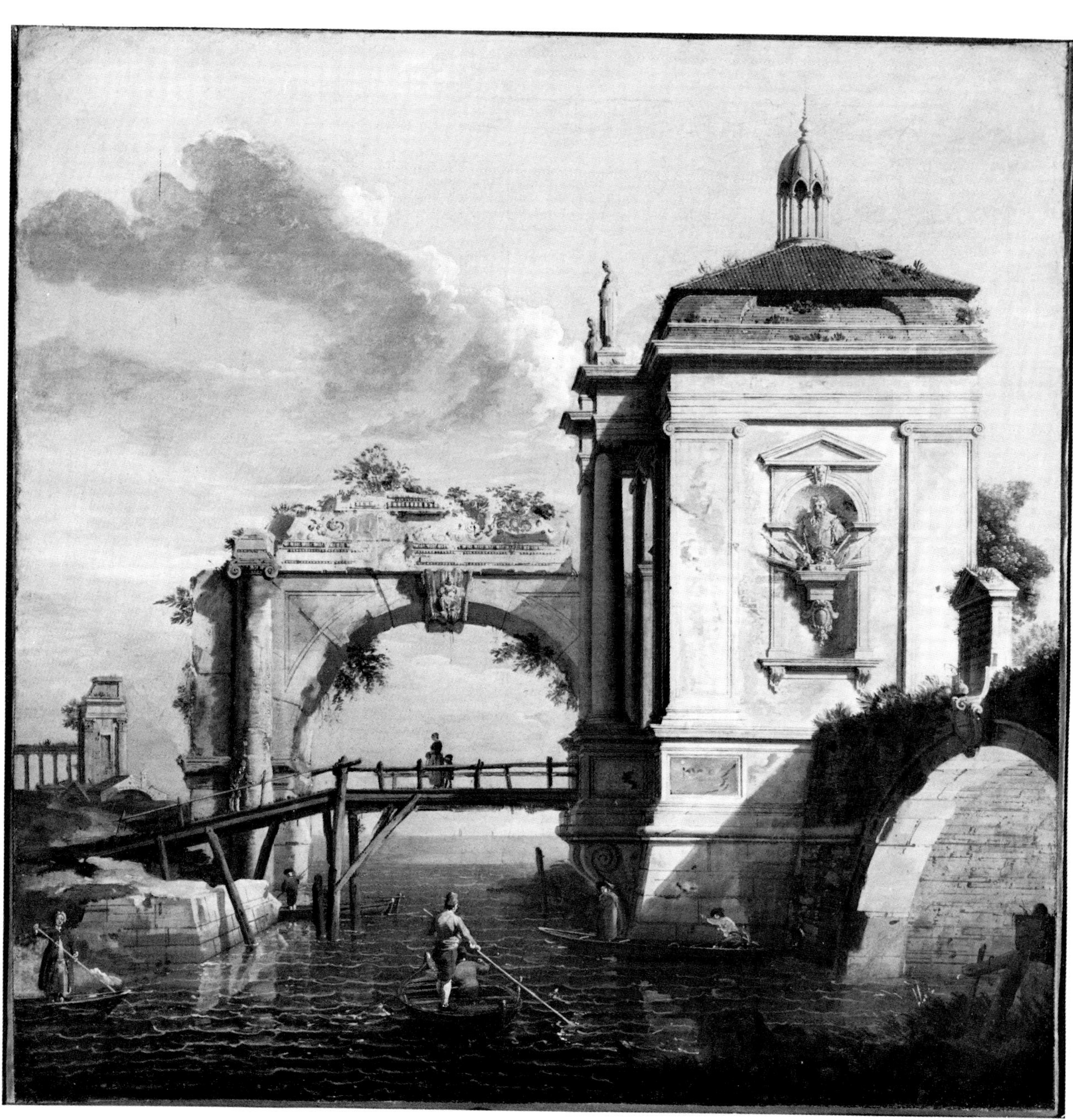

CANALETTO (1697–1768)
(Giovanni Antonio Canal)

---

20. *Architecture in Ruins (Capriccio: A Pavilion and a Ruined Arcade by the Lagoon),* ca. 1754

Oil on canvas. 41½ × 41 inches (105.4 × 104.1 cm.)
The Mary Frick Jacobs Collection (BMA 38.194)

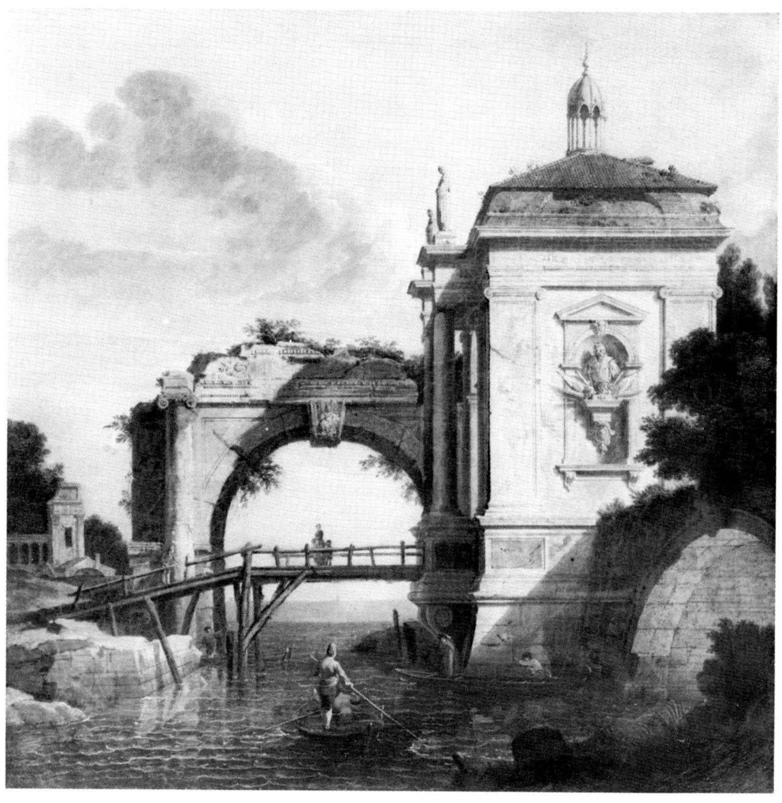

Fig. 1. Canaletto, *Architecture in Ruins,* cat. no. 20, before cleaning

PROVENANCE

Sir Charles Robinson, London

Sold by Sedelmeyer, Paris, in 3rd sale, June 3–5, 1907, no. 108

Acquired by Mary Frick Jacobs, Baltimore, in 1909 from Eugène Fischhof, Paris

Bequeathed to The Baltimore Museum of Art in 1938 as part of The Mary Frick Jacobs Collection

CONDITION

Because of a much darkened varnish Canaletto's *Architecture in Ruins* was cleaned in 1953 by Elisabeth C. G. Packard of The Walters Art Gallery (fig. 1). After the varnish was removed, the painting was confirmed as a work by Canaletto. At that time, it was noticed that several areas were overpainted. The overpainting of the trees at the middle right was removed, revealing a monument with an inscription. The trees at the middle left edge were also easily removed. And at the lower left a man in a boat reappeared during cleaning. The awkward cutting of the boat on the left leads one to suppose that the painting itself had at one time been cut. Though the heavy cloud formation in the left of the sky is not original, it was not removed as the original paint surface underneath no longer exists. An old glue lining, probably applied at the time when the painting was cut down, is still in stable condition and was not removed. After cleaning, the painting was revarnished and put on a new stretcher.

Giovanni Antonio Canal was born in Venice in 1697. Toward 1717, while still a young man, he assisted his father, a scenographer, on stage designs for operas by various contemporary composers, among them Antonio Vivaldi. In 1719 Canaletto left Venice for Rome and "solemnly swore off the theater;"[1] nonetheless, two libretti for operas written by Alessandro Scarlatti and performed in Rome in 1720 bear Canaletto's name along with that of his father as scene designer. In that same year, the young artist was recorded in the "Fraglia," or association of Venetian painters, indicating that his stay in Rome was brief.

Having returned to his native city at about age twenty-three, Canaletto almost immediately began to receive important commissions. He was included among the artists contracted in 1722 by Owen McSwiney, an impresario willing to turn his hand to various money-making propositions, to paint allegorical tomb paintings commemorating twenty-four Englishmen of the seventeenth and eighteenth centuries. Canaletto's contributions to the series were the architectural sections of the two works dedicated to Lord Somers and Archbishop Tillotson.[2] These playful arrangements of ancient and medieval arches in ruin, fanciful Baroque tombs, and ornate sculptural decorations reveal the young painter's ease in dealing with imaginary settings composed of strikingly different structural types all organized according to traditional perspectival rules. Canaletto's early scenographic work had obviously provided him with just the right artistic foundation for these images of fantastic monumentality.

Contemporary with the McSwiney commission, Canaletto began to paint views of Venice in the tradition of two older but still living view painters, Luca Carlevarijs and Gaspar van Wittel. Like their views, Canaletto's early works are large in size and depict the most famous sites of the city. But, whereas the paintings of his two predecessors in the genre are bright in color and sometimes almost chalky in appearance, Canaletto's are somber and dark and often show a dramatic and stormy Venice. But heavy daubs of brightly colored paint describe the little details of daily life, thus enlivening the pictorial image and adding a coloristic richness and tactile luxuriance completely new to the genre of view painting. Canaletto's success with these works was impressive. Non-Venetian and non-Italian patrons, in particular, commissioned works from him, and during the 1720's he produced an enormous number of *vedute* in which he sought to approximate ever more closely the light, air, and movement of the unique experience that is Venice.

By 1730, when Canaletto had clearly mastered all the technical difficulties inherent in representing space and volume, his vision of the city changed; instead of the heavy clouds, deep shadows, and mottled building surfaces characteristic of his first period, bright and sunlit surfaces and broad, powdery blue skies now fill his works. Little figures painted mostly in the primaries—red, blue, and yellow—animate and actively move about his city scenes. Perhaps the painting that best captures this moment in his career is the view of the Basin of St. Mark (*Bacino di San Marco*) in the Museum of Fine Arts, Boston (fig. 2). Here, Canaletto has stressed the amplitude and breadth of the Basin, and the place is presented, in effect, as an enormous bowl of space. The spectator feels himself pulled deep into the city of Venice. Amazingly, Canaletto accomplished this without the use of perspective orthogonals. Clouds and embankments encircle the Basin, opening it rather than delimiting it, and the harmony between the breadth of the view and the crystalline quality of the light is perfect.

Canaletto continued to fulfill commissions during the following years, although his art began to show a somewhat mechanical repetition both in terms of the kinds of views he chose and in his painterly execution. Partly as a result of declining patronage in Venice, he made his way in 1746 to England where, through the offices of McSwiney, he was introduced to the English nobility for whom he produced scenes of London and the

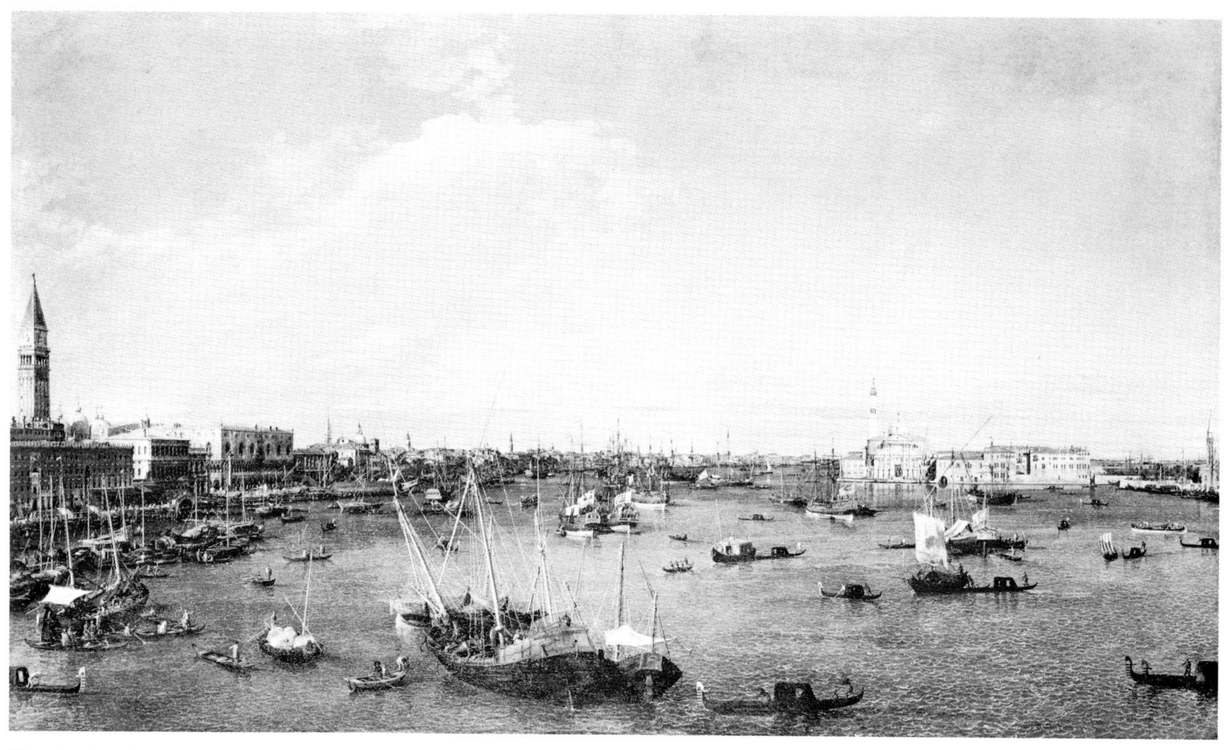

Fig. 2. Canaletto, *Bacino di San Marco,* 1730's. Oil on canvas. 49⅛ × 60¼ inches (124.8 × 153 cm.). Museum of Fine Arts, Boston. Purchase, Abbot Lawrence Fund, Seth K. Sweetser Fund and Charles Edward French Fund (39.290). Courtesy, Museum of Fine Arts, Boston

surrounding countryside.[3] Although he executed several remarkably fine paintings of the Thames and Whitehall for the Duke of Richmond, his total output in England was unsatisfactory in quality. His views of English country houses are flat and unconvincing in their atmosphere, and many of his city scenes, too, were executed in a wooden style. So disappointed were the English in his work that the rumor began to circulate that he was not the "veritable Cannelleti [sic] of Venice."[4] As a result, he placed an advertisement in local newspapers reminding the English public of the availability of his work. In 1755, after an absence of ten years, he finally returned to Venice where he once again painted views of that city, and he began as well to create perspective studies meant to please the new academic tastes of the third quarter of the century. In 1763, after having denied him entrance once, the Venetian Academy of Painting and Sculpture admitted him into their ranks as a perspectivist. Five years later, in 1768, he died, leaving neither family nor fortune.

A pivotal figure in Canaletto's career and decisive for the artist's production of imaginary views was Joseph Smith, an English entrepreneur established in Venice from the beginning of the century.[5] Desirous of turning a profit wherever he could, Smith must have seen as early as the late 1720's that Canaletto's paintings were not only remarkable pictorial recreations of Venetian sites but that they could also be extremely marketable commodities. As a shrewd merchant shipper in contact with wealthy Englishmen, Joseph Smith assumed the role of commercial intermediary between Canaletto and an art-collecting public in and near London. In fact, it was in part with Smith's help that Canaletto made his way into the homes of prospective clients in England. Unfortunately, we have no documentary evidence explaining the exact form of Smith's and Canaletto's relationship, but it is clear that Canaletto's fame and indeed the very nature of his later work reflect his interaction with Venice's most famous foreign resident of the eighteenth century.

During the 1730's, Smith bought and kept for his own collection many of Canaletto's *vedute esatte* of Venice; he also seems to have become particularly interested at this time in imaginary views, or caprices. The imaginary view can be traced back historically to the Renaissance and Baroque traditions of ruin painting and drawing.[6] In the sixteenth century northern artists such as Marten van Heemskerck and Hieronymous Cock came flocking to Rome and expressed their fascination for the remains of ancient Rome by making accurate copies of these overwhelming architectural sights. Seventeenth-century images of ruins, however, unlike their precedents, tend not to reproduce Roman ruins faithfully but rather to reorder them, that is, to bring together buildings of different styles and from different places to form imaginary architectural ensembles. Italian and non-Italian artists produced such works. In the early seventeenth century, Cornelius Poelenburgh and Bartholomeus Breenberg, both Dutch, painted scenes of pastoral life in and among ancient Roman ruins, often transforming and rearranging the relationships of recognizable monuments. Later in the century, Viviano Codazzi and Giovanni Ghisolfi created urban images showing decaying temples, palaces, and obelisks that were meant to recall the once glorious monumentality that we associate with the ancient city.

Scenes of ruins and rubble continued to be produced in the eighteenth century by Marco Ricci in Venice and Giovanni Paolo Panini in Rome. Their works express the fantasy and playfulness often associated with Rococo art, as well as the attentive study of real architectural and sculptural remains that reflects a new archaeological seriousness in the second quarter of the eighteenth century. Canaletto painted several works of this type in the early 1720's, at the same time that he was working on the McSwiney commission, and then again in the 1730's. In a work from the twenties, the flank of a pyramid attached to a wall is placed near both the Arch of Constantine and the Colosseum; and in a work from the thirties, Canaletto capriciously mixes Roman and Paduan elements to create a haunting scene of ruined isolation.[7] Such juxtapositions of architectural elements were hardly new in ruin painting, but Canaletto's air-filled space and dramatic lighting, cutting across worn and uneven surfaces, affirm that for the first time ruin painting was in the hands of a first-rate painter. With Canaletto, the genre became a major landscape statement.

Subsequently, in the 1740's, Canaletto combined elements from the traditions of *rovinismo* (ruin painting) and *vedutismo* (view painting) to create a new type of painting. The combination is, to say the least, bizarre and offbeat. The *veduta ideata,* a term first used by Canaletto himself on the frontispiece of his series of etchings dedicated to Joseph Smith in the mid-forties, is not at all a romantic vision of monumental decay, but rather a projection of an imagined reality. Canaletto turned the full powers of his sober and workaday mind upon the fantasy scenes of ruined architecture, adding prosaic elements and details of daily existence, so that his new image assumes the guise of reality. Before Canaletto, Carlevarijs had experimented with the type; he had grouped together, for instance, a Roman triumphal arch, St. Peter's Basilica, and Castel Sant' Angelo alongside a harbor and port.[8] But Carlevarijs produced only a handful of such works, whereas Canaletto obviously made a specialty of the type during the last twenty years of his life. It is to this genre of the *veduta ideata* that *Architecture in Ruins* belongs; it is a representative example of the new kind of fantasy image that Canaletto began to produce in the 1740's.

Canaletto's creation of the *veduta ideata* can be explained partially by contemporary political events but above all by his association with Smith. During the 1740's the hostilities of the War of the Austrian Succession cut off the usual droves of English tourists to Venice. Having lost many of his patrons, Canaletto found Smith stepping into the void and commissioning him to execute a number of paintings and prints of imaginary views. Smith's extensive art collection, eventually bought in the 1760's by George III of England, already contained several architectural caprices and ruin paintings by Marco Ricci, Carlevarijs, and Canaletto himself. The decision made by Smith in the mid-1740's to ask Canaletto not to continue in the existing tradition but rather to create a different kind of imaginary view reflects the new set of colleagues with whom Smith came to associate in the late 1730's and 1740's. Not only did he begin to frequent the homes of the intelligentsia of the Veneto, but in 1744 he was also named Consul from the Court of St. James's to the Venetian Republic. His status in Venice now altered, Smith very likely began to consider how to express artistically his new position in society. The *veduta ideata,* a genre of intellectual pretensions, most felicitously fulfilled his need. There is, in fact, no doubt that its creation is as much a result of the Consul's new intellectual and cultural environment as of Canaletto's own creative artistry.[9]

Foremost among Smith's commissions were a series of prints and thirteen overdoors celebrating the works of famous Venetian architects of the Cinquecento. In the prints and the overdoors Canaletto dealt extensively with the problems of the *veduta ideata*—that is, with choosing and rearranging critical monuments so as to form new environments and with creating fantastic architecture that would convey the semblance of a concrete reality. In the series of etchings, Canaletto produced a number of imaginary views of small towns on the *terra ferma.* Venetian houses, porticoes, and lone monuments are juxtaposed to create small, north Italian villages amidst mountain landscapes or along the seaside. In the overdoors, eleven of which can still be traced, the artist rearranged famous existing buildings of Venice, and by shifting monuments from one site to another created a "new" Venice. He continued this work in England where he composed paintings in which unexpected mixtures of Venetian and English architectural elements produce bizarre but striking, imaginary urban scenes.[10]

In *Architecture in Ruins,*[11] probably painted some years later, Canaletto produced yet another type of *veduta ideata.* The scene is set not in the English countryside nor in Venice, but in the lonely lagoon between the city and the *terra ferma.* Canaletto's preoccupation with the quiet and isolation found in the lagoon is typical of one aspect of his oeuvre from about 1750 on. He dealt with the theme probably for the first time in a real view, the *Torre del Malghera,*[12] from the prints of the 1740's. Here, figures work in boats that move on the waterways of a lonely part of the city. But with the passing of years, Canaletto seems to have wanted to develop the theme, not utilizing actual sites but creating instead imagined islands with unlikely combinations of monumental and rustic architecture, as in *Architecture in Ruins.* On the right stands a bridge, reminiscent of those in Venice, leading back in space to the side of a monumental entranceway similar to many constructed in Renaissance villas in the Veneto. Placed at a ninety-degree angle to this are the remains of a Roman archway before which stands a rickety wooden bridge that ties the structure on the right to an island where more Roman ruins complete the scene. Small figures animate the picture: a group of boatmen glide their vessels through the water, and on the wooden bridge above, a woman and a young child cross toward a man who looks attentively down over a new handrail. These figures move with a quiet purpose, and they carry out their prosaic chores with a rhythm very different from that of the romantic personages found in earlier and more traditional ruin paintings by Ghisolfi and Ricci.

Other lagoon scenes show similar groupings of temples, arches, and ruins united by bridges, with lone figures moving about and working along the water's edge.[13] In all of these paintings, light rakes across building surfaces and space in a similar manner. Note, for example, how cast shadows on the right are juxtaposed against architectural monuments standing in the brilliant sunlight. This hard, sharp line cutting light from

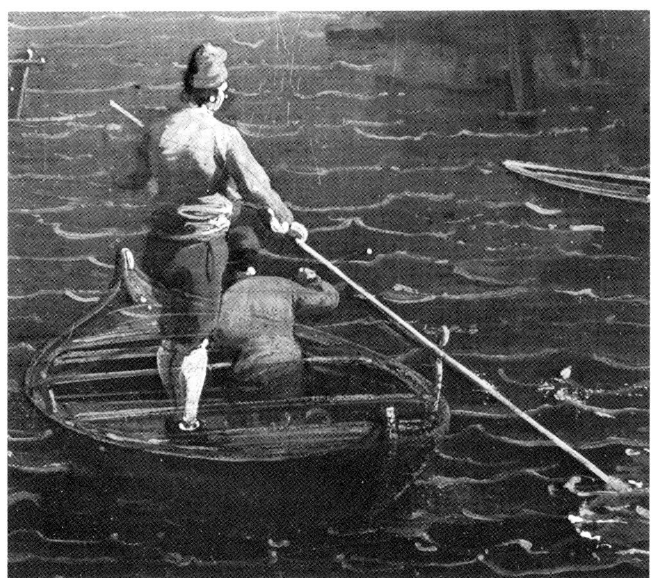

Fig. 3. Canaletto, *Architecture in Ruins,* detail of cat. no. 20

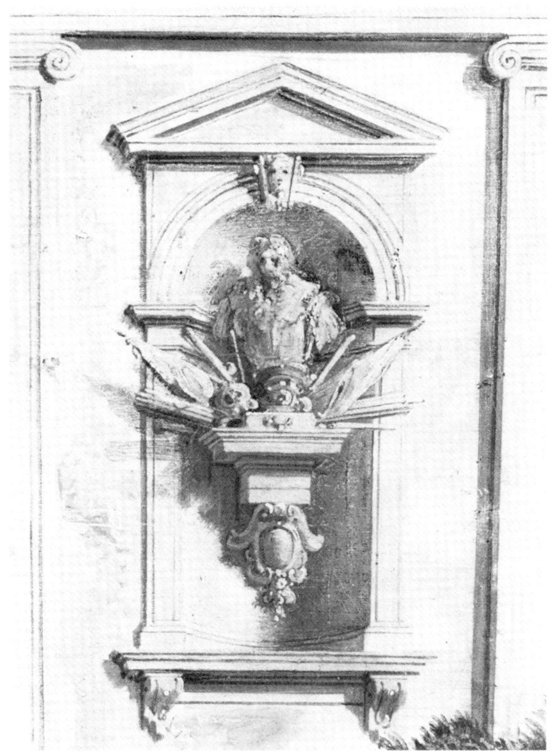

Fig. 4. Canaletto, *Architecture in Ruins,* detail of cat. no. 20

shadow is typical of Canaletto's Venetian style of the 1740's as well as of his scenes of London and the English countryside from the late forties and the early fifties. Indeed, almost the entire organization of these lagoon scenes is determined by the ruled architecture, sharp edges, and right angles so characteristic of much of the artist's work from this period.

The brushwork is also similar to that found in his real views from the 1740's and 1750's. It can in fact be easily distinguished from both his early style of the 1720's extending into the 1730's and his late style of the last ten years of his life. In his early work building surfaces appear mottled, for the paint was laid on in thick and pasty applications. In the thirties, too, draperies and fabrics are still described with rich swirls of color, and painting surfaces seem to flicker with the animation derived from the very active brushwork. Canaletto's late work, on the other hand, is quite different. The handling is calligraphic; short and dry strokes of paint create tiny squiggles of color and little dots of light that dart across the painting surface. The brushwork in *Architecture in Ruins* seems to stand somewhere between these two extremes. The frieze and keystone of the Roman archway, for example, are described by thick paint, and the painterly description of the figure of the boatman in the center foreground is characteristic of a style still tied to the 1730's (fig. 3). Other elements, however, reveal a slow shift to the late style. Canaletto paints the bust in the niche and its accompanying banners and escutcheon more tightly (fig. 4); for the most part, the brushstrokes tend to be tense, and tiny dots of paint are employed in this area to describe light bouncing off surfaces. It must be stated also that the general tonality of the painting is grayish and somewhat dull, not close to the sunlit paintings of the thirties or even to the harder, more brilliant lighting found in many works from the forties. In sum, stylistic evidence would seem to indicate a dating in the early 1750's for *Architecture in Ruins.*

Canaletto executed a number of paintings related to the Baltimore work. Several reproduce this scene with only small variations (Constable/Links nos. 511 and 511[a]). One version, in a private collection in New York, depicts an expanded view with Roman colonnades extended onto the island at the left. Written on the back of the lining canvas is the inscription "1754 Io Antonio Canaletto Pinx v. invenzione." Constable asserts that the notation is "probably inscribed from one on the original canvas,"[14] although he does not explain the basis for this belief. Stating that all the versions are related stylistically, Constable then concludes that they all date from the same artistic moment. Thus, 1754 would be the approximate date for the Baltimore painting also. Although Constable's argument for this very precise dating hinges upon an unauthenticated inscription, pictorial style and architectural morphology do in fact confirm, as we have already seen, that the Baltimore painting dates from the early 1750's.

The existence of the New York painting with its expanded architectural ensemble, and the Baltimore canvas's severed boat and square format, so uncommon for an autograph work by Canaletto, suggest that *Architecture in Ruins* was cut down at some time in the past. Even in its reduced state, it measures 41½ × 41 inches, whereas the New York version, although greater in panorama, measures only 20 × 33½ inches. Certainly the physical impact of the Baltimore painting in its original state must have been impressive. It was, in effect, a new kind of imaginary view. In it, Canaletto merged ruin painting with the Venetian lagoon, and the combination is charming. It is a formula original with Canaletto, and it speaks of the artist's commitment to fantasy constructed out of a perceived reality.

William L. Barcham
Fashion Institute of Technology,
State University of New York,
New York

NOTES

1. A. M. Zanetti, *Della pittura Veneziana e delle opere pubbliche dei veneziani maestri* (Venice, 1771), p. 462.
2. The former work is in the possession of the Earl of Plymouth, Oakly Park, Shropshire; the latter is in a private collection in England.
3. See H. F. Finberg, "Canaletto in England," *Walpole Society* 9 (1920–1921):21–76.
4. G. Vertue, *Anecdotes of Painting in England,* vol. 3 of Vertue Notebooks (1722–1754), reprinted in *Walpole Society* 22 (1933–1934):149.
5. See F. Vivian, *Il console Smith, mercante e collezionista* (Vicenza: Neri Pozza, 1971).
6. See W. L. Barcham, *The Imaginary View Scenes of Canaletto* (New York: Garland Publishing Co., Inc., 1977), pp. 14 ff.
7. J. G. Links, *Canaletto and His Patrons* (New York: New York University Press, 1977), fig. 8, and Barcham, *The Imaginary View Scenes of Canaletto,* fig. 113.
8. A. Rizzi, *Luca Carlevarijs* (Venice: Alfieri, 1967), fig. 64.
9. W. L. Barcham, "Canaletto and a Commission from Consul Smith,"*Art Bulletin* 59, no. 3 (September 1977):383–93.
10. W. G. Constable and J. G. Links, *Canaletto,* 2 vols., rev. ed. (Oxford: Clarendon Press, 1976), 1:pl. 92, nos. 505 and 506.
11. W. G. Constable, *Canaletto,* 2 vols. (Oxford: Clarendon Press, 1962), 2:no. 511(c) listed as "Capriccio: A Pavilion and a Ruined Arcade by the Lagoon"; W. G. Constable, *Canaletto,* exhibition catalogue, The Art Gallery of Toronto, National Gallery of Canada, Ottawa, and Museum of Fine Arts, Montreal, 1964–1965 (Toronto, 1964), no. 108; *Time Magazine* 84 (October 16, 1964):90; L. Puppi, *L'Opera completa del Canaletto* (Milan: Rizzoli, 1968), no. 314 B; Constable and Links, *Canaletto,* 2:511(c).
12. Ibid., 1:pl. 175, no. 8.
13. Ibid., 1:pl. 90; 2:nos. 487 and 488. The fantasy of these scenes lies not in the architecture itself, as in the artist's late caprices, but in the architectural associations.
14. Ibid., 1:147.

SELECTED BIBLIOGRAPHY

Anton Maria Zanetti. *Della pittura Veneziana e delle opere pubbliche dei veneziani maestri.* Venice, 1771.

Hilda F. Finberg. "Canaletto in England." *Walpole Society* 9 (1920–1921):21–76, and 10 (1921–1922): 75–78.

George Vertue. *Anecdotes of Painting in England.* Vol. 3 of Vertue Notebooks (1722–1754) reprinted in *Walpole Society* 22 (1933–1934).

Henry Barton Jacobs. *The Collection of Mary Frick Jacobs.* Baltimore: Prepared and published by Dr. Henry Barton Jacobs, 1938.

Elisabeth C. G. Packard. "The Restoration of Two Paintings in the Jacobs Collection." *Baltimore Museum of Art News* 18, no. 2 (December 1954):3–12.

Age of Elegance: The Rococo and Its Effect. Exhibition catalogue. Baltimore: The Baltimore Museum of Art, 1959.

Eloise Spaeth. *American Art Museums and Galleries: An Introduction to Looking.* New York: Harper and Bros., 1960.

W. G. Constable. *Canaletto.* 2 vols. Oxford: Clarendon Press, 1962.

Time Magazine 84 (October 16, 1964):90.

W. G. Constable. *Canaletto.* Exhibition catalogue. The Art Gallery of Toronto, National Gallery of Canada, Ottawa, and Museum of Fine Arts, Montreal, 1964–1965. Toronto, 1964.

Lionello Puppi. *L'Opera Completa del Canaletto.* Milan: Rizzoli, 1968.

Gertrude Rosenthal, ed. *From El Greco to Pollock: Early and Late Works by European and American Artists.* Exhibition catalogue. Baltimore: The Baltimore Museum of Art, 1968.

Frances Vivian. *Il console Smith, mercante e collezionista.* Vicenza: Neri Pozza, 1971.

W. G. Constable and J. G. Links. *Canaletto.* 2 vols. Rev. ed. Oxford: Clarendon Press, 1976.

William L. Barcham. "Canaletto and a Commission from Consul Smith." *Art Bulletin* 59, no. 3 (September 1977):383–93.

William L. Barcham. *The Imaginary View Scenes of Canaletto.* New York: Garland Publishing Co., Inc., 1977.

J. G. Links. *Canaletto and His Patrons.* New York: New York University Press, 1977.

Burr Wallen. *The William A. Gumberts Collection of Canaletto Etchings.* Santa Barbara: Santa Barbara Museum of Art, 1979.

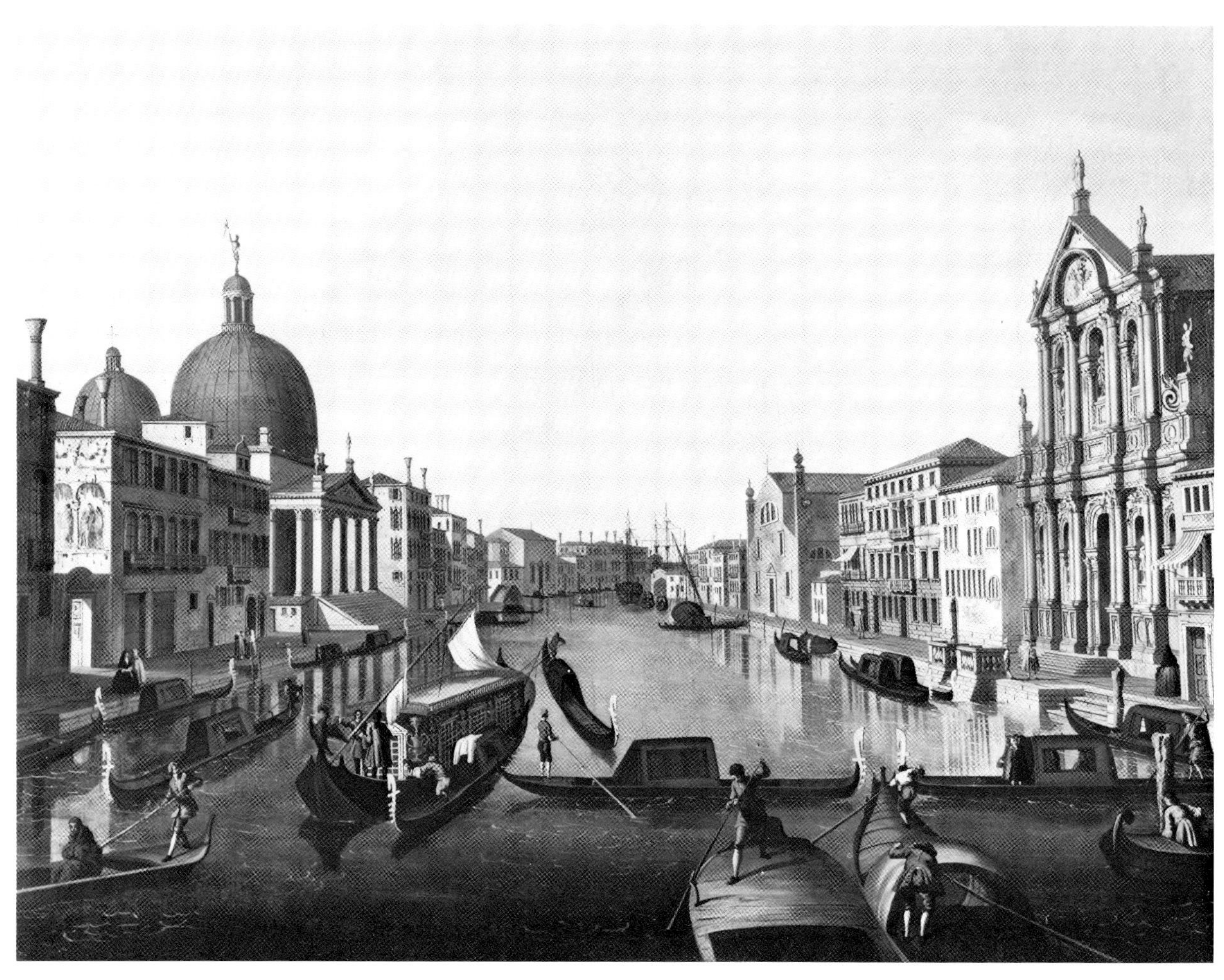

Attributed to
VINCENZO CHILONE (1758–1839)

21. *Venice, The Grand Canal with San Simeone Piccolo and the Church of the Scalzi Looking Toward Sta. Croce,* ca. 1785–1800

Oil on canvas. 44¼ × 56⅞ inches (112.4 × 144.5 cm.)
Gift of Mrs. John Eager Howard, Baltimore (BMA 1980.125)

PROVENANCE

The history of this painting is not documented; however, it can be surmised that this is the picture exhibited at the Second Annual Exhibition of The Peale Museum in 1823 as *View in Venice* by Canaletto (no. 96). At that time it was owned by William Gilmor (1775–1829) of Baltimore, brother of the noted collector, Robert Gilmor, Jr., and father of Jane Grant Gilmor (1801–1890). Jane Gilmor married Benjamin Chew Howard (1791–1872), son of John Eager Howard, the Revolutionary War hero, and great-grandfather of John Eager Howard (1901–1977), whose widow presented the picture to the Museum.

The gift of this painting was made while the present publication was in progress. Limitations of time thus precluded the inclusion of comparative material.

CONDITION

The linen support of this Venetian view is of a medium fine weave. The oil paint, on a light gray ground with a slightly ochre cast, was applied as an opaque paste, smooth in most areas except for some heavier brushstrokes in the highlights of the clouds and some minor impasto visible in the architectural highlights.

Prior to its acquisition by the Baltimore Museum, the picture had deteriorated through natural aging as well as inferior restoration. The design layer shows a pronounced crackle, most noticeable in the sky. The picture was glue-lined, probably in the second part of the nineteenth century. After relining it was torn, which made another restoration necessary. The tear extended from left to right, 8 inches above the bottom edge and almost parallel to it. In this subsequent restoration, when overpainting the tear, a much foreshortened gondola close to the ornate barge was painted out. Probably at that same time the entire sky was overpainted, presumably in order to cover the crackle and minor damages. Prior to its publication in this catalogue the painting was cleaned. Most of the overpaint could be removed. Obvious losses were inpainted, and the picture was given a coat of non-yellowing varnish. Further conservation treatment is contemplated in the near future.

Geoffrey Michael Lemmer
The Baltimore Museum of Art

As the demand for views of Venice reached boom proportions in the first quarter of the eighteenth century, largely to satisfy English tourists intent on souvenirs of the Grand Tour, the repertory of subjects extended from the San Marco area to include several characteristic aspects of the Canal Grande. Canaletto (1697–1768), the greatest of the *vedutisti,* created the prototype of the present composition in a painting of the early 1730's, now in the Royal collections at Windsor Castle.[1] Paintings were, however, already very costly and difficult to transport and most visitors had to content themselves with prints. Canaletto's pictures provided the models for the first major set of such engravings, the volume of fourteen views of which this subject is number XI, a set published by Visentini in 1735.[2] Its success must have inspired another view painter, Michele Marieschi (1710–1744), to produce his own set of twenty-one etched views in 1741.[3] He reproduced several of the subjects done by Canaletto and Visentini, being careful to adjust the angle of view, perspective, and details, especially substituting his own *staffage* of gondolas, boats, and passers-by for those used by his predecessors and competitors. Marieschi's plate VI represents the Grand Canal looking toward Sta. Croce, repeating the vantage point of the earlier print by Visentini, as though he were perched in the rigging of a boat at mid-canal, and reproducing the aspect of this end of the Canal with such other details as his own boats and pedestrian traffic.[4] It is this etching which formed the basis for the present painting which repeats the print's format and most, but not all, of its details.[5]

The authorship of the Baltimore Museum picture cannot, however, simply be described as an anonymous copy based on Marieschi's etching. It is evident that Venetian *vedutisti,* both major and minor, did not work out-of-doors in the manner of the Impressionists more than a century later; instead, they drew on the site and then painted from their sketches and from memory in the comfort of the studio. Since the popular repertory of subjects was already set by the widely circulated prints, they quite often simply took a Visentini or a Marieschi graphic work as their point of departure, making it serve in lieu of their own life sketches. The young Guardi often followed this procedure by transforming Marieschi's etchings into his own unmistakable pictorial idiom.[6] The same process pertains to the Baltimore Chilone, since the composition follows the print in most of its elements, but the painting style has nothing to do with Marieschi's thready impasto, hot color, or scratchy detailing as seen in his rather rare paintings.[7] Instead, here it is the late manner of Canaletto which formed the basis for this painter's approach. A cool, gray tonality accented by touches of lucent blue, yellow, and red complements a crisp, linear definition of architectural detail. Dappled light on the tile roofs and elsewhere, an optical clarity of reflections in the canal, and the calligraphic play of wavelets on the water's surface recall Canaletto's latest paintings. Even the enameled but transparent brushstrokes with which the figures are suggested have some of the creamy impasto and the luminosity of the master's. It is significant that when our painter departs from the Marieschi print in these figures, it is to substitute a standing gondolier at center in a pose taken from Canaletto but not to be found in Marieschi. In sum, an artist trained in the Canaletto tradition has made use of a Marieschi print for the format of the present painting. Just as he was not Marieschi, neither was he Canaletto himself, but he was a competent if not remarkable *vedutista* of the last part of the Settecento.

Among the artists whose names might be considered in searching for the painting's author, several such as Jolli, Battaglioli, or Moretti may be excluded since they either specialized in a different genre, such as the *capriccio,* or painted in a style distinct from that of this picture.[8] Giacomo Fabris would seem a possibility, but he died in 1761, a date almost certainly too early for our painter.[9] The name Vincenzo Chilone does carry some conviction in this context. Born in 1758, Chilone was well enough established to participate in the Papal and Conte del Nord commemorative pictures of 1782 and in the next decade enjoyed the patronage of Venetian nobility, depicted events of the Napoleonic era, and continued to provide visitors with views described as in the tradition of Canaletto up to his death in 1839. He seems to have inherited some of the old master's English patronage and even extended it to include some of the earliest American collectors, such as Robert Gilmor who bought a sizable number of his drawings in Venice in 1835.[10] Chilone's painting style has yet to be given a clear definition, but some suggestions might be advanced on the basis of the few signed or documented works which have so far been identified. His 1782 pictures have not been located, but the three fresco *vedute* in the Palazzo Minotti at Udine are signed and dated 1792.[11] In them, his methodical but frequently halting application of perspective, a dependency on stick-like black lines to define architectural form, a spotted accenting of highlights, and a pallid gray monochrome tonality broken only by touches of bright color in the figures underline his debt to Canaletto. In 1815 he recorded the return of the bronze horses to San Marco in a picture which is more abstract, arid in its perspective scheme, uncertain in its grasp of scale, and distinctly neo-classical in its exclusion of the casual and picturesque from its schematic formula.[12] Finally, a pair of small signed canvases of unidentified houses on the Venetian lagoon are looser, more improvisational in brushwork, and distinctly reminiscent of Giacomo Guardi's small genre views produced in quantity in these same years.[13] They probably date from the last decade of Chilone's activity. Chilone's studies in pen, pencil, wash, watercolor, and gouache now concentrated in the Gilmor collection belong to these same years but are fresher and more responsive to the changes in Venice beginning to be evident in the early nineteenth century.[14] By turns rather exact imitations of Canaletto's precise sketchbook style, or candidly prosy, these drawings suggest an artist of modest talent practicing an outmoded genre with variable skill but considerable charm. The Baltimore Museum painting seems very close to Chilone in its handling of paint, line and decorative conventions, color and tonality, and the use of the Marieschi etching which suggests a certain deficiency of invention. It most closely resembles the Palazzo Minotti frescoes of 1792. If it is by Chilone and not another as yet unidentified Canaletto follower, it may be dated to the last decades of the eighteenth century.

W. R. Rearick
University of Maryland,
College Park

NOTES

1. W. G. Constable, *Canaletto* (Oxford: Clarendon Press, 1962), 2, no. 258, pp. 297–98. Also L. Puppi, *Canaletto* (Milan, 1968), no. 77, p. 97. It is one of fourteen views which came to the Royal collections from Consul Smith, all of them engraved by Visentini. Sometimes dated before 1730, this view was painted by Canaletto before 1738 when the steps of S. Simeone Piccolo, here only partly built, were completed.
2. J. G. Links, *Views of Venice by Canaletto. Engraved by Antonio Visentini* (New York: Dover Publications, 1971), pl. XI. See also Constable, *Canaletto* (1962), 2:605.
3. F. Mauroner, "Michele Marieschi," *The Print Collector's Quarterly* 27, no. 2 (1940):192–93, 203. Also J. G. Links, *Canaletto and his Patrons* (New York: New York University Press, 1977), pp. 53–57.
4. By now this part of the Canal has been much altered.
   Among the details recorded by the painter of this picture are the now lost frescoes by Lattanzio Gambara (1530–1574) in the courtyard of the Foscari Contarini Palace.
5. Almost all architectural details follow those of the print. Many of the figures and boats are identical, but the gondolier at center has been replaced by a more erect figure and the first passenger has been omitted. Some spectators at right are also Canaletto-type insertions. The rendering of the sky and the handling of the canal surface do not follow the Marieschi etching.
6. For Guardi's use of Marieschi's etchings, cf. cat. no. 22 a & b of this publication.
7. Our knowledge of Marieschi's paintings is very scant, but pictures related to his prints have accrued to his name in quantity, although for the most part they are derivations by other artists, as is the present painting; cf. Links, 1977, pp. 55–57.
8. Ibid., pp. 97–104.
9. Ibid., p. 102.
10. There are twenty-one sheets of drawings by Chilone in the Gilmor Collection plus a few others attributed, probably wrongly, to him. One bears the date 1835 and several are annotated in Gilmor's hand *Venice*. It seems probable that all were purchased by Gilmor in Venice, perhaps directly from the artist; cf. W. R. Rearick, "Some Little Known Old Master Drawings in The Baltimore Museum of Art," *The Baltimore Museum of Art Annual 4, Studies in Honor of Gertrude Rosenthal*, pt. 2 (Baltimore: Baltimore Museum of Art, 1972), pp. 80–97.
11. R. Pallucchini, *La pittura veneziana del Settecento* (Venice, 1960), p. 175.
12. On Chilone, see G. Pavanello in *Venezia nell' età di Canova*, exhibition catalogue (Venice: Alfieri, 1978).
    The Metropolitan Museum of Art, *The Horses of San Marco, Venice* (Milan and New York: Olivetti, 1979), pp. 72, 79.
13. Private collection, England. Signed, they are evidently pendants and may be inventions in the *capriccio* tradition. They are unpublished.
14. Other Chilone drawings are in the Correr Museum, Venice, and the Gabinetto Disegni e Stampe of the Uffizi, Florence. Together with the Gilmor drawings, they deserve a more extensive publication. The Gilmor Collection, for almost half a century on deposit with The Baltimore Museum of Art, has recently been transferred to Evergreen House Foundation of The Johns Hopkins University, where, it is to be hoped, it will remain intact and accessible to scholars.

SELECTED BIBLIOGRAPHY

Thieme-Becker. "Vincenzo Chilone." *Allgemeines Lexikon der Bildenden Künstler*. 37 vols. Leipzig: E. A. Seemann, 1907–1950.

Fabio Mauroner. "Michele Marieschi." *Print Collector's Quarterly* 27, no. 2 (1940):178–215.

Rodolfo Pallucchini. *La pittura veneziana del Settecento*. Venice: Istituto per la Collaborazione Culturale, 1960.

W. G. Constable. *Canaletto*. 2 vols. Oxford: Clarendon Press, 1962.

J. G. Links. *Views of Venice by Canaletto. Engraved by Antonio Visentini*. New York: Dover Publications, 1971.

W. R. Rearick. "Some Little Known Old Master Drawings in The Baltimore Museum of Art." *The Baltimore Museum of Art Annual 4, Studies in Honor of Gertrude Rosenthal*, pt. 2. Baltimore: Baltimore Museum of Art, 1972.

Venezia nell' età di Canova. Exhibition catalogue. Correr Museum, Venice. Venice: Alfieri, 1978.

The Metropolitan Museum of Art. *The Horses of San Marco, Venice*. Milan and New York: Olivetti, 1979.

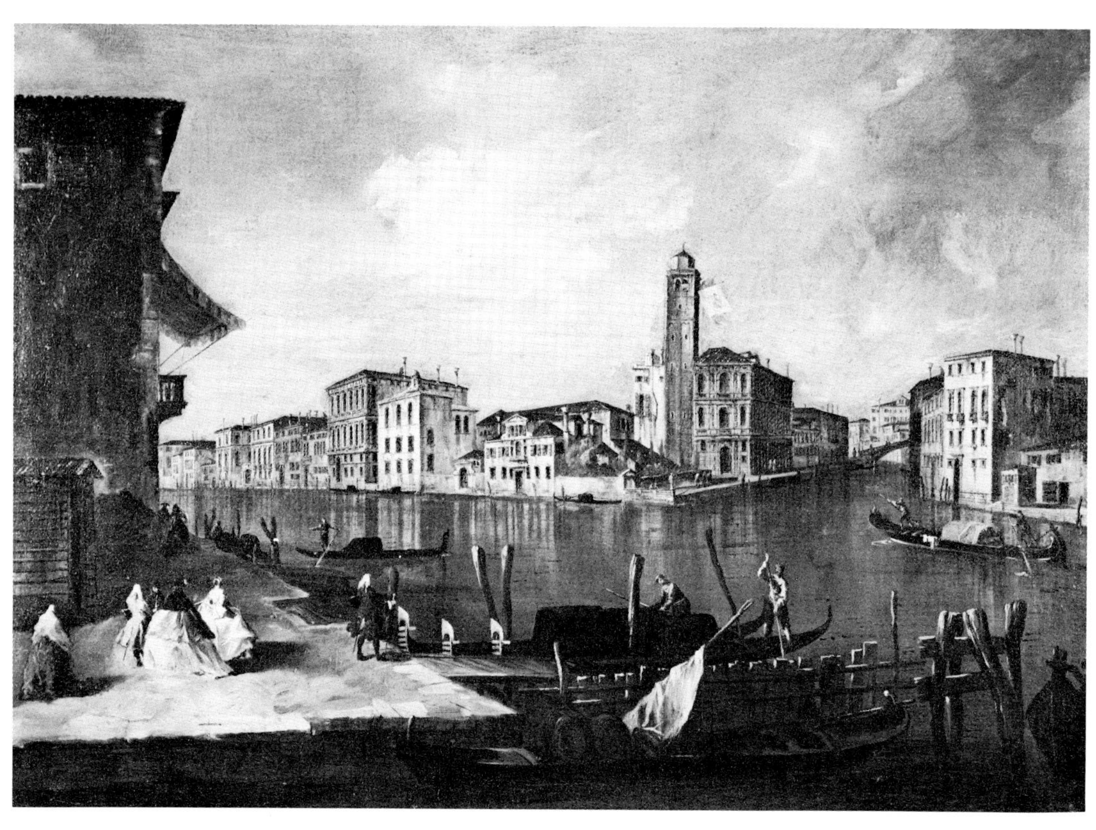

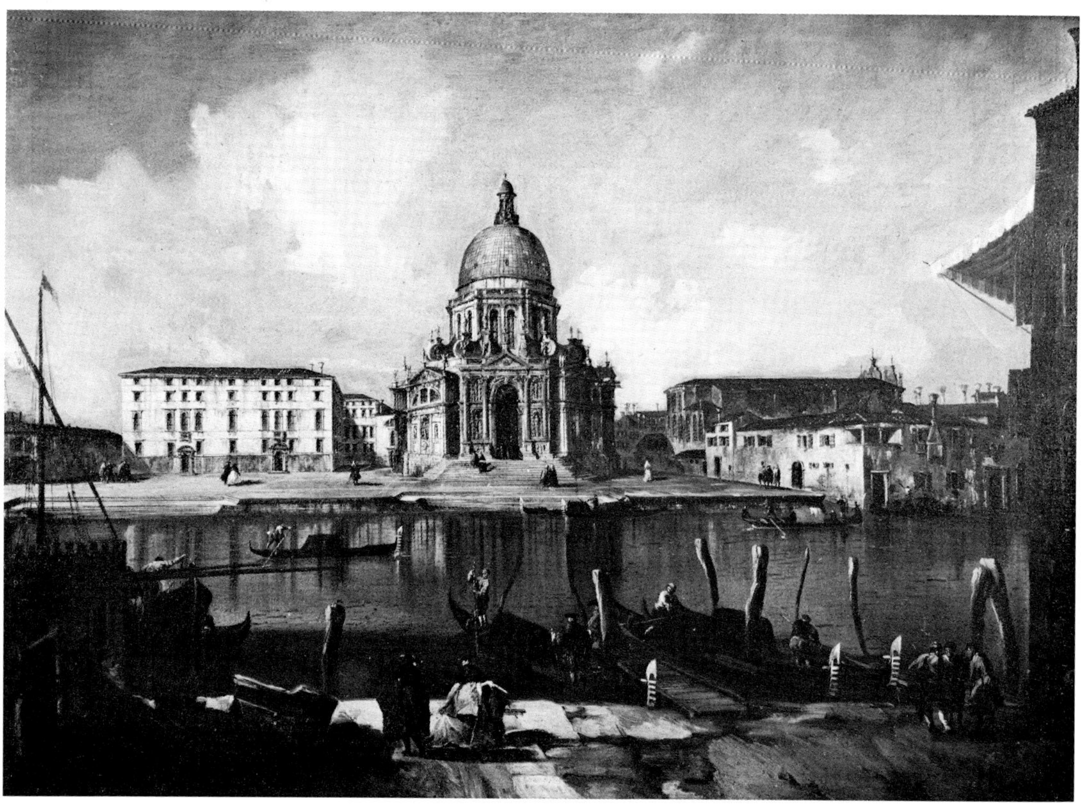

FRANCESCO GUARDI (1712–1793)

22a. *Venice, The Grand Canal with San Geremia, Palazzo Labia, and the Entrance to the Cannaregio,* ca. 1750

Oil on canvas. 36¼ × 51 13/16 inches (92 × 131.5 cm.)
The Mary Frick Jacobs Collection (BMA 38.214)

22b. *Venice, The Grand Canal with Santa Maria della Salute,* ca. 1750

Oil on canvas. 36¼ × 51 15/16 inches (92 × 131.9 cm.)
The Mary Frick Jacobs Collection (BMA 38.215)

PROVENANCE

Palazzo Comello-Montalba, Venice
This provenance could not be confirmed.
Collection of Arthur J. Sulley, Middleton, Berkshire

Acquired as works of Francesco Guardi by Mary Frick Jacobs, Baltimore, from the Blakeslee Galleries, New York, in 1913

Bequeathed to The Baltimore Museum of Art in 1938 as part of The Mary Frick Jacobs Collection

CONDITION

In both *The Grand Canal with San Geremia* and *The Grand Canal with Santa Maria della Salute* the oil paint was applied over the red ground as a thin-to-moderate paste with low brush markings. In many of the thinner passages the weave of the loosely-woven fabric is visible.

Both paintings are in good condition, although minor losses and some abrasions have occurred, especially in the sky area. A fine crackle has developed throughout the paint film of each, and the surface coating has darkened slightly. Actual paint film losses are minor. *The Grand Canal with Santa Maria della Salute* has small losses along the perimeter, mainly at the right side and the lower right corner. There are some retouched losses at the upper left corner and top center.

In *The Grand Canal with San Geremia* a small area of paint loss at the lower left of center can be seen, as well as an old repair at the lower right corner.

At an unknown place and time, before entering the Museum's collection, both pictures were glue-lined. The paintings were treated in 1951 at the conservation department of The Walters Art Gallery where they were cleaned, received some minor inpainting, and were varnished.

These two views of Venice by Francesco Guardi must be considered among the prize possessions in the Italian collection of The Baltimore Museum of Art. Not only are they beautiful visual documents of the Grand Canal in the eighteenth century, they also serve as a much needed fixed point for an artist whose career, although assiduously studied, still presents a number of historical problems. Francesco Guardi was the last great master of Venetian *vedutismo*. He was born in Venice in 1712, the second son of a minor painter and his Austrian wife.[1] After his father died in 1716, Gian Antonio, Francesco's elder brother, born in 1699, maintained the Guardi workshop.[2] By age twenty, Francesco was already a participating member in the family shop; a will of 1731 left by Count Giovanni Benedetto Giovanelli mentions works executed "dalli fratelli Guardi."[3] Although remembered in the twentieth century principally as a view painter, Francesco began his career assisting Gian Antonio in painting religious subjects, usually commissioned by provincial churches in the Veneto.

Two lunettes for the sacristy of the parish church at Vigo d'Anaunia clearly represent the differing styles and individual hands of the brothers.[4] To Francesco one can surely assign the *Vision of St. Francis,* whereas Gian Antonio must have been solely responsible for the *Sacrilegious Communion of the Bishop of Magdeburg*. The vibrant forms, the lack of figural substance, and the brilliant surface quality associate the latter painting with known works by Gian Antonio.[5] In the *Vision of St. Francis,* however, another hand and attitude were evidently in control; there is less sparkle in the paint, the rocks and plants have an emphasis and definition not found in the elder brother's style, and, most important, the dramatic impact is direct and affecting. A signed work by Francesco, *Saint in Ecstasy,*[6] presents notable similarities with the lunette showing St. Francis, particularly in the way the seemingly tangible reality of the saint in each work is presented in terms of a moment of profound religious experience.

Among scholars, some differences of opinion still exist regarding the definition of each brother's style,[7] but the majority would state that those paintings that reveal a more elaborated pictorial surface, a tendency to dissolve three-dimensional form rather than render it palpable, and a taste for refined, even balletic, figures are generally assigned to the hand of Gian Antonio. As the majority of these works are large altarpieces, or extended cycles comprising more than two to three canvases, or ambitious decorative ensembles, it seems reasonable to conclude that Gian Antonio retained full control of the Guardi shop during his lifetime and that he was himself responsible for the major figurative commissions executed by the *bottega.*[8]

Francesco, although he painted religious subjects, was attracted as well to works showing more varied themes. Generally, these paintings show scenes of simple folk or of an observed reality. In this, Francesco was in harmony with one particular aspect of Venetian cultural development of the second quarter of the century. Canaletto's realistic views of the city were, of course, becoming big business as Francesco matured. Giambattista Piazzetta executed during this same period several large paintings, as well as many drawings, of shepherds, peasants, and *popolani.* Moreover, in the 1740's Pietro Longhi and the dramatist Carlo Goldoni initiated an art that clearly mirrored the daily existence of the Venetian lower and middle classes. Francesco Guardi's attempts to fix for himself new pictorial goals, free from those of the more tradition-bound Gian Antonio, followed the lead of these older compatriots. Indeed, two of Francesco's early such works—the *Ridotto* and the *Nuns' Parlatory,* both in the Museo Correr, Venice—are reworkings of themes by Longhi.[9] And even in paintings of monumental ruins, the *Roman Temple with Figures* (Stiftung Kunsthaus Heylshof, Worms) and the *Classical Ruins with Figures* (present whereabouts unknown),[10] Guardi focuses as much on the toiling laborers as he does on their surroundings. Thus by 1750, at age thirty-eight, Francesco must have found himself moving ever further away in his painting from his brother's main artistic interests and market.[11]

It is at this time that Guardi probably turned his hand to *vedutismo*. Although he did not immediately give up figurative commissions, his primary artistic concerns until his death were views of Venice and architectural caprices based on its buildings and sites. He portrayed his native city for more than forty years, but few dates or historical figures can be associated with any of his paintings. Francesco seems to have worked in relative obscurity; at the beginning, the name Guardi more likely than not suggested Gian Antonio rather than Francesco, and inevitably his *vedute* were compared with those by the famous Canaletto.[12] Moreover, he had no patron such as Joseph Smith in his career, as the more fortunate Canaletto had in his.[13] Not catering to a wealthy and art-starved foreign market, Francesco quietly painted for uncelebrated members of the Venetian middle class.[14] And when important public commissions did come his way—the paintings of 1782 commemorating the visits to Venice of the Archduke and Archduchess of Russia, and of Pope Pius VI—Guardi's recompense from the State was meager rather than generous.[15]

Although Francesco did not realize the same prices as Canaletto, he did attain some recognition during the last years of his life. In the 1780's, his art was several times praised to the Venetian Academy, to which he was admitted as "pittore prospettico" in 1784.[16] He died in 1793, leaving a son Giacomo who continued to paint rather simple views of the city until his own death in 1837.[17] During the nineteenth century, Francesco's name was overshadowed by that of Canaletto; it was only in the wake of the French Impressionists that, early in this century, Guardi came to be appreciated in his own right. Further study of Francesco brought attention to Gian Antonio, completely ignored since his death in 1760; and since World War I, scholars have sought to separate the entangled careers of the two brothers. Francesco's view paintings have subsequently won wide popularity, to some extent even eclipsing Canaletto's contribution to the genre.

Following upon Luca Carlevarijs (1663–1731) and Canaletto (1697–1768), Guardi's *vedutismo* extended through the latter half of the eighteenth century and effectively ended the long native Venetian interest in urban topography which had begun in the fifteenth and sixteenth centuries when Venice was pictured in the background of many paintings for the purpose of pinpointing the "Venetianness" of the subject matter. The late fifteenth-century series depicting the miraculous events related to a piece of the holy cross and commissioned of Gentile Bellini, Vittore Carpaccio, Lazzaro Bastiani, and Giovanni Mansueti for the Scuola di San Giovanni Evangelista comprises the most famous of such works, but Tintoretto, Veronese, Titian, and Francesco Bassano continued in the sixteenth century to use the city as a topographical reference.[18]

In the seventeenth century, large religious and historical paintings using Venice as a background were not produced. What took their place were festival paintings that record special Venetian holidays and activities.[19] But independent view painting also began to appear at this time. Viviano Codazzi (1603/04–1670), a Bergamasque by birth but active in both Naples and Rome,[20] painted many views in the latter two cities during the mid-century. And in Venice, Joseph Heinz the Younger (ca. 1600–ca. 1679) seems to have been the first to paint the Piazza San Marco as a totally independent artistic image.[21] Although Codazzi was clearly the superior of the two, both painters had a similar pictorial aim—to present the most famous sites of a city during moments of intense luministic contrast, that is, to dramatize the daily scene.

In the late seventeenth century, the possibilities of the genre were greatly expanded by Gaspar van Wittel, an artist born near Utrecht in 1652 who went to Italy in 1674.[22] Van Wittel's early years in Holland during the 1660's and early 1670's coincided with the period in which the Dutch townscape was developing as a popular form of painting.[23]

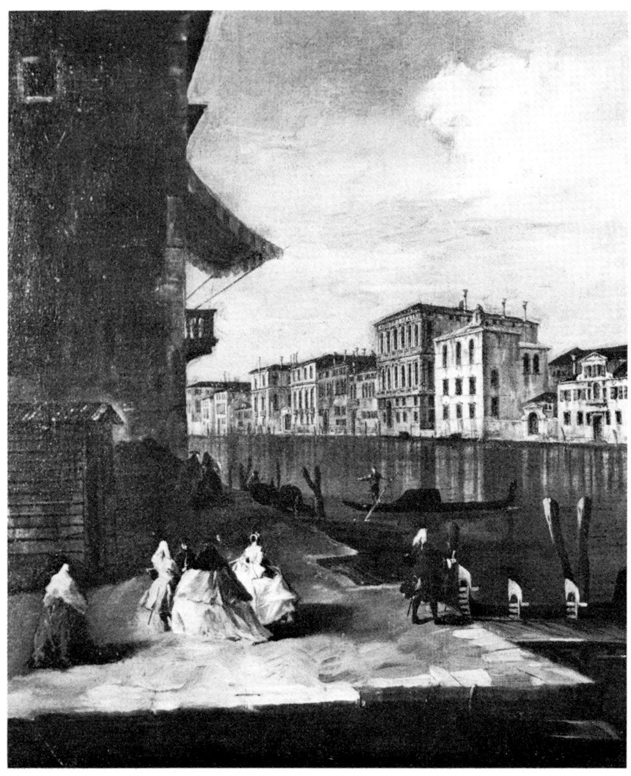

Fig. 1. Francesco Guardi, *The Grand Canal in Venice with San Geremia and the Entrance to the Cannaregio,* detail of cat. no. 22a.

The impression of a tranquil and prosperous city scene, fundamental aspects of Dutch views, became essential to van Wittel's concept of the urban scene. He understood that a view painting was only a conglomeration of buildings and did not really mirror a city's appearance unless the painting was animated by activity in the streets. This plus a pervasive light which, moving across an entire scene, creates an impressive spatial amplitude are the major pictorial contributions that van Wittel left for eighteenth-century *vedutismo* in Italy. Above all, however, his career was a most visible example—he traveled up and down the peninsula, from Venice to Naples—of a painter making a viable, indeed successful, profession of producing topographical portraits.[24]

Luca Carlevarijs from Udine began to produce views of Venice during the first years of the eighteenth century.[25] His first works were prints, which must have been quite successful because soon thereafter, in 1707, he was commissioned to record in paint the arrival in Venice of the Count of Manchester, Ambassador from Great Britain to the Venetian Republic.[26] This fine view represents in the Settecento the first flowering of what would later become for both Canaletto and Guardi a unification of some of the principal pictorial glories of Venetian *vedutismo:* broad, panoramic space joined with a perspectival plunge into depth, frequent transitions from light to dark, convincing architectural renderings, and an interesting variety of *staffage.*

Canaletto's great success in view painting during the second quarter of the century followed upon and was no doubt partially a result of Carlevarijs's earlier example.[27] Two other Venetian *vedutisti* made a mark during this period. Michele Marieschi (1710–1743) painted in Venice for less than ten years, but his work had an important significance for later developments of the genre. Bernardo Bellotto (1720–1780), Canaletto's nephew,

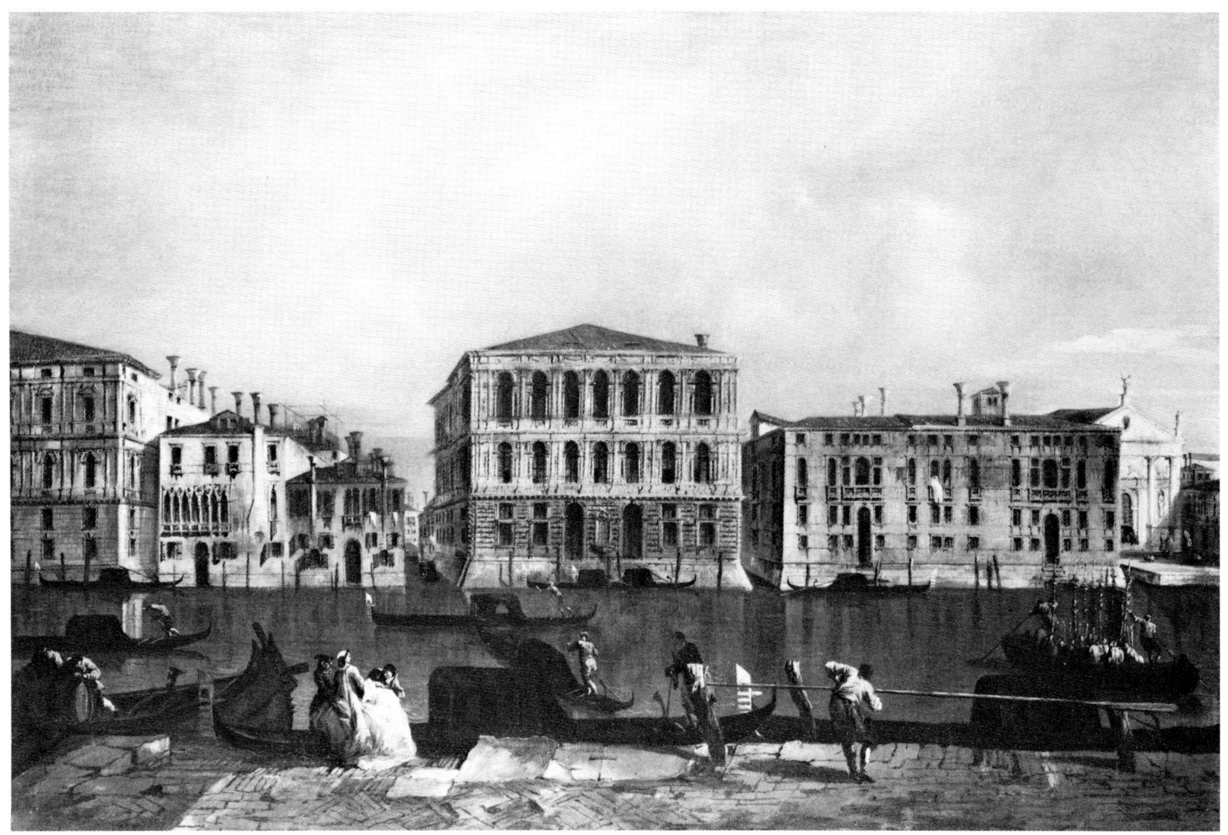

Fig. 2. Francesco Guardi, *The Grand Canal in Venice with Palazzo Pesaro*. Oil on canvas. 36½ × 51½ inches (92.7 × 130.8 cm.). The National Gallery, London. Reproduced by courtesy of the Trustees of The National Gallery, London

studied first with his uncle. He worked only briefly in Italy, leaving in 1747 to unfold his career in Dresden, Warsaw, and Vienna.[28] This rich and pictorially varied topographical tradition stood behind Francesco Guardi's emergence as a view painter around 1750.

Several important characteristics distinguish Guardi's style from those of the other famous practitioners of the genre. Foremost is the lack of precise or fussy architectural rendering. Although the buildings and their urban context are faithfully portrayed, Guardi's mature views rarely suffer from the insistence upon straight, ruled lines that, at times, reduce the pictorial interest of Carlevarijs's or Canaletto's mature paintings. Mottled surfaces or strong shadows or irregularly shaped forms on the ground are often used to fragment architectural outlines and spatial zones, as in the foreground of the Baltimore view of the Salute. One suspects that Guardi learned this fundamentally important lesson from Canaletto's early style of the 1720's and 1730's.[29]

Second, Guardi used paint as no other great *vedutista* did. Blotchy patches and variegated textures make of the oils themselves an active element in the pictorial design: for example, in the *View of the Grand Canal with San Geremia,* the spirited brushwork of both the gowned women at the bottom left (fig. 1) and the stormy sky above balance these zones against the aggressive movement embodied in the embankments of the Grand Canal and the Cannaregio. In his later works, these broadly laid on brushstrokes yield to more minutely applied areas of color. In the famous *Concert of Women Musicians* (Alte Pinakothek, Munich), datable to the artist's old age,[30] tiny flickerings of light bounce over the painting surface. However, unlike Canaletto's own late style, where a similar conception of light exists,[31] Guardi's lights are irregularly shaped and dispersed. Moreover, they do not assert the foreground plane of space, as they do in Canaletto's works, but rather tend to pull our glance into the distance.

Last, Guardi's views portray a Venice that seems at times mutable, even fleeting and impermanent. We view the city through a heavy and moist atmospheric veil that is radically different from Canaletto's brilliant and crystalline sunlight, where all forms and their details are solid and fixed. Decay, in addition, is an important theme in Guardi's mature oeuvre; the worn surfaces and crumbling architecture are a direct result of nature's ungovernable powers—storms, fires, and time itself. Even in such early works as the two Baltimore views, the twisting moorings suggest the perennial force of the Venetian tides; one would search in vain among Canaletto's *vedute* to find an equivalent pictorial use of these mooring posts, though they are in fact found everywhere along the city's waterways.

The two Baltimore Guardis were originally part of a set of four paintings depicting a seventeenth- and an eighteenth-century palace on the upper reaches of the Grand Canal, Ca' Pesaro (fig. 2) and Palazzo Labia, and two churches located where the Canal opens into the Basin of St. Mark, Longhena's Sta. Maria della Salute and Palladio's S. Giorgio Maggiore.[32] The first and last works of the series are presented with oblique views off to one side, whereas both Ca' Pesaro and the Salute are seen straight on, from the opposite embankment of the Grand Canal. All four paintings are characterized by a dark tonality, intensely heavy shadows juxtaposed against brightly lit foreground areas, and broad brushwork.

The two Baltimore canvases, purchased as Guardis, were attributed by W. G. Constable to Michele Marieschi,[33] for the compositions are based on two of his prints from a series published in 1741 (figs. 3 and 4).[34] Constable noted that the handling of the paint, too, approximated Marieschi's, calling it "ragged . . . and applied in small touches, which, joined to the use of sharply impastoed small lights, gives a flickering quality to the whole surface."[35] But in the intervening years further study of Marieschi's style has made it apparent that although his brushwork is indeed broad, as is found in fact in the Baltimore views, rarely does he attempt to create a dramatic view such as we see here. Moreover, his canals are hard, lacking totally the appearance of murky depths characteristic of the Grand Canal in both these paintings. In fact, if we confront the Baltimore *San Geremia* with a version of the same subject by Marieschi,[36] it becomes apparent that the same painter could not have executed both works. In the Baltimore painting the artist was clearly less concerned with fussy handling of detail—note in particular the surface quality of the Grand Canal—but more interested in depicting startling luministic contrasts and heavy atmospheric conditions.

In 1966 Rodolfo Pallucchini restored the attribution of the two Baltimore works to Guardi, and they are universally accepted as autograph.[37] However, those elements that led Constable to substitute the name Marieschi for Guardi—that is, the dependence upon the 1741 prints, the awkward construction of space, and the splotchy brushwork—suggest that the views came early in Francesco's oeuvre. Denis Mahon has demonstrated on the basis of topographical and stylistic evidence that the two Baltimore canvases date most probably from the early 1750's, that in fact they are among the artist's first attempts at *vedutismo*.[38]

Understanding Guardi's early professional development allows us to follow his transformation from *figurista* to *vedutista*. He came of age artistically under the aegis of his elder brother Gian Antonio; thus he was necessarily subservient to the needs of a workshop that specialized in making copies of famous Venetian paintings.[39] And even when striking out on his own, he based his experiments on the works of others—for example, when he painted the *Caprice with Figures* from a composition of Marco Ricci and the *Nuns' Parlatory* from a painting by Longhi. Moreover, both Ricci and Alessandro

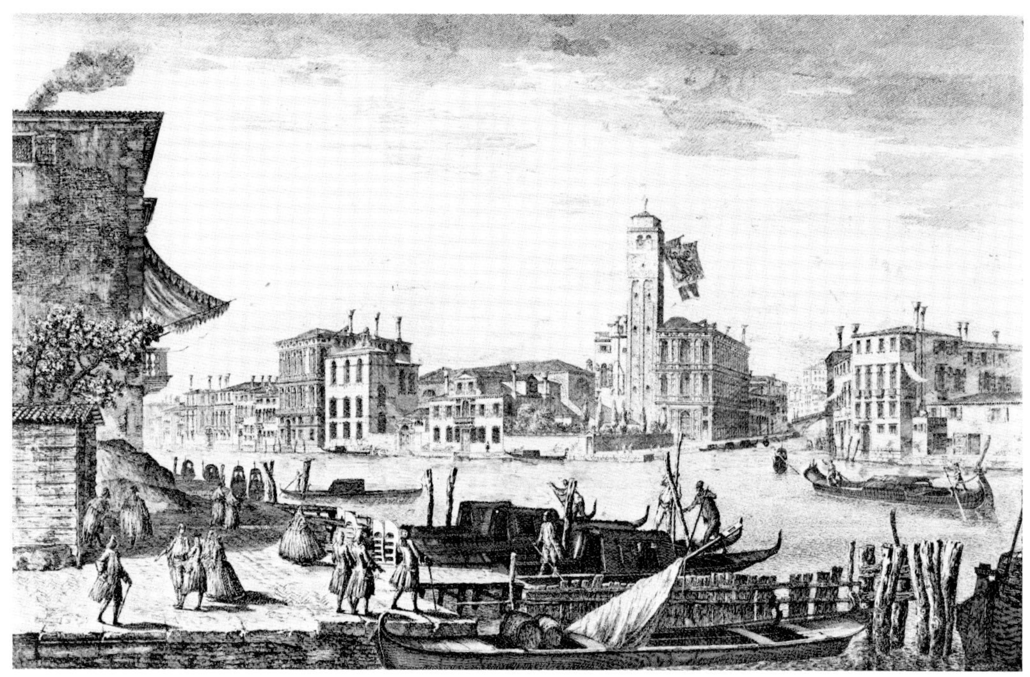

Fig. 3. Michele Marieschi, *San Geremia and Palazzo Labia* from *Magnificentiores selectioresque urbis Venetiarum prospectus* (Venice, 1741). Etching. 12¹/₁₆ × 18⁵/₁₆ inches (30.6 × 46.5 cm.). Prints Division, The New York Public Library, Astor, Lenox and Tilden Foundations

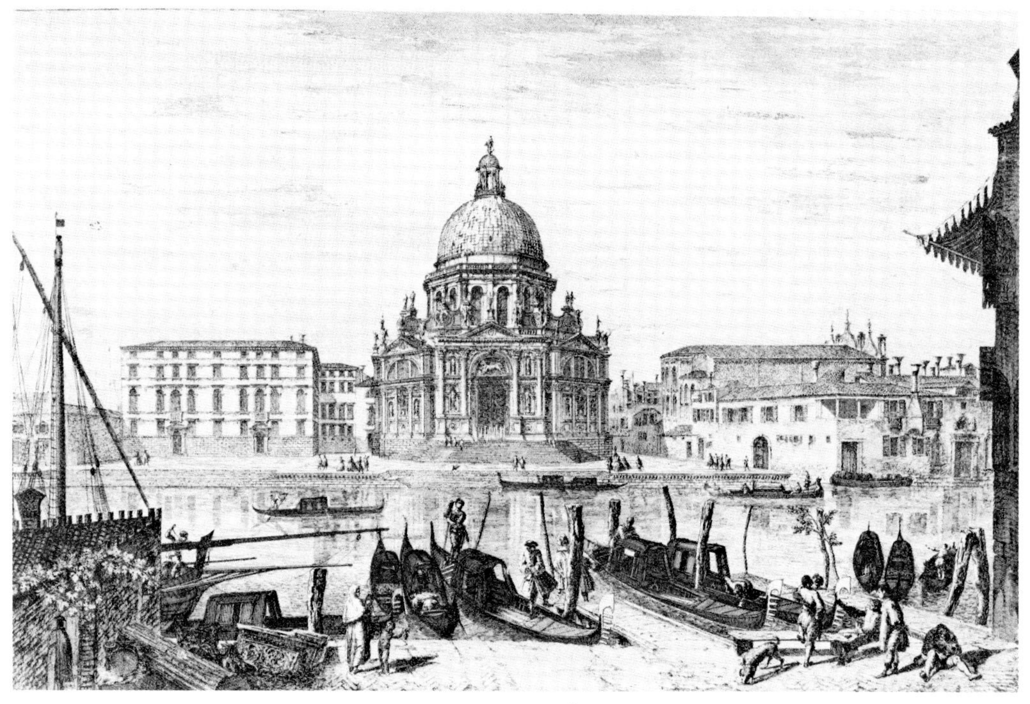

Fig. 4. Michele Marieschi, *Santa Maria della Salute* from *Magnificentiores selectioresque urbis Venetiarum prospectus* (Venice, 1741). Etching. 12³/₁₆ × 18¼ inches (31 × 46.4 cm.). Prints Division, The New York Public Library, Astor, Lenox and Tilden Foundations

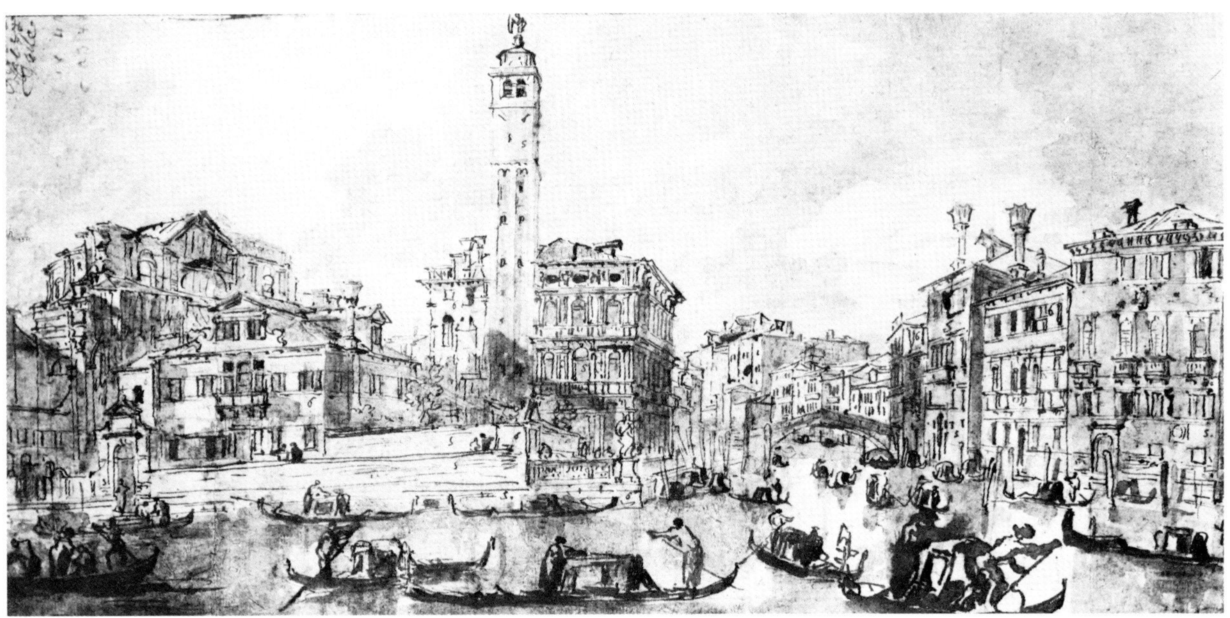

Fig. 5. Francesco Guardi, *View of the Grand Canal at San Geremia, Palazzo Labia, and the Entrance to the Cannaregio.* Pen and watercolor. 10¹/4 x 21⁷/16 inches (26 x 54.5 cm.). Museo Correr, Venice

Magnasco provided a tradition of shipwreck and storm scenes from which Guardi profited; and a Piazzetta altarpiece, the *Saints Hyacinth, Lawrence, and Bertrand* in Sta. Maria del Rosario, Venice, suggested the figural pose for the *Saint in Ecstasy* (signed) in Trent. All of these borrowings would certainly have been recognized in the eighteenth century. It cannot come as a surprise to us, therefore, to find that two such early *vedute* as the *Salute* and the *San Geremia* spring from a study of two elder *vedutisti,* Marieschi and Canaletto.

The compositions are, as we have seen, lifted from Marieschi's 1741 prints, although the figures have been altered, as have a few minor architectural details. The dramatic presentation, however, is a reflection of Canaletto's successful style of the 1720's.[40] Canaletto himself was absent from Venice from 1746 to 1755, and it was during the latter part of this period that the paintings were executed; but his early style could have been studied in works belonging to the English consul Joseph Smith. It thus becomes apparent that Guardi attempted to develop into a view painter just as, during his earlier career, he had pursued other genres—by following contemporary eighteenth-century Venetian pictorial tradition. The Baltimore views document this moment in Francesco's artistic maturation.

No preparatory drawings by Guardi exist for these two paintings: his dependence upon Marieschi's prints precluded the need for such preliminary work. There does exist, however, a drawing for a view of San Geremia and the Palazzo Labia (fig. 5). Rodolfo Pallucchini attributed it to Niccolò Guardi, the younger brother of Gian Antonio and Francesco, but J. Byam Shaw has restored it to Francesco.[41]

A number of pictorial variants for the Baltimore paintings can be found in different collections. One version of the *San Geremia* is identical with the Baltimore work in both style and viewpoint,[42] but two other views of the same site, projected directly from the other embankment so that we cannot look up the Grand Canal, date stylistically from a much later period.[43] In his mature reconsiderations of the subject, Guardi followed Canaletto's less oblique organization of the view rather than Marieschi's.[44] Of the

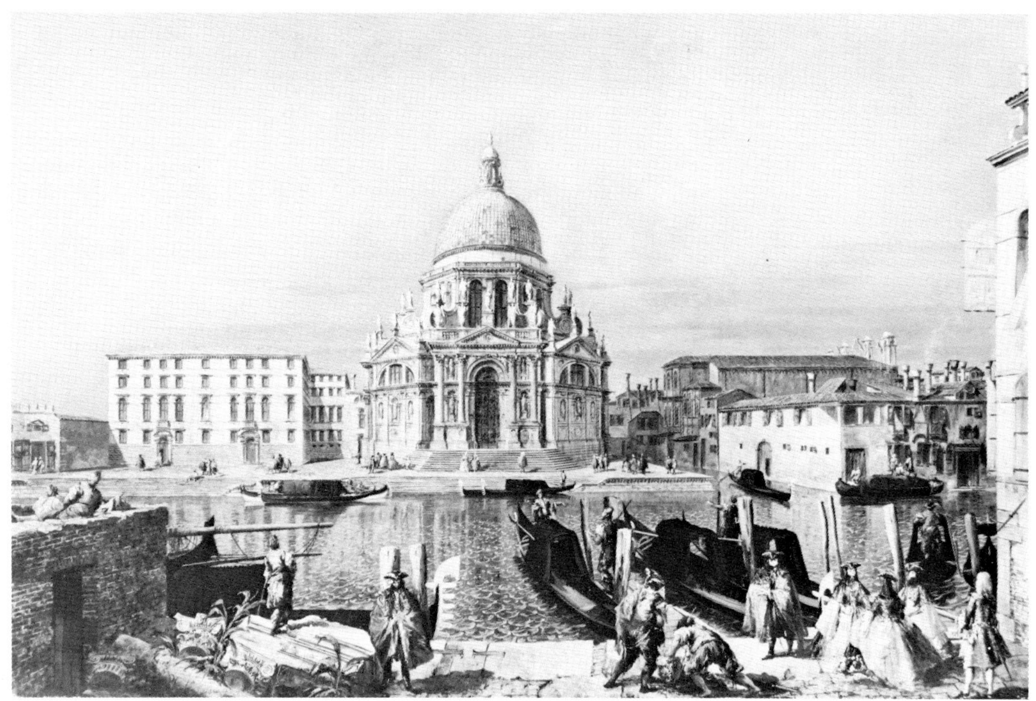

Fig. 6. Michele Marieschi, *Santa Maria della Salute, Venice.* Oil on canvas. 22 × 33¼ inches (55.8 × 84.4 cm.). The Art Institute of Chicago, Charles H. and Mary F. S. Worcester Collection

Baltimore *Salute,* two other versions exist: one in the Gemäldegalerie der Akademie der Bildenden Künste, Vienna, and one in the Institut für Denkmalpflege in Halle.[45] All three paintings are identical in viewpoint and vary only in the disposition of the figures. Later in his career, Guardi more often pictured the Church of the Salute from an angle, either from the right or the left. Here too we can follow his shift from a dependence upon Marieschi to Canaletto. Marieschi produced not only the 1741 prints of the Salute but several painted views of the Church as well (fig. 6),[46] and all are seen from the level of a first floor window on the opposite side of the Grand Canal. Canaletto, on the other hand, invariably depicted the Salute from an oblique vantage point. We might well ask why Guardi became dissatisfied with his first solutions, based on Marieschi, and changed his later views of both San Geremia and the Salute. The answer lies, I believe, in his recognition that Canaletto was the surer master in constructing pictorial space. In his painting and prints of these sites, Marieschi blocks our view into space, whereas Canaletto, in his desire to depict the luminosity and breadth of the Venetian sky, opens our view into the distance. We look past the Salute up or down the Grand Canal or, alternatively, past Palazzo Labia into the full expanse of the farther parts of the Cannaregio.

Guardi's two views in the Baltimore Museum not only confirm that, in *vedutismo* as in other genres, he based his personal style upon recent Venetian painting, but they also establish for us a point of departure from which the artist would soon develop into the last great exponent of view painting in the Italian tradition.

William L. Barcham
Fashion Institute of Technology,
State University of New York,
New York

NOTES

1. For Guardi's life, see "Regesti Guardeschi," in P. Zampetti, *Mostra dei Guardi,* exhibition catalogue (Venice: Alfieri, 1965), pp. xxiii–xxxiv; A. Binion, *Antonio and Francesco Guardi: Their Life and Work* (New York: Garland Publishing, Inc., 1976), chap. 2; and A. Morassi, *Guardi* (Venice: Alfieri, n.d. [1973], pp. 133 ff.
2. See *St. John Nepomuk* in Zampetti, *Mostra dei Guardi,* cat. no. 1, and in Morassi, *Guardi* [1973], cat. no. 52. All subsequent references will be made to Zampetti's 1965 exhibition catalogue as *Mostra* and to Morassi's catalogue of 1973 as Morassi. See also L. Rossi Bortolatto, *L'opera completa di Francesco Guardi* (Milan: Rizzoli, 1974).
3. Cited in Binion, *Antonio and Francesco Guardi,* p. 88, and in *Mostra,* p. xxiv.
4. See *Mostra,* cat. nos. 7, 8; Morassi, cat. nos. 59, 61.
5. See the portraits executed by Gian Antonio for Marshall von der Schulenburg in *Mostra,* cat. nos. 2, 11, 12, 13; Morassi, cat. nos. 118, 121, 120, 122.
6. *Mostra,* cat. no. 66; Morassi, cat. no. 202.
7. The scholars whose attributions differ most from the general consensus are G. Fiocco, in *Francesco Guardi, L'Angelo Raffaele* (Turin: Giulio Einaudi, 1958), and R. Pallucchini, in *La pittura veneziana del Settecento* (Venice: Istituto per la Collaborazione Culturale, 1960), pp. 131 ff.
8. Among these commissions were the altarpieces at Belvedere di Aquileia and Cerete Basso (*Mostra,* cat. nos. 16, 49; Morassi, cat. nos. 63, 65); the series based on Tasso's *Gerusalemme Liberata* (*Mostra,* cat. nos. 45–48; Morassi, cat. nos. 71, 66, 67, 70); the decorative parapet for the organ loft in the Church of the Angelo Raffaele, Venice (*Mostra,* cat. nos. 28–34; Morassi, cat. nos. 15–21); and the ceiling paintings belonging to the Cini Collection, Venice (*Mostra,* cat. nos. 39–42; Morassi, cat. nos. 75–78).
9. See *Mostra,* cat. nos. 24–25; Morassi, cat. nos. 232–33.
10. See *Mostra,* cat. nos. 56–57; Morassi, cat. nos. 702–703.
11. It is generally agreed that the ruin paintings and the views of Venetian interiors are early works by Francesco. The *Classical Ruins with Figures* is after a painting by Marco Ricci, who died in 1734, whereas the *Ridotto* and the *Parlatory* are based on themes developed by Pietro Longhi before 1750.
12. Pietro Gradenigo called Guardi a "buon scolaro del rinomato Canaletto" at age fifty-four (cited in *Mostra,* p. xxx).
13. See my discussion of Canaletto's career in a preceding article (cat. no. 20) of this publication, and my article, "Canaletto and a Commission from Consul Smith," *Art Bulletin* 59, no. 3 (September 1977):383–93.
14. See F. Haskell, "Francesco Guardi as 'Vedutista' and Some of His Patrons," *Journal of the Warburg and Courtauld Institutes* 23 (1960):256–76, and Binion, *Antonio and Francesco Guardi,* pp. 110–11.
15. Binion, *Antonio and Francesco Guardi,* p. 109.
16. Cited in *Mostra,* p. xxxii.
17. See A. Dorigato, *L'Altra Venezia di Giacomo Guardi,* exhibition catalogue (Venice: Alfieri, 1977).
18. For discussions of the history of view painting, see W. G. Constable and J. G. Links, *Canaletto,* rev. ed. (Oxford: Clarendon Press, 1976), chap. 2; J. G. Links, *Townscape Painting and Drawing* (New York: Harper and Row, 1972); and Morassi, 1:210 ff.
19. Particularly active in this field was Joseph Heinz the Younger; see Thieme-Becker, *Allgemeines Lexikon der Bildenden Künstler,* 37 vols. (Leipzig: E. A. Seemann, 1907–1950), 16:312–13.
20. See E. Brunetti, "Situazione di Viviano Codazzi," *Paragone* 6 (1956):65–68.
21. The painting is in the Palazzo Doria-Pamphili, Rome; see Constable and Links, *Canaletto,* pl. 3a.
22. See G. Briganti, *Gaspar van Wittell e l'origine della veduta settecentesca* (Rome: Ugo Bozzi Editore, 1966), and W. Vitzthum, *Drawings by Gaspar van Wittell,* exhibition catalogue (Ottawa: National Museum of Canada, 1977).
23. For Dutch view painting, see W. Stechow, *Dutch Landscape Painting of the Seventeenth Century* (London: Phaidon Press, 1966), chap. 5; also *The Dutch Cityscape in the 17th Century and Its Sources,* exhibition catalogue, Amsterdam and Toronto (Amsterdam: Stadsdrukkerij, 1977).
24. Van Wittel worked for both the princely Colonna family in Rome and the Spanish Viceroy in Naples, Don Luis de la Cerda; see Briganti, *Gaspar van Wittel,* p. 133.
25. See A. Rizzi, *Luca Carlevarijs* (Venice: Alfieri, 1967).
26. Ibid., pl. 3.
27. See my discussion of Canaletto's career in a preceding article (cat. no. 20) of this publication.
28. See F. Mauroner, "Michele Marieschi," *Print Collector's Quarterly* 27, no. 2 (1940): 178–215; A. Morassi, *Michele Marieschi,* exhibition catalogue, Bergamo (Milan: Alfieri, 1966); and S. Kozakiewicz, *Bernardo Bellotto* (Greenwich, Conn.: The New York Graphic Society, 1972).
29. One assumes, of course, that this is exactly the meaning of Gradenigo's phrase "buon scolaro," for it is unthinkable that Guardi began in middle age to paint views in Canaletto's studio.

30. See *Mostra,* cat. no. 141; Morassi, cat. no. 256.
31. See my discussion in a preceding article (cat. no. 20) of this publication.
32. All four works are approximately the same size, varying in their dimensions by about one inch. *Ca' Pesaro* is in the National Gallery, London; see M. Levey, *The Eighteenth-Century Italian Schools* (London: National Gallery, 1956), pp. 65–67; Morassi, cat. no. 463. The whereabouts of the *San Giorgio* is unknown after its appearance in the Solly Joel sale, December 1931; see Morassi, cat. no. 564.
33. W. G. Constable, "Two Paintings by Marieschi," *Baltimore Museum of Art News* 11, no. 4 (January 1948):1–4.
34. The frontispiece bears Marieschi's portrait and the title "Magnificentiores Selectioresque urbis Venetiarum Prospectus. . . ." There are twenty-one views of Venice in the series.
35. Constable, "Two Paintings by Marieschi," p. 4.
36. See P. Zampetti, *I vedutisti veneziani del settecento,* exhibition catalogue (Venice: Alfieri, 1967), cat. no. 115.
37. R. Pallucchini, "A proposito della mostra bergamasca del Marieschi," *Arte Veneta* 20 (1966): 314–18. Pallucchini confirmed his attribution to F. Guardi, according to Zampetti, *I vedutisti veneziani,* cat. nos. 133, 134. Morassi includes the two works in his catalogue, nos. 463 and 571, but he attributes the large figures to Gian Antonio.
38. D. Mahon, "When Did Francesco Guardi Become a 'Vedutista'?" *Burlington Magazine* 110 (February 1968):69–73.
39. A. Morassi, "Antonio Guardi ai servigi del feldmaresciallo Schulenburg," *Emporium* 131 (1960): 147–64, 199–212; and Binion, *Antonio and Francesco Guardi,* pp. 89 ff.
40. Guardi borrowed several of Canaletto's compositional ideas later in his career: the *Caprice View with Portico,* Museo di Castelvecchio, Verona (Morassi, cat. no. 840) is based on a Canaletto composition for a print; and the *Grand Canal with the Rialto Bridge According to Palladio's Project,* Gulbenkian Foundation, Lisbon (Morassi, cat. no. 559), comes from a painting now in the Royal Collection, Windsor Castle. Both originals by Canaletto were commissioned by Consul Joseph Smith in the 1740's.
41. Pallucchini, *Die Zeichnungen des Francesco Guardi im Museum Correr zu Venedig* (Florence: Sansoni, 1943, cat. no. 164; J. Byam Shaw, *The Drawings of Francesco Guardi* (London: Faber and Faber, 1949), cat. no. 18. In a note to G. Rosenthal, the Museo Correr accepts the attribution to Francesco Guardi.
42. Morassi, cat. no. 572 (fig. 545).
43. Ibid., cat. nos. 573 (fig. 550) and 574 (fig. 549).
44. Constable and Links, *Canaletto,* figs. 251 and 252.
45. Morassi, cat. nos. 462 and 471.
46. Other versions exist besides the view in The Art Institute of Chicago: cf. Morassi, *Michele Marieschi,* cat. nos. 1 and 29.

SELECTED BIBLIOGRAPHY

Henry Barton Jacobs. *The Collection of Mary Frick Jacobs.* Baltimore: Prepared and published by Dr. Henry Barton Jacobs, 1938.

Fabio Mauroner. "Michele Marieschi." *Print Collector's Quarterly* 27, no. 2 (1940):178–215.

Rodolfo Pallucchini. *Die Zeichnungen des Francesco Guardi im Museum Correr zu Venedig.* Florence: Sansoni, 1943.

Max Goering. *Francesco Guardi.* Vienna: Schroll & Co., 1944.

W. G. Constable. "Two Paintings by Marieschi." *Baltimore Museum of Art News* 11, no. 4 (January 1948):1–4.

James Byam Shaw. *The Drawings of Francesco Guardi.* London: Faber and Faber, 1949.

Michael Levey. *The Eighteenth-Century Italian Schools.* London: National Gallery, 1956.

Giuseppe Fiocco. *Francesco Guardi, L'Angelo Raffaele.* Turin: Einaudi, 1958.

Antonio Morassi. "Circa gli esordi del vedutismo di Francesco Guardi." In *Studies in the History of Art Dedicated to W. Suida.* London: Phaidon Press, 1959.

Francis Haskell. "Francesco Guardi as 'Vedutista' and Some of His Patrons." *Journal of the Warburg and Courtauld Institutes* 23 (1960):256–76.

Antonio Morassi. "Antonio Guardi ai servigi del feldmaresciallo Schulenburg." *Emporium* 131 (1960): 147–64, 199–212.

Rodolfo Pallucchini. *La pittura veneziana del Settecento.* Venice: Istituto per la Collaborazione Culturale, 1960.

Pietro Zampetti. *Mostra dei Guardi.* Exhibition catalogue. Venice: Alfieri, 1965.

Giuliano Briganti. *Gaspar van Wittel e l'origine della veduta settecentesca.* Rome: Ugo Bozzi Editore, 1966.

Antonio Morassi, ed. *Michele Marieschi.* Exhibiton catalogue. Bergamo: Galleria Lorenzelli, 1966.

Rodolfo Pallucchini. "A proposito della mostra bergamasca del Marieschi." *Arte Veneta* 20 (1966): 314–18.

Terisio Pignatti. "The Contemporaneity of the 18th Century Venetian 'Vedutisti'." *Art International* 11 (1967):20–25.

Giuseppe Maria Pilo. "La mostra dei vedutisti veneziani del settecento." *Arte Veneta* 21 (1967):269–77.

Aldo Rizzi. *Luca Carlevarijs.* Venice: Alfieri, 1967.

Pietro Zampetti. *I vedutisti veneziani del settecento.* Exhibition catalogue. Venice: Alfieri, 1967.

Luitpold Dussler. "Francesco Guardis Bilder Der Alten Pinakothek." *Pantheon* 26 (1968):26–35.

Rolf Kultzen. *Francesco Guardi in der Alten Pinakothek, München.* Munich: Bayer. Staatsgemäldesammlungen, n.d. [1968].

Denis Mahon. "When Did Francesco Guardi Become a 'Vedutista'?" *Burlington Magazine* 110 (February 1968):69–73.

Gertrude Rosenthal, ed. *From El Greco to Pollock: Early and Late Works by European and American Artists.* Exhibition catalogue. Baltimore: The Baltimore Museum of Art, 1968.

J. G. Links. *Townscape Painting and Drawing.* New York: Harper and Row, 1972.

Antonio Morassi. *Guardi.* 2 vols. Venice: Alfieri, n.d. [1973].

Luigina Rossi Bortollato. *L'opera completa di Francesco Guardi.* Milan: Rizzoli, 1974.

Alice Binion. *Antonio and Francesco Guardi: Their Life and Work.* New York: Garland Publishing, Inc., 1976.

W. G. Constable and J. G. Links. *Canaletto.* 2 vols. Rev. ed. Oxford: Clarendon Press, 1976.

William L. Barcham. "Canaletto and a Commission from Consul Smith." *Art Bulletin* 59, no. 3 (September 1977):383–93.

William L. Barcham. *The Imaginary View Scenes of Antonio Canaletto.* New York: Garland Publishing, Inc., 1977.

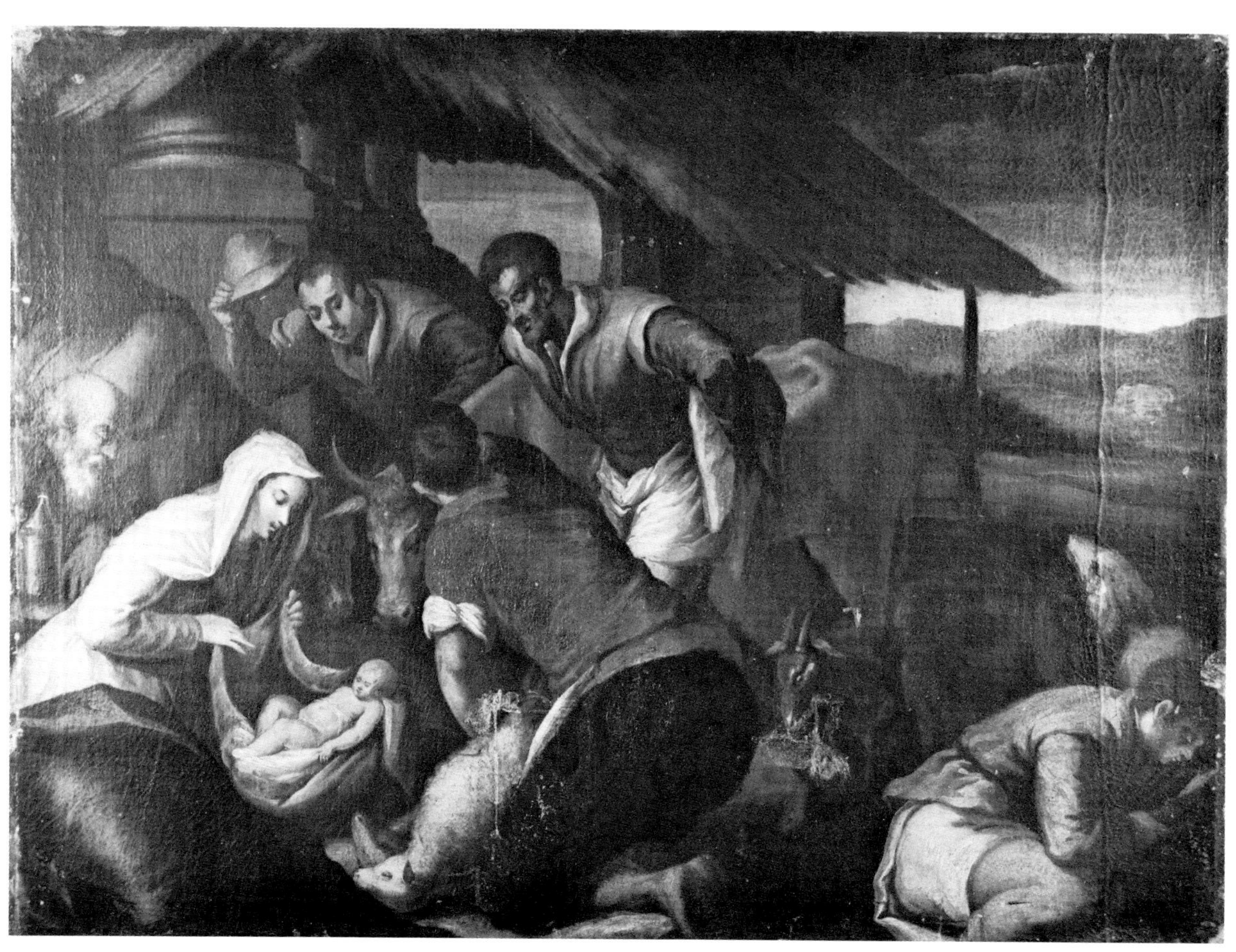

Modified Eighteenth-Century Copy After JACOPO BASSANO (ca. 1517–1592)

23. *Adoration of the Shepherds*

Oil on canvas. 37¾ × 51 inches (95.8 × 129.5 cm.)
The Cone Collection (BMA 50.382)

PROVENANCE

Dr. Claribel Cone and Miss Etta Cone, Baltimore
Nothing is known of the history of this painting before its acquisition by the Cone sisters.

Bequeathed to The Baltimore Museum of Art in 1950 by Dr. Claribel Cone and Miss Etta Cone

CONDITION

The paint of the *Adoration of the Shepherds* is opaque and thickly applied with fairly prominent brushstrokes throughout. The ground is light red. The original finely woven fabric support, suggesting northern rather than Venetian origin, is comprised of two pieces sewn together; the vertical seam is on the right side, approximately 13 cm. from the edge and running from top to bottom. The present dimensions most likely are not those of the original canvas, as edges of the original painting are now bent over the stretcher serving as tacking margins. The top margin consists of a different piece of material, similar in weave and stitched to the main fabric; some of the stitching and parts of the surface of this attached piece are covered by original paint. The other three tacking margins also show some original paint as well as traces of the painting design, suggesting that the picture has been trimmed.

The thick heavy paint layer has cracked and exposes a fine network of fissures, the center section showing much cupping and some flaking. The picture, which has not been treated since it was received by the Museum, was torn in several places, most notably in the lower center area. The various tears were crudely repaired. Losses through flaking exist around all four edges.

The painting had been heavily glue-lined prior to its donation to the Museum, and the surface appearance is obscured by a discolored varnish coating.

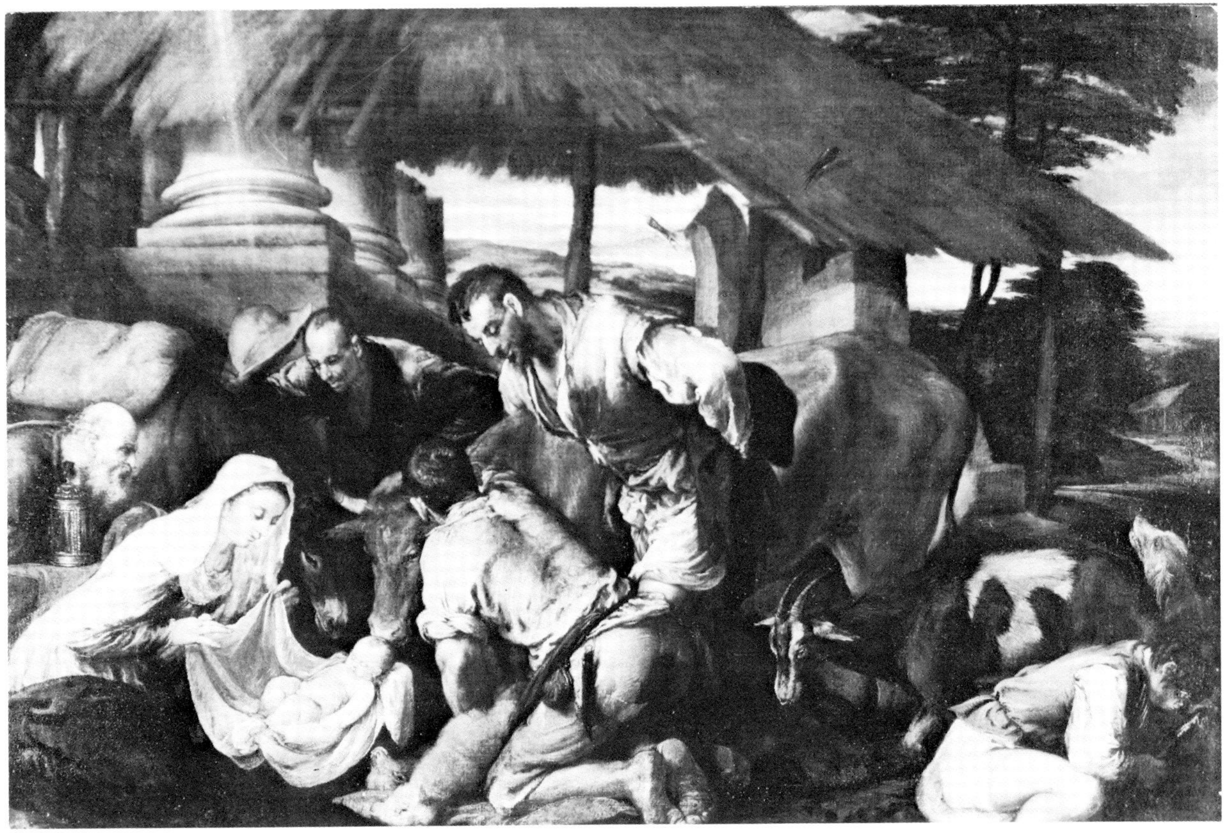

Fig. 1. Jacopo Bassano, *Adoration of the Shepherds,* ca. 1565–1570. Oil on canvas. 40⁹⁄₁₆ × 59⅞ inches (103 × 152 cm.). Oskar Reinhart Collection Am Römerholz, Winterthur, Switzerland

The Baltimore *Adoration of the Shepherds* is probably an eighteenth- or perhaps very early nineteenth-century French copy after a painting of the same subject in the Oskar Reinhart Collection in Winterthur, Switzerland (fig. 1). As such, it poses a number of interesting questions about the role of copyists and about the artistic tastes and attitudes toward Italian Renaissance art in eighteenth-century France.

The earlier picture, one of a number of related paintings of the *Adoration of the Shepherds* created by the Bassano school, has aroused considerable controversy over its attribution and dating, and, therefore, its place within the production of the Bassano workshop. In the *Catalogue of the Oskar Reinhart Collection*[1] the work is given to Jacopo Bassano and dated ca. 1565–1570. Bernard Berenson[2] has also given the work to Jacopo, but he signifies it as an early work of the master. In this he agrees with Pallucchini[3] who felt that because of its "luminosità del timbro cromatico," the Winterthur picture must antedate the version of the *Adoration* in the Palazzo Barberini in Rome, though he gives no clear date for either work. Arslan[4] has since implied that Berenson's dating is incorrect, arguing that the painting in Rome dates from shortly before 1568. Koella[5] supports Arslan's dating by suggesting that the Winterthur picture served as a model for the *Adoration* in the museum in Bassano del Grappa and could therefore be dated to about 1565. W. R. Rearick[6] has not included the Winterthur picture in Jacopo Bassano's oeuvre, calling it a work largely by his son Francesco with Jacopo's collaboration.

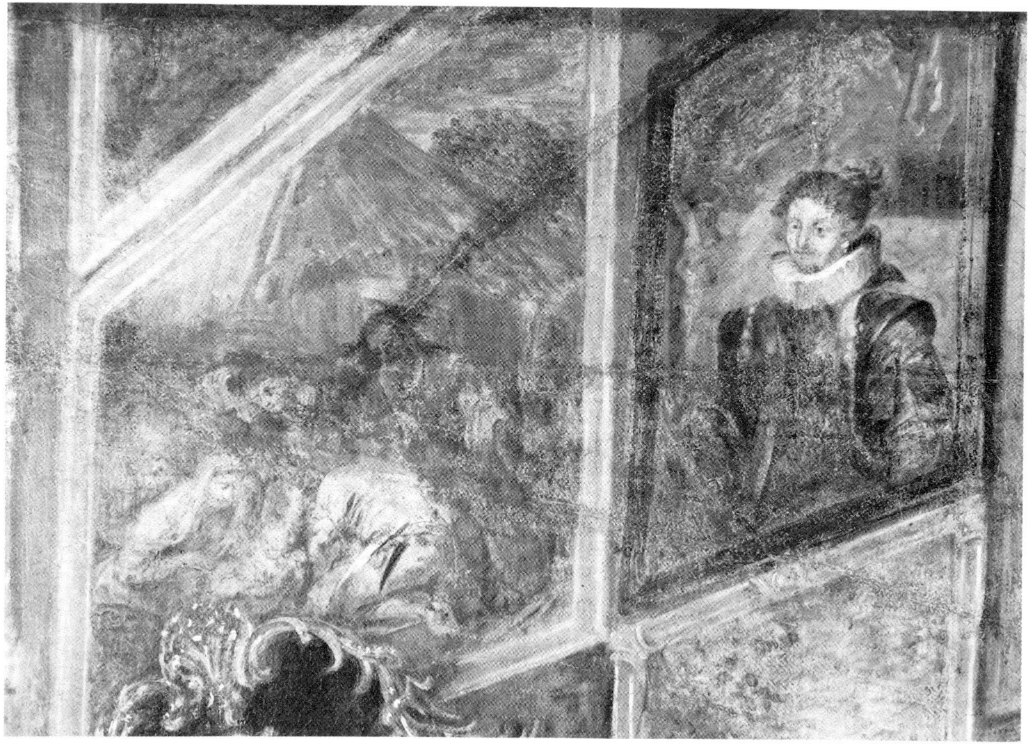

Fig. 2. Jean Antoine Watteau, *Shopsign of Gersaint,* detail. Verwaltung der Staatlichen Schlösser und Gärten, Schloss Charlottenburg, Berlin

In any case, it is the Winterthur picture, or some close copy, which served as the model for the Baltimore work.[7] But where and how did the copyist become acquainted with his model? It has been suggested on stylistic grounds as well as because of the canvas type that the Baltimore picture was probably painted by a French artist of the late eighteenth or perhaps early nineteenth century.[8] It is clear from the color scheme and the handling of the paint that the copyist worked directly from a painted model rather than from any of the engraved versions which were available by that time; however, our lack of knowledge of the early provenance of the different versions makes it impossible definitely to declare any of them as the model.

Yet there is evidence that at least some version of the subject existed in France in the eighteenth century, for on the right wall of the room in Watteau's *Shopsign of Gersaint* (fig. 2) hangs a dimly visible Bassanesque *Adoration.*[9] Since it is not known to what degree Watteau's painting actually reproduces Gersaint's collection, this is not absolute proof that one of the renderings of the *Adoration* was included in the collection; nevertheless, it certainly suggests this as a possibility and confirms the acquaintance of the French with at least some version of the Bassano picture.[10] In fact, Watteau's painting seems to indicate that a work like the Bassano *Adoration* may have held a special place in eighteenth-century taste, since in the *Shopsign of Gersaint* it stands out as one of the very few early religious paintings in a gallery dominated by secular subjects, mostly from the Baroque and Rococo periods. Moreover, the Bassano work with its peasants and animals is the one painting with genre elements in a room whose walls are mainly adorned with portraits and mythological pictures. As such, the Baltimore canvas seems to become a kind of symbol of an underlying artistic trend in eighteenth-century Paris. In this capital of Rococo art there existed a colony of Dutch artists who specialized in genre

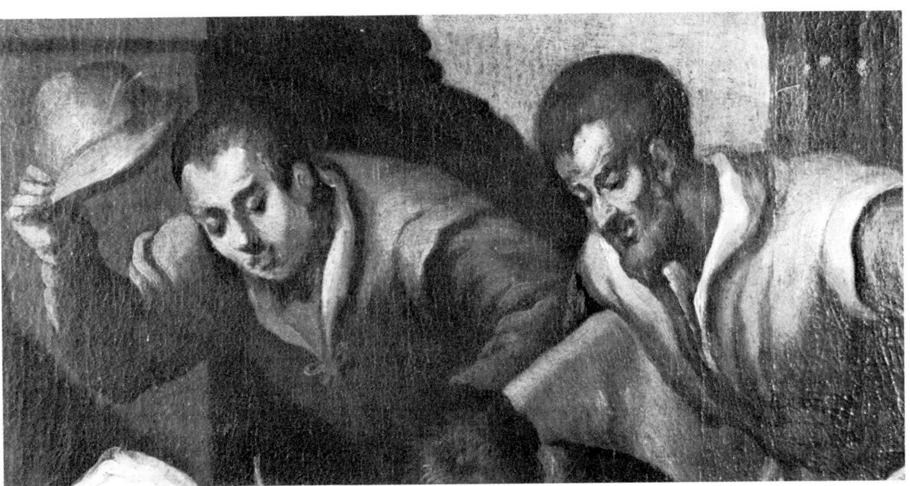

Fig. 3. Modified Eighteenth-Century Copy after Jacopo Bassano, *Adoration of the Shepherds,* detail of cat. no. 23

subjects and had an impact on such leading French painters as Chardin. Their presence would help to explain the creation of a work like the Baltimore *Adoration*. In fact, the Baltimore figures, with their bulky bodies and broad faces (fig. 3), have a decidedly Dutch cast in contrast to the Italianate figures in the Winterthur model, suggesting that the copyist himself may have been associated with this northern group.

The main interest of the Baltimore work, then, may lie in the indication of an often overlooked area of eighteenth-century French artistic taste. Otherwise it is basically a repetition of the iconographic and stylistic concerns expressed in the Bassano model. Iconographically it repeats the traditional Renaissance motifs associated with scenes of the nativity story found in the Winterthur picture. Classical columns and remnants of stone architecture appear frequently in Renaissance pictures with a religious content as symbols of the ancient order of the synagogue.[11] As the architectural elements crumble they are replaced by a thatched hut, symbolizing the young Church which was born with Christ replacing the decaying Jewish law of the Old Testament. The humility of Christ and His Church suggested by the hut is a frequent theme in Adorations of the Shepherds; it sets the tone for the Baltimore picture's other iconographic elements. The ass and the ox, for example, also represent the humble audience to whom Christ addressed His appeal.[12] Other themes appear as well: the lamb which is offered to the Baby by one of the shepherds suggests Christ's Passion, just as the Child's sleeping posture prefigures His death with its significance for the new Church. Another reference to the new Church appears in the figure of the boy crouched at the right of the picture who blows on a coal to ignite a fire, a symbol of the light that entered the world through Christ. The only element in the painting that is unusual in a depiction of the *Adoration of the Shepherds* is the dog which barks, presumably at the star, a motif which appears frequently, however, in scenes of the *Annunciation to the Shepherds*. Its presence in the Winterthur *Adoration* may indicate that this work might originally have been paired with an *Annunciation to the Shepherds,* perhaps the one housed today in the Accademia di San Luca (Rome) as suggested, on stylistic grounds, by Pallucchini.[13]

The colors in the Baltimore picture, though somewhat harsh and darkened with age, generally follow those of the Winterthur painting, yet they lack the depth and richness that characterize the creations of the Bassani. Similarly, the long swirling brushstrokes of the copy trace those of the model, but without the varying impasto with its rich, flickering quality found in true Bassano works. There is, moreover, a general carelessness

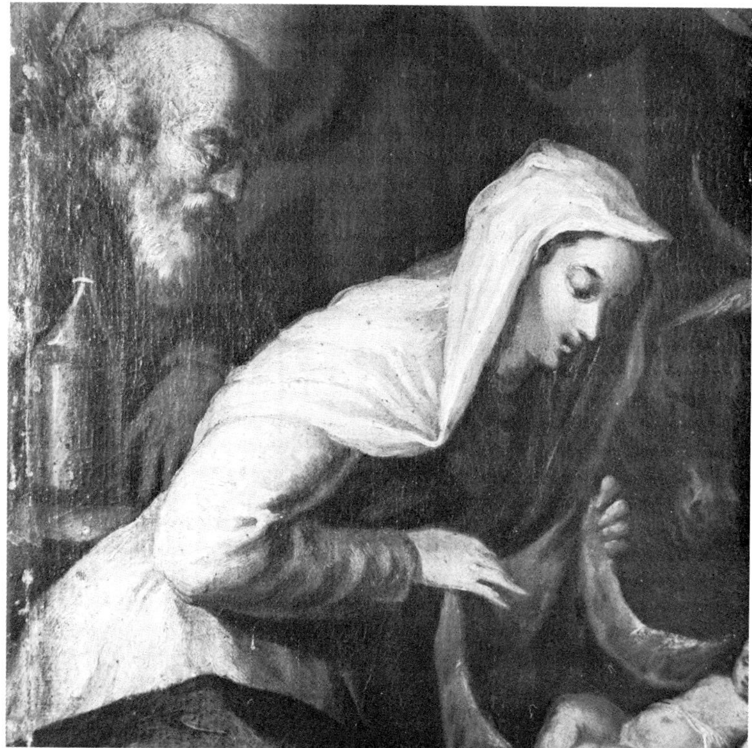

Fig. 4. Modified Eighteenth-Century Copy after Jacopo Bassano, *Adoration of the Shepherds*, detail of cat. no. 23

in execution that departs from the technique of the original: elements such as the feet of the shepherd in the foreground, depicted in detail in the Winterthur version, are undefined in the Baltimore work, as is the landscape background. The Christ Child, who has a natural, baby-like appearance in the model, becomes a lifeless, doll-like form in the copy; and the Virgin's gesture of lifting the veil, delicate and graceful in the earlier work, has a heavy, clumsy aspect in the Baltimore picture. There is, however, one element in the Baltimore painting that stands out as superior to that of the original: the head of Joseph (fig. 4), who stands behind Mary. While in the model he looks out over the Virgin's shoulder, in the copy he bends his head in an introspective attitude and is given a soft, gently modeled treatment; he becomes a sensitive portrait of the somewhat uncomprehending man who was involved if not altogether included in the miracle of Christ's nativity.

The Baltimore picture, although a minor work, offers considerable information about certain aspects of the eighteenth-century French art milieu. It gives a glimpse into a copyist's approach and subject choice, and it also provides insight into the trend toward simple tastes introduced into the predominantly Rococo Parisian art world.

Jane Nash
The Johns Hopkins University,
Baltimore

NOTES

1. *Catalogue of the Oskar Reinhart Collection Am Römerholz* (Winterthur, Switzerland: Swiss Confederation, n.d.), p. 15, no. 1.
2. B. Berenson, *Italian Pictures of the Renaissance: The Venetian School* (London: Phaidon Press, 1957), 1: 21.
3. R. Pallucchini, "Una nuova Adorazione dei Pastori di Jacopo Bassano," *Arte Veneta* 2 (1948):151, fig. 2.
4. E. Arslan, *I Bassani* (Milan: Ceschina, 1960), 1: 107.
5. R. Koella, *Die Sammlung Oskar Reinhart* (Zurich: Verlag Orell Füssli, 1975), p. 76.
6. W. R. Rearick, conversation of May 12, 1978, and note to G. Rosenthal of August 17, 1979.
7. Among the various copies and later versions of the Winterthur *Adoration,* the ones at the National Gallery, Oslo, and at the Musée des Beaux-Arts, Tours, are best known.
8. Rearick, conversation of May 12, 1978.
9. Ibid.
10. J. Sunderland and E. Camesasca, *The Complete Paintings of Watteau* (London: Weidenfeld and Nicolson, 1971), pp. 126–27, pls. 60, 61. Watteau's picture was to hang outside Gersaint's shop on the bridge of Notre Dame in Paris. Although it stayed there only fifteen days before it was sold to Claude Glucq, during that time it received considerable attention. By 1732 the painting had become the property of Glucq's cousin Jullienne, who sold it before 1756, probably to a representative of Frederick II of Prussia who had it hung in his collection in the Charlottenburg Palace near Berlin.

    Exactly which version of the *Adoration* appears in Watteau's picture is unclear. The scene, only dimly visible and distorted by the wall's angle, appears to be slightly different from those in Winterthur and Baltimore; among other changes is the omission of the crouching boy at the right.
11. For a further discussion, see G. Schiller, *Iconography of Christian Art,* trans. J. Seligmann (Greenwich, Conn.: The New York Graphic Society, 1971), 1:78 ff. Since the columns in the Baltimore painting, unlike those in the model, appear unbroken, the theme of the breakdown of the old order is diminished.
12. See Schiller, *Iconography,* 1:87–88, for a further discussion of the symbolism in scenes of the *Adoration of the Shepherds.*
13. Pallucchini, "Una nuova Adorazione," p. 151. This comparison, of course, adds yet another dimension to the problem of attribution already discussed in relation to the Winterthur picture.

SELECTED BIBLIOGRAPHY

Lily Fröhlich-Bum. "Some Original Compositions by Francesco and Leandro Bassano." *Burlington Magazine* 61 (1932):113–14.

Edoardo Arslan. "Di Alcuni Dipinti di Francesco e Leandro da Ponte." *Rivista dell'Istituto d'Archeologia e Storia dell'Arte* 5 (1933):178–87.

Wart [Edoardo] Arslan. "Bassanesque Pictures of 1560–1570." *Burlington Magazine* 65 (1934):214–19.

Wilhelm Suida. "Studien zu Bassano." *Belvedere* 12 (1934–1936):193–98.

Rodolfo Pallucchini. "Una nuova Adorazione dei Pastori di Jacopo Bassano." *Arte Veneta* 2 (1948): 151.

Ludwig Baldass. "Some Remarks on Francesco Bassano and His Historical Function." *Art Quarterly* 12 (1949):198–219.

Bernard Berenson. *Italian Pictures of the Renaissance: The Venetian School.* 2 vols. London: Phaidon Press, 1957.

Lily Fröhlich-Bum. "Some 'Adorations' by Jacopo Bassano." *Apollo* 65 (1957):215.

Michelangelo Muraro. "The Jacopo Bassano Exhibition." *Burlington Magazine* 99 (1957):291–99.

Pietro Zampetti. *Jacopo Bassano.* Venice: Alfieri, 1957.

Edoardo Arslan. *I Bassani.* 2 vols. Milan: Ceschina, 1960.

W. Roger Rearick. "Jacopo Bassano's Later Genre Paintings." *Burlington Magazine* 110 (1968):241–49.

Gertrud Schiller. *Iconography of Christian Art.* 2 vols. Translated from the German by Janet Seligmann. Greenwich, Conn.: The New York Graphic Society, 1971.

John Sunderland and Ettore Camesasca. *The Complete Paintings of Watteau.* London: Weidenfeld and Nicolson, 1971.

Rolf Kultzen and Peter Eikemeier. *Venezianische Gemälde des 15. und 16. Jahrhunderts.* 2 vols. Munich: Bayerische Staatsgemäldesammlungen, 1971.

Rudolf Koella. *Die Sammlung Oskar Reinhart.* Zurich: Verlag Orell Füssli, 1975.

Catalogue of the Oskar Reinhart Collection Am Römerholz. Winterthur, Switzerland: Swiss Confederation, n.d.

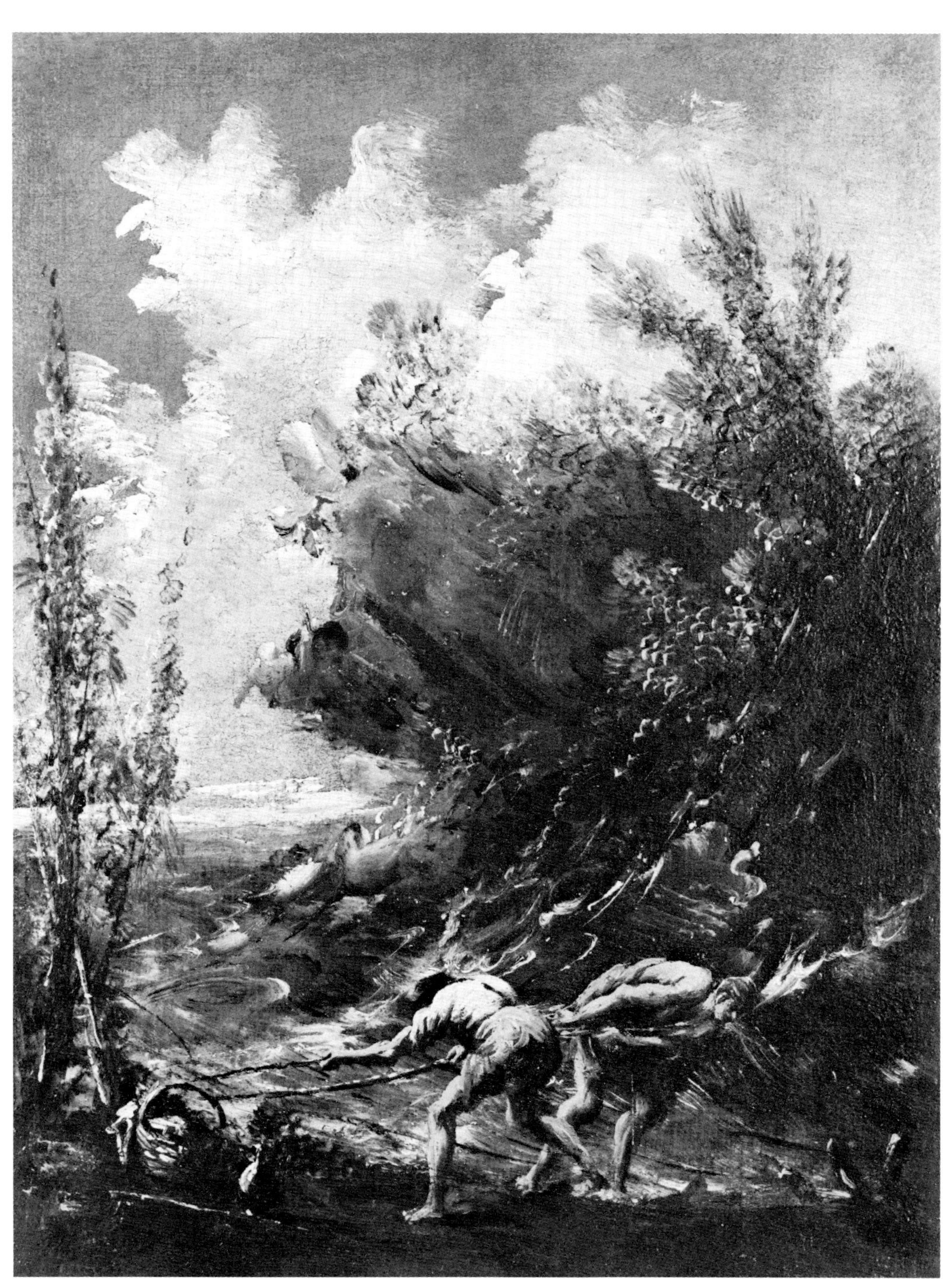

Eighteenth-Century Imitator of ALESSANDRO MAGNASCO (1667–1749)

24. *Two Fishermen Drawing a Net*

Oil on canvas. 15⅞ × 11¾ inches (40.3 × 29.8 cm.)
Gift of Harold M. Landon (BMA 45.54)

PROVENANCE

Harold Bendixson, London
Sale, Christie's, London, July 5, 1929, lot 138

Durlacher Brothers, New York

Acquired by Harold M. Landon, Baltimore, either in 1936 or 1937

Given to The Baltimore Museum of Art in 1945 by Harold M. Landon

CONDITION

The fabric support of the painting *Two Fishermen Drawing a Net* is of medium weight and of a rough texture. The reddish ground shows through in the thinly painted passages of sky and water as well as in some areas of the rock formations. Other passages, such as figures, foliage, etc., are painted in a thickly applied impasto technique.

There is no record of treatment before the picture's acquisition by the Baltimore Museum. However, examination of the painting in 1978, when it was treated at the Museum laboratory, revealed that it had been glue-lined at some time in the past. Presumably during this earlier treatment the top and bottom edges of the design layer were extended by 7 mm. each, while technical evidence suggests that perhaps about 10 mm. were cut off from the right side. These size alterations seem to have been made to have the picture fit an existing stretcher and frame. Upon removal of old fillings and overpaint, old tack holes were discovered on the face of the painting along the top, bottom, and left side—indicating that the picture had originally been painted on a fabric tacked to a board.

The picture is generally in good condition. There are minor losses along all edges and abrasion is noticeable in the thinly painted areas of the sky. After the painting was wax-relined to a semi-rigid support, the losses were filled and inpainted, and a synthetic acrylic varnish was applied.

Geoffrey Michael Lemmer
The Baltimore Museum of Art

It is with reluctance yet conviction that *Two Fishermen Drawing a Net* is here removed from the list of accepted works by Alessandro Magnasco.[1] The reluctance, in part, stems from a hesitation to appear to challenge a half-century's satisfaction with such an attribution, one adhered to by several authorities[2] and echoed in a number of exhibitions. Partly, too, the reluctance is prompted by regret that no alternative name can be suggested as that of the author of this admittedly attractive work. The conviction is based on observable elements in the Baltimore painting that differ significantly from a canon of style that appears uniformly throughout most of the paintings given to Magnasco. It should be noted that the extreme scarcity of documented works by this artist does dictate a special caution in either making or unmaking attributions on stylistic grounds alone.

Since the figures of the two fishermen in the Baltimore painting are its most conspicuous feature, they afford the best evidence for the opinion here advanced. Reference to comparative illustrations of generally accepted works by Magnasco provides the necessary background for the following observations on the figures and on other aspects of the painting as well. To begin, the figures are built up with slightly cursive or wavering brushstrokes which are quite different in appearance and effect from the more angular, staccato handling normally associated with Magnasco. The figures here lack the apparent knitted articulation of muscle and sinew ordinarily visible even at small scale, and also the characteristic wiry vigor seen in the *Landscape with Fishermen* in San Diego (figs. 1 and 2). In the Baltimore painting this weakness is especially obvious in the right arm and shoulder of the figure to the right and in the extended left arm of the other fisherman; there is no sense of any plausible surface modulation nor of any internal structure. The flaccid handling is obvious too in the indifferent, generalized modeling of the breeches of the fisherman to the left and in the streaky rendering of the legs (see fig. 2). The legs do exhibit the exaggerated curvature of the calf which is a conspicuous mannerism in many of Magnasco's figures, but they lack the springiness that the distortion was surely intended to impart. Finally, the feet are far too small and delicate; they are neither long enough nor broad enough across the ball of the foot, they lack any vitality of modeling, and they are missing the highly developed big toe so characteristic of Magnasco.

Similarly, the landscape contains passages that seem careless, if knowingly chosen, paraphrases of typical Magnasco motifs. Chief of these is the rock outcropping in the center. It is difficult to understand in terms of its placement within the landscape and is illegible in its form—this is especially obvious in its left-hand margin, against the sky, which altogether lacks definition. The foliage is thin and tattered, particularly in the passage above the rock cliff and in the little clump of saplings at the extreme left. The clouds are oddly shaggy and angular. And everywhere there is evident a lack of attention to the scale of the brushwork that is yet another argument for assigning the painting to an imitator of Magnasco rather than to the master himself.[3]

The question is, of course, "which imitator?" It is a problem for which there is no solution, at least for the present. That there were imitators is evident from the number of paintings in the style of Magnasco that survive in many private and public collections. But beyond that evidence is the valuable testimony of Magnasco's eighteenth-century biographer, Carlo Giuseppe Ratti.[4] First, it is clear that Magnasco enjoyed a successful, profitable career in Milan, where he lived from 1677 to 1703 and again from 1711 to 1735, and during the intervening years in Florence as well. The example of the elevated and sustained patronage his novel style and choice of subjects gained him cannot have gone unnoticed. Ratti explicitly mentions two of Magnasco's students who were slavish followers of their teacher's manner, but it is a matter for regret that he identifies them

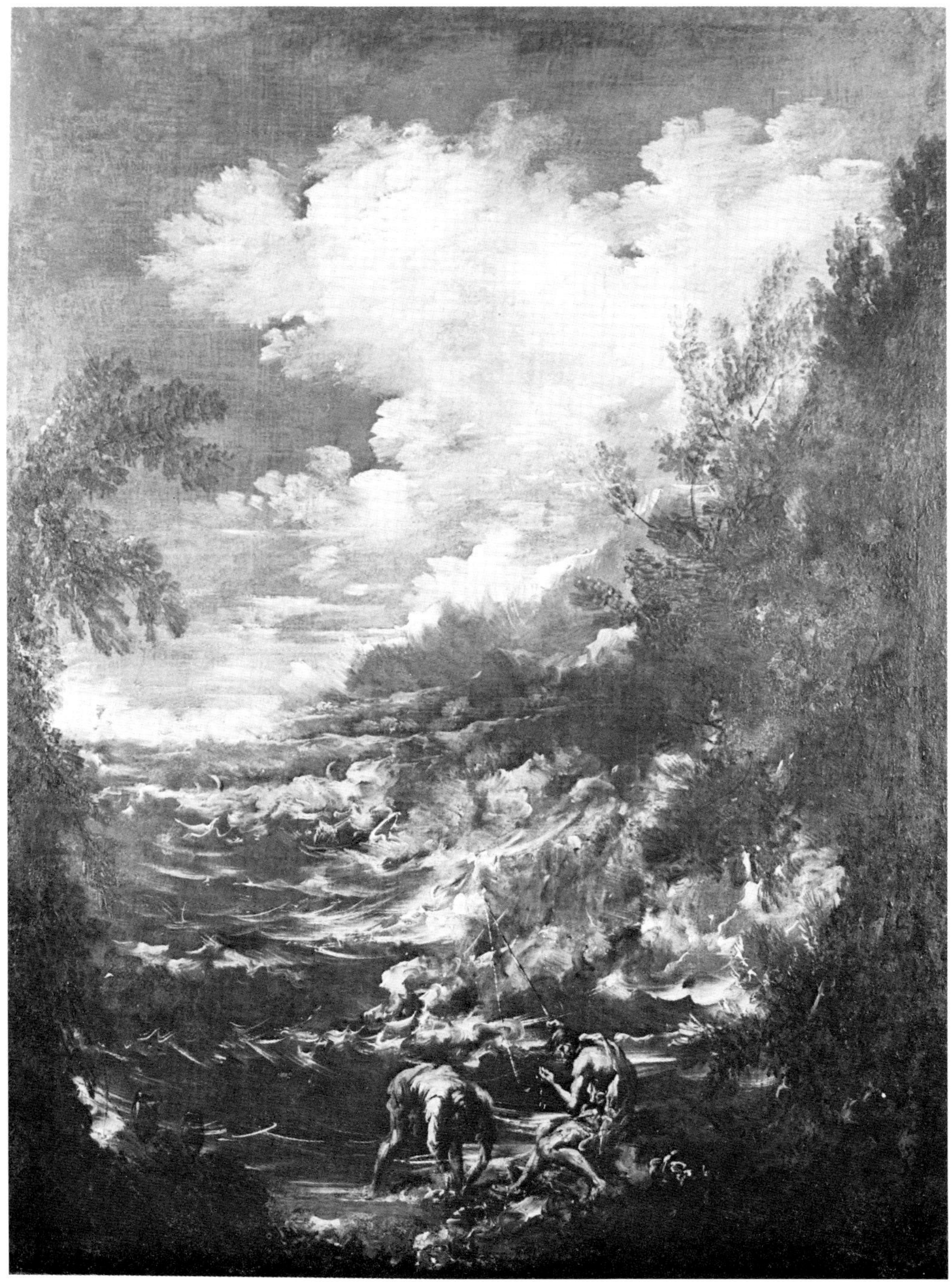

Fig. 1. Alessandro Magnasco, *Landscape with Fishermen*. Oil on canvas. 38¾ × 28¾ inches (98.4 × 73 cm.). The San Diego Museum of Art

only as the Neapolitan, Ciccio, and the Milanese, Coppa, the less able of the two. So here are two imitators whose minimal documentation has deprived them of their undoubted share of attributed Magnascos.

The first serious attempt to pare down the large and too generously defined oeuvre of Magnasco was made by Maria Pospisil in her monograph of 1944.[5] She reassigned a

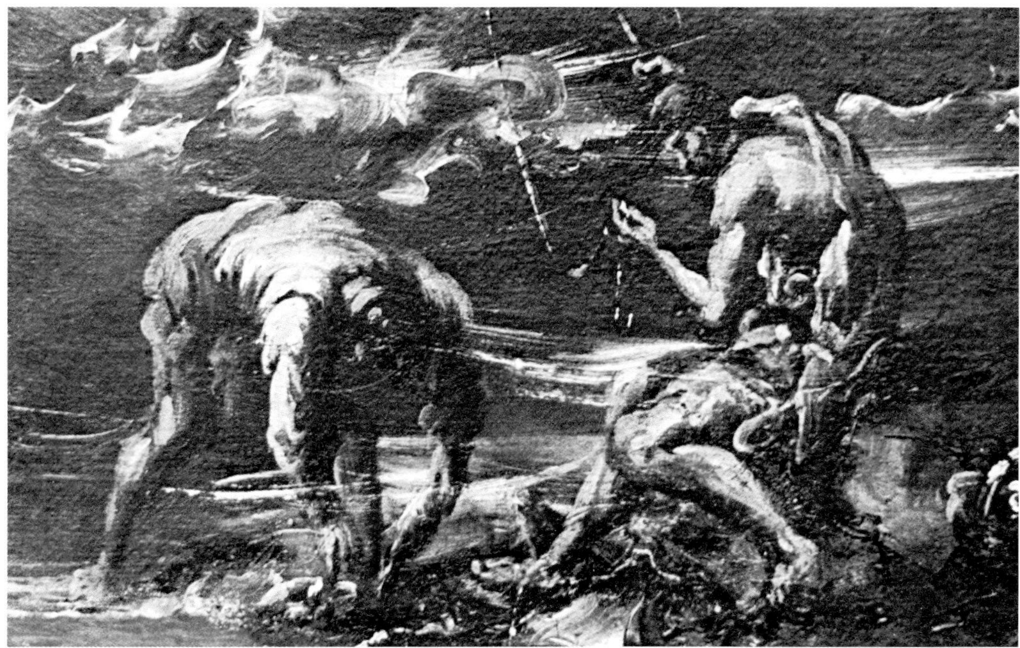

Fig. 2. Alessandro Magnasco, *Landscape with Fishermen,* detail of fig. 1

number of Magnascos to the virtually unknown Giuseppe Zola of Brescia and used as the basis for these reattributions a painting previously said to be by Magnasco but which carried the inscription "G. Zola 1707."[6] This crucial painting was in a private collection and circumstances prohibited its reproduction. Certainly none of the few works that had earlier been identified as by Zola could have prepared anyone to accept him as remotely capable of some of the landscapes with which Pospisil credited him.[7]

It is difficult to perceive any common denominator of style linking the various paintings that Pospisil gave to Zola, and among them are many that to this day seem quite acceptable as works by Magnasco. However, her intention of beginning to create some order within a large and impossibly diverse corpus did succeed in calling attention to numerous canvases that were not likely to be by Magnasco. Such an ambition was and remains laudable, and hardly seems to have merited the attack made on Pospisil by Benno Geiger in his third monograph on Magnasco, published in 1949.[8]

One of the problems that any study of Magnasco's production must deal with is his well-known and frequent practice of collaboration with one or another artist who, usually, would supply the setting, either landscape or architecture, for his figures. That Magnasco was first a figure painter is attested by Ratti, who describes Magnasco's early activity as a portraitist and then as a genre painter whose subjects were customarily interior and rather humble settings. It seems likely that his interest in landscape first developed in Florence (although it clearly had originated in Milan since there exists a signed and dated landscape of 1691) in a collaboration with Antonio Francesco Peruzzini, to whose landscapes Magnasco added small figures.[9] Peruzzini's personality is now well enough established to provide a firm basis of identification: his landscapes are broad and intricately constructed through many changes of level, linked by trails, roads and waterways, and punctuated by small architectural or topographical features. The facture is elegant, delicate, and dense.[10] He clearly had nothing to do with the Baltimore painting although his oeuvre has been extended to include a fairly large group of canvases that have previously passed as Magnascos.[11]

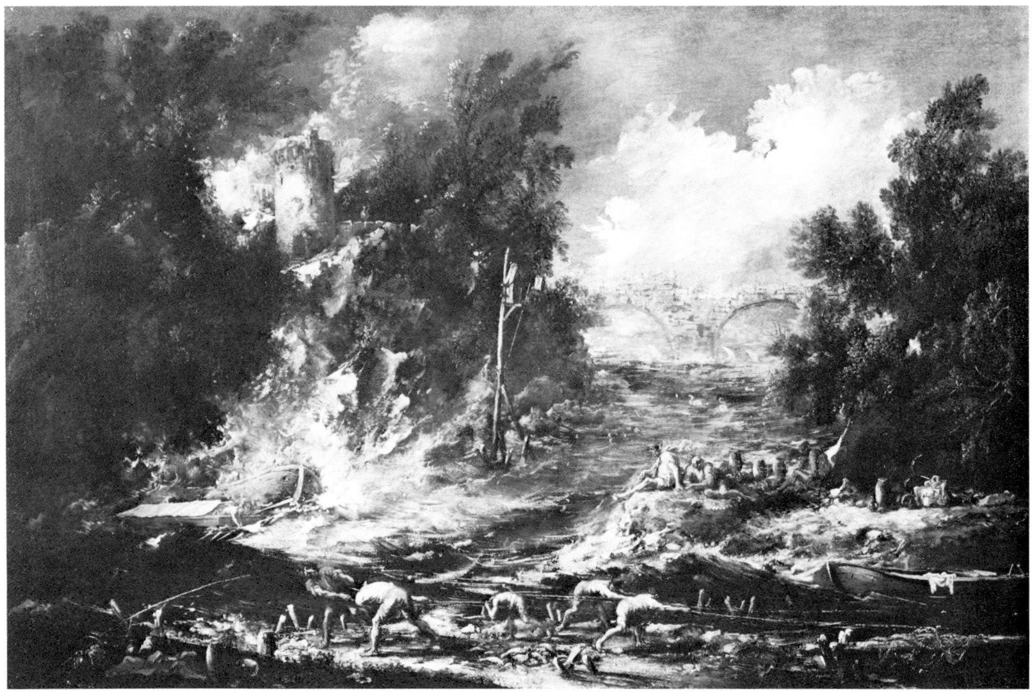

Fig. 3. Alessandro Magnasco, *Bay with Shipwreck* (after 1735). Oil on canvas. 45¼ × 68⅛ inches (114.9 × 173 cm.). Courtesy of the North Carolina Museum of Art, Gift of the Samuel H. Kress Foundation, Raleigh

A second collaborator, Clemente Spera, appears to have furnished extensive architectural settings for Magnasco during some part of his Milanese periods. Spera had rather a reputation as a ruin painter, and pure landscape seems not to have interested him. Pictures with figures by Magnasco in settings considered to be by Spera reveal him as a fine and careful painter whose preferred subjects and technique suggest Roman connections, a solid foil to his partner's contributions.[12] Yet another collaborator, this time in Genoa for the brief period 1735 to 1738, was Carlo Antonio Tavella, like Peruzzini an independently important painter of landscapes.[13] His works, which do appear to range extensively in stylistic derivation, generally owe their character to Salvator Rosa and to Pietro de Mulieribus (called Il Tempesta), whom Tavella knew. These landscapes typically are monumental but simply structured with full, substantial forms. There is a strong element of drama present, and it is not difficult to understand how he might have invited the old Magnasco to add figures to heighten the effect, as Ratti tells us he did. Neither Spera nor Tavella can be thought the author of the Baltimore painting, nor, indeed, does it seem likely that an established collaborator would ever produce a work, however small, that is so patently in the style of Magnasco. However, these extended arrangements of collaboration and other recorded instances of briefly formed teams for the creation of specific paintings must have been common knowledge to Magnasco's students and followers who would have accepted such practices as a matter of course. One is confronted with the possibility that many of the non-Magnascos that exist are in fact the product of two or more entirely anonymous painters working jointly in emulation of their master's method.

What is very much needed before such works can be put in any sort of order is a further delving into north Italian landscape painting in search of minor but definable personalities, and also a complete reexamination of Magnasco. As an instance of the

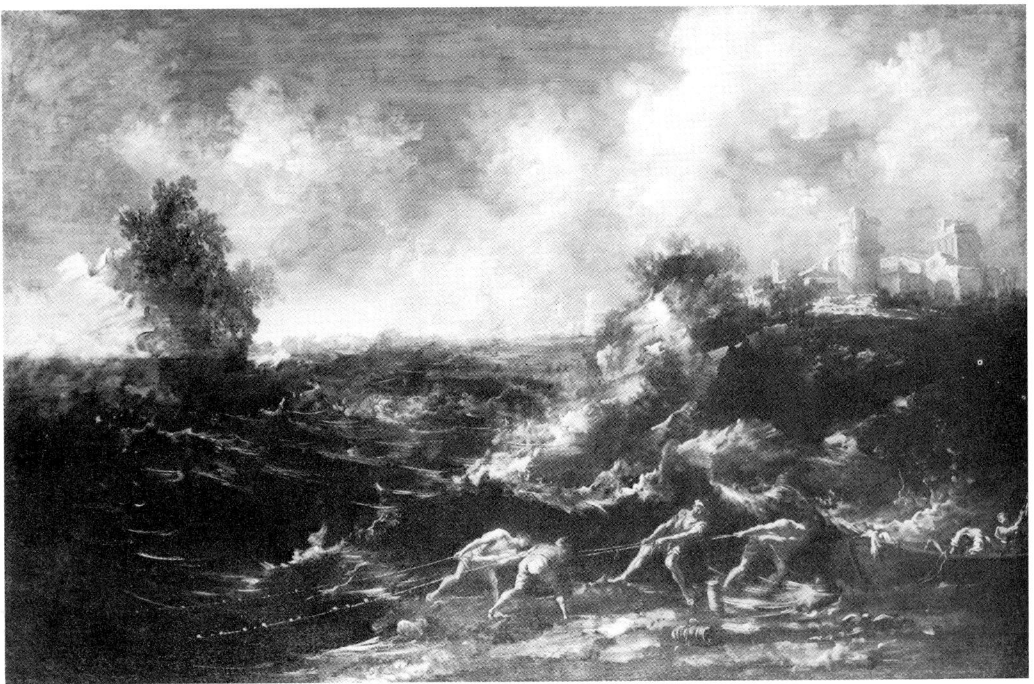

Fig. 4. Alessandro Magnasco, *Seascape with Fishermen Pulling Out Nets.* Oil on canvas. 45½ × 68¼ inches (115.5 × 173.3 cm.). Yale University Art Gallery, The Maitland F. Griggs Collection, New Haven, Connecticut

former type of research there is the recent resuscitation of Giuseppe Antonio Pianca, whose dark, lush landscapes are often compared to and sometimes confused with those of Magnasco. Chief instrument of this rediscovery was the Pianca exhibition at Varallo in 1962 which has been supplemented by useful, later articles.[14] It must be said that the conflation of Pianca and Magnasco seems more an intellectual conceit of Italian art history than the recognition of strong similarities between the two. It has now been thirty years since the last important wave of Magnasco studies, and a new investigation of the accepted oeuvre would be timely.[15] A fresh study could take advantage of such welcome contributions as the rather recent discovery by Jeffery Daniels of a quartet of large landscapes signed "AM" and dated 1711, the important year of Magnasco's return to Milan from Florence.[16] Other similar finds, made either through a closer examination of already known paintings or in works newly brought to light, could surely be expected.

The author of the Baltimore canvas probably intended that it should look like a Magnasco, and in spite of the shortcomings noted earlier, he almost achieved that end. This "anonimo" chose a subject that appears so frequently in Magnasco that Geiger in his division of the total oeuvre into categories based on content recognized an entire "Ciclo Marino," scenes along the shore of some large body of water where fishermen often appear. The *Bay with Shipwreck* from the North Carolina Museum of Art (fig. 3) and the *Seascape with Fishermen Pulling out Nets* from the Yale University Art Gallery (fig. 4) are but a sampling of this extensive group. It has been widely assumed that these littoral scenes must date from after Magnasco's return to Genoa in 1735; however, so far as I know, there is nothing in any of these paintings to suggest an actual view along the Gulf of Genoa. Furthermore, the argument, more implicit than overtly stated, that Magnasco would only have taken up this type of subject under the direct inspiration of his surroundings is counter to the fundamentally anti-naturalistic, imaginative nature of his art. It is unlikely that he drew his inspiration from what he saw before him except in rare and very specific instances. So literal an approach to landscape painting would, in fact, have been most unusual in north Italian landscape representation during the early eighteenth century. And if Magnasco did rely on direct observation of shore and wind-whipped waters, there are always the Italian lakes within a comfortable journey's distance of Milan.

The exclusively Genoese origin of such coastal scenes is worth questioning, since it seems to me that if one is going to venture placing the Baltimore painting in some context more exact than just the eighteenth century, it would be to Milan in the years immediately following Magnasco's final departure from that city. Ratti's testimony of the popularity of Magnasco in Milan argues by implication that this would have been the most likely place for the activity of an imitator. There is no way of knowing what Magnasco might have thought of such a compliment, but he obviously had no objection to at least two of his students trying to imitate him, and his financial success and secure reputation may well have made him tolerant of other copyists. However, the years just after 1735 would have been the most favorable to any such undertaking since he was no longer present either to gratify a continuing demand or to speak out against a too egregious appropriation of his manner.

In preparing this paper, I was struck now and again that a given work attributed to the master tended to look more like the Baltimore canvas than it did a true Magnasco. Admittedly, these observations were prompted by the study of photographs, notoriously unreliable for transmitting nuances of style, yet useful for formal characteristics supporting a Morellian analysis, especially of figures.[17] Among the works that seem closer to the Baltimore picture than to those by the master is a landscape of *Washerwomen and Fishermen* in an Italian private collection, originally attributed to Magnasco but published by Pospisil as by Giuseppe Zola.[18] The figures here are virtually interchangeable with those of the Baltimore painting. Of the washerwomen, Pospisil wrote: "Le braccia sembrano rigonfie come cuoio molle." ("The arms seem to be swollen like soft leather.") Could there be a better description of the arms of the Baltimore fishermen?

It is in such company that the Baltimore *Fishermen* must languish, but it need not be forever. Just as I have suggested a nebulous imitator, a "Maestro dei Pescatori," so would a broader inspection of paintings called Magnasco reveal some six or possibly eight equivalent yet distinct personalities. It is not impossible that an artist's name may yet be found to attach to the Baltimore work.

Barry Hannegan
North Carolina Museum of Art,
Raleigh

NOTES

1. The painting was bought as a Magnasco by Durlacher Brothers. It was the smallest and simplest of four paintings attributed to Magnasco in the Bendixson Collection, yet it realized the highest price.
2. The references in both A. Ferri (*Alessandro Magnasco* [Rome: Ferri & Recchi, 1922], p. 29) and B. Geiger (*Alessandro Magnasco* [Vienna: Krystall Verlag, 1923], p. 49, no. 132) are so vague that it is not at all clear that it is this particular painting in the Bendixson Collection that is cited. However, since Geiger in his later monograph (B. Geiger, *Magnasco* [Bergamo: Istituto Italiano d'arti grafiche, 1949], p. 68) does explicitly assign both his earlier citation and that of Ferri to the Baltimore painting, it seems reasonable to accept them and to include them here. The Baltimore picture was accepted as by Magnasco by most scholars, with the exception of B. B. Fredericksen and F. Zeri (*Census of Pre-Nineteenth-Century Italian Paintings in North American Public Collections* [Cambridge, Mass.: Harvard University Press, 1972], p. 115) who list it as "attributed, uncertain attribution."

3. That the painting does date from the eighteenth century is strongly suggested by visual examination and has been confirmed by technical laboratory examination.
4. C. G. Ratti, *Delle Vite de' Pittori, Scultori ed Architetti Genovesi* (Genoa: Soprani, 1769). Magnasco's *vita* has frequently been republished in works on him, and a thoughtful English translation of it appears in *Alessandro Magnasco,* exhibition catalogue (Louisville, Kentucky: J. B. Speed Art Museum, 1967).
5. M. Pospisil, *Magnasco* (Florence: Fratelli Alinari, 1944).
6. Ibid., p. 26.
7. E. Calabi, "Un paesista del '700: Giuseppe Zola," *Rivista d'Arte* 16, no. 1 (January–March 1934): 84–93.
8. Geiger, *Magnasco,* p. 50. Pospisil had challenged a number of Geiger's attributions.
9. F. F. Guelfi, "Su alcuni 'Paesaggi' di Alessandro Magnasco," *Pantheon* 27 (November–December 1969):472.
10. M. Chiarini, "Antonio Francesco Peruzzini," *Paragone* 26, no. 307 (September 1975):65–69, and M. Gregori, "Altre aggiunte a risarcimento di Antonio Francesco Peruzzini," *Paragone* 26, no. 307 (September 1975):69–80.
11. A candidate for reassignment to Peruzzini may perhaps be the painting attributed to Magnasco, *Wooded Landscape with Monks at a Fountain,* in the Dayton (Ohio) Art Institute.
12. Examples of this collaboration are the *Ruins with Soldier and Musicians* in the Smith College Museum of Art and the *Bacchanal among Ruins* in the Suida-Manning Collection, New York.
13. M. Bonzi, *Il Tavella* (Genoa, 1961).
14. M. Rosci, *Giuseppe Antonio Pianca,* exhibition catalogue (Varallo: Palazzo dei Musei, 1962). G. Testori, "Quattro paesaggi del Pianca," *Paragone* 18, no. 205 (March 1967):87–88. F. M. Ferro, "Inediti del Pianca," *Paragone* 26, no. 303 (May 1975):55–64.
15. In addition to Geiger's and Pospisil's monographs, also published during the 1940's were B. Geiger, *I Disegni del Magnasco* (Padua: Le Tre Venezie, 1945) and A. Morassi, *Mostra del Magnasco,* exhibition catalogue (Genoa: Palazzo Bianco, 1949).
16. J. Daniels, "Pair of Landscapes with Figures," *Connoisseur* 179, no. 721 (March 1972):225–26.
17. The influential Italian art historian Giovanni Morelli (1816–1891) originally worked in the field of natural science. He was the first to establish the method of critical analysis of works of art by comparing details of documented paintings (e.g., the rendering of an ear or a foot) with the corresponding parts in pictures whose authenticity was to be determined. *Encyclopedia of World Art* 7, p. 524.
18. Pospisil, *Magnasco,* p. 26, pl. 300.

SELECTED BIBLIOGRAPHY

Carlo Giuseppe Ratti. *Delle Vite de' Pittori, Scultori ed Architetti Genovesi.* Genoa: Soprani, 1769.

Armando Ferri. *Alessandro Magnasco.* Rome: Ferri & Recchi, 1922.

Benno Geiger. *Alessandro Magnasco.* Vienna: Krystall Verlag, 1923.

Pictures by Old Masters: The Properties of the Most Hon. The Marquess of Linlithgow, K.T. Sale catalogue. London: Christie's, July 5, 1929.

Italian Painting of the Sei- and Settecento. Exhibition catalogue. Hartford: The Wadsworth Atheneum, 1930.

Venetian Painting of the Eighteenth Century. Exhibition catalogue. St. Louis: City Art Museum, 1936.

Alessandro Magnasco. Exhibition catalogue. Springfield, Mass.: Museum of Fine Arts, 1938.

A Loan Exhibition of Paintings by Alessandro Magnasco: 1667–1749. Exhibition catalogue. New York: Durlacher Brothers, 1940.

Contrasts in Impressionism: An Exhibition of Paintings by Alessandro Magnasco, Claude Monet, and John Marin. Exhibition catalogue. Baltimore: The Baltimore Museum of Art, 1942.

Maria Pospisil. *Magnasco.* Florence: Fratelli Alinari, 1944.

Benno Geiger. *Alessandro Magnasco.* Exhibition catalogue. Venice: Ateneo, 1945.

Benno Geiger. *I Disegni del Magnasco.* Padua: Le Tre Venezie, 1945.

Benno Geiger. *Magnasco.* Bergamo: Istituto Italiano d'arti grafiche, 1949.

Antonio Morassi. *Mostra del Magnasco.* Exhibition catalogue. Genoa: Palazzo Bianco, 1949.

Mostra dei Pittori genovesi a Genova nel '600 e nel '700. Exhibition catalogue. Genoa: Palazzo Bianco, 1969.

Burton B. Fredericksen and Federico Zeri. *Census of Pre-Nineteenth-Century Italian Paintings in North American Public Collections.* Cambridge, Mass.: Harvard University Press, 1972.

F. Franchini Guelfi. *Alessandro Magnasco.* Genoa: Cassa di Risparmio, 1977.

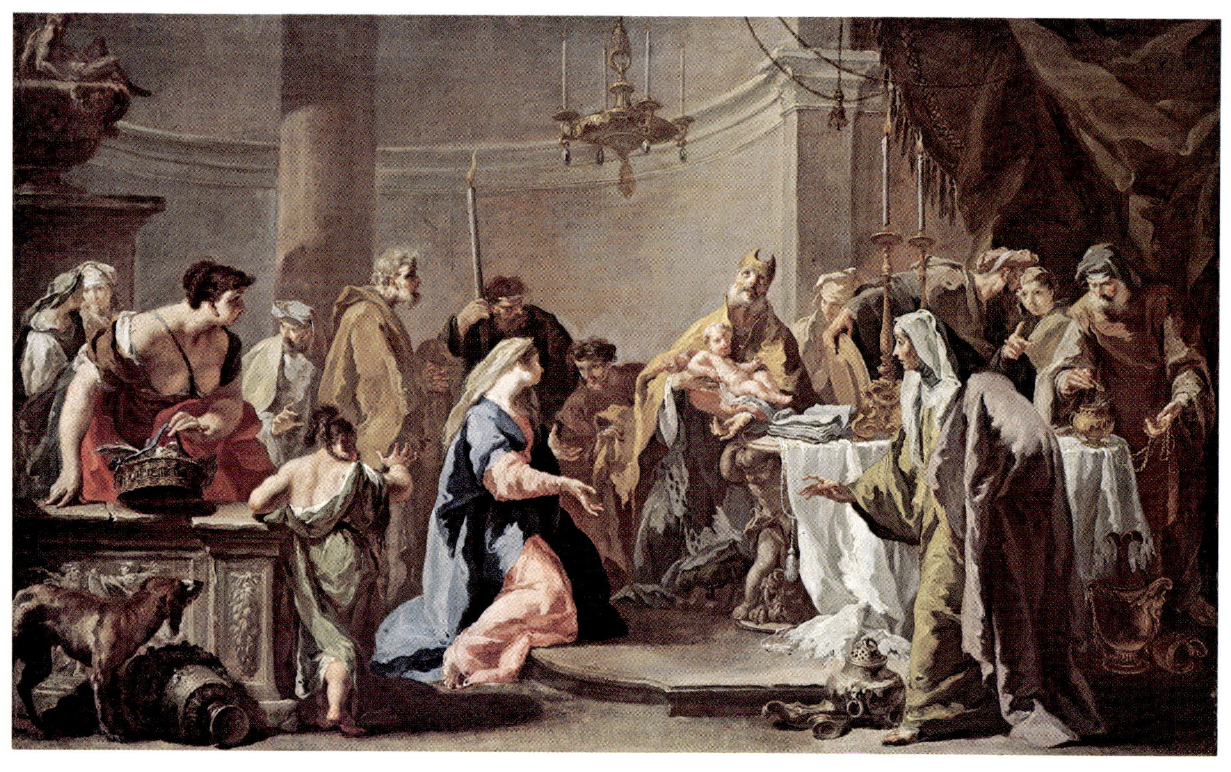

GIOVANNI BATTISTA PITTONI (1687–1767)

25. *The Presentation in the Temple,* ca. 1730–1732

Oil on canvas. 18⅛ × 29⅜ inches (46 × 74.6 cm.)
Museum Purchase (BMA 65.31)

PROVENANCE

Senator Ettore Conti, Milan

Acquired in Florence in 1925. The early history of the painting is not known. Laura Coggiola Pittoni thought that the picture had been brought to Tuscany during World War I.

Italico Brass, Venice

Purchased by The Baltimore Museum of Art in 1965

CONDITION

The support of the Pittoni painting appears to be linen, unevenly spun of thin to medium threads in a plain, loosely woven weave. The ground is light red in color, possibly with a white layer underneath. The paint is applied as a soft paste, opaque except for some thin areas in the details; the fabric pattern is visible through the paint and ground layers.

The painting currently has a two-layer glue lining, but there are indications that the picture had been previously lined. There are slight draws along the top and bottom edges and a few slight bulges along the top edge. These surface defects are minor; the picture is in stable condition, and the existing lining is being retained.

There are no major losses in the design layer. Two small vertical tears, one to left of center in the background, the other to left of the candle, have been repaired. Small inpainted losses are scattered throughout, most of them in the background.

X-radiographic examination shows a large irregular area in the center of the painting that is denser than the surrounding areas. This area is sharply defined and shows signs of abrasion. However, there are no corresponding damages or changes in the surface paint; the increased X-ray absorption may indicate that the central area was reworked by the artist shortly after the picture was started, or it could suggest that Pittoni left some ground on the reverse of the original support, or it could be a mark of residual adhesive from the earlier lining.

The surface appearance is very good. There is a very fine crackle pattern throughout the paint film, but all of the paint is secure. Small darkened residues of old varnish are not disfiguring.

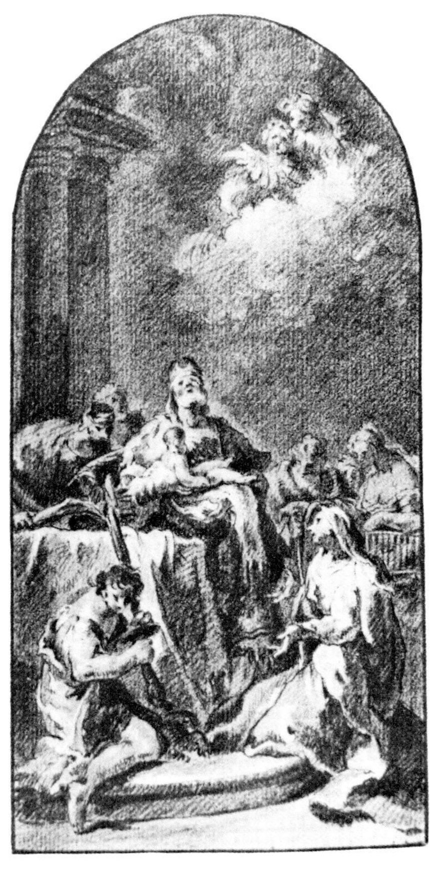

Fig. 1. Giovanni Battista Pittoni, *The Presentation in the Temple.* Pencil, heightened with white. 7½ × 3¾ inches (19 × 9.5 cm.). Correr Museum, Venice

Giovanni Battista Pittoni was born and died in Venice where he is believed to have spent his entire life. Despite his large oeuvre and his great reputation in the eighteenth century, little is known about his personal life or his artistic development. Therefore, few of his works can be dated precisely.

According to the scant recorded information, Pittoni received his early training from his uncle Francesco Pittoni, a minor artist whose pupil soon superseded him in skill and recognition. Antonio Balestra, a Veronese painter who, though with interruptions, worked for many years in Venice, seems to have had a far stronger impact on Pittoni than did his uncle.[1]

In his time Pittoni was considered one of the most outstanding painters of his native city. His artistic stature was compared favorably with that of the great masters of his era, Piazzetta and Giovanni Battista Tiepolo. In the eyes of the eighteenth-century connoisseur, these three painters formed the triad that elevated Venetian art above the creations of any other Italian school of that period. Pittoni's works were sought not only by his countrymen but also by foreign courts and by the princes of the Church all over Europe.

Pittoni painted altarpieces and mythological and historical scenes, almost all on canvas; also oil sketches on canvas; and a few very small pictures on copper. Several hundred extant drawings reveal the excellence of his draftsmanship. Before the establishment in

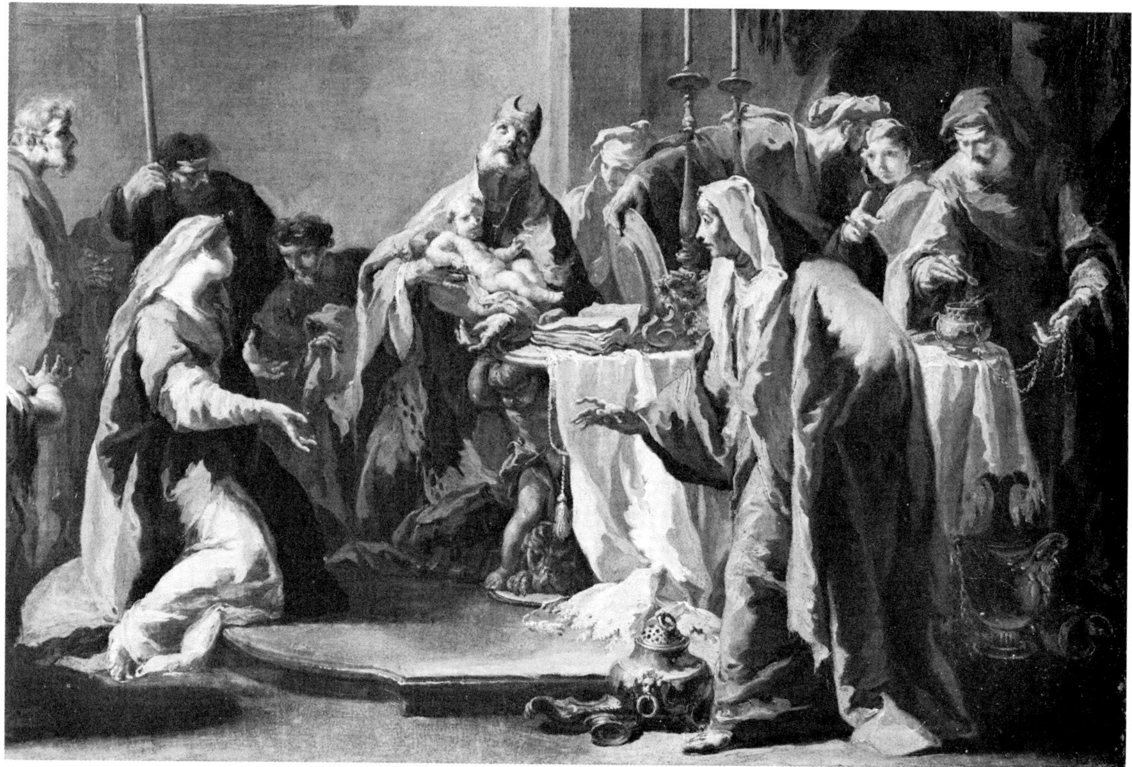

Fig. 2. Giovanni Battista Pittoni, *The Presentation in the Temple,* detail of cat. no. 25

1756 of the Accademia dei Pittori e Scultori of Venice, he acted as President of the Collegio dei Pittori[2] of his native city, where he also made a name for himself as a picture dealer, often advising the collectors who commissioned him on purchases of other artists' works.[3] In 1758 he succeeded Giambattista Tiepolo as President of the Venice Academy, a post he kept until 1765.

Today Pittoni's altarpieces and large mythological or "history" paintings are less appreciated than are his oil sketches, of which *The Presentation in the Temple* is a brilliant example. This picture was first published in 1925, together with its companion piece, a *Circumcision.*[4] The present location of the latter is not known.

Oil sketches had a number of different functions.[5] They were used mainly as models (*modelli*) for the patron who, thus informed of the artist's conception, could decide whether to commission a work based on the sketch. They also may have been intended for the master's assistants who often executed parts of the final painting following the sketch provided by the head of the workshop.[6] Then there are shorthand studies made as notations for the painter's own use, and also those *modelli* that were sometimes kept in the studio for future reference. Moreover, in the eighteenth century, sketches not planned as preparatory stages but as salable independent pictures were much in demand. Since no finished painting related to the Baltimore *Presentation in the Temple* has thus far come to light, it may be considered such an autonomous work, executed for a collector's "cabinet" or as a devotional picture.

A work by Pittoni's own hand,[7] as indicated by stylistic evidence and perhaps suggested by an apparently related drawing (fig. 1)[8], the Baltimore *Presentation* reveals the qualities of his best works: a dramatic conception of the subject,[9] virtuoso brushwork, and an

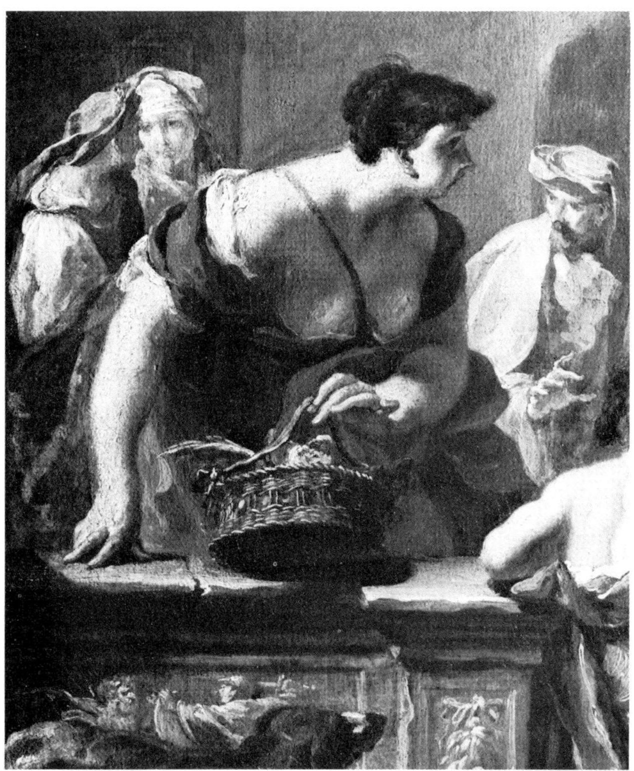

Fig. 3. Giovanni Battista Pittoni, *The Presentation in the Temple,* detail of cat. no. 25

alluring color scheme. Here are the Venetian rose tones, blues in different hues, crimson, some brown and brownish-black, muted whites, grays, and golds, recalling the sixteenth-century Venetian master Veronese, whose color combinations must have inspired Pittoni—even more in his oil sketches than in his finished works. From comparisons with a few datable works by Pittoni,[10] it can be assumed that the *Presentation* was painted in the 1730's, at the height of the artist's powers and fame.

The composition, emphasizing the horizontal, is based on the shape of an ellipse, which allows the painter, without crowding the space, to include a large number of well-defined, lively figures (fig. 2). As in many of his works, large and small, Pittoni adds movement and drama to the scene by placing the major group off center—here the priest Simeon with the Christ Child, the Virgin, and the Prophetess Anna—nevertheless succeeding in making this group the focal point of the composition. While these figures (including St. Joseph, who stands directly behind the Virgin) have a classical air, some of the others, either looking on or occupied with the ceremony, almost appear to belong to a genre scene. Prominent among these is a large woman at the left (fig. 3) who seems just to have dropped in, bringing with her a basket with a pair of turtledoves which are part of the ritual.

The apparently effortless mixture of spiritual exaltation (as manifest in the group formed by the Virgin, the priest holding the Christ Child, and the Prophetess Anna) and of elements of everyday life often occurs in Pittoni's works. Also characteristic of Pittoni's style is the predilection for showing many of the principal figures in profile, as seen in the *Presentation* in the rendering of the Virgin, the Prophetess, St. Joseph, and, on the left, the peasant woman with the basket. Equally typical are the expressive gestures of the figures and the nervous mannerism in the drawing of their hands (hands, once observed, will always betray Pittoni as the artist of a painting or drawing). In the Baltimore *Presentation* the hands seem to link the figures and contribute to the flowing rhythm of the entire design.

A study of Pittoni's paintings will reveal frequent repetitions or near-repetitions of figures, faces, poses, and gestures—a fact that indicates that he, like many of his fellow artists, kept his sketchbooks at hand, noting whole figures or details and making use of them whenever they would fit a new composition. As in his works of the thirties, these "reminiscences" often appear also in Pittoni's later paintings—in his moving *St. Mary Magdalene Repenting* (1745), for example, though in spirit it is removed from the earlier oil sketches.[11]

The artist has invented the architectural surroundings in which the event takes place, combining classical motifs with features from eighteenth-century church interiors. A similar combination, indicative of his interest in ancient remains, can be found in the furnishings of the temple. Here Pittoni, who was admired for his scholarship, has used a Roman altar, a high pedestal topped with a large vessel on which a river god rests, and an elegant Rococo table. This mélange of the ancient and the "modern" is carried further by the inclusion of such paraphernalia as the ancient urns and braziers which contrast with the lamp and candlesticks in contemporary style. It was partly this propensity to blend elements of antiquity with the life of his own time which made Pittoni a favorite with the learned collectors of his era. According to Pallucchini, he must be considered one of the most representative painters of the Venetian Rococo and of its manifestations in the countries beyond the Alps.[12] Today's appeal of Pittoni's works, especially of his oil sketches, lies primarily in the richness of his paint surfaces, his spontaneous brushstrokes, his sure sweeping lines, and his brilliant use of color.

Gertrude Rosenthal
The Baltimore Museum of Art

NOTES

1. A. Morassi points out in "Una mostra del Settecento a Gorizia," *Arte Veneta* 10 (1956):251–54, that Francesco Pittoni played a more important part in his nephew's artistic development than is usually allotted to him; on the other hand, R. Pallucchini, supported by the opinions of earlier and modern scholars, emphasizes Balestra's influence on Giambattista Pittoni at his uncle Francesco's expense. See R. Pallucchini, *La pittura veneziana del Settecento* (Venice: Istituto per la collaborazione culturale, 1960), p. 115.
2. See A. Binion, "The 'Collegio dei Pittori' in Venice," *L'Arte,* fasc. nos. 11–12 (December 1970):92–99.
3. Ibid., p. 98, n. 43.
4. L. Coggiola Pittoni, "Due quadri Settecenteschi inediti nella raccolta del Senatore Ettore Conti in Milano," *Emporium* 62, no. 370 (October 1925): 268–73.
5. See the explanation by the late R. Wittkower of the various uses of a *modello* in his introduction to *Masters of the Loaded Brush: Oil Sketches from Rubens to Tiepolo,* exhibition catalogue (New York: M. Knoedler & Co., 1967), pp. xv–xxv.
6. Another type of sketch, almost always in monochrome and done after the finished painting, served as guide for the transfer of the picture to the medium of graphic art or to tapestry.
7. F. Z. Boccazzi, *Pittoni, L'Opera completa* (Venice: Alfieri, 1979), no. A I, p. 203, fig. 493, attributes

The Presentation in the Temple to Anton Kern (born 1710, Tetschen, Bohemia; died 1747, Dresden). To this writer the attribution to Kern in Mme. Boccazzi's catalogue entry is not convincing. Other experts who have examined the painting —including Alice Binion, Rodolfo Pallucchini, Terisio Pignatti, Federico Zeri, et al.—agree that the work is an authentic Pittoni (see letters and written statements in the curatorial files of The Baltimore Museum of Art).

8. Pittoni, *The Presentation in the Temple,* Correr Museum, Venice, inv. no. 786; in the Correr collection since 1830 (Lugt 1862a). Pencil, heightened with white on brown paper; 7½ × 3¾ inches (19 × 9.5 cm.). See R. Pallucchini, *I disegni di Giambattista Pittoni* (Padua: Le tre Venezie, 1945), p. 105. Also T. Pignatti, *Eighteenth-Century Venetian Drawings from the Correr Museum, Venice,* exhibition catalogue (Washington, D.C.: Smithsonian Institution, 1963), no. 11, p. 37; Boccazzi, *Pittoni,* no. D 50, p. 214, fig. 477. Recently the attribution to Pittoni of this drawing, which is of fine quality, has been questioned.
9. The subject of the painting is based on Luke 2: 22–38.
10. Among the paintings showing some connection with the Baltimore picture are the oil sketches of the *Sacrifice of Polyxena,* Louvre, Paris, which is also an oblong picture (see Pallucchini, *La pittura veneziana del Settecento,* fig. 304) and the *Sacrifice of Jephthah's Daughter,* at Agnew, London, in 1974 (only the finished painting has been reproduced, see ibid., fig. 301).
11. *St. Mary Magdalen Repenting,* oil sketch, Accademia, Venice; see Pallucchini, *La pittura veneziana del Settecento,* fig. 308.
12. Ibid., p. 120.

SELECTED BIBLIOGRAPHY

Hermann Voss. "G. B. Pittoni." In Thieme-Becker, *Allgemeines Lexikon der Bildenden Künstler.* 37 vols. Leipzig: E. A. Seemann, 1907–1950.

Laura Coggiola Pittoni. "Due quadri Settecenteschi inediti nella raccolta del Senatore Ettore Conti in Milano." *Emporium* 62, no. 370 (October 1925): 268–73.

Max Goering. "Zur Kritik und Datierung der Werke des Giovanni Battista Pittoni." *Mitteilungen des Kunsthistorischen Institutes in Florenz* 4 (1934):201–48.

Rodolfo Pallucchini. *I disegni di Giambattista Pittoni.* Padua: Le tre Venezie, 1945.

Antonio Morassi. "Una mostra del Settecento a Gorizia." *Arte Veneta* 10 (1956):251–54.

Rodolfo Pallucchini. *La pittura veneziana del Settecento.* Venice: Istituto per la collaborazione culturale, 1960.

Terisio Pignatti. *Eighteenth-Century Venetian Drawings from the Correr Museum, Venice.* Exhibition catalogue. Washington, D.C.: Smithsonian Institution, 1963.

"Acquisitions." *Art Quarterly* 28, no. 4 (1965):315, repro. p. 319.

"La Chronique des Arts." *Gazette des Beaux-Arts,* ser. 6, 67 (February 1966), supplement no. 1165:54–55.

"Accessions Report." *Baltimore Museum of Art News* 29, nos. 1–2 (1967):43–65.

Rudolf Wittkower. *Masters of the Loaded Brush: Oil Sketches from Rubens to Tiepolo.* Exhibition catalogue. New York: M. Knoedler & Co., 1967.

Alice Binion. "The 'Collegio dei Pittori' in Venice." *L'Arte,* fasc. nos. 11–12 (December 1970):92–99.

Johannes Wilde. *Venetian Art from Bellini to Titian.* Oxford: Clarendon Press, 1974.

Franca Zava Boccazzi. *Pittoni, L'Opera completa.* Venice: Alfieri, 1979.

Alice Binion. *I disegni di Giambattista Pittoni.* Florence: La Nuova Italia, to be published 1981.

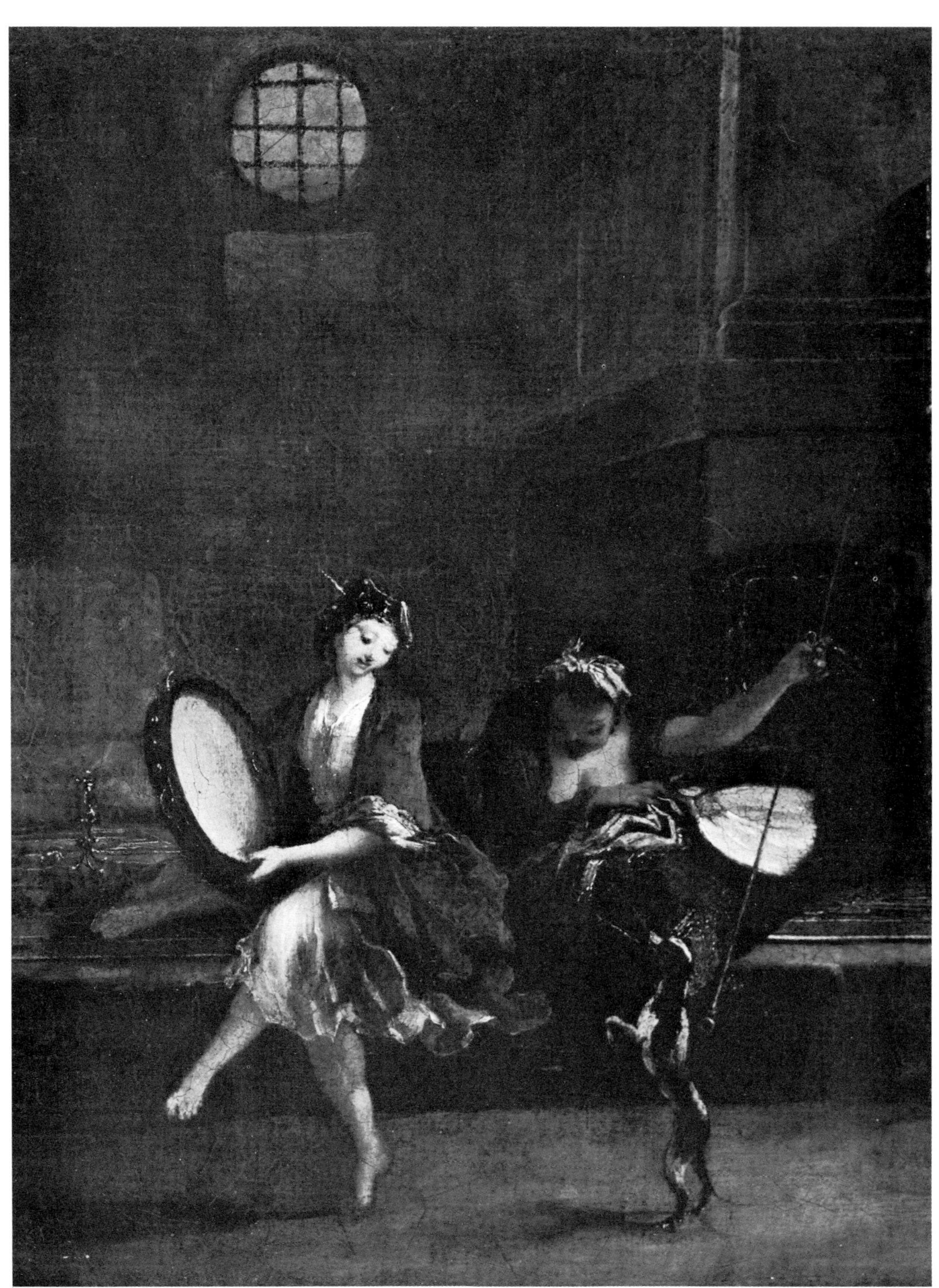

Circle of
GIOVANNI CAMILLO SAGRESTANI (1660–1731)

---

26. *Turkish Scene,* ca. 1720

Oil on canvas. 17½ × 12½ inches (44.4 × 31.7 cm.)
Gift of Morris Schapiro (BMA 44.89)

PROVENANCE

Victor D. Spark, New York

There is no information on the history of the painting prior to the early 1940's when it was in the possession of Victor Spark.

Acquired by Morris Schapiro, Baltimore, in 1944

The picture was purchased by Mr. Schapiro from an exhibition at The Baltimore Museum of Art entitled *Three Baroque Masters,* where it was listed as *Gypsy Scene* by Giuseppe Maria Crespi.

Given to The Baltimore Museum of Art in 1944 by Morris Schapiro

The attribution to Crespi was retained when the painting entered the Museum collection. In 1959 the title and attribution were changed to *Turkish Scene* by Francesco Guardi.

CONDITION

The oil paint on this *Harem Scene* is thinly applied with light brushstrokes on a reddish ground. There is a crackle pattern throughout the design layer, and some of the longer cracks, being fairly wide, allow the ground to show. At an unknown date, before the painting entered the Museum collection, it was lined, probably with glue, and, at the same time, was cleaned by an over-zealous hand. This caused a fine abrasion throughout the dark passages of the design layer, particularly along the ridges on either side of the cracks, making some of them appear wider than they are. Actual losses of the paint film are confined to the extreme edges of the painting. There are also some small losses through flaking in the lower right corner. Essentially, the painting is in sound, stable condition.

Acquired as a work by the Bolognese painter Giuseppe Maria Crespi (called Lo Spagnuolo, 1665–1747), this painting representing a Turkish scene has, for the past several decades, been attributed to Francesco Guardi.[1] However, this ascription has been widely questioned without any resultant consensus on a more likely name to attach to the work.[2] It is hoped that the following remarks may provide a basis for a convincing identification of the author of this picture.

The initial attribution to Crespi had a certain degree of reasonableness to recommend it. The casual intimacy of the subject, the dusky setting, and the soft, rather friable chiaroscuro of the figures all recall Crespi's darkly lambent genre paintings. However, the figure types themselves, the markedly limited range of color, and the overtly exotic subject matter of the Baltimore picture find no parallel in Crespi nor, indeed, in any known aspect of Bolognese painting of the period.

Equally problematic was the attribution to Francesco Guardi. The chief argument here rested on the existence of a considerable number of small Turkish scenes formerly attributed solely to Gian Antonio Guardi, Francesco's older brother, with whom he often collaborated. Antonio Morassi has published thirteen from this series, which originally numbered forty-three and which were painted in 1742 and 1743.[3] The observable variations of style in the known examples indicate that, as was usually the practice in Gian Antonio's studio, the work was shared with an unknown number of helpers and assistants. Since the principal assistant would have been Francesco, and since the Baltimore picture did not exhibit any of the somewhat variable characteristics of Gian Antonio, it was to the younger brother that the picture was assigned. Another possible link to the Guardi studio was provided by the dimensions of the Baltimore Museum painting, which is roughly the same height as canvases of the Guardi series and just half their width. However, the Guardi attribution has not found many advocates, owing mainly to the incompatibility of the picture's style with the Guardi Turkish scenes or, for that matter, with any of the recognized Guardi manners.

In 1975 Federico Zeri pointed out that several paintings of a similar type "bear a traditional attribution to Giovanni Camillo Sagrestani (1660–1731)," a Florentine who, significantly, had much of his training in Bologna.[4] The initial step in what has become a somewhat involved history of the attribution of Turkish subjects to Sagrestani seems to have been taken by Mina Gregori in the catalogue she prepared for an exhibition of later Florentine art held in the Palazzo Strozzi in 1965.[5] Four paintings (nos. 39a, 39b, 40, and 41) belonging to a private collector in Genoa were here attributed to Sagrestani on the strength of an oral opinion given by Roberto Longhi.[6] These four pictures appeared to conform satisfactorily to Sagrestani's customary manner.

That Sagrestani might have been capable of small paintings of a rather unusual type of subject seemed at first unlikely, since he is known—primarily to specialists—for typically Late Baroque works of the conventional literary and religious subjects of the period, works that are to be seen only in the palaces and churches of Tuscany. His style, perfectly devised for the frequently monumental and even colossal scale of his many commissions, borrows heavily from the two great Baroque painters who had been occasionally active in Florence, Luca Giordano of Naples and Pietro da Cortona of Rome. It is especially from the latter that Sagrestani derived his abundant compositions, filled with attenuated figures and brittle, ribbony draperies. The restless, strongly modulated chiaroscuro is his own proto-Rococo adaptation of the expressive shadows of a whole phase of Florentine painting of the seventeenth century (fig. 1).

In 1968, at the Heim Gallery in London, four more small paintings (nos. 28–31), again of Turkish scenes, were exhibited and attributed to Sagrestani on the strength of Gregori's 1965 catalogue.[7] However, the Heim paintings seem to have been quite different from

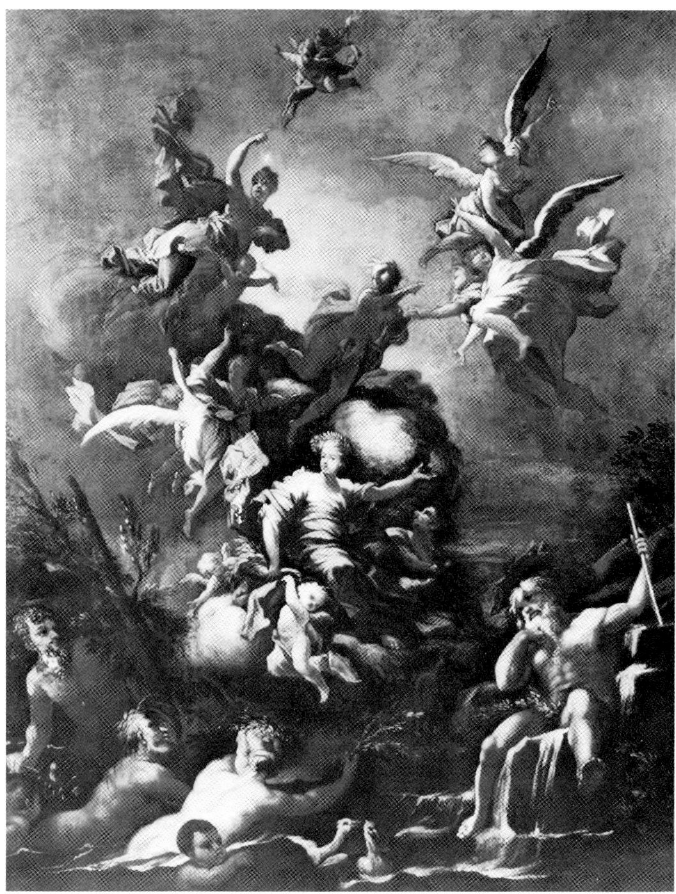

Fig. 1. Giovanni Camillo Sagrestani, *Triumph of Galatea*. Oil on canvas. 45½ × 34 inches (115.5 × 86.3 cm.). Victor D. Spark, New York

the Genoese group in almost every respect. One pair (see figs. 2 and 3; Heim cat. nos. 28 and 29) does rather strongly recall Baltimore's painting, although perhaps not sufficiently to allow complete confidence in the idea that they were by the same hand. The other pair of Heim canvases (nos. 30 and 31) seems to be removed stylistically from its companions and from the Baltimore picture, but the measurements (17½ × 12 inches) are intriguingly close to those of the Baltimore *Turkish Scene*.

The evident source for the idea that similar small paintings of Turkish subjects can be linked to Sagrestani, as indicated by Zeri, was a group of such pictures in the storerooms of the various national galleries in Florence[8]—pictures which apparently can be given without reservation to Sagrestani. Of the Florentine pictures, only one (fig. 4) is known to me from an illustration in a most informative article by Stella Rudolph which touches on the Baltimore painting.[9] Here the Florentine painting is published as Sagrestani, and there is the implication that the attribution is an unquestionable one.[10] To the degree that one is willing to accept, somewhat on faith, the certainty of the painting in Florence being by Sagrestani, one should be equally disposed to accept the Baltimore canvas as being Sagrestani as well since, insofar as one can rely on the reproduced photograph, the two works are by the same hand. The paintings formerly with the Heim Gallery which Rudolph reproduces are given by her to Sagrestani with a question mark.[11]

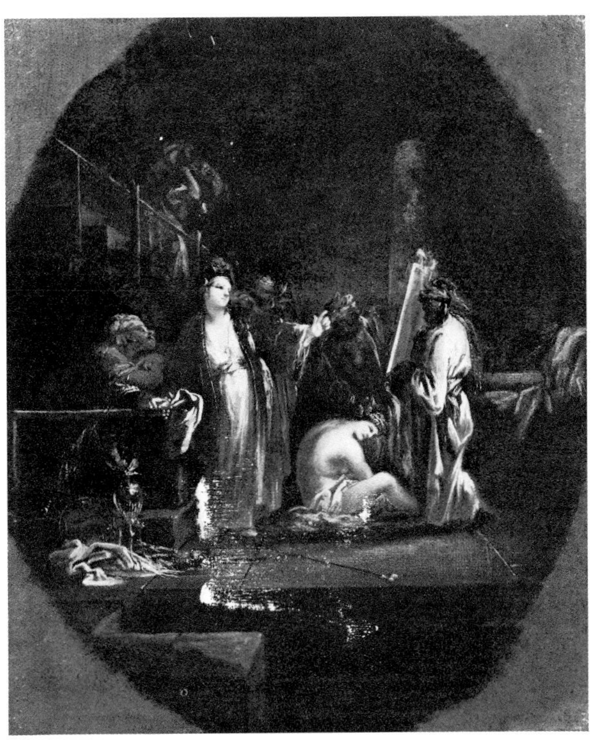

Fig. 2. Giovanni Camillo Sagrestani (attributed), *Harem Scene* (one of a series). Oil on canvas. 19 × 15½ inches (48.2 × 39.3 cm.). Formerly Heim Gallery, London

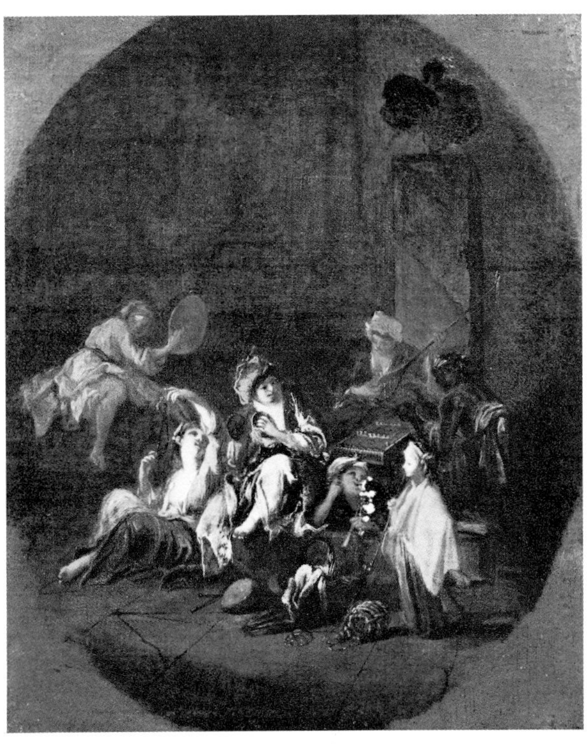

Fig. 3. Giovanni Camillo Sagrestani (attributed), *Harem Scene* (one of a series). Oil on canvas. 19 × 15½ inches (48.2 × 39.3 cm.). Formerly Heim Gallery, London

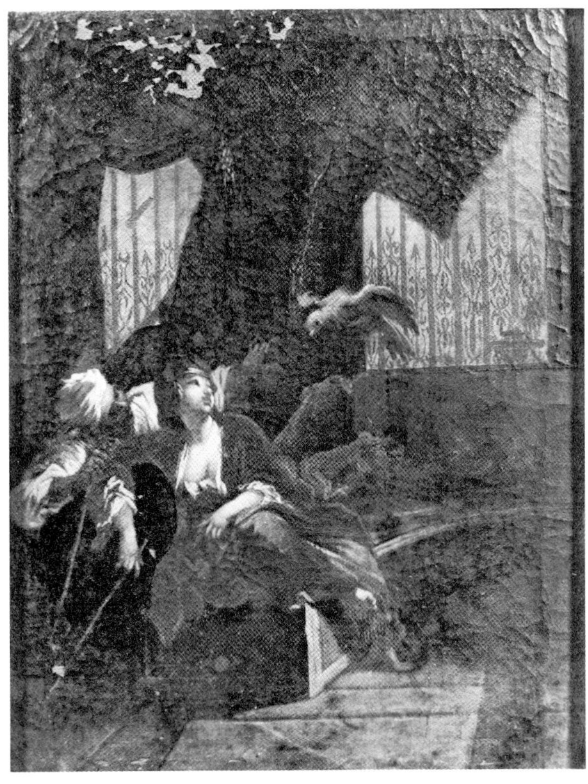

Fig. 4. Giovanni Camillo Sagrestani, *Harem Scene*. Oil on canvas. Gallerie fiorentine (deposito), Florence

As a further indication of the complications that the satisfactory placing of the Baltimore Museum's painting encounters, it should be pointed out that Zeri has tentatively attributed a *Rustic Scene* in The Walters Art Gallery to Sagrestani. It is difficult to see how both canvases could be by the same artist, in spite of superficial similarities, and, indeed, Zeri himself had reservations about the accuracy of this suggestion, also raising the possibility that a certain François Rivière (1675–1746), who is known only through documentary evidence, might have created the Walters picture.[12]

Although the still vexing question of the authorship of the Baltimore painting must wait for further research and discoveries in the relatively newly appreciated field of the Florentine Baroque, the previously mentioned article of Stella Rudolph surely provides the correct context for the *Turkish Scene*. Using the date of the lifting of the Turkish siege of Vienna in 1683 as the starting point, she succinctly touches on the manifold ways a new curiosity and taste for things Turkish appeared in the politics, literature, and painting of the Baroque fin de siècle. Florence shared this fashionable enthusiasm, perhaps prepared for it by the long existing trade with the Levant and more explicitly motivated by the spectacles ordered by the Grand Duke Cosimo III to celebrate the victory of 1683 in which elements of the Tuscan armed forces had participated as units of a great international Christian alliance. Perhaps the most unexpected document of this "voga turca" is the obscure Castello di Sammezzano at Rignano near Florence, discussed briefly by Rudolph. There, dating from the first half of the eighteenth century, is a suite of ceremonial rooms entirely executed in a lavish and, indeed, hallucinatory Turko-Moresque style. Rudolph rightly and sensitively associates this aberration with the series of paintings of Turkish scenes by, or attributed to, Sagrestani which form another if less sensational innovation in Florentine art around 1700.

Certainly it would not be difficult to imagine the Baltimore Museum's painting hung in some alcove or nook of an interior of the period fitted out with Oriental porcelains and stuffs in an approximation of the fully architectural settings of the Castello di Sammezzano. The taste among collectors of the time for small cabinet pictures of many kinds of subjects was extensive and is documented by surviving letters between artists and collectors and by inventories of collections. It was not an unknown practice to set aside a room for paintings of a single, contemporary school or for paintings of kindred subject matter. The existence of a series of paintings on Turkish themes, such as those by Guardi or the group published by Gregori from a Genoese collection, argues that these little canvases were executed for some specific and predetermined setting. With such a function in mind, the artist would extend himself to provide works of decorative distinction. In spite of a deceptive simplicity of means, the author of the Baltimore canvas has done just that. Some features of the picture's character have already been noted at the outset of these remarks, but it is worth observing here how complete the little scene is with its dark earth tones providing the foil for a few glowing patches of warm red and the soft gleam of ivory and white. Similarly, the spare, broad setting forms the backdrop and support for the delicate animation of the two women whose piquant little faces and limbs correspond to the brief passages of color of high value. And finally, how well the artist has been able to convey the peculiar quality of an aspect of harem life, placing this moment of simple amusement and feminine camaraderie against the looming confinement of stone and iron grills.

Barry Hannegan
North Carolina Museum of Art,
Raleigh

NOTES

1. F. Watson, "A Series of 'Turqueries' by Francesco Guardi," *Baltimore Museum of Art News* 24, no. 1 (Fall 1960):3–13.
2. While F. Watson's recognition of a different subject matter, *Turkish Scene* instead of *Two Gypsies in an Interior,* has been generally accepted, the picture's ascription to Francesco Guardi has been rejected by nine experts on Italian eighteenth-century painting. One scholar has supported Sir Francis's attribution (opinions in the curatorial files, The Baltimore Museum of Art).
3. A. Morassi, in *Guardi: Antonio e Francesco Guardi* (Venice: Alfieri, 1972) attributed cat. nos. 103, 104, 107, 108 in vol. 1 to Francesco; see text pp. 61, 113, 114, 117, 121. Baltimore's *Turkish Scene* is not included in Morassi's book.
4. Letter of December 22, 1975, from F. Zeri to G. Rosenthal (curatorial files, The Baltimore Museum of Art).
5. M. Gregori, *70 pitture e sculture del '600 e del '700 Fiorentino,* exhibition catalogue (Florence: Palazzo Strozzi, 1965).
6. Ibid., p. 60.
7. *Baroque Paintings, Sketches and Sculptures for the Collector,* autumn exhibition catalogue (London: Heim Gallery, 1968).
8. F. Zeri, *Italian Paintings in the Walters Art Gallery* (Baltimore: The Walters Art Gallery, 1976), 2: 550.
9. S. Rudolph, "La 'voga turca' nella pittura fiorentina dopo la vittoria sugli ottomani nel 1683," in *Die Kunst des Barock in der Toskana* (Munich: Bruckmann, 1976), pp. 321–24, p. 331, n. 17. Rudolph discusses the Baltimore painting in conjunction with the Heim group (figs. 1-3 and p. 323).
10. Ibid., p. 324, fig. 4. Regarding the illustration for fig. 4 in this paper, we regret the poor quality, but re-photographing the painting was not possible since its exact present location in the Florentine Museums' storerooms is not known, and a better negative does not seem to exist. Nevertheless, we wanted to publish the photograph because of a certain closeness of the work in Florence to the Baltimore painting.
11. Ibid., p. 331, n. 19, where Rudolph indicates that Gregori now feels the Heim pictures are more likely to be by a Genoese painter or, at least, a Florentine working under strong Genoese influence.
12. Zeri, *Italian Paintings in the Walters Art Gallery,* 2: 550–51, no. 439.

SELECTED BIBLIOGRAPHY

Three Baroque Masters: Strozzi, Crespi, and Piazzetta. Exhibition catalogue. Baltimore: The Baltimore Museum of Art, 1944.

Francis J. B. Watson. "A Series of 'Turqueries' by Francesco Guardi." *Baltimore Museum of Art News* 24, no. 1 (1960):3–13.

Mina Gregori. *70 pitture e sculture del '600 e del '700 Fiorentino.* Exhibition catalogue. Florence: Palazzo Strozzi, 1965.

Baroque Paintings, Sketches, and Sculptures for the Collector. Autumn exhibition catalogue. London: Heim Gallery, 1968.

Painting in Italy in the Eighteenth Century: Rococo to Romanticism. Exhibition catalogue. Chicago: The Art Institute of Chicago, 1970.

Antonio Morassi. *Guardi: Antonio e Francesco Guardi.* 2 vols. Venice: Alfieri, 1972.

The Twilight of the Medici: Late Baroque Art in Florence, 1670–1743. Exhibition catalogue, The Detroit Institute of Arts and Palazzo Pitti, Florence. Detroit: Detroit Institute of Arts, 1974; Florence: Centro Di, 1974.

Stella Rudolph. "La 'voga turca' nella pittura fiorentina dopo la vittoria sugli ottomani nel 1683." In *Die Kunst des Barock in der Toskana. Studien zur Kunst unter den Letzten Medici.* Munich: Bruckmann, 1976.

Federico Zeri. *Italian Paintings in the Walters Art Gallery.* 2 vols. Baltimore: The Walters Art Gallery, 1976.

Renato Roli. *Pittura Bolognese 1650–1800 dal Cignani ai Gandolfi.* Bologna: Edizione Alfa, 1977.

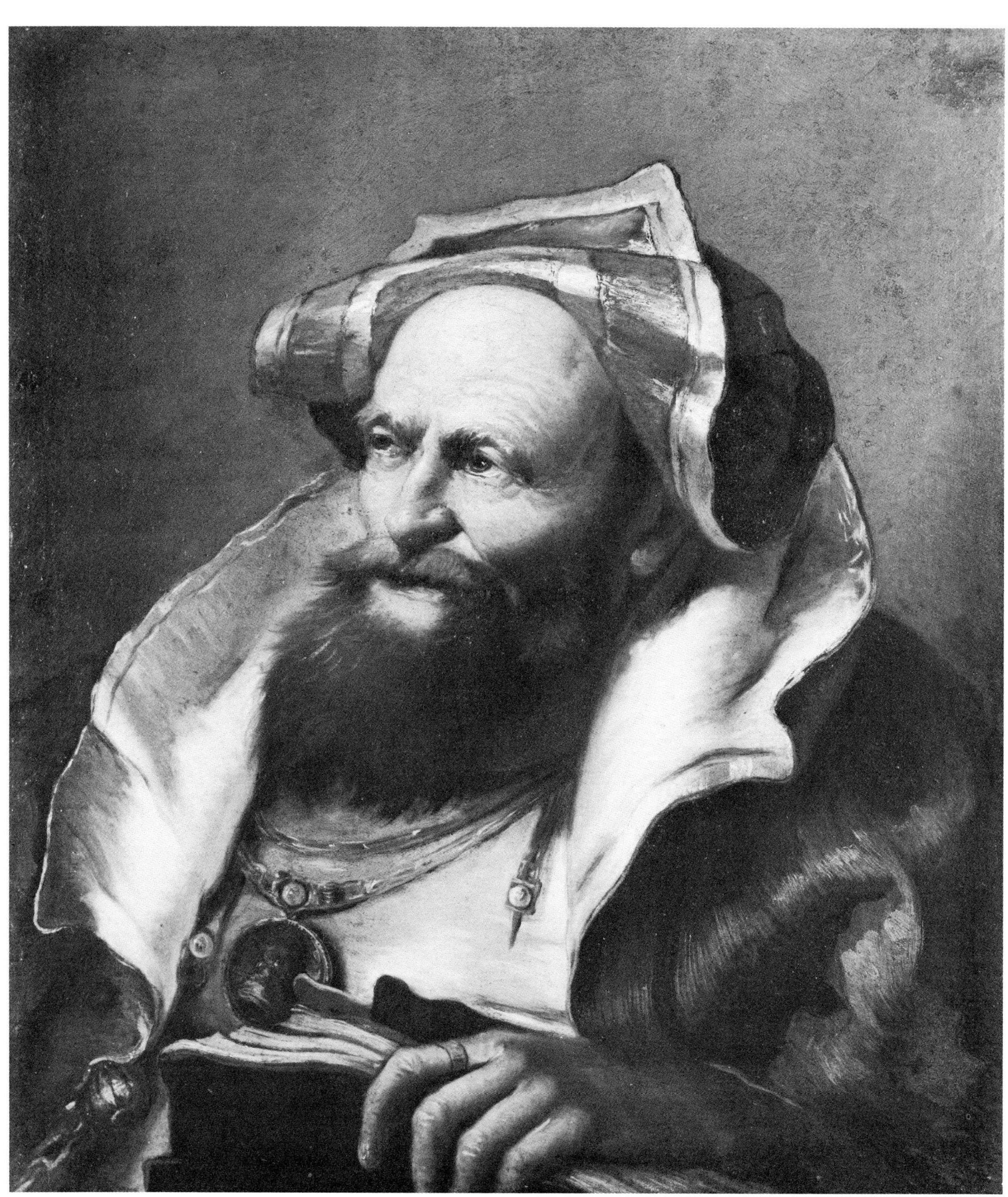

After Giambattista Tiepolo
LORENZO TIEPOLO (1736–1776)

27. *A Philosopher with a Book,* ca. 1754–1757

Oil on canvas. 24⅛ × 20¹/₁₆ inches (61.3 × 50.9 cm.)
The Jacob Epstein Collection (BMA 51.117)

PROVENANCE

Acquired by Jacob Epstein, Baltimore, as a work by Giambattista Tiepolo, from the Collection of Monsieur L. S., in the sale at the Galerie Fiévez, Brussels, on May 26, 1930

Sale catalogue (Brussels: Galerie Fiévez, May 26, 1930), lot 94, pl. 34

Loaned by Jacob Epstein to The Baltimore Museum of Art in 1932 and bequeathed in 1951

CONDITION

The ground applied to the support of the painting *A Philosopher with a Book* is reddish in color and quite thin; the paint film is thick and opaque, except for the dark shadows where it was applied as a glaze.

The painting had undergone major treatment prior to its acquisition by The Baltimore Museum of Art in 1951. It had been glue-lined. During this early lining the tacking edges were removed. Technical examination indicates that the picture may have been slightly reduced in size.

In 1954 surface treatment which consisted of cleaning, filling and inpainting of a few small losses, and resurfacing with damar varnish, was carried out by the conservation laboratory of The Walters Art Gallery. Since this treatment, the painting had again taken on a darkened yellowish appearance from the aging of the damar. In 1978 it was treated in the conservation laboratory of The Baltimore Museum of Art. The picture was again cleaned, inpainted, and resurfaced with a synthetic acrylic varnish.

This painting is in good condition. There are small pitted losses scattered in the background and a few in the face and headdress. Some abrasion losses can be seen along the edges. The paint film has developed a normal aging crackle pattern, especially apparent in the forehead of the man depicted. Though the picture is currently in stable condition, the old glue-lining shows signs of deterioration, and relining is contemplated within the next few years.

Geoffrey Michael Lemmer
The Baltimore Museum of Art

Giambattista Tiepolo dominates Italian history painting of the eighteenth century. His career is comparatively well documented and it has been carefully studied, yet we still have no knowledge of the circumstances surrounding the commission and the creation of his series of philosopher portraits. These were apparently twenty in number and painted in the early 1750's, certainly no earlier than the arrival of the Tiepolo family at Würzburg in December 1750, and no later than the fall of 1757 when they were etched by Giambattista's son Domenico. The project is so far removed from Giambattista's normal sphere of activity that one feels it must have been a special commission. Yet, once completed, this portrait series remained in the studio to be copied, possibly more than once, by the artist's younger son Lorenzo, to be etched by Domenico, and ultimately to be dispersed in a manner which is also still obscure. It is a situation unparalleled in Giambattista's long career, and as a consequence we are faced with a large group of works, variously given to Giambattista, Domenico, and Lorenzo Tiepolo, the attribution of which continues to be a matter of debate. For each design there are a number of variants and copies, many of them recorded only in old photographs, on which any judgment of quality is a precarious enterprise. Of the history of the Baltimore painting prior to its acquisition by Jacob Epstein, little seems to be established except that it passed through the Fiévez sale in Brussels on May 26, 1930. There it was attributed to Giambattista, and the dimensions were given as 24 × 20⅛ inches (61 × 51 cm.), which are almost right.

The portrait was exhibited at The Baltimore Museum of Art in 1939 and in 1954 as by Giambattista, but in the 1962 catalogue raisonné of Antonio Morassi it was attributed to Domenico. It is also listed by Adriano Mariuz in his 1971 monograph on Domenico Tiepolo, with a note that indicates that the writer was none too anxious to become involved in a debate on attribution. Neither Morassi nor Mariuz reproduces the picture, and both get the dimensions slightly wrong, giving them as 21⅝ × 17¾ inches (55 × 45 cm.), which is a matter of not entirely negligible significance. In an article of 1975 I was satisfied that the picture should be given to Lorenzo, and other recent informed opinion seems to oscillate between Domenico and Lorenzo.

In 1962 Morassi was able to make two key observations: first, he showed that the painting was a copy of an original by Giambattista which was formerly in the Orloff collection; second, he pointed out that this design was the subject of an etching by Domenico in the series called *La Raccolta di Teste*. The original appeared, with an illustration, as lot 61 in the Orloff sale at the Galerie Georges Petit in Paris in 1920 (not the Petit Palais as indicated by Morassi); it is now in the Národní Galerie in Prague (fig. 1). Its dimensions are now given as 24 × 19⅞ inches (61 × 50.5 cm.), as compared to 24⅛ × 20¹/₁₆ inches (61.3 × 50.9 cm.) for the Baltimore picture, and its history can probably be traced back to the collecting activities of the Russian art historian Count Gregory Vladimirovitch Orloff (1777–1826).[1] In its present condition the picture in Prague is not as brilliant as it might be. It suffers from undercleaning on the forehead and the hat; there is some heavy craquelure and repaint in the background; and the impasto is flattened. Nevertheless there is no question that this is the original and that the painting in Baltimore is the copy. It is certainly a close and faithful copy for the only variations are some slightly softer outlines here and there, some slightly heavier shadows, and a greater contrast between light and dark areas.

Morassi also notes that there are records of two other copies. One, in the Opuich-Fontana Collection in Trieste, listed by Eduard Sack in 1910, is much smaller than the others, its dimensions being given as 13⅜ × 11¹/₁₆ inches (34 × 28 cm.).[2] The other appeared as lot 310 in the Pepoli sale at the American Art Association in New York City on January 18–19, 1929, with a reproduction, and with an attribution to Giambattista

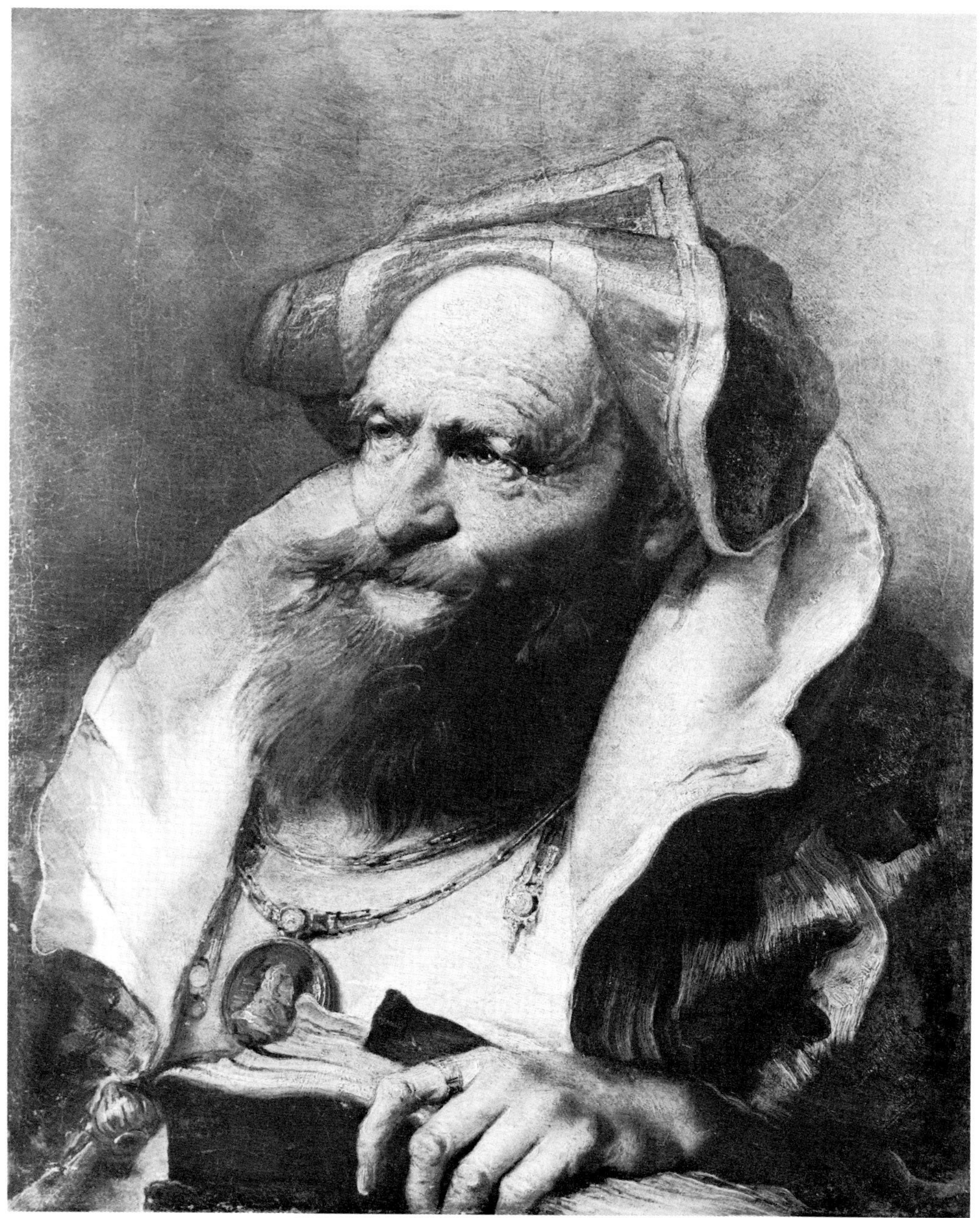

Fig. 1. Giambattista Tiepolo, *Philosopher with a Book* (Testa I.27 A). Oil on canvas. 24 × 19⅞ inches (61 × 50.5 cm.). Národní Galerie, Prague. Courtesy of Národní Galerie, Prague

(not Domenico as indicated by Morassi). The dimensions were given as 23¼ × 19 inches (59 × 48.2 cm.). This painting, again to judge by the photograph since the work can no longer be traced, shows the composition cut down on all four sides. In this version the modeling appears to be far less emphatic than in the Epstein picture.

Thus we have four paintings, three of them approximately the same size—the Orloff, Epstein and Pepoli versions—and a substantially smaller one of which we know little, the Opuich-Fontana version.

In 1970, as part of the Tiepolo celebrations at Udine, and with the kind cooperation of Dr. Aldo Rizzi, I was able to publish a little book with a full set of reproductions of the sixty etchings by Domenico, the *Raccolta di Teste,* with reproductions of the original models or other comparative material wherever this could be found. The etching related to the Baltimore painting appears as *Testa* I.27, together with the Orloff picture as its model.[3] No attempt was made at that point to arrive at any hard and fast decisions about the attributions of the various paintings that were listed in association with each etching, for I had seen few of them, and the photographs, most of them drawn from the invaluable files of the Witt Library, London, were often inadequate for arriving at a proper judgment. However, a little later it began to seem possible to discern an underlying pattern which offered a hope of sorting out much of the confusion that surrounded this group of pictures. My conclusions were published in the *Burlington Magazine* of March 1975.

To put the matter briefly, it appeared that Giambattista had painted a set of twenty "philosopher portraits," of which we seem to have some photographic record of thirteen. This is described as Set A. The Zanetti-Mariette documents in the Bibliothèque Nationale, Paris, discovered by Lina Christina Frerichs,[4] show that the etchings by Domenico after Set A were in process of production in the fall of 1757, hence Set A is probably no earlier than Giambattista's return from Würzburg at the end of 1753 and certainly no later than 1757. While the set was still in the Tiepolo studio it appears to have been copied, either in whole or in part, and in some cases certainly more than once, by a painter who is here identified as the young Lorenzo Tiepolo (1736–1776). Broadly speaking, two sets of copies can be discerned: Set B, of the same size as Set A, of which five examples seem to be extant, and Set C, smaller in scale, though variable in size (generally about 50 × 40 cm.), of which seven examples seem still to exist.

At some date after 1757, Domenico too painted a series of "philosopher portraits," which may be described as Set D; but these, of which ten can be counted, are based upon the etchings. Although they are the same size as Sets A and B, the heads are larger in scale, and hands and other details are often omitted. There is in addition a miscellaneous group, described as Set E, which follows either the etchings or Set D, and which may be given to Lorenzo. These may well have been painted in Madrid.

In the 1975 checklists, the Orloff picture, now in Prague, was listed as *Testa* I.27A, the Epstein picture as *Testa* I.27B, and the Pepoli picture, although it is larger than most of this group, as *Testa* I.27C. No corresponding paintings in Sets D and E seem to be known.

The attribution of paintings to Giambattista and to Domenico Tiepolo can proceed with some confidence, for we have a volume of signed, dated, and documented works to which we can refer, but in the case of Lorenzo things are very different. We are unable to assign to him a single dated or documented oil painting. There is no hard evidence that he ever touched a paintbrush in his life, and yet the result of my analysis is to give him twelve paintings in Sets B and C and ten or more paintings in Set E. With Giambattista's and Domenico's roles established and their characteristics noted, a third person was required, one who not only copied Set A by Giambattista in the years 1754 to 1757, but also copied Set D by Domenico, probably during the years in Spain. Only Lorenzo seems able to fill this role. He was eighteen to twenty-one years old between 1754 and 1757, and he could well have made these careful copies in the final phase of his apprenticeship. His drawings also indicate his preoccupation with the human head, as do his later pastels, and these do not present any stylistic conflict with our attribution of Sets B, C, and E to his hand.

It is certainly difficult in words and photographs to demonstrate the qualitative difference between the painting in Prague and the painting in Baltimore, but when a considerable body of photographic material is brought together, as in the illustrations for

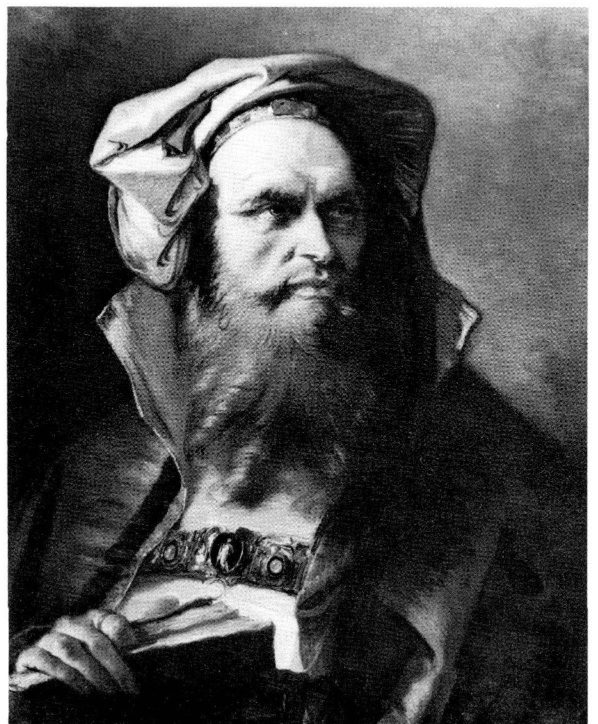

Fig. 2. Giambattista Tiepolo, *Jewish Priest* or *Prophet* (*Philosopher with a Book,* Testa I.7 A). Oil on canvas. 23 × 18⅞ inches (58.4 × 47.9 cm.). Bob Jones University, Greenville, South Carolina. Courtesy of Unusual Films, Bob Jones University, Greenville, South Carolina

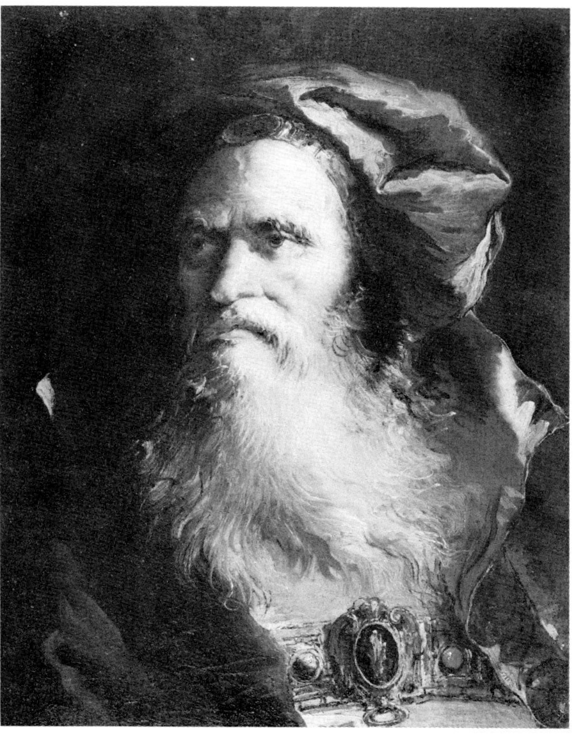

Fig. 3. Giovanni Domenico Tiepolo, *Head of a Patriarch* (*Head of a Philosopher,* Testa I.7 D). Oil on canvas. 23¾ × 18 inches (60.3 × 45.7 cm.). The Art Institute of Chicago, Charles Deering Collection. Courtesy of The Art Institute of Chicago

the article in the *Burlington Magazine,* it is safe to say that the distinctive character of the three artists becomes fairly evident. The ideal solution, and indeed the only proper one, would be to bring together as many of the paintings as possible, to make a direct comparison. This occurred recently on a modest scale in the Tiepolo exhibition at the Birmingham Museum of Art, Alabama, when *Testa* I.7A (fig. 2) and *Testa* I.7D (fig. 3) could be seen side by side, together with *Testa* I.26D. The superiority of *Testa* I.7A, the painting from Bob Jones University, was evident at a distance of twenty feet as well as on closer examination.[5] The painting from The Art Institute of Chicago, *Testa* I.7D, was beyond question the work of Domenico. The painting from the Springfield Museum of Art, *Testa* I.26D, was almost certainly by Domenico, but one would have welcomed the opportunity of comparing it with specimens from Sets B, C, and E.

One final note is perhaps needed to explain why these figures are described as philosophers. Two of them, *Testa* I.17D and *Testa* I.29E, are inscribed *Diogenes* and *Pitagoras,* which indicates that some at least may have been regarded as philosopher portraits in the Tiepolo studio. Further, the number twenty suggests a link with the twenty members of the philosophical family of Dante in the Noble Castle of Limbo.[6] As for the Baltimore painting, we have scarcely a clue to the identity of the philosopher but if the medal worn by him may be said to bear the portrait bust of a young man, and if this could be accepted as an image of Alexander the Great, then our philosopher could be identified as Alexander's teacher, Aristotle.

George Knox
The University of British Columbia,
Vancouver

NOTES:

1. For an account of the Orloff collection, see G. Knox, "The Orloff Album of Tiepolo Drawings," *Burlington Magazine* 103 (June 1961):269–75.
2. E. Sack, *Giambattista und Domenico Tiepolo* (Hamburg: Clarmanns Kunstverlag, 1910), p. 202, no. 403, identified as Opuich-Fontana Collection, Trieste. This is not illustrated but the composition is cut down, for Sack notes that the hand with the book is missing. This picture should not be confused with Sack, 402, also in the Opuich-Fontana Collection, which Sack illustrates as pl. 200. This relates to *Testa* I.17 and seems certain to be the original by Giambattista. However, the picture illustrated by Sack does not appear to be the same as the one now in the collection of Antonino Rusconi of Trieste (see G. Knox, "Philosopher Portraits by Giambattista, Domenico and Lorenzo Tiepolo," *Burlington Magazine* 117 [March 1975]: 147–55. *Testa* I.17A, fig. 39, identified as the original by Giambattista). The upper part of the head is much rounder, and the hand is different in many details. It is also evident that the painting illustrated by Sack, rather than the Rusconi painting, was the model used by Domenico for his etching.
3. G. Knox, *Domenico Tiepolo: Raccolta di Teste* (Udine and Milan: Electa, 1970), *Testa* I.27A.
4. L.C.J. Frerichs, "Nouvelles sources pour la connaissance de l'activité de graveur des trois Tiepolo," *Nouvelles de l'estampe,* no. 4. (1971):213–28. L.C.J. Frerichs, "Mariette et les eaux-fortes des Tiepolo," *Gazette des Beaux-Arts* 78 (October 1971):233–52.
5. E. Weeks, *The Tiepolos: Painters to Princes and Prelates,* exhibition catalogue (Birmingham, Ala.: Birmingham Museum of Art, 1978). The painting from Bob Jones University is no. 93 (color pl. p. 140). The corresponding etching is no. 149 (ill. p. 113). The Chicago painting is no. 89 (ill. p. 102). The Springfield painting is no. 96 (color pl. p. 140). See also Knox, "Philosopher Portraits," *Testa* I.7A and D (pls. 33 and 34), and also *Testa* I.26A and D (pls. 41 and 42) for the Springfield painting and the lost original.
6. See Knox, "Philosopher Portraits," p. 22, for further details on the identified portraits and for notes on the tradition of philosopher portraits in the seventeenth century. I understand that Oreste Ferrari is currently working on a major article on the iconography of "Philosophers" in Italian painting of the seventeenth century.

SELECTED BIBLIOGRAPHY

The Jacob Epstein Collection in The Baltimore Museum of Art. Baltimore: Published by Jacob Epstein, 1939.

Man and His Years. Exhibition catalogue. Baltimore: The Baltimore Museum of Art, 1954.

George Knox. "The Orloff Album of Tiepolo Drawings." *Burlington Magazine* 103 (June 1961):269–75.

Antonio Morassi. *A Complete Catalogue of the Paintings of G. B. Tiepolo.* London: Phaidon Press, 1962.

George Knox. *Domenico Tiepolo: Raccolta di Teste.* Udine and Milan: Electa, 1970.

Adriano Mariuz. *Giandomenico Tiepolo.* Venice: Alfieri, 1971.

George Knox. " 'Philosopher Portraits' by Giambattista, Domenico and Lorenzo Tiepolo." *Burlington Magazine* 117 (March 1975):147–55.

Edward Weeks, Barry Hannegan, et al. *The Tiepolos: Painters to Princes and Prelates.* Exhibition catalogue. Birmingham, Ala.: Birmingham Museum of Art, 1978.

Appendix of Unauthenticated Paintings

The paintings listed in this section were withdrawn from exhibition many years ago. Since some of them have been published and periodically turn up in reference works, it seemed important to record them here. After examination at different times by members of the curatorial and conservation departments and also by visiting experts, it was not possible to establish the authenticity of these works. Several of the paintings have been so overpainted and/or are in such deplorable condition that it is not possible to determine the simple question of whether the pictures under scrutiny were originally genuine before undergoing so-called "restoration." This question may perhaps be answered in the affirmative in the case of the *Madonna and Child* purchased by the donor as by Francesco Botticini. Together with the so-called Perugino *Madonna and Child Enthroned with Four Saints,* the picture thought to be by Botticini is the most challenging of the group; it appears to be partly authentic but repainted in the most essential areas. As both these paintings were accepted as autograph by several well-known experts, they have been discussed here at greater length than the rest of the items. Some of the pictures are pastiches—works executed in the style or styles of famous artists by imitators who have combined parts of several originals to give their work the air of authenticity.

G. R.

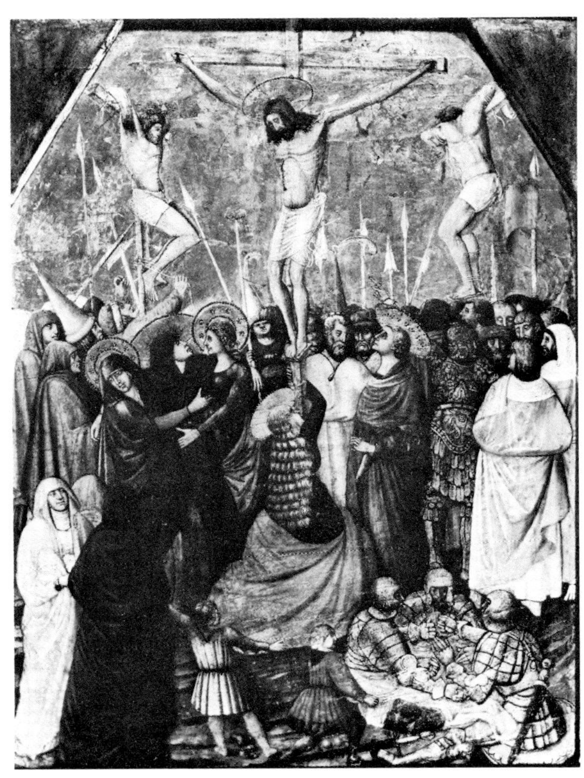

Received as

FERRARA, FOURTEENTH CENTURY

A 1. *Crucifixion*

Oil on wood. 19½ × 14½ inches (49.5 × 36.7 cm.)
Bequest of Saidie A. May (BMA 51.394)

PROVENANCE

Galerie Daguerre, Paris

Acquired by Saidie A. May before 1933

Bequeathed to The Baltimore Museum of Art in 1951

CONDITION

The findings of the technical and stylistic examinations of this painting are extremely puzzling and have not yet been resolved. The support of the picture is not poplar, commonly used in old Italian panel paintings, but appears to be mahogany, rarely found in Italian works of the fourteenth or fifteenth century. When in 1961 the well-known Italian scholars Cesare Brandi and Cesare Gnudi made a visual examination of the painting, they concluded that it was so heavily overpainted and altered that it should be withdrawn from exhibition. Technical investigation did not confirm their observation. However, other technical and also stylistic inconsistencies made the *Crucifixion* seem to be a spurious work, a suspicion which has been shared by various visiting experts who studied it. The Museum's Senior Conservator suggested pigment analysis for which, however, the Museum's conservation laboratory was not equipped. W. T. Chase, Head Conservator, The Freer Gallery, was consulted and he offered to make the tests. The results were on the whole inconclusive. There was no modern Prussian-blue pigment in the Madonna's mantle as had been expected, but neither could azurite or ultramarine, generally used in the fifteenth century, be detected. Microscopic examination of the blue pigment particles seemed to show a mixture of indigo and smalt, which presumably was frequently employed in Spanish painting. Indigo was much used in the fifteenth century, whereas smalt can hardly be found in European paintings prior to the late sixteenth century. A sample of the green taken from the robe of the figure to the right of the Madonna was identified as copper resinate, in use since the beginning of the fifteenth century. Thus, except for smalt, the tested pigments all existed in the fifteenth century and do not indicate a later date than the one which the style of the picture seems to suggest. However, the fact that the medium has been identified as oil—used here not even in connection with tempera—is a strong indication that the painting is not an authentic fourteenth or fifteenth-century work but a pastiche or forgery.

REMARKS

The contradictions found in the condition of the *Crucifixion* also exist in the style of the picture. The dating to the fourteenth century, given at the sale of the panel to the donor, obviously is not supportable, though the composition and the iconography of certain figures occur in fourteenth-century paintings. However, almost every one of the figures—especially the faces—recall a different prototype, an observation that might signify the work as a pastiche. Some are reminiscent of Pietro Cavallini, or Barna da Siena, or Orcagna, and there are certain details that recall Taddeo Gaddi. Motifs such as the swooning Virgin supported by the Holy Women and St. Magdalen (here strangely awkward) kneeling at the foot of the cross can be traced to the thirteenth century and were widely diffused. The children included in the spectacle frequently occur in late medieval works as *staffage*. So do the soldiers dicing for the robe of Christ whose face looks Spanish and of a later period. Perhaps one of the picture's most disturbing shortcomings is the isolation of the various groups that almost seem to be separate entities fitted together like a jigsaw puzzle.

The inconsistencies noticed in the faces of the many participants of the *Crucifixion* can also be seen in such details as the halos. For information we turned to Mojmir Frinta, a well-known specialist on these matters. After mentioning the various types of punchwork occurring in halos, he continues:

> I find most unusual the inconsistent use of earlier and later forms of haloes juxtaposed. The "floating" perspectively inclined haloes are clearly of the fifteenth century but in the provincial schools the round vertical haloes (of an earlier period) may still be found even in the advanced part of the fifteenth century. Their juxtaposition is, however, strange. In addition, the shape of the Virgin's halo is misunderstood and misformed which can hardly occur in genuine works of the period. . . . (Letter of July 24, 1978, curatorial files, Baltimore Museum).

Frinta's observations concerning the halos reinforce the suspicion that the painting is a pastiche. In addition to other disturbing aspects, mentioned before, doubts of the painting's authenticity are first of all based on the use of the oil medium (not mixed with tempera) which hardly occurred in a medieval panel.

Another vague possibility perhaps should be mentioned: the picture has a number of features that may point to a Spanish origin, such as the use of smalt and, in terms of style, the Spanish type of Christ, and the group of dicing soldiers. Could the picture have been the work of a provincial Spanish sixteenth-century artist visiting Italy—or of a rather clever nineteenth-century forger?

G.R.

SELECTED BIBLIOGRAPHY

Rutherford J. Gettens and George L. Stout. *Painting Materials—A Short Encyclopedia*. New York: Dover, 1966.

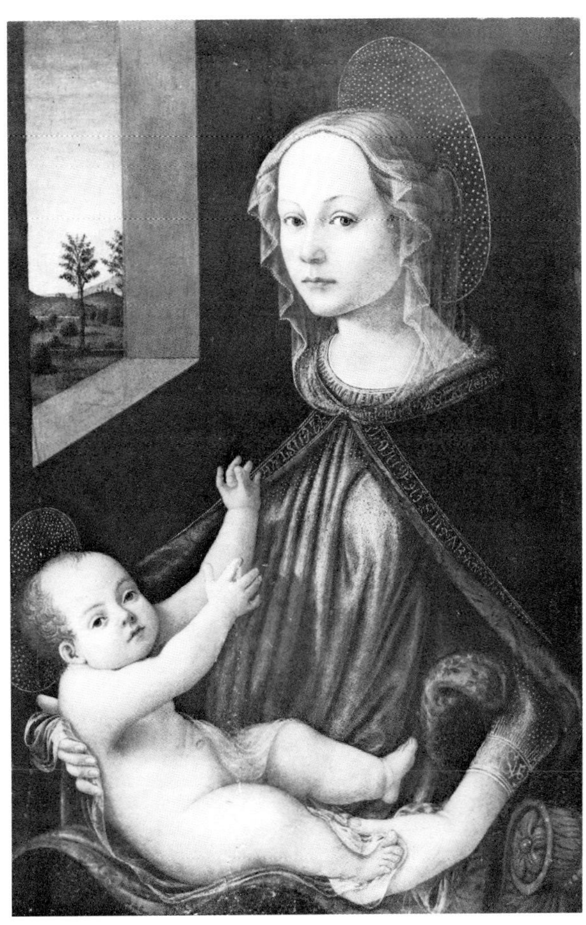

Received as

FRANCESCO BOTTICINI (1446–1497)

A 2. *Madonna and Child*

Oil on wood. 28¾ × 18 inches (73 × 46 cm.)
The Mary Frick Jacobs Collection (BMA 38.224)

PROVENANCE

Said to have been in the collection of a Baron Plumbo [Palumbo?], Florence

Henry Barton Jacobs. *The Collection of Mary Frick Jacobs* (Baltimore: Prepared and published by Dr. Henry Barton Jacobs, 1938), cat. no. 31

Name of Plumbo Collection probably given by dealer; the existence of such a collection could not be confirmed in 1980.

Constantini (dealer), Florence

Acquired by Mary Frick Jacobs, Baltimore, in 1909 from Eugène Fischhof, Paris

Bequeathed to The Baltimore Museum of Art in 1938 as part of The Mary Frick Jacobs Collection

CONDITION

When in 1957 the so-called Botticini painting was sent for examination and cleaning to the conservation department of The Walters Art Gallery, treatment was rejected because major parts of the original paint surface had been greatly altered and not enough remained to warrant restoration of the picture. Elisabeth Packard pointed out that "large areas, especially of the face, had been repainted." At that time the surprisingly light weight of the worm-holed panel was noticed. It was assumed that the original support had been shaved down and attached to a very light, worm-holed panel. However, some shaving at the top and bottom edges—a test undertaken in June 1978 by the Baltimore Museum's Senior Conservator—showed that no previous shaving of the panel could have taken place.

The light weight of the panel perhaps may be explained by a possible transfer of the surface design from the original weakened support to another very light but structurally stronger piece of wood. If such a transfer did occur, it is likely that it was carried out at the time when parts of the paint surface were altered—in any case before the painting entered the Jacobs Collection.

The Museum's examination in 1978 by X-radiography and ultraviolet rays did not show extensive overpainting in the areas where it was mainly expected—the Madonna's face and parts of the Child's body. However, solvent testing produced different results. Micro-spot solvent tests were made in eighteen areas, such as the Madonna's face and hands, her robe with its ornamented border, some of the Child's flesh tones, and the landscape seen through the window. These tests revealed that essential, large areas were easily soluble and thus must have been repainted not earlier than the nineteenth century. Most, if not all, of the Madonna's flesh tones are not original, and parts of the Child's body are also suspect. The veil on which He rests is a later addition. The difference between the results of the X-radiography and the solvent testing is puzzling. One possible explanation could be the occurrence of severe damages which induced the restorer of long ago to eradicate most of the original face and repaint it.

Only very thorough cleaning and comprehensive technical analysis of every inch of the picture could answer fully the remaining questions concerning the past and present condition of this painting.

REMARKS

Despite its problematic nature, several experts have accepted the painting as a work of Botticini. Berenson lists it as such in his *Italian Pictures of the Renaissance* (1932, p. 106); he also includes it in *Italian Pictures of the Renaissance: Florentine School* (1963, 1:39) but qualifies his acceptance by adding the letter "r" which denotes "ruined or restored or repainted." Everett Fahy's approval in 1968 of the attribution to Botticini appears on the back of a photograph of the picture in the files of the Frick Art Reference Library (no. 707-8M). Also cited on the back of the same photograph is the verbal acceptance in 1924 of F. Mason Perkins.

In my opinion stylistic analysis supports the technical examination discussed above; since much of the evaluation of the picture depends on its present state, I shall limit myself here to only a few remarks. The composition recalls traditional Florentine pictures of the second half of the Quattrocento but the Madonna's face seems to belong to another era. Her gaze is directly focused at the viewer, whereas in most Florentine paintings of this period, and particularly in the oeuvre of Botticini, the Madonna's eyes are downcast toward the Child on her lap. In those instances when she does not look at her Child, she pensively gazes into the distance, her eyes unfocused, her expression demure and often sad, but her glance is never assertive nor does she seem to scrutinize the onlooker as she does in the Baltimore picture. On the other hand, the Virgin's red robe with its tubular folds and ornamented gold border is characteristic of Botticini and appears to be genuine. So is the window view of a landscape section with hills and carefully spaced trees which are a hallmark of Botticini.

Determination of the authenticity of the figure of the Child poses special problems. His face and body seem to be at least in part original. His pose, the shape of the fingers, the peculiar rendering of the toes, the short neck, pudgy torso, and heavy thighs are similar to features in Botticini's representations of the Christ Child (cf. paintings such as two tondos, *Madonna Adoring the Child with Infant St. John,* formerly Lady Ashburnham Collection [Berenson, *Italian Pictures of the Renaissance: Florentine School,* 1963, fig. 1067] and *Madonna and Child,* Art Museum, Cincinnati, Ohio [Berenson, 1963, fig. 1068]). However, the body of the Baltimore Infant is even more flaccid, the modeling even more reduced, and the legs, without any muscles, even heavier—characteristics which frequently can be found in copies or repainted areas of originals.

I have no doubt that Zeri was correct when he said: "At one time, this panel may well have been by Francesco Botticini; now it is a wreck, all refixed."

G.R.

SELECTED BIBLIOGRAPHY

Ernst Kühnel. *Francesco Botticini.* Strasbourg: J. H. Ed. Heitz, 1906.

Henry Barton Jacobs. *The Collection of Mary Frick Jacobs.* Baltimore: Prepared and published by Dr. Henry Barton Jacobs, 1938.

Bernard Berenson. *Italian Pictures of the Renaissance.* Oxford: Clarendon Press, 1932.

Bernard Berenson. *Italian Pictures of the Renaissance: Florentine School.* 2 vols. London: Phaidon Press, 1963.

Edward Fahy. Photographic file. Frick Art Reference Library, no. 707—8 M, 1968.

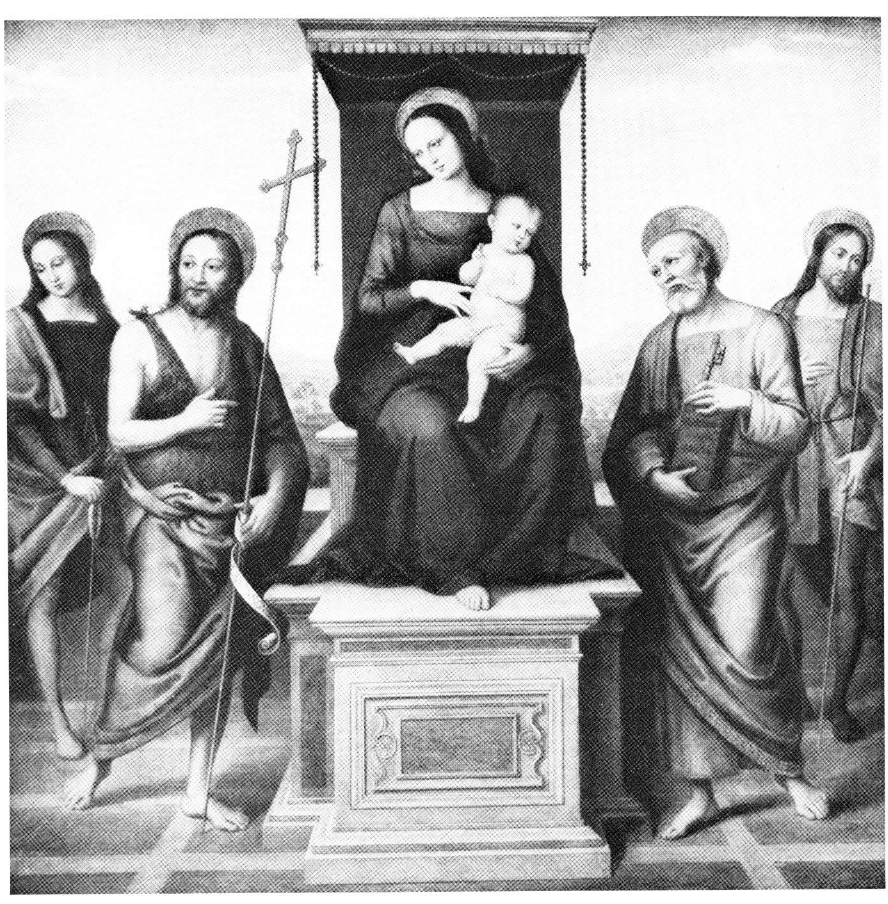

Received as

PERUGINO

(Pietro Vannucci, ca. 1445–1523)

A 3. *Madonna and Child Enthroned with Four Saints*

Oil on canvas (transferred). 80¾ × 80½ inches (205.1 × 204.5 cm.)

The Mary Frick Jacobs Collection (BMA 38.229)

PROVENANCE

Said to have been in several private collections:

Residence of the Cardinal of Lucca

Camesasca, *L'opera completa del Perugino,* cat. no. 223

Collection of Baron Blanc, Ambassador of France, Rome

Edward Cheney Collection, Badger Hall, Shropshire, England

Henry Barton Jacobs, *The Collection of Mary Frick Jacobs* (Baltimore: Prepared and published by Dr. Henry Barton Jacobs, 1938), cat. no. 32

Acquired by Mary Frick Jacobs, Baltimore, in 1909 from Eugène Fischhof, Paris

Bequeathed to The Baltimore Museum of Art in 1938 as part of The Mary Frick Jacobs Collection

CONDITION

Recent technical examinations, made by Geoffrey Michael Lemmer of the Baltimore Museum, thus far have yielded, for the most part, only inconclusive results. At an unknown point in its history the painting suffered considerable damage; it suffered further from attempts by early restorers to conceal this damage. At least twice major treatment was undertaken, during which large areas of the surface were overpainted, and compositional elements were added; the most recent restoration probably occurred during the second half of the nineteenth century. It was presumably at this time that parts of the Virgin's face and hairline were altered, and the faces of the Christ Child and the saints to the right were extensively repainted. The landscape, too, has been changed; the restorer added a mountain peak to the right of the Virgin's throne to conceal a hole in the canvas. The strings of beads ending in crosslike pendants, suspended at either side of the canopy, are similarly a nineteenth-century addition. Certain passages of the composition, however, seem to be original, among them the Virgin's hands and foot, St. Sebastian's face, St. John's drapery, and most of the lower left-hand corner of the picture, but it has not been possible to date even these areas with any assurance. It can be assumed that the picture was executed prior to the nineteenth century, since tests performed at The Walters Art Gallery conservation department indicate the presence of two pigments (orpiment and realgar) unlikely to appear in paintings executed after the eighteenth century.

Additional pigment analysis has established that the picture is not a transferred fresco, as usually stated in the literature, but was originally executed in oil. The *craquelure* further corroborates this fact, indicating that the original support of the altarpiece was non-rigid.

The photograph illustrated here was taken before the deterioration and before the cleaning of the painting.

REMARKS

The *Madonna and Child Enthroned with Saints Sebastian, John the Baptist, Peter and Roch* was purchased by the donor as the work of Perugino, but relatively few scholars have concurred in this assessment. Walter Bombe, Umberto Gnoli, and Fiorenzo Canuti all reject the attribution, and Ettore Camesasca, in his recent monograph on Perugino, excludes it from the catalogue of accepted works (*L'opera completa del Perugino,* cat. no. 223). Yet the painting has not been without its supporters: van Marle implies that at least part of the altarpiece is by the artist's hand, stating that it is, "for the greater part, the work of pupils" (*The Development of the Italian Schools of Painting,* 14:372), and Bernard Berenson, though noting the participation of assistants, considers it genuine (*Italian Pictures of the Renaissance: Central and North Italian Schools,* 1:325). Most recently Konrad Oberhuber has drawn attention to the Baltimore picture. Though he cautions that, because of its condition, "one cannot be sure of its authenticity, date, or authorship," he states that "it must surely reflect an authentic work of Perugino or his circle" ("The Colonna Altarpiece in the Metropolitan Museum," *Metropolitan Museum Journal,* 12:69, n. 40).

The diversity of scholarly opinion concerning the Baltimore picture is, to an extent, justified by the painting itself. A number of awkward passages, even in those sections which are not heavily overpainted, indicate a hand other than Perugino's. Especially troublesome is the rendering of the saints flanking the throne. The face of St. John, for instance, is curiously flat and devoid of bone structure, in sharp contrast with the finely wrought, delicately modeled features of Perugino's saints. Anatomically St. John and his companion, St. Sebastian, are similarly unconvincing. Sebastian's right foot toes in, so that the saint seems both bowlegged and pigeon-toed—abnormalities which never afflict the graceful figures of Perugino. And John's right arm is strangely proportioned in comparison to limbs of similar figures by Perugino himself.

On the other hand, much about the Baltimore picture suggests that its painter was extremely familiar with the work of Perugino: the overall composition, the figure types and drapery patterns, even a number of minor details derive from Perugino and are especially reminiscent of his work of the 1490's. The composition seems to fuse two formulas with which he experimented in the nineties. At first glance the Baltimore altarpiece resembles a panel, *Madonna and Child Enthroned with Saints* of 1493 in the Kunsthistorisches Museum, Vienna (Camesasca, cat. no. 31). In each work the Virgin and Child are presented as regal personages: they are seated on an imposing throne, its fringed canopy recalling the Gothic cloth of honor, and attended by four saints. The two compositions differ, however, in important respects. In the Vienna altarpiece pictorial space is severely curtailed by two devices: the high wall enclosing the figures and the Mantegnesque worm's-eye view from which they are seen. Both the figures and the throne seem pressed directly against the picture plane, restricted to an uncomfortably shallow ledge.

In the Baltimore picture, however, this almost claustrophobic sense of confinement is considerably relaxed. The enthroned Virgin and saints occupy a paved terrace terminating in a low wall, behind which a vast landscape opens. Further, the figures are no longer pressed against the picture plane but stand back on the terrace. Exactly these features—the paved terrace, low wall, vista, and placement of the figures—appear in Perugino's tondo in the Louvre, *Madonna and Child with Saints and Angels,* of about 1492 (Camesasca, cat. no. 28, pl. XVII). Though in the tondo the Virgin has relinquished her regal canopied throne and sits on a humbler backless chair, the similarities are evident. Other, though minor, visual parallels exist between the Baltimore painting and the tondo. In each the Virgin and Child gaze in opposite directions, a device which Perugino first employed in the early nineties and to which he returned repeatedly. Further, in both paintings only one of the Virgin's feet is shown, a detail that Perugino frequently used in the middle and later part of the decade.

Thus the two works in Vienna and Paris, taken together, account for almost every compositional feature of the Baltimore painting; the only conspicuous element not present in either one is the pair of hanging beads suspended from the Virgin's canopy in the Baltimore painting. Though such beads do occur in Perugino's oeuvre, they do not seem to appear until the 1520's, a fact which evidently did not deter the nineteenth-century restorer who added them to the picture.

Not only the general composition but aspects of drapery and physiognomy suggest that the painter of the Baltimore altarpiece had thoroughly assimilated the Peruginesque idiom. The robes of the saints, especially that of John the Baptist, echo a formula characteristic of the master especially in the nineties: the fabric hangs in loops at the waist, clings to the thigh, then breaks into U-shaped folds just below the knee. The Virgin's square neckline, softened by a translucent serpentine veil, and the delicate gold embroidery at the bodice and hem recur frequently in Perugino's work of the nineties. The modeling of the Virgin's face, with its full squarish jaw and slight swelling at the temple, also recalls the features of Perugino's female figures of this period. However, very recent cleaning unfortunately revealed that these features were largely the work of a clever restorer. The extent to which his design was based on original remnants, perhaps still visible at the time of his restoration, cannot be known.

Despite the Peruginesque elements which still survive, the authorship of the Baltimore picture must remain conjectural. It may be a copy of a now-lost original by Perugino or his workshop. It is even conceivable that it was a work of the late fifteenth or early sixteenth century by a Peruginesque painter. But because of its ruinous state, one should not venture beyond Oberhuber's assessment of it as a reflection of a work by Perugino or his circle. Nevertheless, one detail, probably coincidental, should perhaps be noted: the traditional belief that the painting once belonged to a Cardinal of Lucca. Perugino himself is known to have visited this Tuscan town in 1494 (van Marle, *The Development of the Italian Schools of Painting,* 14:304), not long after he executed the Baltimore picture's closest analogues, the works in Vienna and Paris.

Anne Derbes
Hood College, Frederick, Maryland

SELECTED BIBLIOGRAPHY

Walter Bombe. *Perugino.* Stuttgart: Klassiker der Kunst, 1914.

Umberto Gnoli. *Pietro Perugino.* Spoleto: C. Argentieri, 1923.

Raimond van Marle. *The Development of the Italian Schools of Painting.* 19 vols. The Hague: Martinus Nijhoff, 1923–1938.

Fiorenzo Canuti. *Il Perugino.* 2 vols. Siena: La Diana, 1931.

Henry Barton Jacobs. *The Collection of Mary Frick Jacobs.* Baltimore: Prepared and published by Dr. Henry Barton Jacobs, 1938.

Bernard Berenson. *Italian Pictures of the Renaissance: Central and North Italian Schools.* 3 vols. London: Phaidon Press, 1968.

Ettore Camesasca. *L'opera completa del Perugino.* Milan: Rizzoli, 1969.

Konrad Oberhuber. "The Colonna Altarpiece in the Metropolitan Museum and Problems of the Early Style of Raphael." *Metropolitan Museum Journal* 12 (1978):55–91.

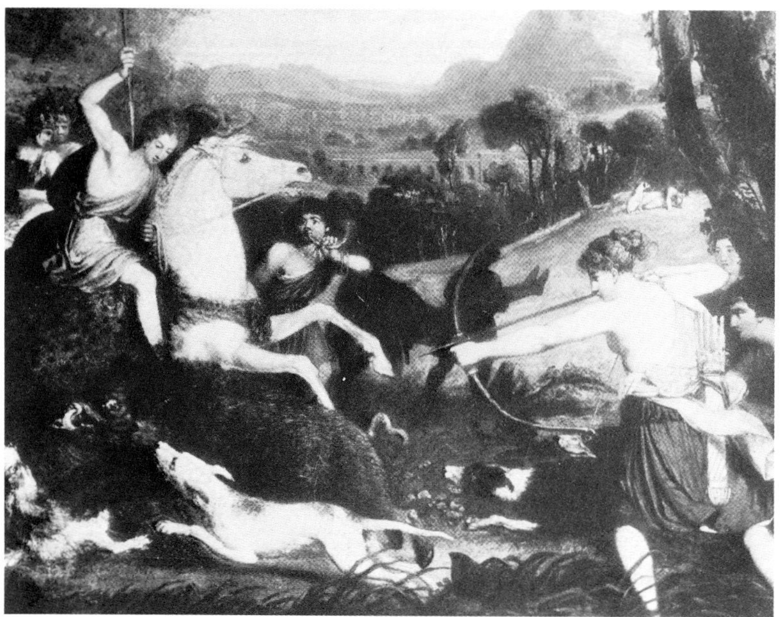

Received as

LUCA GIORDANO (?) (1632–1705)

A 4. *The Calydonian Boar Hunt*

Oil on canvas. 40 × 50⅛ inches (101.6 × 127 cm.)
The Mary Frick Jacobs Collection (BMA 38.197)

PROVENANCE

Said to have been in the collection of General Bulwer, Hayden Hall, Norfolk, England

Henry Barton Jacobs. *The Collection of Mary Frick Jacobs* (Baltimore: Prepared and published by Dr. Henry Barton Jacobs, 1938), cat. no. 35

Acquired by Mary Frick Jacobs, Baltimore, from the Blakeslee Galleries, New York in 1913

Bequeathed to The Baltimore Museum of Art in 1938 as part of The Mary Frick Jacobs Collection

CONDITION

This painting, once tentatively attributed to Luca Giordano, is of poor artistic quality, a fact which suggested that only a limited technical examination should be undertaken.

The original canvas is moderately coarse and has been glue-lined to a fabric of fine weave. The tacking margins had been removed. The paint film is generally thin but has some impasto. Throughout the paint surface there is heavy crackle which in light and medium-light areas seems to have been retouched. The dark passages reveal a lumpy crackle texture probably from the use of bituminous paint (not available until the eighteenth century). Paint losses due to flaking are noticeable along the lower left side. Examination by ultraviolet light shows a small puncture on the neck of the large, leaping dog. Other parts of the surface are obscured by the heavy discolored varnish which is easily soluble.

The type of stretcher can date at the earliest from the beginning of the nineteenth century but is probably later. Visual examination reveals abrasion especially in the dark areas.

REMARKS

The question mark which follows the Luca Giordano attribution in the 1938 Mary Frick Jacobs Collection catalogue—the only atribution to be so questioned in that publication—is well deserved. There is no basis to connect this painting with Luca Giordano whose dramatic representations of images as well as his compositional skill and virtuoso technique are here completely missing. Instead, the figures of Atalanta and Meleager, who both, according to Greek mythology, were famous for their physical prowess, appear strangely static and flaccid without the dynamic movements required by such a scene. Moreover, the composition of the Baltimore picture lacks unity and even basic elements of craftsmanship. Notice that Meleager seems to aim his javelin not at the boar but at his own shoulder. The dogs, supposedly running, are not convincingly depicted as being in motion; the only feature that faintly recalls Luca or his school is the white horse, but when compared with its prototype it, too, appears without strength, a poor imitation of Giordano's fiery animals.

Visiting scholars have tentatively ascribed the picture to nineteenth-century England.

G.R.

SELECTED BIBLIOGRAPHY

Henry Barton Jacobs. *The Collection of Mary Frick Jacobs.* Baltimore: Prepared and published by Dr. Henry Barton Jacobs, 1938.

Michael Milkovich. *Luca Giordano in America.* Exhibition catalogue. Memphis: Brooks Memorial Art Gallery, 1964.

Oreste Ferrari and Giuseppe Scavizzi. *Luca Giordano.* 3 vols. Rome: Edizioni Scientifiche Italiane, 1966.
In this catalogue raisonné the Baltimore painting is not listed nor is it mentioned in *Luca Giordano in America* (see above).

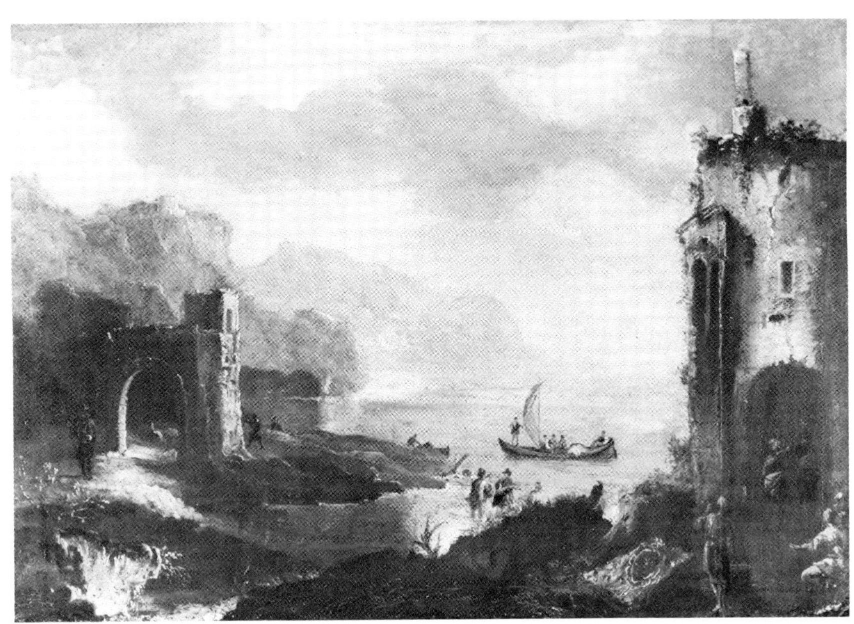

Received as

ALESSANDRO MAGNASCO (1665–1732)

A 5. *Landscape with Figures*

Oil on canvas. 28⅛ × 40 inches (71.4 × 101.6 cm.)
Gift of Miss Eleanor L. Turnbull, Baltimore
(BMA 62.29)

PROVENANCE

For the last few decades of the nineteenth century the painting had belonged to the family of Eleanor L. Turnbull, the donor. Nothing is known about its earlier history.

CONDITION

When in 1978 *Landscape with Figures* was thoroughly examined and cleaning was started, it became evident that the picture had been transferred. One can assume that this procedure had taken place in the nineteenth century when the transfer of picture surfaces was very much practiced. Probably at the same time the entire center including most of the sky was overpainted; when mild solvents were applied to part of the center paint surface, the portion so treated practically disappeared. Further cleaning was stopped, so that some of the later additions such as the boat with its figures and the group of figures in the water are still visible.

The structures as well as the small figures at the right and left of the composition appear to be original. There are small passages such as the faintly outlined buildings in the far distance at left which also could claim to have been part of the original painting.

REMARKS

The Museum never accepted the initial ascription of the picture to Magnasco but it was thought that its attribution to Bartolomeo Pedon (1665–1732), a little known Venetian landscape painter, was a good possibility. This attribution was suggested tentatively from a photograph by two well-known Venetian specialists. Nancy Press of the Museum staff intended to write a brief paper for this publication on the so-called Pedon. However, when she had the opportunity to compare the Baltimore Museum picture with accepted works by Pedon, she realized that the resemblance which had been established through photographs was deceptive. When she pursued her aim of finding the painter of the *Landscape with Figures,* various other artists such as Leonardo Coccorante and Alessio de Marchis were mentioned. The technical investigation of the painting's condition finally clarified the problem.

The curatorial decision to relegate the picture to the storerooms and use it as a study piece was easily reached. The Museum's research has confirmed some valuable lessons—the risk of making attributions only from photographs, and the need for technical examination of works of art.

G.R.

BIBLIOGRAPHY

Painting not previously published.

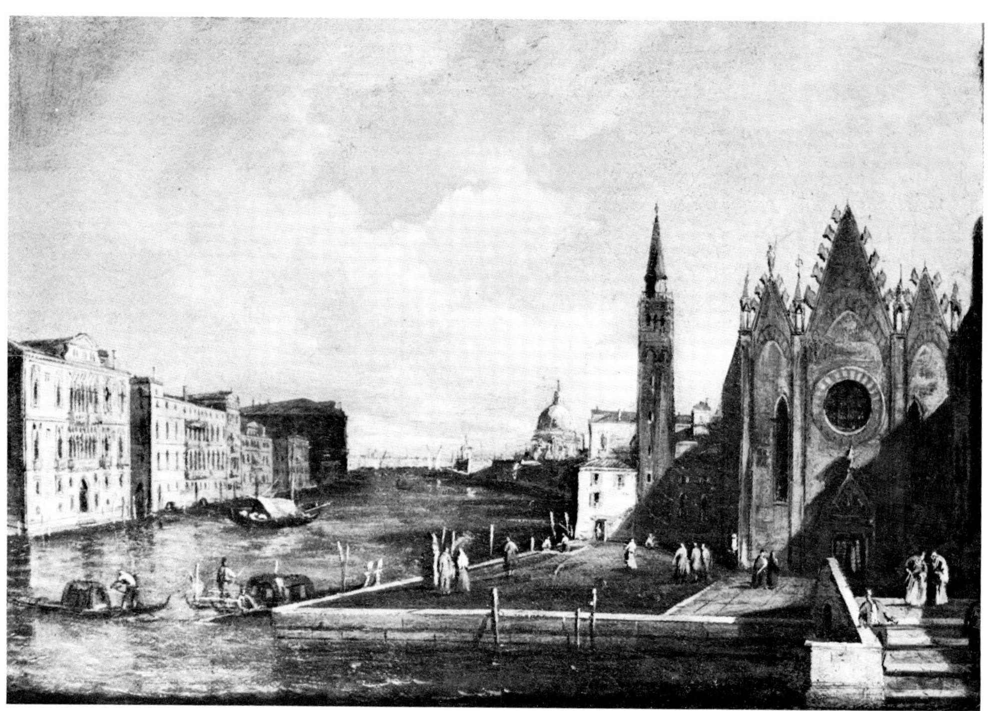

Received as

JACOPO MARIESCHI (1711–1794)

A 6. *Venetian Scene*

Oil on canvas. 16 × 22¾ inches (40.5 × 57.8 cm.)
Elise Agnus Daingerfield Collection (BMA 44.112)

PROVENANCE

The picture was acquired by the donor, Elise Agnus Daingerfield, probably on one of her many trips to England.

CONDITION

The painting was relined in this century prior to its presentation to the Museum. Some part of the original support still can be discerned, showing a coarse open weave, which does not seem machine made. Therefore it can be assumed that the original lining dates from the eighteenth or early nineteenth century. Examination of the painting by ultraviolet rays and X-radiography indicates that the center of the sky and small areas throughout the picture were overpainted. X-radiographs also revealed parts of an earlier design layer beneath—a church steeple, roofs, and a columned doorway are clearly visible; they may suggest details of a view of a northern town.

In a solvent test only the very discolored varnish covering the entire painting was easily soluble, which should date the copy not later than the first half of the nineteenth century.

REMARKS

The painting was apparently acquired as a work by Jacopo Marieschi who is often confused with the *vedute* painter Michele Marieschi. Since attribution and authenticity seemed questionable, a photograph was sent to Federico Zeri who with unfailing expertise responded:

> I feel very doubtful about the period of this canvas. It has nothing to do with Marieschi's quality, and it is reminiscent either of an old copy or of a forgery. Much too poor to be by Tironi, or by some other minor Venetian vedutista. I do not exclude that this is an imitation after Canaletto's "Grand Canal from Santa Maria della Carità to the Bacino di San Marco" at Windsor Castle [see Constable, *Canaletto,* I, no. 196]. In fact, almost all the details correspond very closely. If so, this should be an English *pastiche* from the 19th century (letter of January 27, 1976, in the Museum's curatorial files).

In a later letter Zeri referred again to the picture, stating that "it still looks to me like a 19th century forgery. The forger either worked from the actual picture in the Royal Collection or from the print by Visentini." Antonio Visentini's engraving of the painting at Windsor Castle in the *Views of Venice* was first published in 1735, then in 1742, 1751 and finally in 1833 (republished in 1971).

There can be no doubt that the composition of the Baltimore canvas is a slightly modified copy of Cana-

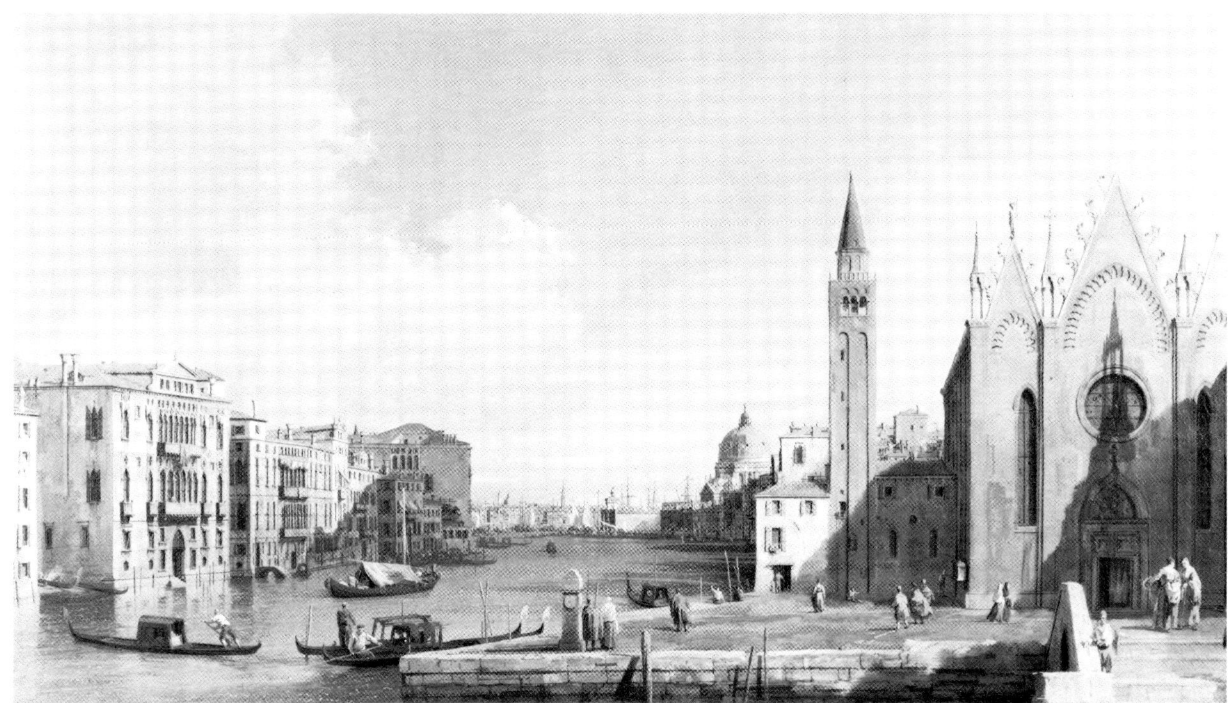

Fig. 1. Canaletto (Giovanni Antonio Canal), *Grand Canal, Venice, from Sta. Carità to the Bacino di S. Marco.* Oil on canvas. 18¾ × 31¼ inches (47.5 × 79 cm.). Collection Her Majesty Queen Elizabeth II

letto's *Grand Canal Venice: From Sta. Maria della Carità to the Bacino di San Marco* of ca. 1730 (fig. 1; see Constable and Links, *Canaletto,* no. 196; also Levey, *The Later Italian Pictures* . . . no. 386). The copy is smaller than the original which measures 18¾ × 31½ inches (47.6 × 80 cm.).

The most obvious compositional changes from the original are that there is a broader area of water in front of the quay (as there is in the Visentini engraving) and that the part of the building at the left corner in Canaletto's painting has been completely omitted in the Baltimore Museum version. There are also some very minor changes in some of the figures. A great difference, however, is easily noticeable in the poor quality of the execution of the Baltimore picture. Compared with the firmly outlined shapes and rich surfaces of the original Canaletto view, the copy with its clumsily defined buildings and mechanically drawn waves looks almost like the work of an amateur.

Since the engravings after Canaletto by Visentini were easily available models, it is impossible to say whether the Baltimore picture was intended as a forgery or simply as a copy of a much admired and popular painting.

G.R.

SELECTED BIBLIOGRAPHY

Francis Haskell. *Patrons and Painters.* New York: Alfred A. Knopf, 1963.

Michael Levey. *The Later Italian Pictures in the Collection of Her Majesty the Queen.* London: Phaidon Press, 1964.

J. G. Links. *Views of Venice by Canaletto. Engraved by Antonio Visentini.* New York: Dover Publications, 1971.

W. G. Constable and J. G. Links. *Canaletto.* 2 vols. Revised edition. Oxford: Clarendon Press, 1976.

Index of Artists

Numbers in *italics* refer to illustrations.

PHOTOGRAPHY CREDITS

Photographers are cited alphabetically. Credits are cited by page number and figure number where applicable. Photographic material not specifically cited was provided courtesy of respective owners.

Jörg P. Anders, Berlin, pp. 63, 278.

Osvaldo Böhm, Venice, pp. 138, 139 (fig. 7).

Bullaty-Lomeo Photographers, New York, p. 46.

Prudence Cuming Associates, Ltd., London, p. 95 (fig. 6).

Gabinetto Fotografico, Florence, pp. 153, 197, 208 (fig. 3).

Gabinetto Fotografico Nazionale, Rome, pp. 36, 38, 124.

Photographic Studios, Bob Jones University, Greenville, South Carolina, p. 314.

Sydney W. Newbery, London, p. 133.

Pfauder, Dresden, p. 166.

John D. Schiff, New York, p. 95 (fig. 5).

Duane Suter, Baltimore, cover and pp. 16, 24, 32, 42, 60, 66, 71, 74, 100, 108, 112 (figs. 2 & 3), 116, 128, 130, 141, 148, 156, 162, 168, 180 (fig. 2), 181, 190, 195, 202, 206, 209 (fig. 4), 211 (fig. 7), 214, 218, 219 (fig. 2), 235, 244, 251, 254, 260, 265, 274, 279, 280, 282, 296, 297, 300, 308, 319, 321, 323, 326, 327, 328.

John Tennant, Washington, D.C., pp. 54, 86, 172, 230, 292.

LIBRARY OF CONGRESS CATALOGING IN PUBLICATION DATA

Baltimore. Museum of Art.

Italian paintings, XIV–XVIIIth centuries, from the collection of the Baltimore Museum of Art.

Includes bibliographical references and index.
1. Painting, Italian. 2. Painting, Gothic—Italy. 3. Painting, Renaissance—Italy. 4. Painting, Modern—17th–18th centuries—Italy. 5. Baltimore. Museum of Art. I. Rosenthal, Gertrude, 1903– . II. Title.
ND614.B28 1980 759.5'074'01526 80-66714
ISBN 0-912298-51-0

Art Museum Drive
Baltimore, Maryland 21218

THIS BOOK WAS DESIGNED BY ALEX AND CAROLINE CASTRO,
THE HOLLOW PRESS, BALTIMORE, MARYLAND

TYPOGRAPHY, SET IN BEMBO, BY MONOTYPE COMPOSITION COMPANY,
BALTIMORE, MARYLAND
TITLING IN MONOTYPE ARRIGHI BY MACKENZIE–HARRIS CORPORATION,
SAN FRANCISCO, CALIFORNIA

COLOR WORK BY PROGRESSIVE COLOR CORPORATION,
ROCKVILLE, MARYLAND

OFFSET LITHOGRAPHY BY SCHNEIDEREITH & SONS, BALTIMORE, MARYLAND,
ON WARREN'S 100 LB. TEXT AND COVER PAPERS

SMYTHE-SEWN BINDING BY ROBERT BURLEN AND SON, INCORPORATED,
HINGHAM, MASSACHUSETTS
END PAPERS ARE STRATHMORE ARTLAID IVORY

THREE THOUSAND COPIES PUBLISHED BY THE BALTIMORE MUSEUM OF ART
MAY 1981